FAITH † AND FRIENDSHIP

BY DAVID O'BRIEN

Prepared for publication
by the Office for Communications,
Catholic Diocese of Syracuse

Captions & sidebar stories
by Ronald D. Smith

CATHOLICISM IN THE DIOCESE OF SYRACUSE
1886-1986

This book is dedicated to

BISHOP FRANK HARRISON
a witness to
Faith and Friendship

ACKNOWLEDGEMENTS

In 1977, shortly after he was installed as bishop of Syracuse, Frank J. Harrison received a letter from an old friend, Father Robert McNamara, historian and teacher at St. Bernard's Seminary in Rochester. Wishing Harrison well, McNamara advised the new bishop that, with the centennial of the diocese only nine years off, he should begin immediately to plan a diocesan history. To the outsider, he admitted, such arrangements might look a bit premature, but the historian knew that at least that much time would be needed to do an adequate job. He had himself been given 10 years to write his history of the diocese of Rochester, a model of thoroughness and accuracy. Five years later in 1982, I was approached by a committee of the Syracuse diocese about the prospects for an anniversary history. I warned the committee that I would have only three summers and what time I could spare from teaching and other oerdue writing commitments. Nevertheless, I took on the assignment, attracted by the committee's interest in a somewhat unusual history, one which would concentrate on the key themes of contemporary diocesan life and bring the story up to date, attempting to show the relationship between the century of experience and the current struggles of the Church. We all recognized that, in the time available, I could not write the kind of detailed history which McNamara had done so elegantly for Rochester. Instead I would have to concentrate on the areas of current interest, and I would need a lot of help.

Some of that help had already been provided by an earlier historian, Thomas Francis O'Connor. Born in Syracuse in 1899, O'Connor graduated from Christian Brothers Academy and Holy Cross College and received a masters degree in history from Syracuse University in 1927. After further graduate study in American history at St. Louis University, he taught for two years at St. Michael's College in Winooski, Vermont. In 1941, Bishop Walter Foery of Syracuse hired O'Connor to write the history of the diocese. Earlier, in 1936, Bishop Duffy had requested pastors to prepare historical outlines of their parishes, and on the basis of this material O'Connor was expected to complete the diocesan history in a year. A tireless researcher, he began detailed examination of archives throughout the country on the early history of Catholicism in the area, particularly examining the work of the French missionaries. A short time later, he agreed at the request of New York's Archbishop Spellman to take on another project, a biography of Bishop John Hughes. He moved to New York, working on both books. Then began a long correspondence with Syracuse officials, looking for their history. O'Connor eventually did write several chapters covering the early years, but he never completed his work. A perfectionist who loved research but always wanted to consult the last documents before writing, O'Connor was plagued by recurrent

V

illness, made worse by his overextended commitments. He was a widely respected historian, serving as president of the American Catholic Historical Association and earning an honorary doctorate from St. Bonaventure University. Well liked by the Syracuse officials, he died in 1950 and was buried in St. Agnes cemetery in his home town. He left behind manuscript materials covering the early Church in the area and a tremendous collection of notes on his research which would prove useful to later historians. In this book, O'Connor deserves credit for much of the material in the early chapters on pre-diocesan history. Indeed, the chapter on the early missions follows O'Connor's text closely, though the interpretation reflects more recent reflection.

A second advantage provided by previous experience was the work of Monsignor David Gildea, longtime secretary of the diocesan building commission, superintendent of schools, and pastor of St. Vincent de Paul and St. Anthony of Padua parishes. Gildea, something of an archivist, gathered materials on the history of the Syracuse Church in the basement of the chancery office. In 1976 he drew up a questionnaire similar to one distributed in 1936 in preparation for O'Connor's work, and with the help of Bishop Cunningham and Bishop Harrison, Gildea succeeded in persuading most parishes to provide an updated outline of their parish history. This material, together with an excellent collection of published parish histories and the uncatalogued papers of the Syracuse bishops provided a basis for constructing a record of the Syracuse Church.

Through newspaper stories and word-of-mouth, a small number of volunteers joined the project to help me in the preparation of the history but also to assist the diocese in preparing for other forms of celebration during the centennial year. These people were generous, warm, talented and deeply com-mitted to the Church and to the diocese. Among those who were so helpful was a group of women and men who for over two years, worked one day a week in the archives and occasionally ventured forth to visit parishes. This group included Margaret Blake, Helen Byron, Elizabeth Gravell, Effie Hughes, Pat Markert, Virginia Millert, Lottie Muchnicki, Margaret and Pat Testa and Dorothy Vecchio. George Eiffe, parish historian of St. Peter's in Rome, organized the O'Connor papers and notes. Sue Good took on a host of research projects, compiled data on priests, and poured over back issues of the *Catholic Sun*. David Fichera joined the project in its last year and completed several research assignments. Particularly energetic was Stephen Podkowinski, who explored the history of Polish, Slovak and other national parishes and furnished detailed outlines of the history of these communities. Father Francis Case offered his unique skills at several crucial points, particularly by computer use to sort out some of the data. These were the core of the volunteer team, but others joined from time to time, including Professor Mark Jackson of LeMoyne, Father Timothy Elmer, Cil Sidone, Joe Michaels and T. Gene Law. Larraine Batey helped organize the archives early in the project.

Innumerable people were equally generous in sharing their stories and ideas. Bishop Harrison and Bishop Costello were always available for advice and to offer their recollections. Father David Barry translated documents from Latin, answered questions about canon law, and smiled when he heard what we were up to. Father Richard Kopp and Roger Shaver provided the resources needed for a project such as this. Kate Anderson of the Bishop's Office, Brother John McGovern and Marion Gleason of the school department, Katherine Kearney of the diocesan staff, and Monsignor Ronald Bill of the community services vicariate, all were ready to help when called upon.

Dr. Richard Lawless, diocesan vicar for education, was one of the men who got me into this position; he was so affirmative and encouraging that he made me believe it could be done.

Diocesan communications director Ron Smith, the other originator of the project and later an orchestrator of events associated with the centennial, was invariably helpful and generous with his time, resources, budget and staff. By the time this book appears, he will have been over it a dozen times — editing, making suggestions, arranging layout and design, and dealing with the thousand problems that surround publication. He has also contributed to the volume by gathering and organizing the photographs and captions and by writing the sidebar stories which accompany the text.

His secretary Kathy Gill McHale, did much of the typing of notes and duplicating of materials; her skill and speed were incredible, her patience beyond the call of duty. Joan Agrasto and Bonnie Cox did much of the typing after Kathy was called to other duties by her first baby. Others who helped type were Pat Gale and Kyle Schroeder. Colin Campbell and Mary Trott assisted in editing the various drafts.

Others in the chancery who joined in from time to time, usually in response to some strange request outside their normal duties, included Sharon Bach, Margaret Dwyer, Tina Janiszeski, Charlene Oppedisano, Mary Osada, Kay Rea, Michelle Fenner, Catherine Vieau, Linda LeStrange, Don Stapleton, Maureen Suatoni, and Sisters Barbara Garland, Gladys Feeley, Bonaventure Hanson, Francine Bauser, Maureen D'Onofrio and Maureen O'Brien; Jean King at the Harrison Center; Wes Brush, Mary Kay O'Brien, Diane Kogut and Jim Murphy at the *Catholic Sun,* and Father James Fritzen, Mary Coates and Kate Smith at the diocesan cemetery office.

Many others shared generously of their time and knowledge. Among those interviewed were Monsignor A. Robert Casey, Monsignor Robert Dillon, Father James Carey, Sister Mary Vera Blank, Frank Woolever, John McRae, Dolores Morgan, Professor William Ehling and Monsignor Joseph Champlin, who also graciously made his summer cottage on Lake Skaneateles available to me for almost a month at a crucial time in the writing process. When members of the research teams visited local historical societies there were assisted by Richard Wright and Violet Hosler of the Onondaga County Historical Society, Douglas Preston at the Oneida Historical Society, Russell Hubbard of the Madison County Historical Society, Margaret Shiel of the Broome County Historical office and the staffs of the Oswego County Historical Society and the Roberson Center for the Arts and Sciences in Binghamton. Mary Ann Kane, city historian in Cortland, generously shared her notes and clippings on local Church history and her excellent slide show illustrating the history of local Catholicism. Mary Fargo, parish historian at St. Malachy's in Sherburne also provided superb professional assistance, as did Rita Hogan of Broome County Community College. Father McNamara, the Rochester historian, read and commented on several chapters. Bill Oley of Pompey made available several of his many scrapbooks. Sylvia Shoebridge of Pompey and Mrs. Alice Folts of Deerfield also assisted with local materials and information. Michael Byron helped research the deaf apostolate. George Loftus, Sister Leonilla Fuchs and Father Laurence Kennedy translated documents for us. More help was found from library staffs at the Onondaga County Library, the Guernsey Memorial Library in Norwich, the Penfield Library at the State University in Oswego, the Rare Book Room at Cornell, the archives of Onondaga Community College, and the Special Collections Room at Syracuse University.

Diocesan archivists in Buffalo, New York and Albany were helpful, as were archivists for the Sisters of St. Joseph, the Daughters of Charity and the Franciscan Sisters and Fathers in Syracuse. When research teams visited parishes, they were invariably greeted warmly by pastors, associates, secretaries and parish staffs, far too many to mention. Particular notice is due to the special help provided by John Krzewinski of Transfiguration parish in Syracuse, Mrs. Vickie Reinhardt of Transfiguration parish in Rome, Adeline K. Chaplo of St. Mary's parish in New York Mills, and Miroslawa Wielgosz of St. Michael parish in Fulton.

Finally and most important of all, there was Carl Roesch, who became my research assistant, supervised the volunteers, and organized the magnificent materials of the diocese into an actual archives, ready for professional use by scholars and Church personnel. He worked at least twice the hours he was asked to, he cared about the project more deeply than any one, and he showed by love for all of us associated with it something of the meaning of the story. In his deep faith in God, his compassion for those who suffer, his sensitivity to people of every stage of life and state in society, Carl embodies the strength, wisdom, and grace which are the marks of a healthy Church. Those who may still wonder about the phrase "faith and friendship" after reading this book might stop by the archives to meet Carl.

David J. O'Brien
Worcester Mass.
November 1986

CONTENTS

x

xiv

FAITH AND FRIENDSHIP

CATHOLICISM IN THE DIOCESE OF SYRACUSE
1886-1986

Words are strange things, coming down to us as they do from far off paths, bearing the marks and colorings of minds and hearts, of thoughts and feelings of long ago. They come to us like fossil specimens, on whose mutilated, fragmentary surfaces we trace the leaves and stems of plants and flowers, of thoughts that grew and bloomed in hearts of other days. A faithful record do they bring, these words so old, so new, of the life that was, of the life that is — the impression of the hearts that touch them and bear them onward as they go in long procession of the passing years. The history of the past is in the very words we hourly use, in the meanings and the forms they bore and took on lips that ages since were chilled, and fell to dust. You have seen how in the rocks and crags that overhang the borders of our streams, are marks and grooves and worn surfaces, the silent history of the mighty flood that once did pour along where now but shallow waters ripple idly by. Even so upon the ancient words and phrases of our familiar speech, left from the days of old, are left traces of the mighty stream of feeling once poured onward to eternity, where now but careless thought and wayward sentiment trip lightly on the hallowed ground.

Rev. Edward Terry of
St. John's Utica,
Eulogy for Pope Pius IX, 1878

"The Catholic Church has divided up the surface of the earth. The larger units are called dioceses, the smaller units parishes." These tongue-in-cheek words of historian Henry J. Brown quite accurately describe the organization of the Catholic Church. Beginning as a small, somewhat obscure movement within Palestinian Judaism, Christianity spread across the Roman world. Local communities of Christians found leaders gifted by the Holy

Spirit, who received authority by the laying on of hands by the Apostles and their successors. The Church was never an abstraction, but a very specific community at a very specific place, like the churches at Corinth or Ephesus or Phillipi to whom Paul directed his epistles. Peter's evangelizing mission to Rome and his martyrdom gave that local Church a primacy over the others, recognized in successive Church councils and confirmed by the eventual conversion of the Emperor Constantine. When that took place, the leaders of local Churches, now distinguished as bishops from their brothers in the ministry, the priests, took on leadership within local communities which increasingly corresponded to Roman imperial administration. By then, bishops were seen as the successors of the apostles, possessing the full power to teach, govern and sanctify which the Catholic Church believed had been given to the Twelve by Jesus.

With the emergence of the modern nation state, bishops of a given national community together governed the national Church. This governance usually was in association with the monarch who, anointed and crowned in solemn ceremonies, also possessed sacred authority. In many cases, the king nominated candidates for vacant sees, and those nominations were confirmed by the Holy See in Rome.

The church depended heavily on royal authority in its struggle against Protestantism and then found itself, more often than not, subordinate to that authority. Monarchs like Joseph II in Austria took to themselves the power not only to appoint bishops, but to define parish boundaries, determine the times at which Masses would be said, and in general manage local Church affairs. In 1773, when the pope was forced by the crowned heads of Europe to suppress the Society of Jesus, seen as his strong right arm in the Church around the world, the power of the pope over local Churches was at an all-time low. Not too

many years later, Napoleon took the pope prisoner and attempted to bend him to his will in order to lend legitimacy to his new order in Europe.

With the overthrow of Napoleon, a new era in Catholic history began, climaxing at the first Council of the Vatican in 1869-1870. At this council, the pope was declared infallible when teaching the whole Church on matters of faith and morals and, equally important, was defined as the primary pastor of all Christians and all local churches. By that time, the papacy had recaptured the power of appointing bishops, though in some states new agreements, called concordats, gave governments powers of nomination. But the trend was toward a more independent Church, an independence confirmed by the close union of bishops with the pope. The local Church was now seen as a division of one great Church, centered in Rome. The bishop, ordained to office in a solemn sacramental ceremony, received his powers to teach, govern and sanctify directly from the Holy Spirit; but his jurisdiction, his ability to actually work as a bishop, depended upon his appointment to a specific see by the Holy Father. A bishop is fully bishop when appointed to exercise jurisdiction over a given territory. When a large diocese requires the assistance of an assistant or auxiliary bishop, he is named as "titular bishop" of a long-suppressed diocese in North Africa or the Middle East, reflecting the fact that the bishop always is connected to a local church. The Church is not an abstraction but a concrete community in a particular time and place.

When the United States won its independence from England, the Catholic community in the new nation found itself isolated from the former seat of ecclesiastical authority which had been with the vicar apostolic for London. The first step to place the new American Church on proper foundations came with the appointment by Rome of John Carroll of Maryland as the vicar apostolic for the United States. Directly under the authority of the Congregation of the Propaganda, the Vatican office responsible for mission countries, a vicar apostolic could perform many of the duties of a bishop, but did not have the power and authority which come from episcopal ordination. This situation worried Carroll and the other priests of Maryland because they only recently had won their freedom from the oppressive penal laws which England and its colonies imposed upon Catholics. English Protestants distrusted the papacy, which they saw not only as the enemy of their religious freedom, but as an ally of oppressive political forces aligned against their country. American Catholics worried that their leader, so dependent upon Roman authority, would make their Church appear as a foreign, dangerous group whose first loyalty was to a foreign power, the pope. Therefore Carroll and the priests petitioned the pope to have their own bishop, with the same authority as bishops in other countries. Permission was granted to the priests to elect by vote one of their number to fill this post. Carroll was chosen. His election was confirmed by the pope in 1787. Ordained in Europe in 1788, he returned to take charge of his nationwide diocese in 1789.

In 1808, unable to administer properly such a huge diocese from his base in Baltimore, Carroll persuaded Rome to establish new dioceses at Boston, New York, Philadelphia and Bardstown, Kentucky. From then on, an ever-expanding body of bishops struggled to build the Church within the areas assigned to them. Because the Unites States was still a mission country, under the direct authority of the Holy See, the ordinary canon law of the Church did not apply here, so that priests were totally dependent upon their bishop. Carroll and his successors insisted upon strong episcopal authority because they feared

that, in the atmosphere of religious freedom, and amid the competition of various churches for the free allegiance of the people, parishes might become too independent and shatter the doctrinal and organizational unity which was one of the distinguishing marks of Catholicism. Later the bishops for similar reasons, secured legal control of all Church property. The American Church, in short, was a very bishop-centered Church, and the quality and character of local Church life closely mirrored the concerns and character of the bishop in charge.

A diocese is an administrative and organizational unit of the Church governed by a bishop. While ordinary Catholics were concerned primarily with their parish, that parish was authentically Catholic when its priest was united with his brother priests and with the bishop, and the community expressed the same faith and celebrated the same sacraments. Parishes together, united with the bishop, constituted the local Church. The union of those bishops with one another, in communion with the bishop of Rome, constituted the Roman Catholic Church. Catholicity, then tended, to be identified with the pope, bishops and clergy.

The task of the American Church was to bring its potential members, mostly immigrants, into parishes, making them "practicing Catholics" by their participation in the sacramental and devotional life of a parish. As the number of parishes grew, dioceses subdivided, with new jurisdictions established to join parishes and clergy into yet another diocese. The bishop was a sign of their unity, and Catholics celebrated the day when their city became the seat of a new diocese. This was a step which marked their growth, expansion and success in preserving the faith and extending the sway of Catholicism over the lives of an expanding people. The bishop sent them priests to serve their parishes, he confirmed their children, and he helped them find the resources they needed to build their churches and schools. In short, the bishop provided services to parishes, he stood forth as their spokesman to the larger society, and he connected them with the larger Church in the United States and in the world.

The spirit of the American understanding of the role of the bishop and his diocese was expressed well by New York's Patrick Cardinal Hayes at the installation of John Duffy as fourth Bishop of Syracuse in 1933. Episcopal consecration had given Duffy "a power not of this world, with light divine, with a courage supernatural, with a wisdom wiser than that of man," Hayes said. The "golden candlestick of the Church of Syracuse went dark" with the death of Duffy's predecessor, Bishop Curley. Now the new bishop was "the light on the golden candlestick of the diocese, a light dispelling darkness, a light guiding to wisdom, a light vivifying, a light celestial." The bishop's main task was to rescue souls "from the dark waters of the stormy sea of the world's iniquity." He "embarks on the barque of Peter," with Jesus as "the master, the pope as the pilot and the apostles and their successors the officers." As "shepherd of souls," the bishop and officers brought them out of that "sea of iniquity" and into the "fold of Christ among the tents of the shepherd priests of the diocese," keeping them united and combatting the effort of worldly forces and powers to "scatter the sheep." As Hayes, Duffy, and their generation saw it, the Church was one organization among many, but an organization which enabled its members to escape from the dangers of the world and enjoy the comfort of grace and the possibility of eternal salvation. By drawing people into herself, the Church helped shape men and women who were productive and responsible citizens, to be sure, but it was into the Church and away from the world that was the direction of pastoral action. In this image, the diocese,

under the bishop, defended Catholics against attack, offered spiritual counsel designed to resist the world, ordered the community itself toward its end of salvation, and provided for the sure routines of Church life which enable members of the Church to find salvation and be, by their faithfulness, a light to the world.

After Vatican II, many of these themes persisted, but they were set in a different context, one which made less of the escape from the world to the Church and more of the mission of the Church to the salvation of the world. Instead of a flock of sheep under a benevolent shepherd, the Church was "a family," a community, a people. This "family" was gifted by the Holy Spirit with faith and called to share in the life and mission of a Church oriented toward personal growth in faith, proclamation of the gospel to all people, service to those in need and leadership in all walks of life. The people of God are the people of God all the time, and not just when they are in church. As Bishop Frank Harrison put it in 1978:

Be it in the sanctuaries of our families, our neighborhoods, our churches; be it in the societies of our cities, our nation, our world, be it in the halls of our schools and campuses, our hospitals, our centers of government; be it on the streets of our ghettos, our marketplaces, our countrysides, the work of the Church is the work of the Lord, a work proclaimed by His word, enlivened by His spirit, sustained by His promise.

This history attempts to tell the story of Catholicism in the diocese of Syracuse from the point of view of the post-Vatican II Church expressed by Bishop Harrison. Its themes will be those he named — community, evangelism, worship and serving the needy. For most of the history of the diocese, those themes were understood within the framework of a heavily institutional, bishop-centered Church. The angle of vision will be from the viewpoint of the diocese as a whole, not that of individual parishes; the emphasis will be on those themes that express the experience of the diocese as a whole. Because this is a history which is to be read by a non-academic audience, footnotes are replaced by brief notes on sources for each chapter. Most of the material on which this book is based comes from the collections in the diocesan archives. There the papers of the individual bishops, committee and department records, biographical information on priests and data on parishes are kept. Unless otherwise indicated, the citations would be to the various collections, many unsorted and all un-catalogued, in the archives located at the Chancery office. No pretense is made that this is a final, exhaustive or complete history of the diocese of Syracuse. Many areas discussed here, like education and charities, are examined only briefly. The records of individual institutions, schools and religious orders all were largely unexamined. There are gold mines of information and many sources available for some future researcher interested in parish life, family life, education, medical care and social services, as well as material for the cultural historian seeking a deeper understanding of the function and meaning of styles of worship, devotion and community life. Still, what is here is a general, accurate and

coherent story of one local Church, with its unique experience and its rich resources of people and possibilities. I hope it can be a contribution to the life of this local Church, and through that local Church to the life of the larger Church of which it is a part. The spirit of the work was captured well by Father J. V. Byrne in a brief history of Catholicism in the area of Tully, New York, written shortly after the turn of the century:

> *It is a task pleasing as it is just to glean here and there a fact concerning early Christianity in these communities, the knowledge of which otherwise would soon be lost to this life with the last heartbeat of its possessor. We have spared no time and left nothing undone to make this little history complete in every detail which appears to us as interesting and proper.... We trust it will provide a source of emulation to our readers and a source of pride to the people...many of whom call the makers of it by the sacred names of mother and father. The only apology we can offer for a paucity of facts, inaccuracy of dates, or omission of names is the lack of resources. With this little preface, while asking the leniency of our readers, we begin this history....*

GOD IS EVERYWHERE

CATHOLIC CHRISTIANITY AMONG THE IROQUOIS
1650s-1700s

The first bishop of Syracuse, Patrick Ludden, had strong views on most questions, including history. Ludden once said that historical knowledge could improve the "enlightenment, refinement, and cultivation of the human race," but there was "no department of human science more liable to error and deception." Ludden was right, of course. Each generation rewrites its history in order to shape a past more useful than that learned in its youth. In the process, each becomes skilled at discerning the motes in the eyes of its predecessors, but is often blinded to the planks in its own. Perhaps nowhere is the subjective, tentative character of historical knowledge more evident than in the treatment Americans give to the Indians who lived in this land for centuries before Europeans arrived. Proud of the accomplishments of their nation, Americans nevertheless have been haunted by the spectre of the thousands upon thousands of natives destroyed by the "March of Progress." On the one hand, Americans have been grateful for the sacrifices of their pioneer ancestors; on the other, they have wondered how the God who so favored the United States could countenance the tragic destruction of whole races of human beings.

Ignored, the Indians have stood as silent witnesses to the price of American success. Patronized, they have provided evidence of the supposed contrast between "civilization" and "savagery" which conveniently justified the record of violence and oppression inflicted upon them. For Christians, the Indians have been remembered most often as unfortunate victims of a mysterious Providence. Those who attacked them were individuals who violated the teachings of their religion, the argument runs, while the churches are thought to have struggled to rescue native Americans from the horrors of their "pagan" religion, while protecting them against the assault of another "paganism" of greed and violence lurking in the hearts of even civilized men and women. Rarely entertaining the thought that Christians and their churches participated actively in the process of destruction, contemporary Christians often do not face the possibility that even the Christian religion, expressing itself in a particular culture, can serve as the motivating force for actions which violate the basic teachings of Jesus. Forgetting Father Simon LeMoyne's message that "God is everywhere," Christian missionaries sometimes acted as if the True God could be found only in their Church. To bring non-Christians to the Church, therefore, was a most noble activity, one which justified the means required. In the twentieth century, when civilized nations systematically have slaughtered whole categories of people because of their race or religion and when the most advanced nations prepare daily for actions which could mean the end of the historical experiment itself, it is less easy to speak of civilization and savagery. This is particularly true when examining the relationship between the Indians and the Christian newcomers who penetrated into the forests of North America in the seventeenth century.

8

The early history of the Church in Central New York, with its drama of heroic missionaries, cruel Indian warriors, devoted Indian converts and vast imperial rivalries long has fascinated Catholics. However, there was no direct link between the mission efforts of the French priests who labored among the Iroquois and the Church which emerged in the nineteenth century. On the contrary, that chain was broken around 1700, and the modern Catholic community finds its origins among small pockets of white settlers more than a century later. Still, Catholics have a special attachment to the place the first priest visited, the spot where he celebrated the first Mass. In the nineteenth century, a mischievous man and boy carved the famous Pompey stone, proving that Mass was said much earlier than previously believed, and their hoax stood as fact for years. Fascination with the missions went beyond antiquarian interest. Learned debates about missionary routes, conversions, martyrdom and persecution all helped Catholic immigrants to Protestant-dominated communities demonstrate that their faith had been there first, that their fellow Catholics were the true founders of

civilized society in the region. Monuments, pageants, markers and reconstructed mission buildings all helped build the morale of latterday Catholics who were determined to place themselves on an equal footing with those who sometimes claimed that only native-born Protestants deserved recognition as authentic Americans. The fact that the missions disappeared a century before the modern Church began was irrelevant; what was important was that heroic, self-sacrificing Catholics brought civilization and "true religion" to the region, and therefore, Irish-, German-, French- and Italian-American Catholics could be fully at home in a world that was not, after all, so new.

In all the local Catholic writing about the missionary period, one fact stands out. Those who wrote about such things regarded the missionaries as agents of Christianity and western civilization who provided the Indians with a chance to emerge from the "darkness" of barbarism into the light of western culture. In a typical address delivered in 1897, Father John F. Mullany of St. John the Baptist church in Syracuse argued that the teaching of the missionaries transformed "the children of

WAS ISAAC JOGUES IN BINGHAMTON?

Was there a Catholic missionary presence in the present-day Syracuse diocese before LeMoyne arrived in 1654? Sparse records and historical conjecture lead some to conclude that there may have been.

Twelve years before LeMoyne's visit, Jesuit Father Isaac Jogues and lay missionary Rene Goupil were taken prisoner by the Mohawk, along with several Christian Hurons. Goupil was killed for making the Sign of the Cross over a sick child — a bloody reaction to the Indians' fear of the Europeans, who along with Christianity also brought disease, death, and destruction. Regardless of the motive, the killing marked Goupil as the first Catholic martyr in the Northeast.

Meanwhile, Jogues was inflicted with the horrible tortures which the Mohawk then reserved for their prisoners. Besides the physical torture, he was treated with contempt and forced into demeaning and heavy labor at the Mohawk village near present-day Auriesville. His captors took him along on a journey to the Susquehannocks encamped near present-day Harrisburg, Pennsylvania, displaying their humiliated European prisoner in a show of strength to other Indians along the way.

Most of the old Indian routes were along river banks, and some conclude that the journey into Pennsylvania brought Jogues along the Susquehanna River into the area of present-day Binghamton. If so, it may have been the first occasion when the faith was preached and the sacraments administered within the Syracuse diocese. But all this remains mere conjecture, for even Jogues own retelling of his captivity does not detail his whereabouts.

That Jogues was a prisoner, there is no doubt. No doubt exists that he also was tortured and mutilated. Yet Jogues himself later explained that he had resolved to live among the Mohawk, because even in captivity he found some occasions to give witness to the Christian faith, to preach and to baptize. It was only after he learned that he was to be burned alive that Jogues consented to escape to Albany with the Dutch — so he might return again to spread the Catholic faith among the Mohawk.

In the end, it matters little whether Jogues actually was in the lands of the Syracuse diocese. What is more important is that his death — and more important, his life of service — sounds even today an echo of the gospel message of unselfish service, forgiveness, and enduring love.

the forest," as he called them, "from savage beasts and ravenous wolves into gentle lambs and docile children of the church." Mullany, one of the period's most intelligent priests, claimed that, when deprived of the Church's ministry, the Iroquois fell "back into the night of paganism from which he was rescued by the Catholic missionaries." For Father Mullany, the noble story of the missionaries of the seventeenth century blended easily into the struggles of the white Catholic communities of the nineteenth, so that the history of the local Church was one to "warm the heart," for, where once the "cruel warwhoop rang in the air," there was by 1897 "a home of quiet voices all attuned to the blended harmony of Christian civilization." For those who look back on the mission years from the perspective of the last decades of the twentieth century, such assurance is less available. The supreme confidence of eighteenth century French and English empire builders and the complacent righteousness of middle class Catholics of the Victorian era seem equally remote, almost as remote as the mysterious world of spirits and dreams that was the imaginative life of those Indians the missionaries came to save.

The first European visitors to Central New York found the land occupied by the Iroquois, whose villages ranged in a slender ribbon from the lower Mohawk river on the east to the Genesee on the west. A confederacy of five tribes, Mohawks, Oneidas, Onondagas, Cayugas and Senecas, the Iroquois nation claimed to hold primacy over virtually all Indians east of the Mississippi and north of the Tennessee. With a genius for political organization unique among the nomadic tribes of North America, the Iroquois were an agricultural, village-dwelling people, cultivating a variety of crops, while depending on the hunt for meat. Their religion centered around omnipresent spirits, animating men, animals and material objects, all under the sway of a great and powerful spirit, Tharonyawagon, the "Sky Holder," or later, Hawenio, "the Thunderer." The spirits communicated with human beings through dreams in which persons received injunctions they must carry out, while a liturgical "dream feast" occupied a central place in their ritual.

FIRST MISSION TO THE ONONDAGAS

The first authenticated record of European presence in the region was an ill fated campaign against the Iroquois by Samuel de Champlain in 1615. However, it was not until 1632 that the golden age of French missions began, spreading across French possessions in Canada and the Mississippi Valley. For three decades, this remarkable work did not extend into New York, but was concentrated among the Hurons, almost all of whom lived across the Niagara river and were bitter rivals of the Iroquois. The Hurons proved receptive to the missionaries, and it was captive Hurons who comprised the basis of most Catholic communities in the Iroquois country. While working among the Hurons, Father Isaac Jogues was captured and brought to the Mohawk country. Tortured and released, he returned to the Mohawks, first on a diplomatic mission, then in an evangelizing effort which led to his martyrdom in 1646.

During that period, the Iroquois engaged in a war of extermination against the Hurons, which concluded in 1650. Approximately 300 Huron Christians were taken to Quebec by the missionaries and many more were taken captive by their Iroquois conquerors. A short time later, the Iroquois invited the French to establish missions among them. Simon Le Moyne, a Jesuit who had been working among the Hurons since 1638, led a delegation into the Iroquois country, arriving at an Onondaga village near latterday Pompey on August 5, 1654. He described his reception:

At a quarter of a league from the village, I began a harangue which brought me into high favor. I told them that Peace was attending my course, that I was dispelling war in the more distant nations, and that joy was accompanying me. Two captains made me their harangue upon my entrance, but with a joy and a light that I had never seen in savages. Men, women, and children, all showed me respect and love.

LeMoyne ministered to some sick children,

10

Mural at LeMoyne College in Syracuse depicts Father Simon LeMoyne on his missionary visits to the Iroquois of Central New York. (Photo: LeMoyne College)

heard the confessions of captive Hurons, and baptized another captive who had been instructed by a Huron woman. The persistence and courage of Indian converts deeply impressed him. He "found that God is everywhere and that he is pleased to work in hearts where the faith has held sway."

At a council meeting, LeMoyne learned that the Iroquois, except the Mohawks, were anxious for peace. They invited him to select a site for a later French settlement. He also recovered some possessions of Jesuits martyred in Huron country and baptized his first Onondaga convert, giving him the name Jean Baptiste. After visiting the shore of Onondaga Lake, where he tasted the water of the salt spring there, LeMoyne left for Quebec. Along the way he visited small groups of Christians at Phoenix and on the shores of Lake Ontario. The next year, Fathers Peter Chaumonot and Claude Dablon arrived at Indian Hill and said Mass on November 14, 1655, "on a little Altar in an Oratory contrived in the cabin of Teotonharason, one of the women who had gone down to Kebec with the [Iroquois] Ambassadors." Under the supervision of the missionaries, the Indians erected a tiny chapel, later named St. John the Baptist, the first Catholic church in New York.

The Indians placed no restraints on the missionaries' preaching, but they proved unreceptive. Dablon noted the problems:

Dreams form one of the chief hindrances to their Conversion; and to those they are so attached that they attribute to them all their past great successes, both in war and hunting. Now, as they well know that the belief in dreams is incompatible with the Faith, they become even more obstinate; especially as they are aware of the fact that, the moment the Hurons received the Faith and abandoned their dreams, their ruin began, and their whole Country has ever since been declining to its final destruction.

Dablon believed this resistance was the work of evil spirits present in Indian religion:

The devil still opposes us with two other enemies, — namely, dreams, as already noted, and the indissolubility of Marriage. Men are told that they will have ill luck if they disregard their dreams; and women, that there will be no more marriages for them if they become Christians, because then they cannot take another husband when they have left a bad one.

Under pressure from the Iroquois to establish a permanent French colony, Dablon returned to Quebec and persuaded the authorities to send a party of 50, who settled on the shore of Onondaga Lake, not far from the salt springs visited by LeMoyne in 1654. There, a stockade and chapel were erected. While Dablon was away, Chaumonot had addressed the great council, distinguishing the religious aims of the missionaries from the economic goals of other Europeans:

Not for traffic do we appear in your country: our aim is much higher. Keep your beaver, if you like, for the Dutch: what comes to our hands shall be employed for your service. We seek not perishable things. For the faith alone have we left our land; for the faith have we traveled the ocean; for the faith have we left the great ships of the French to enter your tiny canoes; for the faith I hold in my hand this present, and open my lips to summon you to keep your word given at Quebec. You have solemnly promised to hearken to the words of the great God: they are in my mouth, hear them.

With the help of new priests from Quebec, the Fathers spread out among the several Iroquois tribes. Chaumonot and Rene Menard visited the Cayugas, Oneidas and Senecas, usually finding Huron captives anxious for their services, while at Onondaga the prospects seemed more promising than in the past. In contrast to the warlike behavior so associated with the Iroquois, the missionaries now found "in the Onnontagehronnons a gentleness in their conversation and a civility which hardly savors in any wise of Barbarism. The children there are docile, the women inspired with the tenderest devotion, the elders affable and respectful, the warriors less arrogant than they seem." As the Christian community formed, so did Christian behavior: "The divine office is recited, the sacraments are administered, the Christian virtues are practiced with as much modesty, care and fervor as they are in the most Catholic and devout provinces of France." Unfortunately, despite appearances, the Iroquois were losing interest in a French alliance, while the number of French troops at the post declined. Friendly Indians brought word of an intended massacre by younger braves, and, on a March night in 1658, the priests abandoned the settlement and returned to Montreal.

SEEDS FOR A SECOND MISSION

The departing missionaries left behind, scattered throughout the villages, a number of captive Frenchmen and Huron Christians, and, at Onondaga at least, a few Iroquois who had embraced Christianity. The Onondaga Christians found a protector in the person of a truly remarkable man, Garacontie, an influential Onondaga, who apparently had visited Montreal during the negotiations of 1654. He remained there for a time as a hostage, acquiring an unusual knowledge and appreciation of the French. He was credited with saving more than 60 French captives

12

SEEKER OF PEACE

Three-and-a-quarter centuries ago, Garacontie, a leading chief of the Onondagas and a renowned peacemaker among the other Iroquois tribes, traveled up the waterways to Quebec on a mission of peace among the French. While there, he surprised Indians and French alike by publicly professing Christianity. Garacontie was received into the Catholic Church by the bishop of Quebec, with the governor of New France as his godfather and Indians from throughout the St. Lawrence valley as his witnesses.

"Daniel" Garacontie's was not a conversion of convenience, nor was it done on a whim. He long had been familiar with Catholic Indians in his own tribe and the prisoners-of-war from other tribes living among them. It was Garacontie who had welcomed Father Simon LeMoyne in 1654 and later the first missionary priests to the Onondagas, building for them a rustic bark chapel. It was Garacontie who urged the Jesuits to instruct children and adults, and it was he who helped the priests escape when their lives were in danger.

Finding the mission without pastors, Garacontie stepped into the void. Though not yet a member of the Church, the chief called Catholic Indians to morning and evening prayer, and on Sundays he held feasts to give them an occasion for devotions and fellowship.

Garacontie's full embrace of the Catholic faith in 1669 sparked the conversion of many of his fellow Iroquois, including eventually his wife. And despite opposition from some tribesmen, he rose to even greater esteem among his people.

The chief long had been a peacemaker among the Indians. He had helped negotiate the federation of the Onondagas, Oneidas and other tribes of the Iroquois and, on at least one occasion, he influenced another tribe not to start an inter-Iroquois war. When he was baptized, Garacontie announced that he would be guided in tribal affairs by his Christian beliefs, and he continued even more earnestly in his peacemaking efforts. He worked to establish peace between the Indians and the French. He even made a venture among the English along the Hudson — but his peace mission ended when he denounced the English for selling liquor to his Indians and for kicking him out of a Protestant church for praying his rosary.

Eight years after his baptism, Garacontie made his last confession, urged nonchristians in his tribe to accept faith in Jesus Christ, and counselled all of his people to pursue the ways of peace. He died a few days after Christmas in 1676, reportedly with a prayer on his lips and a rosary in his hands. Today, Daniel Garacontie stands in history as an extraordinary leader of the Iroquois federation. For Catholics in the diocese of Syracuse, he is an inspiration for the persistence of faith and the pursuit of peace.

from death. An early historian of New France wrote of him, in the superior tone characteristic of the French: "Garacontie was the Indian only in birth and education, and with all his good qualities that it is impossible not to recognize in his nation, he has an excellent disposition, great mildness, a superior intellect, and great uprightness."

Although not yet baptized when the French left the Onondaga in 1658, Garacontie nevertheless became the protector of the Christians and an earnest advocate of friendly relations with the French. Unable to prevent the outbreak of hostilities, he labored to mitigate the sufferings of French captives, bringing 24 to Onondaga, where he gathered them and the Christian Indians twice daily for prayer. In 1660, Garacontie persuaded the Onondagas to open negotiations with the French. A delegation led by Saonchiogua, a Cayuga friend of Garacontie, went to Quebec, bringing along four French captives as a gesture of good will. Saonchiogua urged the return of the missionaries as a condition of peace. French authorities had good reason to be skeptical, but they ultimately asked Father LeMoyne to return to the Iroquois country. He was received well by Garacontie at Onondaga and spent several months ministering to the spiritual needs of the French captives and of the Huron and Iroquois Christians, then returned to Canada with the French captives who had survived their stay in the Indian villages. Soon after his departure, the war was renewed, and finally a large French force succeeded in pacifying the region.

The resumption of mission work followed quickly. Julien Granier, the first Jesuit ordained in Canada, went to Onondaga, where he was received kindly by Garacontie, who helped build a chapel and then went to Quebec, where he persuaded two more missionaries to return with him. The new missionaries still found the going hard among "those Barbarians" but, as the *Jesuit Relations* record, "that did not prevent the Onnotaguez from respecting the Faith of God's Commandments." Some were "touched by the example of the Christian Hurons" such as Jeanne Ascerraguehaeon, who came all winter to hear two Masses and, in the evenings, conducted prayers in her cabin for those unable to reach the chapel.

The faith and courage of these new Christians, almost all Hurons, not only served as an example to the skeptical Iroquois, but at times moved the missionaries themselves, as Father Pierre Milet noted in one of his regular reports:

I admire in respect to some, the remote and secret ways by which God's providence has led them, in order to make them gain a knowledge of the sovereign good, in others, the marvelous efficacy of the grace of Baptism in preserving them in the purity of the Faith and in the innocence of their morals, in the midst of such general corruption. There appears in them a certain character of piety, and a conduct so holy that it is clearly seen that God animates them with his hand. Their assiduity in attending Chapel to pray there in public, when they can repair thither, and their faithfulness in performing their devotions in the cabins or in the fields, when necessity, work, or old age make it impossible for them to come to Church, exceed all that can be told of them. We have one Cabin among others wholly Christian and occupied exclusively by Huron women....They have always kept themselves, amid all the disorders of the country, in a regular life and innocence that charm our Barbarians; and God,—who watches, without ceasing, over those who serve him with fidelity,—in order to crown, even in this life, the virtue of these good Christian women, so protected them against....maladies that, at the time when these were making unusual ravages in the neighborhood of their Cabins, they never did the women any injury. It may be said that, as these Huron women, formerly belonged to the church at Quebec, and as they have dwelt in the bosom of piety, they have taken care to become formed and so firmly established in the practice of all the virtues that neither the pains of extreme poverty, which they often suffer, nor the bad example of the idolaters, nor all the efforts of the Demon, have ever been able to make them waver, or to promote them to make a single request contrary to what they owed God.

The priests themselves persisted in their effort to win over the skeptical Iroquois, using some innovative evangelizing techniques described by Father Milet:

For a week, I put before their eyes various strings of porcelain beads, to mark the number and variety of the things I taught them. And during the following week I stretched a cord, and attached it to various collars, made of twine, with which the Savages fasten and chain the captives taken in war, to conduct them thus to the fire which is prepared for them. By this symbol I represent to them the cruel chains of sin wherewith the Demon loaded them to drag them into the fires of hell. At other times, I hung to the same cord (1) a handsome porcelain collar, before my Chapel Altar, to teach them that there was only one God; (2) a map of the whole world, to show them that he made all things; (3) a little mirror, to signify that he knew all things; (4) some strings of glass beads, to express the liberality with which he rewards all good actions; also some instruments of human justice, to express to them that which God exercises in the flames of Hell. I tried, above all, to make

them conceive, by the excess of Jesus Christ's sufferings, how terrible God's Justice is; and what torments must await a sinner, for the punishment of his crimes, since the Son of God had suffered so great pains for the expiation of ours. Then I showed them that the Savior, the Master of our souls, could not have given us more striking proofs of his love, than by taking upon himself the burden of our sins, and purchasing for us, with all his blood, an eternal happiness.

As these quotations from the records of the Jesuit missions indicate, the Fathers saw conversion as a step which brought the new Christian into a new way of life and a new civilization, different in almost every respect from Indian culture, which the missionaries regarded as barbaric, corrupt and perverted. Jesuit mission teaching suggested the need to respect Indian traditions and assimilate, where possible, native language and customs. The early missionaries even hoped for the integration of French and Indian cultures through intermarriage. By the time of the Iroquois missions, however, this prospect had dimmed considerably because of the resistance of both the Indians and the French to marriage with each other, while the missionaries' own attitudes toward Indian culture became increasingly negative. The missionaries still believed that "God is everywhere," alive even in native religion, but He could be hard to find. On the other hand, they also knew that French culture was not, in itself, Christianity. The Indians need not become French, yet neither could they remain among other Indians. Indeed, as Milet's reference to the community of Huron women indicated, they had little hope that their converts could persevere in the faith unless they were separated from their corrupting environment.

Elsewhere, in California and Paraguay,

contemporary missionaries, led by similar considerations, established separate communities where Christian Indians could be insulated against the temptations of their old Indian traditions and the influence of family and friends, and not incidentally, protected from the dangers of exploitation and corruption which came from contact with white settlers and trappers. The French Jesuits followed suit, establishing Christian villages on the St. Lawrence River where Huron, Mohawk and Oneida converts could be relocated. The results were promising. In a report of 1683, the Canadian Jesuit superior claimed that:

> It is difficult to find better Christians than are the Iroquois, when they have overcome the obstacles that hinder their conversion. This we observe in those who are at the mission of Sault de Saint Francois Xavier three leagues from Montreal...This mission is composed of all the most fervent Christians among the five Iroquois nations; they have left their country, their kindred, and their friends, to avoid occasions for offending God, and to lead a truly Christian life. Nothing better shows to us the strength of grace than the change that it works in these Barbarians, in whom is no longer seen that pride and arrogance which make them unbearable before they are converted....Their most shining virtues are devotion and charity...They display so much modesty in going to church and at prayer that those who have known them in their own country, and who see them now, have much difficulty in restraining their tears. They prepare themselves for the festivals by more scrupulous Confessions; by longer and more fervent prayers before the blessed

> sacrament, which they come to visit several times a day....They seem to possess nothing for themselves when it is a question of succoring the poor and the sick... There are also some among them who truly possess the spirit of the Cross, and whose sole joy consists in sufferings and austerities that would shame many Religious. Iron, ice, bloody disciplines, fasts, and long prayers are very common among them, — with great submission, however, to those who direct them and whose sole care is to prevent this fervor, which has lasted several years, from proceeding to excesses that might greatly injure their health.

It was to this Christian village, eventually composed of more than 1,500 converts, that Kateri Tekakwitha fled, there to live her life out as "The Lily of the Mohawks," her faith, holiness and charity a challenge to her French protectors as much as to her Iroquois brothers and sisters. Few Onondaga reached these villages, because few, in fact, were converted. Prospects became even less favorable when anti-French sentiment reawakened in the late 1670s, first among the Cayugas and Senecas, later spreading to the other tribes. Garacontie died in 1676. With his death, the missionaries lost their most powerful native protector on the Onondaga Mission. Father de Lamberville gained the friendship of Garacontie's successor, who joined the Church. But conditions continued to deteriorate especially as European rivalry for the fur trade, brought the scourge of alcohol into Indian life. The Canadian superior reported in 1678:

> Our Fathers suffer great persecutions... both from the Savages addicted to liquor, who are becoming more and more unbearable; and from those who

try to renew the war against the French. Both carry their insolence so far that our missionaries are frequently struck, pursued in the streets, driven from the cabins, and threatened with cruel massacre, in order that war may be brought on by their death....

Nevertheless, the missionaries still did not retreat. They quite probably would have continued indefinitely had not a combination of circumstances made mission work impossible. Gradually the English were gaining the upper hand in the competition for the fur trade. In 1683, Thomas Dongan arrived in New York as governor. Although a Catholic, Dongan quite correctly regarded the presence of the Jesuits as an important factor in strengthening French influence among the Iroquois. The missionaries were naturally sympathetic to French claims, while the practice of sending converts to missionary villages in Canada presented a very real challenge to English prestige. Dongan was disposed kindly towards the missionaries, but he represented a nation in which, as a Catholic, his every action was subjected to the closest scrutiny. He told the governor of Canada the English would provide priests in the Iroquois towns, and then tried to persuade the Christian Iroquois living in the Canadian mission villages to return. Rising English power strengthened the hand of the anti-French party among the Indians. When a French party escorting a cargo of merchandise to the Illinois country was plundered by a group of Senecas, the inexperienced governor of New France, De la Barre, decided to invade the Seneca country. In August 1684, De la Barre's army arrived on New York soil, but a large number of his soldiers soon fell ill. The governor urged Father De Lamberville to persuade the Onondagas to send a delegation to meet him. A party of Onondagas went, but when they saw the weakness of the French

forces, they forced De le Barre to accept humiliating terms of peace.

De la Barre soon was recalled. His successor, the Marquis de Denonville, arrived from France with instructions to humble the Iroquois. As he prepared to invade the Iroquois country, he called Father Jean de Lamberville to Quebec and instructed the missionary to tell the Iroquois to send deputies to negotiate a treaty, while secretely planning to take the Indians captive. De Denonville wrote to the French minister of marine on November 8, 1686, "That poor Father, however, knows nothing of our designs...I am very sorry to see him exposed, but should I withdraw him this year. The storm will, without doubt, burst sooner upon us." De Lamberville, deceived by the governor, carried out his commission and some prominent Iroquois set out the following spring. When they arrived at Cataroqui, they were seized and sent to France to serve as galley slaves. Jean de Lamberville was, by this time, the only Jesuit remaining in the Iroquois country. The older Iroquois knew the missionary was not to blame for the treachery, but they feared the anger of the younger warriors. As a precaution, they conducted him to a French outpost. His departure from Onondaga in the summer of 1687 marked the close of the second Onondaga Mission.

A MISSION TO THE ONEIDAS

Meanwhile, French missions had continued elsewhere. After several false starts, Father Jacques Bruyas established a mission among the Oneidas in 1667. The Indians frequently charged the French priests with pride, while the priests in return described the Iroquois as arrogant and almost always noted the "humility" and "docility" of converts. Bruyas, unlike many of his fellow missionaries, admired many qualities of Indian character and, even

17

This monument marking the site of Father De Lamberville's mission was erected in the 1930s near Jamesville. (Photo: Chancery Archives)

meditating upon the Canada mission in one's oratory, and finding oneself exercising the duties of a Canadian missionary...But the principal thing is that [superiors] need not expect to see thousands of unbelievers converted.... Often a year is occupied in the conversion of five or six families, and this is not considered a loss of time. For my part, I apply myself especially to the instruction of the children, waiting to become better acquainted with the language before working for the instruction of the adults.

The ministry of Father Bruyas at Oneida lasted until late 1671. There as elsewhere, Bruyas reported, liquor raised havoc with the work.

People return from trading, with sixty kegs of brandy brought from New Holland. A drunken man breaks in the door of my chapel, reproaching me for the insolence of our Frenchmen. Another strikes my companion, with such violence that he bears the marks of it. I take occasion to go on a trip toward our lake, where there are some fishermen,—although I am still very weak from a certain fever which, by the grace of God, has not stopped or hindered me from working for the instruction of my little flock. The heaviest cross that I have is that of the drunkards; and I have need of all my little virtue to bear it patiently. It breaks up all our exercises, and all our teaching; and prevents the people from coming to the chapel to say their prayers, morning and evening,—each one thinking only of running away and hiding, in order to avoid the violence of these furious men.

more unusual, he knew his own shortcomings. Progress was slight, he reported to his superiors, not only because of "the opposition the Iroquois feel toward the Gospel," but still more on account of "the weakness of him who announces it to them." He did not know the language and had converted only a few adults, although he had baptized numerous children of Christian Hurons. Evangelization was a more complex task than his superiors at home could imagine:

There is a great difference between

The latter part of Bruyas' ministry at Oneida

was saddened further by the deaths of some of his most fervent Christians. "God," he writes, "tries these little churches in an admirable manner, by depriving them of the principal pillars which seemed to sustain them."

In 1671, Father Bruyas was appointed superior of all the Iroquois missions and Father Milet was transferred from Onondaga to Oneida. Milet reported the prevalence of intemperance, debauchery and superstition but also commented on the edifying confessions of the Christians. He also recorded that the Christians were "very exact in observing Sundays, when they decorously assist at Mass, at which they generally pray in two choirs, some in Huron, the others in Honneyout, and instruct one another." Those he baptized were from families where someone already had become Christian. When children died, he hesitated to remind their parents of the child's baptism "for fear of confirming them in the idea which they generally entertain, that the Faith and baptism hasten death." He was impressed by the visit of a "Huron captain, Louis Thaodechoren," who "always wore his rosary and crucifix around his neck," safeguarding him "against all invitations to feasts and other occasions for sin, which are only too frequent here." He asked Milet "to confess him and give him communion, in order that God might fortify his mind in this country of infidelity, and inspire him with the words of life and of salvation when he should speak to the other Savages." On Sunday, this Indian convert gave "an instruction to the Christians during mass; and to his private exhortations in the cabins he added gifts,—both to withdraw some from evil ways, and to strengthen the others in doing good." Apparently such Indian evangelists were especially effective, for the missionary described "two Christian women who are of great use to me in instructing the faithful, and for the advance-

ment of this Church." Felicite had received from the Ursulines in Quebec "so sound a knowledge and so excellent principles of piety, that, through her virtue, she was able to assume and ever to maintain a certain ascendancy over all the other Christians." She knew "all the prayers, the chants of the Church, and the mysteries of our Faith" and explained "them so clearly that the men themselves willingly listened to her as their teacher." Another young woman "distinguished herself by the skill that she displayed in bringing back to the right path one of her friends, who was straying from it." One problem was the marriage bond, which "among savages, is dissolved on the slightest disagreement between husband and wife." Under the influence of such exemplary Christians, however, marriage was becoming "more stable," while the Indians' "worship of the divinity, whom they call Agriskoue, has greatly diminished." Many were "no longer so attached to their dreams as they were." Such "favorable tendencies" led Milet "to hope that, in a few years, the majority of the Iroquois of Onneiout will have embraced Christianity. Drunkenness, for which all these poor savages have a great weakness, is probably the sole obstacle that now hinders their conversion."

Assisted by such lay leaders, Milet's work among the Oneidas was unusually successful, his converts including an emotional chief known as "Hot Ashes" who became a leader in the Christian community. Even among those Oneida leaders who resisted his preaching, Milet enjoyed respect. As the Canadian superior reported in 1683:

Although Father Milet is not free from the Annoyances of the drunkards at Onneiout, He has, nevertheless, the consolation of seeing every day very remarkable fruits of his labors in the conversion of many savages, who there publicly profess Christianity. He has inspired them with such esteem for the Cross that even those who are not Christians look upon it only with respect. All the principal families have vied with one another in erecting very fine ones, without the Father speaking to them of it.

Milet's departure from Oneida resulted not from Indian hostility, but from De Denonville's invitation to serve as interpreter at the treacherous peace conclave that doomed the Onondaga mission as well. The governor's deception meant the end, at least temporarily, of Milet's usefulness among the Iroquois, but his missionary career was far from over. In July 1689, a party of Iroquois arrived at the French outpost at Cataroqui requesting the services of a doctor for their sick and a priest to minister to the dying. Milet and a surgeon responded to the request. They were captured, tortured and turned over to a group of Oneidas who were present. Some were old acquaintances of the priest, and they quickly took him to an Oneida village where Christian converts defended him against pro-English chiefs who wanted him put to death. His life was saved by their offer to substitute him for a long-dead warrior and he was adopted formally into the tribe, working for five more years in these unusual circumstances. Milet's presence and influence irritated the English, who made several attempts to capture him until, in 1694, during a brief peace between the French and Iroquois, he was released and returned to Montreal.

THIRD ONONDAGA MISSION

As Milet's experience indicated, the struggle between the English and French for the allegiance of the Iroquois intensified as the century entered its last decade. In many villages, there was a pro-French party and a pro-English one, and the Iroquois proved adept at manipulating the European rivalries. Priests visited the tribes occasionally, but the balance of forces was working against the missions. In 1700, Father Jaques Bruyas went to Onondaga to receive prisoners and, in the summer of 1702, the governor of New York complained to the Onondagas that "some of your people are gone to fetch a Jesuit from Canada." He ordered them to "either send the Jesuit back again to Canada, or bring him hither," but the only reply the governor could extract from the Onondaga envoy was to the effect that he would have to go home and think about it. The Jesuit was Father de Lamberville who had returned to the Onondagas and been received well, while two other priests visited the Senecas. The French governor reported that a pro-English chief "presented a belt from the [English] government to the Onontagues," forbidding them to receive de Lamberville and "ordering them to convey that Jesuit and his French companions to Orange [Albany]." The pro-French Indians refused. Instead they built a house and chapel "and the Te Deum and Mass were sung."

Little information survives of these new missions. English pressure was not relaxed and, when active hostilities resumed in 1709, the mission fell prey to the war. The final tragedy was described by the Canadian governor on November 14, 1709:

The English sent Abraham Schuyler to Onontague with four Dutchmen and some Englishmen to sing the War song in the Villages, and to present the hatchet to the Nations on the part of the Queen of England. Abraham Schuyler, having a long conversation with the Reverend Father de Lamberville, and having likewise expressed to him his regret at being obliged to present the hatchet to the Indians, and managed so well that he persuaded

20

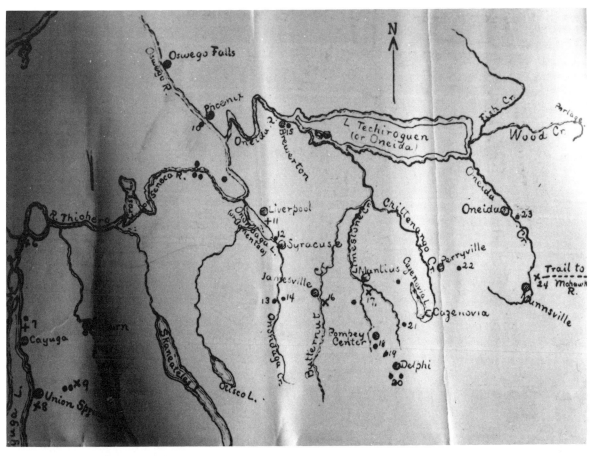

Jesuit missions to the Iroquois, shown on this segment from a larger mission map, include (11) Mission Ste. Marie de Ganentaa near Liverpool, (16) the final Onondaga mission near Jamesville burned in 1709, (17) Mission St. Jean Baptist at the main Onondaga village near Pompey, and (24) Mission St. Francois Xavier at the main Oneida village near Munnsville. (Photo: Chancery Archives)

this good father to come himself to Montreal to give me an account of what was passing, and as he desired nothing better than to send off Father de Lamberville, of whose influence over the minds of the Onnontagues he was aware, he took advantage of his absence, as soon as he saw him depart and told the Rev. Father de Mareuil, who had remained, that his life was not safe, insinuated to him that the only means of extricating himself from certain danger to which he was exposed was, to accompany them to Orange [Albany], which this good Father complied with.... In order to engage the Onnontague the more to declare war against us, Abraham Schuyler immediately made some drunken Indians set fire to the Father's chapel and house, which he first caused to be pillaged.

By an act of deception similar to that practiced by De Denonville 22 years earlier, the third and last Onondaga Mission ended.

VICTIMS OF THE NEWCOMERS

Historian Thomas O'Connor, after recording these events, noted that the missionaries had only one object, "the Glory of God through the conversion of souls." Convinced beyond all else that only through the grace of the sacraments could men and women earn eternal salvation, the priests delighted in recording the baptism, perseverance and happy death of virtuous Christians. Like their Spanish counterparts, the priests who served in New France were among the most energetic and enlightened men of their generation. Blocked in France by the suffocating embrace of royal absolutism, the passion for a renewed missionary church was extended overseas, reaching into the forests and river valleys of New York. Yet, as O'Connor pointed out, the number of converts was very small and, when the missionaries left the region early in the eighteenth century, "no permanent body of Christians remained on New York soil." Like the missionaries themselves, O'Connor attributed the result to the tenacity of "native superstition," the Iroquois' aversion to Christian marriage and their "weakness for intoxicants" which "released the most violent of savage passions."

This last factor pointed to the fur trade and the imperial rivalries to which the Indians fell victim. The missionaries could not extricate themselves from their dependence on French civil authorities. The reigning theory of church-state relations was Gallicanism, which placed the government of the Church in the body of French bishops and the king, with papal authority reduced to a minimum. This made the hierarchy de facto officers of the state and the clergy dependent upon civil authorities, a dependence radically intensified by the frontier conditions of the new world empire. In many cases, the Church opposed or resisted the policies of imperial officials, but the distances involved in communicating with France and the pressures of life in New France made such protests, at least in the short run, ineffective. The missionaries were regarded by most of the Indians and by the English as agents of French power and, willing or not they were. Left undisturbed by Dutch or English competitors, the French might have mounted enough force to break Iroquois resistance and the missions might have flourished. But the example of the Spanish colonies leaves little reason to believe that French imperial victory would have increased the odds on Indian survival, though they might have died Catholic, a prospect even the missionaries would not have found altogether Christian.

There was more to it than that. As the mission records indicate, and as was clearly evident in the establishment of Christian Indian villages, conversion was a matter of Europeanization as well as Christianization. Despite the theoretical Jesuit commitment to respect Indian culture, in practice, converts were expected to adopt Christian patterns of personal and family behavior and to become conversant with western civilization, of which the French thought theirs the ultimate expression. Originally the missionaries hoped to blend the French and Indian cultures through intermarriage, but both sides resisted. Instead, Christian Indians occupied a cultural no man's land. Life in the Christian villages necessarily required abandonment of Indian language, customs and traditions. It meant for individuals a sharp sense of separation from family, friends and the land, a whole way of life. Incorporated but not assimilated into a colonial civilization, at best only remnants of the old ways could survive. If that colonial civilization itself was defeated and driven from the scene, survival of Indian Christianity would become precarious, if not impossible. Unwilling to leave their converts in their villages, fearing they would lose their faith, reluctant to expose them to the exploitation of traders and officials over whom the clergy exercised diminishing influence, and unable to assimilate them to the best of French culture, the missionaries, to keep them Catholic, brought them to the villages. There they were suspended between two worlds, rejected by Indians and French alike, strangers in their own land. Later perhaps, that very distance might allow them to speak wisdom to both cultures. But for a moment which would last centuries, they were isolated and alone.

The Iroquois, caught up in the struggle for empire, could not win. They were among the earliest victims of the expansion of Europe; and the missionaries, in spite of themselves, were agents of that cruel process. As a nation in control of its destiny, the Iroquois were doomed. Allied with the English against the French, they found victory as deadly as defeat. Gradually they were driven from their land, some to perish to the north and west, others to survive in reservations on both sides of the border. Ironically, political and economic decline occasioned a remarkable religious renewal. In the early nineteenth century, under the inspirational leadership of Handsome Lake, the Seneca renewed the traditional faith and created a religion which came to dominate much of Indian culture in North America. Three centuries and more after Simon LeMoyne tasted the salt water near Onondaga Lake, some Americans began to think there might be a wisdom worth knowing in the religious traditions surviving in "the Old Way of Handsome Lake."

The story of Catholicism in upstate New York would begin again after 1800. It would be a new history made by men and women coming from countries far removed from the forests and valleys where the heroic missionaries and their struggling converts once celebrated the same Mass and preached the same Gospel. In time the newcomers would wish to know more of LeMoyne and Garacontie; they would honor the memory of the missionaries, venerate the martyrs, take pride in the faith of the holy Indians. They would invent a story of early Catholicism which would enhance the prestige of their own church, bent on vindicating itself in a hostile world. It would remain for their children and grandchildren to rediscover that story and read it in new ways amid the rush of historic events, among which would be the worldwide awakening of dominated native people and the cry of the poor for justice. Chastened by the tragedies of their own history but inspired by the power of the Gospel to reveal a vision of human dignity and a sense of the possibilities of human history, that generation would perhaps find in the Indians and their missionary companions some insight into the mysterious ways of Providence. For, as Simon LeMoyne discovered on his first visit to the warlike Iroquois, God is, after all, everywhere, and God works "in hearts where the faith has held sway."

A BAND
OF BROTHERS

EARLY SETTLEMENT AND PARISH BEGINNINGS
1800s-1850s

Most American Catholics think of the history of their church in terms of bishops and priests. This is natural enough because Catholicism in the years following the Protestant Reformation became a very clergy-centered Church which emphasized the ordained priesthood rather than the priesthood of all believers, the authority of the Church rather than personal interpretation of scripture, the significance of sacraments, especially the Eucharist, rather than the direct relationship between God and the individual human soul. Of course, at its best, Catholicism attempted to strike a balance between these poles of belief. However, in practice there was a natural tendency to identify the Church more and more with those elements which made it unique, especially the hierarchy of priests, bishops and pope.

This tendency toward a nearly exclusive identification of the Church with the clergy quite accurately reflected the conscious experience of American Catholics, who, in fact, often evaluated their parish in terms of the quality of pastoral services the priest provided. Historically, strong priests did unify congregations and mobilized their resources around the great constructive work of building the church, establishing the parochial school and raising the money needed to sustain these institutions. But, interspersed in the parish record of the first Mass, the visits of itinerant clergy and the often short-lived tenure of successive early pastors, is a record of lay initiative and leadership. Among the early Irish and German settlers of Central New York, later when Italians, Poles, Slovaks and other groups repeated those earlier experiences, almost always a group of lay people began the process, gathering for prayer or mutual assistance, then searching for a priest to serve them. It was they, "a band of brothers" and sisters in the faith, who had to buy the land, raise the funds to erect a church and demonstrate their capacity to support a priest. All this before their embryonic community could become a parish, a moment which happened when a resident priest arrived. After all, there were few priests in the United States. The American Church, unlike its continental European sister-churches, had no large endowments, no support from the state and no rich aristocrats to provide money. If there was to be a Church in the United States, or in Central New York, or in Utica, Binghamton or Deerfield, the Catholic people would have to create it. In short, the Church had to grow from the bottom up. While a visiting priest might plant a seed before moving on to the dozens of other villages awaiting his arrival, the people he left behind for a few weeks or a few months would have to cultivate that seed and make an organized Church where none had been before. That they did so again and again is remarkable testimony to the strength of their faith, to the ever-renewing vitality of Christianity in general and Catholicism in particular, and to the rich possibilities opened to the Church by the freedom of the new nation.

Between the close of the last Indian mission and the American Revolution, Catholic activity in Central New York all but ended. The wars which concluded with the treaty of Paris in 1763 established English control over the entire region. During the same period, powerful French factions harassed the Society of Jesus and, in 1773, the Jesuits were supressed, eliminating the most energetic agents of mission work in Indian country. The English, by the Quebec Act, guaranteed the continued work of the Catholic Church in Canada, but there was little likelihood that mission efforts would be welcome south of the border. New Yorkers remained unsympathetic to Catholics, even as anti-Catholicism eased elsewhere. Later the all but universal support of Catholics in other colonies for the Revolution and the new nation's alliance with Catholic France encouraged several states to move toward religious liberty. The Constitution's first amendment, adopted in 1791, provided that "Congress shall make no law respecting the establishment of religion or prohibiting the free exercise thereof." This was binding only upon the new federal government, not on the states. It was not until 1808 that New

York removed its constitutional provision requiring officers to swear an oath "abjuring all foreign allegiances ecclesiastical as well as civil," in effect barring Catholics from public office.

The history of formal Catholic activity in New York during these years was largely the record of the passing ministry of individual priests. The first priest known with certainty to have visited Central New York after the departure of the missionaries was Father John McKenna, an Irishman who arrived near present day Rome in 1773 with a company of 300 Catholics, mostly Scots and a few Irish. Their passage was arranged by Sir William Johnson, on whose land they settled. The hostility of their neighbors and the anti-Catholic spirit of the New York Assembly made the newcomers unsympathetic to the American cause when what Father McKenna called "the first Commotions and general rising of the Rebbels" took place in June 1775. By then, William Johnson was dead and his Tory son had fled to Canada. With the arrival of Revolutionary troops, McKenna and his Catholics followed. Once in Canada, many joined the British army with McKenna as their chaplain. After several unsuccessful campaigns, including one to Fort Stanwix, the priest returned to Ireland in 1778.

The New York Catholic Loyalists were unusual. Elsewhere their co-religionists supported the revolution. The Jesuits of Maryland reconstituted themselves as secular clergy under the vicar apostolic of London after the suppression of their order in 1773. One of their most prominent members, John Carroll,

---

A BISHOP AT ONEIDA

As the Catholic Church was beginning to take root in the newly independent United States, a curious proposition was put forth to Pope Pius VI: Would his holiness send a bishop to the Oneida Indians?

Peter Pinet was a French-born merchant out of Philadelphia who traded with the Oneida. He had convinced the Indians that he was personal envoy of the king of France and received from them a grant of 10 square miles, apparently for royal use. In 1787, he persuaded the Oneidas to ask the French ambassador to the United States to send them a priest. A Father Perrot arrived two years later, residing at Oneida Castle and incurring the criticism of the Rev. Samuel Kirkland, a Presbyterian missionary there. But historians have been unable to uncover any other information about this priest. He may have come from the French West Indies or somehow not been listed on Church or civil records; or he may have been an impostor.

Meanwhile, another French adventurer, Jean de la Mahotiere, calling himself an agent for the Oneidas, presented a petition to Pius VI through the papal nuncio at Paris. "We have built a church in the city of Oneida," said his document. "We have provided it with sacred vessels, bells, books and everything necessary for divine service." Mahotiere then asked the pope to appoint as bishop "the Rev. John Louis Victor Le Tonnelier de Coulonges, a man full of merit and good works, whom the Oneida nation and the chiefs of the Six Nations have nominated Bishop of Oneida and Primate of the Six Nations, and presented to your Holiness in that quality; he has expended at least two-thirds of his fortune in works of religion and benevolence; he has obtained of the Oneida nation the expulsion of the Episcopalian and Presbyterian ministers, as they have no longer among them either church or flock." Furthermore, Mahotiere told the pope, this would-be bishop was planning to bring six Capuchin friars with him to Oneida as soon as he was consecrated.

Nothing more is known of this project, nor of Father Perrot or Father Tonnelier because the pope apparently never replied to the request for a French bishop supported by the French king to an American Indian tribe on United States soil and within the territory of the new diocese of Baltimore. Perhaps the reason for no response is self-evident. As one historian has observed, "Had the endeavors of these individuals been realized, the Catholic history of this State might have had to record the story of a particularly unfortunate blunder perpetrated at the very beginning of organized Catholic life in the United States."

was appointed vicar apostolic for the new United States in 1784. When this arrangement proved unsatisfactory, Carroll and his priests received permission to elect a bishop. Carroll was chosen, and after consecration in Europe, he took charge of a diocese extending from Maine to Georgia and from the Atlantic to the Mississippi. Among a population of three million, there were between 25,000 and 30,000 Catholics served by 26 priests, most advanced in years. While still vicar apostolic, Carroll visited his prefecture as far north as New York City. There, Father Ferdinand Farmer of Philadelphia occasionally visited the city's small Catholic congregation of a few residents, diplomats and foreign visitors. This was the state's only Catholic church. Carroll reported to Rome that there were "at least 1,500" Catholics scattered through the state; "would that some spiritual succor could be afforded them," he added.

In 1793, a layman, Thomas Barry, laid the cornerstone of St. Mary's Church in Albany, the second church in the state and the first outside New York City. From that tiny beginning would spring the Church of Central New York, but first, as Carroll recognized, the Church had to be organized. Alone, he could hardly provide "spiritual succor" for Catholic fellow citizens like Barry. He worked hard to find priests, first establishing Georgetown College in hopes it would generate candidates for the priesthood. Then, with the help of Sulpician priests driven from their homeland by the French Revolution, he began St. Mary's seminary in Baltimore and Mount St. Mary's in Emmitsburg. At the same time, he persuaded Rome that his huge diocese needed more bishops. In 1808, new jurisdictions were established in Boston, New York, Philadelphia and Bardstown, Kentucky. For New York, a Dominican, Luke Concanen, was selected. Concanen asked Anthony Kohlmann, a former Jesuit recently arrived in the United States, to serve as his vicar

general. When Concanen died before reaching his diocese, Kohlman was appointed administrator. He in turn appointed Paul McQuade pastor of the tiny church in Albany, a parish which extended as far west as Buffalo. In 1814, another Irish Dominican, John Connolly, succeeded Concanen. When he arrived in the United States a year later, he found six priests to help him. Four of them, including McQuade, soon left for other posts. Connolly labored for a decade to find priests to serve his scattered congregations, which soon included a parish in Utica, but when he died in 1825 the situation had not improved much. The new bishop, appointed in 1826, was John Dubois, a Sulpician and founder of Mount St. Mary's. Under his administration, a rapidly expanding population in Central New York began to generate its own resources, erecting churches to serve as places of worship when an itinerant priest could visit and, perhaps, settle among them.

The most important single factor promoting the growth of the central portion of the state was the Erie Canal. Construction began in 1817 and navigation opened over its first section in 1820. The editor of a New York newspaper published a vivid account of the country through which the canal passed:

The country...from Rome to Salina was wild. The canal pierced the wilderness at Rome.... The land almost the entire distance was low, marshy and cold. The forests most of the distance were deep and dark and the advancing settlers had eschewed the region as unfit for cultivation, but the clearing for the canal let in a stretch of daylight, which enabled people to see more distinctly. The marshes and swamps were to a considerable extent drained by the canal; and its banks, instead of the shores of a gloomy forest, now for the most part refresh the sight by the prospect of a well settled country smiling under the hand of well rewarded industry.

Irish immigrants in large numbers worked in the construction of the canal, and later on the railroad along the Mohawk River. Upon the completion of the work, many of them settled in the towns and villages in the vicinity.

Serving these scattered communities were itinerant priests who grew used to horseback rides, mud roads and considerable hardship. Jesuit Father John Grassi, describing Catholic life in the United States, captured the experience of the New York missions:

> I shall say nothing of the services in city churches, because they are the same as in Europe, so far as the number of priests will permit: but it will not be without interest to say something of those which are held in the country churches situated at a distance from any dwelling house, which are by far most numerous. On Saturday, the missionary leaves his residence, and goes to take up his lodgings with some Catholic family near the church. Having arrived at the house, he puts the Blessed Sacrament in some decent place, and also the Holy Oils, without which he never sets out on a journey. On the following morning he rides to the church, and ties his horse to a bush. The whole morning is spent in hearing confessions: meanwhile the people from distances of four, six, ten miles, and even more, are coming in on horseback, so that often the church is entirely surrounded with horses. Mass begins towards noon; during the celebration, those who can read make use of prayerbooks, and pious hymns, for the most part in English, are sung by a choir of men and women. The sermon comes after the Gospel, and it is preceded by the Gospel read in the vernacular. The preacher either reads or delivers his sermon, according to inclination and sometimes it is deferred until after Mass to enable the priest to take some refreshment, which the faithful never fail to supply.... Vespers are not said, as the people live so far off and are so scattered; and so when Mass is over, the children recite the cathecism [sic], infants are baptized, or the ceremonies are supplied in the case of those already baptized in danger, prayers for the dead are recited or the funeral services are performed over those who have been buried in the churchyard during the absence of the priest. Finally, one must attend to those who ask for instruction in order to join the Church, or who wish to be united in the bonds of holy Matrimony.

THE MOTHER CHURCH: ST. JOHN'S, UTICA

Missionary visits were not frequent. Many early settlers retained the memory of childhood faith and family devotions. In all-male labor camps, few occasions arose to call forth religious practice. In towns and on farms, however, Catholic families were more inclined to renew the practice of their faith. As might be expected, more prosperous and settled lay people took the lead in gathering their scattered fellow Catholics to begin the process of establishing a church. Among the trustees of St. Mary's in Albany, elected in April 1813, were two such men, John C. Devereux of Utica and James Lynch of Rome. At their invitation, Father McQuade, the pastor, visited their towns to offer Mass and collect

BIRTHDAY LETTER TO MY DEAR WIFE

Nicholas Devereux was a devoted husband and father, and his correspondence with his wife, Mary, is filled with testimony of faith and love. While in Albany on business, he shared with his Protestant wife an important religious experience.

June 8, 1823.

"My dear wife, how very anxious I am to see you and my little family. I never had so much anxiety to see home before, for my dear Mary, my heart blood is concentrated on you and my dear little children. May God guard and protect you. Yesterday — 7th of June — was my birthday. I felt remarkable gloomy all day, that I have spent thirty-two years on this earth in so unworthy a manner, but I yet put my confidence in God that hereafter I will lead a better life for the time He is pleased to leave me on this earth. I never before had such a knowledge of our total dependence on our good God, as I now have, and, my dear Mary, join with me in prayer that this knowledge may be ingrafted in our minds, that we may hand it down to our little children, that they may have cause to bless their parents when we shall be no more. In fulfilling my duty in the world, my dear wife, it becomes necessary that we should be separated from each other, but my Mary, it will be but short; let us join with our united minds that hereafter we may meet in that happy country where time will have no end, and to look on this transitory life in the light we should do. We must join with fervency of prayer, begging of the Almighty God to grant us His blessing and protection — the spirit of prayer as that of faith is a gift from God which we must ask for with confidence and humility. I regret that you could not have gone with me to Montreal — it is a very interesting place — to see so many as I saw them in the constant service of their God, who devote their lives (as my dear sister Catharine does) to prepare for another and a better world. How happy must that mind be who, clear from the trouble of this world, can say with confidence "O Lord, I am Thine, do with me as you will. They will be done."... I am delighted to hear by Brother John's letter that Mr. Hurley will baptize my dear little John C. before he leaves Utica. Kiss my dear little Hanna and John for me, my dear Mary, and rest assured that I shall always be your affectionate husband, N.Devereux."

funds for his huge parish. Between visits, as Devereux's son recalled years later, the lay people expressed their faith and constituted themselves as a Catholic community, a church:

There were very few Catholics in this village and it is in the recollection of several persons that one of the Devereux parlors would easily contain all the Catholics..... Indeed it was their regular place of meeting every Sunday to hear one of their number read Mass prayers and a sermon. In this way the faith was kept alive and there grew up a bond of Sympathy and Union which kept them together like a Band of Brothers which was probably in the hands of God the reason of their great success in planting and establishing so soon afterwards a permanent Church Establishment....

John Devereux was born in 1774 in Ireland of mixed French and Irish stock. He spent a year in France studying dancing and learning to play the violin before coming to the United States in 1796 or 1797. He worked for a time in New England as a dancing master. He told his grandchildren he "danced $1,000 out of the Yankees" before moving to Albany, where he met and married Ellen Barry. By 1802 he was settled in Utica, where he opened a dry goods store and soon was joined by his brother Nicholas. The Devereux brothers were among the city's most prominent citizens. John served as incorporator of the first bank and later was the first elected mayor. Nicholas Devereux was among the major promoters of the Erie canal and a leading figure in a group which purchased the massive holdings of the Holland Land Company. He invested in local businesses, particularly in woolen mills. Nicholas was devoted to the scriptures, from which he read for 15 minutes each morning. His family claimed he completed the testaments 17 times before he died. He also purchased plates in Europe for the printing of the first Catholic Bible in the United States and worked actively for its distribution. Like his brother he taught children their Sunday school lessons, with great emphasis upon reading and memorizing scripture texts. In later years, he helped the Franciscan friars establish themselves in Western New York and launch St. Bonaventure College. In 1855, he offered to donate $1,000 for the new American College in Rome if 99 other Catholics would do the same, a fundraising appeal that was counted a great success.

As they developed the Church in Utica, local Catholics received help from Protestant friends. In return they made frequent donations to the building and charitable projects of Protestant congregations. In 1819, they brought together a small group of laymen from as far away as Rochester and incorporated themselves as "the first Catholic Church of the Western District of the State of New York." In January 1819, the first public Mass was celebrated at the Utica Free Academy, a non-sectarian school the Devereux family had helped start. Nicholas Devereux's wife, at that time still a Protestant, wrote her mother describing the event:

> *I was very much surprised to find so many Catholics in this part of the country, Some came 50 miles, and some two days journey to partake of the sacrament. This will show you how much attached they are to their religion. The canal has brought many Catholics to this place.*

Shortly after, a child was baptized and the ceremony was attended by many of the Protestants in the community. Mrs. Devereux reassured her mother of her attachment to her own church, but two decades later she herself became a Catholic.

Impressed by the progress of the community, Bishop Connolly sent Father John Farnam, recently arrived from Ireland and then assisting Father Gorman, the pastor in Albany, to reside in Utica. Father Farnam was to "teach, preach, administer Sacraments and perform all other Ecclesiastical functions" throughout the state, save for the areas covered by the New York City and Albany parishes." Recognizing that a lay-led community was well established, Connolly added that the "Catholic Gentlemen of Utica" had not given him "a discretionary power of sending them a priest," so Father Gorman should "request" that they accept Farnam. Apparently they did so gladly. The new priest celebrated Mass in Utica in March 1821, and then left on visits to communities across the state. With generous financial assistance from the Devereux broth-

First St. John's church in Utica, 1821 (Photo: St John parish)

ers, and with land donated by a non-Catholic woman, work began on a church which was dedicated as St. John's in August 1821. Two years later, Farnam left for New York and the parish then was served by a string of pastors, none of whom remained more than two years. In 1833, less than three months after his ordination, Walter J. Quarter was appointed to take over the direction of St. John's and its missions. The number of calls made on the pastor from outlying villages and hamlets was greater than ever, although another resident pastor now was located 50 miles away at Salina. The growth of population had secured for Utica its city charter in 1832. While the rate of increase of the Catholic body was less than that of the general population, the little congregation soon outgrew its first church, so Father Quarter set to work to raise funds for a new and larger structure.

On May 1, 1834, three Sisters of Charity arrived in Utica to open St. John's Asylum and School in a small wooded building adjacent to the church, another project largely financed by the Devereux brothers. When Father Quarter was transferred to New York City late in 1839, his place was taken first by the Rev. Francis Ferrall, then after Ferrall's death, by Thomas Martin, a Dominican. Father Martin aroused controversy by his strong support of temperance and his attacks on the authorities at the state asylum where, it was charged, Catholic employees and inmates were required to attend Protestant services. Patrick Stokes succeeded Martin, and like all his predecessors, he was plagued by problems with the trustees.

In Utica, the bishop and priests faced a problem common throughout the United States — trusteeism. State laws provided that, to secure tax exemption, churches had to be owned by lay trustees elected by the congregation. Church law and practical circumstances led the bishops to claim the right to appoint pastors, while the trustees controlled the purse. This set the stage for conflict and misunderstanding if the pastor proved unacceptable to the congregation or if the laity attempted to control his behavior, deprive him of support or deny him use of the church. In most accounts of trustee problems in Utica and elsewhere, the argument is made that the hard-working priests were unjustly treated by the trustees, who seem vaguely heretical, as if they believed that they, and not the priests and bishop, were responsible for the Church. In some cases, trustees were in fact less than responsible in their approach to Church affairs. Yet, in the early history of Utica, while the trustees of St. John's are pilloried for their treatment of the early pastors, John and Nicholas Devereux are celebrated as deeply pious, dedicated, generous and loyal Catholics. Throughout the period of conflict, John and Nicholas Devereux were also active members of the parish and, surprisingly, for much of the period they were also trustees. Record books indicate that the trustees were assiduous in their efforts to raise funds. They stood at the door of the church at all Masses and vespers to collect pew rentals, instructing the sexton to make sure that those who had not paid for their pews were not admitted to the church proper, and they appointed committees to call on

their Protestant fellow citizens for donations for the new church. They hired an organist and arranged his conveyance to the church; they hired others to clean the church, and at one point, voted to make a large donation to the orphanage from their personal funds. They even sent an annual contribution of $50 to Bishop John Hughes after he assumed charge of the diocese in 1838. Regularly, they voted to pay the pastor a salary, $600 for Father Quarter in 1834, $700 for later pastors.

Why then, did the disputes arise? One clue is found in the record books. People did not contribute as they should have, or at least as they had promised to. Again and again the trustees appointed committees to call on pewholders who had failed to fulfill their obligations. In some cases, the trustees resented the fact that the priest was less than energetic in supporting their appeals. If, as in one case, the pastor also antagonized the local non-Catholic community by charges of prejudice or by assaults on the liquor trade which alienated important members of the congregation, the trustees may well have been irritated. One leading parishioner, Paul McCabe, known for his generosity to the poor and second only to the Devereuxs in his support of the orphanage, owned a brewery and a distillery. The Devereuxs, for their part, devoted large portions of their fortune to the orphanage. They might have wondered about clergymen who disputed over a portion of their salary when the needs of the parishioners were not being met fully. In addition, the priests paid by this congregation were absent often, ministering to missions and stations at a great distance from the city, and collecting from the people there. In these circumstances, the trustees' resistance to paying full salaries, set at a level comparable to those in New York City parishes, at least becomes understandable.

For their part, priests were adjusting to new conditions in the United States, where the entire support of the Church rested upon the congregations. One historian has argued that, in the late eighteenth and early nineteenth century, the Protestant ministry moved "from office to career" as the minister, who once could depend upon "the church" to find him a pulpit after he had received the proper education, increasingly had to find for himself a congregation which would accept him and pay his salary. Priests, who understood themselves somewhat differently in the more corporate and sacramental life of the Catholic Church, undoubtedly found it hard to accept the idea of dependence on the people for their income. They naturally desired a more secure and dependable "living" and resented the suggestion, found in early Utica history, that to some degree at least they were accountable to the trustees and to the people who paid their salary. It would not be too much to suggest that any desire the lay trustees had to "control" the clergy by decisions about the time and length of ceremonies, the disposition of church funds and the services expected was matched by the desire of both clergy and hierarchy to limit, if not eliminate, accountability to the congregation. They feared with good reason that direct accountability might lead to the compromise of doctrine or morality. Less admirably, they worried that it might limit their ability to determine the shape of the Church. That the clergy eventually were successful in establishing such authority was, in part, a result of their control of the sacraments and the sources of Catholic legitimacy, and also a result of the fact that they were able to transcend community divisions and draw people together around common objectives which priests and people shared. It was unfortunate that, in doing so, they were led to exclude the laity from any formal role in, or responsibility for, the life and mission of the organized Church.

The experience of St. John's, where lay leadership preceded arrival of a pastor, was repeated in other communities in Central New York. Nicholas Devereux had a hand in the formation of the second English speaking Utica parish, St. Patrick's. He helped organize a string of steam woolen mills in West Utica and, in 1849, 13 Catholics gathered in the office of the Globe mill and decided to approach the curate at St. John's, Father Patrick Carahar, to ask his help in founding a new parish in that part of the city. The bishop consented and Caraher agreed "to settle down in a congregation so poor with no hope of improvement." Carahar, with the help of his parishioners, constructed a small wooden chapel, installing a few pews and small melodeon and offering the first Mass on St. Patrick's Day 1850. Two years later, a permanent church was built on a site formerly occupied by a tavern and a Lutheran church which had been destroyed by fire. Devereux personally purchased land for a rectory. The church, rectory and school left the parish with a large debt, but the community flourished until these financial problems caused a major crisis many years later.

AN EXPANDING NETWORK OF MISSIONS

Rome's Catholic history may have predated that of Utica, because there is one indication that as early as 1798, an Irish Capuchin, Father Thomas Flynn, served near Fort Stanwix. In 1786, Dominick Lynch, a Catholic and New York City merchant, purchased a large plot of land in the area. Later, he added other land purchases and, in 1796, the village of Lynchville was laid out. Lynch and his wife donated a portion of the land to the board of supervisors of Oneida County for the purpose of erecting a "Church and School house." Over the next few years, the area was served by traveling priests. Benedict Fenwick, later bishop of Boston, made at least one visit to the town, now known as Rome. Connolly, on a visit upstate, was received by the Lynch family, and the community was attended from St. John's after its formation in 1819. In 1837, Father William Beecham, after battling with the St. John's trustees, received permission to move his residence to Rome. There probably was already a temporary church, but it was only with Beecham's arrival that legal steps were taken to form a congregation.

Unusual in his energy and longevity, Father Willian Beecham served in Rome from 1837 to 1876 and became a legend, so secure in his authority and in the confidence of the people that he was known good naturedly as "the Pope of Rome." After a year at Rome, he described his work to the bishop:

The churches which I attend are three, viz. St. Peter's at Rome, St. Mary's Verona, Irish Ridge, and St. John's, Turin, Lewis County, all of which are dedicated, together with a Meeting House in Vienna built for that purpose since my appointment to this Mission. We have a private chapel in Florence where we expect after a short time to build a Meeting House, though not yet commenced. Along the Black River Canal now in operation we have three places built as temporary meeting houses where we have Service occasionally in order that men on the public works may have an opportunity of complying with their duty.

The Verona Church and St. Peter's were served on the first two Sundays of each month, the others less regularly. Beecham thought there were approximately 900 Catholics under his jurisdiction, not counting those on the public works "who have no fixed residence." Beecham was a regularly appointed pastor, so the bishop thought he might send in a contribution for diocesan needs, but Beecham thought otherwise. He told the

bishop that, when sent to Utica, he had been promised $400 a year. In eight months at St. John's he "never received as much as one cent from the congregation" and, since coming to Rome, he "did not receive as much as would be sufficient to pay for board and other expenses attendant on a clergyman, viz, the keeping of a horse." He also owed for his board, because there was no rectory and he lived at a private home. All his parishioners promised "they will be liberal towards me and the erection of our church," but for the present they were unable to pay because of their own problems "procuring and building shanties." Beecham was nevertheless optimistic. Two of the trustees were honest, he thought, and Lynch had given him "possession of the lot," and promised "one hundred thousand of bricks and some stone to the church."

In 1838, the Lynch family deeded to the new church the property set aside earlier for that purpose. Unfortunately one of the provisions of the original agreement was that this should be done in accordance with the "direction and appointment of a majority of the freeholders" of the town. Opposition grew in the largely Protestant community as a contract was let and building materials gathered for the Catholic Church. Finally Jaspar Lynch suggested that, in return for the contested site, the church should take the space formerly occupied by the state arsenal. There St. Peter's church was completed in 1841, when Bishop John Hughes visited. Hughes recorded the event:

Standing on an eminence that overlooks the railroad and the town [is] a beautiful church of Grecian architecture, erected on the ground that was gratuitously given by Jaspar Lynch, Esq., the original proprieter [sic] of the village. Not only did this gentleman give the site, but he also most generously contributed toward the erection of the building, the beautiful portico of which was entirely at his expense.

When John Devereux went on to lead the formation of St. John's, one of its original trustees was Thomas McCarthy of Salina.

Born in Ireland, McCarthy came to "Salt Point," opened a small store and soon became an influential citizen. On a trip to New York City, he persuaded James Lynch to come to Salina. When DuBois became bishop in 1826, he soon had a letter from McCarthy assuring the bishop that he and his associates had half the money for a church and he himself would

THE POPE OF ROME

Father William Beecham was born in Denmond, Queens County, Ireland, on November 12, 1805. He was baptized into the Established (Anglican) Church, but later his entire family joined the Catholic Church. While still a boy, Beecham entered the College of Carlow. Coming with his parents to the United States in 1836, he settled in New York City. Within months, he was ordained a priest by Bishop Dubois and assigned to St. Mary's parish in New York City. He later was appointed assistant pastor of St. John's parish in Utica.

In 1838, at the age of 33, he built St. Peter's church in Rome and was named pastor of a widespread congregation. When he died 38 years later in the same parish, Rome shopkeepers closed their stores and three bishops and 64 priests from throughout the state attended his funeral. In his obituary, the New York *Freeman's Journal* wrote:

"In about nine months afterwards he was sent to administer to the spiritual wants of the Catholics living in the northern and southern portions of Oneida County, and scattered over the territory now embraced in Lewis, Jefferson, St. Lawrence, Madison, Onondaga, Chenango, and Broome Counties, with permission to make his home in Rome, Carthage or Ogdensburg. He selected Rome as being easy of access from the different points of his vast mission, and also, no doubt, on account of its close proximity to Utica, where he could avail himself of the wise counsels of a most prudent priest, and where

Father William Beecham (Photo: Chancery Archives)

donate the site if they could have a priest. Dubois had only 22 priests in the entire state, but when the laymen finished their church in 1830, he sent Francis O'Donohue with jurisdiction over Onondaga, Oswego, Cortland, Tompkins and half of Madison counties. With the new St. John the Baptist church in Salina as a base, O'Donohue and his successors roamed that vast area. In July 1839, Michael Haes arrived and reported to the bishop that church buildings were now available in a number of towns, including nearby Syracuse, where the Catholics had purchased a former Episcopal church and renamed it St. Mary's. In 1843, Haes took charge of the Syracuse parish. Between that

he could go to fortify himself with the Sacraments.... From Rome he traveled over this vast extent of country, baptizing the children of the early emigrants, blessing marriages, anointing the dying, hearing confessions, and administering the Bread of Life day after day, encouraging and exhorting all to repentance and a life of holiness, till from Rome to Rochester, from Binghamton to the Adirondacks, the name of Father Beecham became a household word, at the very mention of which blessings and benedictions without number were bestowed upon him, as no doubt numerous and fervent prayers will now ascend to God for the repose of his soul.... Those early settlers, when they wished to make remittances to Ireland and other parts of Europe, gave him the money and requested him to secure a draft and forward it to their relatives. And as he passed along through his mission, he not only announced the glad tidings of the Gospel, but also very frequently carried welcome news from the fond friends whom the emigrants had left in the dear old home. Thus this good priest was more than a father to the early settlers, and we need not wonder that he was their joy and their pride.... Over twenty years ago the death of his brother, Mr. Joseph Beecham, and his estimable lady (sister of Bishop Quarter, first Bishop of Chicago), brought upon him the responsibility of caring for, and educating their six orphans, and of economically administering their estate. He was not untrue to the trust committed to his care by the dying wife of his deceased brother. He had the consolation of having his last days made joyous by those same children, and was consoled in his last moments by their tender care and pious attentions, by their sympathy and prayers... When he took charge of the mission there were not ten Catholic families in what is now known as the city of Rome, and even the few that were there were very poor. In such circumstances it was almost impossible to succeed, and no wonder the Archbishop told him that even if he succeeded in building it would be sold for debts. Still Father Beecham was not discouraged... He had the satisfaction in 1840 of seeing his efforts crowned with success in the completion of the church and in the liquidation of nearly all claims against it. We may now build more stately temples, more pretentious edifices to the glory of God, but we must not forget the circumstances — we must remember that in those days the building of St. Peter's was a work of far greater magnitude than the erection of more expensive and elegant churches in these days."

date and the appointment of William Bourke as pastor in 1877, St. John the Baptist was served by 11 pastors whose average tenure was less than four years. This was an indication of the pressure that a growing Catholic community placed on the resources of the diocese and the pervasive instability which plagued Catholic life. Meanwhile, Haes and the lay leaders of Syracuse moved into their frame wooden church for their first Mass on Christmas Day 1842. From then until 1858, Haes ministered there and throughout the area, multiplying missions and stations, sowing the seeds of many other churches.

While the leadership provided by the Devereux, Lynch and McCarthy families was dramatic, other towns also often found a particular family, more settled and a bit better off, who became the focal point for the initial organization of Catholic communities. Stephen Prendergast in Phoenix, for example, gave over his home for Mass during his lifetime, and when he died in 1879, he left land from his farm to construct a church and contributed $2,500 to the cost, with his surviving relatives matching that amount. Prendergast also assisted the congregation in Baldwinsville, donating lumber for the construction of the first church there. Mass was first said there in 1845 in a private home; five years later two hundred persons were showing up for Mass in a converted band room. When the priest could not come, legend has it, the Irish parishioners in a group walked 14 miles to St. John's in Syracuse, sometimes encountering the hostility of their Protestant neighbors. In 1851, land was purchased, the congregation dug the foundation and the new church was built with Prendergast's lumber. The parishioners then paid an admission fee of 50 cents to attend the dedication. While 116 persons rented pews and the people looked after the property, weekly collections were small, going over $10 only three times during a three year period preceding appoint-

Thomas McCarthy (Photo: Onondaga Historical Society)

ment of the first resident pastor in 1867.

Settlers came more slowly to the southern portion of what later would become the diocese of Syracuse. Until the completion of the Chenango Canal in 1837, Broome County was less accessible from the north than from the south, via the Susquehanna River valley. Bishop Francis Patrick Kenrick of Philadelphia was one of the first priests to visit the area, pausing there while on a visitation through his diocese in 1833. He was followed by occasional mission priests, including Arthur Wainwright, whose visit was described in a contemporary account:

On Sunday an altar and canopy were erected on [a small lawn at the residence of a Catholic family] as also benches to accommodate some hundreds of persons, all of which were occupied during the divine service and the delivery of a sermon; and in the afternoon, when the Rev gentleman preached again, amongst those as-

38

sembled were the principal citizens of the place. At the early service, a piano was judiciously placed, the performance of which, accompanied by a few voices, added not a little to the interest of a scene so novel in Binghamton.

Kenrick returned in 1836, staying with the family of Edward White, one of the original settlers of the area, and the major organizer of the community. The Catholic families occasionally gathered for prayer and the religious instruction of the children while constructing a church, collecting money for that purpose from Irish railroad workers. Thomas G. Waterman, a leading Protestant, offered a piece of land, but it was declined in favor of what was regarded as a more appropriate site. However, Protestants contributed to the drive, and the Catholics also received help from Ireland and Cuba, not unusual at the time, as settlers appealed to friends, acquaintances or simply communities which they had heard might be generous to such mission appeals. According to a local source, the "self-constituted committee" that undertook the project included a blacksmith, miner and student; their "stock of faith (was) disproportionate to their stock of cash." Father Quarter from Utica began visiting the new church of St. John's fairly regularly. When he went to New York to collect for the church, Bishop Dubois refused to allow the subscription, but assumed the mortgage debt of $1,000. After his death, his vicar general had the balance taken up by the trustees of St. Peters church in the city. In 1843, Andrew Doyle was appointed the first resident pastor; he was succeeded after a year by John J. Sheridan. In 1847, when James F. Hourigan arrived, he found a handsome small church and a school conducted by two Catholic ladies. He soon began plans for a cemetery and a new and larger church.

IMMIGRANTS OF A DIFFERENT MOLD

Germans had been in the Mohawk Valley since the early eighteenth century, when settlers from the Palatinate were encouraged to come to America by Queen Ann. When St. John's of Utica was organized, a handful of Germans worshiped there and the number grew slowly through the 1830s. Visiting missionaries reported their presence and complaints sometimes were heard of their difficulty listening to English sermons and making themselves understood in the confessional. As in so many immigrant communities, lay people took the initiative in forming Catholic organizations. By 1835, when German clergy began to visit the city on a regular basis, the community had provided itself with a "house of prayer" near St. John's. In 1839, the St. Joseph's Society, organized to visit the sick, began seeking the permanent services of a priest. A year later, this group named a committee of trustees, purchased a Methodist church and moved it to a new site. Having done so, the committee tended to see themselves as responsible for the welfare of the community. Like other trustees, they were reluctant to turn financial affairs over to the priests who came to serve them. Still they were anxious to have a priest. They tried to recruit Father Francis Guth, then serving in a short-lived New York seminary. He wrote the bishop in 1841, letting him know he had no sympathy with lay control:

I hardly think I would...have troubled you with a letter were it not for the step I understand the Germans of Utica have taken concerning me. When some weeks ago I visited them they insisted very eagerly that I should come to stay altogether with them. I told them I had no wish for it, nor any reluctance, that I am, without any reserve or restriction, at the disposal of the Bishop.

In 1842, the church received its first pastor, not Guth but Joseph Prost, a Redemptorist priest. A distinguished Viennese traveler, Dr. Joseph Salzbacher, describes the parish of Father Prost's time:

The little church is a frame building,

PEDDLER MURPHY AND THE DODGE FAMILY

When Francis Murphy was born in 1800 in Ireland, English occupation law prevented Catholics from receiving formal religious education. Francis learned his faith from his parents and his parish priest. As a 26-year-old immigrant, he brought to Utica his deep-but-simple Catholicism. Murphy and others like him would have blushed at the thought of being counted among the Catholic missionaries, but that was what many of the early settlers were.

In March 1835, near the end of what was later called "the winter of the deep snow." Murphy got lost in a storm while travelling in his peddler's cart from Syracuse to Cazenovia. He found himself at the home of the distinguished Captain David Foote Dodge, a wealthy farmer near Pompey. Murphy was given shelter for the night. During the supper conversation he acknowledged that he was a Catholic, the first the Dodge family had ever met. His hosts were members of the Presbyterian church, where Captain Dodge was a deacon. They shared the suspicion toward Catholicism that was common in those days. Nevertheless, the Dodges' allowed Murphy to remain for the evening, and their conversation revolved on the beliefs and myths about the Catholic Church. Ada Dodge showed some interest in religious beliefs and practices different from her puritan heritage. David, while he appreciated the sincerity of his guest, expressed sorrow that such a sensible young man would believe in the Catholic Church. "Do not pity me, sir," answered Murphy. "...If you only knew what the Catholic faith is, you would have a better opinion of it."

On leaving the next morning, the peddler offered his hosts some books to explain the faith better than he could. In the coming months, Ada and David read these with interest, along with other books which Murphy dropped off when his trade brought him near Pompey. Soon the Dodges' were telling friends about their attraction to Catholicism. This led to a heresy trial in the Presbyterian church, from which both were expelled. "My belief, my whole belief, is in

Francis Murphy (Photo: Bill Oley, Pompey NY)

40

and was formerly the property of the Methodists, from whom the parish bought it for the sum of $1200.00, but   *still owes half this sum. Under the active and zealous cooperation of Father Prost the Church is already*

whatever the Roman Catholic Church teaches," testified Mrs. Dodge. "All whatever that Church teaches, I believe firmly. All whatever that Church condemns, I disbelieve and reject. Now this is my faith, and I bid you farewell."

Soon, less than 16 months after she encountered Catholic Christianity in the person of Francis Murphy, Ada Dodge joined the Church. After another one and a half years of prayer, Catholic reading, and correspondence with some of the leading priests in America, and continued contact with Murphy, Captain Dodge also became a Catholic. Eventually, the Dodge children and other members of the family (including an Episcopalian priest) also were received into the Church.

The Dodges' conversions were noted in publications in England, Ireland and France. Several Irish immigrants sought out Pompey because of Captain Dodge, and the Dodges offered their home for services of visiting priests until the growing Catholic community built a church on land given by Captain Dodge. Murphy, meanwhile, married a Protestant woman who later became a Catholic. The couple is counted among the founders of St. Lucy parish in Syracuse. Dodge and Murphy remained friends, and both saw their daughters join the Sisters of Charity.

In the Church's pre-diocesan infancy of the 1830s, many Catholics were poor on book-born doctrinal information, but rich in belief and enthusiasm for the Church. One-and-a-half centuries later, the Catholic Church is the largest religious community in this area of New York State. The Church continues to grow because of people like Francis Murphy — with faith bright enough to attract, gentle enough to invite, simple and honest enough to inspire. And the Church is enlivened by people like Ada and David Dodge — with curiosity, integrity, a willingness to hear God and respond to His call through the Church.

David Foote Dodge (Photo: Bill Oley, Pompey NY)

*furnished with everything necessary
and is well kept up. I said Mass in
this church in a beautiful vestment.
The congregation numbers about 80
families or 400 souls, very good
Catholics who sincerely love their
Pastor and pay him an annual salary
of $300.00 despite their poverty and
small earnings.*

This idyllic picture of German Catholic life in Utica was not to last long. In 1843, Adelbert Inama replaced Prost and within months reported to the bishop that the church was "the private property of several citizens who wished to resell it." Inama moved on to Syracuse. When Florian Schwenninger arrived in 1844, he reported to his superiors in Europe that "the trustees think they are the legal superiors of the priest and therefore have the right to watch over the pastor's actions, his work, his housekeeping." Father Florian would have none of it, denouncing the trustees as thieves and scoundrels from the altar and irritating the saloon keepers among them by preaching against hard liquor and Sunday drinking. When Hughes ordered the trustees to turn over control of church funds to the priest, the congregation divided sharply, with about two thirds following the pastor and one third a wealthy saloon keeper, Joseph Masseth. Several times Schwenninger had to say Mass at St. John's. On one occasion, he slept there because the dissidents threatened his safety. On another occasion, he celebrated Mass in the school, because the trustees locked him out of the church. Law suits followed, but in a short space of time several of the "goats," as the dissidents were called, died, one committed suicide and the pastor's supporters got the best of a fist fight outside the courthouse, all of which the pastor saw as signs of divine favor. Undaunted, Schwenninger built another German Church in Rome

over the objections of Father Beecham, the pastor there. But all was not yet settled in Utica, where more law suits were filed. Even a visit from Hughes and a mission preached to unify the parish failed to bring the factions together. Father Theodore Noethen of Syracuse, at Hughes' behest, tried to mediate the dispute. He thought that the Benedictine's extremism was making things worse. He offered to switch parishes with Schwenninger and this was done, but the latter became convinced Noethen had gone over to the dissidents and the two priests became bitter enemies, a conflict that became public when they disputed in the German press over temperance. St. Joseph's remained torn by public disputes until the arrival of Franciscan pastors in 1860.

When Father Inama moved west, he discovered numerous German settlements along the way and near Salina, "eight hundred souls" made up "largely of people of no wealth, farmers in Manlius, saltworkers and laborers in Salina and Syracuse." In contrast to other communities, lay leaders had not appeared. In fact, according to Inama, "on account of the lack of a priest of their own, the reception of the holy sacraments, and in fact, nearly all religious practices, had almost ceased among them." It was "highest time," Inama thought, that "something be done to save them from formal apostacy or complete indifference." Inama successfully appealed to Europe for financial assistance, noting that with a priest among them, the people's "enthusiasm begins to reawaken." By the end of 1845, Inama had completed work on the Church of the Assumption.

Like other early pastors, Inama had trouble getting paid, but he was understanding. It bothered him that, for 16 years, Catholics in "Constableville, Salina, Syracuse, Manlius, etc." had waited for a priest. In Constablesville, he found a "very numerous but poor peasant-community...waiting in vain for

First St. John the Baptist church in Syracuse, 1831–1874 (Photo: Onondaga Historical Association)

a promised priest." So far "no one has had compassion on these poor people," he noted, contrasting their situation with the Protestants who had their own mission societies, salaried itinerant preachers and Bibles printed in German. He advised the people of Manlius, who were "good (and) pious" but felt "neglect and sadly deserted," to turn these "Protestant" Bibles over to him but definitely not to burn them, as they were tempted. He feared that "ordering the Word of God to be burned would doubtless have given me a notorious name in all the journals of North America." Inama was referring to an incident in northern New York in 1843 in which an overzealous priest had destroyed Protestant Bibles distributed to his people and aroused a national outcry.

American Protestant proselytization was not the only danger among the Germans, because not all German immigrants were Catholics; Many were Lutheran and Reformed and their churches could provide an alternative for disenchanted Catholics, although historical

European animosities, regional as well as religious, inhibited such transfers. Yet the option was there, as a story in the *Syracuse Standard* in December 1855 indicated. A prominent citizen died and three of the large German societies gathered to accompany his body to Assumption Church, of which he was a member. However, the pastor refused to perform the ceremony because the man was a member of a secret society condemned by the Church. As the newspaper reported, "the German Protestant clergyman was called upon and officiated, and interesting remarks were made at the grave by...other German citizens."

Bishops only reluctantly accepted the separation of German communities, like those in Utica and Syracuse, from English speaking congregations. As early as the 1790s, caught in a dispute between a French pastor and a predominately Irish congregation, John Carroll had told a group of trustees that the Church in the United States should not have "German, Irish or French parishes" but "Catholic and American parishes." However, it was not to be, at least not yet. German immigrants thought themselves as Catholic and American as anyone else, but they also wished to be German and would not settle easily into congregations without a clergyman of their own. Establishment of national parishes — first for the Germans, then for others — was never easy. Based on language, not territory, they were regarded as temporary and often had problems dealing with pastors of neighboring territorial parishes. To the minority nationalities, the behavior of Irish priests and bishops often appeared as prejudice against their language, customs and traditions. However, there also were practical reasons as well for Irish American bishops and priests to regard the formation of nationalities within the Church as adding further complexity and cost to the already staggering task of evangelization. Father In-

43

ama wrote his superiors in Austria that Irish bishops were his chief obstacle. He said they "naturally" desired to integrate German settlers so they could do without German missionaries, while the English speaking pastors would "suffer considerable pecuniary loss" by German withdrawal. Indeed, he thought the congregation at Salina, St. John the Baptist, might not survive the formation of his new parish of Assumption in Syracuse. By 1845, he believed most priests and bishops had become convinced of the need for "special care for the German Catholics," but they regarded it as a "bitter necessity."

BUILDING FROM THE BOTTOM UP

Ethnic problems and the problem of trustee control of Church property were met head on by John Hughes, who took charge of the New York diocese in 1838. Hughes was the great organizer of Catholic life in the state of New York. A militant and determined man, he guided the Church through years of conflict with non-Catholics that threatened to destroy the relative good will seen in the generous support of many Protestants for the original church building campaigns in places like Salina, Binghamton and Utica. For Hughes, the rapid increase in Catholic population created by the influx of Irish immigrants exiled by famine and German refugees from revolution required a different approach from that of his predecessors like Carroll and Dubois, who wished as quickly as possible to integrate Catholics into community life. Hughes emphasized instead the thorough organization of the Church, the discipline of the clergy and the multiplication of institutions under Catholic sponsorship and episcopal control. He did this to ensure the unity of Catholics, their loyalty to church authorities and their ability to shape their own destiny.

The most dramatic example of this separa-tion came in 1841 when Hughes organized his own slate of candidates for the New York State Assembly elections. He wanted to demonstrate the ability of Catholics to act independently of the Democratic party and thus win greater attention to their needs by politicians and government officials. The occasion was the first dramatic appearance of the school question, as the Church, apparently with the blessing of Governor William Henry Seward, sought public assistance for its schools. Failing this, the bishop did succeed in extending the common school system to the city, while at the same time persuading many Catholics to educate children in their own schools. Similarly, in dealing with outbreaks of anti-Catholicism, Hughes aggressively defended the rights of Catholics and threatened at one point to protect the city's Catholic churches with arms. In fact, Hughes was inclined to welcome the hostility of Protestants. As he told a Roman correspondent after nativist riots in Philadelphia in 1843, "I have reason to think that what has occurred will serve, instead of injure the Catholic cause" because the riots would unify Catholics and demonstrate the futility of seeking security and acceptance by minimizing or abandoning their faith.

Hughes' pugnaciousness reflected the feeling of at least some Catholics resentful of perceived discrimination. In November 1851, for example, Catholic inmates of the Albany almshouse were put on a bread and water diet for refusing to attend Protestant church services, though the punishment was ended when drawn to the attention of the local officials. In 1853, a student was whipped and expelled from school for refusing to read the "Protestant testament," although once again the state superintendent of schools condemned such actions as "barbarous." Catholic perceptions of injustice persisted; they were suspicious of arson when a church burned down in Palmyra; they believed that poor children confined to public institutions were being raised Protestant; and they regularly complained of the injustice of being taxed for support of schools they felt they could not in good conscience have their children attend. In 1853, Oswego Catholics followed Hughes' earlier effort by petitioning for a share of the school fund.

Hughes was equally firm in dealing with the major internal problems of the church. Trustees had solid ground in both civil and canon law for asserting their right, having built the church and provided for its pastors' support, to nominate clergymen to serve them. However, the practice of this right threatened to deeply divide the Church. The bishops became convinced that trustee ownership of church property, translated into the right to accept or reject a pastor, threatened the doctrinal unity of the Church, reduced the priest to a mere mouthpiece of the parishioners, and most importantly, led to a basically congregational form of organization in which each parish would be practically independent of every other. After numerous efforts at compromise, the bishops decided to end the practice and insist that deeds to church property be passed over to the bishop before a church would be dedicated or a priest named to serve the parish.

This was easier said than done, however, because many state laws provided for ownership by elected lay trustees, and these laws were not changed easily. In New York state, the 1784 act governing incorporation of churches provided that elected trustees should have "the sole disposition and ordering of all payments of the monies belonging to the said church, congregation or society." No provision was made for the representation of the priest or bishop on the board of trustees. Amended in 1833, the intent of the law, according to an 1854 legal opinion, was:

To place the control of the temporal affairs of these societies in the hands of the majority of the corporators, independent of priest or bishop, presbytery, synod or other ecclesiastical judicatory. This is the inevitable effect of the provision giving to the majority, without regard to their religious sentiments, the right to elect trustees, and fix the salary of the minister.

By the time the first Diocesan Synod of New York was held in 1842, it was clear that the Church could not accept such a system. The synod noted "the cares and troubles" and "the abuse" to which "the system of trustees" had given rise, and then attempted to reform that system. In a pastoral letter of September 1842, Hughes explained the new regulations designed to consolidate the authority of the clergy:

We have directed and ordained....that henceforward, no body of lay trustees... shall be permitted to appoint, retain, or dismiss, any person connected with the church - such as sexton, organist, singers, teachers, or other persons employed in connection with religion or public worship, against the will of the pastor.... We have ordained, likewise, that the expenses necessary for the maintenance of the pastors, and the support of religion, shall, in no case, be withheld or denied, if the congregations are able to afford them. It shall not be lawful for any board of trustees, or other lay persons, to make use of the church, chapel, basement, or other portions of ground, or edifices consecrated to religion, for any meeting, having a secular, or even an ecclesiastical object, without the approval, previously had, of the pastor, who shall be accountable to the bishop for this decision. And, with a view to arrest the evils of the trustee system in expending inconsiderately, or otherwise, the property of the faithful, it has been ordained, as a statute of the diocese, that no board of trustees shall be at liberty to vote, expend, or appropriate for contracts, or under any pretext, any portion of the property which they are appointed to administer without the express approval and approbation of the pastor in every case. And it is further ordained, that even thus, the trustees of the churches, with the approbation of the pastor, shall not be at liberty to expend an amount larger than one hundred dollars in any one year, without the consent of the bishop.

This was legislation for a well organized church, but Catholicsm in upstate New York was still in a missionary situation. There were simply not enough priests yet to take charge of congregations in the way Hughes wanted. As Hughes found on an 1841 trip upstate, sheer growth outstripped the structures and facilities of the church. In both city and countryside, immigrant Germans and Irish hoped to build churches, and the process for doing so from the bottom up, was already evident. First, St. John's had served all of western New York, with representatives from as far away as Auburn and Rochester on its trustees. Then gradually communities appeared at Salina, Oswego, Rome, Binghamton and Clinton. Ordinarily, the initiative toward formation of these communities came from the laity who gathered for prayer, then sent word to the nearest priest that they would welcome his visit. His visit would occasion gathering a larger group which, if substantial enough, might arrange for regular visits from the priest and for a place to worship, a home, rented or borrowed civic hall, even an unused Protestant church. If the group was large enough and if there were some members with means, the lay leaders, possibly working with the priest, would arrange to purchase some property and provide a church. To do so, they had to elect trustees to receive the protection and benefits of the law.

While the priest might lend encouragement, this work almost always was carried out by the lay leaders in the local community and often surprisingly with the support of local Protestants. Sometimes the Catholics purchased a former Protestant church. The Germans in Utica began in a former Methodist church. In Florence, Catholics purchased a former seminary from Protestant leader Gerritt Smith, who also donated the land for St. Paul's in Oswego in 1840. In Camden, a former Methodist church was purchased and moved to a new site in 1852. The first French church in Syracuse was located in a renovated Baptist church; in Chittenango, it was a Baptist church which had been owned for a while by Presbyterians; in Fabius, a Universalist church served the tiny congregation for nine years. While churches were obviously easy to renovate, almost any structure would do. Many were residences, others stores. In Fayetteville, it was a former hotel; in Marcellus, "Deacon Rice's tavern" on whose second floor the community had worshiped before they purchased the building. The Italians of Cortland who later began in an abandoned spaghetti factory stood in a long and honorable tradition.

At this point, provided with a building and the regular attendance, but not residence, of a priest, the station became a mission, with the elected trustees responsible for the upkeep of the property and the collection of funds to provide the priest with a stipend. The next step would be to become a parish, with a pastor formally assigned to the service of the congregation. Two factors determined this step, the availability of priests and the ability of the parish to maintain a priest by paying his salary, providing his housing and keeping the property in good repair. The former was a constant problem, as the bishops of New York and later Albany struggled to find the clergy needed by their expanding Church. French and German congregations in particular were difficult to serve, while even among the English speaking congregations, the number of priests seemed never to catch up with the expansion of population. Bishops did all they could to recruit priests from abroad, and they welcomed the services of priests who came on their own from overseas or from other dioceses. After a number of damaging experiences, where such priests turned out to be educated poorly or afflicted with one or another vice, the bishops diligently checked the credentials of such itinerant clergy. But even with the most careful examination, the time required to correspond with other bishops or overseas churches led to unfortunate experiences. All American bishops longed for the day they could provide first an American-educated clergy, later a clergy native to the diocese. The availability of clergymen was crucial to the resolution of the control problem because the trustees, who had sacrificed themselves and begged money from their fellow Catholics, were unlikely to surrender control of funds or property to a priest who visited the congregation only irregularly, as the Utica experience demonstrated. Only when the bishop was able to negotiate the parishioners' desire for a permanent pastor into their submission to diocesan regulations would the trustee system be replaced by one of clerical and episcopal control of property and resources. Until that time came, successful implementation of diocesan regulations depended on the forcefulness and pastoral skill of the individual priest.

The other factor that determined development from mission to parish was the economic status of the congregation. In Europe, parishes were often benefices, provided by a landlord or wealthy patron with an endowment for the priest's support. After 1815, in many cases, the government provided a salary for the clergy. In America, there were no such endowments or government support, so the money to build and maintain churches and support pastors had to come from the community itself. In some cases, a single family might make the difference. In others, help might come from better off Protestants, anxious to assist their Catholic fellow citizens. In a setting of considerable anti-Catholicism and even more anxiety about community order in the face of massive immigration, it was no small thing for a Protestant lay person to assist the Catholics. Abolitionist leader Gerritt Smith responded to an appeal by Father Beecham by authorizing the priest "to draw on me a total of $100," but noted that some of his friends complained of the help he was giving the Catholics. Later, when he offered to sell the Florence community a building, he wrote one of the leaders of the local Presbyterian church:

I am aware that my reputation has suffered somewhat from my course of action...I should be sorry to see the building in question used in a manner contrary to the feelings of the people in Florence. But I hoped that they would take pleasure in seeing the poor Catholics of their town assembled for divine worship in it.

In Florence and elsewhere, Catholics had reason to complain of their treatment, but the negative experience was not more characteristic than the generosity of Smith. The immigrant priest Father Inama found much to admire in the religious culture of Protestant dominated America, even in the evangelical stronghold of Central New York. When Utica Catholics protested the dismissal of Catholic servant girls from the state asylum for their

AN END FOR THE DEERFIELD HILLS MISSION

History shows a Church that is fluid, moving with settlers into new areas, letting go of buildings that are left behind. Over the years, several church centers in Central New York withered as populations moved or as they were absorbed into other parishes.

St. Bridget's at Solon, for example, in 1849 became the first Catholic church in Cortland county. It was abandoned within two decades as Catholics moved to Cortland and built a new church. In the late 1800s through the mid-1900s the St. Francis mission served the settlement of Little France in Oswego county; later both the town and its church were left behind as the residents moved elsewhere. Missions at Hawleytown, Nineveh and Harpersville in Broome county ended when settlers moved to other towns. And in the 1870s, German Catholics built their short-lived St. John Chrysostom church at Hawkinsville in Oneida county, soon to see it absorbed into other, larger parishes.

The most important abandoned mission was that centered in the Deerfield Hills of Oneida county. Irish Catholics were among the settlers in the town of Deerfield, which for a time rivaled Utica as a population center. As early as 1808 — before the first Mass in Utica — missionary priests were in Deerfield celebrating the sacraments in farmhouses, with worshipers coming from areas of Oneida and Herkimer counties north of the Mohawk River.

In 1838, Father William Quarter of New York City bought a farm on Bell Hill for his sister, donating an acre for a church. Neighbors cleared timber and put up a frame building, calling it the Church of the Holy Cross at Deerfield Hills. Quarter (who later became the first bishop of Chicago) celebrated the first Mass in the new church that summer, using

refusal to attend Protestant services, Inama endorsed Catholic resistance to "this unexampled interference with their sacred rights." And he went on to note that "the force of public opinion, which is all powerful here" was "entirely upon the side of the Catholics." The reason was clear, Inama thought.

The American people is without question deeply religious and the preservation of religious freedom (is) one of its greatest desires. The Catholic Church owes its rapid spread and quick growth to this precious freedom.

Germans, both Catholic and Protestant, were used to celebrating Sunday in what was known as the "continental fashion," with picnics, recreation and even beer drinking, practices which directly conflicted with the Puritan practice of keeping the Sabbath quietly with church and family. This often led to clashes, but once again, Inama found much to admire in the American way and in the general respect for religion in a country which many of his friends at home regarded as hopelessly Protestant and irreligious:

It is indeed edifying to see how differently from in Europe Sundays are spent here. The President of the United States in his message, first gives honor to God, and the governors all set a common week-day, December 14, as Thanksgiving Day for the blessings of the past year. Sundays are

*Holy Cross mission church at Deerfield Hill
(Photo: Fr Michael Dwyer)*

an altar donated by his brother, Father Walter Quarter of St. John's in Utica. Over the next three decades, visiting priests and, for a brief time, resident pastors served Holy Cross, where 500 worshipers would attend Sunday Mass in good weather.

But settlers began moving away from Deerfield Hill during the Civil War era, while new churches built north of the Mohawk further reduced the number of Holy Cross parishioners. Finally in 1868, a priest from Herkimer said the last Mass with the remnants of the once-thriving Holy Cross congregation.

The old church itself was abandoned; the cemetery became overgrown; by 1904, the tower had fallen and the rest of the building was near collapse. Today, Holy Cross mission is a footnote to history — a pioneer community that ended as people moved to new towns and began new parishes, a gentle reminder that the Catholic Church is not buildings, but people both settled and on the move.

not days of amusement, but of quiet devotion. Instead of going to the theater or the saloon, here one goes to the church. No ships sail on Sunday, it has even been decided not to run trains on that day. In many respects in regard to religion, and especially Catholicism, matters appear much better here than in many European countries. The missionary in his wanderings and on all carriages to and from church travels free of turnpike-toll. On steamers and railroads the missionary travels free.

Even the carrying of mail on this day is disapproved. On Sundays the towns are as if dead; everyone is in church;

in one of the best hotels I could not even obtain warm food on Sunday. The fact that he had traveled on Sunday damaged Henry Clay greatly as a presidential candidate. No meeting of Congress is opened in any of the states without a solemn prayer. In short, there is religion aplenty here, only the deviations from the true one are to be regretted.

Still, however open the society was to the formation of churches, and however sympathetic individual Protestants were to the organization of Catholics, the money for the church had to come for the most part from the incomes of Irish workers, small shopkeepers and merchants, German tradesmen and farmers, French factory and dockworkers. Not surprisingly, it was the settled families in these communities, usually married with children, steady employment, and some degree of security, that provided the backbone of Catholic parish development. Not only did such families have the income to share with their church, but they had the stability to follow regular patterns of church attendance, and to become the "practicing Catholics" who alone could make Catholic congregational life viable in the new United States. Baptisms and marriages featured the names of persons whose families remained in the neighborhood from one census to the next. This was a sign of economic progress which broke the pattern of itinerant unskilled employment and too frequent alcoholism, pauperism and family breakdown so marked among the canal workers and itinerant laborers who constituted the raucous crowd that so worried native-born Americans. Nor was it surprising that Church life, once organized, seemed aimed as much at achieving improved behavior, security and respectability as holiness. When Bishop Hughes visited the area in 1841, he noted how the formation of the church with a resident pastor influenced the behavior of the congregation and won the favor of the respectable Protestant majority. In Little Falls, for example, he was "happy to state that improved habits, in consequence of temperance, prevail and are rapidly gaining for them the regard and kind feeling of the neighborhood in which they are employed." In Salina the priest reported he had not erected a temperance society because even without one "his flock has become remarkable for sober and abstemious habits." The great Irish temperance reformer, Father Matthew, visited Utica and 1,000 men took the pledge. In the wake of his visit, the Father Matthew Temperance Association became one of the most popular parish societies. Its Utica chapter, at one time, listed 1,500 members.

Hughes felt from the beginning of his work in New York that his statewide diocese was too big to provide adequate pastoral care and the growth of population justified its division. In January 1845, he wrote Rome requesting establishment of a new diocese at Albany with his coadjutor, Bishop John McCloskey, as its bishop. In his letter, he indicated that the state eventually should be divided into four separate jurisdictions, with additional sees at Plattsburg and Rochester. Fully aware of the vague knowledge of American geography in the Roman Curia, he enclosed a map of the state with the proposed division clearly marked. Still, he concluded that "at present" the Albany diocese would be sufficient. Rome, as usual in such cases, delayed a decision and eventually the question was referred to the sixth provincial council of American bishops in May 1846. The assembled bishops recommended that two new dioceses be established at Albany and Buffalo, recommending McCloskey and John Timon as bishops.

Rome acceded to that request and McCloskey was appointed to preside over a still vast territory extending from the boundaries of the state on the east and north, to the forty-second degree latitude in the south and to the eastern limits of Cayuga, Tomkins and Tioga counties to the west. The Albany diocese embraced 23 counties, comprising an area of nearly 30,000 square miles. The Catholic population of approximately 60,000 was in 50 churches. There were two orphanages, St. Vincent's Orphan Asylum in Albany and St. John's Female Orphan Asylum in Utica; and there were two Catholic schools, one at Troy under lay direction, the other connected with St. John's at Utica.

In the portion of the diocese which later would comprise the diocese of Syracuse, there were still only 11 parishes with a resident pastor in 1846. Nevertheless, the Church was well situated for a period of rapid expansion when priests could be provided to serve those missions which were prepared to take the next step. Credit for the progress that had taken place in such a short time must go to the bishops and to energetic clergymen like Beecham and Inama, but most of all to the lay leaders who kept the faith alive and began the process of providing a Church. Men and women on the move, they had come to New York to build new lives for themselves. They did not forget their ancestral faith, nor did they neglect their responsibility to pass that faith on to their children. Rather than allow their religious life to lapse under the pressure of providing a living for their families and securing a place for themselves, they reached out to each other to form new friendships and found new organizations through which they could carry on the task of becoming secure and successful Americans, while remaining loyal to their Church. They did so because they wished to live with integrity, to maintain their beliefs and live according to their principles, while making their own the freedom and personal responsibilities which were at the heart of the American experiment. They refused to allow their Catholicism to drive them to the margins of community life, and they refused with equal determination to accept the argument that true Americanism required the surrender of their faith. Instead, they determined to be both Catholic and American, and to do so they needed the help of one another and the presence and support of their Church. Soon, the leadership of that Church would pass more completely into the hands of the clergy, but new immigrant groups would repeat their experience of starting again, from the bottom up. Most of all, these lay people, with only the occasional services of clergy and religious, constructed a Church because they wished to live as free and responsible men and women. They confirmed in the process both the strength of their faith and the possibilities of freedom, leaving a record of self-help, personal responsibility and community loyalty. This record could serve as a model for later generations who might face as they did a time when priests would not be available to live among them, but when the challenge of living with integrity in an age of freedom would be as real and demanding as ever.

A NEW CHURCH MUST BE BUILT

PARISH EXPANSION AND DEVELOPING ORGANIZATION
1850s-1880s

The era of lay leadership which marked the formation of many American parishes was followed by a period dominated by strong pastors. Born abroad, but often educated in the United States or Canada, these priests were filled with dreams of the future that were uniquely American. They arrived in cities and towns to find small wooden churches, struggling congregations, limited financial resources and communities largely composed of poor, working-class people. Somehow, they saw beyond the uncertainty evident around them to a vision of proud, respectable congregations, worshiping in large stone churches the match of any Protestant churches in the community. That vision included schools to educate the children, societies to meet a variety of human needs, and ceremonies to demonstrate the faith and loyalty of men and women who were Catholic and proud of it, and as good Americans as anyone else. A century and more later, Catholics looked back in wonder at the growth in the second half of the nineteenth century — parishes with expensive buildings, cemeteries, schools, hospitals, asylums, with debts being paid from ever increasing income — and wondered how it all happened so fast. Legends grew around the memory of that generation's leading priests, Barry in Oswego, O'Hara in Syracuse, Hourigan in Binghamton and McLoughlin in Cortland. They seemed the Catholic equivalents of such "captains of industry" as Andrew Carnegie, men who shaped history to their transcendent vision of American possibilities. They set forth great plans, challenged their people to respond, praised them when they succeeded, nudged them along when they became worried, persisted when the recurrent depressions of the period threw fear into the hearts of wealthier men. And apparently, as far as we can tell, they never lost confidence that their dreams would come true.

The bottom-up lay initiative of the formative period continued in towns and rural areas, and among newer immigrant congregations. But in the older parishes and in new ones spinning off from them, the priests now took charge. Through the force of their personalities and the compelling power of their vision, backed now by Church and civil law, they unified communities often divided by income, dialect or expectations. "A new church must be built" became the rallying cry; the project of the pastor became the common ground. He set standards of behavior, defined the terms of religious membership, established the goals for which they would work and the criteria to measure success and failure. Like the political bosses, the pastors earned loyalty by their single minded pursuit of their people's welfare. Eventually, their domination would be challenged and modified, not by rebellion from below but by administrative control from above. This phenomenon occurred as bishops made in the same mold as these pastors attempted to unify their widespread congregations, mobilize the church's resources, and allocate them in ways best suited to realize the dreams of bishops, priests and people.

In the years following the Civil War, Central New York hummed with activity, as canals and railroads connected New York and Albany to Utica, Syracuse, Rochester, Buffalo and points between. This transportation network serviced a hinterland of small farmers growing a variety of staples for the markets of eastern cities and, eventually, for shipment abroad. The bulk of the early population of upstate New York had come from New England. Along the route of the great canal, later along the subcanals connecting the Erie Canal with Lake Ontario and the Susquehanna River, then along the plank roads built first in this area, and still later along the railroads, villages sprang up where there had been construction camps. The pioneers were eager for the fires of revivalism which spread across the region, leaving behind Congregationalist, Presbyterian, Baptist and Methodist churches. So receptive to evangelism were upstate New Yorkers that the region became known as the "burned over district." From it came some of the nations' most vigorous preachers and a steady stream of reformers anxious to see that the Lord's will was done, the nation was purged of sin and the promise of a Christian democracy was fulfilled.

America might be composed heavily of Christians, but they were not exclusively Protestant; that was clear in upstate New York by the Civil War. In Utica alone, St. John's, St. Patrick's and St. Joseph's soon were joined by St. Mary's which began to worship in a formerly Lutheran church in 1870, and St. Francis de Sales organized in 1877. Even that was not enough and another parish, St. Agnes, was authorized in 1887 to serve the Irish in East Utica. Similar growth took place everywhere. No problem posed a greater challenge than finding priests to serve this expanding population, and no desire was greater than to develop a native clergy. Bishop John Dubois established a short-lived seminary at Nyack on the Hudson, another was attempted at LaFargeville and later at Fordham. Lacking diocesan priests to staff the seminary, Hughes closed it and persuaded his fellow bishops to open a provincial seminary at Troy in 1864. The new seminary survived and prospered. While by no means the united body of native born and locally educated priests that most bishops desired, there was by 1870 a corps of priests, almost all Irish or Irish-American, who shared a common background and a similar education and faced similar pastoral challenges. The nature of their calling and the pioneer setting of the Church nurtured a sturdy independence, but it also required some degree of mutual support. This support was evident in the way Father James O'Hara of Syracuse loaned other priests books from his library and in the joy with which they welcomed occasions for meeting together, as at Forty Hours devotions. They fought one another when they thought their rights were at stake, sometimes carrying those fights to the public press or the courts; but they were brothers, and they knew it. Their fate was bound up with that of the Church, and their devotion to its welfare and to that of their people was remarkable.

Father Leopold Moczygemba (Photo: Assumption parish)

THE FRANCISCAN CONTRIBUTION

It was already clear that this largely Irish-American group of priests could not do the job alone. The German community was growing far too rapidly to be served adequately by the occasional German-American diocesan priest. The first three priests to serve the German people were a Redemptorist, Praemontratensian and Benedictine. In 1859, Bishop McCloskey found a more permanent solution in the Conventual Franciscans. This community had come to the United States in 1851 in response to an appeal from the bishop of Galveston, Texas. After taking charge of several parishes there, the superior, Father Leopold Moczygemba, left because of ill health, eventually settling in Philadelphia, where Bishop John Neumann was particularly hospitable to German Catholics. There the

order took charge of a formerly Redemptorist parish and assumed the spiritual direction of a community of German speaking Third Order Franciscan sisters. In 1858, Bishop McCloskey asked the Franciscans fathers to take charge of German parishes in Utica and Syracuse. His request arrived at an opportune time because Moczygemba was anxious to establish a novitiate to recruit American members. He found Philadelphia too expensive and filled with "too much noise and turmoil" for a novitiate, while the parish they had been assigned was burdened with a large debt. After visiting upstate New York, Moczygemba decided to transfer his community to Utica. McCloskey ceded the Utica and Syracuse

MISSIONARY AMONG THE LEPERS

Mother Marianne of Molokai
(Photo: Mother Marianne Cope Archives)

"Mother Marianne's name will live as that of a woman whose noble self-sacrifice ranks with the death-defying devotion of the martyrs of old. No woman ever went out of Syracuse on a greater mission, none from Syracuse ever gave more than she did," wrote the Syracuse *Post-Standard* in 1918.

A century ago, leprosy was a disease that turned most people to fear. Lepers were outcasts — forcibly separated from their families, often banished to isolated settlements to fend for themselves. The contagious disease itself was pitiable — open sores, rotting flesh, mutilated noses and fingers, nauseating stench. It also ate away at the soul and left its victims despondent, with the certain knowledge that only a slow and painful death would free them from their outpost of hell.

It was into such a den of despair that Marianne Cope walked when the king of Hawaii sought American nursing sisters. "I am hungry for the work," wrote the Franciscan sister, "and I wish with all my heart to be one of the chosen Ones, whose privilege it will be, to sacrifice themselves for the salvation of the souls of the poor Islanders... I am not afraid of any disease, hence it would be my greatest delight even to minister to the abandoned 'lepers.'..."

Mother Marianne was a former Utican who knew responsibility from working in a factory to help support her family, a leader who headed St. Joseph's hospital in Syracuse before twice being

parishes to the Franciscans, with the provision that they also serve other German Catholics until he could provide diocesan priests.

McCloskey, nearly desperate for help, had not been entirely candid with Moczygemba because he praised St. Joseph's, riven by

internal divisions and constant bickering between priests and trustees, as the "best organized German community in the diocese." Moczygemba and his Franciscans had been in the United States long enough to know how to handle such situations. The elected as provincial of the Franciscan Sisters. She had a strong sense of ministry to the poor, desiring to imitate her patron, St. Francis of Assisi. Francis himself had overcome revulsion to embrace a leper during his spiritual conversion, so it seemed fitting that a sisterhood following in his footsteps would minister among lepers.

In 1883, Mother Marianne led six Franciscans to their first Hawaiian mission, a leper hospital near Honolulu. She soon helped establish a nearby home for the daughters of leprous parents.

A remarkable man had preceded the sisters to the islands. Father Damien de Veuster had spent his life among the lepers and contracted the disease himself by the time he met Mother Marianne, who helped care for him in his final years. In 1888, Mother Marianne led the sisters to open a home for girls on Molokai, the leper outcast colony where Damien worked. Five months later when the priest died, she took charge of his boys home there as well.

Mother Marianne's years at the leper settlement were difficult ones. She cared daily for the victims of the dread disease. Amid the physical decay, she also had to deal with the drunkenness, violence and sexual immorality which was rampant among the doomed victims. But the sisters' quiet virtue helped change lives. They were a force for good, and gradually the moral and spiritual climate improved. Through it all, Mother Marianne treated the lepers with a respect which others denied them, and she helped many appreciate their God-given dignity.

On August 9, 1918, 35 years after she left Syracuse for the mission to Hawaii, Mother Marianne died peacefully at the age of 80. She was buried among her beloved lepers on Molokai.

Despite bureaucratic problems with government officials and considerable bigotry against Catholics, Mother Marianne had gained the respect of many Hawaiians. Before her death, she had received the title of "lady companion" of the Royal Order of Kapiolani, an honor given by King Kalakaua. Queen Kapiolani befriended and supported her early work. Robert Lewis Stevenson wrote a poem celebrating her ministry on Molokai.

Today, the Franciscan Sisters of Syracuse have completed extensive research into her life, documenting her heroism with a view to her eventual canonization as a saint. However the Vatican handles this case for sainthood, Mother Marianne Cope of Utica, Syracuse and Molokai stands today as a figure of heroic Christian service, an example of Christ-like compassion shining before the Church of Syracuse.

trustees, unhappy with the more independent Franciscans, refused to submit to their authority. The friars simply withdrew, leaving the trustees with their church, and began offering Mass and other pastoral services elsewhere. Impressed by their mildness and simplicity, the majority of the people gravitated to the new priests until the trustees finally gave them the keys. Construction of a new church began in 1869 and was completed at a cost of $100,000 four years later. However, Moczygemba decided to locate his novitiate and motherhouse not in Utica, but at Assumption in Syracuse. With the support of the prosperous German community there, construction of a new church, built around the old one, began almost immediately.

In both parishes, knowing well the passionate desire of the German people for their own schools, the Franciscans moved quickly to provide for the education of the young. Even before moving to the area, Moczygemba appealed for help to the Third Order Franciscan Sisters he was working with in Philadelphia. With the permission of Bishop Neumann, the community agreed to staff his schools. Shortly after arriving in Utica, Moczygemba sent a telegram asking the superior to send four sisters. Although Bishop James Wood, who had succeeded Neumann in 1858, was away at the time, Mother Francis did not hesitate to respond on the basis of Neumann's earlier approval. Accompanying the sisters on their journey, she agreed that more were needed. Wood, learning of all this, was incensed. He told Mother Francis that the sisters sent to New York state were separated from his jurisdiction and her community. He then wrote McCloskey that the sisters were now his responsibility. Mother Francis was furious with this arbitrary treatment that divided her community, but she was powerless. McCloskey welcomed the eight sisters and three novices and, in 1864, purchased for them a motherhouse and novitiate in Salina, where in 1871 the sisters elected Mother Bernardine Dorn as their superior general and Sister Marianne Cope as secretary. Central New York had a religious community of its own. It also now had strong schools at its two most important German parishes. And for now, it had Sister Marianne. She served faithfully in schools, convents and especially at the fledgling hospital in Syracuse before assuming leadership of the community. Later she would follow the call of the Holy Spirit to Hawaii, to Molakai, to serve lepers,

there to win the love and respect of all whose lives she touched, and to achieve remarkable sanctity.

The work of these sisters was staggering. In addition to their work at Assumption, in 1869, they opened St. Joseph's Hospital, the first in Central New York, on Prospect Hill in Syracuse. Begging door-to-door for money and supplies, they occupied two small buildings, a former saloon and a dance hall. In Utica, the sisters opened a school at St. Joseph's under Mother Bernardine, who also visited the sick poor after school hours. Distressed by the needs she saw, Mother Bernardine received permission to begin a hospital. Thomas Devereux, a lay Third Order Franciscan, provided a building and St. Elizabeth's Hospital opened in 1866 with one patient. In 1868, the old building was removed to make way for a new church and the hospital moved to the original church building, now with room for 30 patients.

Not everyone welcomed the Franciscans into the diocese. Father Theodore Noethen, McCloskey's only reliable German-speaking priest, took a strong dislike to Moczygemba. He resented the intrusion of a religious order to whom the bishop had turned over title to his most prosperous German parishes. He wrote a strong criticism of the Franciscan leader to Moczygemba's superiors in Rome. McCloskey, who counted on the friars to get control over the restive German Catholics, hastened to assure Moczygemba that Noethan had acted without his knowledge. The bishop thought it "neither fair nor generous" to criticize when they had barely time to become established.

He urged Moczygemba to communicate his hearty appreciation to his general in Rome, and signed himself "your sincere friend and brother in Christ." Well he might have because the Franciscans were to prove indispensable in the years to come.

The Franciscans reached out beyond their

First Assumption church in Syracuse, completed in 1845 (Photo: Assumption parish)

own parishes to pockets of German Catholics in other parts of the diocese. In Oswego, for example, a small German community had long worshiped at St. Mary's where, at the laying of the cornerstone in 1849, sermons were preached in that language as well as French and English. After visits from the Franciscans in 1859, the German community organized the St. Boniface Society to raise money to purchase land and erect a church, which was completed and dedicated in 1863. In 1870, the Franciscans turned the parish, St. Peter's, over to the diocese with a diocesan priest as pastor. The problems with German Catholics, however, were far from over. St. Mary's in Rome, built by Father Schwenninger over Beecham's objections in 1848, remained a diocesan parish under the charge of a long series of religious priests until Noethen, the trouble-shooter of German parishes, arrived in 1870. Finding both church and rectory in poor condition, he determined to build a new church. Faced with opposition regarding a site, Noethen reorganized the parish under the authority of the bishop and proceeded with a majority of the parishioners. The division was not healed when the new church was completed. A dissident German Catholic group continued in existence, worshiping in the old church and later in other buildings with the help of itinerant priests of questionable standing. Father Noethen provided the Albany bishops with a running account of "apostate" and excommunicated priests, their "sacrilegious" performance of ceremonies, and their "manifestations of familiarity" with women of "loose character and easy virtue." At one point, the dissidents accepted the services of an Episcopalian priest until, some years later, they sold the old church to Polish Catholics.

Such problems demonstrated the persistence of trusteeism. Establishment of clerical and episcopal authority required a combination of forceful personality and pastoral skill. Father John Ludden had the former in abundance. When the owners of the vast expanse of land along Lake Ontario, known as the Holland Patent, offered farm land for sale at low prices, some Irish settled there around the town of Florence. In 1845, they purchased land formerly owned by local Baptists and converted a former trade school conducted by Gerritt Smith into a church. Father Robert Kelleher served them for three years, but he was upset by the lay people's insistence that, as owners of the property, they would hold the keys to the church, determine the time of services and generally set church policy. Kelleher's successor, faced with these demands, withdrew to Camden and told the people they must come to the new church there for baptism, marriages and funerals. A lay committee consulted with the bishop, who told them they would have to surrender the keys to the priest. Only when they were promised a new pastor, Father John Ludden, did they agree. Unfortunately, when the committee returned home, the people repudiated the agreement. On his second Sunday, Ludden announced that he would say Mass the following week at 9:00 rather than 10:30. When he arrived for that purpose the following Sunday, the doors were locked securely. When two requests for the keys were denied, Ludden broke down the door with an axe, said Mass and departed for a Forty Hours ceremony in another parish. The people brought suit and Ludden consulted a lawyer in Utica, who told him he was liable to two years in jail for breaking and entering the property owned by the parishioners. On the street, Ludden met Roscoe Conklin, a young lawyer destined for later political fame, who took the case. By subpoenaing hundreds of farmers from the Florence area and scheduling testimony at inconvenient times of planting and harvest, Conklin won numerous postponements and eventually the case was

dropped. Ludden remained as pastor for many years and eventually the church was deeded to the bishop.

The Florence case made clear the need for state legislation. In 1863, after a long struggle, a new law allowed the Catholic Church to constitute parish corporations composed by the bishop, vicar general, pastor and two lay "trustees" named by the other three. Older parishes quickly took legal steps to reconstitute themselves in accord with the new law, although a few resisted. Legally, the bishops and clergy were now on solid enough ground to exert full control over the property, income and personnel of the Church. Lay people no longer had the legal or canonical right to share in Church decisionmaking, while priests were clearly at the disposal of the bishop, to be sent where he thought their talents could be used best. For reasons good and bad, the American Church and the Church in New York became the most centralized in Christendom.

THE ERA OF STRONG PASTORS

The new law coincided with the appearance of a new generation of pastors in the Irish-American parishes, men able to unify expanding congregations and make clerical authority popular and effective. The dominant figure in Syracuse, for example, was the "gifted but controversial" James A. O'Hara. Born in Ireland and educated at Villanova University, O'Hara came to Syracuse in 1859. He found his little parish, St. Mary's, struggling and in debt, but there was no limit to his sense of what the church could become. Within a few years, he paid off his parish debt, helped the Sisters of Charity begin St. Vincent's orphanage for girls, and purchased property and developed support the House of Providence orphanage for boys. In 1870, he purchased 56 acres, had it surveyed for a cemetery and began selling lots, a move which soon brought

Father James A. O'Hara (Photo: Chancery Archives)

him into sharp conflict with McCloskey's successor, Bishop Conroy. That dispute reached the press and the courts. But O'Hara again challenged the bishop when he took part of St. Mary's for a new parish, St. Lucy's. O'Hara resigned his pastorate, refusing to "preside over half a parish." The bishop refused the resignation and the argument went to the ecclesiastical courts. O'Hara told a local reporter that he thought the bishop "vacillating, procrastinating and hardly the person to occupy his exalted position," causing the bishops' supporters to denounce the prominent pastor for his "flippant and impotent tirade" filled with "falsehoods and other nonsense."

The great project of the independent pastor's life was to build a new church. It was, as it turned out, the project of a lifetime. He paid a huge price, $35,000, for prime real estate at the very heart of the city, close by its Protestant churches and public buildings. Then in February 1873, he announced, "A new church must be built." He called on the men of the parish, "especially those who are

unemployed," to join him in digging the foundation; the boys helped dismantle a barn at the rear of the property. Under his enthusiastic leadership, walls were built and the cornerstone laid with great ceremony in the spring of 1874. But the depression of the mid-1870s forced suspension of construction and the partly finished church stood as an embarrassment; some called it "O'Hara's folly." The pastor refused to give in. Sunday after Sunday he urged his people to redeem their pledges. He announced visits to their homes, when contributions would be expected. He appealed to their pride and occasionally again sought their physical assistance. In January 1881, for example, he asked them to bring their "teams" to help draw stone from nearby quarries, adding a prayer that the men who helped and their families would "live long and prosper and their horses be spared to them." His church, which eventually cost a quarter of a million dollars and left a debt of $120,000, was not quite a nickel and dime operation. It actually was a matter of a quarter and 50 cents, the usual price paid by parishioners for seats at concerts and entertainments. This was the size of the gift expected when O'Hara met them in their homes and, as the project neared completion, the weekly donation O'Hara begged from them. In January 1885, he announced that this special collection would end in June; after that, "the people of the parish will decide how to manage the future." In December, the great day of the dedication arrived, with tickets available for one dollar, and bishops, monsignors and local dignitaries on hand. The personal triumph of the priest, remarked upon in the sermons of dedication day, was without question a day of collective achievement for his people. However often they had battled with each other, and lost confidence in each other and in O'Hara, they came together in the end to bask in the glow of a day when their magnificent church, the match of any in

61

the city, stood in the name of that same parish begun by lay people from nearly nothing only 50 years before.

O'Hara was only one of the new breed of pastors appearing throughout the diocese. Irish laborers had begun to trickle into Cortland County in the 1830s and in 1852, General Samuel Hathaway sold a piece of land to the Albany diocese on which St. Bridget's in Solon was erected. Two years later, he conveyed another plot to the Church for use as a cemetery on the condition that they "shall make and forever maintain a good substantial fence." In 1854 St. Patrick's in Truxton was established, served from Cazenovia. When the original church burned in 1878, Mass was said in the Methodist church until a new building could be erected. In the towns of the area visited by Father Haes and other pioneer priests, Mass was said in private homes, rented rooms or, as in Homer, at the Homer Academy or Mechanics Hall. In the 1850s, Mass was being said in Cortland itself for the Irish there and, in 1867, Bartholomew Francis McLoghlin, a native of Ireland educated in the United States, came to serve at its new parish, St. Mary's of the Vale. Father Mac, as he was known, was the equal of O'Hara in energy and vision. He purchased land for a larger church in 1868 and built a beautiful church, seating 920 people. Larger than seemed necessary, the church was a monument to the pastor's vision of the possibilities of Cortland and its Catholics. He was assisted first by one nephew, Thomas McLoghlin, and then a second, John J. McLoghlin, who succeeded him as pastor in 1888. Father Mac was buried after a large Irish wake and funeral in the basement of the church. His estate included $2,500 to erect a large monument on his grave in St. Mary's cemetery. In December 1896, a 25-foot-high granite monument with a 10-ton base was erected in his honor and his remains were transferred from the church.

Father James F. Hourigan (Photo: Chancery Archives)

Father James Hourigan dominated the life of the Church in Binghamton and Broome County. When Hourigan arrived in Binghamton, he was 32 old, but had been ordained only six months. He was a strong temperance advocate known for his denunciations of drink and his willingness to enter saloons and, with the help of his blackthorn cane, drive errant husbands and fathers home to their families. Like so many others priests of this constructive generation, he seemed to have a vision that far transcended the tiny church and struggling community he found on his arrival. He quickly snapped up land around his church, adopted a school for young girls conducted by two lay women, invited the Sisters of St. Joseph to take charge of a

Father Michael Barry (Photo: Miss Frances Barry, Oswego)

came to dedicate the new church in 1873, he and the pastor were calling it St. Patrick's, not St. John's, and this name stuck.

Oswego on Lake Ontario seemed at mid century to have a future as bright as any city in the state. In 1850, its population was the equal of that of Syracuse and Buffalo; the lake trade was booming as were lumber, flour milling, iron and starch industries. Unfortunately, the city was not serviced well by the railroads. As the national rail network matured, the lake trade declined and Oswego never fulfilled its early promise. Nevertheless, as a Catholic center, the city moved ahead rapidly. The opening of the Oswego canal brought in Irish laborers in the 1820s; others followed, as did numerous French Canadians. Traveling missionaries served the community, and in 1840, the Catholics purchased land from Gerritt Smith. On an 1841 visit to the area, Bishop Hughes noted that the Oswego community had "with becoming zeal, commenced a new church which when completed will rank among the best in the diocese." In 1869, Michael Barry arrived to take charge of this parish, St. Paul's. Stories of Father Barry still fill the air when older Catholics of Oswego get together. One resident can recall singing in "priory hall" which Barry opened under the church. His parents would spend Sunday afternoon and evening there, taking part in parish activities and in the evening listen to Barry as he narrated slides about far off lands. Others remember his strolling through the neighborhoods on Sunday with his big cane, telling the men to go home to their families. He did not believe in roller skating, one recalls, and would call out from the altar on Sunday morning the names of those who had been at the roller skating parlor on Saturday night. He would walk through the park "with his high hat and flowing white hair, long tailed coat and his cane," and "the kids would run yelling 'here comes Father Barry.'" From the point of view

63

combination day and boarding school, and eventually opened a co-educational parochial school in the old church building. In the 1880s, he purchased an abandoned orphanage and persuaded the Franciscans to take charge of St. Mary's Home for orphan boys and girls. Once again, the great project was the new church, built for $170,000. When the bishop

St. Patrick's in Binghamton included a new church built in 1873, a day and boarding academy, and a parish school housed in the old St. John's church building. (Photo: Roberson Center, Binghamton)

of boys and young men, "he believed in going to church, home, and that was it." If he saw youngsters standing on the street corner talking, he would "give them a whack on the behind and say 'get home and rake up the yard or wipe the dishes for your mother.'" In 1886, Barry publicly denounced baseball, a pastime he felt attracted "shiftless vagabonds whose only qualifications are strong legs and arms and thick heads." This charge drew some well stated opposition from newspapers in the area and from local ballplayers. Undaunted, Barry reiterated this position and many others, while striving mightily to lift his flock to new visions of its own possibilities. Most notably he worked at his school, trying not only to instill in the students a sense of discipline, but to lift up a vision of the world and themselves which could bring them to

leadership and distinction. His method was sometimes hard, but his parishioners had some idea of what he sought. As one elderly lady recalls, "he put fear into some of the school children. They still loved him and they always respected him, but he did put fear into them to be just the best."

French Catholics in Oswego were fewer than the Irish, but gradually their numbers required special attention. Most had come from Quebec and the Church there, beleaguered within a rising sea of English speaking Canada and the United States, struggled to make of that province a hospitable home for French speaking Catholics. As a result, priests discouraged emigration and bishops were reluctant to release French speaking priests to serve congregations in New England and upstate New York. That policy eased a bit after mid-century, although priests tended to retain their ties to the homeland and Catholic societies remained associated to larger parent societies north of the border. The first church established for French speaking Catholics in Central New York was St. Mary's in Oswego, where land was purchased and a building begun in 1848. By the time construction was completed in 1850, however, the new congregation had become bilingual, with half its parishioners English speaking. At the laying of the cornerstone in 1849, sermons were preached in English, French and German. In the early years, the poverty-stricken French, used to public support of churches and schools in Quebec, were slow to contribute toward the support of the parish. On the other hand, the Irish, who provided most of the money, became resentful of French claims. Some began attending St. Paul's on the opposite side of the Oswego River, so that the second pastor, leaving after only a year, pleaded with the bishop to define clearly parish boundaries and force those on his side of the river to attend St. Mary's. In 1852, Father Joseph Guerdet arrived and temporarily pacified the conflicting groups. In 1859, tragedy struck when, during a heavily attended mission, a portion of the floor collapsed, carrying a large number of parishioners into the basement. While no one was killed by the fall, the ensuing panic caused five fatal injuries. Father Guerdet kept things peaceful until 1867, but by that time only 54 French names remained on the pew rent rolls. When Louis Griffa arrived that year as pastor, enthusiasm was rekindled and French membership swelled to more than 400. Griffa persuaded J.F.S. Pelletier of Quebec to come to the city to organize a separate French parish. St. Mary's purchased a hall for St. Louis Church and paid the old parishioners $7,500 for their rights in the older parish. In 1863, the Germans also left St. Mary's to form St.

Peter's and, in 1869, another division was made to form St. John the Evangelist.

With John F. Lowery as pastor, a temporary frame church was quickly built for St. John's, but an early photograph showing 259 families with 592 names on the back indicated the inadequacy of the building. Fairs and other fund raising efforts began. Subscriptions came in generously and the construction of a new church moved ahead quickly, surviving even a great storm in October 1871, the effects of which shook Lowery's characteristic optimism:

They were ready for the roof. I contemplated the finished walls of my new church with delight and started for a distant parish to preach a sermon next evening. A fearful storm arose that night which swept along the Great Lakes doing incalculable damage, and, alas, blowing the finished walls of my new church to the ground. As I was descending the pulpit of the distant church...a telegram was placed in my hand which I quickly opened on the altar to read the sad news of the sudden demolition of my large and beautiful church. Surely this was poor encouragement for my sermon but I said nothing and did my preaching as best I could. Hastening homeword I found on my arrival a multitude of my beloved flock, in tears and sadly weeping over the ruined walls of their Jerusalem. I have stood in the Holy City of a Friday when I heard the Jews mourn and wail and utter their lamentations over the ruined walls of Jerusalem but I can truly say that the sights of my people weeping and wailing that day impressed me more than the sights of Jerusalem.

Nevertheless the church was completed

speedily and dedicated in July 1872. Father Lowery, whose loving description of the people, building and grounds of his church reflected his rare delight in the parish priesthood, was transferred in 1875 to Fonda, then later to Johnstown and Cohoes. In each place, he either developed a former mission to parish status or founded a new parish. Late in life, he confessed that he had always "loved to build churches."

Surely he did, and so did many others. Storms, such as the one which threatened the Oswego church, were only one of the obstacles to be overcome. There were also the periodic panics and depressions which could set back even the most energetic pastor, as O'Hara discovered. In smaller towns and rural areas, parishes depended upon the meager income of small farmers increasingly left behind by agricultural advances to the west, or on income from employment by a single industry vulnerable to the fluctuations of that industry. In Fulton, Father Patrick Kearney served Immaculate Conception parish, which had received its first resident pastor in 1854 and worshiped in a former female seminary. By 1886, he was at work with plans for a new church, but he noted that "it was a rather difficult undertaking" because the "congregation were all poor, depending solely for their support on the woolen mill." A "few poor farmers" scattered through the countryside, were "willing workers," ready to lend the use of their "teams and men." When asked, "they came like one man to excavate the basement, and draw building material." But before the church was completed, the factory closed down and many were forced to seek employment elsewhere. Not until the plant reopened a few years later could work on the church resume.

While this new generation of priests was building new churches, smaller communities were struggling to reach parish status. During the period of administration from Albany, 41 new parishes were established in the seven counties which eventually would form the Syracuse diocese. The pattern established earlier held firm, with stations and missions served by parishes, services becoming more frequent as new parishes were established closer at hand. In 1876, for example, Father Patrick Beecham, nephew of William Beecham, became resident pastor at Camden and was able to serve missions in the area more easily than his aging and distant uncle. However, the lay community still had to provide the church. Catholics who had been worshipping together in Camden since the 1840s decided it was time to build a church on the land they had acquired. On Sundays, the men gathered to drain a fish pond on the property, dig the foundation and lay the stones, and finally to erect the small church. Each week, the women of the parish would prepare Sunday dinner to be served at the site.

Irish settlers in North Annsville in Oneida County had built a small church in 1847. They each contributed $10 for materials, then framed the building with spruce and hemlock, cutting and squaring the logs with broad axes and making shaved shingles for the outside. When they opened the church, they had two pews made from planks nailed to empty nail kegs. One craftsman made wrought iron candle holders in his blacksmith shop. In the years that followed, German and Irish settlers came to the area, and by 1870 there were 60 families nearby, needing a larger church. A dispute developed over whether to locate in North Annsville, where the old church stood, or in Taberg. The following year the Taberg faction purchased a local Methodist church. This eventually became St. Patrick's, while the other group, unreconciled to the Taberg site, built its own church near the old one.

There was far more to these parishes than construction, but the building of "the new church" was the great project of the day. The

66

priest was the catalyst, gathering around him men and women who could put aside their differences to join in a common project. This project would provide a visible, concrete symbol of so many things in their lives — their religious faith, their loyalty to their homeland and to the parents and grandparents they had left behind, their defiant devotion to a Catholicism their neighbors often despised, their faith in themselves and in the future they were building for their children, their assurance that they — Irish or German or French as they might also be — were Americans, equal citizens, participants in the common life with rights and responsibilities the same as their more respectable neighbors. Whether it was a lovely tiny white wooden church in the valleys of the Oswego or Susquehanna rivers or among the hills of Oneida county, or the massive churches built by Father O'Hara in Syracuse or Father Mac in Cortland, these buildings were monuments to the incredible confidence and determination of a generation remarkable for their faith in God, the Church and the future.

A FOOTHOLD
FOR CATHOLIC EDUCATION

In Central New York, Catholic priests and lay people still were primarily concerned with establishing parishes, building new and larger churches, and finding the money for such projects. Aside from the Germans, few were interested in building parochial schools. In 1884, the Third Plenary Council of Baltimore decreed that there should be a Catholic school in every parish within two years. The argument of the pro-school forces, led by Bishop McQuaid of Rochester, was that, unless children were formed from an early age in the tenets and duties of their faith, the survival of American Catholicsm would be in jeopardy. Bishop McNeirny of Albany, likewise tried to convince his priests, preoccupied

as they were with building churches, that the school should come first, for reasons of self-interest as well as religious idealism.

Better not build the church and leave it unfurnished - better still, as you have often heard me remark, build the school house first and temporarily use it as a church - than neglect the Christian education and religious training of the little ones. When they shall have been thoroughly imbued in the school with Catholic faith and doctrine, they will not fail to do their share in the erection and preservation of the material edifice. But if they are deprived of the blessings of a Christian Catholic education, they will learn to look upon religion with indifference and do little to sustain and support the church.

In Utica, Oswego, Syracuse and Binghamton, this message was not heard fully if, for no other reason, than the enormous investment required to keep up with the demands of rural and small town stations and missions and the rapidly expanding population of the cities. Nevertheless, the impulse towards building schools received several boosts forward. One boost came from the desire to assist orphans and abandoned children, which led to the provision of orphan asylums with schools attached. The schools not only instructed the young inmates, but often drew paying students, providing some badly needed income. In 1834, the Devereux brothers and Father Walter J. Quarter had brought the Sisters of Charity to Utica to open an orphanage and school for girls and infant boys. The brothers donated an initial $5,000, provided temporary lodging for the sisters when they arrived and contributed heavily each year to their support. With this help, St. John's Asylum opened with 30 children and a tuition free school. In 1848, it was incorporated independently and, in 1864, a new brick building was erected. In 1854, St. John's under Father McFarland opened a school for boys, Assumption Academy; tuition was charged until the debt was paid. In the 1860s, concern for older Catholic orphan boys in the public asylum led to formation of another orphanage for boys, launched with a fair in 1865 which, with the governor and other notables present, brought in $10,000. The new orphanage received some public funds for the care of children who were public charges, but its costs were heavy. In 1876, chagrined at mismanagement by a lay board, the Christian Brothers withdrew and the bishop purchased the home at public auction. The Brothers returned in 1877 and in 1885, they purchased the property and reincorporated as St. Vincent's Industrial School. Boys between six and 14 were admitted and received instruction in ordinary school subjects, religion and industrial arts.

In Rome, Father Beecham persuaded the Sisters of the Holy Names of Jesus and Mary to send four sisters to open St. Peter's school in 1865. In 1873, they added a select school for girls intended, in the bishop's words, to prepare young women "for the station in life to which they may aspire or be called." Among other things, each girl was taught "to cultivate the Christian virtues and acquire the womanly accomplishments indispensable to the true mistress of the home." When Father James Hourigan arrived in 1847 to take charge of the church in Binghamton, he found a similar school already opened under the charge of two Catholic women, Ellen White and Miss Dodge, sister of the famous David Dodge of Pompey. Miss White wanted to establish a new religious community of women to instruct the "children of the Catholic poor," but neither Hourigan nor Bishop McCloseky were interested. Instead the pastor opened a parish school for girls with these ladies in charge. In 1851, the

Sisters of St. Joseph of Carondelet arrived and the school, now called St. Joseph's Academy, attracted both Catholic and Protestant students and took in boarders as well as day students. Not until 1876 was a boy's school, St. Patrick's Academy, opened in the city. Later when Hourigan took a homeless child to the convent, the community decided an orphanage was needed. In 1881 the priest purchased a large former Methodist property recently used as a college. The Franciscan Sisters arrived to help. They begged door to door, and St. Mary's Home, serving girls through their teens and boys through childhood, opened, assisted by county support for public charges.

The first sisters to arrive in Syracuse were three Sisters of Charity invited to open an orphanage for St. Mary's and St. John the Baptist parishes. A joint fair was held, but the diocese decided to attach the institution to St. Mary's. In the early days, the sisters had difficulty finding adequate quarters and income. As one of the early sisters wrote later of another: "I've known her to go on foot for hours when every step was like a dagger going through her and nothing but her courage kept her from dropping in the street." Once again the sisters were allowed to care for boys only until the age of 10 or 12 years, so Father O'Hara and Father Guerdet of St. John the Evangelist persuaded the Christian Brothers to open a home for boys, the House of Providence. They vigorously appealed for help to non-Catholics and to local government for support. Also in 1869 the brothers took charge of the school at St. John's which had begun in 1854. In 1881, the Sisters of St. Joseph came to St. John's to assist with the primary grades, and a few years later the parish opened a high school, St. John's Academy. St. John the Baptist opened its first school under the Sisters of St. Joseph in 1877. They also launched a high school, Sacred Heart Academy. By 1877, 500 students were

SISTERS FOR RURAL EDUCATION

Several times in 1852, Ellen White and Cynthia Dodge of Binghamton wrote to Bishop McCloskey of Albany about forming a religious congregation with its motherhouse in New York's Southern Tier. They hoped to work in rural education, teaching boys under age 14, as well as girls. In one such letter, Miss White included the following overview of such a community:

"Inclined toward the Rule of St. Francis of Sales for the Sisters of the Visitation.

"The end and aim of the order to be the preservation of the faith among the children of the Catholic poor, by establishing for them in the *country towns* schools so good in every respect, that the parents will not be tempted to send them to those seminaries of infidelity, the district schools, and by giving to the farmer in a measure the character of pay-schools, to foster a spirit of honest independence even among the poorest of the poor.

"The members are never to have the charge of hospitals, orphan asylums, or boarding schools. The higher branches of education not professedly taught; but if in the neighborhood of those schools are respectable Catholic families in poor circumstances who are desirous to have their children educated for teachers, it will come within their rules to teach (these) accomplishments for a moderate compensation, and thus keep them from the cheap protestant schools.

"But the children of the rich are not to be taught if their parents can be prevailed upon to send them to convent schools...

"When time and number shall permit it, the members are to visit the sick amongst the scholars and their parents, bringing them any little comforts they can procure for them.

"This order must make it their business to ascertain the districts most needing their services & with the Bishop's permission, *offer* themselves accordingly. They are to *offer* their services (when their numbers will permit) instead of waiting to be invited as in other orders, for this reason, that these schools are intended for places in which the inhabitants consider themselves too poor to attempt establishing an order, with the expense which generally attends such an undertaking.

"A house and play ground must always be supplied them. The house large enough to lodge four persons and accommodate 150 scholars. They will also require about two hundred dollars for the first year. They will require no pastor to make any positive agreement, further than this. The school department to be fitted up neatly. The part occupied by the sisters with rigid economy.

"The order must never receive money from government aid in carrying on their school."

For some reason, perhaps because of the lack of encouragement by her pastor and the bishop, or perhaps because she lost interest in the idea herself, Miss White did not follow through with her intention to form a religious community. Letters later that year speak of her interest in joining the Sisters of Notre Dame de Namur in Cincinnati.

enrolled in the parish schools.

In Oswego, the beginning of Catholic school education came in 1851 with a school at St. Mary's, taught by two lay women and a lay man. The Sisters of St. Joseph of Carondelet made their first eastern foundation there in 1858, the sisters traveling from Missouri by boat, wagon train and railroad. In 1867, the Sisters of St. Anne came from Canada to serve a new school in St. Paul's. A few months after they arrived, the pastor died. His successor, Father Barry, was unsympathetic to the sisters' methods and wished them to leave the school; but the parishioners backed the sisters, and what one sister called "a fourteen year war of nerves" ensued until the school closed temporarily in 1881. Barry believed in Catholic education, but had his own ideas. He opposed the sisters because they refused to recognize his authority, submit to examinations he would administer, or work with lay teachers. Meanwhile, another group of these sisters had come to work at St. Louis, the French parish in the city, arriving in 1872. Their service there helped that shaky parish survive. In the early days the sisters begged door to door in Albany and other cities to save the parish from bankruptcy.

But it was the German parishes which were the earliest and most tenacious supporters of Catholic schools. At Assumption in Syracuse, a lay schoolmaster, often assisted by the pastor, instructed youngsters from the founding of the parish. When Francis Baumer arrived in 1848, he took charge of a school of more than 40 boys; later other lay teachers were added, while Baumer became organist and choir director. St. Joseph's in Utica hired its first schoolmaster in 1851. At the small German parish of St. Mary's in Manlius, there was also a schoolmaster; control of the small school was a bone of contention between pastors and the trustees. The great turning point for these German schools came in 1860, when the Franciscan sisters arrived. Their

services secured these German Catholic schools at Assumption and St. Joseph's Utica, which were the most stable and successful in the diocese. When St. Joseph's German parish opened in Syracuse in 1882, Father Joseph Pickl hired a teacher "who came from Germany with high ideas," but left because he "could not do the schoolwork." The pastor pleaded with the Franciscan Sisters to help him and they promised to do so, finally sending the first contingent in the spring of 1883. The superior announced this good news to the pastor, adding that she would "give you and the sisters the joy of accompanying them," which would be "a great help to you and them in preparing for this new assignment."

Obviously these few struggling schools and academies could not meet the educational needs of all Catholics. In urban areas, most Catholic youngsters attended the common schools. New York state's system of common schools had been in existence since the 1830s and, in most communities, prayer and Scripture reading were part of the daily routine. In some cases, the priests persuaded local authorities to excuse the Catholic children from such exercises. In 1871, for example, the priests of Syracuse requested that Catholic children be allowed to leave the room during prayer and scripture reading, but the more self-confident pastors were not satisfied with this arrangement. It was "not a just rule," O'Hara told his St. Mary's congregation; they should keep their children home until the matter was settled satisfactorily. "This is not a request but a command," he told them; "those who are negligent will be deprived of the sacraments." Apparently the matter was settled temporarily, but it kept returning. In 1873, O'Hara once again told his people to insist that their children be excused and, if refused, to boycott the school. Bible reading ended that year, but it was back in 1883, when the priests again reminded parents to have their children excused.

Yet not all was conflict. In many communities the priests lived comfortably with the public schools. In Utica, St. Patrick's school was leased briefly to city authorities who allowed the pastor to appoint the teacher, an arrangement similar to others around the country. However, such cooperation was becoming more rare. In theory, if not yet in practice, the Church sought schools where religion could be a vital part of the curriculum, but only if it was Catholicism and not a watered-down, nondenominational Christianity. The Albany diocese reflected the new self-confidence and assertiveness of the Catholic population by petitioning, along with other dioceses, for state support of Catholic schools in 1869. Bishop Conroy wrote his priests, urging them to get signatures for passage of a law to secure a "fund for the permanent aid and support of our Catholic schools," while warning them to keep their effort "free of any political party." When this action caused a firestorm of controversy in the Albany press, Father Patrick Ludden defended the Church, arguing that it was the state's task to ensure equal educational opportunity, and it was the right of parents and guardians to make a free, unrestricted choice in the selection of schools. The bill proved unsuccessful. However, Ludden, Bishop Conroy and others shared the conviction of Bernard McQuaid, recently appointed the first bishop of Rochester, that if the Irish and German Catholics of the state could be mobilized, "we shall obtain what we want."

THRESHOLD OF A NEW DIOCESE

For Bishop McQuaid, as for John Hughes four decades earlier, unity could be achieved best by unified Catholic people, who would demand their rights and, through their own schools, ensure the survival of a distinct Catholic subculture, segregated to some degree from their neighbors. The goal and the means were the same — the organized unification of the Catholic community. Bringing about unity was the major responsibility of the bishop. In most communities, the diocese and its bishop were distant, hardly noticed save at confirmations or when a pastor was needed. But diocesan administration also was changing. The new legislation on parish corporations ensured the bishop's control over property, making it possible to begin implementing the sweeping powers over parish funds called for in the last days of the Hughes era. McCloskey, however, was a mild, somewhat bookish man, little inclined to run things from Albany. During his administration, the strong pastors of the city parishes had close to a free hand.

In 1864, McCloskey succeeded Hughes as Archbishop of New York and his vicar general, John J. Conroy, became bishop of Albany. Conroy had a difficult administration, plagued by personal problems and internal dissension. He was forced to accept a coadjutor bishop against his will in 1874. The new bishop, Francis McNeirny, presided until the formation of the new diocese of Syracuse in 1886. Both Conroy and McNeirny were centralizers, attempting to follow in Hughes' footsteps by bringing a greater degree of order and discipline to the Church. For example, each parish previously had attempted to provide cemetery space for its members. Indeed, provision of sacred ground for burial was a strong motivating force in the foundation of Catholic parishes. Rapid expansion and lack of planning soon rendered these small cemeteries obsolete, and a variety of alternatives were adopted, including the one in Syracuse where Father O'Hara and some laymen founded a cemetery independent of the diocese and parish. Conroy ordered O'Hara's cemetery closed to all but those who had purchased plots. Later he placed an interdict on it, so that it no longer was "sacred ground." This led to a long drawn out battle with the crusty Syracuse pastor and a law suit with O'Hara as the embattled defendant.

Conroy's plan for diocesan cemeteries to replace the patchwork of parish and ethnic units was not very successful. However, it provided a clear indication of the direction of diocesan policy, attempting to bring greater efficiency and order to a Church long composed of more or less autonomous congregations. While formally the bishop's authority over the pastor was nearly total, practically great distances, the loyalty to the pastor of his own congregation, and the sturdy, independent character of these mission priests rendered that authority less than perfect. Conroy and McNeirny struggled mightily to make their diocese into one Church in organization, as well as in faith, but their demands reflected anxiety about their priests' compliance. Indeed, other New York state bishops occasionally complained of the lack of discipline in the Church in Central New York, complaints which contributed to the division of the diocese and the formation of the See of Syracuse in 1886. One of those incidents, whose outcome showed the shape of things to come, took place at St. John's in Utica. Father Edward Terry was assigned as assistant to Father Thomas Daley in 1876. Although ordained only a short time, the young priest had to take almost entire charge of the parish because of the pastor's physical incapacity. Terry was instrumental in saving the local orphanage from bankruptcy, and he won wide popularity for his thoughtfulness, refinement and oratorical gifts. In fact, he served as the attractive Catholic clergyman in *The Damnation of Theron Ware,* a novel written by the editor of the local newspaper. By 1880, it was clear that Father Daley would not return to good health and an acting pastor would have to be appoointed. The diocese selected James M. Ludden, then

pastor of St. Mary's in Little Falls, and transferred the younger Father Terry to St. Ann's in Albany. Leaders of the congregation, who admired Terry, clamored for his return and made things uncomfortable for Ludden. Some even withdrew entirely from the church, bringing about a sharp drop in parish revenues. The battle continued for a year and a half until finally McNeirny intervened, promising to make a change provided there was clear recognition of his authority to make pastoral assignments. A lay committee then wrote him stating:

> *If in the course of the discussion that has unfortunately arisen on this subject, any of us have given expression to any sentiment questioning your authority as Bishop to appoint and remove the priest of the parish in accordance with the statutes governing the diocese, or your authority or right to be obeyed as our bishop, we hereby in the most unqualified manner, retract the same. That there may be no doubt of the position we now occupy in the matter, allow us further to say that we do now accept and recognize the Rev. Fr. Ludden in the position to which you have appointed him.*

McNeirny was satisfied, telling the committee that as his rights were now "clearly and distinctly recognized," he would "probably" take their petitions into consideration. Ludden was then transferred and J.S.M. Lynch was appointed pastor. Tired of the controversy, the parish acquiesced in this move.

McNeirny's understanding of his leadership went beyond control of appointments. He was the founder of modern diocesan administration, inaugurating new policies with the help of his vicar general, Patrick Ludden. McNeirny systematized the work of the chancery, set up schedules for parish reports, convened synods and theological conferences for the

Bishop Francis McNeirny of Albany (Photo: Assumption parish)

clergy, and made confirmation ceremonies every three years occasions for canonical visitation of parishes, when he carefully examined parish records and inspected the property. He was particularly anxious to establish better control of church finances. One consequence of the abolition of the old trustee system and the now near absolute control of church property by the bishop, through his appointed pastor and trustees, was the need for the bishop to be informed fully about the financial situation of parishes. In 1883, McNeirny told his priests that he "keenly felt the necessity" to develop "a system which would bring under control the management of the pecuniary affairs" of the diocese and "place clearly and distinctly before the observing eye of the ordinary of the diocese ... the financial condition of each and every mission within its precincts." This was especially needed, he wrote, because of the "overflowing vitality" of the Church, its rapid expansion and the generosity of the people. It was this concern which led him to push the priests so zealously for annual reports from their missions. "The intimate knowledge the bishop should have of everything that pertains to his diocese" could not

but bring "happy results," he told them. Surely they could have avoided some of the problems and "embarrassment of the past" if such information had been available. Now that the affairs of the diocese "have assumed better shape," he wanted to take steps to "obtain a more perfect knowledge of all that relates to the diocese." He announced formation of a "diocesan bureau of accounts" and "an audit of diocesan accounts." Pastors were required to submit a signed statement of all parish financial accounts, their mortgage, debts, insurance, and a diagram showing the parish property and buildings. At Christmas 1883, McNeirny asked the priests to submit a form containing detailed information about their parishes although, as he noted later, it was far from what he could have asked for according to Church law; he thought it would make a good start. He was attempting to make parish operations more efficient and responsible:

We all know with what care and vigilance affairs are managed in business houses of good standing. Every detail is noted with minuteness, and every item of receipts and expenditures accounted for by a corresponding voucher, a reference to which easily dispels any doubt that may arise as to the nature of business transactions. Such is the wisdom of the world in its commercial relations; and it certainly behooves the church not to be less wise in what effects its material and temporal interests. Anyway, the pastor who enjoys the confidence of his people through a careful accounting wins their increased generosity. In the future, therefore, you will pay no bills exceeding the sum of one dollar without exacting receipts therefore. These receipts will be retained to serve as vouchers. In like manner, you will

73

give receipts for money paid to credit of church account, pew rents, etc.

He added a copy of a letter of praise from the cardinal prefect of Propaganda at the Vatican, in order to encourage in his priests "a willing, cheerful and prompt compliance with the requirements of your bishops."

Clearly this cooperative spirit among the priests required not only orders from the top, but respect for their dignity and attention to their needs. In other dioceses, arbitrary transfers and removals inhibited that sense of clerical-episcopal solidarity. Even more damaging were incidents in which bishops treated aged or infirmed priests or those subject to some vice with less than generosity. McNeirny was determined to avoid that problem. He established a clerical fund to be paid from parish revenues or special collections for the care of retired priests, those who were ill, or those in any other way unable to perform their ministry. His program was notable because it admitted the bishop's responsibility for such cases, including those who were disabled by "human frailty," a provision some friends like John Farley of New York thought most generous and one which the clergy would appreciate deeply.

Bishop McNeirny's efforts to unify his priests and improve the management of the diocese were still a bit premature. because the priests themselves were just taking charge of their parishioners. The work of building churches in the setting in which they found themselves required a high degree of independence and single-minded force of personality. A new generation of self-confident priests, Franciscan German and secular Irish, by 1886 had solidly established the Church in the cities of Central New York. They were equivocal about other projects. While they gave their full support to orphanages in Utica, Syracuse and Binghamton, most still tended to think of schools as appropriate only for more prosperous and established communities. In addition, most still had confidence in the basic good will of public school authorities. They had not yet reached the conclusion that social segregation, rather than social advancement and integration, was the best way to ensure a faithful and unified Catholic Church in years to come. Yet it would be wrong to think of these men only as builders, and neglect the pastoral skill which was at least as important as their forceful personalities. In building churches, they were also building communities and assisting their people to discover the presence of Christ in one another and in their world.

MEMBERS OF THAT WONDROUS CHURCH

CATHOLIC LIFE CENTERS ON PARISHES
1850s-1880s

Catholic communities in Central New York took shape around apostolic lay leaders and became organized as churches through the leadership of a remarkable generation of commanding, energetic priests. By the end of the third quarter of the nineteenth century, there was a growing, even flourishing Catholicism in the region, large and complex enough to give rise to talk of a new diocese under its own bishop. The Catholicism that was emerging in Central New York appeared, at first glance much like that found elsewhere, especially in Ireland. However, the United States was not Ireland, and this Church was not the same as any other. It was a new Church, built from experiences that encompassed people's memories of churches left behind and a faith learned in their youth, but formed as well to the living realities around them, and expressing their own longings for the future.

Churches fulfill many functions other than worship. Catholicism found in this place, New York State, at this time, the nineteenth century, included tenets of faith, principles of morality, church buildings and much else. Most notable was a fabric of relationships among the "members of that wondrous church," knit around common objectives which led to common activities. The parishes of Syracuse, Utica, Binghamton, Rome, Oswego and dozens of smaller towns and villages were centers of fellowship, networks of mutual assistance, focal points for shared memories and energizing centers for the pursuit of shared hopes. To ask the question why it happened, why this surprising phenomenon appeared, is to probe beneath the surface, there to find few clear answers, but perhaps to expand one's understanding of what is and might be.

—>·÷·<—

In a small notebook kept between 1869 and 1873, Father James O'Hara of St. Mary's Church in Syracuse jotted down the following random thoughts:

What necessity for this society
the world has become degenerate
did God make it so
God made man right God's laws are
onerous
so thinks unthinking man
he must submit to human law
he calls for freedom and becomes more
servile
men who speak most of freedom
enjoy least of it
no freedom out of God's laws
to do wrong is not freedom
knowledge true is freedom
you are willingly under obligation
everything is plain and full of light
you assemble to injure no man
you assemble to improve yourself and
do good
in this society should be one heart and
one soul
you should fulfill obligation
pay your dues
you have many benefits here
enjoyment, good books and papers
promote religion
sanctify and instruct yourselves
pacify society.

Perhaps intended for a talk to a young men's society, these notes highlight many of the assumptions around which nineteenth century American Catholicism developed. O'Hara asks the "necessity" for this society, the Church. Why does it exist and why should people sacrifice for its provision? The answer begins with pessimism, "the world has become degenerate," a seeming paradox when stated by an ambitious priest at the center of an aspiring community in a booming industrial city. Yet, the consciousness of many immigrants, especially the Irish, was often dark and foreboding. The dramatic changes which had taken place in their own lives left a strong sense of the fragility of life, lived always, despite appearances, at the edge of poverty and powerlessness. In Ireland, ruled by an alien English elite, facing a future with few prospects, people had experienced the possibility of starvation. In urban, industrial America, the transplanted Irish saw themselves as "strangers in the land." Freedom was a heady experience, at once exhilarating and frightening. Freedom could bring new possibilities of dignity, but it also might cost them their children or their souls. In the priest's mind, freedom might mean escape from the demands of God in order to pursue money, pleasure and worldly gain. The Church knew better, O'Hara thought. In the Church, one learned the requirements of God, and on that basis alone, could there be a secure foundation for the enjoyment of that wider freedom offered by the new land.

"To do wrong" was not freedom, but only "knowledge true," the kind of knowledge no longer automatically available from the integrated village culture of Ireland, Quebec or Bavaria, but preserved and made available through "this society," the Church. If they could establish in this new world a separate, Catholic world, freedom and order might be combined. By placing themselves willingly "under obligation," "everything" could become "plain and full of light."

Thus the Church established a center of order, authority, stability and continuity. It was an anchor and guide in the midst of rapid change, in an American setting filled with people hostile to the faith, suspicious of traditional customs, and seemingly anxious to exploit the newcomers and their children at every turn. The Church was a community, a "society," which faced in two directions. It faced backwards toward the old world, preserving the best that the newcomers had brought with them. It also looked forward toward the American future, ensuring that the new freedom did not make people "more servile" and assisting them to build new lives with integrity, to become Americans while remaining true to themselves.

Rebutting the charges of nativists and anti-Catholics, O'Hara told his people they "assemble to injure no man" but "to improve yourself and do good." Through the Church and its programs, Catholics could "sanctify and instruct" themselves, lay the foundation for secure advancement and prepare for the judgment to come at death. Here, too, they could "do good," assist one another, provide help for the poor, the orphans and the widows, "promote religion" of such obvious benefit to the community and, by establishing order among the sometimes disorderly immigrants, contribute to civic harmony and "pacify society." "Enjoyment, good books and papers" suggest one of the ever-present groups of young adults whose meeting rooms were also libraries, and whose fellowship provided the young with opportunities "to sanctify and instruct" themselves. To be successful, the Church needed the support of its members, they must be united, "one heart and one soul," and they must contribute to its support — "fulfill obligation, pay your dues."

These were the themes of Catholic development, explaining why it was important to be part of the Church, why the growth of the Church helped the larger community and nation, why the Church required unity and submissiveness to God's will, and why it was so important to provide the financial support which alone could make it successful. All over the world, the nineteenth century Church was in a process of reorganization, aimed at unifying the Catholic population around a disciplined diocesan clergy, serving through a regular network of parishes centered upon the provision of the sacraments. Men and women whose village Catholicism had featured a variety of family and local saints, household devotions, festivals, pilgrimages and holy day celebrations were becoming "practicing Catholics" who attended Church, confessed their sins, listened to instructions and assisted at Mass. Under Pope Pius IX (1846-1878), a whole host of prayers and devotions (some new, others long present in informal popular practice or promoted by religious orders) were given official recognition. To the practice of these devotions, indulgences were attached which could be won after the performance of certain obligations, including, in every case, reception of penance and holy communion. At the same time, veneration of the Blessed Sacrament spread widely and gained in intensity, drawing the attention of Church members to the place where the Blessed Sacrament resided, the church, and to the clergy who made it available.

BRINGING CATHOLICS TO CHURCH

Evangelization was aimed primarily at bringing people whose background included little experience of frequent church attendance to church practice and instructing them in the elementary teachings and moral obligations of Catholics. Church-centered piety and clear moral rules stood at the center of Catholic consciousness and at the heart of the Church's ministry. Together they provided a valuable and appropriate foundation for the community life immigrant Americans so badly needed.

In 1875 and 1881, the pope declared jubilee years. In New York, a plenary indulgence could be earned by six visits to specially designated churches, fasting on a day other than those assigned by the Church, almsgiving to the poor, and confession and at least two communions beyond those needed to fulfill the Easter duty. Like many popular devotions, this one centered attention on the Church, ensured the practice of the sacraments, educated Catholics to the rules of fasting, and brought to practice convictions which flowed from a piety which emphasized sin and the means the Church offered to overcome sin and earn eternal salvation. At a more popular level, such events helped the American Church break down the influence of popular religious practices subject to abuse when carried on outside the Church's control. In 1882, for example, a Syracuse pastor declared from his pulpit that "blessing graves by laymen is not permitted." In his notes for the announcement, under the heading "Dust thou Art," he wrote that such practices might be permitted "at an infidel or freemason burying ground," but not at a Catholic cemetery, where the blessing must be given by a priest. People might pray privately, he wrote, but public "prayer should not be conducted by a layman."

Parish missions were another important technique for bringing immigrant Catholics to the practice of their faith. The first English speaking mission band, a group of Redemptorists, included Clarence Walorth, George Deshon and Isaac Hecker. The band preached to huge crowds at St. Patrick's in Utica, a poor Irish parish, six years after the tiny community was founded. A few years, later they were at the larger parish, St. John's, and they returned frequently after they had founded the Paulist Fathers. Jesuits, Lazarists and Passionists also gave missions in the area. Always the opening sermons, in Isaac Hecker's words, aroused "fear in the most hardened sinner." The sins denounced threatened personal lives, family welfare, and the reputation and good name of all Catholics. In a mission sermon for the women of St. Patrick's, for example, Father Angelo, a Passionist, described the sins of "Mrs. Scandal," whose licentious behavior damaged her own soul and the reputations of her fellow Catholics:

This city is darkened by the foul crime of scandal even more than by the black clouds of smoke that hang over it and shut out the light of day. Doubtless there are here young girls whose earliest memories have been associated with drunkeness and debauchery, young women who have been driven to infamy and despair by the shameful conduct of parents; aged mothers have seen all their love and self-sacrifice turned into bitterness and despair by the saloon, the gambling den, the dance hall, houses of infamy.

A typical mission in 1865 opened on Monday evening, the feast of All Saints. A sermon on penance was followed by Benediction of the Blessed Sacrament. Four masses were held each morning at five, six, seven and eight o'clock, with a brief instruction following the first and last Mass. The early Mass was intended for "working and business men" who could not make it at another hour. Evening services, with sermon and Benediction, were scheduled for 7:30, while confessions were available from eight to 12 in the morning, two to six in the afternoon and following the evening service until 10 o'clock. Three priests were offering the mission, but five others were available to assist with the sacraments. As with a jubilee year, indulgences were available for those who attended, contributed to a charitable enterprise, and received penance and communion.

Catholic missions were the counterpart of Protestant revivals, aimed at making faith a matter of personal conviction by bringing about a real conversion from sin and an awakening to the need for God's grace. This evangelicalism was Catholic, however, because the converted sinner was directed toward the sacrament of penance as the means to free

GOING FORTH FROM ONEIDA

The story of Catholicism in the United States is filled with the sacrifices of men and women who have left the comforts of American towns to serve as missionaries among people of other continents with different ways of life and other understandings of God. These messengers of the Church took with them a faith to share and a desire to serve the needy.

In the 1850s and 60s, St. Patrick's parish at Oneida prepared one of its own as such a missionary. As a young boy, Theophilus Mayer had come to Oneida from Montreal. His French-Canadian family was devoted to the faith, and Theophilus seemed drawn to the priesthood. Later parish histories would call him "an esteemed favorite and protege" of the pastor, Father William Fennelly, who himself once had been a missionary in the South. At St. Patrick's, Theophilus grew in faith and yearned for mission service. When he was 25, he studied at seminaries in Montreal and London — becoming the first priest from the Oneida parish. Theophilus was noted for his piety and zeal in everything pertaining to missionary work. He was the only American among four priests selected by St. Joseph's Society for Foreign Missions to go to what was then British India.

Mayer arrived there during a severe famine that began in the 1870s and began his work among the Hindus. After recovering from smallpox, he devoted himself to caring for the ill, especially those suffering from cholera, smallpox and other diseases aggravated by the famine. The British government appointed him to head relief efforts distributing supplies to the Indians, and Queen Victoria herself wrote of her admiration and thanks.

When famine subsided in 1880, Father Mayer was named to head a Catholic mission covering 11,000 square miles. He mastered five native Indian languages and converted many Hindus to Christianity. He later headed a Catholic college in Madras and was named vicar-general of the Madras diocese, the first American missionary to receive that important position.

Theophilus Mayer apparently never went home to St. Patrick's where fellow parishioners once had nurtured his missionary dreams. But years later, he was remembered with pride — a product of Oneida who had served his Church well in the mission field of India.

oneself from sin and make things right with God. Attending Mass and receiving communion completed the process of conversion, while continued attendance at the sacraments and participation in the life of the Church were means by which one persevered in the new-found moral life. Conversion to the life of grace was, at the same time, bringing people to participate in and support the church and its pastor, for it was only in church and through the priest that the sacraments could be secured. As one newspaper report put it, "every Catholic in the parish makes it his duty to attend the services...the object of the mission is to bring the lukewarm to a sense of their religious obligations and to instruct the people in the faith."

The themes of the mission sermons carried over into the regular preaching. One typical sermon described in the bleakest terms the period that intervened between the sin of Adam and coming of Jesus, with appropriate lessons drawn for the modern age. The degradation of the human race left to its own "depressed powers" was evident again in modern times, when some would "turn back the hand of the dial of civilization twenty centuries by establishing, as the only lamp for man's course, limited, closed and perverted reason." Now, as then, "man wallowed in the mire of iniquity." But, "having drunk to the dregs of every pleasure," people "began to feel that this was not the end for which they were created" and demanded something "more noble to satisfy their soul." What John the Baptist had announced to such seekers, the Catholic Church made available here and now. No effort was spared to evoke the ancient power and glory of Catholicism. However excluded and exploited they might feel at the moment, Catholics were part of an ancient, universal, historical communion. The sentiment of Catholic exclusivism, the idea that the Church was both the means of salvation and the guardian of civilization, filled sermons and lectures, items in bazaar booklets and announcements of social events. One eloquent expression can be found in a sermon preached by Father Edward Terry of Utica on the death of Pope Pius IX in 1878:

It is no spirit of reflection upon any man, or upon any other conscience, but with a sincere charity for all, that we own with honest pride that it is a great glory of our lives to be members of that wondrous church — to be born into that fold that holds for us the food of heaven, the precious sacraments whose grace may make us worthy of the great reward. All the dignities of earth, the crowns and plumes and laurel wreaths of victory, the pride of birth, the pomp of station, the fawning praise and service of the entire globe, were empty baubles all in the presence of this one supreme privilege of being faithful members of the holy Catholic church.

Amid the great movements of history and the rise and fall of nations, the "wondrous church" persisted. "Rough waves roll and lash her yielding form and storm clouds gather and lower in her path," Terry said, but Pius' "whitened locks flung streaming on the winds were contrast with the darkness; the grasp of the old man's hand was a grasp of enduring youth, and not all the power the earth could have availed to wrest the helm from the hand of that sainted old pontiff."

Nowhere was that sense of ancient glory and present power evoked more wonderfully than in the massive churches of the period and the ceremonies celebrated within them. Assumption church in Syracuse was among the most magnificient, and its celebrations invariably drew detailed press attention in an age when newspapers sent "stringers" to cover Sunday services and report the musical program and the sermon on Monday morning. For the closing cermonies of May devotions to the Blessed Mother, for example, the Mary altar was richly decorated with fresh flowers, with candles interspersed among them. The Syracuse *Journal* described the scene:

A magnificent canopy was erected in front of the high altar, which was also decorated with flowers and ablaze with lights, and this was carried in the procession around the church, under which was the Sacred Host, borne by priests and their attendants, preceded by cross bearers and acolytes dressed

Christmas decorations at St. James church in Cazenovia (Photo: Chancery Archives)

in white and bearing lighted wax tapers. They were followed by the 'children of Mary,' girls dressed in white with wreaths upon their heads and flower baskets in their hands, from which they scattered floral tributes in the line of procession over which the Blessed Sacrament was borne. The fine choir, which was very effective under the leadership of Professor Baumer, the efficient organist, with its sweet and powerful organ, rendered 'Ave Maria,' the Litany of the Blessed Virgin, the Sublime Cantical of the 'Magnificat.' The decorations, the long line of acolytes bearing burning tapers, the priests in surplices, stoles and capes and the church in white all contributed to the making of an imposing religious display.

First communion was also an event everywhere, but again nowhere more than at Assumption, where it was occasion for yet another procession, this time a public parade in which all the parish societies and some from neighboring parishes marched in full uniform. In 1875, 123 children were ready for their sacramental reception, and so were their elders:

As early as 9 a.m. the various German societies attached to the church of the Assumption were out in full regalia and formed an imposing procession in front of the church, with rich banners interspersed with the national colors and headed by Pierson's fine band. The procession included St. Joseph's Benefit Society, St. Francis, St. Michael's, St. Stephen's, St. Boniface,

*and St. Fidelius Benefit Society, all
with their respective banners in blue,
white and other colored satins, trimmed in gold and silver fringe and
bearing various scriptural devices. Boys
and girls neatly dressed passed through
a double file and entered the church
where services of the day commenced.
The High Altar still wore its Easter
decorations and was loaded with wax
tapers, as were the subaltars and the
effect was dazzlingly beautiful with the
floral display and the rich ornaments.
Schafford's Grand High Mass in D
was the one sung by the full choir and
organ and aided by a fine orchestra. At
the Gospel, Father Dehm ascended the
pulpit and preached a discourse from
the first chapter of St. Luke and the
following verses: 'My Soul Doth Mag-
nify the Lord.' The Mass proceeded,
and the boys and girls received their
first communion. Father Dehm then
addressed them and they were dismissed for the morning.*

The Irish, of course, came to America with
less liturgical background, because the public
celebration of the Mass was forbidden until
the early nineteenth century. Country stations
and missions in the United States naturally
lent themselves to simple ceremonies.
However, urban Catholics, particularly as they
became more settled, wanted to impress their
neighbors with the grandeur and richness of
their Catholic tradition. Music was one way to
do that. One of the first actions taken at St.
John's of Utica after the parish was organized
was to hire an organist and "arrange for his
conveyance to and from church." Even an
extremely poor parish like St. Patrick's in
West Utica announced proudly when it
opened its tiny church that it had a melodeon.
When St. Mary's of Syracuse dedicated a new
church in 1861, the newspapers announced a
full musical program open to the public,
along with a "most intellectual feast" in a
sermon by a visiting priest. Later, praising
Father O'Hara, the paper placed him in "that
useful class of Pastors, who, while they edify
and instruct the interior do not forget to
adorn and embellish things that are external."
They were not wrong, for his parish opened a
mission with the singing of Mozart's twelfth
Mass and regularly featured major musical
presentations at Sunday Vesper services. For
example, when the service was sung with
antiphonal voices, there was a boys' choir in
the front of the church and a men's choir in
the loft.

Forty Hours devotion was another major
event in every parish. Introduced in the
United States in 1853, it proved a useful way
to center attention on the Eucharist. The
priest reminded his people of the privilege of
having the Blessed Sacrament on the altar.
Opening ceremonies often featured a major
musical presentation and a sermon by a
visiting priest. Many clergy from the surrounding community attended the closing
Benediction, which was often followed by a
dinner given for the visitors by the pastor.
This event provided one of the few occasions
when priests could meet together, discuss
common problems and catch up on ecclesiastical gossip. For the parish the Forty
Hours was a time of renewal, with daily
Masses at five, seven and nine, confessions in
the afternoon, and Benediction and sermon in
the evening.

Another element of Church discipline was
fasting. In 1869, Lenten regulations provided
that everyone over 21 should take only one
full meal a day, except Sundays. Coffee or tea
could be taken in the morning and light
nourishment in the evening. Meat was allowed
on Sundays and at one meal three days a
week. Meat and fish could not be used at the
same meal, even on Sundays. Eggs, butter and
cheese were not prohibited. Dispensation

from fasting, though not from abstinence, was granted to the sick and infirmed, "laborers and mechanics and others whose duties are of a very laborious and exhausting nature," pregnant and nursing women, and the poor "who are not sure of even having one meal a day." Lent was also a time when there were many special "ceremonies, instructions and lectures," including the Stations of the Cross, Benediction of the Blessed Sacrament and recitation of the rosary.

FORMING A BETTER COMMUNITY

In a free and pluralistic society, the state no longer enforced religious uniformity and the larger culture did not reinforce but even challenged Catholic identity. In this environment, "practicing" Catholics were men and women who had decided voluntarily to join a particular church, follow a prescribed routine of Church practice and adopt a mode of behavior which conformed to Church teaching. It meant, in short, the acceptance of discipline which made "good Catholics." At the same time this discipline helped Church members develop the qualities of sobriety, industriousness and dependability required if they were to be successful in the urban, industrial society in which they now lived. When O'Hara told his congregation that "spitting in church is not allowed" or when he complained after a visit from the bishop that his parishioners were "spitting in pews [and] eating peanuts," he was demanding a decorum, order and respectability as important for their social and economic advancement as for their eternal salvation. When Bishop McNeirny of Albany announced the special indulgences of a jubilee year in 1875, he told the priests to teach the people:

To be sober, to avoid the widespread vice of intemperance, which leads to

degradation, ignominy and to shame. Teach them to despise the perverse maxims of a conceited and misled world, to avoid its vain and frivolous and sinful amusements. Teach them not to be slaves of, but to overcome all false human respect in the faithful performance of duty. Teach them to guard unceasingly and unswervingly against the false teaching of liberalism, of indifferentism, and of infidelity. Teach them that the truth can make no compromise with error, and that it is base and cowardly to sacrifice truth and principle to the expediency of the hour. Teach them to value their holy faith above all else, and to seek, constantly, in its practice, that which alone can bring peace to them here and secure it for them eternally hereafter, the testimony of an unsullied conscience.

For Irish pastors, in particular, building up the Church also meant disciplining the Irish immigrants. There was, in fact, a disproportionate share of crime, alcohol abuse, violence and pauperism in Irish communities, and there was a real need to establish standards of personal behavior and family life and persuade Irish men to live up to them. The priests attempted to bring community affairs under Church surveillance, as with St. Patrick's day, which became a celebration largely organized around the Church and its lay organizations. The first celebration in Oswego in 1834 featured a banquet at which the church choir sang and a priest delivered an address. In Norwich, the papers reported that the "quiet holiday" had no parade, an event which often became near riotous. Instead it had a musical program at the church and a lecture at a local hall by a prominent visiting priest. In Syracuse, the parade continued but under the auspices of the Church, with priests and parish societies prominently participating. As early as the 1850s, newspapers reported the day marked by Mass, a parade of societies from the two Irish parishes of the city, and an evening of lectures and entertainments at Shakespeare Hall followed by dancing. In 1860, the press praised the "fine spectacle" of that year's events, with a parade of societies to the grave of Father Haes, where prayers were said by the priests, then back to St. Mary's for Mass, followed by another parade with colorful banners and uniforms to another evening of lectures and musical programs.

The major Irish clergy of the area were all strong supporters of Irish nationalism, a stance which undoubtedly strengthened their efforts to gain control over Irish activities. Barry in Oswego, Martin Hughes in Oswego and Binghamton, and O'Hara in Syracuse loudly championed the Irish Land League and the efforts of Charles Stewart Parnell to win home rule. Meetings and lectures were announced from the pulpit, the priests themselves sprinkled their lectures on Irish history and devotion with political commentary, and every major Irish fundraising event won their endorsement. In 1883, a meeting was called in Syracuse to respond to a new wave of repressive legislation consequent on the assassination of Lord Cavendish and Thomas Burke, the chief secretary and under secretary for Irish affairs. The day before the Syracuse meeting, Joseph Brady was executed for the crime. O'Hara, elected chairman of the meeting, stated: "Poor Brady, he died a martyr for his country. Never will the name of Brady be forgotten and the name of his noble mother will live with that of the mother of the Maccabees and the Gracchi." The statement caused a fire storm of criticism. The *Utica Herald* claimed that clergymen who commended such a "cowardly and degrading crime" brought "discredit on their religion." The New York *Telegram* pointed out that O'Hara's actions placed him in opposition to

Pope Leo XIII, who had warned the Irish clergy to abstain from political interference. O'Hara replied that he had said nothing of the guilt or innocence of the executed parties, but knew enough of English justice to believe that the judge and jury were "brought in to convict." As for Leo XIII: "We owe spiritual but not civil allegiance to the Pope. In civil matters we are responsible as American citizens to the constitution of the United States. Let the Pope legislate as far as he can legislate for Italy. He has no authority to legislate for us. In case he had issued such a letter, I don't know that the people of Ireland would be much to blame for refusing to pay Peter's Pence."

These same priests also were bent on uplifting their Irish communities, so such radical statements were rare. None expressed sympathy with the Fenians, who advocated armed revolution. At home, they were alert to every slight upon Irish honor. One pastor responded to the charge that there was a disproportionate number of Irish men in local jails. He argued that the reason for this was that Protestant exploitation naturally had given the Irish a suspicion of law and taught them, out of deep suffering, the occasional need to steal to support their families. On the other hand, they wanted the Irish to take pride in themselves. While they sponsored Irish literary and political figures, they had little use for the "stage Irishman" popular in the late nineteenth century. Forbidding his people to attend a vaudeville performance by "Murray and Murphy," Martin Hughes told them to respect exhibitions of "wit, humor and the nobler traits of Irish character," but treat with scorn performances that connect Irish with "vulgarity and drunkenness."

No activity of the Irish parishes received more notice than the work of the temperance societies. In Oswego, Father Barry of St. Paul's organized a "Sacred Thirst" society of men who swore off drink during Lent. St.

Funeral of a young sodality member at St. Mary's church in Oswego (Photo: Chancery Archives)

Mary's in Syracuse received a big boost by the mission of 1869, when the preachers strongly addressed the evil of drink. The press regularly reported meetings of the parish temperance societies, which featured the singing of temperance ballads by the glee club and lectures on "the destructive tendencies of the wine cup" particularly upon the "domestic circle." The size, vigor and attractiveness of the temperance group helped set a tone for the parish. No organization better illustrated the influence of the desire for self-improvement on the life of the local parish. At one meeting in January 1870, a speaker noted "a great improvement in the morals and conduct of a class that perhaps had given the police docket the most cases." The stories which surround Barry, Hourigan and Beecham, using their canes and religious authority to throw fear into the hearts of men prone to drink in saloons away from their families, reflect deep anxieties in the Irish-American

community and real needs among families. Long-standing evidence of the devastation wrought in Irish communities by drink adds to the conviction that these legends were not mere inventions. The evidence also says the emphasis on temperance and sobriety was neither an accident nor a reflection of a puritanical or Jansenistic morality.

In the German community, temperance was another matter. Saloon keepers and brewers were often prominent in the congregation, and drinking customs were different and generally more restrained. What conflicts there were arose more around violation of the puritan sabbath by German parties and picnics on Sunday than by public drunkenness and desertion. The occasional German priest who advocated temperance, like Father Florian Schwenninger in Utica, met tremendous resistance in his congregation.

Temperance societies were only one of many auxiliary organizations developed around Catholic parishes. The Catholic Mutual Benefit Association offered insurance benefits while promoting Catholic solidarity. Devotional societies flourished, with regular meetings for prayer, instruction and the practice of a particular devotion. Many parishes also organized sodalities for younger, unmarried men and women. At the end of his life, Father John F. Lowery, speaking of his years at St. John's in Oswego, recalled that the formation of sodalities for young women was "a labor of love." He always found them "ready to labor night and day to help the pastor in every good work, especially in adorning the church and altar, and in collecting funds to build churches." In contrast, forming sodalities for young men was "the only difficulty I have experienced in the sacred ministry." Twice in Oswego he had tried and failed, finally commeting:

What a pity that our young men do not second the labor of their pastors. It is easy, indeed, to induce young ladies to band together for religious purposes, a fact which is largely due, no doubt, to their emotional nature. But our young men! They prefer, unfortunately, to organize themselves in worldly associations. They are quite ready to form debating clubs, literary societies, lyceums; quite ready to organize brass bands, and drum corps, become firemen or soldiers for dress parade, but are unwilling to become humble, faithful sodalists. They begin with alacrity, but they do not persevere. What a pity!

To draw young men to church, O'Hara, Barry, Hughes and others organized debating clubs, lending libraries and a variety of self-help projects. They had not turned yet to athletics and were unprepared to organize the bands, marching societies and cultural groups popular in the German parishes.

Among the most successful parish programs was the St. Vincent de Paul Society. Founded by the saintly French layman, Frederick Ozanam, as a means of serving the poor, the organization was brought to America in the 1850s and spread rapidly, the first local chapter appearing at St. John the Evangelist in Syracuse in 1861. Composed of men of the parish, the St. Vincent de Paul chapter collected money, used clothing, food and other necessities for distribution on a confidential basis to the poor. In Central New York, these parish societies initiated efforts to open homes for orphans and raised funds for the sisters and brothers who served them, but their central focus was on the parish.

One major function of these societies was to generate teachers for the Sunday School, which was still in most parishes the major form of religious education for children. Pastors pleaded with parents to send their children and to check to make sure they attended. They regularly praised the performance of the children and organized picnics for them in the summer. In smaller parishes or missions, it was the priest's task to instruct the children during his visits. However, since John Devereux brought the children to his home to teach them the scriptures, lay persons had been needed to help with religious instruction. These classes were harder to organize in towns and rural areas, where the numbers were small, the families scattered, and the organization of sodalities for men and women where teachers could receive the proper training was almost impossible. One sign of the growth of these efforts was a parade of Sunday School teachers and students held in Syracuse to convey the children on a picnic. The papers reported 1,200 children and teachers participated.

In a large and well organized urban parish like St. Marys of Syracuse, Sunday School was almost as important as a training ground for young adult teachers as it was for the children. On January 28, 1885, a meeting was called to organize a permanent association of Sunday School teachers. The members bound themselves to teach for at least a year, to comply with the rules contained in the class books and, in the case of absence, to provide a substitute, while doing all they could to add efficiency to their classes. Soon there were 60 members, male and female, and committees were drafting a constitution and planning a public lecture to raise money. Father John Grimes, assistant pastor, spoke at each meeting, at one urging them to give the Sunday School paper to deserving students, at another urging the teachers to receive communion with the children in order to give their society "standing" within the parish. When a child was absent, the teacher would visit the home and familiarize the student with the lesson for the coming week. Grimes urged them to be alert for good voices for the choir, and the teachers planned the summer picnic, a highlight of the St. Mary's year. They planned entertainments and programs for ceremonies opening the new church. Music was such an important part of the program that the decision was made to hire a music teacher. At the meetings, religious topics were examined. The minutes record a "lively discussion" of "foreordination" in mid-1894. In other parishes, the Sunday School teachers organized libraries, reading rooms and debating clubs. Only a few parishes offered religious instruction for high school-age children. More common was outreach to young people beyond the reach of the Church. At St. Mary's, the St. Vincent de Paul men visited the homes of children who did not attend, while one parishioner offered classes in his home for "children who live near the quarry." At St. John's, the work of the St. Vincent de Paul in holding classes in a poor neighborhood led to the purchase of a building, the offering of services and, eventually, a new parish.

The German parishes were even more notable for a wide range of lay societies for devotional charitable and educational purposes. Almost every major religious event at Assumption parish in Syracuse provided an occasion for a parade. Parishioners marched through the streets to picnics, church dedications, and Confirmation and First Communion ceremonies. Always they arranged themselves according to societies, for example, the Knights of the Holy Cross and the St. Boniface, St. Francis and other devotional societies dedicated to a particular saint. Each of these groups raised money for the Church, offered support for its own members during illness, unemployment or bereavement, and celebrated the feast of its patron saint with appropriate devotions.

It should be recalled that both Irish and German parishes were in competition with other groups for the time and energy of their people. Some of that competition came from other churches. Father Michael Clune in East Syracuse warned his people in 1884: "We are not to go to Protestant services. We can feel kindly, but we are not to attend services." In the German community, there were many cultural and political organizations, the *Vereins,* as well as competing Protestant churches. Americans were a nation of joiners, and the late nineteenth century saw the growth of fraternal organizations, many modeled on the Masonic Order, with its rituals and secret oaths. These, too, could compete with Church-related organizations because they offered aspiring Catholics opportunities for contact with non-Catholics which could prove beneficial in business or professional life. The Church had long been wary of "secret societies" and had forbidden the taking of oaths. However innocent they might appear in the United States, the Masons were regarded as enemies of the Church. In Ireland, the Ancient Order of Hibernians was once a secret society which usurped the prerogatives of the priest. In 1893, the pope warned the American bishops against allowing Catholics to join non-denominational organizations. Instead, they should encourage them to "associate as much as possible with Catholics." Local pastors, determined to draw their more settled and secure members to active involvement in the Church, needed no such instructions. In addition to multiplying their own forms of social and recreational activity, they did all in their power to prevent people from joining other groups. In 1853, there was an uproar when a German pastor refused to bury a prominent member of his congregation who belonged to a forbidden society. Father Barry, with his usual directness, decided to do the same when a member of his parish who was a member of the Eagles died. Locally this organization might have seemed innocuous, even useful, but in fact it was on a list of organizations prohibited by the Church, a list which had not been given wide circulation. Barry's motives were clear:

> *With me it is a matter of principle. A halt must be called and the time is now auspicious. We have too many so-called fraternal societies. Many of our young men cannot afford to contribute to the support of the Church, but they find no difficulty in contributing to societies whose influences are not elevating, but in many instances positively demoralizing and a menace to the best interests of society. I, for one, propose hereafter to follow strictly the rule of the church in such matters. In the past we have been too lenient in our liberal construction of the rule .... It will not be so in the future.*

RAISING MONEY FOR PARISHES

While all priests, of course, preached and celebrated the sacraments, the overwhelming task was to secure the foundations of the parish. At stations on the route of the missionary priest, pressure mounted to buy land, provide a building and secure his regular services. Once that was done, the community worked to provide sufficient income to guarantee the support of a resident pastor, who once appointed almost always began planning a new building. With that secured, plans might start for a school. At the same time, there were demands for charity; in urban areas hospitals, orphanages and other Catholic institutions were springing up, sometimes before adequate financial support was assured. The priest depended on the parish for his housing and his annual stipend (originally $600 and raised to $1,000 in 1880), and for the additional personal income provided by the Christmas and Easter collections, weddings, funerals and special Masses said for a particular intention. No wonder, then, that the parish seemed preoccupied with raising money. Yet it should be noted that, in the days before radio, television and movies, Church activities were a major form of social life and many events designed to raise money were also occasions for entertainment, courting and simply enjoyment.

On financial matters, bishops and lay people demanded a strict accounting of the use of funds. The trustee episodes often had originated in concern about financial accountability, and these concerns did not disappear after ownership was lodged securely in the bishops' hands. Lay leaders who had purchased the land and contributed to the Church were not inclined to leave all material concerns to the clergy. Trustees were there to ensure that money was spent wisely and to share responsibility for generating the income needed for parish projects. Almost every parish issued a detailed annual report, listing all expenditures and often listing, as well, the names of the parishioners and how much each had given to the Church during the year. Similar lists of individual donations were posted often for special collections and for the funds taken in for the pastor on Christmas and Easter. These reports were extremely detailed. One reason why can be found in the frequent complaints appearing in the public press about the misuse of funds. There were, almost everywhere, lay persons alert to financial transactions and ready to criticize if even the smallest error or misjudgment was made. As for the priest, his reputation with his congregation depended as much on his honesty and competence in managing funds as on his spiritual and pastoral skill. Father James O'Hara echoed the sentiments of most pastors when he assured his people: "This congregation will be conducted on purely business principles. Every dollar you pay will be used without discount."

The major source of income in most parishes was the rental of pews, a practice used throughout the American Church in the nineteenth century. At an annual auction, church members rented pews for which they paid in quarterly installments. A chart indicating pew holders was posted in the church. In some cases, the poor were instructed to see the pastor privately to arrange a seat. Those occupying pews had exclusive claim to their use during high Mass on Sunday. Children, visitors and non-pew holders had to find space in unrented pews or in the gallery, often for an admission charge of 10 cents. In its earliest days, St. John's of Utica paid its sexton $100 a year to, among other things, "keep non-pew holders from seats." Pew rental was a concrete sign of commitment as O'Hara told his people: "The taking of pews is the best way of continuing the work of the missions."

Pews were regarded as the property of those who rented them and law suits were fairly common among Protestants. When Catholics went to court, however, they usually

Pew rent sign (Photo: St. John Church, Utica)

found the judges unsympathetic. A parishioner sued the pastor of St. John the Baptist in 1867 for "trespass" because he took away the man's pew when he failed to meet an increased minimum charge. The pastor won the suit. In another church, the pastor asked a man to surrender his front row seat and accept another further back. When he refused, the pastor simply dismantled the pew. The following Sunday, discovering his pew removed, the parishioner brought in chairs and placed them on his spot. When the priest appeared for Mass, the man denounced him "in the most obstreperous manner," for which the priest had him arrested.

The pressure to rent a pew was very great. O'Hara accused families of "injuring the children" by renting only a few seats and then crowding their children and relatives into space rented by others. Moreover, for many pastors, pew rental was a sign of church membership and, therefore, a claim on the services of the priest. While all recognized the need to minister to the poor, and while even divisive parishioners deserved care at time of death, the ordinary ministry of the priest was directed at families who held pews. "Any person in the parish not having a pew has no claim," O'Hara noted in his announcement book in 1873. Competition for pew holders among churches in urban areas was relatively common. In Syracuse, Father Guerdet of St. John the Evangelist was scrupulous in respecting parish boundaries, but O'Hara regularly announced that "those who wish my services must attend my church, no matter where [they live] in the city." He assured his pew holders that he would "attend them in life and death if they have a pew in my church."

Strong pastors minced few words in denouncing those who could afford a pew, but neglected to rent one. In 1873, O'Hara spoke of 40 families in his parish who did not hold pews, though several were "owners of two horses." Failure to support the Church was the surest sign one was a bad Catholic. O'Hara claimed that those who "give nothing are generally the most talkative" in criticizing the pastor. He announced from the altar that, while visiting homes to collect for his new church, he found a "great many unworthy Catholics." His warning was clear but unexceptional given the importance of voluntary support to the life of the American Church: "They will expect every attention in case of sickness and death. We will know how to treat them."

Pew rents provided the regular, dependable income for the Church, but there was a never ending stream of special collections. The American bishops insisted that annual collections be taken in all churches for the support of the Holy Father, and others were added. The bishop asked once a year for a collection for the education of clergy. In the parish, a special need might arise, as when Father O'Hara held a special collection to pay for repaving the sidewalk outside his church.

When his special envelopes were not returned in adequate numbers, he announced that he would take up a plate collection himself the following week. A similar plea was heard during the especially cold winter of

1881. Some parishes had weekly plate collections, seeking support from non-pew holders or additional contributions from regular church members. Almost every event had a small charge. At St. Joseph's in Camillus in 1880, parishioners paid 50 cents to attend confirmation. When the French and German population opened their own churches in Syracuse, the other parishes marched in parade to the new edifice for its dedication and paid an admission on entering. When St. Mary's opened its new church, tickets to the opening ceremonies were one dollar, and even the tiny congregation in Baldwinsville charged 50 cents for tickets to the dedication of its church in 1852. Palm Sunday brought a charge for palms, while the priest expected a stipend for baptisms, weddings and funerals. Parishioners brought candles to the church to be blessed once a year, but the pastor always had proper candles available for purchase. First Communion, confirmation or Forty Hours all brought added expenses, and occasions for special collections. No effort to raise money was unappreciated, and no amount raised was too small. In 1875, when construction of his beloved church was stalled, O'Hara told his people: "Two little girls, Maggie Woodward and Mimmie Barry, handed me $15.50 realized from their little entertainment at Miss Mulcahy's. I will with pride put it on the church."

In missions struggling to become parishes, in new parishes seeking funds for an adequate building, or in established parishes attempting to erect a larger, permanent facility, the priest would solicit his parishioners where he could find them. When mission priests like Beecham and Hourigan began their work in Rome and Binghamton, they were known to visit construction camps, farms and neighborhood gathering places to ask Catholics to join in supporting the Church. When O'Hara announced his new church, he made several rounds of home visitation, the first in 1875

First St. Mary's church in Syracuse (Photo: Onondaga Historical Association)

when he told his people every family was expected to contribute at least a dollar during his visits. He asked the families to be at home between six and 11 in the evening for his visit. Husbands who had to work were asked to leave money with the wife or children.

Priests were not at all shy about pleading for generosity in the Easter and Christmas collections intended for their personal use. They announced the collection weeks ahead of time, urged generosity, appealed to parish pride by comparing the results of the previous collection with those of neighboring parishes, and sometimes outlined their own financial problems. A list of donors, with the amounts contributed, was posted in the church or read at vespers. The priest regarded the collection as a test of the parish's appreciation of his services. In appealing for generosity in 1874,

O'Hara told his parishioners: "I hope before my God that I have done my duty to you and your families." A few years later he noted in his announcement book for Easter Sunday: "Collection - I need it." In the larger parishes, the collections could be quite substantial. O'Hara received from $500 to $600 in the late seventies and early eighties, while newspapers reported that Dean Michael Barry of St. Paul's in Oswego received $2,000 a year from these special collections. Neither seemed strapped for funds, because their salary was paid regularly. Barry occasionally contributed his Easter and Christmas collections to the school in his parish, while O'Hara turned his collection over to the fund for the new church. In 1869, he donated his Christmas collection to the orphan asylum and suggested: "Let other churches follow the example." Between the regular salary, the special collections and the stipends for special services, priests in larger parishes received a fairly substantial income during that period. When O'Hara organized a special solicitation of the priests on the occasion of the renovation of the Albany cathedral, he collected more than $14,000 from 134 priests, many of whom gave more than $100, one $350 and another $500.

Yet many priests served in parishes where not only was the Christmas and Easter collections small, often less than $20, but the annual salary was not paid. Even in larger parishes, income could be a problem when hard times hit. During the depression of the mid-seventies, for example, a Syracuse pastor told the bishop he had received only half his annual stipend and no longer could support the assistant who had been sent to him. Clearly, the prosperity of congregations gradually established a hierarchy of parishes, with the wealthier parishes serving as rewards to eminent clergy, while others where ordinary expenses were a problem occupied the bottom rung of the diocese.

One of the most common, lucrative and apparently enjoyable forms of fundraising was the fair. Throughout the century, fairs were held to support church building projects, schools, orphanages and charitable institutions. They lasted from a day to two weeks and were advertised throughout the community, aiming to enlist the support of non-Catholics as well as Catholics. Each night, a supper was prepared and served by a group of volunteers, and a musical program or other entertainment was presented, all in the midst of a variety of booths offering homemade baked goods, handsewn or knitted items, and handicrafts. Raffles and auctions of donated goods were a major source of income, with parishioners and supporters being given books of tickets to sell, while individuals and merchants were solicited for gifts. In 1877, St.

Mary's of Syracuse, at a fair to benefit its building fund, disposed of a list of items which included gold pieces, greenbacks, women's and children's hats, a box of cigars, skates (donated by the pastor), blankets, lamps, framed mottos, handmade ships, bed-spreads, pieces of furniture, even an expensive case of imported wine and a set of five silver forks. The wine brought in $58, the forks $30.50. Altogether the parish raised $1,400, small compared to the $10,000 raised for the Utica orphan asylum in 1865 at a fair opened by Governor Horatio Seymour, or the $9,000 raised by St. John's parish for its new church in 1869.

The enjoyable social character of these fairs was evident in the description of an Oswego fair in 1887. The fair opened on a Saturday night with 1200 tickets sold at the door. Tables and booths were manned by "young ladies" who also served a supper from five to seven, featuring oysters of every variety, roast chicken, roast beef, tongue, ham, ice cream, and delicious baked goods, all for 25 cents. The newspaper reassured those who might want to attend during the week that visitors were not accosted at every step by "canvassers and solicitors of votes." The merry-go-round was "very amusing for the children," while attractive door prizes were available, including a gold watch, ton of coal and barrel of flour. Fairs like this challenged the creativity of the organizers. In 1876, a Syracuse fair featured nightly dancing, which later was forbidden at these events, and a New England kitchen where women in "full Puritan costume" served dinner. Among the new fundraising devices at this fair was a contest to determine the city's most popular undertaker, with each vote costing 10 cents, and a popularity contest in which votes were cast for young women, for a price, with the winner to receive an expensive tea set. An indication of the numbers involved can be seen in the outcome, with the top two finishers receiving 4,662 and

3,516 votes. The importance of these events was evident in the parish announcement books, filled with references to committee meetings and solicitors' reports before and after the event. One pastor simply wrote in large letters across a page "FAIR FAIR FAIR," presumably to remind himself to exhort his parishioners to the most strenuous activity.

Fairs, like so many fundraising events, had more than one function. Beyond the obvious purpose of raising money for worthy endeavors, they provided opportunities for socializing for the young, they brought priests and people together in informal ways, and they allowed the community to honor its more prominent and generous citizens, while providing them with a chance for community recognition and the status and prestige that brought with it. The larger fairs for hospitals and orphanages brought lay people from many parishes together in ways which expressed their shared identity as Catholics and enlisted their support in community institutions which served them all. Not least, these fairs, regularly and flatteringly reported in the public press, increased the visibility and respectability of the Catholic population, a process well expressed in the tendency of local officials to attend the event, their visits announced ahead of time and reported faithfully the next day in the fair journal and in the newspapers. On the other hand, the fair could be a test of loyalty. After an 1884 fair, O'Hara announced that "many parties who had made great boast of their generosity had been enemies of our fair and our new church," even though "our fair has been patronized by all the most respectable people of this city." He and the people of his parish, he warned, knew these enemies and would "know what to do with them in the future."

Another, more controversial social event which helped raise funds was the picnic. Parishes seemed to enjoy organizing excur-sions to parks, lakes or scenic places. Tickets were sold ahead of time, reservations made for cars on the railroad, and committees assigned to prepare food, organize entertainment, contests and recreation for all ages, and to sell tickets. There were picnics for particular societies, for altar boys, for the Sunday School children, for the benefit of charities and for the entire parish. In some communities, picnics became controversial, because they might serve beer and fill the park with immigrants singing strange songs and playing unfamiliar games. Even respectable Catholic pastors sometimes joined in community complaints at the behavior of citizens in local parks, and they were determined to keep picnics and festivals under their control.

Priests regularly announced that no picnics, bazaars or fairs could be held, even if for the benefit of the Church or a Catholic institution, unless approved and directed by the priest. As early as 1867, O'Hara announced that "fairs, festivals, excursions and picnics were prohibited" unless approved by the bishop and announced from the altar. These warnings eventually found their way into Church law. The Third Plenary Council of Baltimore met in 1884 and the New York State bishops were quick to promulgate its decrees within their jurisdictions. One area covered was "forbidden ways to collect money." Only societies serving a public purpose could appeal for funds through the Church or hold picnics, festivals, suppers or lectures on church property. In addition "all kinds of round dancing, night dancing, dancing in halls or ballrooms" to raise money for Church purposes or public charities "was strictly, unqualifiedly forbidden" as was "the sale of wine, beer or any kind of intoxicating liquors at church picnics, excursions, festivals, suppers, etc..." Also banned were "moonlight excursions, picnics continued after nightfall, meetings of the people where morals or good

Altar boys at St. Patrick's church in Truxton (Photo: Chancery Archives)

behavior are endangered." Once all that was covered, Bishop McNeirny made clear that, for any picnic or excursion, the bishop's permission was needed. The regulations were to be read from the altar, and any groups which violated them would "forfeit their religious character, prestige and privileges." Enforcement of these restrictions proved difficult, but the intent was less to eliminate these affairs than to bring them under the control of the clergy.

Public lectures were another form of Catholic fund-raising, instruction and evangelization. Aimed most often at the Catholic population, they also offered the general public intelligent speakers capable of explaining controversial points of Catholic doctrine or, more frequently, the Catholic position on questions before the general public. In January 1871, for example, when newspapers were filled with stories of the conflict between the Vatican and the state of Italy, the priests of Syracuse held a public meeting at St. John's to arouse support for the pope. Bishop Lynch of Charleston lectured on Bismark in 1873. Well-known Catholic apologists like Isaac Hecker, Louis Lambert and Edward McGlynn spoke on religious controversies, and Catholics were urged to bring their "separated brethren." Visiting Irish politicians were also popular. For most lectures, a small admission was charged. Often the pastor himself conducted regular lectures, not always on topics of directly Catholic inspiration. Father Barry of Oswego was famous around the area for his Sunday night presentation of illuminated lectures featuring stereopticon slides taken of various parts of the world. Father O'Hara presented a lecture on a Sunday night in January 1874, featuring "nineteen views of the New Testament," followed a week later by additional pictures of Palestine and Egypt, all narrated by the pastor and open to the public for a charge of 25 cents. Lent, advent and other occasions often brought a weekly lecture series, either by the pastor or neighboring clergy.

FINANCE: MEANS TO AN END

The record of financial exertions in individual parishes makes clear several things about nineteenth century Catholic life. First, provision of financial support was the single most important factor in determining church membership and defining the quality of that membership. Of course, baptism made one a Catholic and no one was refused confession or denied Christian burial, unless in the latter case they had been a public sinner. The poor were provided for, but they were in a very real sense outsiders, second-class citizens. Widows, orphans and the unemployed usually were treated with compassion and generosity, but they had little share in the organized activity of the parish. Yet they ranked far above those who had the means to support the Church, but did not do so. Priests and lay leaders agreed in regarding such persons with contempt. Posting parish reports, listing donors to special collections, public reading of delinquent contributors at vespers, references to malcontents and critics and what would happen to them when they needed the priest, all signaled the role assigned to nominal Catholics who did not practice their faith, not only by coming to the church but by contributing to its support.

Second, and more important, the Church had become a self-conscious human project. Irish and German Catholics may have thought they simply were reconstructing churches like they had known at home, but the very process made them different. In the old country, there was little tradition of financial support for the

Church from ordinary parishioners, even less for the priest's dependence on their support rather than on that of wealthy patrons. At home, to varying degrees, the Church was so integral to the life and history of a community that it could be taken for granted. Now there would be a Church and a priest only if the people were able to provide one. Led by better-off lay leaders, Catholics of every nationality initiated the process of providing for the Church, first by organizing themselves, seeking the services of a missionary or a neighboring pastor, perhaps purchasing land for a cemetery, then seeking land and a building for worship. From then on, provision of a church building and a priest, later his assistant and sister-teachers in the school, depended upon the ability of the community to provide the resources to maintain the church and support the staff. The priests and religious had no other source of income than the donations of the people. The people had no other source of Catholic services than the priests and religious. Out of mutual necessity, sometimes amid considerable bickering, they joined their energies to build the Church.

The Church, then, was not only a place where young people could "improve themselves," it was itself a self-help project. The result of the deliberate and purposeful actions of people and priests, it could not help but be different than the Church which had existed in other places at other times. While the law of the Church anchored membership in baptism, the people could not help resenting those who sought the Church's services without contributing to its support. Those who succeeded in providing a church for themselves were apt to wonder at other groups who did not do so, and to find the claim that "The Church" should provide for them unjustified. The same process which made of the self-constructed parish a tight network of relationships which provided identity, confidence, strength and assurance

The generosity of parishioners built beautiful churches throughout the diocese. St. Stephen's church in Marathon was a Presbyterian academy before it was purchased and renovated by the Catholics. (Photo: Chancery Archives)

for its members could, at the same time, insulate them from the struggles and agonies of those outside. There was a natural tendency toward parochial self-centeredness, to locate and test all the claims of the Church in the parish and to become impervious to wider evangelical and missionary responsibilities. At the same time, for all its apparent dependence upon the leadership of the clergy, the American Church was closer to being a people's Church than most other times and places in the history of Christianity. Invested in buildings and instilled in the spirit was the hard earned money, the time and talent, often the sweat and suffering, of the people themselves.

Finally, the financial development of Catholic parishes was an educational experience of considerable importance. Priests and people together learned through experience the need to establish clear and attainable goals. Extravagant hopes often proved disastrous, as when O'Hara planned the rapid construction of a huge church, stumbled over the depression of the 1870s and waited 13 years for the church to be completed. Several hospitals and orphanages almost collapsed for lack of support because of rapid and unplanned initiatives. Gradually, groups learned the necessity to keep objectives limited to goals which could unite the congregation, could be met by available resources and left room for expansion. The same organizing skills, the same deliberate process and careful action would serve in later efforts to develop trade unions, political coalitions, ethnic associations and community organizations. It was something of a Catholic style, reflective of the communal traditions and pre-industrial realism of immigrant communities. It was also altogether appropriate to an open and fluid country with few institutions interested in, or capable of, providing support to individuals and families caught in the midst of urban-industrial expansion. This Catholic style of development carried within it the organizing skills and the realistic assessment of prospects to the service of high ideals which provided a legacy of great value to later generations.

The cultural framework set forth in James O'Hara's lecture notes provided something of a blueprint for parish development in Central New York. The emphasis was on the conscious construction of a world in which people could come together to establish a center of order and authority in their lives, and integrate the heritage they had brought with them with the opportunities they found in the United States. By the 1880s, when word began to circulate that the region might become a diocese independent of Albany, a patchwork of parishes was clustered around four urban centers and scattered across seven counties. Among the clerical and lay leadership, there was a mature satisfaction with what had been accomplished in such a short period of time, and an optimistic anticipation of the future as population expanded and Catholic institutions multiplied. In each community, the struggle to make a people of "one heart and one soul" was far from complete. Between parishes and nationalities, there were tensions far from resolved. But the unity of the parishes themselves, and the solidarity of the Catholic body and its clergy in dealing with those outside the Church, mirrored a deep process. In this process, new devotions and old rituals were blending with a theology of salvation which echoed from the immigrant experience to form an American Church different from those in Europe but clearly and deliberately Catholic.

Together, the Catholics of Central New York stood at the threshold of a new beginning, one as significant as those earlier new beginnings of Simon LeMoyne and John Devereux. It was a sign that this would be a major turning point, that the next beginning would be a bishop, for the first time a bishop of Syracuse.

97

KEEP THE LINES TIGHT

SYRACUSE WITH ITS OWN BISHOP
1880s-1890s

In 1840, Bishop John Hughes met and took a liking to a remarkable Dutch-born Jesuit, Peter Havermans. The priest joined Hughes in his travels around the sprawling New York State diocese, visiting among other places tiny St. Peter's Church in Troy, where Bishop Dubois had been plagued by trustees. By then, Hughes had persuaded his new friend to become a diocesan priest, and he placed him in charge of the Troy parish. Leaving for New York, Hughes told him: "Father Havermans, I leave you here as pastor and all I have to say is 'keep the lines tight.'" Havermans did so, though not without difficulty. When Patrick A. Ludden, vicar general of the Albany diocese, arrived in 1880 to take over the parish from his illustrious predecessor, Havermans was still in residence. He would live to be well over 90. His new colleague, Ludden, already had learned well the lesson Hughes taught all priests who would listen. In his 10 years at St. Peter's, he added expensive stained glass windows and a new altar and built a parochial school. He kept careful accounts, published regular lists of donors to special collections, and accounted for paid and unpaid pew rents. He borrowed money at good interest, collected enough from his parishioners to meet interest payments and ordinary expenses, and made considerable progress in paying the debt. As vicar general, he shared responsibility with Bishop McNeirny for tightening the lines between bishops and pastors. In his travels around the diocese, he proved the very model of the new diocesan administrator. More than McNeirny, he was able to support clerical authority under episcopal control, while winning the respect and admiration of most of his fellow priests. Remarkably, in that day of independent and often contentious clergy, his appointment as the first bishop of Syracuse drew almost unanimous praise. As he took charge of his new diocese, he knew well the need, and the way, to "keep the lines tight."

In the rapidly expanding post-Civil War United States, both Rome and the American hierarchy spent considerable time and effort establishing new dioceses. The archbishop within whose jurisdiction a growing population seemed to require closer attention consulted with the other bishops of the province, particularly those whose jurisdictions would be reduced by division. Boundaries had to be determined, a matter not only of assessing present population, but of anticipating future growth as well. Next, a site for the see city had to be selected, a matter that could cause considerable maneuvering. Finally, candidates for the proposed bishopric had to be nominated by the bishops of the province, who selected three names for presentation to the Holy See. Since 1820 the American hierarchy had guarded jealously its prerogative to nominate candidates for American sees. In making their recommendations, they emphasized pastoral experience in the United States as a prerequisite for high office.

Generally, until the 1890s, Rome bowed to the will of the American bishops, but the Holy See was far from passive. As a missionary Church, the United States fell under the supervision of the Congregation of the Propaganda, which kept in close touch with American Church affairs. In addition to regular reports and visits from American bishops, the congregation had its own informants, often priests who had studied in Rome. After the Civil War, large numbers of American priests appealed to Propaganda for relief from the arbitrary power of the bishops. Similarly, as we have seen, property holding arrangements varied across the country with differing state laws, none of which fit the forms common in Europe and familiar to Rome. Accordingly, the Holy See was compelled regularly to respond to complaints received from the United States. Rome usually asked bishops for explanations and advice, but sometimes ordered the bishops to act

against their better judgment. The bishops, for their part, while deeply respectful of papal authority, often felt that Rome was unfamiliar with American conditions and therefore unqualified to judge disputes or make decisions for the American Church.

All these factors played a role in the complex negotiations which led to the establishment of the diocese of Syracuse. Rapid expansion of population along the Erie Canal had led to creation of the dioceses of Albany and Buffalo in 1847. Later, the Holy See responded to concern about the vast size of these jurisdictions by dividing each diocese, separating the eastern portion of Buffalo into the diocese of Rochester in 1868, and the northern portion of Albany into the Ogdensburg diocese in 1872. Even with these changes, Albany remained the largest diocese in the state and, by 1886, the diocese with the largest number of churches in the province of New York.

Naturally, speculation about a new diocese in the western reaches of Albany increased with the growth of its major cities. As early as 1852, Syracuse newspapers referred to the new St. John the Evangelist Church as a future "Catholic Cathedral." Later, Father Barry of Oswego indicated his concern that Oswego county might be detached from Albany and given over to either Rochester or Ogdensburg. The recurrent conflicts with parishioners, together with a series of scandalous public controversies involving diocesan priests, gave rise to speculation that a new diocese was needed to ensure the maintenance of ecclesiastical authority. In addition, some methods of fundraising, most notably picnics conducted without clerical supervision, raised concern. In 1881, Michael Augustine Corrigan, coadjutor bishop to New York's Archbishop McCloskey, told his friend, Bishop McQuaid of Rochester: "There is need of strong discipline in the Diocese of Albany." By the early 1880s, expectation of a new diocese had grown to more than newspaper talk, as priests began meeting to express their views on the subject. In fact, few diocesan establishments were carried out amid as much public debate and comment as that of Syracuse.

In January 1882, Cardinal Simeone, prefect of the Propaganda, inquired whether a division of Albany should be made. The news leaked out, leading to renewed comment in the newspapers. The question was to be discussed at a provincial synod planned for 1883, but this meeting was postponed because Rome and the American bishops agreed to hold a national Plenary Council at Baltimore in 1884. In his "letter of instruction" about the national meeting, Simeone included the division of the Albany diocese as one of the items for discussion. However, this information was omitted from the copy of his letter sent to the other bishops by James Gibbons, the archbishop of Baltimore who was to serve as apostolic delegate at the council. The omission was made so that Albany's Bishop McNeirny could "still move first." Nevertheless, there was some informal discussion of the issue at the council, although McCloskey's absence because of declining health kept the matter from being considered formally. Word from Rome was that Propaganda had decided already to make the change and opposition had become "useless and displeasing."

The delay, and McCloskey's reluctance to move on the matter, arose from the opposition of Bishop McNeirny. The latter believed a division was needed, but opposed it for the time being, fearing it would weaken, not strengthen, episcopal authority. In notes prepared for the provincial synod, he argued that separation from Albany would please the malcontents in Utica and Rome. Nor did he appreciate outside interference in his diocesan affairs, such as McQuaid's lobbying for the change. Moreover, McNeirny had the backing

of all the leading priests in the area. In 1883, they gathered in Syracuse and petitioned McCloskey to prevent the division. McCloskey hesitated to act without McNeirny's approval, but the New York bishop died in October 1885 and was succeeded by Corrigan, who agreed with his friend McQuaid on the need for action. Within a month of the change in New York, Simeone wrote Corrigan a strongly worded letter, indicating that the proper response to the "deplored troubles" in the diocese of Albany was division and that this should take place immediately.

THE DIOCESE OF SYRACUSE

Events moved forward rapidly. In April 1886, the bishops of the Province of New York met to put the decrees of the Plenary Council into effect. They also began the process of complying with Rome's will on the Albany matter. In May they met again, decided upon the boundaries of the diocese and nominated a list of candidates for the new see. Immediately thereafter, McNeirny, accompanied by Father James Ludden, left for Rome. Over the next three and a half months, newspaper speculation reached fever pitch, as rumors of the new diocese and its bishop spread wildly. James Ludden's presence on the trip worried Syracuse area priests, who met and notified the archbishop of their opposition to his appointment, as well as their continued opposition to a new diocese. Letters were going to Rome from groups in Central New York arguing for and against the division and in favor or against one or another candidate. Press speculation centered on well known local personalities like O'Hara, Barry, John Moriarty of St. John the Evangelist and numerous others.

In fact, McNeirny, now resigned to the change, proposed his own vicar general, Patrick A. Ludden, Father James S. M. Lynch of Utica and Monsignor James Farley of New

SEVERING THE TIES

On February 24, 1887, Bishop McNeirny of Albany wrote his last official letter to priests in the new Syracuse diocese:

"Our Most Holy Father, Pope Leo XIII, was pleased to create on the twenty-sixth day of November last, the new diocese of Syracuse, and to appoint as its first Bishop, on the eighth day of December following, our Vicar General, the Very Rev. Patrick A. Ludden, pastor of St. Peter's Church, Troy.

"The new diocese comprises the counties of Broome, Chenango, Cortland, Madison, Oneida, Onondaga and Oswego, hitherto under our jurisdiction.

"The Right Rev. Bishop-elect has signified to us that, in deference to the expressed will of Christ's Vicar on earth, he will not shrink from the shouldering of the burden imposed upon him, and that, on the first day of March next, he will take up his abode in his Episcopal City of Syracuse, and assume jurisdiction over that portion of the Church wherein the Holy Ghost hath placed him to rule.

"On that day the close spiritual ties which, during many years, have united us, will be forever severed.

"In this, our last official communication to you, we may be permitted to add that our best wishes and most earnest prayers will ever accompany the Bishop and priests and the faithful of the new diocese. May the Giver of all good gifts grant them His choicest blessings, and may the Great Shepherd of souls ever watch tenderly over them, that, when He shall appear, they may all receive a never-fading crown of glory.

"We remain, Rev. Dear Sir, very devotedly,

Francis,

Bishop of Albany."

York, later to become cardinal archbishop of that city. After discussion, the bishops unanimously agreed to submit Ludden first, Lynch second and, by majority vote, Father Thomas M. A. Burke of Albany third.

Finally, on September 13, Corrigan received word that the previous day the Holy See had erected the new diocese at Syracuse and appointed Patrick Ludden as its first bishop. The news was communicated immediately to the press and to the priests in upstate New York. On November 22, the diocese was erected formally and, on November 26, the brief of erection was issued. The Holy Father, Pope Leo XIII, solemnly confirmed Ludden's appointment in a consistory December 8, and the brief of appointment was issued on December 14. Ludden, meanwhile, went immediately to New York to ask Corrigan to intervene to prevent his appointment. He also wrote to Rome asking to be left in Albany, but received no reply. Ludden's pleas were by no means merely formal; he was not resigned to the outcome. Father O'Hara sent his congratulations on September 16, stating that "of the many names mentioned in reference to this appointment I am heartily glad that yours is the chosen one." In reply, the new bishop expressed his gratitude, but was strangely uncertain about the future. In

November, he wrote Corrigan again, appealing for help in revoking Rome's decision and telling the archbishop that, if news arrived, he would be vacationing "down South on the Negro Plantations."

His vacation was not interrupted, but his requests went unheard. On January 10, 1887, Corrigan informed Ludden he had written for the proper papers. They arrived in New York on the 25th of that month. One month later, on February 25, Ludden wrote his letters of acceptance to the Holy Father and to the cardinal prefect of Propaganda. On March 1, he assumed administration of the diocese and two days later arrived in Syracuse to take up residence at St. John the Baptist Church. On April 18, he moved into an episcopal residence and, on May 1, he was consecrated solemnly at the Church of the Assumption, the only church with a sanctuary large enough for the ceremony. Ludden chose St. John the Evangelist as his cathedral.

The delay of more than six months between news of the new diocese and Ludden's formal installation simply heightened interest in Syracuse. When the day arrived, the whole city was ready for the celebration. Corrigan presided, with McNeirny and Bishop John Loughlin of Brooklyn assisting. Bishop Michael O'Farrell of Trenton preached the sermon, and there were 10 other bishops and almost 100 priests in attendance, while approximately 2,000 spectators paid one dollar apiece for the privilege of attending the solemn ceremonies. Thousands more outside watched the splendid procession led by a torch bearer in a golden cope, followed by such lay organizations as the Knights of the Cross, Societies of St. Joseph, St. Boniface and St. Francis, and the Catholic Mutual Benevolent Association, all in full uniforms, "the metal ornaments of which, all in line, flashed and sparkled like a river in the sun." Then came the priests, the monsignors in light purple and the bishops in dark. It was, it would seem, a day of great pride for the Catholics of the city, the public display marking their emergence to prominence, their new bishop symbolizing their permanent foundation, their growing respectability, and their pride in what they had accomplished.

If Patrick Ludden needed confirmation of his instinctive desire to "keep the lines tight," O'Farrell provided it in his homily in which he argued that the unity and power of the Church depended upon obedience to the bishop. "The duty of every child of the Church is to obey the order established by Christ and the duty of the priests above all is to be the helpers and cooperators of the episcopacy," O'Farrell said. "If the Church be compared to a ship, the bishop is the captain ... under the admiral, the Pope." The welfare of the local Church was in the bishop's hands. "Though manned by able sailors, the (ship's) safety may depend on the wisdom, prudence and sanctity of the captain," O'Farrell argued. "He may make the ship avoid the rocks and the quicksands, or the ship may be lost if he fail." Since the earliest days, therefore, the Church said to the priests, "obey the bishop as the Apostles obeyed Christ himself. Obey the bishop as Christ obeyed his Father in Heaven." All this was for the sake of the people. Turning to Ludden, O'Farrell instructed him to "lead the people and keep them from poisonous pastures into which they might be tempted to stray, and from wolves that might attack them."

This emphasis on discipline and near total identification of the Church with the hierarchy reflected powerful currents in the contemporary Church. The First Vatican Council of 1869-1870 had defined the infallibility of the pope on matters of faith and morals and the authority of the papacy over every church and every Christian. Bishops were instructed to find support for their authority in their intimate identification with the Holy See. In the United States, episcopal

A BISHOP'S DUTY

When Patrick A. Ludden was consecrated bishop of Syracuse on May 1, 1887, bishops were seen much as vassals of the pope, personal agents for the bishop of Rome. This view of the bishop's role was evident in the "Oath of Duty" which Ludden made immediately following his Profession of Faith:

"I, P.A. Ludden, elect of the church, will be from this hour henceforward obedient to blessed Peter, the apostle, and to the holy roman church, and to the most blessed Father, Pope Leo XIII, and to his successors, canonically chosen. I will assist them to retain and defend against any man whatever, the Roman Popedom, without prejudice to any rank. I will take care to preserve, defend and promote the rights, honors, privilege and authority of the holy Roman church, of the Pope, and of his successors as aforesaid, with my whole strength. I will observe and cause to be observed by others the rules of the holy fathers, the decrees, ordinances of dispositions and mandates of the Apostolic See. When called to a synod I will come, unless I be prevented by a canonical impediment. I will personally visit the Apostolic See once every ten years and render an account to our blessed Father, Leo XIII, and to his successors as aforesaid, of my whole pastoral office, and of everything in any way appertaining to the state of my church, to the discipline of the clergy and the people and to the salvation of the souls entrusted to my care; and I will humbly receive in return the apostolic mandates and most diligently execute them...."

authority was a serious problem. Protests by priests at their exclusion from any significant role in ecclesiastical government led the Third Plenary Council of Baltimore to enact changes in the law which would designate the pastors of some parishes as "irremovable," so that they could not be transferred without grave reasons. Even then, they would have the right of appeal to ecclesiastical courts. Moreover, bishops agreed to appoint diocesan consultors, whose consent would be required for certain diocesan decisions, for example the disposal of property and acceptance of debts. At the same time, the council showed the bishops' concern with priestly discipline by legislating on such matters as absenteeism, attendance at the theater, gambling and requiring the use of the clerical collar when appearing in public. Ludden assisted McNeir-

ny in implementing this legislation, and in introducing the system of diocesan accounts and reports from parishes. He also was something of a troubleshooter, attempting to settle disputes that arose. In 1886, he was still only 50 years old, but he had both pastoral and administrative experience. He knew the priests of the diocese well, and he needed no time to learn about the problems and possibilities of his new assignment.

Born Patrick Anthony Ludden in County Mayo in 1836, he was the oldest of eight children; three of his sisters became nuns. In the summer of 1861, he joined his cousins, three of them priests, in the United States. That fall he entered the seminary in Montreal and was ordained for the Albany diocese in 1864. After only three months in a parish, he was appointed chancellor and secretary to

Bishop Conroy. He accompanied Conroy to the Vatican Council in 1869. In 1872, he became vicar general and rector of the Albany cathedral. Later, McNeirny appointed him pastor of St. Peter's, but he remained vicar general and took an active role in developing the policies by which McNeirny attempted to modernize the diocese. He was known as an independent man, dedicated to the Church, intelligent and able, but reserved in manner. One newspaper reported he was "a pleasing conversationalist, though distinguished more for business than for oratorical ability." Another said he was "not a man who displays marked gifts of the oratorical kind in the pulpit or on the platforms," though accurately noting that he was "outspoken" and "a man on whom flattery is wasted."

While cordial and gracious with outsiders and devoted to the welfare of the community and the nation, Ludden was very much a man of the Church. His faith in the Church's teaching and its organization was complete and his respect for outsiders, Protestants and non-believers was limited at best. He had more in common with the combative and sometimes arrogant John Hughes than the reasonable, reconciling John Carroll.

He saw himself as a realist, who understood that "most of our country is without religion and quasi-pagan. There are 40,000,000 non-baptized and 20,000,000 heretics in diverse sects whose baptisms are uncertain and doubtful." His conclusion was clear. The Church could only hope to safeguard its faith by depending on its own resources, its churches, its schools and, especially, its priests.

ORGANIZING A NEW CHURCH

The new diocese spread over seven counties and encompassed a Catholic population estimated by the New York State bishops at 62,664 (a vastly exaggerated figure). Approx-imately 35 percent lived in the Syracuse area and almost two-thirds lived in the five major cities of Syracuse, Utica, Oswego, Binghamton and Rome. There were 50 parishes, 24 missions with churches but no resident pastor, and approximately 45 stations where Masses were said occasionally in private homes or rented halls. The bishop had 70 priests to serve these communities, including 61 secular priests and nine Franciscans. There were 17 schools of varying size and quality. There were parish schools at the two German parishes in Syracuse, Assumption and the recently established St. Joseph's, and at St. John the Baptist and St. John the Evangelist. In Oswego, there were four schools at St. Paul's, St. Mary's, St. Louis, the French church, and St. Peter's, the German church. In Utica, St. John's had two schools, Assumption Academy conducted by the Christian Brothers, and St. John's School under the Sisters of Charity of St. Vincent de Paul. In Rome, St. Peter's and St. Mary's both had schools, while St. Patrick's in Binghamton had a parochial school and St. Joseph's Academy, the latter a combination boarding and day school for girls, both conducted by the Sisters of St. Joseph. Outside the cities, the only school was a small one at the German speaking mission of St. Francis in Durham-ville. Religious orders also staffed the impressive series of orphanages, with the Sisters of Charity conducting St. Vincent and the House of Providence in Syracuse and St. John's Asylum for girls in Utica, the Christian Brothers St. Vincent Industrial School in Utica and the Sisters of St. Joseph the recently established St. Mary's Home in Binghamton. The Franciscan Sisters, who also served the German-language schools, conducted two small but growing hospitals, St. Elizabeth's in Utica and St. Joseph's in Syracuse.

Ludden moved quickly to organize his new diocese, summoning a synod which adopted statutes long operative under Albany. Father Lynch of St. John's was brought from Utica to serve as vicar general and rector of the cathedral, while Father Patrick McEvoy was appointed chancellor and secretary to the bishop. Ludden also summoned his priests to a retreat and announced that these events would now be annual, not bi-annual affairs. He scheduled regular clergy conferences to keep them informed of diocesan policy and provide for their continuing education in theology, morality and Church law. While settled for the moment at St. John the Evangelist, Ludden clearly saw this as a temporary arrangement made necessary by the fact that a heavy debt remained on St. Mary's new church in the center of the city.

In Bishop Ludden's mind, the biggest problem facing the diocese was "ecclesiastical discipline." As the term was used in the discussions which took place prior to forma- tion of the diocese, it encompassed problems with both the laity and priests who created scandals and sometimes resisted episcopal directives.

Examples of problems with the laity in- cluded the trustee conflicts which had punctu- ated its early history and the rebellion of the parishioners at St. John's after the removal of Father Terry. In fact, by the time Ludden took charge, the laity were relatively passive. Far more pressing were a series of conflicts with clergymen, few of which were settled to Ludden's satisfaction. One of the most bitter, the case of Father O'Connell at St. John's in Oswego, who had become embroiled in a factional dispute among Irish Democratic politicians, had been settled earlier by O'Con- nell's removal to a parish in Cooperstown in the Albany diocese. Far worse was the problem of Father John E. O'Sullivan of St. Joseph's in Camillus, who had been convicted of rape, though he vigorously proclaimed his innocence. The case fascinated area news- papers and deeply embarrassed Church au-

thorities. And it would not go away, because the priest was determined to vindicate his honor. Ludden attempted to disclaim respon- sibility, arguing that it was a matter for the Albany diocese, but that proved impossible. In 1888, the civil courts finally overturned the charges against O'Sullivan, who then initiated a long litigation in Church courts to win back pay and restoration to a parish. This process, again well publicized by leaks to the news- papers, dragged on for years. The process included a scandalous effort by O'Sullivan to retain control of the Camillus church, legal wrangles over parish property, and hearings in New York and Rome which ended only in 1895 when O'Sullivan was more or less exonerated of the original charge.

Another controversial priest who tested Ludden's orderly life was James L. Meagher. While at St. Mary's in Oswego he earned the enmity of the highly respected pastor, Louis Griffa. Griffa charged that the "wicked" priest "infatuated" local women and per- suaded one nun to seek dispensation from her vows so she could tour the country selling religious books he had written. There was even talk that he might form a new religious community. When Ludden arrived, Meagher was pastor of St. James in Cazenovia. Accused by parishioners of stealing money belonging to the parish, Meagher's case was before the ecclesiastical courts. The local people would not have Meagher's services, and the bishop could not remove him while his case was pending. As a result, Ludden told Archbishop Corrigan, Cazenovia Catholics were going elsewhere, even to Protestant ministers, for religious services. When Meagher attacked the popular local postmaster, the latter sued him for slander. Before that civil case could be settled, the postmaster died and his family refused to allow Meagher to perform the funeral. Instead, Father O'Hara, a friend of the deceased, came out from Syracuse to officiate, leading to a confrontation with the

A DIABOLICAL DEED

Oct. 9, 1889 (Oneida *Democratic Union*)

"The Rev. Father James Kelly, the beloved priest of St. Patrick's Church, now lies seriously ill at his residence on Mulberry street. The circumstances connected with his illness point unmistakably to a crime most diabolical and fiendish, which calls for a prompt, thorough investigation that the guilty party may not escape unpunished for the cowardly, murderous act. Yesterday morning, while Father Kelly was celebrating mass at the rink, in the presence of his congregation, and as an appropriate and sacred part of the service, he partook of about two teaspoonfulls of wine, when he was immediately seized with excruciating pain and a burning sensation in his stomach, which he instantly regarded as symptoms of poisoning. He quickly repaired from the altar to the drug store for an antidote.... Father Kelly was deathly sick when conveyed to his home, but all rejoice that his condition is regarded as much better... One of the trusty parishioners yesterday, went to Syracuse to have the wine in the bottle analyzed and returned last night. Several tests were made, and each disclosed the presence of arsenic in large quantities."

Oct. 12, 1889

"Father Kelly is fast recovering from the effects of poison, and probably might have been able to be about by this time, had he not suffered an attack of his old malady Thursday afternoon.... It is evident that a would-be murderer is lurking in our midst, and nothing should be left undone to bring the guilty party to justice. Some three weeks ago, an attempt was made to poison a span of horses belonging to John F. Ryan, the gentlemanly proprietor of the Chestnut Street coalyard. He is very friendly to Father Kelly who has kindly assisted him. A similar unsuccessful experiment was tried on the same team a week later...."

(No further mention is made of the "diabolical deed" or about its perpetrator. The explanation which comes down through oral history in Oneida is that the attempted murder was committed by a person, thought to be mentally "off," who felt it improper for a priest to be involved in gambling by owning race horses.)

Father James A. Kelly (Photo: Chancery Archives)

pastor, recorded verbatim by local reporters. Ludden reported that when Meagher came to see him, he was "half crazed." The bishop threatened to call the police to oust him from his office. Once again, the clerical courts found in the priest's favor and Meagher remained at his post until 1895, when he removed to New York where he won some reputation as a writer and publisher.

Ludden was frustrated even more by the outcome of another well publicized case. The division of the Albany diocese cut in half the parish at Deposit, depriving its pastor, Martin Stanton, of much of his income. He resigned his post and demanded justice from the new bishop, who made him pastor of neighboring parishes, St. Patrick's in Chittenango and St. Agatha's in Canastota. Unfortunately, those two parishes could not pay his salary and the Christmas collection was half what it had been in Deposit. The parishioners, who were rebuilding the burned out church at St. Patrick's, took an understandable dislike to Father Stanton. In 1892, he took his grievances to higher authorities. Eventually, the new apostolic delegate, sent from Rome to handle such cases, worked out a compromise by which Stanton agreed to resign his pastorate if the bishop provided him with an annual stipend of $400 and the right to preach in the diocese until given another assignment. Soon after, Stanton returned to St. Patrick's, but the people refused to accept him. The bishop then appointed William Slavin pastor of the two parishes, though Stanton had not been paid his $400 or assigned elsewhere. Slavin called on the parishioners to boycott Stanton's Masses, the two priests clashed publicly and the entire dispute was covered thoroughly in the press. The bishop, forced to uphold the agreement with the delegate, intervened to ensure Stanton's right to say Mass and preach. Finally the priest moved to another diocese and Slavin was transferred. His successor in

Chittenango, Father James Collins, was no improvement. Described by the press as "a robust individual of pugilistic tendencies" who had "worsted the strongest men in Chittenango and left some minus their teeth when they crossed his path," Collins was arrested for stealing some "choice chickens" from members of his congregation. He jumped bail and returned to Ireland. From there he wrote letters defending his honor and attacking the bishop. These events nearly bankrupted the parishes. No wonder Ludden seemed grateful when he visited St. Agatha's in 1905 and praised Father William Flynn, who had restored peace to that parish. Ludden praised Flynn for rescuing a "ramshackle institution" which five years before had "belonged almost entirely to the banks."

Ludden himself had suffered from impetuous and arbitrary treatment by Bishop Conroy and was not unsympathetic to the priests' desire to be treated in ways which respected their dignity and accorded with basic principles of fairness. Yet these experiences taught him that the formal requirements of ecclesiastical law designed to protect priests might make good sense on paper, but in the still unformed and rapidly expanding Church of the United States, they could not easily be "reduced to practice." Understandably, he resented the apostolic delegate's support for dissident priests, predicting to Corrigan that, having "commenced by sowing the winds," he would soon begin "to reap the whirlwind" created by weakening episcopal authority. Ludden told Corrigan in 1895 that ecclesiastical discipline in his diocese was still "very much relaxed," but by then the disputes he had inherited from Albany or discovered during the first days of his own administration were all but over. There was little he could have done to resolve them more amicably. In cases where he did have some room to act decisively and effectively, he did so, with the result that a decade after his arrival his authority was established quite well.

At St. Mary's in Oswego, for example, he decided to appoint a highly educated French Canadian priest, Father Founier, as pastor, rather than promote the Irish assistant, Father Mahon. A delegation complained to Ludden and some withheld their contributions to the Christmas collection in 1888. Ludden, taking charge, visited the parish and upbraided the parishioners for their behavior. Mahon was transferred and Founier remained. Equally decisive action was taken when Ludden learned quite accidentally that the Franciscans at Assumption had raised $60,000 in loans on their Syracuse church and turned the money over to a Buffalo parish in difficulty. Ludden threatened to place an interdict on their parish if the money was not returned in three days. It was.

In Binghamton, he acted with similar decisiveness, providing to his priests a clear example of that power of which Farrell had spoken. Nicholas J. Quinn was born in Ireland and came to Binghamton with his family at the age of seven. There he was educated under the direction of his uncle, Father Hourigan, the pioneer pastor of St. Patrick's. Ordained in 1868, he served briefly in Albany before joining his uncle as assistant, serving under him for 25 years. Hourigan was among the acknowledged leaders of the diocesan clergy, chosen to chair several of the clerical meetings held before the diocese was established. His was the largest donation contributed to the purse for the new bishop. His parishioners, worried about his management of affairs in later years, had established a committee to assist with parish finances. Irritated, Hourigan made over his will to leave his substantial fortune to Father Quinn.

In 1892, Hourigan died and the huge crowd at his funeral fully expected that the popular, eloquent Quinn would succeed him. The new bishop had other ideas. Determined

Father Nicholas Quinn (Photo: Chancery Archives)

to establish firm control over his pastors, he surprised Binghamton Catholics by transferring Quinn to Utica, there to preside over St. Patrick's, whose church recently had burned to the ground. In his stead, John J. McDonald, a trusted friend of Ludden, was brought to Binghamton from the Utica parish. Parishioners protested, as did many other Catholic and non-Catholic residents of Binghamton. One paper reported that "smoldering fires of indignity and protest are not extinguished yet and only require a breath to fan them into flames." But times were changing and Quinn knew it. He told the bishop he fully accepted his will as law and, to prove it, prevented an appeal by the parishioners to the apostolic delegate. The *Catholic Sun* sympathized with the parishioners, but showed that the bishop's point was well made: "When the bishop has decided on a removal, the cause is finished. 'Rome has spoken.' It is the groundwork of faith, without it we are nothing. The Bishop is Rome, Rome is the Church, the Church is God, whom we are bound to obey in all things." This was what Ludden wanted to hear, for this was the way his motto, "Justice and Peace," could be obtained best.

As the long discussion of the establishment of the diocese and the treatment of several scandals indicated, the Church fascinated contemporary newspapers. Shortly after Ludden's appointment, for example, the *Utica Observer* reported at length on the priests in the running for important appointments, quoting one priest who claimed a "political machine" of local clergy were plotting to take control. Ludden, no shrinking violet, sent a note to the paper accusing the reporter of being a "sewer, a squirtgun, a conduit of slander." Like many bishops, Ludden felt himself at the mercy of these papers, but he was ever ready to defend the Church, and sometimes himself, in public controversies. After 1893, he had help, because that year a Catholic paper appeared — the *Sun,* owned and edited by prominent Irish Catholic laymen. Appearing weekly, it featured news of parish and diocesan affairs and commentary on politics and social issues. In the heated atmosphere of the 1890s, it was alert to violations of Catholic rights and interests. Still, it was not an official paper, and Ludden took the occasion of one disagreement to praise the editors for "doing the best they can," but warned that, as laymen, they were not authorized to teach:

No matter what the acquirements of a layman, no matter how much a

scholar, no matter how much worldly and scientific knowledge he may have, even as a profound theologian, he is not a teacher. He has no authority to teach because...he does not participate in the divine mission to teach all nations. That must come down from God. Let no man take upon himself the honor except him who is called of God.

The key to keeping the lines tight lay precisely here, in an understanding of the priesthood as central to the life of the Church. If only the priest could teach, then his authority to teach had to be upheld. The best way to uphold that authority was to recognize what the *Sun* stated so clearly in the Quinn case, that "the Bishop is Rome, Rome is the Church, the Church is God, whom we are bound to obey in all things." If this was true, the lay people should obey the priest the bishop sent them, and the priest would find his authority and his ability to do his work best supported by obedience to his bishop, as Farrell had argued at Ludden's installation. Ludden fully accepted, and by now his priests all but fully accepted, the idea stated clearly by McNeirny in his last pastoral before the division of the diocese: "On the continuation and perpetuation of God's priesthood on earth every good work depends. Without a priesthood, there can be no altar, without an altar, there can be no church." The pioneer pastors who had taken charge of the parishes after mid-century had embodied that belief. What was added to it after 1886 was the realization that this belief was supported best by the intimate union of these priests with their bishop.

Even administratively, the same conclusion emerged. In other large national institutions during this period, new forms of transportation and communication were producing larger organizations and greater centralization of power and authority. McNeirny's modernization of diocesan administration reflected a similar understanding of the importance of centralized control if there was to be efficient use of resources. Yet the Church remained a highly decentralized organization, because the "branch managers," the pastors, controlled the delivery of services and in a democratic environment in which religious affiliation was a matter of choice, they had to lead through persuasion, not coercion. Moreover, unlike his secular counterpart, the bishop did not have enough priests to replace easily those on the spot. Finally, he did not yet have the resources at his disposal to act adequately upon the information he received. In Syracuse, only Father McEvoy, the chancellor and secretary, and the bishop himself, worked full-time for the diocese.

Even the vicar general was also rector of the cathedral, while other diocesan officers were also pastors. For several years, Ludden kept diocesan accounts in a notebook small enough to be carried in his pocket. A briefly kept diary for 1888 showed that his major official actions involved consulting with pastors and trustees, regularizing ownership in badly managed parishes, celebrating confirmation and preaching in the cathedral.

Accordingly, the truly critical matter was to build a strong relationship with and among the diocesan clergy. This required not just the visible use of the bishop's authority, as in the Quinn case, but less tangible efforts to enlist their cooperation by inviting them to share at least some of the responsibility for important decisions. To raise the required funds for diocesan administration, Ludden formed a committee of respected priests to decide on assessments for parishes. Another committee helped establish a clerical fund for aged or infirmed priests similar to the one McNeirny had created in Albany. Appointed consultors acted as a body of advisors on the establishment of new parishes, setting parish boundaries, assessments for special collections and, even in some cases, suggesting appointments to major parishes. In 1896, this body, slightly expanded, was established legally as the diocesan corporation. On a number of matters this group engaged in rather extended debate before making recommendations to the bishop. In 1906, it elected a vicar general by secret ballot. Later the consultors approved loans taken out by parishes, while filling vacancies in their own ranks. Thus, rather than ruling arbitrarily, Ludden took steps to ensure that many of the most prominent and respected priests in the diocese were involved in the decision making process and thus bound to support its results. At the same time, he regularly demonstrated his personal dedication to the diocese. For example he deeded his episcopal residence to the diocese as a gift. Later he acquired St. Mary's Cemetery at a cost of $43,000 and gave it over to the corporation.

By the turn of the century, Ludden, by such means, had drawn the lines tight. He was assisted by the New York State legislature which, in 1895 at the behest of the hierarchy, amended the religious corporation law to ensure that parish trustees could transact business only with the consent of the bishop of the diocese. In a letter at the end of 1904, Ludden summarized his expectations regarding the management of parish affairs. The bishop reminded the pastors that trustees were "trustees and administrators, and in no sense owners or irresponsible agents." He added that "business methods" demanded of "trustees and administrators in purely secular matters" were required as well in "the management of Church revenues, receipts and expenditures." Indeed, "the very nature and sacred uses" of church income "demand most emphatically stricter, more conscientious, and businesslike methods than the former." Regular meetings of trustees and committees should be held, for even if the advice received did not coincide with the pastor's own views, "it may modify them to great advantage and satisfaction and secure their success and general approval." The "faithful people" were "loyal and generous" and "when they are fairly treated, as they deserve to be, they will always respond more liberally and generously to all reasonable appeals and demands."

For his part, Ludden made clear to the laity at every opportunity their responsibility to support their pastor both personally and financially. When Nicholas Quinn arrived at his new assignment at St. Patrick's in Utica, he found an unusual situation. Father Patrick Caraher, who had served as pastor for almost 40 years, had allowed the parish debt to bring the community to near bankruptcy. When the church was sold at auction, Caraher bought it and attempted to persuade the people to provide for him in his retirement. When acceptable arrangements were not forthcoming, the community and its new pastor, Father McDonald, withdrew to another parish building and outfitted it as a church. This was the building which burned to the ground shortly before McDonald and Quinn traded places. Quinn soon was at work raising money for a new church, and he was aided by a visit from the bishop in 1893. During the confirmation ceremony, Ludden told the people:

> Unfortunately there are some very sad pages in the history of this congregation.... You have passed through trouble and through fire.... For a number of years you have scattered. For one reason and another people have been fault-finding and when a congregation grows dissatisfied, it is sure to run down financially and spiritually. The people of this congregation have not contributed enough to support a church and hence it is they lost confidence in the management of things.... It is true business

> matters were not managed according to law. Sometimes they were managed only by the whims of individuals and this is not a safe rule to follow.

COORDINATING SOCIAL SERVICES

All that went in the diocese under the Catholic name was subject to Ludden's authority. Charities carried on by religious orders were independent of parishes but accountable to the bishop. Shortly after arriving in Syracuse, Ludden learned that the property of the House of Providence orphanage was "dilapidated, unhealthy and unsafe." Assured that repairs would be futile, he began plans to erect a new building. He put aside his dislike of appeals to the public and organized a union fair, with city parishes ordered to cooperate. Although it was "largely successful," more money was needed and a general collection was taken in the parishes. All these efforts almost came to a tragic end when, in December 1907, the House of Providence was destroyed by fire. No lives were lost, but the damage was nearly total. The children moved to temporary shelter. A "committee of 100" set about raising money, ground was broken in June with 5,000 people in attendance and, in February 1910, 27 months after the fire, the children moved into their new home.

A major unmet need in the city was the care of unwanted infants and small children. A Catholic laywoman, Mrs. John Toole, recognizing this need, began taking such children into her home and then established, quite on her own, a foundling home. Many saw this institution as unnecessary and indeed as an encouragement to the evil of extra-marital sex and pregnancy. When Mrs. Toole solicited support, Ludden hesitated. Then, in the letter announcing the general collection for House of Providence in 1891, he made an admission. Without mentioning Mrs. Toole by name, he wrote of "a very earnest and devoted woman" who seemed to have "a special adaptation for this most uninviting and sadly neglected department of human miseries." He had refused his help, he said, because she was "a woman, partially a stranger, and wholly without means or influence, undertaking a most disagreeable work, whose magnitude, owing to reasons not farfetched, was altogether an unknown quantity." For Ludden it was almost equally important that "this good woman was only an individual, not an institution: individuals pass away, institutions, if they are useful, ought to live on." Having said all this, Ludden then launched into a long reflection on the Catholic philosophy of life, constrasting it sharply with other reigning world views:

All the combined wisdom and learning and refinement and poetry and philanthropy of paganism never built an orphanage or produced a foundling asylum. The oldest and wisest philosophies of the world taught and still teach that helpless and unpromising infant life would be most wisely treated after the manner of the supernumerary offspring of domestic brutes, dumped alive into ditches and canals.... In genteel terms, this is called the law of the natural environment. It is the savagery of refinement. Call it scientifically "the survival of the fittest.

Fortunately, Christianity long since had rejected such ideas, said Ludden. The Church held fast to traditional values of human dignity and human worth in society where others, including Protestants, were slipping into pagan naturalism. "We alone, the children of the faith, have a philosophy that teaches us that even unwelcome fortuitous waifs, these derelict scraps of humanity, are each and every one the purchase of an infinite price," Ludden wrote. Whatever the pretext, "we place on his brow the murderer's brand who dares to destroy human life even in its most fragile dependent and helpless state." After these strong words, Ludden's closing sentence was almost anticlimatic. The foundling institution he had referred to recently had been incorporated, was under the supervision and patronage of some of the best known and most charitable citizens, and the bishop now recommended it "cordially to the generosity and charity of our people."

By the end of the decade, St. Mary's, now under the management of the Sisters of Charity, was receiving approximately 75 children a year, of whom 13 were city or county charges. At the age of six, the children were placed in Catholic orphanages or put up for adoption.

During Ludden's administration, new buildings and expanded facilities were provided at the other orphanages in the diocese, an addition and nursing school were added to St. Elizabeth's hospital in Utica, and a modern surgical pavilion was provided for St. Joseph's in Syracuse. In 1905, philanthropist John Dundee helped place the Syracuse institutions on a sound foundation with legacies of $180,000 to St. Joseph's, $130,000 to the House of Providence, $100,000 to St. Vincent's and $50,000 to St. Mary's Infant Home. Despite this evident progress, Ludden remained cautious about expansion and jealous of his authority. When the Sisters of Charity planned a new building for St. John's orphanage in Utica, Ludden attempted to force them to adopt more modest plans:

We all knew the struggles and unseemly schemes that are used to meet debts on our institutions, picnics, lawn festivals, excursions, dances, fairs, festivals. Sisters leaving the security of

A SLIP OF THE TONGUE?

In March 1888, St. Patrick's parish in Norwich was celebrating the funeral for one of its founding members. Shortly after the service ended, the small wooden church went up in flames — victim of a coal stove used to heat the building. Sixteen weeks later, Bishop Ludden made his first episcopal visit to Norwich to lay the cornerstone for an impressive new church for St. Patrick parishioners. The bishop marked four crosses on the stone, blessed it with holy water, and proclaimed that the new "St. Paul's church" was under construction.

Was it a slip of the tongue that led to the renaming of St. Patrick's church? Some people later felt it was. The event had been advertised as a dedication service for "the new St. Patrick's church," and the preacher referred several times to the "new St. Patrick's" which would be built. Parishioners were pleased that among the few items saved from the fire's debris was a statue of their Irish patron.

Intentional or not, the new name stuck. Neither the bishop nor the pastor ever explained the name change, and for years the original St. Patrick's church was called, not by name, but simply "the old church." Later church and public documents refer to the Norwich parish as St. Paul's as if that had always been the name of the parish.

their convent house, begging and importuning the faithful to meet the interest on those debts. I repeat my advice—revise your plans. Construct a very plain house suitable for orphan children and the means at your disposal and within the reach of reasonable expectations.

CIVIC AFFAIRS AND EDUCATION

Parishes and charities were at the heart of the diocesan enterprise, but they did not exhaust the bishop's responsibilities. He was also the most visible Catholic leader in the area, regarded by both Catholics and Protestants as a spokesman for the Church, a role he accepted fully. Local Catholics once had felt themselves to be a beleaguered minority, tempted to keep silent about its grievances. But men like O'Hara and Barry had begun to change that. The presence of a bishop, reflecting the growth and maturity of an ever

more prosperous Church, deepened Catholic self-confidence and ushered in more aggressive defense of Catholic rights and a more vigorous participation in public debate. Even the appearance in the 1890s of the American Protective Association, riding a wave of renewed nativism and anti-Catholicism, failed to dampen this new aggressiveness. The *Catholic Sun* challenged every manifestation of prejudice and denounced the Republican party when it failed to disassociate itself from the APA. The combination of renewed attacks on immigrants and Catholic interests, especially in education, combined with the new assertiveness of Catholic leadership to deepen intergroup divisions and erode much of the good will and cooperative spirit evident in non-Catholic support for many early parishes and charities. Renewal of conflict took place in the 1890s, when a severe economic depression, widespread labor unrest, and the influx of the so-called "new immigrants" from southern and eastern Europe caused considerable anxiety among the largely Protestant middle classes about the stability of American institutions. This lead to more self-conscious organization of native Protestants and movements for civic reform and social improvement which sometimes were barely disguised efforts to control the behavior of poor and working class Americans. These social and cultural strains contributed to an increasingly bitter tone of public debate and to an intensified group consciousness among Catholics. This reinforced the instinct of Ludden and other Irish-American priests that the survival and progress of the Church depended upon its own strength, solidarity and resources.

The new Catholic assertiveness was evident from the time of Ludden's arrival in Syracuse. When parishioners of St. John the Evangelist cathedral were annoyed by the passing of railroad engines during Sunday services, they called upon the local alderman and threatened to take action against the railroad, contending that it was deliberately harassing the church. Ludden himself organized property owners in his East Fayette Street neighborhood to protest extension of noisy surface transit past their houses.

When plans for a new fire station in the old City Hall across from St. Mary's church threatened that parish, Father John Grimes, the pastor, charged that this project of a "few petty politicians" would interfere with church services, endanger Sunday school children, and insult his congregation and all the Catholics of the city. At the same time, he denounced the building of a public bath house at the rear of the church, a project continued despite offers by the church to provide comparable property elsewhere. Grimes' conclusion reflected the growing determination and self-confidence of Syracuse Catholics: "Concentrated bigotry and prejudice of Syracuse may place deformity before and behind the church but its extension shall

not be prevented or retarded when the 100,000 or more Catholics of the diocese of Syracuse see fit to improve it or enlarge its dimensions." The moment came in 1904 when Ludden purchased the property, tore down the bath house, expanded St. Mary's sanctuary over the site and made the church his cathedral.

Ludden's most constructive intervention in public affairs came early in his term. Syracuse still was receiving water from Onondaga Creek, pumped into a reservoir and through the city in antiquated and unsanitary wooden conduits, all controlled by a privately owned water company. The wealthy could and did buy bottled water, but even they were worried about inadequate fire protection. Reform groups proposed drawing upon the water of Skaneateles Lake under the control of a municipally owned water company. Ludden threw his support behind the proposal, despite charges that it was "socialistic." Many observers believed his public championing of the cause in letters to the press and public meetings was a critical factor in its success.

In the fall of 1907, when political controversy over the corrupt ballot was stirring the city, the bishop spoke out: "We are not to simply condemn the person who sells his vote," Ludden said.

This condition exists among the poorer classes in society, the idle class and the men hanging around street corners and saloons. They are willing when tempted to sell their votes. Another class is the poor foreigners. They come from a country where they did not have the vote. Our criticism should be reserved for the better class who do the buying.

Portions of that better class may have agreed. The well-to-do reformers, bent upon bringing Syracuse politics into the progressive era, formed an association to fight corrupt prac-

115

tices, and Ludden was elected vice president. The hard-bitten bishop was frank: "I am in sympathy with this organization but, to speak candidly, I have not much faith in its success. I was chaplain of the Senate in Albany during the time of Tweed and I prayed for the Senate but it did not seem to do any good."

Like most conservatives Ludden regarded politicians as greedy, self-seeking men who contributed nothing to the public good. He had an almost puritan leaning toward sobriety, thrift and decorum and hated extravagance, display, and enthusiasm. In 1903, invited to offer a guest editorial in the Syracuse *Telegram*, he expressed sentiments in keeping with his self-image as a respectable citizen hostile to hypocritical politicians, ruthless business men and social agitators of every stripe:

Syracuse should be cleaned, both physically and morally. Commerce alone does not make an ideal, virtuous city. A city having no higher aspirations is doomed. What Syracuse needs most is contented and industrious people, virtuous home and family life with low taxes and a greater consideration for the taxpayer and a lesser for the tax consumer. Let there be no sinecure offices for the mere seekers— suckers I would say, if you pardon a solecism—no political pap, no public extravagant monuments for the erection and maintenance of which small property owners, laborers and merchants are mortgaged out of their humble homes and driven to poverty or the poorhouse. Don't take on metropolitan airs. Syracuse is an inland city, not a metropolis. You can't execute the airs of an eight keyed flute on a penny whistle. Let there be no more expansion. Our city is big enough now geographically for half a

million people.... Pay as you go and if you can't pay don't go at all....Posterity, if it be permitted to come into existence, will have enough to bear its own burdens without the superimposed inheritance of puffed-up pomp and the extravagance of fancies, fads, and fakes.

Such words were not likely to attract reformers or the working class to Ludden's standard. His approach to school issues undoubtedly alienated conservatives who might have shared these social views. One of their projects was to retain the long-disputed practice of having the Bible read at the opening of the day in the public schools. Ludden regarded the practice as "a religious exercise that is an injury and insult to parents and Christians not of the Protestant faith." When editorials in local papers suggested that the churches get together and agree on scriptural readings acceptable to all Christians, Ludden was at his most scornful:

Well! The millenium must be here. We have, the Syracuse Post *informs us, a non-sectarian Bible for the schools.... What efforts, what ludicrous efforts, will people make at contradictions and impossibilities, the frantic, futile efforts on the part of the state to introduce into the public, secular state schools that meaningless, shapeless intangible, non-existent thing called a non-sectarian religion. The state cannot teach religion. The Church of God alone can teach religion.*

Ludden was equally candid, and equally sarcastic, in expressing his views on the widely debated school question. As a young priest, he told the *Albany Evening Journal* he was "opposed to the public school as it now exists." Instead, Ludden favored a division of the school fund among the denominations, an arrangement similar to that in Canada and parts of Europe. He explained these views to an inquiring Protestant in 1894:

I am in favor of public universal education. I am not in favor of an irreligious or godless education. I am anxious that our schools exceed the secular requirement. But since the State is incompetent to teach religion, it ought not to prevent from teaching it those who are divinely authorized to do so.

I would rejoice in paying taxes to the public school fund if I knew that every sect and denomination, in sharing it would add to the secular, a religious education of their children.

On another occasion, when an official said he would not tolerate any remuneration of teachers in Catholic schools because of the distinctive dress of the sisters, Ludden called the man "bigoted." He supposed that "if they came to school on bikes in short skirts and read the Protestant King James Bible, they would be on the common ground nearest (his) narrow minded soul."

One possible compromise of the school question, widely debated across the county, was to distinguish sharply between the secular and religious content of the curriculum and provide public support for the former while leaving religious instruction in private hands. An experiment of this kind had been in place for years in Poughkeepsie, and in fact had been tried for a time at St. Patrick's in Utica. However, in the 1890s, when Archbishop John Ireland praised the nation's public schools and advocated such an arrangement, Catholics divided sharply. The German Catholics and New York bishops like Corrigan and McQuaid, who were committed deeply to schools, opposed the plan. Ireland, whose energetic championing of active citizenship

and rapid assimilation of the immigrants made him a controversial figure in the Church, enjoyed considerable popularity in Syracuse. Yet it was necessity as much as ideology which led to an effort to implement his school proposals in the city. In 1890, Father Kennedy of St. Lucy's and his parishioners decided to build a school. Kennedy visited schools around the country and hired the leading local architect, Archimedes Russell. When completed, his school had 12 large modern classrooms, a gymnasium and a fine assembly hall. Unfortunately, as soon as it was completed, the depression of 1893 hit Syracuse and Kennedy decided that his people could not afford to maintain the school. He wrote to the board of education, offering to rent the building to the city for one dollar a year, with the teachers to be employed by the board which would have full control of the building during school hours. It was an opportune time because there were increasing demands for a new public school in that section of the city. Protestant leaders lobbied vigorously against the proposal, however, while even some Catholics were opposed. In the end, a canvass of the board showed a majority in opposition, and Kennedy withdrew his offer before it came to a vote. The following year, he engaged the Sisters of St. Joseph and opened his school with 200 children in attendance. The episode indicated that, even at this late date, the school question was not settled entirely. Eventually, Catholics did become convinced that separate schools were the best, if not the only, way to ensure the proper religious education of their children. Catholics believed this in part because of the inability of their neighbors to consider any alternative to a public school system which excluded religious considerations. The hope of some Catholics, like Ireland and Kennedy, that people of good will could find a way to respect religious convictions and respond to pluralism without violating anyone's freedom, proved unavailing. They could locate no common ground.

Yet Syracuse was hardly a bulwark of parochial school education. In 1893, at the height of these controversies, there were 3,000 children in Catholic schools in the city, 1,000 of whom were in the German parish of Assumption. Already, the Polish people were demonstrating their adherence to the German position on schools, as Sacred Heart, the city's first Polish parish, had 150 in its new school. But two years later, in a letter to Archbishop Corrigan, Bishop Ludden noted that "except in the larger congregations in cities," there were "no parochial and Catholic schools," and those that did exist had "a hard struggle for support." Although Ludden felt there was no immediate prospect of increasing the number of schools, he believed strongly in Catholic school education. He told Rome that the small time available for Sunday school instruction hardly could compensate for the damage wrought by the atmosphere of the public school, so that there was "no hope of safeguarding the faith if Catholic schools are destroyed or their efficiency is notably diminished." Given the obstacles of inadequate income and lack of lay support, the goal of full Catholic education could not yet be realized. However, Ludden lost no opportunity to teach his people that eventually this commitment would be necessary if they were to fulfill their religious duty. To do so, they would have to depend on their own resources, because the larger public was unlikely to accept a denominational system. Any other form of government assistance was unlikely to be forthcoming and, because of the restrictions it could bring with it, probably would be unacceptable. Like John Hughes a half century earlier, Ludden may have found the conflicts with public school authorities and Protestant critics useful. These conflicts deepened the conviction that public schools were inadequate to the demands of parental re-

sponsibility and were conducted under auspices hostile to Catholic interests and insensitive to Catholic symbols and values, this in spite of the fact that, as the *Sun* pointed out, a majority of the teachers and a growing number of principals were Catholic. Of "lady teachers" in 1893, according to the *Sun,* 119 were Irish, 112 "American," 42 German, eight Jewish, three French and two English. While the *Sun* told the Catholics among them to give good example and Ludden defended their right to a job, no one asked if their presence might modify the Church's antagonism.

Yet not everyone agreed with the single-minded defense of Catholic schools in every discussion of education. In Utica in 1901, a proposal was put before the voters which would make free textbooks available to all students, replacing a system by which families had to demonstrate their need in order to receive the books without charge. Father Lynch of St. John's opposed the legislation vigorously, arguing that the students in Catholic schools, particularly in his Catholic Free Academy, would be unable to benefit from the law, which therefore discriminated against Catholics. One of his leading parishioners, Henry Coupe, publicly opposed the pastor on the issue. Coupe argued that the bill in no way disturbed Catholic schools and the injustice of their position was not pertinent to the legislation, which in his opinion brought a greater degree of justice to the public schools. Lynch and the opposition prevailed, and the law was defeated soundly.

BUILDING RELATIONSHIPS

Ludden's sometimes crabby and contentious attitude on public affairs and inter-religious disputes also contrasted with the more progressive civic-mindedness of priests like Michael Clune, who became pastor of St. John the Evangelist in 1891. Clune, one of the most popular Catholic clergymen in the history of the city, argued the case for the Church with more restraint than his bishop. In 1894, for example, he pointed to the services provided to the city by Catholic hospitals and orphanages, and the money the city saved because so many children attended Catholic schools. Catholics, he argued, were patient with the unjust burdens they bore because they believed there was a latent sense of justice in the American people that in time would rectify such anomalies. Addressing local Protestant ministers who opposed assistance to such Catholic institutions, Clune asked these "good and true men" to join in abandoning the "hatreds and bitterness of the past." Pointing to recent statistics which indicated that in poorer sections of Syracuse many were outside any Church, he argued that both Catholics and Protestants were not "in touch with humanity at enough points." At a time when the nation increasingly was concerned about racial and religious conflict — conflict intensified by immigration and class strife, occasioned by industrial expansion and economic depression — Clune presented a view of religion's role which was not far removed from what was becoming known among Protestants as the "Social Gospel," a commitment to human betterment that could unite Christians across religious and social barriers:

I believe that teachers of religion could learn something from physical scientists. These scientists take the abstract principles of Euclid and transfer them from paper to the stars. They have given us the theory of navigation by which on the darkest night our steamers find a safe passage through the sea. In the same way, the teachers of religion should take the principles of the Gospel and apply them to the service of humanity. They could con-

struct a roadway over which the now helpless and criminal, capitalist and anarchist could walk in peace.

Clune took a similar attitude toward problems of public morality. In contrast to Father Barry's sharp condemnation of baseball a decade earlier, Clune responded to complaints about games on Sunday by arguing that "the sabbath was made for man," not the reverse. The day was one for rest and "innocent social amusements" and a golden mean should be found between the puritan and continental treatment of Sunday. Baseball he found "a clean, healthful, interesting and intellectual game" and, provided it did not interfere with religious services, was played in "country places" and surrounded with adequate safeguards, he thought it "delightful both to player and spectators."

Clune's reasonable, conciliatory approach, which would have been familiar to John C. Devereux, Father Michael Haes and Father O'Hara, at least in his early days, was being bypassed by Ludden's more polemical tone, which reflected single minded concern with the Church, its ideals and its interests. The tone of Catholic polemics reflected the growing strength and self-confidence of the Catholic community and its leadership. Sensitive to every slight, Catholics were now almost contemptuous of Protestants. The *Catholic Sun* was amused when the Presbyterian church attempted to discipline a teacher of theology whose views of Scripture violated traditional orthodoxy. "They scorn the claim of the infallible authority of the Catholic church and yet set themselves up as infallible in dealing with their own dissenters," the editors wrote. "From being a ship, Presbyterianism is fast becoming a raft. The shipwrecked will drift to the Catholic Church which, like a stately cruiser, is guided by the compass of infallibility." The "Episcopalian pleasure yacht" was little better off. When a

119

group of ladies from that church went on a retreat with "the most severe order" in that church, the *Sun* laughed editorially: "In Catholic retreats fasting is strictly observed for a part of the time, but these Episcopalian sisters could never stand that while the strawberry season is on." Still, it was a good sign they were seeking such experiences because it demonstrated that Catholics "have set the style in the religious world."

Ludden occasionally strolled with the Episcopal bishop, but he had no more respect for Protestants than the editors of the *Sun,* as his comments on Bible reading indicated and his private correspondence confirmed. Moreover, unlike Clune, he saw little to admire in the "spirit of the age." In Oswego, praising Father Barry's educational projects, he told parents that they need have no fear that children educated by the Church would become "innoculated with the spirit of the age, detestable egoism and independence of all legal and moral authority." He contrasted the present situation with what the parents had known in Ireland: "now it is dollars and cents which command all the attention; then it was the trinity that was worshipped."

Ludden considered himself deeply patriotic, but he reflected an emerging ideology of American Catholicism. He argued that the truths taught by the Church corresponded with authentic American ideals, ideals now found in the past and in danger of being abandoned by non-Catholic Americans. On the occasion of the centennial of Washington's inauguration as president, the bishop called upon Catholic pastors to participate in the national day of Thanksgiving scheduled for April 30. In his letter, he contrasted the "illustrious founders of this government," men "who were responsible to conscience and believed in God," with the "grasping, trading politicians seeking their own individual aggrandizement," presumably widespread a century later. To redeem the promise of American life and be worthy of God's gifts, Americans had to discipline themselves in freedom, finding the law of God and "knowledge true" in the Church. Thus by being the Church, teaching its doctrine and morality to its members, asserting its truths forcefully in public debate, the Catholic Church trained good citizens and offered the nation a way to recover its authentic traditions and built the orderly, sober, law abiding citizenry that alone could make the experiment in freedom work.

Ludden's private life was generally hidden from view. He walked regularly through the city, patronized the same barber for years, eventually welcoming the man into the church, and was reputed to be a good shot at billiards. He continued his earlier practice of vacationing in the south, where he fished and hunted. On these trips, and his *ad limina* visits to the Vatican, he usually was accompanied by some prominent clergymen. His priests were generous. When he left on his *ad limina* visit in 1895, they subscribed $8,275. A testimonial on his behalf in 1904 netted more than $10,000, another in 1909 brought $12,000. When he died, he left $47,000, half to the diocese and the other half to needy relatives and local Catholic charities.

Ludden, as bishop, adopted the motto "Justice and Peace." These words reflected no passion to bring about justice in the world, a world he viewed with a profound pessimism and about whose projects for human betterment and social improvement he was always skeptical. Rather, they reflected the need of a maturing Church to organize itself for more effective service to its members, convinced that a smoothly functioning Church (worshiping, educating, providing good example and upholding ancient truths) was the best contribution Catholics could make to society. Ludden's major means to that end was to insist that each priest do his job well, work closely with the bishop and his fellow priests, and stick to his assignment. As the fourteenth anniversary of his installation approached, the *Catholic Sun* noted that his method seemed to be found in the advice of St. Paul to Timothy "Attende Tibi." Loosely translated, this means "Mind your own business." Forgetting some of the early problems, the *Sun* claimed that Ludden's 14 years had been marred by no unpleasant incidents in his dealing with priests and people, a record the *Sun* believed resulted from "his practical viewpoint of ecclesiastical affairs." During the bitter conflicts among other bishops which stirred the Church in the 1890s, the *Sun* noted that Ludden "has been quietly attending to his business." Minding one's business was not a passive matter, but an active struggle to build the Church, defend it against attack, carry on its religious work, and serve as an example to others. O'Farrell had emphasized unity and power at his installation and Ludden understood the message. "In union there is strength," the bishop told the national convention of the Catholic Mutual Benefit Society in 1903:

> *We as Catholic citizens have passed the swaddling clothes stage and have grown into a panoply of strength and numbers and we are not scared by the cry of a "Maria Monk" or other fanatics who burned our convents. All we ask are our rights.... We shall no longer tolerate any infringement of our rights.... United we should stand shoulder to shoulder against proselytizing and intrusion or interference with our religious affairs on the part of state or people.*

Peace and justice, it seems, was a matter of building an orderly family. In this family, there would be due order under proper authority and respect for the rights and dignity of every member, and the sturdy defense of that family against assault. Given this goal, set forth in his motto, all Catholics, or at least the Irish among them, could agree that an earlier description of the Syracuse diocese was now quite accurate. It had indeed become "a well disciplined household under its first Bishop, the Rt. Rev. P. A. Ludden."

NOW YOU ARE A PEOPLE

THE IMMIGRANTS ARRIVE
1890s-1920s

Bishop Patrick Ludden organized a strong diocese which, in many ways, resembled a family, but not everyone in that family was happy. In fact, the struggle to build a Church of "one heart and one soul" living in "justice and peace" had only begun primarily because, as Irish and German Catholics matured, new groups of Catholics were gathering among more recent immigrants from southern and eastern Europe. Pluralism always has been a reality in the Christian Church since the days of Paul's ministry to the Gentiles. In the United States, the Church has had a unique experience of this pluralism. People from many lands created parish communities intended to preserve old world traditions and enable newcomers to adjust to American conditions. Seen from the outside, these ethnic groups and their churches appeared conservative, bent upon resisting adaptation to American ways by separating themselves from other people, thus, the word "ghetto." Yet, many within the community were learning to speak English, working hard to acquire money, homes, and standing among their fellow citizens, and dreaming of American futures for their children. Some groups, of course, insisted on traditional ways and condemned everything American. Others were so anxious to shed old ways that they changed their religion, their language, even their names. But most immigrants were more moderate. They believed there was much they had brought with them that was valuable, and they wished to pass those things on to their children. They felt ties of family and blood to the homeland and, in many cases, they longed for its liberation. At the same time, they believed with equal passion in the possibilities of America. They insisted that they were already good citizens and were contributing to the welfare of their adopted nation. They looked forward with hope and backward with pride, and they had the audacity to believe that such dual loyalties were not only acceptable, but fully in accord with the American commitment to freedom and self-determination. They also believed that it was possible to become free citizens and successful Americans, while remaining proudly Irish, German, Polish or Italian, and while remaining proudly Catholic.

The ethnic group was neither an island of resistance of Americanization, nor a suicidal staging ground for the gradual abandonment of traditional values. Rather, it was a means by which ordinary men and women organized themselves to support each other through a difficult transition. It was also a means to uphold family and communal values, not only for a moment, but for the future, and to provide a foundation for effective participation in American life. Similarly, the Catholic churches such people formed were not temporary holding pens where they could practice an outmoded and archaic religion. Nor were they vehicles through which American, or Irish-American, Catholics could mold them to new forms required by a future they would control. Rather, ethnic parishes were communities of people redefining their identity as Catholics. The people of Polish, Italian and Slovak parishes before World War I were expressing in community, in organization, in worship and in buildings their experience of God. Churches, after all, are simply one of a variety of ways in which men and women organize themselves as a people, and establish the relationships which allow them to answer the question "who are you?" They meet very real human needs for the public expression of shared values and beliefs. They provide one means by which the diversity of religious experience can find concrete human expression. As Bishop Ludden told one proud congregation as it dedicated its new church, "now you are a people."

Irish and German Americans constituted the overwhelming majority of Church members when the diocese of Syracuse was founded in 1886. Their churches had arisen out of the adjustment of immigrant Catholics to local conditions, one result of which was the national parish. Defined formally by language, it was the form given to a developing sense of identity as first the Germans, then other groups, discovered that they were a distinct people. The process was not without pain, but the formation of national parishes represented a creative pastoral response to the American experience of pluralism. In 1886, the process had only begun.

In addition to the Germans, French-Canadians in Oswego already had created a parish for themselves. Soon there would be new groups, as the sources of American immigration shifted dramatically after 1890. Educational reforms in the Austro-Hungarian Empire, Russia and Prussia awakened new aspirations among young men and women in the villages of eastern Europe. Economic and political institutions, changing less rapidly, could not meet these new aspirations, while population pressures and new forms of agriculture were transforming rural life. Beginning with a small but steady stream of emigration in the 1880s, the movement of Poles, Czecks, Slovaks, Hungarians, Ruthenians and a dozen other eastern European nationalities to the United States grew to flood proportions after 1890. At the same time, large numbers of Italians began to enter the country, pushed by similar forces of modernization. This immigration from southern and eastern Europe added a bewildering array of new national groups to America's already polyglot population, and greatly complicated the work of the American Church.

What historian Luciano Iorizzo has written of the Irish in turn of the century Oswego could have been said for all of Central New York:

> *Indeed, the Irish, the earliest immigrant group to come en masse to Oswego, were working their way into the American native-stock 'establishment.' They had come a long way from the squatter days on back lots and waste patches, when their tenements in Pea Soup Flats were sometimes destroyed on order of the city health officials for fear that such substandard housing would be detrimental to the health and welfare of Oswego residents.*

Such hard won progress did not necessarily make the Irish sympathetic to newcomers. Utica's Monsignor Lynch, more understanding of non-Irish ways than most, wrote in 1912 that the Italians, Poles, Lithuanians and Slovaks were "for the most part ignorant of our ecclesiastical laws and customs and many of them [held] ideals utterly at variance with the true spirit of the Catholic church." Of course, many of these immigrants were relatively uneducated in their faith and unfamiliar with Church law, as the Irish once had been. But what Lynch meant by "the true spirit" was submission to the all but total control of church property and income by the clergy, regular sacramental practice and the restriction of devotions to those officially recognized by the Church. These were the standards by which the newer immigrants were judged. In April 1914, Father John F. McLoughlin of St. John's in Oswego reported

he had Italians in his parish and had brought in an Italian priest at Easter time hoping "to induce them to approach the sacraments," but his efforts had not been very successful. "The Italians are industrious, though wanting in generosity to church or school," he wrote. Their "morals are good, especially that of the women and girls," but they "were not well instructed in their faith" and aside from "a few good reliable Italian men who speak the language of the Country," they came to church seldom. Men came only on the occasion of the "great feast days," a situation made worse by the presence of a few "Free masons given to ridicule of religion." Similarly, in Jamesville in 1916, Father P. J. Sloane presided over St. Mary's parish, which included by his estimate 606 Catholics. Of those a little more than half were English speaking and the rest composed of six French, 12 German, 28 Hungarian, 92 Poles, 21 Slovak, 14 Syrian and 91 "other foreigners." Only approximately a third of his immigrant population was "devout and well instructed." The rest were not regular in attendance, partly because men had to work on Sunday.

While pastors like McLaughlin and Sloane had problems with immigrants, Bishop Ludden was reluctant to encourage separate parishes. With his orderly concern for unity and discipline, he disliked national parishes and hoped those already established would give way before the assimilation of immigrant children. This was clear in a letter written to pastors in April 1899, calling attention to diocesan statutes dealing with the foreign born. Children born in the United States of non-English speaking parents were not obliged to remain attached to the parish to which their parents belonged, the bishop noted. These American-born Catholics, as well as Catholics born abroad who spoke English, were not obliged "to subject themselves to the jurisdiction of the rector of churches of their

Bishop Patrick A. Ludden (Photo: Chancery Archives)

National parishes were needed at least temporarily, and Ludden approved their formation whenever a community demonstrated its ability to provide the funds to build a church and support a pastor. The one condition was that the parish abide by the "American" system of turning ownership of the property over to a corporation controlled by the bishop.

The Germans, in fact, provided a model for other national groups because they, by now, accepted fully the need to support their parish, while cooperating with the bishop. Many Irish pastors had been incensed when German pastors began offering services in English. The *Catholic Sun* condemned the practice and some priests angered German Catholics by their efforts to force English speaking Germans to attend territorial parishes. Ludden wisely ignored the problem, perhaps sensing that, in the long run, the use of English would weaken national bonds and erode the distinctiveness of ethnic communities. In fact, he encouraged German expansion.

When 286 Catholic families of German origin living in the Schiller Park area of Syracuse told Bishop Ludden they wanted to build a parochial school because of the long walk to Assumption, he responded that if there was need for a school, there was need for a parish. By the summer of 1890, a Holy Trinity Society of former Assumption parishioners purchased three lots in an area known as Kaiser's Grove and, in 1891, work began on a combination church and school. Many Assumption parishioners, upset by the division of their community, would not speak to people from the new parish. However, when a second and larger church was build in 1912, feelings had subsided and Assumption donated a large crucifix for the new edifice. Another new German parish, St. Joseph's, was established in Oneida during the early years of Ludden's administration.

own nationality." If there was any doubt about Ludden's views, he eliminated it: "It is clear that the motives of this legislation are to discountenance as far as possible the multiplication and perpetuation of different religious rites and nationalities in this country."

At the same time, Ludden was a veteran pastor who understood the need to provide religious services in native languages if the faith of the immigrants was to be preserved.

POLISH CATHOLICS

The Germans provided a home for the next group to organize as Catholics. The earliest Polish settlers in the diocese were, for the most part, from German and Austrian areas of Poland and thus gravitated toward the German churches. Nevertheless, they and their priests at home had resisted the efforts of Prussia to enforce the use of the German language in education and in public business. Even under the milder rule of Catholic Austria, the Polish clergy were conscious agents of Polish nationalism. As a result, familiarity with the German language was not enough to persuade Polish Catholics to assimilate into German parishes.

With the Poles, as with earlier communities, parish formation came from the bottom up, but it required the help of the clergy to move to the consolidation and unification of growing congregations. As early as 1875, there were Polish immigrants working in the salt industry. Gradually, friends and relatives arrived and the community expanded and worshiped at St. Joseph's German church, where Father Pickl knew enough Polish to hear confessions. In 1891, a group of laymen organized a mutual aid society. Polish priests from Pennsylvania visited occasionally and a decision was made to form a parish, Sacred Heart. Father Francis Kolazewski served as Sacred Heart's first pastor, saying Mass first in a rented hall, then, in August 1892, in the first church. The laying of the cornerstone was a grand event. Brightly uniformed societies from as far away as Rochester assembled in front of the bishop's residence for a great parade to the site, where Father Reuland of Holy Trinity spoke in English, German and Polish. The highlight of the day was an address by Father Michael Clune, the much admired rector of the cathedral. Clune's was a somewhat paternalistic appeal to the Poles to follow the Irish and German example:

You Poles have crossed the west sea to gather the golden fleece. You do well. By industry and sobriety the fleece will be gathered. Yours is a noble nationality. It has but one failing. It lost its prestige by disunion. Leave disunion in Europe. Find union and struggle here. Set your ambition to become American. As Americans you may yet be able to do something for your fatherland. You have a glorious example in the Germans and the Irish. The Irish are the real winners of Home Rule in Ireland. A few years ago [during Bismark's Kulturkampf] the German Catholics were strengthened by words of sympathy and approval that reached them from America. So you may yet obtain a just autonomy for Poland. To win the love of your fellow citizens here you have only to be upright, industrious and obedient to the law. If you make your lives conform to the spiritual law as expressed by your bishop and to the civil law as expressed by the civil magistrates, you lay the cornerstone of happiness and prosperity in your lives.

Kolaszewski, who had come to the city from Cleveland, was very popular. In addition to his Church work, Father "Colly" organized a society to encourage Poles to register to vote. During the election of 1894, the society's 625 members sponsored debates between Republican and Democrat politicians. By the end of 1894, however, he was back in Cleveland, the leader of a schismatic Polish Catholic movement. He was denounced by Catholic organizations and vilified in the local Catholic press, particularly when his lieutenants attempted to attract followers in Syracuse. The *Sun,* which earlier had described Kolaszewski as "a good and practical leader of his people," now accused him of taking money in exchange for Polish votes, persuading Catholics to buy from a grocery store he owned and stealing $10,000 when he left the diocese. In fact, the schism reflected deeper problems of immigrant adjustment to Irish-American Church priorities, because not all Poles agreed with Clune that the best way to fulfill Polish aspirations was to become Catholic and American on his terms.

Kolaszewski was followed by a series of pastors, none lasting more than a few months until, in 1896, Father Francis Rusin arrived, fresh from his ordination, to take charge of the community as forcefully as his Irish predecessors. Like Hourigan, O'Hara, B. F. McLoughlin and other builders of the pre-diocesan years, he saw in this far from promising community with its divided congregation, small wood church and $10,000 debt the possibility of magnificent achievement. The young priest first won the respect of his congregation by taking up residence in the damp basement of the church. In 1902, the bishop met with the pastor and trustees. The *Sun* reported innocently that the meeting was arranged to clear up "some slight misunderstanding owing to a lack of appreciation on the part of the trustees of American business methods." Some Poles, unreconciled to "American business methods" which gave all financial control to the priest, drifted to small schismatic churches like Kolzsewski's. However, most accepted Rusin's leadership, partly because it worked. Before long he opened a school, persuading the Felician sisters from Buffalo to serve in it, and cleverly guided his people through the tortuous process of acquiring a parish cemetery.

From the start, Rusin wanted a new church, one which would express his vision of what Polish-American Catholicism might become. Pushing his people hard, he drew up plans, begged door to door, encouraged every fundraising device developed over the past decade, oversaw construction and, in 1910, completed one of the largest and most impressive churches ever erected in the diocese. Rusin was not finished. The old church building now was used for the school. When it was destroyed by fire in 1916, the pastor directed the building of a two-story brick school with 17 classrooms, a hall with a capacity of 600, two clubrooms for use by parish societies and bowling alleys. By this time, he was the undisputed leader of Polish Catholics in the diocese, guiding the development of new parishes in Syracuse and other cities. He also investigated problems that arose, maintained Polish ties with the diocese while ensuring their autonomous development, and the oversaw his expanding parish, church and school.

Francis Rusin was a man of enormous energy, expansive vision, deeply loyalty to the Church and his homeland, and a healthy dose of self-centeredness like that of his Irish counterparts. He was an immigrant and a "self-made man." Born in Poland, he worked his passage to the United States while in his teens and won acceptance to the Troy seminary. He was an amateur carpenter of some skill and a powerful writer and preacher. Handsome, with dark hair and prominent eyebrows, he has a determined, commanding look in surviving photographs. When his new church opened in 1911, Rusin published a memoir. In addition to recording all contributions, he added his personal recollections, written in the third person. When he arrived in 1896, he recalled, the parish was "in a deplorable state" and "it was necessary to clothe oneself in holy patience to conquer these difficulties and troubles." It took six years before the people began to trust him, a time when the pastor "suffered greatly because of a lack of a home." Living under the church "like a church custodian," he endured "much discomfort and noise, since his living quarters were connected to the school." Finally in 1910, a rectory was built, and Rusin turned over his uncomfortable home to the sisters. After two years, they told the long-suffering pastor they would no longer live there. Out of "his savings of ten years" of admittedly "dedicated service," Rusin purchased a nearby home and donated it to the parish as a convent. "With this praiseworthy deed" Rusin wrote modestly of himself, "the Reverend Pastor united the hearts of his parishioners so much that there was a generous outpouring of offerings." Rusin was also as proud of the cemetery. He admitted that landscaping still was needed, but added good naturedly "even Krakow was not built immediately."

Around 1906, Rusin continued, parishioners began complaining that ther church was too small, and the pastor concluded they were right. Together priest and people excavated the site for a new church, saving $2,000 with their own labor. By 1910, it was ready for dedication by Paul Rhode, the first Polish bishop in the United States. An enormous crowd from all over New York state attended the ceremony. So many clergy, military and civic officials and fraternities marched that the beginning of the parade reached the church, while the rear guard was just starting, a mile and a half away. A Gothic structure bonded to a steel frame, the church had steeple walls four feet thick and foundation walls under the steeple 12 feet thick. A $7,000 organ capped the magnificent decorations. It was, as Rusin saw it, "outstanding not only in the Syracuse diocese but almost in the entire state of New York. Not only is it the pride of the local Polish community, but Americans are proud of it as the most beautiful structure in the city." So in 15 years of hard work, the pastor's sufferings had been crowned with success. It had not been easy, as he concluded in his memoir:

It should be mentioned that Father Rusin [he wrote of himself] from the

Father Francis Rusin (Photo: Chancery Archives)

very beginning of his stay in Syracuse has had several dissatisfied parishioners. He never had a moment of freedom. Always he had to struggle, knowing full well that the life of a person is not peaceful but a struggle. A person must struggle his entire miserable life. Whatever activity the Rev. pastor began with the counsel of the majority favorable, he always found his adversaries who wanted to wreck his noble plans. However, by his energy and courage, he overcame all and reached his noble goal, for the glory of his parishioners, with the help of the grace of God.

Fathers Hourigan, Barry and O'Hara could not have said it better.

Sacred Heart was, in fact, a great success story, but it was not alone, because Poles around the diocese moved quickly to organize parishes. As early as 1898, some Poles had begun settling on the east side of Syracuse. Unskilled laborers, they worked in the manufacture of radiators and boilers, on the railroad or at the Solvay Process Company. For 10 hour days and six-day weeks, they received an average daily wage of $1.70. Many families took in boarders, while women found domestic work in hotels and office buildings. They traveled four miles to Sacred Heart until Rusin called a meeting in the neighborhood in 1911 to propose formation of a new parish, Transfiguration. A committee was elected, purchased some land and arranged for incorporation. Door-to-door collections, raffles and dances helped generate funds and a temporary frame chapel was ready for the first resident pastor, Father Stanislaus Linisky, in 1912. Like all Polish communities, Transfiguration did not stop with the church, but, in 1913, built a two-story, cement-block, four classroom school and a basement convent to house the Felician sisters. The parishioners contributed food as well as money, and the school opened in the fall with 130 children in kindergarten and three grades. A number of the characteristic Polish societies also were organized, each with its own banners and uniforms, further cementing the parish. In the summer of 1916, a convent was built at a cost of $7,000. The school that fall had 210 children, 70 of them in the kindergarten. Thirty children were turned away for lack of room. An annex, with two additional classrooms and an auditorium that could be converted into two more, was built, covered by a mortgage of $10,000.

The bottom up process was repeated again and again, as poverty-stricken Polish Catholics made almost unbelievable sacrifices to provide churches and schools. The Polish community in Binghamton formed around families drawn to the area from Pennsylvania to establish farms in the rolling countryside of the Southern Tier. They were visited occasionally by Father Rusin and with his help, organized the Holy Trinity Society in 1911. The group purchased a vacant lot and erected a platform on which Mass was celebrated. Outdoor dances helped raise money and, in 1914, St. Stanislaus Kostka parish was organized with 45 families and Father Michael Dzialuk as pastor. Walls were erected around the platform and a roof added for a temporary church, then work began on a permanent church and school building. Once again, the people provided much of the labor, digging the foundation, hauling stone and lumber. Finally in 1916, the new building was ready. That first year, the Felician sisters taught 154 students — Slovak, Russian, Hungarian and Polish. When Dzialuk left in 1920, the parish had added a rectory and convent and its membership had swelled to 250 families.

In 1889 in Utica, a Benevolent Society of St. Stanislaus was established. In 1896, the society purchased land and a frame building to serve as a church. The new parish, Holy Trinity, was incorporated the following year with newly ordained Simon Pniak as pastor. Beginning with 50 to 60 Polish families of German origin, the parish grew rapidly as Poles from the Russian partition flooded to the country to escape service in the Russian army. In 1905, work began on a new church, which was completed by Pniak's successor. Costs ran beyond estimates, leading to some serious court suits. Nevertheless, an additional $30,000 was spent on church furnishings. In 1899 Pniak had begun a school in the basement of the first church. In 1901, two lay teachers were instructing 135 children. Seven years later, there were four teachers and almost 200 children and plans were underway to enlarge the school as soon as the new church was completed. In 1910, the new pastor transformed the old church into an eight-classroom school and brought in six Sisters of the Holy Family as teachers.

Another Polish community took shape in New York Mills, near Utica. Lay people there, who had been attending Holy Trinity, taught the children their catechism in private homes until, in 1910, they formed Our Lady of Czestochowa, later known simply as St. Mary's, and purchased a lot with a barn which they quickly transformed into a place of worship. The next year they received a pastor, Father A. Figaljowski, who began work on a school which opened with 156 children under the Felician sisters in 1912. By 1917, its student population reached 360 children in eight classrooms in a new building erected two years earlier. Fijalkowski remained as pastor for 46 years, a diocesan record.

In Oswego, the Polish community developed a bit later, but by 1907 there were at least 500 Polish residents, most unskilled laborers. Housing conditions were crowded, with many families taking in boarders to make ends meet. Farmers in the old country, many families set up small gardens around their houses and had sheds to shelter chickens, hogs and cows. In February 1908, a meeting was held at St. Louis French church for the purpose of establishing a Polish parish. With the help of Father Rusin, the group rented the third floor of the Hennesey building and, in April 1910, began work on a church.

In Rome, a Polish community appeared in the mid-1890s and, in 1909, a Catholic society purchased a private home, remodeled it, built an altar and bought a small confessional and organ. Visiting priests said Mass there until the appointment of the first resident pastor in 1911. The small congregation of 80 families was not an attractive post and priests were much in demand, so five pastors served in five years. In 1920, John Tarlowski built a new

brick church and rectory and the old building was converted into a school. Here as elsewhere, the evident progress obscured a complex reality because many remained beyond the reach of the Church. For one thing, in this community, there was a large number of single, unmarried adults, few of whom were active in or contributed to the Church. Those who were married often did not send their children to school, but encouraged them to go to work at an early age. The pastor estimated, in 1913, that there were in the area 187 children under 16, but only 14 attended one of the Catholic schools in the community. He also had been told there were only 21 in public school, of whom 12 attended religion classes at his church.

The Polish people won the admiration and respect of their Irish co-religionists by the speed with which they developed their own institutions and the sacrifices they made for their support. On July 16, 1906, Ludden confirmed 500 children at Holy Trinity in Utica. A huge parade featuring 14 uniformed Polish societies brought 2,000 people to the church to watch the ceremonies. Ludden complained about the length of the service, but waxed eloquent praising the people for their splendid success. "You are an energetic people and you have an energetic pastor," he told the throng. "A few years ago you were a few scattered communicants. Now you are a people. These young children here are growing into useful citizens. I urge you to hold fast to your pastor. Help him in all his projects."

Yet it was more difficult than the large parishes indicated. Poland was not yet a nation, and the newcomers struggled to develop a Polish identity from the deeply divided remnants of partition. In Utica, for example, one neighborhood was labeled Prussian Avenue, another Galicia and a third Russian Poland. These divisions damaged the parish, where the Galician born Father Pniak found himself in constant conflict with his

Prussian-born parishioners. His successor was, like Rusin, the embodiment of the type of Polish priests who brought order and unity to the flourishing congregations around the country. Ludden appointed Louis P. Muczynski pastor on December 1, 1909, and said he would "hope and pray that you may bring peace and order to the long distracted and much scandalized good Polish people." On his first Sunday, the new pastor was blunt:

I am sent here by the Most Reverend Bishop Ludden. My name is Father Ludwig Muszynski. I am your pastor. I am not afraid of you. You will not call each other Pruss, nor Galician, nor Russ nor anything else. You are all of one mother—one country—one Poland. Most of all, you are one parish.

And one parish they became. By the time Muszynski left in 1920 to visit his family in Poland, never to return, he had finished the church, built a permanent rectory, added the old rectory to the school facilities and brought in the Sisters of the Holy Family of Nazareth to conduct the flourishing school. Like Rusin, he knew how it was done.

DISCRIMINATION AGAINST ITALIANS

If the Poles, like the Germans, were a great success story, the Italians, from the Irish point of view, were a great failure. Between 1880 and 1920, approximately 5,000,000 people came to the United States from Italy. Many had little sense of national identity. Their self-understanding was formed by their province or region. In the "Little Italys" which took shape in upstate cities, it was common for the Italian colony to be subdivided into neighborhoods or blocks according to home village or province. Eighty-five percent of the Italian immigrants to upstate New York came from central and southern Italy, the poorest and least educated areas of the country. A later study showed that, in the decade before World War I, 75 percent of the Italians in Syracuse were unskilled laborers. They had a very strong sense of family loyalty. Indeed, the family was the primary social institution and the authority of the father far surpassed that of the priest. While the Italian community had the same problems of crime, dependency and alcohol abuse as other migrating groups, their sense of family buffered the pains of migration and poverty.

Italian immigrants came from a country whose people were nominally Catholic, but had been torn for a century by the conflict between the Church and the movement for national unification. In 1870, the new Kingdom of Italy seized Rome and the papal states. The pope became a "prisoner in the Vatican" and Italian Catholics were forbidden to participate in the new government, an order widely ignored. Furthermore, Italian Catholicism did not experience the devotional revolution which swept much of western Europe in the nineteenth century. For the most part, Italians were not practicing Catholics who regularly attended church or contributed to its support. Their faith instead centered on family and home, on religious feasts and festivals. In some sections of Italy, as many as 30 festivals in honor of patron saints might punctuate the year. In the United States, communities tended to develop one festival as peculiarly their own, marking the feast day with a variety of religious and community observances. In Binghamton, it was the feast of the Assumption; in Utica, the feast of Saints Cosmos and Damian; in Cortland, the feast of St. Anthony. In addition, for centuries, the Church had depended upon income from Church lands and assistance from secular rulers. There was no established tradition of popular financial support for the clergy or of voluntary church organization among the Italians. In the United States, faced with an English speaking hierarchy and clergy who placed a premium on regular religious practice and generous financial assistance, the Italians were not drawn easily to the Church. As a result, Church leaders often regarded them as far less than ideal Catholics. The fact that some Protestant churches and charitable organizations did attempt to assist them and to evangelize among them made "the Italian problem" increasingly prominent in the American Church.

Perhaps the least understood feature of Italian life has been the question of leadership. In upstate New York communities, particular individuals enjoyed enormous prestige and could make or break a parish or pastor. Their power was based upon an intimate relationship with the community, secured by helping people get jobs, deal with public agencies, find a place to stay and rescue the children when they ran into trouble with the law. In Syracuse, for example, Thomas Marnell recruited Italian laborers in New York, helped them find jobs and became himself a contractor bidding against American builders, as well as a banker, financing his own projects and those of others. Marnell also guided many Syracuse Italians into the Republican party. He enjoyed the respect of non-Italians and the loyalty and admiration of many of his countrymen. He helped organize and contributed greatly to the support of St. Peter's church. When he was killed in a freak accident preparing the societies of St. Peter's for the annual parade in 1906, he was mourned by the largest outpouring for a funeral in the city's history.

In Syracuse, it was Marnell; in Binghamton, Nicholas Gallo; in Cortland, James Comando and James Adessa; and in Oswego, Antonio Russo and his son-in-law Rosario D'Angelo. In every case, these men were trusted by their fellow Italians and by the local political and business leadership. They helped settle disputes in factories and rendered a variety of personal services, all the while building substantial businesses and invariably spearheading drives to build and maintain the Catholic Church in the Italian-American community. Only in Endicott, where employer and philanthropist George F. Johnson preempted their function by lending money, renting houses, paving streets, and providing medical and recreational facilities, did such a leader fail to emerge. The seeds of more episodes of lay/clerical conflict, like those that had first emerged in the Utica of the Devereuxs, were present.

Bishop Ludden was well aware of the large numbers of Italians in his diocese. With the help of the apostolic delegate, Ludden persuaded Father Nicola Menella to come to Syracuse in 1894 to serve Italian Catholics, using the basement of the cathedral and visiting small Italian groups in neighboring parishes. The following year, Father Francesco Becherini, a member of the Missionary Society of St. Charles, arrived in Syracuse. He organized a society of prominent Italian leaders and secured a bank loan to purchase, for $12,000, a former Lutheran church which was renamed St. Peter's Church. Serious financial problems arose, and some lay people refused to contribute until a priest who could preach in English, as well as Italian, was appointed. They got their wish when Father Sevilla became pastor in 1900. He urged the community to adapt to American ways.

In Italy we have different rules. To you who have children I say: they are Americans, and naturally they will adapt themselves to the customs of the country! I see them in Sunday school and I see that they have the spirit of American independence and I admire them and I will do my best to capture

*their spirit. I do not wish to drown
the memory of our dear country where
most of us were born and received our
education, but we are here in the
providential country from which we
receive all benefits; it is but just that
we should obey its laws. In doing so
we will prove ourselves good citizens
and shall be more respected.*

The pastor's words reflected deep divisions. Marnell and other dissident lay people charged the priest with demanding excessive stipends for his services. He responded that they wished to use the Church to make money. When Sevilla denounced one layman from the altar, dissension became heated, with Marnell telling the press that the people wished a new pastor. In July Sevilla suddenly disappeared and was replaced by Eugene Ostino. The trustees claimed they had elected Ostino as the new priest. Ludden stated that Sevilla had returned to Italy for his health and had recommended Ostino as his replacement. Whatever the case, both sides could claim victory and things settled down for a few years. In 1904, a two-story rectory was built. Before that time, the priest had lived in the tower of the church. Faced with financial problems again in 1907, the lay leaders demanded that the pastor, now Father Morassi, return to the tower so they could rent his house and use the income to meet expenses. Ludden was furious, telling the press:

> *I have charged Father Morassi to make
> his people understand that here we are
> not in Italy, and if they wish to
> remain Catholics, they must support
> their own church. In the future, I shall
> not permit any priest to live in the
> tower of the church so long as there
> are Italians capable of supporting him.*

Similar problems existed in Utica, where the Italian population had been growing since the first Italian railroad workers arrived in the 1870s. In 1893, there were 200 Italian families in the city, most attending St. John's church. Monsignor Lynch took a great interest in them, as did Mrs. Elizabeth Kernan, the Italian born wife of Thomas Kernan, grandson of Nicholas Devereux. She organized a number of St. John's women to visit Italian homes and provide charitable assistance and Sunday school instruction for the children. Father Louis Griffa from Oswego and Father Doyle, a Franciscan from St. Joseph's parish, occasionally held services and heard confessions for the Italians until Father Antonio Castelli arrived as first pastor of the new St. Mary of Mount Carmel church. Local bankers and businessmen made donations, as did a large number of Irish Catholics and building began in April 1895. Costs ran beyond estimates, construction was suspended, and the basement was roofed over and became the temporary church. In 1901, Bishop Scalabrini of Italy visited the community, laid the cornerstone of the church and attended a huge banquet in his honor. The following year, the building finally was completed. At the dedication, Ludden told the congregation, "the Italians now look forward to an era of religious progress and advancement." Ludden shrewdly recognized how important it was for the Church to become identified with Italian nationality and win the competitive struggle with non-Catholic Italians to define the form the Italian community would take in the United States. In that competition, what the Church had to offer was order, discipline and, ultimately, acceptance and respectability:

> *In the Catholic Church there is no
> nation and people. You may become
> infidels and join secret societies, which
> will destroy your faith and divide you
> into cliques and classes instead of one
> united people in God's church. Teach
> your children to be generous and then*

Bishop Scalabrini of Italy blesses the cornerstone for St. Mary of Mount Carmel church in Utica in 1901. Scalabrini founded the Missionary Society of St. Charles, whose priests staffed the Italian immigrant parish. (Photo: Chancery Archives)

you bring them up to be respectable citizens. There will be no murders and suicide among you. Follow the instructions of your pastor. Then you will be happy in this life and in the life to come.

The following year a second priest arrived and, in 1904, the Franciscan sisters opened the first school for Italian Catholics in the diocese. In the early days, three sisters were available for six grades, two taught 45 students each, while the third attempted to manage almost 175 in the four lower grades until a fourth sister arrived late in the year.

Despite the progress of Mount Carmel, Utica Italians still were not being served adequately and were tempting targets for non-Catholic efforts at conversion. Again Elizabeth Kernan extended the Sunday School program and organized 150 families, most non-Italian, into the St. Anthony Society to provide support for a chapel in an Italian neighborhood in West Utica, some distance from Mount Carmel. She enlisted the support of Archbishop Falconio, the apostolic delegate, for the "St. Anthony's chapel movement." These pressures became so strong in 1911 that the governing board of the diocese agreed to establish a new parish. A German priest who spoke Italian, Alfred Roth, was appointed pastor. Roth built the basement of the church, occupied a rented rectory and gradually accumulated a building fund of $68,000, though his plans were sidetracked by the war. In 1914, some in the community complained to the apostolic delegate that Roth was not fluent in Italian, a charge the Bishop denied, citing the testimony of parish trustees. The petition received by the delegate had come from a dissident group centered on a schismatic Italian priest. Ludden claimed that a number of these priests had caused trouble previously in the community. Several were preaching in Protestant churches and it was their efforts which had spurred the diocese to action.

In Oswego, the Italian community found remarkable leadership in Antonio Russo, his sister, Sarah, and her husband, Rosario D'Angelo. Sarah was a gifted musician, the organist at St. Mary's in Oswego and, for a time, at St. Joseph's German church in Syracuse. She was also a composer of church music and a gifted music teacher. She and her husband ran a grocery store, steamship agency and bank, and helped build up the Republican party among the city's Italian residents. Together they helped build institutions which could maintain traditional customs, while they urged their fellow immigrants to adapt to American ways. Still, in Oswego as elsewhere, life was hard. One life-long Italian resident recalls her mother getting her a job at a local mill at age 12, then arranging a marriage at 15 with a boy she had never met. Her mother ran a store and took in boarders. As many as 22 people might be living with them at one time. At the mill, the Italians worked the night shift to avoid conflicts with Irish and native workers and, when quarrels did arise, one of the local priests was summoned. Italians worshiped at all three territorial parishes and the French national parish until 1915, when Father Fiomene Germia was assigned the task of forming a parish. After worshiping for a year in a rented hall, the community purchased a former Universalist church for $10,000, dedicated it as St. Joseph's and, over the next decade, added another $20,000 in improvements. In a rare show of community support, Father James Collins of St. Paul's and P. J. Cullinan, a local funeral director, built an altar for the church, St. Louis donated a tabernacle, and a local music store contributed a small organ. In 1920, the community purchased a rectory and, about the same time, the men began construction of a social hall underneath the church, beginning the work by digging under the building by hand.

The history of Italian Catholicism in Binghamton was identified for more than 30 years with Father Matthew Pellegrini. In 1912, he asked the diocese for an assignment and the bishop suggested he go to Binghamton and explore the possibilities of a parish there. Pellegrini reported that, with only 1,500 Italians in the city, the time was not ripe. At that time, priests were reluctant to initiate Italian parishes because of the rather bleak record of priests who could not meet expenses. Nevertheless, in the summer of 1913, an Italian-American banker, Nicholas Gallo, asked for a priest to celebrate Mass on the feast of the Assumption. Pellegrini arrived a few days early to hear confessions. Turned away from St. Mary's rectory, he boarded at a hotel and received a "good offering" from Mr. Gallo. In October, Assumption of the

Blessed Virgin Mary parish was incorporated. Gallo sold the parish a piece of property for $12,000, two nearby houses were rented and, with the help of volunteer Italian laborers, excavation began in January. An April bazaar raised $2400, St. James in Johnson City donated altars and statues, and a basement church opened for services in August 1915.

Years later, Pellegrini recalled the problems of those early years. The pastor of St. Mary's had been unsympathetic and the bishop, who had expressed reservations about the parish's prospects to the apostolic delegate, refused to help him raise loans with the banks. Equally important, conditions within the Italian community were not favorable. Many residents were transients, he said, who came into the area to do summer work on surrounding farms. Others had relatives in the old country to whom they sent support, while large families drained their resources. Factions in the community worked against the success of the parish. "An Italian American Socialist club," encouraged by local Protestants, distributed handbills attacking the priest. As a result, before the war, less than five percent of the local Italian community attended church.

If Binghamton Catholics first organized around the field day held in honor of the Assumption, Cortland Catholics first expressed themselves in the annual festival of the feast of St. Anthony on June 13. In 1892, there were only two Italian families in the community, but the 1915 census listed 697 persons. The major employer was the Wickwire Wire Company, where the unskilled Italian laborers earned 15 cents an hour. The leading figures in the community were James Comando, a saloon keeper and grocer, and James Adessa, first a helper to Comando, and later a banker and labor contractor. Legend has it that one young boy, asked by his teacher to name the President of the United States, responded "Jim Adessa."

As the community grew, so did the St. Anthony's day festival. The Cortland *Standard* described the 1906 procession through the streets of "all the men, women and children, arrayed in their best clothes." The day became an occasion to express Italian unity and respectability, as well as traditional religious beliefs. Uniformed Italian societies, bands and children's groups surrounded banners of St. Anthony, to which money was attached as they passed through the streets. Boys dressed as monks represented each of the 13 miracles attributed to the saint. It was a Catholic saint and celebration, but the local clergy were not so sure. In 1910, Father Robert Boga, assistant at St. Mary's, told the marchers that "the band, new uniforms and fireworks were alright, but to attend Mass only once a year" as he feared was the case with some of them, "was far from right." In 1914, a mission was held to awaken interest in forming a parish, but nothing came of it. Four years later, Father Donahue of St. Mary's asked the bishop to send Father Parolin from St. Peter's in Syracuse to survey the situation. By then prospects were more promising. In 1912, a former public school had been sold for use as a spaghetti factory. In 1917, James Comando purchased the building and donated it for a church. St. Mary's donated an altar and the new St. Anthony's parish was underway.

Despite the support of individual lay leaders, organized lay support, such as marked the early days of other communities, was slow to develop. A few Italian community leaders and priests, many from outside the diocese, struggled to establish a solid foundation, but they needed the help of apostolic non-Italians like Elizabeth Kernan. Even then there would not have been many parishes if Bishops Ludden and Grimes had not wanted to avoid criticism from the apostolic delegate. The bishops and other Irish-American priests resented the fact that the Italian community did not generate lay or clerical leadership and did not contribute adequately to the support of the Church. Ludden's speech on the occasion of the dedication of Mount Carmel reflected the ethnocentric attitude of most Irish-American Church leaders. He told Italian Catholics to be faithful to their Church and wipe out the "defect" which had become attached to them in the United States. In words reported by the local newspapers, he spoke frankly of their failure to support the Church:

If you look all around you in this country, which is made up of many nationalities and various kinds of people, habits and traditions, whose history you have learned, you would find that you would not have much to boast of if you had an elegant church.... I know you will tell me that you came here poor. A hundred years ago [the Irish] came here with nothing but poverty and yet they hung together and struggled and reunited and built their log cabins and lived there and were devoted to the interests of their children...and now they have magnificent temples to worship in. If you will look at your Polish brethren you will find that they are comparatively poor, much poorer than you Italians, yet they build their churches and support their pastors.

He went on to describe in detail the problems of St. Peter's in Syracuse. Only with great exertion had he been able to prevent its being sold for nonpayment of interest, although some members of the congregation were "well off" and all earned "good money." Worst of all, their pastor, "a very humble, learned, modest, eloquent, pious and holy man," had been living in the tower of the church. The comparison with other groups was harsh:

It is comforting when I look at other

nationalities. Even the Greeks have a congregation in Binghamton, and a little piece of property. The Lithuanians have no church of their own and are allowed to worship in St. Patrick's but when a priest is provided for them they will have their own church. Yet, these Italian people, with their glorious record and tradition, who are of such a race coming down from history...from the Ciceros and Ceasars...these people are slow compared to others to take proper care for their churches and support for their priests.

There was, of course, some truth in the bishop's charges. German Catholics had come to the country with considerable resources, found immigrant priests to serve their religious needs and drew upon a rich cultural tradition in erecting their churches. Irish, French-Canadian and Polish immigrants all came from countries where they lived under foreign and, aside from Austrian-ruled sections of Poland, non-Catholic rule. The Church stood at the heart of the national tradition and was a strong supporter of linguistic and cultural survival. While each of these groups had more radical socialist and liberal leaders who also claimed to uphold the national standard, they were generally of urban backgrounds and highly educated. In the struggle to dominate the immigrant communities, heavily composed of people from the villages, they quickly lost out to the Church. In those groups, community leaders recognized that the Church was the surest vehicle for restoring order and discipline to the community. Furthermore, the better-off members of these communities decided quite early that they would remain in the United States, a decision which encouraged them to make substantial investments like churches and schools. Little of this was true among the

Italians. Instead of integration of religion and nationality, the Church and the national movement had been at odds with one another, so there were strong anti-clerical and anti-Catholic elements in the Italian-American community. Little in their background encouraged intimate association with the clergy or popular financial support for the Church. Moreover, many community leaders planned to return to Italy after acquiring some capital. They were as proud and resentful of slights as any other group, so statements like the bishop's became something of a self-fulfilling prophecy, confirming the suspicion that the American Church was hostile, prejudiced and unsympathetic. This impression was intensified by individual experiences of Masses in church basements and incomprehension, if not ridicule, of festivals and veneration of statues and saints, all of which could not be offset by the generous work of lay women like Mrs. Kernan or understanding, if paternalistic priests, like Monsignor Lynch and Father Clune.

Far worse discrimination, poverty and inter-group tensions plagued the Italian community outside the Church. The Syracuse *Herald* ran a series in 1899 describing "little Italy" on the city's north side. Italians were described as "a simple minded, child like race, primitive in their emotions and passions, yet with strong religious feelings and ardent in their patriotism." The Italian woman was very pretty, but "matured too early," as "fully formed and developed" at 14 as her "American sister" at 21. The Catholic press was not immune from such stereotypes. When rumors circulated that the Vatican thought the American Church was ignoring the Italians, the *Catholic Sun* editorialized that "the average Italian emigrant seems to have but one ambition in life and that is to 'make the mon,' procure a watch and chain and return after a few years to his native land." The editorial argued that "there is little hope of reforming these people in

America. There are various reasons for the indifference of Italians toward the Church," among them the "total indifference of the church in Italy toward the people." Forgetting their own history, the Irish editors spoke of Italian rioting on Sunday, "dissecting each other by the wholesale" and advised them to "drop the stillete (and) not segregate so much."

In 1913, tension between Italians and others burst into violence. Italian laborers, carpenters and construction workers went out on strike over low wages. Gangs of strikers roamed the city, calling upon Italians to cease work. Negotiations were taking place when a pitched battle occurred between 500 strikers and police in St. Mary's Circle in front of the cathedral. Across the street, the former rectory was being demolished to make way for a new diocesan office building. Police were ordered to protect the men working on the church project, considered "scabs" by the strikers. The surging crowd of laborers, shouting at the workers, pushed against a police line of 40 men. Stones were thrown and finally shots rang out. Fire hoses were turned on the strikers, who eventually dispersed, leaving one man dead and 20 strikers and police wounded. Respectable opinion was outraged, the *Post Standard* editorializing that "Italians who have found here liberty of action so novel and stimulating that they at times become drunk with it must be taught that there will be no compromise with lawlessness." The funeral of Giuseppe Vesta, the dead striker, attracted a crowd of 1,000 people to St. Peter's church in a tense city. Father Michael Cuneo, who said the funeral Mass, joined with Father Clune to calm the strikers and promote a solution to the labor dispute. The mayor and Clune arranged negotiating sessions.

The strike undoubtedly stimulated concern about the welfare of the Italian community and, in 1915, a group of Catholic women in Syracuse organized the St. Anthony's society which opened Madonna House as a social service center, with Father Alexis Hopkins as spiritual director. It added St. Anthony's communal home in 1919 and Immaculata House in 1920. In addition to Sunday school programs conducted by sisters from neighboring schools and convents, the houses offered kindergarten classes, gymnastics, music, sewing and domestic arts classes, and taught English and citizenship for adults. Gradually, sisters trained in social work became full-time staff members and the work received support from lenten collections at St. Peter's Italian church and at the cathedral. While undoubtedly motivated by sincere concern about the welfare of the Italian people, this work arose from a need to encourage Italians to conform to American ways. As Hopkins put it, "Now that the Indian warhoops are silenced and civilization has been established, the slogan of peace comes to Syracusans: Americanize the immigrant." Americanization could not be forced, he argued. Growing up without religion and attending public schools, the Italians would bring disaster upon their own souls and destroy their usefulness as citizens. By the time World War I was over, Syracuse Catholicism had entered a new era. But the legacy of discrimination and paternalism, coupled with the internal problems of the Italian community, made the fate of the largest of the new immigrant communities an open question.

LITHUANIAN AND SLOVAK PARISHES

Internal divisions, discrimination and unwillingness to submit to clerical control also limited the advance of other groups. In many communities, Lithuanians often blended into Polish or German parishes. Despite efforts by Prussia to make them German, and efforts at home and in several American cities to make them Polish, Lithuanians retained a sense of their distinctiveness. Most Lithuanians came to the area from Pennsylvania where many had been miners. By the time they arrived, their religious and national consciousness had been sharpened by hard struggles with Irish bishops and Polish priests. The first Lithuanian parish in Pennsylvania was established in 1874. After the first priest left, the bishop sent a Polish pastor who, with the support of the growing Polish population, took control. Because the bishops believed that the Lithuanians were actually Polish, the same process happened often, sometimes leading to violent battles and court cases to settle control of church property.

Lithuanians in Binghamton settled in the first ward, where at least 10 churches eventually would spring up along Clinton Street. In 1905, a number of them formed St. Joseph's Mutual Benefit Society. Almost a decade later, in 1914, St. Joseph's parish was organized. It was the largest local Lithuanian organization, divided between those who wished to erect a cultural center and those who wanted a church. The cultural group won out, while the religious group seceded and formed St. John's Society. A church was built, but before getting a pastor, the committee had to turn the deed over to the bishop. One faction refused to do so and brought suit. Their opponents charged that they wanted to establish an independent Catholic Church, though there was no evidence of this. The long court case resulted in the victory of the orthodox Catholic group. The opponents were not reconciled and some joined the schismatic Polish National Church in the city, while others drifted to other congregations. In 1916, Joseph Osip became pastor. He was an authoritarian man who gave the laity no role in Church finances whatsoever. In later years, he was praised for maintaining ethnic identity through his strong leadership, which sharply distinguished Cath-

olic Lithuanians from the other Lithuanian groups, including socialist and radical organizations. He created a strong parish, but the divisions among local Lithuanians were not healed.

A small Lithuanian congregation appeared in Utica, where a visiting priest found 100 families in 1893 and assisted them to form the St. Casimir Society. Previously, they had worshiped at the German church which occasionally provided the services of a Lithuanian priest to hear confessions. In 1911, a resident priest, Father Deksniui arrived and organized a parish corporation, St. George's, which worshiped at St. John's school until purchasing a residence to serve as a temporary church in 1911.

Among the Poles, strong pastors succeeded in winning the trust of their congregations and establishing their authority over the laity, at least for a time. As the disputes among the Lithuanians in Binghamton indicated, the American system which placed the ownership of the property in the hands of the bishop and excluded the laity from a formal role in handling church finances could make the life of the priest very difficult. This was particularly true if there were schismatic or separatist groups insisting on more democratic procedures and more public accountability. The Slovak community in particular was plagued by such problems, in part because of the difficulty of finding talented priests whose personal magnetism could overcome the formalities of the law and integrate power and authority, and in part because Protestant Slovak congregations provided both a more democratic example and a religious alternative. With the Slovaks as with other groups, the desire to preserve their customs, ancestral language, and religious faith and symbols bound together a fabric of family and community life. Through the 1880s and 1890s, Slovak priests from Pennsylvania occasionally would visit the Binghamton area and offer services for their people. In 1902, the first organization took shape. With Bishop Ludden's approval, they purchased land incorporated as Sts. Cyril and Methodius parish and began construction of a church. In 1905, the community began to worship in its own building and work started on a rectory, but soon after the first signs of dissatisfaction appeared. Windows were broken mysteriously and the pastor's sermons were drowned out by coughing and the shuffling of feet. The priest left in disgust and was replaced by Father John Porubsky, who was determined to establish firm control. He immediately excited opposition by ending the annual meetings between pastor and people held to discuss the financial reports, asserting that he alone would keep the books and take responsibility for parish finances. Some discontented parishioners protested to the bishop and others left the parish, but Porubsky remained on until 1917.

Older residents of Binghamton still recall the growth of the Slovak community at the turn of the century, the tension between the Slovaks and the Irish when the newcomers attended St. Patrick's church, and the relatively good relations between the Slovaks and those other newcomers, the Italians. Most settled in the first ward, near the factories. Even before the first parish was organized, national and Catholic clubs or "sokols" were organized to perpetuate Slovak traditions and strengthen community solidarity. There were many picnics, often beginning with a parade through the city to the railway station, where extra cars would be ready to take them to nearby picnic grounds and parks. They recall with genuine nostalgia the ginger cakes, cabbage rolls, sausages, fried dough with powdered sugar, rolled nut pastries and jellied pigs feet that would mark these celebrations. During Lent a "bassa" or bass fiddle would be buried, to be resurrected at Easter. On Easter Sunday, too, the "kerbach" or Easter

whip of willow twigs would be used symbolically to "whip" the women, "to remind them to behave" as one elderly resident put it. On Easter Monday, as a major holiday, it was the men's turn. Happier symbols came during the winter holidays, as on the feast of St. Nicholas, December 6, when the children would set our their shoes at night. If they had been good during the year, they would find them in the morning filled with oranges, cookies and walnuts. If not, they might find potatoes and coal.

In Syracuse, Slovak families who worshiped at Sacred Heart church organized a society under the patronage of St. Stephen in 1909. The next spring they bought lots and invited Father Joseph Martincek from Pennsylvania to preach a mission. They petitioned the bishop to allow them to form a parish. Father Porubsky, who was consulted, opposed this move. He told the bishop that he had worked with the group to help them to improve their situation and "to teach the Slovaks how to obey." The lay people, now with 100 families, persisted. The bishop finally appointed Father Francis Horack to serve the parish. Steps were taken to build a new church. After promising to work with a committee of 12 the pastor confined his consultation to the two trustees and two collectors, while allowing several opportunities for raising money to pass. Frustrated, a group of four parishioners, including a trustee, requested his removal in the fall of 1916. Horak remained and dissension plagued the parish for the next several years. As Francis Sladicak explained to the bishop, the Slovaks had organized their society to work for a parish because of their inability to worship with people of other language groups and their alarm at what they saw as the denationalizing effect of the public schools on their children. Without a parish of their own, they feared for the survival not only of their culture, but of the bonds across the generations in their own families. From

LETTER FROM A SLOVAK CATHOLIC

Amid problems between the pastor and parishioners at St. Stephen's in Syracuse, Frank Sladick (Sladicak) wrote to Bishop Grimes, recounting the determined beginnings of the Slovak community in Syracuse:

February 17, 1917
Right Reverend and dear Bishop:

The Slovaks began to locate here about 20 years ago. The population was gradually rising. The people in most instances work in factories doing hard work. Most all of them were Catholics. Before we had a church and a pastor the Slovaks, owing to the fact that they could not understand the language of the other churches, did not attend church for that reason. During that time the people called upon a Slovak priest from another city for missionary purposes, especially at Lent when our people attended at large to confession and communion at the Sacred Heart of Jesus church, or the church of the Assumption. At this time the Slovak organizations and societies issued confessional tickets to the members, to know who went to confession and who did not. This rule was strictly carried out....

Due to the fact that the fathers and mothers were so over-burdened with their everyday work, they could not teach their children the essential elements of the christian religion as they should be taught and their national history.... At last they have decided in order to overcome all the evils which hindered, namely: to promote christianity, national honor, protect good morals of the children, and to build a firm foundation of the catholic church in Syracuse, about October, 1909, the Slovaks took immediate steps in forming a permanent organization with the intention to build a church and a school.

the time they organized the society until the arrival of a pastor in 1914, Sladicak served as president of the organization. Monthly meetings were held, permission was obtained from the Church and the city to raise money, collectors were chosen, committees appointed and fundraising activities organized, all in a society with elected officers, open books and full public accountability. Sladicak himself had located Father Horak and persuaded him to come to Syracuse. On assuming the pastorate, he had, to Sladicak's satisfaction, assured the parishioners he would "favor and execute the demands of the majority of the people." Sladicek did not have in mind Church doctrine or sacramental services, but the financial problems of the parish.

The grievances of the people were over just such matters. They charged that the pastor changed the building plans and refused to hold ceremonies which brought in funds for the cornerstone laying or the installation of bells. Failure to hold these ceremonies, common in other churches, also damaged the honor of the Slovak people. After the church was built, the organist, who had donated his services for several years, was replaced. Finally, the priest told them they had no right to the parish property. He was free to act as he thought best. Those who complained were told to take care of their families.

The bishop, who had not wanted to send a pastor in the first place, ignored Sladicak's appeal to remove Horak, and things got

At the same time selecting the name for the parish and electing me as Trustee and President of the organization. They gave me all the powers to govern the affairs of the organization, which office I held for five years and until a priest was assigned to our parish in Syracuse. At the time I was elected president of the parish I was empowered to go to the Bishop and demand recognition of our parish, to go to the city authorities to get the right to collect money for the church, to prepare books which were to be used for recording money received from collections, to take proper steps to have the parish incorporated....

(Sladicak continues his letter, recounting numerous complaints of parishioners about ill-treatment and reckless spending by their pastor, whose resignation they already had sought without success.)

...The people came to me as the old organizer of the parish and trustee and requested me to see if I could end all of the comedies so that they would not be discouraged and fall away from the parish.... From the above facts your Excellency can readily see the danger the congregation is in. Some of the people already have left the parish. Some are to leave if a change is not made. The rest are angry and dissatisfied all on account of the acts and treatment which they receive from Father Horak. If a change is not made soon I am sure the people will take action.... I therefore in the name of the members of the whole congregation request that which all the members of the parish voted upon, namely: that the Rev. Francis Horak be withdrawn and another priest substituted, as I think that is the only way to save the congregation from breaking up.

Your most humble servant,
Frank Sladick

worse. Rumors of violence against the pastor led to the stationing of police at services the following week. After they left, the people gathered outside began to attack the lay treasurer, who was rescued by Sladicak. The priest then requested a parish meeting to air the grievances, but he failed to attend. The people passed resolutions asking the bishop for permission to elect trustees "because they knew them better by character." They also asked for permission to replace the present treasurer, with the understanding that if income was not doubled in two months, the position would revert to the incumbent. With insults, the priest rejected these requests. But by now, Sladicak could not be ignored. A few weeks later, Horak left and was replaced by an Irish priest. This temporary solution did not resolve the problem. Once again in 1918, the parishioners, headed by Sladicak, reminded the bishop that he had promised them a priest who understood their language when they had completed their church. Three Slovak priests from Binghamton were available. They requested appointment of Father Pochily, who had been an army chaplain. Apparently an incident took place on May 11 because a letter came to the bishop protesting the pastor's calling the police and having protesting Slovak women arrested. "As we was told that we got to be Americans," one parishioner wrote, "so we say that we are but we want to pray to our Lord God in the language we understand best." A few days later, the bishop appointed Pochilly administrator. For the moment, peace came to St. Stephen's.

By 1919, problems such as those at St. Stephen's and rumblings in a half dozen other eastern European parishes made the diocese wary of establishing any more. The Code of Canon Law, brought together in 1908, appeared to limit, if not forbid, such parishes. However, the law always had been bent to meet pastoral needs in the past, as when the bishops wisely decided to ignore the practice of offering services in English to appeal to those no longer conversant with the German language, although such persons were supposed to move into their territorial parishes. In 1919, a committee approached Bishop John Grimes, who had succeeded Ludden in 1912, asking for a Slovak parish in Endicott, where an estimated 700 people lived, most

working at Endicott Johnson. They pointed out that they had already organized several benefit societies and that in either the English speaking or Italian parishes, the people could not understand the word of God. They needed a parish of their own to protect them against "enemies of the faith, atheists, Protestants and the like." Father James McPeak, pastor of St. Ambrose, explained to them that the law no longer allowed the formation of such parishes. He found them good people and "very tractable." The bishop responded that McPeak should continue to remind them that his hands were tied and he could do nothing for them, given the state of Church law. For the moment, the age of ethnic expansion was over and the Slovak Catholics of Endicott would not have the chance, at least for now, to hear the words of Bishop Ludden "now you are a people."

The conflicts which marked the early days of parish formation in these new immigrant communities reflected the strains arising from pluralism. Irish Catholics, who had taken charge of the local Church in the nineteenth century, tended to see things from the standpoint of their own experience. As a result, they judged other groups on the basis of their ability to organize, raise money and enter into the routine of sacramental practice. Using phrases like "American ways" and "the true Catholic spirit," they demanded conformity from peoples whose experience was quite different. There was merit in their position because the Church was and had to be a self-help project. The bishop did not have the money to buy land and build churches for the newcomers. They would have to provide these things for themselves. Furthermore, the bishops had learned from experience how important it was to have a united and loyal clergy to counteract the fragmenting pressure toward independence built into America's system of religious liberty. The bishops also learned that unity could be secure only if the priests were free from the financial control of lay trustees. Yet a heavy price was paid for the unwillingness of pastors and bishops to compromise with the understandable desire of new communities for a degree of financial accountability. Their willingness to leave room for a greater variety of national traditions of faith and devotion, coupled with their emphasis on the central role of the priest, the control of Church life by the clergy and the almost exclusive role of the sacraments as channels of communication with the divine, meant that the American Church and the Church of Syracuse risked identifying the community of God's people with the forms built out of the unique circumstances of urban, industrial America. Later, when ties of nationality weakened and Catholics lost the unity which came with their shared experience of immigration, it would be very hard to face the need to change. Every revision of liturgy, organization and community life could appear as a challenge to "the true spirit of Catholicism" and "American ways," rather than another episode in the continuing process of community formation required of a people on pilgrimage through the always changing experience of human history.

A LADDER FROM EARTH TO HEAVEN

A WAY OF LIFE FOR AN IMMIGRANT CHURCH
1890s-1920s

O n his first visit to upstate New York in 1841, Bishop John Hughes was pleased to find that wherever a Catholic congregation had been established, there was an evident improvement in the behavior of the people. Priests and community leaders told him that practicing Catholics became more steady in their habits, more sober, industrious and law abiding, more attentive to their families and more dependable in their work. This was an American answer to the question of the purpose of the Church. As early as the first decade of Puritan settlement in Massachusetts, preachers worried about the dangers posed by free land, with men and women "running off into the woods" in search of their own farms, leaving behind the social controls of family, church and community. Evangelism on succeeding frontiers became the characteristic form of American religion, with circuit riders, camp meetings and revivals of religion reminding people of their dependence on God, their need for grace, and the importance to personal welfare and national glory of accepting the moral requirements of Christianity.

The Irish in Boston, Lithuanians in Pennsylvania and Slovaks in Binghamton learned the same lesson. The heady atmosphere of freedom, combined with the disintegrating effects of migration, whether across oceans or across mountains and plains, endangered human souls and social stability. How could men and women be persuaded, in freedom, to follow a moral discipline, build stable families, educate their children, and accept the various inequalities of income and status from which society could not escape? One answer was to remind them of the truths of Christianity by preaching the gospel message they had heard in their youth, as with the Protestant revivals. Another answer among immigrant Catholics was to restore the Church which had been the center of community life and source of moral authority in the villages left behind. Churches could civilize and discipline the people, stabilize community life and make American institutions more secure. Irish immigrant John Hughes and Austrian immigrant Adelbert Inama knew from experience what could happen when their people suddenly found themselves outside the traditional institutions of family, church and community. They were delighted to find that the tiny churches of Utica and Syracuse were islands of order, sobriety and respectability to which men and women could rally. And, like their Protestant revivalist counterparts, they understood that the result could be brought about by organized, systematic effort. Evangelization, the building of churches and the organization of religious work were thus a contribution to Catholicism, forming a new Church in the expanding nation of the United States, and a contribution to society, helping extend the voluntary restraint and moral discipline required by a free society.

The paradox of Catholic life in the United States was that the evangelistic message emphasized the transcendent significance of religion and the relative unimportance of worldly success. In other words, religion provided a "ladder from earth to heaven." Yet the more the Church expanded, the more successful Catholics became. Or, to state the paradox another way, Church leaders appeared to believe that, if people became too successful, their loyalty to the Church might slacken. In fact, the reverse was true. The more they rose in the world, the more generous they became in their assistance to the Church. The more they became American, it seemed, the more they became Catholic. This suggests that, once again, things were not as they appeared. The apparently pessimistic message about sin and the need for the sacraments did not distract from, but supported, people's effort to make a place for themselves. The Church was not an alternative to other non-religious activity, but an expression of the same determination to achieve a secure and respected place in society that stimulated hard work, self-discipline, and the hardheaded pursuit of economic success and social status. Living the moral life, participating loyally in the Church, working hard at one's job and becoming a responsible citizen were all parts of the single, larger project of taking one's life and future into one's own hands.

Religion, like everything else, was a matter of self-help, requiring personal responsibility, mutual assistance and cooperation, and voluntary acceptance of institutional restraints. The road which led from earth to heaven was one along which the way stations of freedom, prosperity and civic participation were quite as appropriate as those of domination, poverty and exclusion from public life. Indeed, the American path to salvation along a route of economic and social equality might be even more in accord with Catholic and Christian truths than those more depressing situations which had marked the lives of previous generations. In any event, through quite traditional belief and conservative practice, Catholics and their Church believed one might reach liberating conclusions.

In the early days of the Syracuse diocese, the basic religious teachings of the pioneer days did not change. Pastors and preachers at parish missions still testified almost unanimously to the corruption of human nature, the judgment of God, the need for repentance and conversions, the grace available through the sacraments, and the test of such conversions in faithful participation in the Church and persistent efforts to keep the commandments and fulfill the duties of one's state in life. Alone and unaided, no person could find God and win salvation. Only with the help of God's grace, available through the Church, could hell be avoided and heaven won.

Sacramental reception was a necessary, but not exclusive, means of salvation. One also had to consistently follow God's will as expressed in the commandments and the moral teachings of the Church. Acceptance of this moral discipline meant qualities of sobriety, self-discipline and responsibility, making a person a better spouse and parent, a more reliable employee and a more valuable parishioner.

There was, in short, a Catholic "gospel of success." Church teaching affirmed and sanctioned the ambition to make a better life and ensure better prospects for one's children. A religious world view which emphasized the sinfulness of men and women, the dangers of the world and the exclusive nature of the Church's role in salvation did not lead to retreat from the world. It led to a disciplined pursuit of worldly success, moderated to be sure by warnings against an overly one-sided pursuit of wealth and a self-righteous attitude toward the poor. One should approach worldly goals with what earlier puritan preachers called "weaned affections," with one eye always turned toward God, so that the heart never became bound up exclusively with possessions or prestige. And one should look upon the poor with the attitude that there, but for the grace of God and the gift of

God's Church, go I.

All of this suggested that building up the Church contributed both to the salvation of souls and the improvement of society, for the Catholic on the road to heaven also was likely to be a good citizen and a productive and stable member of the community. This, in turn, would make Catholics more respected and their Church more accepted, as non-Catholics saw the value of the Church in the virtues of its members. Its place in America would be more secure, and its ability to do its work more assured. The Church project and American project were one. Pastorally, making the immigrants Catholic and American was a single task. Nowhere was this expressed more dramatically than in the integration of Catholic and American symbols. One spring Sunday at St. Joseph's church in Oxford in 1893, the men of the parish were to receive communion. The local newspaper reported that "the church was neatly trimmed with bunting and flowers," while a large American flag hung "over and around the high altar...so arranged to represent a tabernacle." In addition, "a large heart of red and white rested at the foot of the crucifix." At 10 o'clock, the procession formed:

First, the standard bearer, who carried a large beautiful crucifix draped with the stars and stripes, and festooned with red and white roses. He was assisted by two small boys each holding large bouquets. Next came twenty four altar boys, each holding a flag and bouquet of roses; then in double file marched the gentlemen. There were one hundred and eighty one in line, each wore white gloves. The procession was a new and novel one for our streets on Sunday, but not out of place or character. After all had partaken of Holy Communion, Father Mahon preached a sermon upon "The

Good Catholic, a True American."
After Mass, the procession returned to
the rectory and were dismissed.

The natural next step from arguing that being a good Catholic was, in itself, being a good American, was to argue that Catholicism made better Americans than other churches, or to contrast Catholicism's success in making good Americans with the failure of other religions to do so. In a sermon at the dedication of the cathedral in 1904, Jesuit Father Thomas Campbell stated that the "instinct for worship" was absent in modern society. He linked, "as cause and effect," statistics showing that many Americans had no religion, with the "awful corruption that exists in modern society, commercial life and the political world." When the law of the land no longer was seen as "an expression of divine will," there was "no power to control the people save the power of the police" and the "whole machinery of government is paralyzed." When worship disappeared, he insisted, there could be little hope for the individual or the nation. Campbell then argued the Catholic case that the Mass, the Eucharistic sacrifice, was the form of worship given by Christ. The cathedral was evidence of the desire of Catholics to worship God and, in doing so, "we are not only serving God but making ourselves better able to serve our nation." There was no better way to bring about "submission to authority and to the laws of the nation" than by spreading knowledge of God and bringing people to worship. What Catholics had done for the country in building their churches now climaxed with the dedication of their common church, the cathedral:

> *You have made your Cathedral splen-*
> *did and the spirit of Jesus Christ is*
> *within its walls. The cross above it is*
> *a lesson every day and every hour to*
> *the whole community. It is a declara-*
> *tion that recognizes the laws of the*
> *land as God's laws and which makes*
> *you better defenders and lovers of the*
> *laws of your country. Your Cathedral*
> *is a barrier against the enemy and at*
> *the same time a beautiful gate be-*
> *tween heaven and earth.*

KEEPING GOD'S COMMANDMENTS

The success of this argument depended upon the internalization of the morality of the Church and its public display in the behavior of the congregation. Thus, there was a tremendous emphasis on morality in Catholic preaching and religious education, even a moralism which elevated moral requirements to the center of Church life and pastoral expectation. Poor and working-class people, generally, rarely were attracted to optimistic understandings of the economy of salvation. They knew from experience that there was injustice and unfairness in the world, and they tended to be realists about human nature. This was true in the peasant cultures which lay in the backgrounds of most Catholics, who had come from villages where life was hard and piety centered upon the rewards that could come to all men and women. They knew the rewards would come, regardless of their status in this world, if they kept the commandments and followed the teachings of their Church. The Irish especially, after the horrors of the famine, carried deep in their consciousness a sense of the precariousness of life and the limitations on the human prospect. In Europe, this often led to a profound fatalism, because people born to poverty could do little to change their conditions. In the atmosphere of freedom in the United States, however, these same ideas could lead to strenuous activity. If one, indeed, was able to achieve a better life through hard work and self-discipline, then one also could choose to live morally, to become a good Catholic, to earn salvation as one earned daily bread.

Thus, in the United States, sermons tended to emphasize life as a moral battleground where decisions were made which determined one's ultimate destiny.

Father (later Bishop) John Grimes, for example, in a 1915 sermon, argued that preparation for eternity was the major task of human life. The "whole business and duty of man," he wrote, is "to fear God and keep His commandments." Everything would disappear with death, yet the majority of men and women spent their days in pleasure, pursuing honors and riches. He urged his parishioners to awaken from this "sleep of indifference," to look to the martyrs and heroes of the early Church, and to focus attention on the important things which "lay beyond this life." He spoke not of heaven, but of hell, though the word "has a harsh sound to the elite of this world; it is kind of vulgar and not used in good society." Yet Jesus had spoken of hell and, if there were no hell, God was not a God of justice. To avoid hell, to make the "other choice," required Christians "to show ourselves at all times the loving and reverent children and loyal subjects of our Father and King." It meant praying before going about one's daily affairs, keeping God present throughout the day, and being "upholders of justice and lovers of truth." The moral message was clear and direct. Facing a just and judgmental God, men and women carried on their own shoulders the responsibility for their eternal destiny:

> Let us remember that our souls are immortal, that we are the architects of their eternal abode, whatever structure we now build for them, in that they will live forever. If, heretofore, we have lived in conjunction with God, if we have been his loving and devoted children, his loyal and faithful subjects, let us pray to him to continue to bless us and to strengthen us by his grace, that our last breath may be a profession of loyalty to his eternal majesty. If, on the other hand, we have been unfaithful children, if we have dishonored and denied our parent, if we have given ourselves up to works of darkness, let us take to ourselves this morning the words of St. Paul, let us rise from this sleep of indifference and petition God to restore us to his friendship and to enable us by his grace to live forever more in his love.

In the context of a Catholic community still beset by considerable poverty and social stress, the Church offered a principle of order. It demanded submission of individual passions to moral and religious discipline, not in a purely personal moral reformation, but in a concrete acceptance of the responsibilities of Catholic Church membership. As one priest put it in a eulogy for a departed pastor:

> The cross before which we kneel must not be a cross of our own making, nor a Christ of our own imagination. We hear so much today of the Christ of history, the Christ of fact, and the Christ of the Gospel, as if in our imagination we had power to change the eternal truth of God. The cross before which we must kneel is the divinely established priesthood in its glorious hierarchy, from the personal representative of Jesus Christ to the humblest priest in his jurisdiction, for that priesthood is the living continuation of the death of Christ on the cross.

To become a Catholic was to accept the leadership of that priesthood in the regular routine of sacramental practice and reliable support for the Church.

People could choose to be moral and to go to heaven, just as they could choose to work hard and achieve worldly success. The two struggles blended together. At the end of a mission in Oswego, the preacher combined moral realism with the assumption of personal responsibility in a sermon reported in the local press:

This broad earth, he said, was a battleground and we all have a battle before us. Our life is a warfare. We must fight under the standard of our divine Lord or under the standard of the devil. If we keep the commandments of God, we are assured of eternal life. Our enemy, the devil, is always on the alert with new temptations to tempt us. Although we think we are able to defeat him, he is ever on the watch for the weak spots in order to attract us. (He) made an earnest appeal to young men to shun bad company, and pointed out the dangers that arise from such. In this broad land, he said, poverty was no barrier to success and he urged all young men to keep good company or none. Good company and good character were the stepping stones to success. To the young women he gave a word of warning: modesty is your gem, your crowning virtue. Let no one tread on forbidden ground, and no one will when the fences of immodesty are

152

THE INIQUITIES OF THE MODERN DANCE

In a lenten pastoral letter in 1892, Bishop Patrick Ludden issued a strong denunciation of dancing, forbidding any Church-related activity to sponsor a dance. Following are sections from that pastoral letter:

"Many things recorded in the scriptures are for our instruction rather than for our imitation. David, it is true, did dance. But there are few Davids now-a-days. Again, he danced a solo, and before the Ark. This is not the sort of a dance that we see advertised from 10 P.M. to 2 A.M. It is a poor subterfuge then, in order to cover up the iniquities of the modern dance to refer to King David. There is still later and nearer our christian code of morals another example of a dance recorded in Holy Writ, not for our imitation but for our instruction and caution. The incestuous King Herod got up a state dance or ball at which were present "the princes and tribunes and chief men of Gallilee," and the daughter of Herodias danced, and, it seems, danced elegantly, for she so pleased the lecherous King Herod that he became dazed and in his bewildered excitement swore that nothing short of half his kingdom should be at the damsel's request. Here was an occasion for Madame Herodias to be avenged of John the Baptist, who though a rude, uncouth, uncultured denizen of the desert, knowing nothing of the habits and ways of society, the better element, yet dared to rebuke her adulterous and incestuous concubinage with her husband's brother, King Herod. It is a dangerous business to run counter to the habits of good society....

"It is a psychological marvel and a paradox how fashionable customs sanction familiarities and sanctify vulgarities that of their very nature shock decency and modesty *not let down. He urged them to beware of familiarity as familiarity begets contempt. In this age, he said a man could go away and society would receive him, but the woman must stay at home and bear the disgrace. Watch and pray, and never be discouraged.*

Where Hughes had delighted earlier in the sobriety, self-discipline and economic progress of the small communities, preachers like this one now were concerned about somewhat different values. Chastity and parental responsibility became central elements of Catholic preaching. Grimes regularly preached to the cathedral congregation on the duties of parents and the evils of divorce, immodesty and sexual promiscuity.

Missions began to be offered separately for men and women, and boys and girls, another indication that the moral life centered more and more on relations between the sexes.

Ludden's moralism was legendary. Not only did he strictly enforce regulations requiring clerical control of picnics, festivals and fairs, but he waged a near crusade against dancing. In 1892, he warned that these Church events were too often "occasions of sin and scandal," sometimes with the consent of the pastor. Often "Saturday night was selected for these carousals," Ludden wrote in his most sarcastic tone, perhaps "by way of preparation for divine service on Sunday morning when the pastor will preach to the dancers on 'justice and chastity and the judgment to come.'"Noting in one pastoral that it was not the place to discuss the "ethics of the dance,"

153

at first sight and first experience. The manners approved and adopted in the modern dance as graceful, artistic, would not be tolerated outside of the dance and its accompanying sensuous music by persons of the simplest and crudest notions of good morals and decorum. The man who would elsewhere so demean himself would be exposing himself to an angry husband's or brother's six-shooter or to some other physical violence not pleasing to the senses but healthful and chastening to morals.... It is primarily and intrinsically an unintellectual, animal, and sensuous form of amusement, instinctively indulged by the grossly superstitious and untutored savages of every country and clime. Still I do not urge or even suggest a crusade against the dance. I know nice people and good people and, in fact, all sorts of people dance, and do so on all occasions. In fact, you cannot trust your presence in any social gathering unless you are prepared to be unceremoniously brushed into some useless and obscure corner to make room for the dance. It were imprudent then and to no purpose to inveigh against a habit so universal. You cannot successfully swim against a strong current. Better remain on dry ground and industriously try to save from the torrent the driftwood that turns aside in its eddies or is tossed up by the violence of the swollen stream. Moreover, dancing is not in itself an evil and cannot be universally condemned as such. But since it is most certainly a profane and dangerous amusement because of its accompanying fashions, forms and familiarities, the Church forbids it in connection with any christian, charitable, or Catholic name. And no society honored with the name Catholic can honestly or lawfully bring the name into dishonor by connecting it with a ball or dance."

he proceeded to do so at length. He used scriptural texts, classical allusions and class resentment to convince his people that dancing was "primarily and intrinsically an unintellectual, animal and sensuous form of amusement, instinctively indulged by the grossly superstitious and untutored savages of every country and every clime." Several years later, the Syracuse *Herald* headlined "Bishop Ludden Forbids Dancing Among Catholics....Turkey Trot and Grizzly Bear Hug Suggestive of Lewdness and Indecency." As for the "Turkey Trot," Ludden asked why it was not "The Sultan of the Barnyard Trot," which would "add considerably to the suggestion of barnyard morality." The *Catholic Sun* joined in eagerly, arguing that the use of the word "hop" by some Catholics "to designate a certain species of dancing entertainment is not in Catholic taste and is suggestive of light heads." Somehow, young women were peculiarly at risk, the *Sun's* editors thought: "Dancing by moonlight may be very enjoyable and real romantic, but wheeling home from a summer resort at the small hours is hardly compatible with the Catholic idea of what a Catholic girl should be." As late as 1912 the bishop became incensed by plans for a charity ball for the benefit of St. Mary's Infant and Maternity Hospital. He wrote through the chancellor to the sister superior, forbidding her to accept any money from the affair. At the same time, he laid down a general rule against any Catholic institution receiving funds from dances and announced that Catholic chaplains would be withdrawn from organizations which defied this regulation.

The emphasis on this new moralism increased during the later years of Ludden's administration. The bishop attacked local authorities for failing to crack down on prostitution and Grimes denounced well known streetwalkers from the pulpit of the cathedral. Grimes warned young women against keeping company with married men and against long courtships, and he lamented the trend of women's fashions. One pastor following Grimes' lead, deplored thin "chiffon" dress material and recommended muslin. Taking their cue from the bishop, pastors like Father Doherty spoke more often of the moral problems confronting young people and urged a more zealous effort to control young adults by their parents. Even Father Clune, who was clearly no puritan, warned young people against frequenting skating rinks. Later, he was concerned about cosmetics. "Who loves a painted woman?" he asked, and then answered his own question: "not the husband, not the child, not the brother. To the priest it brings thoughts of the poorhouse and prisons of broken hearts."

At first glance, such themes of personal morality, with their emphasis on sexuality, seem to have little to do with the economic and social problems of the working-class Catholics who filled the pews. Yet, in retrospect, it is clear that there was an intimate relationship between stable family life, educational achievement and economic advancement. Irish, German, Polish and Italian pastors knew from pastoral experience that the family breakdown, occasioned by migration which often forced the separation of unmarried young people from their families and placed immense strains upon those families who moved together, led all too often to alcoholism, lawlessness, pauperism and misery. It was men and women from settled families who seemed not only to do better financially, but also to become the most reliable Church members. What the Church taught and what society required were also what people needed in their personal lives — order, stability and emotional support. There was little the Church could do to correct public injustice and immorality, but much it could do to assist its own members to make their way in the world and, in the process, perhaps correct social wrongs. The emphasis

Monsignor James P. McPeak (Photo: Chancery Archives)

on sexual restraint and traditional family values, therefore, corresponded with the needs of Catholics and could relate positively to their hopes for the future.

Yet, deep ambivalence ran through Catholic piety and pastoral life. On the one hand, people with no religious faith were likely to be poor citizens and serious sinners. As so many Americans were irreligious, or affiliated with weak churches, the country, according to the preachers, was becoming ever more materialistic and was in danger of submersion in sensuality. Thus, it seemed, Catholics should shun the world and rely on the Church, for there alone could be found true religion and the means by which one could overcome sin and the world and reach eternal salvation. These ideas suggested a profound pessimism about human nature, as when Grimes argued that, given the enormity of human sinfulness and the greatness of God, the Incarnation was God's humiliation and "supreme debasement."

Yet the churches also were filled with works of art which suggested that the world, especially when shaped to human purpose through art, music and human creation, was itself good. Behind the buildings, organs, choirs and colorful stained glass lay a distinctively Catholic understanding of the relationship between creation and the creator, less moralistic, more authentically sacramental. While preachers stressed sinful human nature and the need for sacrifice and repentance, and while Ludden and Grimes often sounded almost puritanical in their denunciations of sex, dancing and even sports, the buildings manifested another tone to the faith, one which saw in nature, in the body, in the work of human hands, evidence of the glory and grandeur of God. As Monsignor James McPeak put it in a long, scholarly sermon delivered at the blessing of a set of church bells in Clinton in the spring of 1914, "God created this world to know, love and glorify Him." The Incarnation of God in human flesh, in Jesus, meant that material things could glorify God through human beings, and human beings through Christ, so that "the universe joins in a glorious concert of praise which is as infinite as the majesty of Him who is its object." The message of church bells for those who saw the world through the eyes of faith was to "recognize in the various harmonies of earth not the voices by which sin calls it votaries from the service of God, but to recognize in them echoes of those melodies which sound before His heavenly throne, to contemplate the glories of created nature which appear during this pleasant season of the year, and turn from them to praise the great God who gave them."

McPeak was a priest of his age, so he made sure to note that bells, and other reminders of God's creation, should "make us loyal and sincere in the practice of our religion." He reasoned that "it is our own fault if we permit the voices of worldliness and irreligion to lure our footsteps from the straight and narrow path or to lessen by the least shade our enthusiastic devotion for the cause of Jesus Christ and His Church." But he also insisted that the Church was more than a gathering of an elect people standing in judgment on their neighbors, or a beleagured island of sinners clinging to the priest and sacraments to release them from the bondage of sin so they could escape the world for heaven. Rather, the beauties of churches, like the sound of the bells, could enable "us (to) learn that each object of sense...may become a bond to knit the soul with God, a ladder, like the Patriarch's, reaching from earth to heaven, the glass of the Apostle through which Divinity is darkly discernable."

THE COST OF CHURCH MEMBERSHIP

The ambivalence of Catholic moralism did not end there. Preachers regularly denounced "worldliness," but those preachers' churches were very worldly projects, requiring large amounts of money for their construction and maintenance. As the youthful editor of a parish fair journal put it elaborately in 1887: "In this country, where the wealth of religious corporations is not entirely coextensive with the increase in the church-going population, and where it is the desire of pastors to furnish for their respective congregations beautiful and commodious places of worship, it often becomes necessary to make extra-ordinary efforts for the collection of church revenues." It surely did. The invited preacher at the dedication of the new church of the Immaculate Conception in Pompey Hills in 1893 put the matter bluntly. The ceremony was not intended to be "a mere public demonstration of our faith," he said. "This church is your home. We can in truth call our homes our own only when they are paid for." During the early years of the diocese, no goal was more persuasive than paying for the church and, in many cases, the school, and the rapid expansion in parishes ensured that. This would remain true for years to come.

While stories of parish expansion cannot be told for all parishes, a revealing example was the construction of the new St. Mary's church in Cortland. After his death in 1888, the founding pastor, the remarkable Batholomew McLoughlin, was succeeded by his nephew, Father John McLoghlin. Over the next 18 years, John McLoghlin expanded the cemetery, built a rectory, paid all debts and left $32,000 toward the new church. In 1907, Father McLoghlin was sent to St. Patrick's in Binghamton, then the second largest parish in the diocese. The next pastor was as remarkable as his predecessors. Patrick Donohue was born in Ireland in 1864 and achieved some fame as an athlete before leaving for the United States, where he studied for the priesthood at the Troy seminary. He never lost his passion for competitive sports. During his years at Cortland, the parish sponsored many teams, including a semi-pro baseball team which toured the state and country. Donohue proved an adept fundraiser. Parishioners held the usual food sales and fairs. One year the parish sponsored a motorcycle race which raised $10,000. Construction of the new church began in 1909 and the parish had to borrow only $50,000 to meet the $181,000 cost. At the laying of the cornerstone, Bishop Ludden was met at the railroad station by a procession of 800 men who marched, four abreast, to the construction site. The following year tragedy struck. As Donohue and John Harrison, the contractor, inspected the building's progress, the scaffolding collapsed, sending Harrison to his death and leaving Donohue clinging to the support. In 1913, the building was dedicated, with services marked by a sermon by Archbishop (later Cardinal) John Glennon of St. Louis, a boyhood friend of the pastor. The old St. Mary's of the Vale was converted into a parish hall, the transept became a basketball court, and space was made for a game room, locker room and handball court. In 1918, when an additional

$39,000 was needed to meet the cost of furnishing the church, a drive netted $42,000.

Fundraising of this sort remained the major preoccupation in every parish. It required constant effort by the parishioners, under the lash of the pastor's pleas and threats, to pay the bills. It cost money to be fully a member of the Church. In East Syracuse, working-class parishioners paid a dollar or two per quarter for their pews. At the more prosperous St. Patrick's in Binghamton, a parish committee raised pew rents to a scale ranging from $18 for seats near the wall, to $48 for seats on the aisle.

When John Grimes succeeded O'Hara at St. Mary's, he began a system of issuing tickets to pew holders. Without a ticket, one could not be admitted at High Mass. When people did not pay, they could expect a rebuke. Father Bernard Quinn at the tiny parish in Deerfield spoke of parishioners "defrauding" him and the parish by failing to take seats. In East Syracuse, Clune blasted non-pew holders as dishonest. A decade later, at the far more prosperous cathedral, he told his parishioners "pew rent is very backward" and warned that they could not fulfill their responsibilities with the newly installed system of door offerings the "payment of $.10 instead of having a sitting or sittings in the church."

In the larger parishes, pew rent offerings accounted for as much as 80 percent of parish income. In smaller parishes, pew rents were sometimes surpassed by income from fairs, festivals and special events. At the parish at Pompey, the weekly collection in 1916 averaged $21, with another $11 from the mission at Lafayette. However, parish socials were held almost weekly with a bewildering variety of fundraising gimmicks, for example, the auction of a donated horse. These socials often produced $100 for an evening. Immaculate Conception at Pompey Hill received $585 in pew rents in 1896, but took in another $500 on the parish fair. At St. Patrick's in

Binghamton, a creative move was to pay for life insurance policies on 10 leading men of the parish. Unfortunately, they proved long-lived and the benefits did not materialize in time to help with church construction. Rural churches could be equally creative. The 1903 report of tiny St. Mary's church in Jamesville contains a mysterious reference to a "cooperative" which, every two or three weeks, returned between $3 and $6 to the parish. At St. Joseph's in Oswego in 1916, two women sold eggs outside church. Unfortunately this practice seems only to have broken even, leaving the church no revenue. Raising money was a matter of such small items. In 1901, the pastor of St. Mary's in Clinton reported on his building fund: "Five parishioners gave $1 weekly, two gave 75 cents, 96 gave 50 cents, and 414 gave 25 cents or less." Yet from such small amounts, the fund gathered $2,500 during that year and, by 1910, totalled almost $40,000 — the result of a decade of the pastor's pleas and the people's sacrifices.

Priests may have worried about the scandals and sins of the world, but they needed money for their churches and their salaries. The Christmas and Easter collections measured the pastor's popularity and the size and prestige of his parish. Father Grimes, reminding his parishioners about the collection in Easter 1891, asked them to be generous. He said "we take pride in announcing a big one." Grimes described these collections as "magnificent," often reaching more than $1,000, the standard set at other large parishes like St. Paul's of Oswego. Things were very different in the small parishes in rural areas beset by declining population, poverty and the tendency of parishioners to go off to the larger city churches for the elaborate holiday ceremonies. When Father Quinn came to Deerfield in 1890, he found that the Franciscans, who once had served the parish, had a $300 claim against the parish which he was able to reduce to $100 by leaving his own salary unpaid. After serving 13 years, Quinn described St. Peter's as "a very hard and sickening mission." More than half the people in the area failed to provide the "honest assistance they ought to have given." The priest had to "do all and pay all and write all — sometimes more than five clerks — leave all things in perfect order but not trouble the people to pay for himself or money in general." When he arrived, approximately 36 persons, half of them children, attended the church. By 1903, attendance was up to 125-150, again half children, but few would come if he mentioned the problems of finances. Even then, more than half the Catholics attended church in Utica or Newport. Quinn's bitter notes reflected the struggle facing pastors of poorer congregations at a time when finances and buildings defined successful ministry. At St. Patrick's in Jordan, the pastor's bookkeeping accounts listed income and expenditures and each year his salary was entered at the end of December, never reaching the $600 level set by diocesan policy. Sometimes there were other donations that were acceptable, as at Immaculate Conception in Pompey where the pastor told the parishioners one fall Sunday that his cellar needed stocking with preserves.

Most priests believed, as Quinn did, that financial success was the dominant factor in evaluating pastoral performance. When Martin John Hughes was made pastor of St. John's in Oswego, local papers were filled with praise of this energetic young priest who quickly put parish finances on a sound foundation. When he was transferred to another troubled parish, St. Mary's in Binghamton, he quickly placed all financial records before a lay committee and promised to consult them on all decisions. He dramatically cut expenses, held a successful fair which raised $12,000 and soon had a new church under construction. This remarkable ability to unite divided congregations and stabilize

shaky finances made Hughes a remarkably valuable priest. His difficult assignments were far from ended.

The priests, in turn, tended to pass this measure along in their parishes by publishing reports of all collections, listing individuals and their contributions. In announcing a subscription campaign in 1894, Clune told the people of St. John the Evangelist: "What we do will be for God." But he quickly added, "Names will be taken and published afterward." Hughes made even these reports an opportunity to make money, placing them in a small booklet and soliciting advertisements from local and neighborhood businesses. These reports were favorite reading. When posted in the back of the church, a crowd gathered quickly. One year Clune noted that his people had been "a little rude" the previous year. He hoped now they would be "ladies and gentlemen." Occasionally, the ever-present concern for money could interfere with pastoral practice. Clune announced one Sunday that donations for Mass intentions need not be given when the priest came on a sick call. When some questioned that decision, he explained: "It was not intended to discourage Masses being said, only to discourage the feeling that sick calls must be paid for."

FOCUS ON THE SACRAMENTS

There was, of course, more to the Church than fundraising. Concern with money was balanced by religious practices which captured the paradox of this sometimes too worldly religion. Lenten fasting rules were eased in 1889, when meat was allowed at every meal on Sunday and the principal meals on Monday, Tuesday, Thursday and Saturday, with the exception of ember days. Fasting, the abstention from food between meals and reduction of two meals to a minimum, was required each day. However, large categories

DIOCESE OF SYRACUSE

REGULATIONS FOR LENT

1st. All the week-days of Lent from Ash-Wednesday till Easter Sunday are fast days of precept, on one meal, with the allowance of a moderate collation in the evening.

2nd. All the faithful who have completed their twenty-first year, are, unless legitimately dispensed, bound to observe the fast.

3rd. The precept of fasting implies also that of abstinence from the use of flesh meat.

4th. By authority of the Holy See, the use of flesh meat is allowed in this Diocese, at every meal on Sundays and at the principal meal on Mondays, Tuesdays, Thursdays and Saturdays, with the exception of Saturday of Ember Days and Saturday of Holy Week.

5th. It is not allowed to use fish with flesh meat at the same meal, even on Sundays.

6th. The use of eggs, milk, butter or cheese, is tolerated.

7th. In the morning some liquid as tea, coffee or chocolate and a cracker or small piece of bread, are allowed.

8th. Lard may be used in preparing fish, vegetables, &c.

9th. The Church excuses from the obligation of fasting (but not of abstinence from flesh meat, except on special cases of sickness) the following classes of persons: First, the infirm; Second, those whose duties are of a laborious or exhausting nature; Third, persons who are attaining their growth; Fourth, women in pregnancy or nursing infants; Fifth, those who are enfeebled by old age.

10th. Persons exempt from the obligation of fasting are allowed to use flesh meat at all meals, as on Sundays, on days on which its use is granted dispensation.

11th. When the principal meal cannot be taken at noon, the order may be inverted, and the collation taken in the morning and the dinner in the afternoon.

12th. The faithful are reminded that they should sanctify their fast by seclusion from wordly and profane amusements, by constant earnest prayer, by generous almsgiving, by sorrow for sin and by serious preparation to celebrate, through the worthy reception of the Sacraments, the great festival of Christ's Resurrection.

13th. The time for performing Easter duty extends from the first Sunday in Lent till Trinity Sunday.

PATRICK,

Bishop of Syracuse.

Syracuse, Feast of St. Matthias.
1889.

were excluded, including the sick, those whose work was of a "laborious or exhaustive nature...persons who are attaining their growth," pregnant women or women nursing infants, and the elderly. Significantly, Ludden added to his list of Lenten regulations an exhortation to honor the penitential season "by seclusion from worldly and profane amusements." Seclusion could mean attending a variety of Lenten services, especially during Holy Week. Holy Week services at St. Mary's in Syracuse in 1891 began with vespers, benediction and recitation of the rosary on Palm Sunday afternoon. Holy Thursday featured a Solemn Mass and procession at 8:00 in the morning, with the Blessed Sacrament exposed the remainder of the day and through the night for the adoration of the faithful. No evening services were held because "everything is left free for your private devotion." On Good Friday morning, the procession returned with the Blessed Sacrament, followed by adoration of the cross. That evening stations of the cross were followed by a sermon on the passion. The lengthy Holy Saturday service began at 8:00 p.m. and the congregation was urged to participate in order to bring before their "minds vividly the sufferings of our savior." On Easter morning, Masses were held at 7 and 8, with the 10:30 High Mass having orchestra accompaniment. Advent had not been noted much earlier in the century, but by the 1890s it joined Lent as a period in which the priests expected the people to make substantial efforts at penance and spiritual renewal. Father Grimes' prescriptions at St. Mary's were not much different from those for Lent: "All amusements, all public gatherings, no matter for what purpose other than worship of God, should cease. Above all public balls, etc. No Catholic of any standing would be found in a public ballroom during lent or advent. They are penitential times."

Christmas, like Easter, was time for major celebration after the period of penance. Parties were held for the Sunday School children. There were elaborate preparations of the altar, choir practices and reminders about the special collection. Parishioners were invited to bring friends, including non-Catholics, to Christmas services, and the pastor urged them to be kind and hospitable to these strangers. In 1900, for the first time in many years, midnight Mass was allowed. Grimes told his people this was "a great favor and all should show their appreciation by being present and assisting devoutly at Mass."

Ludden's passion for order and regularity extended to the religious life. In October 1903, preaching at the cathedral on the subject of devotions, the bishop emphasized that the sacrament of the altar was the only "real devotion" and he warned that "the multiplication of religious fads, apparitions and pilgrimages tend to obscure that devotion." While Ludden did nothing to check the growth of those new devotional practices, which were under pastoral control and direction, he did encourage the replacement of popular devotions characteristic of old world churches with a more Church-centered piety. Moreover, he had little patience with claims of miracles or apparitions. When he administered confirmation in Oswego in 1903, he referred to reports of apparitions in the city and stated that "the age of signs and wonders had long since passed." Local priests liked to tell the story of Ludden addressing another priest in whose parish there were such reports and telling him there were to be no more miracles in the diocese. The story is undoubtedly apocryphal, but it reflects a perception of Ludden as an organizer and devoted churchman who had little patience with the irregular or the unpredictable.

But Ludden's hopes were not realized yet. While considerable progress was made in drawing people to the sacraments, traditional devotions retained their hold on immigrant

The chapel at St. Vincent de Paul orphanage in Syracuse is decorated for a special liturgy (Photo: Chancery Archives)

communities and popular new devotions proved attractive in Irish and middle-class parishes. The mission priests often brought with them a new devotion. The Jesuits had their devotion to the Sacred Heart and the the Apostleship of Prayer. In St. John's in Camden, Father Joseph S. Tiernan launched this devotion in June 1915:

Next Friday the Feast of the Sacred Heart, the Holy Hour for all First Fridays 7 to 8 P.M. will be inaugurated and the parish consecrated to the Sacred Heart. All parishioners are requested to receive Our Lord Friday at 5:30 or 8 o'clock Mass....The grand consecration sermon, the inauguration of the holy hour with exposition of the Blessed Sacrament, the conferring of diplomas, crosses and badges on all promoters and members of the League of the Sacred Heart, will take place at 7 o'clock in the evening. The like has never been seen before.

The Vincentians had the Holy Agony Confraternity, organized at one of their missions at St. John the Baptist in Rome. Father Dougherty promoted a variety of novenas at St. Vincent de Paul in Syracuse. His favorite was the novena to St. Ann and an annual pilgrimage to her shrine. In East Syracuse, the Novena of St. Joseph was popular, perhaps reflecting the working-class composition of that congregation. Finally, there were the Marian devotions, namely the Novena of the Miraculous Medal, May processions and, most of all, the rosary, already growing in importance as an element of Catholic life. Many parishes responded to Leo XIII's appeal for daily recitations of the rosary in October. Yet all these devotions had in common one major difference from older practices. They took place in the church, sponsored by the priests and controlled by them, and almost always they incorporated the Blessed Sacrament into them by beginning or ending with Benediction of the Blessed Sacrament and by requiring attendance at Confession and reception of Holy Communion in order to receive the full benefits which the novena made possible. Thus, Ludden's goal of making the Eucharist central to Catholic life, while not fully achieved yet and sometimes apparently contradicted by the popularity of devotions to saints, medals, scapulars, statues and non-eucharistic services, was in fact coming more and more to unify and give coherence to Catholic belief.

Other memorable ceremonies marked milestones in the life of the parish, as when the new bell for St. Vincent de Paul parish was blessed in solemn ceremony in 1902. The bell was placed before the altar, the pastor washed it with a special salt and water solution inside and out, while the choir chanted psalms, seven crosses were made on the outside of the bell, four in the inside, a burning censer filled with incense was placed under the bell to fill it with smoke, and the bell then was rung three times. St. John's in Utica had an equally elaborate ceremony to introduce a new electric light system. The dedication of a new church always had been a special event, marked by processions and solemn services. Some churches held similar ceremonies to consecrate the church when all debts had been paid. The bishop had to perform this ceremony and, once consecrated, a church could not be used for any other purpose. In 1900, Ludden consecrated St. John's in Utica and the newspapers reported the elaborate ceremony in detail. Relics, a small parchment containing information about the church, and incense were placed in a silver case the evening before the ceremony, while the office of the day was chanted. An overnight vigil was kept in the church. The next day, 12 crosses of brass were placed on the inner walls of the church, evidence that the church had been consecrated. The bishop processed three times around the outside of the church, blessing the ground and walls with Holy Water. On entering the church, he paused at the threshold, tracing a cross on the floor and saying "Behold the Sign of the Cross. Flee ye all Phantoms." Ashes then were placed in small piles throughout the church, as were the letters of the Greek alphabet. The bishop said prayers of consecration over the altar, placed the silver box in its location and concluded the ceremony, all the while accompanied by a choir and orchestra.

There was an extraordinary amount of interest in the quality of church music at ceremonies at the turn of the century. Newspapers in Syracuse, Oswego and Utica regularly featured the musical programs planned and reviewed the music and the sermon on Monday morning. The Oswego *Palladium,* for example, recounted the elaborate musical presentation at St. John's church at Easter, 1889. One of the soloists was described as a "magnificent bass voice" who

always would be "a welcome visitor to the music loving people of Oswego." The same article praised Father Hughes' new sanctuary lamp, describing it in great detail. That same Sunday, the services at St. Mary's were "on the usual grand scale," while at St. Paul's the musical director, Professor Favreau, was the "subject of many complimentary remarks." St. Paul's, in fact, was the musical center of the diocese, best known for its expensive organ, purchased at a cost of $7,500. It took almost six months to install and opened to rave reviews. Newspapers described it as the "equivalent of an orchestra of 100 pieces." Nineteenth century Masses, vesper services, and solemn opening and closing of Forty Hours devotion and missions occasioned musical presentations by orchestras, string quartets, and choirs of varying size and quality.

By the last decades of the century, however, concern was widespread in the hierarchy over the chaotic variety of musical accompaniment and, especially, the introduction of "secular" music into sacred ceremonies. Once again Ludden was the agent of reform. When newspapers reported that Miss Frankie Hunt sang "Heaven is the Prize" as an offertory song at a cathedral funeral, the bishop told Father Grimes: "'Heaven is the Prize' may be pretty popular and pious, 'Lead Kindly Light' is universally acknowledged to be. But neither is liturgical and each and all are forbidden in our Catholic services." He admitted the newspaper clipping might be inaccurate, but he suspected not because "organists and choir leaders are not generally particular in matters of church liturgy." He asked Grimes to speak to his organist and instruct him in the decrees and statutes which "do not permit anything to be sung in the vernacular during Mass." A papal decree of 1903 confirmed Ludden's views. A "black list" of forbidden music was prepared and women were banned from singing at Mass.

AN EXPANDING ROLE FOR WOMEN

In fact, the role of women became a public question in the years before World War I. The brief but heated controversy indicated further tensions between a pessimistic piety, which emphasized a traditional morality threatened by a sinful world, and the optimistic and energetic life of the growing Catholic community. The Catholic Mutual Benefit Association long had been a successful parish organization, placing small insurance policies within the reach of all. In March 1903, the first branch of the Ladies Catholic Benevolent Association appeared at St. Mary's, approved by Father Grimes. Two years later, another chapter began at St. Lucy's, headed by a woman physician, Theresa Bannon. The *Catholic Sun* warned against this new organization on the grounds that "woman's place is in the home and man's place is to provide." Father Clovis Thibault of St. Joseph's French church was incensed even more. "The place of a good wife or mother is not in the dodge of insurance, nor of labor, nor of politics," he wrote. "Just think of a lady sitting in a meeting hall for two long hours every week, discussing money and trifling matters, then tramping home alone at night, when her male half is supposed to be lonely at home, rocking the baby by the fireside." Response was surprisingly negative. One woman simply noted that the society had the approval of the bishop and pastor. Another thought it highly unlikely that husbands would be rocking the baby while wives were at meetings. Most telling was a comment that reminded Father Thibault of a hard fact: "A woman tramping home alone at night the Reverend would approve if it was from a fair, but not from a society meeting." Father Clune would have agreed with that argument because he tried to shame the men of his parish into working on the parish fair by telling them they should not "in America

let the women do all the work, as in Turkey."

The battle in the letters column of the *Sun* raged for months and spilled over into wider areas of women's rights.

Margaret Moore argued the cause of women's rights more forcefully than ordinarily found in the Catholic press. If men have a right to a voice in making the laws under which they lived, so too do women, she argued. Only through the work of women like Susan B. Anthony had women obtained the "meagre liberties" now enjoyed. Women asked nothing more than their right as "intelligent reasonable beings to have a voice in making the laws which we uphold." Such arguments were challenged by a man who argued that, if women wanted equality, they should grab the sledge or enter the machine shop, appealing to the "spectacle" of women "marching in Salina Street wearing heavy shoes and swinging a dinner pail."

Yet many women, in fact, were working in factories, and the Irish Catholic community had been built in large part by women in domestic service, a fact of which Ludden and the *Sun's* editors were well aware. A Syracuse newspaper derided "Bridget" for sliding into church for the four o'clock Mass on Easter Sunday and then returning to her employer's to prepare the potatoes for breakfast. The *Sun* responded saying that it was such "Bridgets" who had done "what the money of the Vanderbilts, the Astors and that horde of plutocrats have not yet done, the building of a cathedral which is the glory of the Catholicity in New York." Indeed, "Bridget" was "a model woman" from whom "the fair butterflies of society might learn virtue and maidenly modesty." A few years later, visiting his home parish in Ireland, Ludden warned Irish men against immigration because they would find industry closed to them. However, he said, the "Irish maidens" had brought the faith and Irish morality to America because "the American maiden will not do what in

WOMEN'S VIEWS

In the first volley for women's rights — the turn-of-the-century campaign to gain the right to vote — Central New Yorkers were ambivalent. Some were outspoken advocates for women's rights, but many more were quick to defend the traditional view of the subservient housewife. Much of the suffrage discussion focused on marriage, as is evident in these two commentaries from the *Catholic Sun*:

GROUND DOWN BY CUSTOM

"I have been told, (needless to say by a man, and a married one,) that the foundation of happiness in marriage, at least for the man, is a sense of dependency on the part of his wife. No true woman ever married a man for the sake of becoming his dependent. In marrying, a woman certainly gives as much, if not more than she receives. Is it as a dependent that she cheerfully bears and rears his children, makes the home neat and pleasant, cooks his meals, and performs the thousand and one other prosaic acts which constitute the average woman's life? If so, marriage is indeed simply the union of animal passions. But I deny this. Rather, does not the wife earn her right to the home and income by labors greater even than the husband's? Is it not as an equal companion she expects and has a right to be greeted?" — (Margaret Moore of Syracuse) June 23, 1893.

HOW I HELD MY HUSBAND'S AFFECTION

"Assuming that your husband must go to work at 7:00 AM do not let him get his own breakfast but arouse yourself and be 'on the job' with him and when he returns in the evening meet him with a pleasant smile and that dainty pinkness that pleased him so well before marriage. Have flowers on the table, white clean linen and shining china. Rather than gadding about at lectures listening to 'How to Tame the Brute' it is more important to learn 'How to Feed the Brute.' The kitchen is the secret key for holding his affections at home. Equality of the sexes is not in the nature of things. The woman's place is in the home and the difference between mens and womens vocations are that one is active and the other passive. If a woman does her best to please her husband he will be happy and she successful in holding his love." (Unidentified letter writer) July 11, 1913.

America is called housework," but instead entered stores and offices. Yet, he had no sympathy with women's rights, arguing that he favored "home life ... wherein the father is the protector and the mother the queen and mistress."

At times, the *Sun's* editors made light of the new phenomenon of women's emancipation, particularly when they argued that it was unnecessary for men to rise to allow a women to sit on the inner seats of a church pew, a practice they said went back to Indian times. They noted with approval Cardinal Gibbons' denunciation of woman suffrage, yet they argued that the Catholic Church had done more for the rights of women than any other institution. By 1898, the paper was admitting that women had won respect and deserved equality in the workplace, but worried that when women "went back to abomination in dress" they would "lose all, and deserve to, that privilege and independence and self support which the church and society have made such pains to secure for her."

In fact, the whole episode showed strains in the community, which badly wanted to uphold an ideal of middle-class household life which only a few had experienced in the past. Irish women saw in that ideal a way to shame men into fulfilling their responsibility to their families, and the Church was a useful ally. However, many non-Irish families still had more complex and less well defined "roles" than the romantic ideal of father and mother held by Ludden and Thibault. The very Church which had its doubts about women's rights, of course, was providing women with a variety of experiences in which they exercised responsibility and contributed to collective projects, nurturing that sense of dignity and of a public role upon which the movement toward suffrage and equality drew. If the Church and most of its women did not become active in the movement, and even opposed it, their reasons were complex. They were concerned about family stability, the disciplines and responsibilities of family roles, and the dangers of an unchecked individualism. But, at the same time, the arguments showed the continuing conflict between the pessimism about human nature so widespread in the piety, and the optimism and assertiveness evident in Church life.

TOWARD LIBERATION

A final example of how the energetic and quite worldly activity provided a "ladder" to heaven, but also to a better life, is St. Vincent de Paul parish in Syracuse. In 1889, Lillie Burns gathered in her home children from the desperately poor neighborhood known as Grove's Tract for catechism classes. Monsignor Lynch, rector of the cathedral, heard of this work and one of his assistants, Bernard

Quinn, began visiting the area. The people lived in "frightful poverty," he recalled years later, in "dirty old rooms and houses and...in shanties hardly fit for dogs." Many were "ashamed to send their children to school or catechism till the weather and roads became better, as they could not afford to buy shoes or decent clothes," while the women had "no decent dress or shoes" and the furniture in their homes "was not worth ten dollars." In 1891, the cathedral's St. Vincent de Paul Society took over the Sunday School and purchased a small house which soon became a mission with occasional Masses. In 1892, a mission chapel was erected and, in 1894, Father William Dougherty took charge of a little parish with 100 families. The parish immediately began raising money for a new church. Dougherty was vigorous, announcing that the prize to be raffled off at the first parish picnic, worth at least $25, would be "a life size picture of your pastor." Parish societies were organized, each raising small amounts of money. The poor were asked to participate as best they could, even if their contribution was only one to six dollars a year. Soon there was a fair. Through all activities, Dougherty explained that he hoped "to stimulate now and always a parish pride." By early 1897, they were worshiping in the basement of their new church and, in September, he announced plans for the dedication on November 7. He knew his work and his people, and how the public presentation of their new church created by their hard work and dedicated sacrifices marked a moment of pride in what they had accomplished and hope for the future. There would be 56 altar boys and 100 male voices in the children's choirs. Those boys not involved in that way could help prepare the grounds. There would be an orchestra, a one dollar admission to the dedication and $.50 for vespers.

The announcement book of St. Vincent de

Paul provides a window into parish life in the Irish community in the years before World War I. In 1910, there was a Corpus Christi procession, a novena almost every month to St. Joseph, the Sacred Heart, the Miraculous Medal and others. On Sundays, there was vespers, replaced by rosary and benediction during the summer months. A purgatorial society played a major role in organizing the parish picnic, as well as collecting sacrificial offerings of five cents a week for the parish debt. The parish was divided into districts or neighborhoods and, during the spring and summer, there were regular lawn parties held at private homes in individual districts sponsored by the parishioners of that district. The whole parish and neighborhood were invited. There were numerous societies and sodalities. Each Sunday, one or the other was having its special communion Sunday. In July, there was a novena to St. Ann, a favorite of the pastor. Later there would be an annual pilgrimage to her shrine in Quebec. The July parish picnic was the biggest social event and major fundraiser of the year, with contests, music, games, meals and entertainment, netting $2,000 in 1910. In September, the altar society had its annual party, with drawings, entertainment and refreshments. Later that month the Holy Name Society joined others from the city in a parade through the streets, ending with vespers at the cathedral. October brought a mission, held almost every year. In the pastor's words, the missionary priests were given "entire charge of the spiritual life of the parish." In the fall of 1910, Dougherty introduced a new system of tickets for seats at ten cents, to protect the pew renters and "insure that each person paid their due." The poor were not forgotten. A ladies aid society collected clothes, shoes and winter items for distribution to the poor of the parish.

In later years, the parish added other social and fundraising events. Although many Catholics once had regarded cardplaying as just short of dancing among the world's evils, St. Vincent's was among the first to introduce card parties, beginning first with whist and euchre. In 1914, the parish's 20th anniversary was designated as a special jubilee year, with the beginning of a serious drive toward a school. In addition to the regular collections, Dougherty hoped to raise $20,000 with $2,000 from the purgatorial society, $1,000 from the mother club and parish societies, $5,000 from the picnic and fair, a $2,000 surplus in ordinary collections and a special drive asking every member of the parish to contribute one day's pay every quarter to raise $10,000. Originally he planned to begin with a gym and clubrooms, but by the middle of 1914 he decided to go ahead with four classrooms and a home for the sisters, making the picnic and the street fairs in the districts which preceded it even more important. He pleaded for his people's support:

> *The purpose for which it is held should appeal to all—a school and sisters in the parish. Don't bolt, don't lose interest, don't oppose, don't discourage, don't knock, in our jubilee year. Look on what twenty years has meant to our homes, our children, ourselves. Thank God for it and help the jubilee building fund.*

The scope of these district fairs can be seen in one week preceding the picnic of 1915. On Monday, there was a lawn social in one district, and a dutch supper and piano concert in another; on Tuesday, a euchre party and a benefit concert; Wednesday, one district sponsored a performance at the Lincoln theater, another had a lawn social and a third a "fancy dress party;" Thursday, there were two lawn parties and a musical performance; and on Friday, another concert. This was an unusually crowded week, but these district parties went on for five weeks. When final returns were in, the programs cleared $5,000.

In retrospect, it was a bewildering combination. One week Father Dougherty complained that people were not paying their pew rents and promised to publish the list in full because silence had not served any purpose. A few weeks later he praised his congregation for their Christmas contribution of more than $1,000. Soon after he promised that everyone would be called upon to pay their ten cents for a seat. Then he asked them not to go to "expense or extravagance" in dressing their children for first communion, because this is "contrary to the spirit of the parish." Then he announced proudly that, during 1914, he had distributed 11,264 communions.

At the turn of the century, preaching emphasized the weakness of human nature and the dangers of the world, suggesting the need to escape from that world to Church and eventually to heaven. But the Church itself was filled with projects to make money. Here, as elsewhere, people joined to build churches that were monuments to religious faith, but also to worldly accomplishment, sources of pride for the people and symbols of success for the pastors. The key to the paradox was that, in the Church, men and women did indeed learn self-discipline and self-help. The routine of religious practice instilled habits of order and restraint, while at the same time, opening horizons of new possibility. It was a fact that, in the religious ceremonies and social activities of parishes, people were important. The Church did depend on them. Learning in the concrete experience of parish participation a sense of their own dignity and worth, they were empowered to take responsibility that they could accept what the Church taught, that they were responsible for the outcome of their lives. The quality of their family life, their success at work and their satisfaction with themselves depended upon their own efforts. Some might find that incredible, but parishioners got a sense that it might be true by their participation in Church, where they learned that they could be full participants in what they learned was the oldest, greatest and most patriotic Church of all. They could have their sins forgiven and could become virtuous by attending services and receiving the sacraments. By their hard work and sacrifice, they could help build a magnificent building, admired by everyone, later a school with sisters, where their children learned to be good citizens. The piety which, at first glance, was world-denying, in practice was a kind of pastoral theology of liberation. If it taught anything, it taught that, what had been need not be any longer, that age-old notions of deference and status could give way to a new vision of personal responsibility and self-making. And the evidence of the truth of these new ideas was right there in the progress of this Church of which that person was a part.

TO SUPPORT
OUR OWN

PROVIDING FOR CATHOLICS' NEEDS
1890s-1920s

Bishop Ludden and the great pastors of the nineteenth century were the ecclesiastical equivalent of that American ideal, the self-made man. Immigrants themselves, they forged successful careers within the Church, loved by their parishioners, respected by other eminent men in the community. Only Ludden owed his success to his relationship with the bishop. The others had come to small, struggling congregations, developed bonds of community with and among their people, taught them the central doctrines of the Church, persuaded them to practice their faith, and built churches which were impressive monuments to their energy and dedication. Along the way, they defended their people and the faith against attack and established relationships of mutual respect with Protestant church and civic leaders. By force of will and hard work, they united and won the trust of their people, mobilized the resources of the community and led it to the achievement of its objectives. If it was not exactly "rags to riches," it surely was a success story.

In many ways, the Church in Syracuse, under the leadership of Ludden's successors, was another. Like the self-made man, the local Church took pride in what it had accomplished, insisted on providing for its needs out of its own resources, and deeply wished to enjoy the respect of its fellow citizens, without surrendering, in any way, its hard won independence and integrity. If Catholics once had been objects of charity, looking to others for help, they now would be donors of charity. The Church now was able to provide for itself, "to support our own" as Bishop Grimes put it. It did not plead for public support, but demanded respect for its rights and recognition of its public contribution. Independence, civic cooperation on an equal basis with others, efficiency, businesslike administration and Americanism, these were the characteristics of the Church in this period.

In this the diocese reflected the evolving character of American religious pluralism. Once the majority of Americans may have taken it for granted that theirs was a Protestant country, but by the turn of the century it was clear, at least in the northeast and much of the middle west, that the religious leadership of both the nation and its local communities would have to be shared with Catholics, if not yet with Jews. With World War I, this increasingly institutionalized Christian pluralism was accepted more or less. For the Catholic Church, this achievement brought almost as many problems as did its earlier exclusion. The Church still would have to demonstrate its ability to manage its own affairs, and absorb its still not fully organized immigrants. At the same time, it would have to prove its devotion to the public good by joining with others to fulfill common civic and national responsibilities. Pluralism implied both a degree of separation, as each church maintained its own distinct institutions, and a degree of cooperation, as each was called upon to meet such public needs as education, social welfare and wartime mobilization. For the Catholic Church, with its exclusive claims and still fresh sense of minority status, this was no small challenge. Its leaders had to maintain and expand a set of institutions at once Catholic and American. To do so, they would have to persuade their people to support their own churches and schools, while helping them fulfill their responsibilities as increasingly successful and respectable American citizens. The immigrant Church would have to become an American Church, but an American Church still clearly and unmistakably Catholic.

John Grimes was born in Ireland in 1852. Educated as a young man by the Jesuits, he received his seminary training in Quebec and Montreal and was ordained by Bishop McNeirny in 1882. He was assigned as assistant to Father O'Hara at St. Mary's in Syracuse, where he lent his considerable talents to the completion of the long-awaited church. He left briefly to serve at Whitesboro, but returned to become pastor of St. Mary's after O'Hara's death in December 1889. In 1904, when the move of the cathedral took place, Grimes stayed on as rector. In 1909, at Ludden's request, he was made coadjutor bishop and thus automatically became bishop when Ludden died in 1912. Grimes was a well educated man, with a taste for nineteenth century Irish and English history. His priests joked about his avocation for billiards, with

his assistants summoned for games in the evening on the third floor of the cathedral residence. He owned a farm in Jordan and had an interest in scientific agriculture. His financial acumen was evident at his death, when he left a substantial personal legacy to the Grimes Foundation, established before his death to manage various forms of church property. He genuinely loved children, especially orphans for whom he established a summer camp near his farm. He also was adept at ecclesiastical politics. On one of his three trips to Europe, he befriended Archbishop Cerretti, later papal nuncio in France. He sustained this valuable contact with regular gifts, including Tiffany silver and products from his Jordan farm.

During Grimes' 10-year leadership of the diocese, he was guided by a single theme, the need to secure the independence of the Church by strengthening its ability to support its work from its own resources. Clearly, those resources were increasing. Two annual diocesan collections, one for administration and another for seminary education, regularly brought in approximately $12,000. With the backing of a special appeal, Grimes constructed a new chancery office to house his small but growing diocesan bureaucracy. Annual collections for home and foreign missions, for maintenance of the Holy Places in Palestine and for the papacy generated increasing amounts of money. The Holy See also received a steady stream of donations from special appeals and fees for permissions and appointments. On each of the bishop's ad limina visits to Rome, Grimes presented the pope with a purse which helped put his diocese on the ecclesiastical map, no longer as a mission church, but one carrying its full weight with the other churches of the world.

Funds for diocesan use and for contributions to the larger Church had to come from the parishes. Pastors, so involved in fundraising of their own, were now also objects of appeals, and expected to demonstrate the loyalty of their congregations by meeting diocesan assessments. At the sixth diocesan synod, priests were told they would not be considered for "promotion" unless they responded to these collections promptly. At the same time, the increasing prosperity of the Church was reflected in the rise of priests' salaries, which reached $1,000 for pastors in the Ludden years. In 1914, the diocesan council raised the pay of assistants from $500 to $600. Five years later, after the rise in prices occasioned by the war, a committee of priests requested that pastors' salaries be raised to $1,500 and assistants to $720. The bishop and consulters sought a plan to reach that goal by allowing pastors to hold some legitimate fund-raising event or special collection and take from it $500 plus another $100

Bishop John Grimes (Photo: Chancery Archives)

for each assistant, while avoiding any possible dissatisfaction among the faithful.

The basis of a self-reliant church rested in the parishes over which the clergy presided. Ludden's understanding of parish life was shaped by the formative years of the diocese of Albany. He admired strong independent pastors like Barry, Clune and Kennedy. Grimes was the product of a more mature Church. When he named Father William Howard to succeed Barry at St. Paul's in Oswego, he warned him of the dangers of replacing a dominating pastor, as he had replaced O'Hara two decades earlier. "Be not quick to recast (the parish) on modern lines,"

171

he wrote. "This will have to come slowly."
What he meant by "modern lines" was
evident in his own approach to parish
ministry. At St. Mary's, Grimes had been a
businesslike and self-confident pastor who
expected his people to quietly and dependa-
bly support their Church. Unlike O'Hara, he
did not threaten them from the altar or visit
their homes with his hands outstretched.
Instead, envelopes replaced fairs and bazaars,
pew rents were raised to a level appropriate
to the prosperity of the congregation and
collection of these rents was placed on a
semiannual rather than quarterly basis. The
Church no longer would be the disciplinary
agency for the "wild Irish," nor would it
depend on the personality of the pastor.
Instead, it would be a community of respectable citizens, accepting their responsibility to
provide for their own needs without appeals
to others, embarassing internal disputes or the
use of gimmicks. Avoiding fairs and "appeals
to the public," the parish, in Grimes words,
was able now "to bear our own burdens, to
support our own Church."

At the same time, Grimes wished to
broaden the services of the Church, so that all
the religious and social needs of its people
could be met without having to turn to other
agencies. When he appointed his intimate
friend, Father George Mahon, to establish the
new parish of Most Holy Rosary in Syracuse,
they planned to build church and school
together. Eventually they hoped to have a
parish with a full range of religious, social and
cultural services, fully organized and adequately funded by the congregation.

As the *Catholic Sun* put it a few years later,
Most Holy Rosary was to be "an institutional
church with its various features for instruction
and recreation." In fact, that is what the
whole diocesan church aimed to become, so
that all the private and personal needs of its
families could be met within church-related
associations. In other words, it would be a
subculture which would enable people to
participate fully in American life, while
remaining completely and integrally Catholic.

A similar concern for self-help was evident
in Grimes' treatment of ethnic minorities.
When they demonstrated their ability to
support a church and pastor, Grimes and his
successors were prepared to help. Until that
moment came, it was futile to try to organize
the Church from the top down. When the
apostolic delegate asked why he had sent
Father Roth, who was not Italian, to serve at
St. Anthony's, which "the Italians had built,"
Grimes responded in some heat that not more
than 10 percent of the money came from the
Italian community. The remainder came from
neighboring parishes and from the Irish ladies
in the St. Anthony's Society. "We have to rely
entirely on people outside the parish," Grimes
wrote. "The adult Italians in general will not
support the church."

The Italian people were pleased with Roth's
work with the children and his visits to the
sick, and his replacement by an Italian priest
would be a "calamity":

> *The Italian clergy seems to me to be
> unable to cope with the difficulties
> which we encounter in church build-
> ing. They lack energy and vigor and
> do not appear to have much zeal in
> their countrymen's welfare. I have just
> established a parish in Binghamton
> under very favorable auspices, to
> which I have appointed an Italian
> priest, but I have great doubts as to
> his ability to cope with the difficulties
> of the situation dependably.*

EDUCATION AND CHARITY

Grimes' dedication to self-reliance and
independence was most evident in education.
Bishop Ludden regularly had appointed a
diocesan school board, which occasionally

consulted with pastors. However, schools were the exclusive responsibility of the parish or, in the case of the orphanages, industrial schools and private academies, of the sponsoring religious community. At a synod in 1914, however, Grimes announced formation of a new, all-priest school commission. After a study, the commission found that much progress had been made since Ludden's pessimistic assessment two decades earlier. There were now 27 parish schools with 12,000 students. Two more were under construction. Twelve of the 16 parishes in the city of Syracuse had schools, three of eight in Binghamton, three of seven in Oswego, and seven of 12 in Utica. In addition, Immaculate Conception in Fulton, St. Mary's in New York Mills and two parishes in Rome had their own schools. Parish schools were free, supported by the parishes and the service of women religious. Classrooms were extremely crowded, with 70 children in a class not uncommon. The orphan asylums educated another 1,200 children, while St. Vincent's Industrial School in Utica trained 150 "wayward boys."

High school education still was regarded widely as a luxury because the number of students able or willing to pursue advanced studies was limited. St. John's and Sacred Heart Academies in Syracuse, Utica Catholic Academy at St. John's in Utica and St. Joseph's Academy at St. Patricks in Binghamton offered classical studies for boys and music, art, French and "finishing school" studies for girls. Only two were chartered by the New York Board of Regents. In addition to parish schools, there were several academies conducted by religious orders, which often saw such institutions as a means to raise funds to support the bulk of their work with parishes or the poor. The Franciscan Sisters in 1914 opened an expensive, high quality boarding and day school for girls. In Rome, the Sisters of the Holy Names of Jesus and

Mary conducted another independent academy for girls. Christian Brothers Academy opened in 1904, offering "a practical and Christian education" for boys, with both academic and commercial subjects. The Christian Brothers also taught for many years at Assumption Academy in Utica, but shortly after formation of the commission, a puzzling sequence of events led to their withdrawal from that school. The diocese conducted the school for two years until Xaverian Brothers arrived in 1917.

"Rather than rest on our oars and merely drift with the stream," the commission intended to seek "the highest state of efficiency in buildings and teaching staff." Under the leadership of a new superinten-

CONVENT SCHOOL GIRL

GRACE, her distinguished note,
    Poised as a cameo—
Modest her lovely throat,
    Chaste as the Long Ago.

Proudly she rears her head,
    Daughter of Christ the King;
On His Love banqueted,
    Food of His winnowing!

Compassionate, gay withal,
    Eyes schooled to pure delight;
Held in faith's radiant thrall,
    Blithe are her dreams at night.

Image of Mary's life
    Graven on mind and soul,
Smiling through joy and strife,—
    Queenly, she plays her role.

                    —*A Sister of St. Francis*

dent, Charles F. McAvoy, the school board became the most active committee the diocese had seen. Plans for new buildings or alterations of existing ones were submitted to the board for approval. A uniform list of holidays, including holy days of obligation and feasts of the patron of the community serving the school, was established. The board sought to establish "a uniform course of instruction" and to ensure the use of uniform texts ordered through the diocesan office.

Uniform examinations were prepared, with upper grades taking those of the state board of regents. Polish language schools were told to hire teachers fluent in English. The board decreed that English should be the sole language of instruction between 9 a.m. and 3 p.m., a rule that was not enforced fully. Because the board had responsibility for "Christian education," it reminded pastors of their obligation to organize a Sunday School for public school children, even if there was a parochial school in the parish. Taking an interest in public policy, the board opposed legislation prohibiting children under 12 from working during vacations. It also opposed free text books for the public schools unless they also were given to Catholic school students.

Grimes saw parochial schools as essential to the preservation of the Church, and he was convinced that their independence was assured by reliance on popular support. The earlier denial of public funds for church-related schools had been "a glorious decision," the bishop told a crowd gathered to celebrate the opening of a school at the cathedral in 1915. Public support would bring public supervision. Parochial schools then no longer would be "our schools," but would be "punctuated with fads" and subordinated to governmental policies which made "the system more important than the results." He could envision no possible compromise that Catholics could entertain. As far as Grimes was concerned, the long-debated school ques-

tion was settled.

Catholics would take care of their own needs without outside assistance of any kind. They would do so in part because what was available outside the Church was unacceptable. As Grimes put it in urging his people to support the Catholic University in Washington, "the atheistic, Godless and anti-Christian teaching in non-Catholic universities makes it especially urgent for us Catholics to support our own." Far from being a withdrawal into an isolated ghetto, this self-help approach was linked to a very optimistic view of the future, when Catholic success would demonstrate to the rest of the community the wisdom and value of Catholic teaching. That witness could not be ignored because the growth of the Church was rapidly bringing it new power in the community. In 1919, James A. McCormick, a Catholic employee in the Syracuse School Department, confidentially shared with Bishop Grimes the results of a study of local birth rate for the years 1914-1918. In 1918 approximatley 55 percent of the 4,566 births in the city were to parents both born in the United States, a goodly percentage of Irish and German extraction. Six hundred and nine were of Italian parentage, and another 654 were from parents born in Austria, Russia or Poland (some of these may have been Jewish, but the bulk were undoubtedly Polish or Slavic Catholics). McCormick was confident that "within 20 years the population of this city will be more than 50% R.C. — a figure that those who come after us may find satisfaction in contemplating, as I do in anticipating."

Self-help and independence also characterized Grimes' approach to charity. He was as moralistic as Ludden, attacking prostitution, gambling, political corruption, immodest dress, dancing, intemperance and divorce. Less typical was what Grimes saw as the corollary of this moralism, a powerful emphasis on charity. In one sermon, Grimes described in great detail the demands in both the Old and New Testaments for the rich to relieve the plight of the poor. God "has commanded under frightful penalties all those to whom He has given a sufficiency or more to aid the needy and the poor," he argued. The "fires of hell" awaited those who "deafened their ears to the cries of the needy."

"This frightful punishment" did not mean that it was a "crime to be rich." Far from it, because "riches is one of the great blessings of heaven, one of the powerful means God has given us to obtain eternal glory." Unfortunately, failure to share their riches was the "disgrace of Christians." "What have our wealthy Catholics done for the forwarding of the works of the Gospel, at least in these regions?" Grimes asked. "Absolutely nothing." Pointing to local hospitals and orphanages, Grimes claimed that these "monuments represent the public charity of the people" because they long had depended on the generosity of non-Catholics. In contrast, few Catholics left money to the Church in their wills. They remember "everybody but God into whose presence they must go." He concluded that, in charity as in education, the gospel demand binding on conscience was "to support our own."

Local orphanages and hospitals in fact had relied on broad non-Catholic support, as Grimes claimed. Catholic resources still were limited, and charitable institutions served people regardless of faith, so these public appeals remained appropriate, if regrettable. Over Ludden's objections, the Sisters of Charity carried out such an appeal in Utica for a new St. John's orphanage, which opened in November 1912 in a building that cost more than $200,000. In 1918, the New York State Board of Charities found the facilities of St. Mary's Hospital and Infant Home inadequate and dangerous, and the bishop was forced to lead an emergency campaign in

which he successfully appealed to "the generous citizens of Syracuse." In these drives, one underway before he took office, the other a sudden emergency, Grimes appealed to the public. But, on his own projects, he challenged his people to take up their responsibilities themselves. His first goal was to provide a home for the aged, "the only link now wanting in the charitable chain" of hospitals, maternity homes, infant homes and orphanages. Many older Catholic couples had no home and "to send them to separate institutions would be cruel in the extreme." He described the plight of widows and widowers who, even when cared for by children, could not avoid feeling "simply tolerated."

"In the name of these," he called on Catholics to help him build a home "in which these brothers and sisters of ours in faith shall be housed." Property was purchased, but the collection was less than expected and, when enough money was in hand, the war increased the price of labor and materials and construction had to be postponed.

The home for the aged was not the only missing "link" of Catholic charities. The Church made little provision for single young men and women living alone in the city. Like all their contemporaries, Catholics were concerned most about the dangers facing a young woman new to the community and lacking the shelter and support of her own family. Grimes lived in the cathedral residence and the diocese had full possession of Bishop Ludden's home on Lafayette Street. In March 1915, Grimes brought together 25 prominent Catholic women to serve on the board of a new institution to be called the Ludden Home for Girls, where single women working or studying in Syracuse could be assisted to "attain the standard of Catholic womanhood." The board raised funds, hired a house manager, solicited donations of furnishings and began accepting residents.

Much was changing in the world of charities. Many dioceses established charitable bureaus to centralize social service work and make it more efficient. They made it more efficient by eliminating duplication, coordinating resources and personnel, and placing fundraising on a firm foundation with a single, annual charities appeal to eliminate the sometimes competing appeals of a variety of Catholic institutions. Instead of organizing a diocesan charities office, however, Grimes established a foundation empowered to receive property and donations for charitable purposes. He saw it as a vehicle through which the diocese eventually could provide its own institutions, like the home for the aged. When he died, he left substantial amounts of money and property to the foundation, including land and money for a home for boys over the age of 16 to be located at the House of Providence. He also left the land on which the camp and cottage at Cross Lake stood, with instructions to maintain it as a summer place for the sisters and children of St. Vincent's Asylum.

PUBLIC ISSUES

While urging Catholics to "support our own" in parishes, schools and charities, Grimes knew quite well that his increasingly prosperous, secure church was now also responsible to provide moral leadership on public affairs. As pastor and bishop, he welcomed this public role which became increasingly important with the outbreak of war in Europe in 1914. An ardent champion of Irish freedom, Grimes was deeply suspicious of England and therefore had little sympathy with the Allied cause. In late November 1916, he held a Mass of Thanksgiving at the cathedral to express gratitude that American young men were not "maimed and lying dead upon the bloody battlefields." Grimes denied that the war was being fought

for "any great idea." A few months later, however, Woodrow Wilson took the United States into the war to "make the world safe for democracy." Grimes, like most Americans, now indeed saw the war as one in which great ideals were at stake. In 1915, Grimes had turned down an invitation to appoint priests to serve on a civic committee for Belgian relief with the excuse that his priests were too busy. But with the outbreak of the war, he placed his entire church at the nation's disposal. Writing to the mayor of Syracuse, Grimes said:

I wish to place, through you, at the service of our country the institutions of the diocese. These institutions consist of hospitals, schools and asylums, with their corps of nurses, attendants and teachers, to be used for any purpose the government may require. We also offer ourselves as emergency may demand, for while we are not very warlike in times of peace, we stand ready to bid our heart's blood flow when an insult is offered our flag.

He offered prayers for victory and called upon his people to participate actively in national mobilization. "Our God and our country are the watchwords of our creed," he told his priests. "They are emblazoned over our altars; they are frescoed on our schools, and they are written on the heart of every loyal Catholic." To nurse, feed and house the soldiers, those at home had to "sacrifice our pleasures ... restrain our appetites, and give liberally of our means." Perhaps concerned like the government about less-than-enthusiastic support from the Irish and German population, he spoke strongly:

Let there be no slackers among us, no critics of the methods employed. These are always subterfuges to escape our

176

obligations, cloaks to cover our un-patriotic souls.

War brought a convergence of energies which led to unprecedented cooperation across denominational lines. The American bishops formed the National Catholic War Council and agreed to join in a single fundraising campaign with Protestant and Jewish agencies to cover the costs of services to soldiers. In a letter introducing the county campaign managers of this national drive, Grimes told the priests to instruct their people that their generosity would be the "gauge of their level of Americanism ... any American citizen who refuses to subscribe to this American-wide appeal is unworthy to be sheltered beneath the Stars and Stripes." In that same letter, Grimes noted the revolutionary effect of the war experience on interfaith relations:

Up to the time of the war, we all know how bitterly the religious question was discussed and how exclusive were some religious organizations. But no sooner had the trumpet of war sounded, than every vestige of this ancient wrangle disappeared and our boys, regardless of creed, stood forth shoulder to shoulder ready to die in defense of the Nation. So completely was this question obliterated that the man who would now dare to raise this issue, under any pretext, should be looked upon as a traitor to the Country's cause, a defamer of the American soldier, and a sacreligious calumniator of the copious streams of blood that flow from the veins of American citizens in defense of liberty ... O may that blood, comingling with the sands of the battlefield, wash out forever the blots of religious bigotry from this country in which such soldiers are bred.

Wartime hysteria, added to systematic efforts by the Wilson administration to sell the war to the American people, led to efforts to end German-language teaching in the schools. It was a new prejudice against German-Americans and a general concern to make sure that "foreigners" supported American ideals. In Syracuse as elsewhere, "Americanization" committees promoted patriotism and loyalty. Father McEvoy's cryptic report for 1919 showed that this pressure was felt:

Explanation was made to the local Americanization League concerning the work of our schools, in particular our so-called foreign schools, as a factor in Americanization. We should assert we have no 'foreign' schools in Syracuse; they are all American. The Polish pastors of the local churches have been anxiously responsive in their cooperation in this work.

The Americanization League grew out of a similar committee formed by the Chamber of Commerce in 1916. Eventually Italian, Polish, Jewish, Greek, Armenian, Syrian, Albanian and Ukranian groups allied with the league to promote Americanization through language instruction and citizenship training. With the help of Father McEvoy, two such programs were established at Catholic schools, taught by specially trained Catholic public school teachers. Work among the Italians by Mrs. Helena Foley at St. Anthony's settlement and Madonna House was taken as a model by state officials. These and other examples of Church cooperation with citizenship programs undoubtedly helped defuse the renewal of anti-Catholicism which followed the war. McEvoy stated in his 1920 report that, while hostility to parochial schools was evident in Florida, Georgia and Michigan, there was "comparatively little agitation adverse to our schools" in the diocese and "no opposition ... among the more intelligent members of the community."

If the war forced the Church to modify its previous exclusivism, it also brought benefits. Catholics at all levels proved without question the depth of their patriotism and the exact correspondence between the demands of their faith and the requirement of citizenship. In November 1918, priests and people gathered at the cathedral on Thanksgiving Day to celebrate with Bishop Grimes the end of "this wicked war." Grimes had no illusions about the peace. "Democracy for the world, the unfurled banner of President Wilson, has been accepted outwardly by the nations, but to have it written into their constitutions is another story," the bishop said. "The kings with their ancient twaddle of divine right are not so easily removed from the world." While giving thanks for the war's end and the "glorious part our soldiers have taken," joy should be "confined to our own land" and prayers directed toward the peace conference. Meanwhile, there was the work of reconstruction. There was a Victory Loan campaign to care for the wounded and ease the return of soldiers to civilian life, another "great index of the true American." In March 1919, the bishop asked the pastors to select two or three influential parishioners to call on employers and ask them to "give the soldier boys returning home the first opportunity to take their place again in the business world." This was yet another cooperation with a government-sponsored campaign.

One measure of the success of the war was Ireland. In January 1919, Grimes told the priests the armistice was "by no means the end of the war." The "most important part ... rearrangement of the countries of Europe" was yet to come. One nation "in particular which cries to us at this time," Grimes thought, was Ireland, "the oldest and purest nation in Christian civilization." Though Ireland had been for "eight hundred years in captive bonds," she was not listed among the

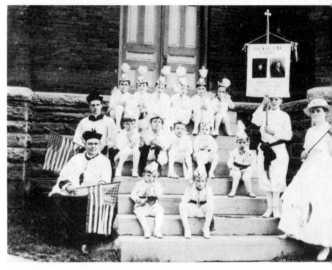

Miss Kate E. Quinn poses with her Victory Boys at St. Paul's church in Norwich after a Thanksgiving service on June 13, 1919. The patriotic event was sponsored by the Catholic Soldiers Field and Home Bureau. John Curley, a captain with the Victory Boys, holds the banner proclaiming the hope of Catholic Americans: "Peace on earth to men of good will." (Photo: St. Paul's, Norwich)

"enslaved nations" who were to be liberated. England, "her unfriendly master," when "in dire distress" had been the "loudest declaimer of democracy and freedom for small nations." However, now England was trying "to overthrow the fourteen propositions which, in the days of distress, [England] cheerfully accepted from our great President." In May, Grimes presided at a Mass for the Irish heroes executed for the Easter rebellion of 1916. In August, he joined 8,000 people in welcoming Irish leader Eamon de Valera to Syracuse. When the Irish question failed to win a hearing at Versailles and England set its face against independence, Grimes urged his people to pray that the Irish people would be patient and that God would loosen the grasp of the "iniquitous tyrant." Grimes and many of his priests made substantial financial contributions to Irish organizations and made no apology. Irish freedom, like the Allied war effort, was a cause that was religious, patriotic and just.

The war clarified the situation in which American Catholics found themselves. On the one hand, they were proud of what they had accomplished and were determined to provide their own churches, schools and charitable institutions to meet their own needs. On the other hand, the Church and its members were now very American. Their enthusiastic support for the war reflected more than a need to answer charges of disloyalty. They believed in the nation's ideals, were grateful for the opportunities it provided and insisted that they were not "foreigners," but loyal citizens. Yet their Americanism had to be tempered if they were to avoid seeing the Church as merely one element of national religious life, to be tested and evaluated in terms of its contributions to public welfare. This might lead to a tolerance and good will which could erode the distinctiveness and solidarity needed to ensure continuing support for Catholic institutions. Catholics would have to be convinced that the sacrifices they made for the Church were, at the same time, contributions to civic and national well being. Being a good Catholic also would have to be good Americanism. One answer lay in an increasing emphasis on the decadence of American culture, especially the decline of traditional values of marriage and family life. By promoting and defending its own teachings on marriage, sexuality and the family, Catholics were defending traditional American ideals as well.

CATHOLIC CHARITIES

Grimes died in 1922 and, in February 1923, Daniel J. Curley, pastor of Our Lady of Solace church in the East Bronx in New York City, was named the third bishop of Syracuse.

Born in 1871, he was Syracuse's first American-born bishop. He attended St. Michael's parochial school and St. Francis Xavier Jesuit High School in New York City, studied for the priesthood at the Troy seminary, spent two years studying in Rome and was ordained in 1894. For the next six years, he served as assistant at Holy Name parish and then became secretary to Archbishop Corrigan. When Corrigan died a year later, his successor, Archbishop John Farley, asked Curley to remain, but he preferred parish work and was given a new parish, Our Lady of Solace in a working class neighborhood in the East Bronx. The parish grew rapidly. When Curley left as a bishop 21 years later, Our Lady of Solace had a church, school, rectory and convent sitting on 23 city lots, with the buildings free of debt and a balance of $30,000 in the bank. Curley was an extraordinary example of a new breed of clergyman suited for a fully developed and increasingly confident Catholic community. He was a careful man who wrote out every speech, even the most informal, kept careful records and studied all the new methods of organizing Church work. Presiding over a diocese in the midst of rapid expansion, he showed the same concern for sound development, total trust in the Church and confident engagement with the wider community he had demonstrated as a pastor.

Curley was as devoted as Grimes to independence and self-reliance, but he brought to Syracuse modern methods of administration. His first chance to show his priorities came with Catholic Charities. When the Syracuse Community Chest was organized in 1922, Grimes enrolled several Catholic agencies and gave the drive his personal support. During the first year, Catholic institutions received only $45,000, a sum many regarded as unfair. When Grimes died, Monsignor Albert Hayes, the administrator of the diocese, appointed Father Alexis Hopkins director of Catholic Welfare in Syracuse to protect Catholic interests in Community Chest. Hopkins helped double the allocation, with one grant given for a local Catholic welfare office staffed by Hopkins and an assistant to provide a central office for Catholic relief work. When Bishop Curley arrived, he appointed Hopkins diocesan director of charities and moved quickly to establish a modern department. Curley authorized Hopkins to survey local needs. His report showed that institutional services were strong, but many programs common elsewhere had not developed yet in Syracuse. Only 23 percent of the 102 parishes had organized relief societies. There were 24 parish conferences of the St. Vincent de Paul Society, but five were inactive and there was no central clearinghouse for case records of people moving from one locality to another. Sixteen ladies aid societies worked independently of St. Vincent de Paul. The Church had no trained parish visitors, and no social workers assigned to public or non-Catholic hospitals or homes for the aged. Only one hospital had a dispensary. There was little follow-up on children leaving orphanages. Only two had a social worker to deal with adoption or placement. There were no resources to find foster homes or safeguard adopted children. There were no day nurseries, and only one diocesan and four parish summer camps, though the demand for camping was growing.

About one-third of the children appearing in children's court were Catholics, and 77 Catholic boys and girls were on probation, but only one organization in the city provided a social worker to deal with them. There was no Catholic Big Brother program, although 10 Catholic men were enrolled in the nonsectarian program. Only two parishes had Boy Scout troops and only nine had any organized recreation for boys, while there were two Girl Scout troops and 12 parishes with recreation

for girls. In contrast, there were 100 non-Catholic Boy Scout and 60 Girl Scout troops in the diocese which, together with the Campfire Girls, were drawing Catholic children away "from Catholic associations and Catholic guidance." So were the YMCA and YWCA, one-third of whose members were Catholics. The Church was "doing practically nothing" for the 20,000 Catholic children in public schools "on their playtime," although it was "generally recognized that this is the most dangerous time for the adolescent boy and girl and that juvenile delinquency and spare time are closely related." There were 13 theaters, 75 movie houses, 57 dance halls, 71 pool rooms, 35 playgrounds and 15 swimming pools in the diocese. "To offset these we have only nine non-parochial clubrooms and halls." There was no room registry to help Catholic girls and women find "safe quarters." There were three settlement houses under Catholic auspices to serve a total immigrant population of almost 38,000. "Only one Catholic organization is promoting citizenship regularly; and two are engaged in teaching English; while one is preventing exploitation of immigrants. The immigrant problems of the diocese are unusually great and present a large field for social workers to cultivate. But this requires goodly funds."

The needs were great, and the new bishop was fresh from New York, which recently had raised millions of dollars for charity. Curley decided to do the same, and launched the first diocesan-wide fundraising campaign in 1924 with a goal of $1,200,000. To run the campaign, Curley turned to a professional fundraiser, Harvey Hill, who had helped run the national Red Cross drive at the beginning of the war, was loaned by the Red Cross to the American bishops and represented them in the United War Work Campaign of 1918. After the war, he ran the $5,000,000 charities campaign in New York. With these credentials, Hill said privately that Syracuse would

Bishop Daniel J. Curley (Photo: Chancery Archives)

be "apple pie." Advanced gifts were solicited from businesses and wealthy donors, and parish committees were organized and trained. Eventually, 6,000 volunteer workers visited between 10,000 and 15,000 homes.

Curley understood that this drive was a new and important step forward for the diocese. To this point, the people had been called upon for money, but most of the time for parish projects. Fairs and other fundraising events for orphanages and hospitals had depended heavily upon the support of non-Catholics, at least until Grimes' drive for the aged. Now the whole diocese was being challenged. Religious orders had produced the "magnificent work of the past," but that work had been mostly along "parochial lines" because there was neither the occasion nor machinery for close cooperation. Now there were agencies and structures to better allow them to ease suffering, safeguard morality and

provide Christian education. All of this had become more costly, but also more susceptible to cooperation and diocesan-wide activity. As Curley put it, the campaign "has lifted us up from the narrow and critical confines of parochialism, giving us a broader, more liberal vision." He said it "furnished the leaders of the laity with greater facilities, not only of becoming better acquainted with each other, but of entering into a more intimate relationship with the bishop and clergy of the diocese," making them more "of one heart and one mind."

The campaign was a great success. Hill reported that more than 50,00 Catholics contributed, pledging $1,700,000, 50 percent above the original quota. With financial support assured, Curley relegated the Grimes Foundation to a holding company and obtained a new charter for the Bishop's House of Charity, a diocesan office of Catholic Charities. Parishes were ordered to establish St. Vincent de Paul conferences to provide food, fuel, shelter and clothing. A central clearinghouse would investigate cases served for more than three months and assist families or individuals moving from one parish to another. The central office also provided training for parish volunteers in interviewing and recordkeeping techniques. This welfare bureau took over the work of the community centers serving Italian immigrants and provided services for Catholics in state penal institutions. Two social workers were hired to handle family problems, adoption and foster home placement.

The Church had become a recipient of Community Chest funds and, therefore, had a responsibility to support this drive and account to the public regarding the use of those funds. At the same time, Curley wanted to unify and expand the Church's own social service agencies and programs. Doing both might be difficult. In May 1924, the bishop asked the pastors to support the Community

Chest drive "whatever our personal sentiment may be." There had been criticism of lack of support the previous year and the bishop felt that "this attitude, or even the appearance of it, would be injudicious." At the same time, he enclosed a private memorandum. While insisting that there was no intention of "underestimating or discrediting the public charities system," he expressed concern that many non-Catholic programs were "merely philanthropic" and might "become altogether heartless, cold and calculating," especially considering the "meager means" at their disposal.

In his public letter backing Community Chest, Curley tried to provide the appearance of active support, while in no way reducing support for the Church's own charitable work. As he told the priests:

While no doubt you observe the meaning running throughout the article, in relation to the lack of character and ennobling motive in the administration of public and much of the protestant variety of charitable and welfare work, and the reasons that prompt the Catholic church to impose such sacrifices upon its members, to erect and control its own institutions of charity and education, yet it was intended ... so to state these facts as not to offend the sensibilities of our non-Catholic brethren. A veil is thrown upon it, yet thin enough, I think, to make its meaning discernable, at least to the initiated.

CENTRALIZATION

Fulfilling public responsibilities while maintaining Catholic support for the Church's own institutions was only one problem. Another was that new professional methods could lead to conflict with previously autonomous re-

ligious communities and with pastors unconvinced that changes were needed.

Catholic Charities and non-Catholic social service had in common a desire to make the relief of social problems more efficient and effective. In January 1926, Father Joseph L. May, a young Syracuse priest completing a masters thesis in social work at Catholic University, wrote that "the modern problems of social welfare work are so numerous and so complicated that it has long been seen that they cannot be dealt with except in a scientific manner and through well functioning and properly directed organizations." Unfortunately, many in charge of Church-sponsored charitable agencies were unfamiliar with these new methods and had little business experience. However, the local Church, as Hopkins had found, had yet to expand its services to cover the wide range of individual and family problems. In addition, the institutions owned by religious communities had "a certain independence of the diocesan authority." The Grimes Foundation, followed by the bishop's House of Charity, represented an effort to establish "diocesan control" in order to modernize and expand social services.

Centralization and the use of professionally trained social workers would displace, to some extent, the amateurs who previously had managed charitable activity and limit the independence they hitherto had enjoyed.

The reorganization of relief work was carried out under a commission of the most talented and influential priests in the diocese. Each parish was expected to provide basic relief for its members, but the new central office would handle interaction with other public and private agencies. New offices would be established, beginning with Utica, not to provide relief, but to make its provision more practical and effective. Any case requiring actions with courts or public social agencies would be handled through

Catholic Charities. Many priests were upset with these new developments, with the large quotas assigned during the 1924 campaign, and with the costs associated with Loretto Rest, the diocesan home for the aged planned by Grimes and finally opened in October 1927. Planners attempted to avoid the atmosphere of an institution and provide the comfort and warmth of a home. But expenses were high, and the deficit absorbed a large portion of the annual diocesan budget.

These problems, and the independent style of Father Hopkins, led to a devastating report by the chancellor in January 1928. Hopkins was accused of making "many mistakes, some of a serious nature," delegating responsibility to "inexperienced subordinates" and expanding social service beyond diocesan resources. The report gave evidence of deep hostility to the whole diocesan charities project. It complained that much of the work was "useful but unnecessary," that the professional social workers hired by Hopkins were impractical and idealistic, and that their case work and scientific methods appealed "rather to Protestant and humanitarian than to sound Catholic principles." The diocese had gotten along well before the office was established, the new program had grown without the agreement and support of the priests, and it now needed to be cut back drastically. Beyond a widespread dislike of Father Hopkins, this report reflected the tension which existed, and would persist, between the professional style of social workers and the more personal style of pastors. It also reflected the resentment which a growing diocesan bureaucracy created among pastors strapped for funds and unconvinced that the benefits of Catholic Charities merited its costs. The charities office was not dismantled, or even seriously reduced, but efforts were made to bring the budget at Loretto Rest under control and Hopkins was transferred to St. Ambrose parish in Endicott. More impor-

tantly, the extensive youth programs, family services, probation work and other programs called for in the 1924 report were not developed until a decade later.

If Curley preferred to maintain and develop a full network of social services under Church control, he knew the complexities involved, and the need to remain part of Community Chest and cooperate with government agencies. It was strategy the wisdom of which was confirmed when the depression and World War II led to a vast expansion of public welfare services. On education, however, there were no ambiguities and few compromises with the public sector. Curley, more than his predecessors, was committed fully to Catholic schools. On the fifth anniversary of his leadership, Curley stated that he found the diocese "exceedingly well equipped with elementary and high schools" and was pleased with their "exceptional method and efficiency." To the extent this was true, it was a result of the work of the sisters, pastors and people, but also of the leadership of Charles McEvoy. The school office was one of the first efforts in Syracuse at modern, centralized administration. In addition to working to develop uniform texts, curriculum and calendar, McEvoy and his successors did what they could to improve the quality of instruction, and guide the building of new schools and the expansion of old ones. Many rules limited parish autonomy and pastoral authority. The board, for example, centralized the purchasing of textbooks and set salaries for teaching sisters "not subject to change by any pastor." No "religious articles, flowers, wreaths, veils, medals, prayer books (or) uniforms" could be sold in the schools. Complaints against any superior or sister were to be taken up with the school superintendent, who would consult with the superiors of the community and report to the executive committee of the board. Neither pastors nor parents were to communicate with religious order superiors directly, in spite of the fact that the pastor had recruited the sisters, paid them and was explicitly responsible for the teaching of religion. Finally, parishes without schools were responsible for tuition charges for their children enrolled in a Catholic elementary or high school outside their parish.

Here again there was grass roots resistance. In February 1929, revised per capita assessments to meet the expanded work of the education office were sent to the pastors and opposition to this centralization came into the open. In Syracuse, Binghamton and Utica, priests objected to the per capita tax and suggested that a budget be prepared and assessments made on the basis of the parish's financial standing, as was done with other diocesan fundraising. In addition, priests objected to the rule that parishes with students attending schools outside the parish pay a charge of $12 for grammar school and $25 for high school. Instead they suggested that parents be billed directly and that only charity cases be referred to the parish for payment. On June 5, a committee of priests met with the board, which then voted to retain the per capita tax. However, several weeks later, at the bishop's direction, the board rescinded the rule requiring pastors to pay for their students attending schools outside the parish.

The caution with which the leading priests of the diocese approached the formation of a central Catholic welfare office, the criticism of Hopkins and the emerging professional elite of social work professionals, and the resistance of the priests to expansion of the diocesan school office all indicated that Curley's vision of a fully organized diocesan church could not be carried out as long as the energies of most priests and lay people were focused on the parish. The bishops and more professionally oriented priests understood that, in the long run, the goal of the Church "to support our own" could be achieved only if the Church matched the quality and efficiency of public institutions of education and charity. Pastors undoubtedly agreed in principle, but they were pressed by the costs of services at the parish level, and they resented the imposition of policies and financial assessments made without their participation or consent. In theory, of course, the bishop's authority was absolute. But in practice, his ability to act effectively depended on the support of his priests, especially the pastors.

Yet, in this area too, Curley's efforts at centralization met opposition. The power of the bishop had centered always on his control of the appointment of priests. He alone determined who became pastors and the parishes to which they were assigned. Early in the history of the diocese, priests were allowed to apply for parishes which had been named to have irremovable rectors. Even after the new code of canon law ended that requirement, Bishop Grimes continued to accept applications for vacancies, but Curley ended this practice. In March 1925, he told the priests that he always would give attention to meritorious service in making appointments, but his first concern would be to "select a priest best adapted to the character of the parish and the temperament of its laity." While priests might let him know if they were satisfied with their current assignment, he no longer would accept applications for vacancies which were a source of division among the clergy and, at times, embarassed the bishop. Drawing once again on his New York experience, Curley intervened more directly in parish work. He ordered that the first sermon at 40 hours devotion be on vocations. He ordered every pastor to establish the St. Vincent dePaul Society, the Propogation of the Faith and the Sodality of the Holy Childhood. He decreed that the last Mass on Sundays, Christmas and Easter would be at 11 a.m., ending the practice in some parishes of a 12:30 p.m. Mass. He combined his appeal for charities with some not-very-subtle criticism of his priests. "Some of the most zealous, most loyal and most religious pastors in the world are, without realizing it, very narrow and selfish," he told the clergy during the 1924 campaign. Later he described their support of music reform as "loyalty of the bluest type," but he took note of resistance to charitable and educational changes by asking the priests: "for whom are you laboring in your parish, your own personal glory or the glory of God?" However justified this implied criticism may have been, it was bound to irritate pastors and limit their cooperation with diocesan projects. Because he was from outside the diocese and determined to build a more centralized administration, Curley lacked Grimes' fraternal closeness to local priests. To make matters worse, his image of diocesan organization which compared the priest's relationship to the bishop to the bishop's relationship with the Holy Father, seemingly excluded personal friendship and intimacy. When Father Hopkins, exiled to Endicott, presumed on his service to the bishop to complain about his assistants, Curley quickly rebuked him, leaving Hopkins angry and bitter. Yet, Curley could not easily compel pastors to cooperate with diocesan policy, or with one another. In Norwich, Father Joseph Tiernan simply ignored a series of efforts by Grimes and Curley to limit his public statements on prohibition and on local, state and national politics, and to force him to treat the lay leaders of his parish with greater respect. In Utica, Father Charles Oley regularly attacked neighboring priests, who responded in kind. In such cases, the bishop could rebuke a priest for extreme language, but there was little he could do if the priest ignored him, except to remove him from the parish, an extreme step which might divide the clergy and, by encouraging dissidents,

undercut all clerical authority. The centralized administration Curley thought required by modern conditions could not be forced from above, especially when both money and popular support depended on the parishes which, in turn, were controlled almost competely by the priests.

MUSIC REFORM

Curley made one other effort to reform the Church from the top down. This was more successful, at least on the surface. Pope Pius X had decreed that the Church should revive the use of sacred music, particularly Gregorian chant. Curley was determined to implement these directives in the diocese. Recognizing that voluntary compliance would prove self-defeating, because one parish resisting the reforms could ruin efforts of a neighboring parish to comply, Curley told the priests that the new rules would be enforced throughout the diocese. There would be no exceptions. Curley put the matter directly to the pastors:

Now be kind enough to approach this subject with an open mind, no matter how limited may be your opportunity. Your people will probably not be favorably disposed toward it at first, and you, yourselves, may be inclined to be discouraged, because it will take considerable time to bring the employment of the method to that efficiency where you will be satisfied and where your parishioners will see its great advantages over the more secular and modern methods .... So be good enough to understand that this is a diocesan decree, and is universal and, when every parish is making an honest effort to carry it out, there will be no cause for criticism or irritation by neighboring pastors and adjoining congregations.

185

A PASSION FOR MUSIC

As Bishop Curley embarked on his campaign to reform Church music, he could draw on a long line of priests and lay people who believed that music can lead people in devotion to God, helping them find beauty and culture along the way.

Dean Michael Barry of a previous generation was one such man. As pastor of St. Paul's parish in Oswego, Barry spent much of his personal funds to rebuild the magnificent organ at his church, making it one of the finest instruments in the country. For the 1894 dedication concert, he invited a musician he had met in Paris — Alexandre Guilmant, one of the most renowned musicians in the world.

On Guilmant's recommendation, Barry hired as parish organist Auguste Weigand, a Belgian musician who had become a church organist at the age of seven. After Weigand died, Barry obtained the services of another accomplished Belgian organist, Dr. Charles Courboin. A decade later, Courboin left Oswego to become organist at St. Patrick's cathedral in New York City.

Today, the organ which Barry rebuilt stands in the new St. Paul's church, rebuilt a second time and still leading people in devotion to God and enjoyment of the transforming beauty of music.

In 1905, Alexandre Guilmant, a famous organist from Paris, visited Oswego to give his second concert on the organ at St. Paul's church. Pictured here (left to right) are Dean Barry; Father John Lindsman, associate pastor; Guilmant; and Charles Courboin, parish organist.

The reasons for the reform were clear. Since late in the last century, the Vatican had been disturbed by the variety of musical accompaniments in the liturgy, and particularly by the use of what was regarded as "secular music." Earlier "white lists" of acceptable music were published, but only sporadically enforced. Explaining the Vatican decrees, Curley noted that the Mass was "our greatest ritual act and the most solemn function of our holy faith." In worship, the Church attempted to help the human community "find language appropriate to the One whom it adores," including music which would "be not a tawdry imitation of the music of the mundane world" but "inspired by the sacred liturgy itself." Gregorian chant, in particular, met this test. Relatively easy to learn, and able to be sung even by untalented voices, it had been and could be again a popular music which would encourage the widest possible participation in the liturgy. Of course, Curley argued, there would be resistance to "such a radical departure." But he was sure that "the proper conception of loyalty to Holy Mother Church," which on such matters "never errs," would lead to compliance. To secure conformity, Curley went about a systematic program. Pastors, organists and music directors were summoned to a diocesan convention in June 1925. They were informed of the spirit of the decrees and told that a newly established diocesan music commission would hold workshops throughout the diocese, with the help of the Pius X School of Liturgical Music in New York.

Over the next few years, large public ceremonies became occasions to demonstrate the progress made and the potential of the music reform. The change was evident in the programs for such celebrations printed in the *Catholic Sun*. In Ludden's day, despite his concern about popular music in church, the musical programs were dominated by orchestras and by music drawn from the major modern composers. By the 1930s, Curley's reforms had taken root and programs were dominated by references to "Vatican Chant" and Gregorian chant. When Curley died in 1932, the *Sun* noted the contribution he had made and that the "matchless beauty and sincerity of the strictly liturgical chants were demonstrated again in the singing of the Bishop's funeral mass."

Just as ethnic pastors looked to American-born children to bring about the kind of participation and support required by American parishes, music reformers saw the future in children educated in Gregorian chant. The board of education in 1929 endorsed the bishop's objective "that the children of our diocese may know and love the sacred music of our Church and thereby enjoy as much as possible the melody and harmony that gave such comfort and consolation to the millions of our forefathers in the faith." Father John J.

Corbett was placed in charge of music education. He arranged to have a teacher from the Pius X School visit the city to offer courses in the Ward method of instruction in Gregorian chant, visit schools and give model lessons. Nine sisters qualified for certification to teach other teachers and repeated the process throughout the diocese. By 1932, the new director of music, Joseph F. Prendergast, could report that the teaching of music in the schools had been revolutionized thoroughly. Every child in grades four through eight was receiving preliminary instruction in chant and the only complaint was that the children had too few opportunities to sing at liturgical services, in large part because the retraining of organists was lagging behind. A priests' choir performed well at Holy Week services in the cathedral, while at Easter in the parishes, "all the masses sung were liturgical, without exception." In short, Prendergast concluded, "the liturgical movement has struck firm roots in our diocese, and great things can be expected in the near future."

Prendergast was undoubtedly overly optimistic because the improvement of choirs and the purging of profane music was not always matched by congregational participation. Outside the major urban parishes, widespread dissatisfaction with liturgical music was evident throughout the period. The ideas which shaped the liturgical movement elsewhere, particularly the theology of the Mystical Body of Christ which reoriented attitudes toward the Church and toward the role of the laity in the Church, was not discussed much in Syracuse. The relationship between the liturgy and the social mission of the Church, in which the experience of participation, community and mission emerging from communal worship spilled over into concern for the common good of society, seemed to make almost no inroads in the diocese. Instead, music reform seemed something required by Church authority, often bringing about more beautiful and impressive liturgical performance, but with little impact on the basic pastoral dynamics of the community at large. On the other hand, unlike efforts at reform in education and charities, music reform brought no overt resistance at first. However later, many of those involved believed that pastors often had complied only formally, while never enthusiastically backing the changes.

Liturgy was, of course, central to the diocesan effort "to support our own." The self-help ethic of Grimes and Curley, reflecting the experience of a self-made Church, continued to inform the life of Syracuse Catholicism. More than anything else, the Mass was the central common thread uniting the people and giving them a sense of their distinctiveness. This, in turn, provided a basis for the effort to broaden Church services, so that, as much as possible, the private and family side of people's lives would be organized around the Church and informed by the Church's faith. There was little concern with public education, only a bit more with public welfare. The Church remained primarily concerned with supporting its own programs and building its own life. This internal preoccupation reflected a deep commitment to the Church on the part of the people, a commitment which gave their culture a distinctive sense of optimism and hope in the years between World War I and World War II.

In April 1931, Curley suffered a mild heart attack and was unable to attend a provincial council held later that spring or to preside over lenten services. In November, he had to ask his friend and classmate, Bishop Walsh of Charleston, to help with confirmations. By this time, the role of the bishop was so central to the life of the Church and especially to the life of the priests that a serious illness quickly generated rumors. The *Syracuse Journal* reported that Curley was to be made an honorary archbishop and that Monsignor John J. Sheridan, pastor of St. Lucy's, would be appointed administrator. On August 3, 1932, Curley died and, once again, speculation centered on Sheridan. Born in Binghamton in 1875, Sheridan had been educated at St. Bonaventure University and St. Bernard's Seminary, where he became a close friend of Bishop McQuaid. Although ordained for the Syracuse diocese, he served for many years at St. Patricks in Owego at the request of McQuaid. There he gained some fame for his large and well organized school, the parish camp at Cazenovia Lake and his work with Italian immigrants which won him commendation from the government of Italy. Sheridan was the very embodiment of the intelligent, ambitious pastor of a major urban congregation. He befriended politicians like Governor Franklin Roosevelt. He helped people get and keep jobs with the city government and was known for his clout with local politicians, police officers and city employees. He entertained lavishly and was very popular with many of his brother priests, several of whom wrote on behalf of his appointment to Cardinal Hayes. Unfortunately, a *terna* was submitted every two years and it was from that list that the next bishop was selected. Hayes undoubtedly could have intervened, but there is no evidence he did so. In December, John A. Duffy of Newark, New Jersey, was named bishop of Syracuse. While Sheridan welcomed the new bishop, oral tradition suggests that the energetic pastor was shaken badly by the result. He became inactive, parish records were not kept and two years later he was dead, some thought of a "broken heart."

The period which followed World War I was for American Catholics the age of great organizing bishops like Cardinal William O'Connell in Boston, Cardinal Patrick Hayes in New York and Cardinal George Mundelein in Chicago. These men gained respect for the American Church in Rome and won admiration among other American leaders for their organizational genius and fervent patriotism. They were churchmen first of all. They saw the welfare and progress of their Church as their first priority and understood that Church largely in organizational terms. Their great contribution was in centralizing administration, and ensuring greater efficiency, while building more coherent systems of education and charities. Loyalty was a key virtue — lay loyalty to the Church expressed in financial support and personal participation, clerical loyalty seen in dependable fulfillment of priestly responsibilities, loyalty of religious communities in their unquestioning acceptance of the bishop's leadership. This organizational change reflected the attitudes and priorities of a self-made Church, ready to use its own resources to meet its own needs, defend its achievements against threats from without, and insist that its own work was, in and of itself, a contribution to national and civic welfare. Bishop Curley brought something of this style to Syracuse. He, more than any of his predecessors, demanded the unquestioning loyalty of his priests, but neither priests nor people were yet ready to turn beyond their parish to accept larger responsibilities. Charitable and educational organization proceeded cautiously, while no substantial effort was made to enlist lay people in diocesanwide organizations. But there was solid achievement in the parishes, steady progress in charities and spectacular growth in education.

The choices made by the Church had significant public impact. Catholics retained a strong sense of themselves as a minority in a basically Protestant country. This feeling was accentuated by attacks on foreign language groups during World War I, by Americanization campaigns during and after the war, and by the defeat of Alfred E. Smith in 1928. Yet in Syracuse, like many cities, Catholics were a very large minority. One study estimated that, in 1906, Catholics constituted almost 40 percent of the Syracuse population and two-thirds of those in the city who belonged to a church. The bishop's report to Rome in 1929 stated that Catholics were 34 percent of the population of the region and 45 percent of church members. The decision of the Church to develop a separate parochial school system could not help but weaken support for public education. Conversely, the decision to participate in the Community Chest and open Catholic charitable institutions to public considerations could only strengthen the voluntary sector in health care, child care and social services. In discussing such matters, Church leaders were at pains to explain and justify Catholic policy, and at times they may have seemed to put Church interests before the public good. But, given the size of the Catholic population and its relatively high degree of organization, Catholics and their Church could not avoid responsibility for the overall quality of public life in their community.

Curley thus had some success in modernizing diocesan administration. But mobilizing diocesan resources for charity, missions or even improved music proved difficult. Unifying the church, ensuring the faith of its members, intensifying loyalty and regularizing religious practice were still the most important needs of the diocesan Church. The pursuit of goals beyond its own institutions would prove difficult. Bishop Curley and Bishop Duffy found success when they articulated the values which distinguished Catholics from other Americans, identified those values with American ideals, and then called upon their people to express those ideals in their own separate world and champion them in moral crusades in the local community. Not charity or missionary work, but combating birth control, immoral movies and communism, would provide a direction to the energies of the maturing Catholic Church in Syracuse, as in the rest of the United States.

THE HAPPIEST
AND MOST PEACEFUL
SOCIETY

CATHOLIC CONFIDENCE IN THE INTER-WAR YEARS
1920s-1940s

I n his brilliant study of American Catholic culture in the period 1920 to 1940, *The Survival of American Innocence,* William Halsey argued that the Church in the United States was a self-confident, optimistic community, convinced it had escaped the pessimism, even despair, which gripped others in the wake of World War I. The war's devastation and disappointing outcome left many in Europe wondering whether the human community had the resources to sustain democratic ideals and institutions. The rising power of communism and fascism lent powerful support to such pessimistic conclusions. Even in the United States, the failure of the Versailles conference, the resurgence of the Ku Klux Klan, the cynicism of many writers, and the decline of movements for social reform gave rise to a similar mood. In that atmosphere, Halsey suggests, Catholics found themselves with an expanding and increasingly prosperous Church, leaders who manifested immense confidence in organizing their communities, massive buildings and impressive displays of unity, such as a huge Eucharistic Congress in Chicago in 1926.

As they looked around them, Catholics saw a world increasingly estranged, it seemed, from Christian values. Anti-Catholicism remained strong enough in 1928 to damage one of their heroes, Alfred E. Smith, but in their own communities they knew that their strength and unity now made them immune from the harsher forms discrimination they had known in the past. Yet loving America, they yearned to redeem its promise by demonstrating that its traditions and values still had defenders, Catholics, and still had a home, in the Church. In the 1920s they appeared on the defensive, but the stock market crash and the depression that followed provided a new opportunity to announce the good news that American ideals still lived; and there was a way out for the nation. If there was a touch of innocence about all this, as Halsey suggests, there was also a charm, as Catholics experienced their unity, and their enormous possibilities. Bishop Curley put it best in

1925 when he told the Catholic Daughters of America that "the church is the happiest and most peaceful society that history records and the most perfect organization the world has ever known."

The diocese of Syracuse was very well organized during the years between the World Wars, despite the limits of Bishop Curley's efforts to modernize its administration. Social action and liturgical movements which stirred the Church elsewhere had little impact in Syracuse, while the absence of a Catholic university contributed to a lack of theological controversy. Bishop Curley's critical references to parochialism suggested a certain complacency which his appeals for charities failed to overcome. Curley also tried to stir enthusiasm for home and foreign missions, ordering each parish to establish mission organizations for adults and children. But this too made little headway. At one point Curley even assisted a devoted priest, Jeremiah O'Mahoney, to establish a seminary for delayed vocations aimed at providing clergy for home mission territories in the American south and west. But this project, too, collapsed, partly because of lack of support within the diocese. Instead Catholics in Central New York devoted most of their attention to their families, parishes and schools, seemingly content with a Church solidly organized around its priests, caring for its own and hoping that, eventually, others might come to see the value of the Church and the wisdom of its teachings.

By now Catholics were well instructed in the basic elements of Curley's "happiest and most peaceful society." Local Catholics identified the Church with its organization and its hierarchy. As the fourth bishop of Syracuse, John Duffy put it, "when we once are there, on the other side of 20 centuries of intricate and confusing history, it is wonderful how simple it all is." Jesus preached the gospel and revealed the doctrines and sacraments needed for eternal life, "not as scattered seeds of truth but permanently established in a Church, under a divinely chosen vicar — the pope." "The teaching of Christ was not left to drift with the centuries," Duffy said; instead "the Savior promulgated a complete organization — a Kingdom that should be stopped by no frontier in space and should withstand the corroding action of time." Kingdom of God and Church were one, and at the center of this "complete organization" was the hierarchy. The Catholic Church was "the only one that has kept inviolable the direct revelation that God gave personally to it in the person of his first priests, the Apostles," Bishop Curley wrote. "This is our belief, and we are absolutely certain that we are correct in this belief."

Bishops saw themselves as delegates of the pope, sharing with him this mandate given to the apostles. What the pope was to the Church in the whole world, the bishop was to the Church in his part of that world. In a very real sense, he was the local Church. Just as the pope shared his mandate with the bishop, the bishop in turn shared his with his priests, so that they too were the Church in the still smaller parts of the world to which they were assigned. All the bishops shared this conviction that priests were the heart of the Church. Bishop Grimes told his priests that only they could enable people to "recognize the Church as the mouthpiece of Jesus Christ, the only commissioned teacher in the world to speak in God's name, and to point out the road to mortal man that leads heavenward." Ignoring the contribution of nuns, brothers, and Sunday School teachers, he wrote: "the instructing of the people rests almost entirely with the clergy." They must, at least, "take the initiative if success is to be won, and where they do not lead in this regard, little advance is made by the Catholic Church." Bishop Curley agreed, arguing that "the divine character of the priesthood" was "the secret of the church's power and her world-wide influence." Bishop Duffy, often reminded his priests of the "tremendous responsibility" that came with ordination, with its powers "never otherwise bestowed on mortal men."

You are the mediator between God and man. You are the dispenser of his grace, not merely through the sacraments, but, if I may say, even in a greater degree through your priestly sanctity, your priestly zeal and your priestly decorum, because, through these externals, Christians should see the alter Christus, *and in this there is an irresistible appeal to sanctification. The lack of these qualities repels and even weakens the faith.*

HOME-GROWN CLERGY

Given the extremely elevated view of the priesthood, the recruitment and training of the clergy was the bishop's most important responsibility.

In the early days, bishops were caught between their desperate need for priests and their equally pressing need for unity and discipline, a problem that persisted in national parishes through the interwar years. One solution was to accept priests for service in foreign language parishes without incardinating them into the diocese, thus allowing the bishop to dismiss them if problems should arise. Father Joseph Martincek, for example, served Slovak parishes in the diocese for almost a quarter of a century before receiving official recognition as a diocesan priest. Several other Polish, Italian and Slovak priests were accepted only under stringent conditions and were later relieved of their assignments with no grounds for appeal to Church courts.

The goal of every bishop was to obtain priests born in the United States, later priests born in the diocese itself. Syracuse was remarkably successful in developing a home grown clergy. In 1886, when the diocese was founded, 39 of it 79 priests, were born abroad; of those, 30 had been born in Ireland. Eighty-seven percent of the priests serving in the diocese were secular priests, directly under the bishop's authority; only the Franciscans were a major group of religious engaged in parish work. By 1900, 60 percent of the 109 priests in the diocese were American born, a proportion that held steady even as the diocese worked hard to recruit foreign born clergy for its national parishes. By 1917, there were 58 foreign-born clergy in Syracuse, including 10 Polish and eight Italian priests, yet the number of American-born recruits increased even more rapidly. Between 1917 and 1930 the total number of priests grew from 148 to 226, an increase of 60 percent, but the proportion of foreign born dropped to 25 percent and by 1940 it was down to 15 percent. At the same time, the percentage of those born in the diocese rose from 32 percent in 1900 to 49 percent in 1930 to 60 percent in 1940. By the Second World War the Syracuse clergy was relatively young, with an average age of 39, and home grown. A similar trend is evident in the seminary education of the diocesan clergy. Of the 30 priests in 1886 for whom evidence of education remains, 11 were educated at St.

Joseph's Provincial Seminary in Troy. By World War I, St. Bernard's in Rochester had become the favorite training ground for diocesan priests, as 42 of the 114 were trained there; another 18 graduated from St. Joseph's. By 1940 one-third of the priests came from St. Bernard's and another 25 percent from St. Bonaventure's or Our Lady of the Angels seminary in Niagara.

At St. Bernard's, the academic program consisted of a prescribed series of courses in dogma, scripture, moral theology and church history, all taught in Latin. Theology was "manual" theology, consisting of expositions of basic doctrine drawn from conciliar and papal statements, with prescribed refutations of objections. Scripture study similarly consisted of official interpretations of scripture. There was little room for doubt or discussion. Promising students from other dioceses were sent to study theology in Rome or Washington. Occasionally a Syracuse seminarian or young priest slated for diocesan leadership received specialized training in Washington in education or social work, but Syracuse was known as a diocese which sent few men for such advanced study. Their horizons were largely shaped at St. Bernard's, where the emphasis was on a regular regimen of prescribed spiritual exercises including morning and night prayers, examination of conscience and spiritual reading. Silence was required during evening study time, visiting rooms was forbidden, no newspapers or magazines were allowed without the permission of the rector; radios were banned. During walks or visits to the city, students were forbidden to visit homes, restaurants or ice cream parlors. Inside the seminary, students wore the cassock at all times, except during exercise or athletic events. They were urged to mingle with all other students and warned against too close friendship with any one person. Visitors were allowed from 3:30 to 4:30 on the fourth Sunday of each month.

Card playing and drinking were forbidden, and letters were mailed and received through the seminary authorities. All these rules were surrounded by warnings of dismissal or postponement of ordination, evidence that increasing applications allowed greater selectivity and the more universal imposition of standards of conduct aimed at making the priest "another Christ," but also, in the words of the rules, "a gentleman":

At all times and under all circumstances the students must conduct themselves so that everything about them, manners, gestures, speech and appearance, will be such as to prove them to be gentlemen, and command the respect due to the clerical state.

For parish priests of this period, the standards of such respect reflected the values and aspirations of a lower middle class culture whose heroes were men like Knute Rockne, George M. Cohan, and Babe Ruth. There was little room for doubt, even less for curiosity. The mild cultural inquisitiveness of new magazines like *Commonweal* or *America,* and the enthusiastic passion for mission of Maryknoll, marked the limits of clerical imagination. Few shared even this degree of intellectual excitement. Their passion was for the Church, their tasks to uphold its claims, maintain its institutions and serve its people. No longer pioneers who would ride on horseback through the countryside or forge community out of divided, often rough and tumble immigrant congregations, they were to maintain and carefully expand an already existing, increasingly well established Church.

Young priests received little practical training and had no parish experience; they had to learn on the job. First appointed as an assistant, they were subject to the authority of a pastor, who was expected to provide "fatherly guidance." Relations between pastors and assistants were sometimes strained,

Father James McGee, pastor of St. Patrick's church in Syracuse, was a frequent and enthusiastic baseball fan. He was known to delight crowds with his verbal battles with umpires at area games. In 1923, McGee posed for this photo with Babe Ruth and two young players — Fred Cadey and E. A. O'Hara Jr. A local newspaper said of Father McGee and this photograph: "Nothing could have delighted him more unless it be the Beatific Vision Itself." (Photo: St. Patrick's, Syracuse)

especially as the period between ordination and appointment as a pastor lengthened in the 1930s. Duffy told young priests to take no initiative without consulting the pastor, quoting the "old adage, if you want to know who is boss around here, start something." In the rectory, the pastor was master of the household; he hired the housekeeper, enforced diocesan regulations including an 11:00 curfew, and determined the menu. The pastor's reports had much to do with the career patterns of the new priests, while any

income beyond his salary and direct stipends for sacramental services depended on the pastor's generosity. Some enjoyed reputations for the quality of the "table" or their broadmindedness, while other were legendary for their domineering ways. Most stories of extreme mistreatment, as that of the pastor who regularly ate steak while assigning pork chops and hamburg for the curates, were apocryphal. There were, however, some near violent altercations, including one in which the pastor charged the curate with physical intimidation, and the curate responded with complaints of ethnic slurs. There were cases in which concerned curates reported the financial and personal misconduct of the pastor to the bishop, and others where unsubstantiated charges by a pastor badly damaged a curate's reputation. More frequent were simple personality clashes, as when the hyper-nervous Alexis Hopkins complained that one of his curates, energetic and enthusiastic, caused him constant pain, while the other, bookish and sophisticated, was a valued companion and constant support. Yet, severe conflicts were rare and, despite its obvious flaws, the system worked fairly well.

Once appointed a pastor, the priest took on vast new responsibilities. The seriousness with which this position was regarded was evident in the letter of notification, which reminded the priest of his canonical responsibility to celebrate Mass in his parish on every Sunday and major feast, unless given specific permission not to do so. He was also summoned to the chancery to sign, under oath, usually in the presence of the bishop, two important documents. One was a "profession of faith" by which the priest swore his "firm faith" in a long series of Catholic doctrines, from the trinity to purgatory and the veneration of saints and including all teachings defined at Trent and at Vatican I, "particularly with regard to the primacy and infallible magisterium of the Roman pontiff," concluding with the general vow to "maintain and profess...with firm constancy until the last breath of my life, this true Catholic Faith, outside of which no one can be saved." The second document, the "Oath Against the Errors of Modernism," prescribed for all pastors in 1910, once again pledged the priest to condemn errors and uphold "in the same sense and always in the same meaning the doctrine of faith handed down to us by the Apostles." Finally the new pastor was required to prepare a will carefully distinguishing between personal property and church property, and file a copy with the chancery office.

In 1924, Rome warned that American priests were growing "lax" in matters of dress. Black was the prescribed color for clerical dress, but many priests had adopted "grays, striped and other more or less worldly colors." In too many such cases, Roman officials charged, "the cut of the priest's clothes suggests rather the man of fashion than the man of prayer." Responding to this warning, Curley told the priests to wear black suits and the clerical collar at all times; otherwise, the Holy Father might order a change in dress, presumably to the cassock, which would be "decidedly unpleasant for us all." The distinctiveness and dignity of the clerical state was a matter of considerable importance. Bishop John Duffy told priests they must be "gentlemen in every respect." They should never discuss rectory affairs with outsiders, even their family. In the confessional, they should not ask unnecessary questions and should show no appearance of curiosity, especially in matters regarding sex. They should work hard at sermon preparation and engage in good reading in order to improve their literary style and "give inspiration to high and noble sentiments." The sick should be visited until out of danger, but otherwise priests should "never make any other visits within the parish to which they are assigned, except those of an official

Life in the seminary was very strict in the early part of the century, with an emphasis on spirituality and self-discipline. For these young men ordained in 1936, learning parish work would be an "on the job" experience when they received their first assignments as assistants to a pastor. (Photo: Chancery Archives)

nature," as when taking the parish census. Social visits were "in bad taste and invite trouble," as lay people were "alert to special friendships and envious of those who receive them." Most important, they should guard against "even the appearance of intimacy with women." Duffy, like Curley before him, warned priests not to enter an automobile with a women, even a member of their family, for fear of causing scandal.

The most visible moment in the priest's life came during Mass, when he stood before the entire congregation. Seminary education and common practice emphasized the grace-giving power of the ceremony and reinforced an assumption that every detail of the Mass was prescribed, and had been for centuries. The character of the celebrant was irrelevant; the Mass was always the same. Liturgical training emphasized rubrics, the proper performance of each prayer, each action, every gesture. Something of the spirit of this was captured in a 1926 letter from Father Charles McEvoy, at the time chancellor of the diocese, to a young priest. McEvoy pointed out "abuses" which made Masses take longer than they should. One was moving the paten 10 or 12 times around the front of the corporal after communion, when one or two movements would suffice; another was purifying the paten several times, when only one movement was needed. Pauses for the memorial prayers for the living and the dead, leaving time to remember particular intentions, usually took far longer than necessary. Most common, McEvoy thought, was the practice of many priests of standing for a long time with hands joined and head bowed, after taking their own communion; "a relatively great delay is caused and without any good reason," McEvoy wrote.

LAITY UNITED

As for lay people, they were to support the projects of their priests. "Your pastor is giving everything — his time, his labor, and suffering many privations to promote the honor and glory of God, and help you...save your souls," Curley told parishioners: "Do all you can, therefore, to help your pastor meet the expenses and relieve him of unnecessary anxiety." Neither priest nor bishop could fully carry out his assigned task without a Church united with him. The saving message of faith could only be credible and effective if it was manifested in the lives of Catholics. They witnessed to their faith primarily by being the Church. As a worshiping, believing community, united with one another and their clergy, they gave testimony to the truth and value of Christianity. Unity was essential, and given the history of poverty and discrimination, the internal tensions of trusteeism, and ethnic conflicts, Catholics were justifiably pleased with what they had achieved. "The Catholic Church has never been stronger in her internal life, especially in this glorious country of ours, than she is today," Bishop Curley wrote. The source of that strength, he was convinced, was the Church's unity centered on the clergy and hierarchy:

One of the Church's most vital sources of stability and influence is that she is a people made one with its priests, a flock clinging to its shepherd, and never before in the entire range of the Church's history has this marvelous unity been more complete and more splendidly conspicuous. Never before has the laity united itself more thoroughly and heartily one with the body of clergy than it is today. Never was this same body of clergy more united with the episcopate. Never was the episcopate more united with the Pope, and never, so far as the Church's members are concerned, was the authority of the Apostolic See, as center of unity, more clearly asserted and more loyally sustained than at the present time.

Another source of this unity was a simple theology based on phrases like "the Church is the ordinary means of salvation" and scriptural texts like that in which Jesus presents to Peter the keys to the Kingdom of God. Curley argued that Jesus came into the world "not to tell men to follow only what would appear to them truths consistent with their individual powers of understanding" but "to present them with divine truths and divine precepts to which they were to conform in their daily life as the earthly children of God." His was not "a religion of convenience," to be accepted in part, but a complete set of doctrines to be accepted and obeyed in its entirety under pain of eternal damnation. The test then was the practice of the faith. "A Catholic sincerely practicing his religion cannot be guilty of grievous sin, either to himself or others," Curley argued; "but one who is merely a nominal Catholic is not only an unprofitable citizen, but he is a reflection upon the church of God, he is a

NEW PASTOR FINDS FAITH AND FRIENDSHIP

In 1928, Father John Butler traveled from Little Flower church in Munnsville to attend a benefit for his fledgling parish held at the Central Opera House in New York City. It was an occasion for Irish-Americans there to help a struggling young upstate parish.

Father Butler told his benefactors of the progress he found after only two years at Munnsville:

"When I went there about two years ago, the flaming cross of the Ku Klux Klan was burning on every hillside. A Catholic priest was a curiosity. Long before the first white settlers arrived, two Jesuit priests ministered to the Indians in that locality. The Catholic tradition had vanished, and my arrival was hailed with suspicion and distrust. The members of the faith were few and far-between. There had been little opportunity for them to avail themselves to the sacraments of the Church, and as a consequence, there had been a corresponding laxity in their attitude toward her. Mixed marriages added to the complexity of the situation. The children of these people had not even the most rudimentary concepts of the Catholic faith....

"Considerable change has taken place in the short space of time that I have been there. The Protestants who looked upon me with suspicion then, are now my friends and I am theirs. When I hold my little card parties and other social affairs, they constitute more than 50 percent of those present. The little children in school, who heretofore knew nothing of their religion, now spend a goodly portion of their lunch hour with me in devotional exercises and learning their catechism and it gladdens my heart every Sunday morning to see their parents coming from afar to hear Mass, in much the same fashion as I have seen it myself in sparsely settled sections of *the Old Land*."

menace to others and an unfortunate enemy to himself." Lest there be any doubt, he insisted on the central truth that it was church membership which was the key to eternal salvation: "There is, therefore, but one true Church, there is but one code of morals of divine origin and that code is for all; in your earthly existence, there is only one way to everlasting life."

Despite the easing of discrimination which followed World War I, there were still social factors at work reinforcing the unity, solidarity and assurance which was reflected in the rhetoric of the bishops. One was the revival of the Ku Klux Klan, now anti-Catholic and anti-Semitic as well as anti-

Negro. The Klan was present in Central New York, its activities stirring reminders of the long intolerance. Binghamton, for example, was plastered with KKK posters and handbills in the early twenties and became known in some circles as the "Klan Capital of the North." However, an over enthusiastic member of the order threatened to boycott George F. Johnson's shoes because he employed so many foreign-born workers. Aided by his brother-in-law, William H. Hill, editor of the Binghamton *Sun* and Republican leader of the area, Johnson launched a scathing counterattack which drove the Klan underground and all but destroyed overt intolerance in the area. Similarly, signs of renewed antagonism with

Protestants proved short lived. When Syracuse school officials reintroduced Bible reading in the schools in the early 1920s, Bishop Grimes, who was ill, did not respond and Bishop Curley, when he arrived, simply ignored the practice.

When Alfred E. Smith first ran for governor in 1920, Syracuse's Republican press pulled out all the stops to favor his opponent, Nathan Miller, a resident of the area.

On the eve of the election, a group of 20 Protestant ministers published an appeal calling for Miller's election. Miller won but, beset by recession and reaction against intolerance, he became very unpopular and Smith swept to victory in 1922, carrying even Miller's home ward in Syracuse. In 1928, during Smith's presidential race, Syracuse provided evidence of his ability to mobilize the immigrant vote which enabled him in defeat to bring the large cities in the country into the Democratic column for the first time since 1892. Aside from strong party and labor union support, Italian and Polish neighborhoods witnessed rallies sponsored by pro-Smith clubs. Bishop Curley wrote a letter to be read at Masses shortly before the 1928 campaign urging women in particular to vote. "The majority of them, no doubt, would have preferred the more ancient method which left the decisions and solutions of national civic problems to the other sex, and they still appear reluctant to share these burdens and responsibilities," Curley wrote. This was unfortunate, he said, urging all Catholics, "especially the women," to "devote a little more sober thought to the conduct of government and to the solution of issues vitally affecting the moral and physical welfare of our national life."

The Smith campaign, like the Klan, helped Catholics maintain a sense of themselves as a distinct group, one which included all the diverse nationalities of the Church. In resisting Klan intolerance and supporting a man like Smith, they were defending not only themselves but authentic American ideals and values as well. Another center of that combination of defense of the Church and promotion of Americanism was the Knights of Columbus, by now a powerful national organization which on the local level assisted the bishop with his projects and provided almost the only means of organizing Catholic men beyond the parish level. Bishops welcomed the K of C not only for its generous cooperation with Church authorities but also because it provided an alternative to other civic and social clubs. However the fraternal spirit and active patriotism of the organization could also lead it to blur the lines between Catholics and others in ways unacceptable to the hierarchy. In 1924 Curley was embarrassed by a K of C project to ally with the long condemned Masons to fight bigotry; the following year he again had to warn the Knights against fraternizing with the Masons, a practice the apostolic delegate told Curley was "dangerous."

As much as possible, Catholics were to associate in their private, non-working life, with other Catholics. One reason was simply the fact that contemporary Catholic believed that theirs was indeed the "one true Church," as Curley called it. "We are bound to regard all other conceptions of God as false, an insult to his divine majesty," Curley wrote. One should be charitable toward non-Catholics, but "we must unequivocally condemn the errors themselves and neither by word or conduct manifest any approval or compromise with their doctrine or form of worship." No associations should obscure the responsibility to "stand resolutely and unflinchingly in defense of...our faith," Curley argued. Catholic doctrines were "the keystone of the arch of all sound morality" and as such a bulwark against what he called "this materialistic, unholy, Godless world." He told a Knights of Columbus audience that the majority of

Americans were obsessed with aquiring wealth and pursuing pleasure, while legislators, playing to "minds devoid of religious conviction," were "sewing the seeds of revolution." Nowhere was this more evident than in what Curley and many other preachers regarded as the rising tide of sexual immorality in the 1920s. Curley told one high school audience: "The ramparts of Christianity all around us are weakening and breaking down."

In the interwar years problems of sexual morality along with anti-communism best allowed Catholics to express to the non-Catholic public their distinctive values. From the earliest days of the American Church, complaints were heard about such cultural problems as the reading of novels, the frequenting of the theater or, later, the promiscuous availability of dangerous reading material. But Catholics took little part in campaigns for enforced morality, such as those mounted by Charles Comstock in the 1880s. In part this was due to inter-religious hostility, with Catholic leaders unprepared to admit the merits of a basically Protestant claim upon public morality. In part too it was due to the realization of immigrant, urban, working class Catholics that vice was due as much to poverty and the disintegrating effects of migration as to the immorality or weak character of the people involved. It was not until the period before World War I that Catholic preachers began focusing on the public moral climate as a danger to Catholic souls, and not until the twenties that they hit upon the theme that Catholics could be defenders both of the Church's morality and of traditional American standards of family, marriage, and sexuality. Blasts at a "spirit of evil" corrupting the morals of the people became common. Dress, the theater, "places of diversion and amusement," as well as movies, books, and magazines, all created an atmosphere of "pagan sentiment and pagan morality," preachers charged. From this posi-

tion to one of vigorous counterattack was a short step. In the thirties, some Catholic leaders claimed that the Church's social teachings, contained in the papal encyclical, could solve America's economic problems; Catholic scholars argued that Catholic philosophy could answer the despair which gripped intellectuals caught between a meaningless relativism and the brutal realism of communism. Neither argument was as popular as the constant claim that Catholic personal morality could show the nation the way out of a growing culture of hedonism and permissiveness.

Bishop Ludden had denounced birth control and abortion, but it was not until 1924 that the issue, simmering for years, burst into the open. The mayor and city council of Syracuse passed a resolution in January making it a misdemeanor for any group to congregate for the purpose of disseminating information on birth control. Protesting this decision, the Protestant Ministerial Association charged that officials had acted under pressure from the bishop. Curley responded by admitting he had made his views known to the mayor, but he made no apology. "As a matter of concern for the welfare of our common country and its future stability," he felt compelled to use "all the influence of my official position and all the persuasion of my personal endeavor and my citizenship to thwart the efforts of those who, by disseminating the knowledge of practices so manifestly against the very law of nature itself, are not only advocating the violation of the law of God...but are endangering the very foundations of our Republic." He regretted that by doing his duty he might set "creed against creed," but concluded that he was "amazed that any minister who preaches either the Gospel of Jesus Christ or the morality of Judaism should take his stand on the principle of Birth Control, which is the modern scientific method of practicing that for which Jehovah, in his divine wrath, slew the first unscientific practitioner of this terrible sin."

Curley drew praise not only from Catholic leaders like Cardinal Hayes but even from some non-Catholic leaders like Dr. C. Bertram Runnels. In thanking Runnels for his contribution to mounting an "aggressive attitude" toward establishment of a birth control clinic in Syracuse, Curley told him that "apart from all the dreadful results of this Birth Control Propaganda" he and Runnels knew that "the fear of public ignominy has been a most valuable support to the religious convictions of maidens when their virginity has been place in jeopardy," an "aspect" of the issue which "we unfortunately cannot discuss publicly." Despite all their efforts as clergy to "safeguard the morals of such maidens," Curley added, "we can but faintly picture the appalling consequences of their knowledge and possession of contraceptive methods." As "Watchmen of the Tower of Israel," they would have to exert their full energy, with the help of God's grace, "to exterminate this human reptile of Birth Control, before its venom destroys the morality of our people and the life of our nation."

In a 1930 pastoral Curley became almost hysterical in his description of national corruption. The contemporary Church confronted "pagan practices" and "pagan morality" worse than that faced by the earliest Christians, Curley thought. One danger was "a putrid stream of the most despicable, the most iniquitous and the most dangerous variety of literature and of prints and pictures that were debaching the minds and morals of the young." Another was the "neo-paganism of birth control," based upon "lewdness and self-indulgence of the most degrading kind," and bringing about "a lustful perversion of the marital relationship" and "prostitution of motherhood." This was promoted by yet another danger, communism, whose "agents

spread sedition and unrest," "created conflict between capital and labor," and undermined national institutions, assisted by "callous employers" who forced people to live in misery while they built "swollen fortunes."

Living in such an environment, Catholics would be in no "grave peril" if they respected God's law, prayed and received the sacraments. Countless Christians had laid down their lives rather than allow the "maxims of the world (to) contravene the law of God." Those who would be "numbered among the elect" must not "walk in the path of self-indulgence, of luxury and sin" but "in the mortification of the senses and evil inclinations."

The moral lesson was thus closely linked to the requirements of this voluntary Church in a competitive environment. Loyalty to the Church, submission of its requirements of faith and morality, and an attitude of humility and deference before priests who embodied God's presence in the world were the way to earn salvation. The sin of sins was pride, placing one's own thoughts, judgments or needs before those of God's Church. Curley told a cathedral congregation in Lent 1927 that it was "foolish pride" which explained the defection of "foolish Catholics who banish from their minds the light they have received."

Contemporary Christians thus lived in a pagan environment. The response was to create an alternative environment — one in which Catholic and American values were honored and supported.

As Curley told Catholic students attending Syracuse University: "You cannot live among the icebergs without feeling the cold." Only by staying close to the Church and staying close to each other could Catholics remain safe from the dangers around them. The Church, then, was a source of truth and grace and at the same time a set of associations, family, friends, companions; it protected one from the pagan environment and sustained one's own faith and will. In an often used confirmation address, Curley told the children that they might not be asked to lay down their life, but they would meet spiritual dangers because they were forced "to associate with those who know very little of God, know practically nothing of his commandments, of their obligations to him, and the spiritual rewards of his sacraments." They could not follow this bad example without endangering their souls. They should therefore be wary of their companions, of their places of amusement, and the sources of their reading — presumably joining Catholic groups, spending time in Catholic halls, and reading Catholic books and magazines, all because they were living

> *in a dangerous atmosphere, in a period of irreligion and paganism. There never was a time, in the history of the world, when there was a more diabolical effort to dethrone God in the minds and hearts of his creatures! Never, therefore, when there was greater danger of worldly contamination to the Christian soul! Never, when there was greater need of constant prayer, of communion with God, of his strength and protection.*

MORAL REFORM

It was a sign of the times that, even when appealing for a wider sense of mission, Church leaders emphasized not the positive responsibilities of Christians but the enemies of the Church and the nation which Catholics had to confront in order to demonstrate their loyalty and commitment. In 1936 mission appeal Bishop Duffy claimed that "at no period in modern history has it been more necessary to have mission activities than now," for the Church stood as the "sole

barrier" to the triumph of forces hostile to Christian and American civilization. "The sinister influence of communism, raising its ugly head in all parts of the world, polluting the minds and hearts of men with its Godless doctrines, has but one opponent...the Church of Christ," the bishop insisted. Missionary activity was not only needed abroad "where God and Satan wage a relentless warfare," but at home as well, where indifference and irreligion were undermining belief in Jesus Christ and threatening the very existence of democratic institutions.

The way to build organized Catholic consciousness was to emphasize such enemies and mobilize Catholic resources to combat them. One means was the Catholic press; Curley endorsed the *Catholic Sun* as an official diocesan paper and urged priests and people to subscribe. He believed that the *Sun,* like all the Catholic press, was attempting to create "a more enlightened Catholic thought and a more militant Christianity to combat the pagan and immoral literature and the degrading and lascivious theatrical productions of the present day." It remained for Curley's successor, Bishop John Duffy, to mount a counter-attack on what both regarded as growing immorality. Curley had been preoccupied with consolidating the Catholic subculture through its own organizations, and he directed his moral messages mainly to Catholics. Duffy had a more assertive sense of the bishop as a public figure and of the Church as a potential agent for reform of the social order. If Curley sometimes seemed to suggest that Catholics could overcome the evils of society simply by being good Catholics, Duffy spoke for a more vigorous Catholicism which would save America from its largely self-imposed dangers by showing that the basic values of the American tradition, now upheld almost alone by the Church, could be drawn upon to combat secularism, moral decay and communism. Indeed he saw the episcopal

Bishop John A. Duffy (Photo: Chancery Archives)

office in terms which suggested that all people, not just Catholics, found in the bishop their moral leader, pointing the way to the restoration of an integrated Christian social order. Speaking at his installation, Duffy said that the presence of "representative of every race and every form of religious belief" provided evidence of "public veneration" for the Catholic bishop, regarded by "thoughtful men" as a "representative person" whose appointment was "a matter of public concern and of common interest." As a successor of the apostles, he carried with him "a spiritual and august prestige" and an authority unlike that of "other officials, local and temporary." The bishop led his Church in the struggle with "that vast mass of human ignorance, human misfortune, human folly." But he also brought to everyone "the dream and the reality of a unified religious society." The bishop protected the "common interests of religion"; he was "the spokesman for God and the representative of Christ."

Born and raised in Jersey City, Duffy was educated for the priesthood in Rome. He had considerable administrative experience, having served as chancellor and vicar-general of the Newark diocese, where one of his major accomplishments was the organization of a diocesan Holy Name Society to 125,000 members. While serving in these diocesan offices, he was also pastor of St. Joseph's in Jersey City, a huge parish with a school with 1,134 students and 27 teachers. Duffy was not as unequivocal a prophet of doom as his predecessor. At a sermon delivered in St. Patrick's cathedral, he noted amid the suffering and growing violence of society a widespread respect for human beings, a yearning for human rights and a determination to find greater happiness in human affairs. During the depression, he recognized that "the social question is in the saddle," and thought it was "not a mere demand for changed social conditions but an enlightened protest against human inequality." Duffy argued that Christians should help introduce the humanitarian reforms required by the times. He approved of President Roosevelt's New Deal because it aimed at a larger measure of industrial reward for working people. "Who wants the national prosperity of the past?" Duffy asked — "prosperity that maintains wealth in the hands of a few who control the whole industrial and social life in America and in the world?" He urged a convention of social workers to back Roosevelt and not "let panic or stupidity wreck a hopeful experiment in social justice." "Capitalism, with its principle of profit in dollars and losses in humanity is definitely a failure," Bishop Duffy told the Syracuse Optimist Club in December 1933. "We have had the civilization of great national prosperity, of great material improvement; but we want back the civilization of the heart, the civilization of mutual respect and mutual sympathy. We want back in our own country and in the world the only real civilization, the humanity of man for man."

Duffy's support of social reform was limited, however, by his distrust of government regulation. In mid-1935 he reiterated the long standing opposition of many bishops to the child labor amendment to the Constitution which he feared would lead to massive bureaucratic intervention in family life. He believed that the way to social reform was not through government action but through personal moral conversion. There was a crying need for leadership in society, he argued, and it would have to come from a "moral revolution" of Christians who had decided to practice their religion. "Christian faith and practice could establish the reign of law.... Peace and social well being are attainable through Christianity but not until the obstacles to their attainment, personal sin, is conquered through the reign of Christ." In a world of freedom, the reign of Christ could only come about by appeals to conscience; the task of Christians was first of all to change their own life by living according to their principles, showing by their example the way these principles contributed to decent life. Only then would the time come to apply these principles to public problems.

Duffy believed that the search for "moral revolution" gave the Church opportunities for a wider public role. This mood was evident in changing relationships with non-Catholics. Father Tobin, pastor of St. Catherine's in Vernon and Our Lady of Good Counsel in Verona, for example, began writing regularly to local newspapers defending Catholic leaders like radio priest Charles E. Coughlin and generally attempting to explain Catholic positions. Misconception could be overcome, he thought, but only if Catholics vigorously set their beliefs before the public. To make the point, he told a story of a big game hunter who visited a museum which featured a series of scenes in which a lion was the central figure. In one the lion was caged, in another chained, and in a third he lay dead with a man with a gun standing triumphantly over him. "As the hunter said," Tobin wrote, "it's easy to see the lion had not drawn the pictures." Similarly, it was clear that what people read about Catholicism was not written by Catholics. He invited people to visit his church so that they could experience it as they might view stained glass. Seen from the outside it appeared as "meaningless lines and splatches of color, whereas from the inside, with the sunlight pouring through, the eye beholds a beautiful picture."

In a similar spirit, Father David Cunningham and Father David Gildea in 1930 established a "Catholic bookshelf" at the Syracuse public library. Later in 1937, with the bishop's blessings, Father Martin J. Whately began a 14-year career of weekly radio broadcasts aimed at explaining Catholic beliefs and building inter-religious understanding; similar programs were launched in Utica and Binghamton. When Syracuse attorney Fred G. Dutton reported to the bishop that a group of Presbyterians and Jews who had been meeting at Elmwood Presbyterian Church hoped to arranged a larger good will meeting, Duffy surprisingly gave his blessing and even attended the first session. There he suggested that, while they differed on "essentials," Christians could join in the "vast field of endeavor wherein religious beliefs do not conflict." On what would later be called ecumenism, Duffy was not advanced. But like many other priests and bishops he felt a new sense of self-confidence spurred by the Church's evident success. This was enough to lower slightly the tone of inter-religious discussions.

Still, the best way to promote moral reform was not gentle discussion with other faiths but mobilization of the Catholic community for action. Duffy was energetic in this regard, bringing to Syracuse the growing national effort to organize the Catholic laity under the heading of Catholic Action, defined as "the participation of the laity in the apostolate of the hierarchy." The laity, organized under Church auspices with priests and bishops in charge, could enable the Church to act with greater strength and speak with greater credibility. The way to organize for Catholic Action was to make Holy Name societies universal in every parish, then organize them along county lines, then into a diocesan federation and ultimately into state bodies affiliated with the National Council of Catholic Men under the National Catholic Welfare Conference in Washington.

The Syracuse diocese had long had Holy Name societies or their equivalent, organized exclusively on a parish basis. Under Duffy's direction diocesan-wide organization began. In April 1934 he named priests as county directors and instructed them to organize county meetings. A year later he summoned delegates to the first diocesan-wide meeting. Some pastors wrote indicating that local Decoration Day events or religious services on the feast of the Ascension would prevent their attendance and that of their lay delegates. Duffy was serious. The chancellor responded to all who had written their regrets:

The bishop has directed me to tell you that he will be looking for you personally to attend the federation Holy Name meeting at 3:00 on May 30th at Cathedral school hall and he will expect that you will bring with you two lay delegates from your parish Holy Name Society.

They did; 400 delegates from 126 parish units attended. They renewed their pledge of filial devotion to the pope and their loyalty to the principles and practices of their faith, sent off a telegram to this effect to the apostolic delegate, and received his congratulations in return.

The county federation was the action arm, of Holy Name. Each had committees whose functions were described in the diocesan handbook:

1. The exercise of vigilance over public entertainments on the stage, screen or otherwise, to the end of safeguarding public morals. (Standing Committee on Public Morals)
2. To answer attacks appearing in the press against the teaching and practice of the Church; to prevent the sale and circulation of salacious literature and pictures; to promote interest in Catholic literature (Committee on Truth and Literature)
3. To arouse and sustain interest on the part of Parish Units in the work of the Diocesan and County Federations and to secure their moral support in all movements of local concern (Standing Committee on Extension)
4. To protect the civil rights of Catholic against invasion and to secure the consolations of religion to Catholic inmates of penal and correctional institutions (Standing Committee on Civics and Legislation)

Federation meetings were public forums on such subjects as "The Situation in Mexico," "Federal Bureau of Education" "Sterilization and Birth Control" and "The Situation in Russia." A speakers bureau aroused the interest of Holy Name men in similar subjects and stimulated local units to cooperate with the legislative committee "in opposition to offensive legislative measures." To meet emergencies, as when the state legislature was considering a bill on birth control, 50 men were trained and sent out to speak to local units. Each year a program was selected, speakers trained, and programs held in local parishes.

Holy Name leaders became outspoken representatives of the Church in public controversies. In June 1935, for example, William E. McClusky, first president of the diocesan federation, wrote a public letter to Dey Brothers department store protesting the opening of a "Mexican Mart." Speaking on behalf of 50,000 Syracuse area Holy Name men, he detailed the persecution of the Church in Mexico, which he called the "first totalitarian state in the New World"; he urged Dey's to follow other large stores by taking Mexican goods off their shelves. Similarly in January 1936, McClusky, as Broome County chairman, protested a speech by the local commissioner of public welfare allegedly advocating sterilization, birth control and "race suicide." These and many other incidents showed a new assertiveness by Catholics and demonstrated the potential of a well-organized diocese.

It should be noted that there was no serious effort in Syracuse, as there was in other dioceses, to organize a federation of Catholic women. The female counterpart of the Holy Name Society in most parishes was the Altar and Rosary Society. If the records of one such society, at St. Peter's in Utica, are at all typical, the contrast between the two groups was marked. The women rarely had talks or forums. Most often the monthly meetings were taken up with plans for fund raising events, bake sales, teas, covered dish suppers, lawn parties, card parties, raffles. The proceeds were used to buy items for the church, a baptismal font, a rug for the altar, flowers for major feasts, catechisms and choir books. They sent Mass cards to members on the death of a loved one and held parties to welcome a new priest or say farewell to an old one. Membership was never large and meetings were usually small enough to be held in the home of a member. One suspects all was not well, as younger women found more meaningful service in non-church programs. In December 1931 the St. Peter's group debated a motion to send a committee to meet with the pastor to ask "just what we are working for." That motion was defeated, as was a proposal the following month to ask "the men of the parish to do their bit, at least once a year."

Women, it seemed, were not yet called to action. In welcoming the Catholic Daughters of America to Syracuse, Curley reflected the manifest male chauvinism of the Catholic subculture by defining the role of women in terms of home and children. Every one had the responsibility to do what was right, Curley told them, and when Catholics attempted to bear witness to their principles, they contributed to "civic righteousness and ethical rectitude." Women's influence was "most potent," but indirect. When men were "chivalrous, her will is the social law"; to use that power to make a better world was a "noble ambition." As Catholics, their faith should "not only adorn your own person, that God may detect it, but it should also diffuse its heavenly perfume among those with whom you are engaged in family and social relations."

Women could assist at home and in the parish with the major project of Holy Name, the Legion of Decency, launched at a communion breakfast of the Cathedral Holy Name in 1935. In a speech broadcast on the radio, Duffy called for a united effort of all good citizens to fight the scourge of immoral films. He added to that appeal with a pastoral letter. Using the newly federated Holy Name societies as a channel, pledge forms were distributed and the bishop made it a "matter of conscience" for Catholics to promise to abstain from seeing all moving pictures of an immoral or indecent character. He left no doubt of the seriousness with which he viewed the problem: "I make it a test of the sincerity of your faith in the moral teachings of Christ and his Church." Pastors were encouraged by a special letter, Father David Gildea began enrolling all children in Catholic schools, and the Knights of Columbus, the Catholic Daughters of America, as well as the Holy Name all pledged their support. Surprising support also came from outside the Church, with promises of cooperation from the Syracuse Council of Churches, the Womens Christian Temperance Union and the American Legion.

The campaign received a boost and demonstrated its potential power in a "short but bitter fight" over the scheduled appearance of Sally Rand, the "fan dancer," at Syracuse's Loew's Theater. In a letter to the local press, Duffy called the "presence of the Rand woman...an act of public defiance of the moral sentiments of the Catholic people of Syracuse." He called the theater a "public enemy" and described a planned welcoming committee as "a worthy object of contempt." Theater managers rather lamely responded that Rand was a "poor little working girl" and that reports of her appearances elsewhere indicated her act was "not so bad," arguments which led the bishop to charge that "the theater has entirely lost the notion of decency and morality." Pastors were told to call the theater and inform its owners that they would denounce the appearance at Mass.

Faced with rumors of a boycott of the theater, the management surrendered and the Rand show was canceled. The national Catholic press hailed Duffy's courageous stand and clear victory, and the Legion of Decency became a household word. By the end of the year over 75,000 Catholics had signed the pledge.

While the Legion of Decency campaign was waged as a private fight through which the organized pressure of Catholic opinion attempted to clean up the stage and films, area leaders recognized the existence of local statutes prohibiting nudity, lewdness and, as in Utica "any indecent or immoral play or other representation." Father David Cunningham, Duffy's secretary, called the attention of local police to what he considered indecent advertising of a film and later thanked them for their cooperation, while Duffy wrote the mayor's office praising local officials for their support of the Legion of Decency campaign. Later Church officials pressured Utica leaders to enforce local ordinances by preventing the showing of offensive films. The cooperation of Legion activists with Catholics in police departments and city halls was evident when a group of Liverpool firemen were publicly reprimanded for attending an immoral show in Salina, an episode brought to public attention by the secret cooperation of a pastor and the state police. In 1939 diocesan director Father James Shanahan reported that the Legion had forced a Utica theater to cancel a particularly coarse program of burlesque and, after an appeal to the governor, forced cancellation of a presentation at the State Fair by Planned Parenthood. In addition they had mounted an enormous protest against the showing of the condemned movie "This Thing Called Love."

The classification system, together with education of the community, constituted the basic and very successful strategy of the Legion of Decency. Duffy called his lead-ership "necessary work for the moral betterment of our civic community," and Shanahan worked hard to arouse public opinion by means of parish and diocesan committees and the cooperation of priests, teachers and Catholic lay leaders. Behind the classification system and its enforcement lay the threat of boycott of theaters that showed condemned films, just as behind the program nationally was the threat of economic pressure against the major film making companies which led to self-imposed censorship, which by the 1940s made condemned movies extremely rare. As the Syracuse leadership stated boldly: "This office makes no secret of the fact that constant check is kept on the pictures being exhibited by theaters in the Syracuse area. This check or score card will serve the purpose of showing the cooperation that Syracuse theaters are giving or not giving to the program of clean movies."

By 1940 the bishops were concerned that the gains made since 1934 were slipping away. They urged pastors and editors to subscribe to the Legion's weekly lists, to post them in prominent places and comment on them. They were especially concerned that Catholic writers and editors give further reasons for the classifications, showing that "the Catholic position on films is informed and sane." Movies "often present pernicious philosophical principles and attitudes which can form in audience habits of thought contrary to the true Christian outlook on life." Competent writers could deal with pictures that offended truth or good taste as well as give special attention to propaganda films, yet the bishops emphasized the need for both reviewing groups and "vigilance committees" to commend good films and not just condemn bad ones.

Duffy also was concerned about the dangers of much reading material. In a 1935 letter, he warned against the "real danger" of "the printed filth that is being peddled today on nearly every street corner." Like so many of the movies, these readings were occasions of sin. He urged Catholics to avoid literature which "portrays crime, appeals to sex and fosters irreligion," keeping their minds "free from such contamination so that the hardness of an ugly and cynical smartness will not tarnish the fresh beauty of God's grace in the soul." More positively he called attention to Catholic books, pamphlets, magazines and especially newspapers like the *Sun*. Two years later he said that the Catholic press "spells Catholic thinking." Never in history had the Catholic press been so needed, he wrote in 1937, as "irreligion and atheism is entering our homes and poisoning the souls of our people; its diabolical fury in other lands must be exposed to the light of day, and only a strong, uncensored press can accomplish this."

In 1939 the national crusade expanded to include magazines, as the bishops launched the National Office for Decent Literature to combat literature which "glorifies crime or the criminal; is predominately 'sexy'; features illicit love; carries illustrations indecent or suggestive; and carries disreputable advertising."

In Syracuse Father Shanahan was placed in charge of the literature campaign, while regional priest leaders were appointed throughout the diocese. In every parish the pastor was told to organize his parishioners to draw up a list of stores, visit them and urge the owner to sign pledge cards not to sell magazines included on a list prepared by the national office. Once this was done and the cards returned, the parish should establish a "vigilance committee" to check on dealers to make sure they had not backtracked. Pledges similar to that of the Legion of Decency were administered. People promised not to purchase, read or tolerate forbidden magazines and to read only those that were "free from harm and had definite value" and "to help form public opinion against those who make light of religion and morality by publishing or selling periodicals which do not meet our moral standards."

The Holy Name Society joined actively in the effort to free the area of "dirty magazines," receiving support from the Council of Churches and district attorney offices in several cities. In 1939 leaders of the movement indicated that 183 stores in Syracuse were cooperating, 43 were not and 17 were as yet undecided. In Utica the score was 114, 15, 13; in Binghamton 72, 17, and 8; and a perfect 25 in Cortland. A misunderstanding with a large Syracuse store was cleared up and an announcement of compliance made from local pulpits. Meanwhile Shanahan had been asked to be reviewer for the national office and sent regular reports. One typical story concerned him because it "discusses childbirth very frankly" and another because it was "predominately sexy." He was particularly incensed by a story in one magazine in which an Italian widow lived as mistress with an Italian man, estranged from his wife because "his Church does not believe in divorce." "The sinful alliance is terminated when the lover is murdered by the woman's fourteen year old daughter," Shanahan reported.

The writer unfortunately made only a "very half hearted attempt to draw any lessons from the story."

In retrospect one is struck by two features of these crusades and of the pervasive sense of moral decay which filled the rhetoric of bishops and priests. One is the concentration on issues of sexual morality during a period when much of the rest of the country, and even large portions of the Catholic church, were most concerned about economic injustice and by the rising tide of Fascism abroad. Too strong support of social reform, especially when it became political or associated with the more radical union movement of the CIO, could risk dividing the Catholic population and bring on serious conflict with the leaders of local institutions. In addition, lacking a strong working class movement in the local community and the local Church, Syracuse had little exposure to arguments which associated Catholic teaching with trade unionism and trade unionism with American democratic values. On the other hand, they found in birth control and indecent films and literature issues which united Catholics, won considerable support among others in the community, and could reasonably be associated with American national ideals and the common good of the community as a whole. At the time, only anti-communism could compete as an issue which at one and the same time manifested Catholic distinctiveness and promoted patriotic action. Secondly, there was the overwhelmingly negative character of these crusades. Both the Legion of Decency and the National Office for Decent Literature argued that they wished to promote worthwhile productions as well as oppose immoral ones, but little enthusiasm was generated by the positive part of their message. The negative tone of the rhetoric suggested that more was at stake than purging theaters and magazine racks. Rather, the presence of external forces threatening Church and society could unite the Catholic community, enhance its morale, give it a strong sense of purpose and provide specific things for people to do to demonstrate their commitment to their Church and their loyalty to the nation. The genius of these movements, in contrast to many appeals for social justice, was that they gave each person in the Church — rich or poor, educated or not — something to do, something immediate, personal and real, which could ground commitment and express dedication. They helped clarify the boundaries between Catholics and other groups and provided solid reasons for being a Catholic and being proud of it. If in the long run they proved ineffective in accomplishing their stated objectives, the crusades against immorality achieved other, less visible goals by enhancing morale and drawing Catholics together around a larger vision than that possible in the parish. That strength was also their fatal weakness, for they also hardened negative attitudes toward American culture, limited impulses to join with other citizens on public problems, and hinted at pride and self-righteousness. Heedless of appeals regarding civil liberties, Catholics appeared more concerned with manifesting their own virtue than finding common ground with others.

For all its early promise, the diocesan Holy Name society never became an effective force for exerting Catholic influence on the larger society and culture. It continued, of course. But under Duffy's successor it seldom became involved in the public activities planned for it in the 1930s. Similarly, the Legion of Decency and the local decent literature campaign passed their peak well before World War II. Catholic interest remained focused on their parishes; for now, at least, moral crusades like social action would take second place to the religious, cultural and educational activities of parish churches. Harvey Hill may have lifted Catholic sights to new horizons, and Bishop Duffy may have given Catholic energies a specific, if temporary, focus. But intelligent, energetic pursuit of either missionary goals or public responsibility would have to wait.

THE MULTIPLICATION OF NATIONALITIES

A NEW WAVE OF IMMIGRANTS
1920s-1940s

From the outside, the Catholic Church in the United States in the years between the wars appeared to be a remarkably unified Church with strong direction, common faith and liturgy, and growing power in society, politics and culture. In its parishes, schools, hospitals, orphanages and old age homes, it provided impressive evidence of the ability of Catholics to provide for themselves. Their public image of submissive obedience to their leaders seemed to confirm the argument that the Catholic Church was "the happiest and most peaceful society." If non-Catholics sometimes feared Catholic power and resented Catholic influence, there was one achievement all respected — the assimilation of immigrants into American society. Here the Church was credited with an enormous contribution to public welfare and social stability. It instilled morality, loyalty to American institutions, and habits of hard work, sobriety, thrift and self-discipline. These virtues, in turn, prevented conflict, eased anxieties and seemingly confirmed the dream of the American melting pot.

Yet, within the Church, that project of Americanizing the immigrant was far from complete. Tensions among ethnic groups remained an important aspect of American Catholicism, while immigrant resistance to the policies of the hierarchy had not ended yet. Bishops bent upon unifying the Church found their biggest challenge in the continuing existence of distinct ethnic communities, some still suspicious of "American" practices of clerical control and voluntary financial support.

Given the self-help ethic which arose from the experience of Irish, German and other successful Catholic groups, organization had to come from below. It had to come from people who wanted the services of the Church and had learned that they could have those services only if they provided the personal support and financial contributions which made them possible. Churches and schools could not be built from above, not only because few Catholics were able to provide the money, but also because experience seemed to prove that, in the long run, parishes could not survive, much less prosper, unless they had the backing of the people. On the other hand, even when that support was forthcoming, it had to be channeled in ways which maintained the unity of the Church, especially by conforming to the authority of the bishop. The bishop would have to be flexible enough to make room for the newcomers. They, in turn, would have to decide to move in to the room provided. Accommodation of the people's needs and organizational demands shaped the drama of parish formation and development in the interwar years in ways at once similar to, and different from, the ways such development had taken place earlier in what were now more settled and established Catholic communities.

After World War I, the United States finally closed the "golden door" and restricted immigration. By that time, there were, according to federal census figures, 6,756 Italian-born residents in Syracuse, more than 8,400 in Utica, 2,462 in Rome and 1,231 in Binghamton. Germans were the second largest group in Syracuse with 4,751, and 2,000 more in Utica. There were more than 4,500 Poles in Syracuse, more than 4,000 in Utica and approximately 900 in Binghamton. Slovaks were concentrated heavily in Binghamton, where the population was 2,892, with only 155 in Syracuse. In Oswego, the numbers were far smaller, with 900 Italians, 780 Poles and 147 French Canadians. These were the major Catholic immigrant groups, though it should be noted that Irish immigration had continued because there were more than 3,800 foreign-born Irish in Syracuse, and more than 1,400 in Utica and Binghamton.

Bishop Ludden's attitude toward immigrants was paradoxical. He disliked national parishes, and regularly noted that even non-English speaking immigrants and their English speaking children had the right to attend territorial parishes. In his mind, the reason that right was guaranteed by Church law was

"to discountenance as far as possible the multiplication and perpetuation of different religious rites and nationalities in this country." At the same time, Ludden was a veteran pastor who knew well the need to provide religious services in native languages if the faith and loyalty of the immigrants was to be preserved, and the possibility thereby kept open of securing the allegiance of their children. National parishes, therefore, were temporarily necessary. Their provision depended on the ability of the community to organize, raise sufficient funds to build and maintain a church and support a pastor, and abide by the "American system" of turning ownership of the church property over to the bishop. By 1920, as we have seen, many national parishes had been established. In the years between the wars, only a few new ones appeared. Instead, during these two decades, ethnic groups in a bewildering variety struggled to secure their foundations, while wrestling with the problems posed by the gradual Americanization of their members.

GERMANS IN THE MAINSTREAM

The latter problem was most acute among

the Germans. In Syracuse, they were a well organized and quite powerful ethnic community. They dominated the second, third and part of the fourth ward of the city and, by 1900, their organized voting power made them a dominant force in local politics. Between 1900 and the First World War, although only 19 percent of the city's population, German-Americans held seven of 19 seats on the city council and filled, at least for a time, all major city posts. Two served as mayor during the period. Institutionally, Assumption church stood at the center of the community, with its large, prosperous parochial school and the motherhouse, novitiate, college and convent school of the Franciscan Sisters. Yet there were already signs of trouble. A fight was waged for the right to preach in English, intended to maintain a hold on the second generation. This signaled a desire for respectability, status and assimilation that was bound to weaken community solidarity in later years. More important, the influx of Italians into the north side of the city gradually eroded the stability of once German neighborhoods. No new "Germantown" appeared elsewhere. Rather there was a slow scattering of Germans throughout the city and suburbs.

Finally, World War I dealt a severe blow. Responding to war-time hysteria, the public school committee ended the teaching of German in local high schools. German political power waned as people stopped voting for people with German names. Three Germans were elected to the school board between 1914 and 1917. From 1918 to 1928, none were elected. Two ran for mayor and were defeated. Syracuse newspapers were strongly anti-German during the war, referring to the "enemy" as "Huns" and to local Germans as "Northsiders." In response, Germans were silent. Many local ethnic organizations did not meet during the war. When they resumed, the earlier pride in German culture

and the strong sense of a bond with the old country were greatly reduced. The German community survived and indeed remained an important component of both Church and community. But its organizations and churches entered a long period of decline. In 1909, Assumption claimed 6,350 parishioners and St. Joseph's 1,162. By 1924, the numbers had dropped to 4,990 and 872. Both began receiving into membership people from the neighborhoods which surrounded them, so that by 1943 the pastor of St. Joseph's could state that the word "German" in his church's title had lost all significance.

St. Peter's, the German parish in Oswego, never developed as strongly as its sister German churches in the diocese. During the 1890s, its supporting German population eroding, the parish school closed and the sisters opened a day nursery for working mothers. In 1917, support for St. Peter's was so limited that it became a mission without a resident pastor. The small German population was dissatisfied and, in 1923, St. Peter's again received a resident pastor, Father Muller. He restored German services and worked hard to expand the parish. In 1928, the archbishop of Honduras, Muller's personal friend, visited the church amid great ceremony. He was greeted by a young girl with a German speech and spoke to the congregation in both German and English. In 1929, Muller raised $25,000 to reinforce the foundation and refurbish the outside of the church, which, by that time, was German in name only. Irish and French families from the neighborhood joined a scattering of Hungarians and Italians. By 1936, all services were conducted in English. One parishioner described St Peter's as "a veritable league of nations, descendants from many European races, all cooperating in a wonder spirit of religious unity, proclaiming the universality of the Catholic church."

In Oneida, St. Joseph's German church also found it increasingly hard to maintain itself as a national parish. In 1928, the pastor, Father John P. Lauer, petitioned that the parish be denationalized and serve as a territorial parish for that section of the city. The petition was opposed strongly by Father McGraw of St. Patrick's, a church that would find its base severely reduced by a territorial division of the city. A difficult situation was made worse by bad feeling between the two pastors. Lauer complained that McGraw refused sick calls from his parishioners who lived near St. Patrick's, and tried to collect stipends for services at St. Joseph's when he thought his parishioners were involved. Lauer encouraged his people to send their children to the school at St. Patrick's, but complained that McGraw made them members of the parish sodalities and used this to persuade them and their families to attend his church.

Most important, he charged that McGraw

A COMMUNITY WITH MANY ROOTS

The Church within the Syracuse diocese long has been a community of people with different ethnic and national backgrounds. This diversity has been one of the strengths of the diocesan Church.

In the past, many parishes were organized for immigrants from a particular country, especially for those who did not speak English. These ethnic parishes include:

GERMAN
Colosse: St Anne mission (closed)
Durhamville: St Francis of Assisi
Hawkinsville: St John Chrysostom
    mission (closed)
Minoa: St Mary
Oneida: St Joseph
Oswego: St Peter

Rome: St Mary of the Assumption
Syracuse: Assumption of the Blessed Virgin
    Mary
Syracuse: Holy Trinity
Syracuse: St Joseph (closed)
Utica: St Joseph
Utica: St Mary

FRENCH
Colosse: St Anne mission (closed)
Little France: St Francis (closed)

Oswego: St Louis
Syracuse: St Joseph (merged)

IRISH
(Because the Irish generally were the first immigrants to settle in communities, they established no parishes on the basis of Irish nationality. But for decades, many parishes retained their strongly Irish flavor. Most other national parishes were established as a foreign-language alternative to the generally Irish parishes.)

ITALIAN
Binghamton: Assumption of the Blessed
    Virgin Mary (merged)
Cortland: St Anthony of Padua
Endicott: St Anthony of Padua
Norwich: St Bartholomew
Oswego: St Joseph

Rome: St John the Baptist
Syracuse: Our Lady of Pompei
Syracuse: St Peter
Utica: St Anthony of Padua
Utica: St Mary of Mount Carmel

and the sisters in the school regularly distinguished between the "Catholic church" and the "German church," telling a child who did badly in religion class, for example, that this was expected from "those who attended the German Church." After long deliberation, the diocese decided against Father Lauer's petition. Instead, he was given responsibility for the city's small but growing Italian population.

ITALIANS SETTLE IN

The Italian community remained plagued by a shortage of priests. At St. Anthony's in Utica, embattled Father Roth served until his death in 1923. He was succeeded by Father Victor Rossi, who immediately began construction of the church, completing it in 1924 at a cost of $107,000. With the help of several American assistants, he built a strong youth program centered on athletics, but the debt

LITHUANIAN
Binghamton: St Joseph
Utica: St George

POLISH
Binghamton: St Stanislaus Kostka
Endicott: St Casimir
Fulton: St Michael
New York Mills: St Mary, Our Lady of Czestochowa
Oswego: St Stephen the King

Rome: Transfiguration
Syracuse: Sacred Heart
Syracuse: Transfiguration of Our Lord
Utica: Holy Trinity
Utica: St Stanislaus

SLOVAK
Binghamton: St Ann
Binghamton: Sts Cyril & Methodius

Endicott: St Joseph
Syracuse: St Stephen

As the diocesan Church matured, and as immigration slowed, the Church was more able to help meet the needs of newcomers without having to form separate parishes, which held the risk of becoming segregated from the mainstream of Catholic life. In recent decades, the diocese has refrained from opening national parishes, preferring instead to integrate people into neighborhood churches while supporting particular ethnic apostolates. These apostolates which have emerged within the diocese include:

BLACK
Syracuse: Office of Black Ministry

IROQUOIS
Syracuse: Native American Apostolate

HISPANIC
Binghamton: Hispanic Ministry
Syracuse: Spanish Apostolate
Utica: Hispanic Ministry

proved a heavy burden. In January 1927, Rossi was summoned to Rome. A month later, he notified the bishop he would not return, so Curley sent Father Penta from Cortland to Utica and asked Father John Marchegiani of Mount Carmel for help in finding an Italian speaking priest. He recommended Father Bindo Binazzi, then serving as an assistant in Boston. By this time, diocesan officials had learned to be cautious, and Binazzi was not officially incardinated into the diocese. The Cortland parish had heavy debts, the result of Penta's improvement program. While Binazzi was able to maintain the parish, problems arose with the trustees. Hardworking and devoted, Binazzi could not speak English well, so after four years, the bishop suggested he seek a place in another diocese. Binazzi complained to Rome and the apostolic delegate made inquiries. The bishop had to explain that Binazzi had been administrator, rather than pastor, no promises of incardination had been made, and his inability to speak English limited his ability to provide catechetical instruction. Rome was satisfied and Binazzi eventually left the diocese. But Rome's interest increased the diocese's caution in dealing with foreign-born priests, and highlighted the continuing difficulty in finding personnel able to serve the large, but still heavily uninstructed, Italian population.

Yet there was progress after the war. The end of open immigration and the return of prosperity reduced the tendency of so many Italians to move back and forth between the two countries and thus to make little investment in local institutions. In 1921, Father Formia returned to Italy and was succeeded at Mount Carmel by the talented Scalabrini, Marchegiani, who began visiting families and rekindling interest in the parish. He reorganized parish societies and began plans to enlarge the church. When Bishop Grimes came for confirmation, there were so many ready that two ceremonies were needed, one

for 308 boys and another for 381 girls. With the help of an assistant, Marchegiani personally completed a corridor between the church and the rectory, winning respect among the men of the parish for his skills as a mason, carpenter and electrician. A new heating plant was installed. The basement hall, years before dug by hand from under the church, was remodeled, electricity added and a moving picture projector purchased. Successful bazaars and minstrel shows and enlarged parish organizations led to an increase in annual receipts from $15,000 to $22,700. A mission that year lasted 16 days, eight days each in Italian and English, and income jumped again to $31,000. In the next few years, the old mortgage was paid, a new convent constructed and the school enlarged. Here, at least, Italians had learned "to support our own." When Marchegiani left to become regional superior of the Scalabrini Fathers, he reported at a banquet held in his honor that during his pastorate they had erected buildings costing $166,000 "without having recourse to the charity of strangers."

In 1924, Father John Robotti took charge of St. Anthony's Home, the 10-year-old settlement house on the north side of Syracuse, and began organizing a new Italian parish, Our Lady of Pompei. A year later, a new church and school opened and the parish made steady progress.

It would be a mistake to think that only foreign-born priests could serve successfully in such parishes. William Walsh was born and raised in Utica, and educated at St. Bernard's and later at the North American College in Rome. He became a student of Italian language and culture and, when he returned, served Italian parishes, becoming pastor of Our Lady of Pompei in 1932. He immersed himself in the lives of his people, and achieved an enviable reputation as both a caring pastor and remarkable fundraiser and administrator. With the help of his assistants, most notably Charles Borgognoni, the parish developed a dramatic group, the Pompeian Players, whose Broadway musicals drew huge crowds and won critical acclaim from the local press. Walsh, like most successful American pastors, was admired for his learning and respected for his parish's healthy attendance and for encouraging the construction of new buildings, but loved for his readiness to be with his people in the crisis moments of life and in play and celebration. As newspaper reporter Mario Rossi described him years later, he was "many things — father confessor, friend, teacher, moderator, story teller, preacher, and even singing and bowling companion. Above all he has been and remains a source of reassurance."

Other Italian parishes made slow progress. At the sprawling St. Anthony's in Utica, Father Penta redecorated the church, installed new pews, a pulpit and confessionals, constructed a bell tower and formed the first football team. In Rome, however, Father Joseph Panesi of St. John the Baptist never overcame the lack of income and the overwhelming social needs of his congregation. Father Pellegrini at Assumption parish, the mainstay of the Italian church in Binghamton, in the mid-1930s estimated that 40 percent of the Italians in his community now were attending church, compared to five percent before the war. Unfortunately, many attended neighboring churches. Pellegrini estimated the number of families in this parish at no more than 700. While Father Pellegrini established something of a record for longevity, his power was by no means unquestioned. When the depression struck, parish revenues were badly hurt, income from the Assumption festival dropped sharply, diocesan assessments went unpaid and plans for a parochial school were scrapped. In 1930, the trustees voted to assess every family $12 a year, to be paid monthly, and to refuse "the rights of the Church" to any who failed to pay this amount, either

directly or through pew rental. Despite severe divisions, the parish reduced its debt, which stood at $41,000 in 1915, to less than $5,000 by 1935. At the same time, it paved the roads around the church, finished the basement, built a rectory, decorated the church and installed stained glass windows. In the depression year 1935, Pellegrini began a subscription drive for $15,000 to bring five nuns to the parish for social work, home visiting and religious instruction. However, his hopes stalled when less than two-thirds was collected because of the continuing unemployment in the city.

Internal divisions and personnel problems also plagued St. Anthony's in Endicott. In June 1926, a "grievance committee" wrote the bishop a long series of complaints against the pastor, Rocco Machiavera. His door-to-door visits to collect a dollar a month from each family, his high fees for such church services as funerals, baptisms, marriages and novenas, and his failure to preach at Sunday Masses jeopardized support for the parish, the committee claimed. Four years later, similar charges were sent to the apostolic delegate, who inquired of Curley. The bishop defended the pastor, but clearly was not satisfied. The bishop personally arranged for a summer school of religion and provided sisters to staff it, while sending an English speaking priest, Father Joseph Osip, to assist with Masses and provide Sunday school instruction for the children "in the only language they know." Unfortunately, instead of accepting the bishop's advice, Machiavera, according to Curley, persuaded the people to resent Osip's presence. Curley was very angry:

I am chiefly responsible for the souls under your spiritual jurisdiction. I have been aware for a long time of your inadequate care for them. I have suggested methods of improvement. You have always met these with

APOSTLE TO THE ITALIANS

When Kate E. Griffin died in 1937 at the age of 70, the pastor of St. Bartholomew's parish in Norwich draped the sanctuary of his church for mourning, celebrated an unusual Sunday funeral and preached a special eulogy — "unusual things that they, by their very rareness, may pay tribute to our dear friend and benefactress."

"Kate Griffin loved the poor because she saw in the poor the image of Jesus Christ. She was not a philanthropist because the love she had for the poor did not stop at the poor. It elevated itself to the supernatural, because the commandment of love taught her to love Christ's unfortunates for God's sake. The poor then were the brothers and sisters of Jesus Christ, and that was the secret of her patience and perseverance when she suffered rebuke and ingratitude at the hands of those she was serving. Kate Griffin did not stop at her desk and write a check to alleviate want; she sought want in the homes of the poor and by her personal contact made the burden lighter. She brought the poor to her very home to her table and did for them the most menial service; she begged for them and did not blush to ask alms and take alms that suffering might be lessened. Hers was Christ-like charity....

"For 17 years I was associated with her, but for twice 17 years and more she had been gathering about her the Catholic children of Norwich to teach them the Christian doctrine. First at St. Paul's in the Sunday School and then looking over the little colony of Italians here in our fair city she saw a field white to the harvest and no laborer willing to gather it in. 'Souls, Souls,' they tell us was the constant cry of St. Francis Xavier, the Apostle of the Indies. And 'Souls, Souls' was the cry of this woman, The Apostle of the Italians of Norwich. It was the valiant woman of the Scriptures that went into that field; those that should have reaped sat by; the Italian emigrant was left to his own devices and God raised Kate Griffin to do the work. There is not an Italian child or man or woman who came into contact with her during the last 40 years but who is the better for the contact. If the Italians amount to anything today in Norwich, the glory belongs to her; if Jesus Christ is loved today in our little colony and His church occupies first place in the thoughts of our thousand Italians, after God the work is that of Kate Griffin.... (Her) religion was not emotionalism or tinged with sentimentality. Her religion was a working religion, a live religion.... Discouraged she was often, a quitter never; she fought the good fight and the soul of the least Italian child was worth all her effort. And today the Italian children of Norwich call her blessed...."

(From a eulogy by Father Walter A. Sinnot, June 27, 1937)

evasions and with no apparent effort to carry out my suggestions. I have found it necessary, therefore, to make other provisions. You will follow my instructions regarding Father Osip, and encourage the support of your people in this respect, especially regarding the children, and bring peace and concord among all your people. And if you do not carry out my instructions in this respect, I will certainly appoint a priest to supplant you. Italians have been going for some time to a Protestant Italian church in your neighborhood. If they continue to do so, and increase in numbers in their attendance there, the sin will be upon your soul. Deus te adjuvet.

Yet Curley's hands were not so free because he had few reliable Italian priests. When his threats had little effect, Father Rocco was replaced by Father William Walsh, just back from Rome. Two lay trustees then submitted their resignations. Later Walsh would turn out to be an excellent pastor, but in this first assignment, his nationality was against him. The former trustees, their friends and their children now indeed were attending the Presbyterian church, they told Curley. They vowed to engage in house-to-house "propaganda against the support of the Catholic church and its pastor, your countryman Father Walsh."

Know, also, that we have taken recourse to Rome, explaining our reasons clearly, because only with Italian sweat was the church paid for, and not American contributions. You have no right to send among us an American foreign to our language, our customs, our ideals, when you know we all want Father Rocco, who knows us and understands us. You are a bishop, but you have no conscience; you have the effrontery to dismiss our pastor after sixteen years of service without giving him another position; you put him out without means and without future, because he cannot return to Italy. Luther with his reform certainly must have been right.

The formation of the Italian parish of St. Bartholomew in Norwich was another case study of the problems facing Italian-Americans. The beginning of the Church in the area followed a pattern that went back to the Devereaux family in Utica so many years earlier. This pattern recently had been repeated at St. Anthony's in Utica and St. Vincent's in Syracuse, where Sunday school instruction by lay volunteers laid the foundation of parish life. In Norwich, the leader was a remarkable public school teacher, Kate A. Griffin, who organized catechism classes for Italians.

With the help of Father Clement Shaughnessy, assistant at St. Paul's, a vacant store was rented and classes were full. Soon the Italian families purchased the building, hoping it would become a mission of St. Paul's. The pastor, Father Joseph Tiernan, offered only sporadic services, but he took charge of all collections despite the fact that the Italian parishioners and not the parish corporation held title to the property. The Italians thought that, once they had bought and paid for the church, they would receive an Italian pastor. Bishop Grimes procrastinated and relations grew tense, with petitions reaching the apostolic delegate. Father Walter A. Sinnott, who had replaced Shaughnessy as assistant to Father Tiernan, tried to reconcile the parties, but with little success. When the apostolic delegate inquired about the matter in 1921, Grimes responded somewhat defensively that Father Sinnott, who spoke Italian, had charge of the community. Grimes said problems arose from a small group of older Italians who wished to "dictate policy and control the pastor." He denied that he had any "personal feelings whatsoever against the Italians of Norwich." He had 50,000 Italians in his diocese and had "done everything possible for them." Nevertheless, said the bishop, now that Rome had indicated an interest, he would let them have their own priest and parish, even though other nationalities would demand similar treatment. Grimes did not move, however, and the matter remained for Bishop Curley, who received respectful petitions from the Italians and strong letters on their behalf from non-

221

Italians, both Catholic and non-Catholic. Curley was decisive, sending Father Sinnott to form the new parish on the condition that a rectory was provided. When this was done, Sinnott took charge, with the understanding that he was to serve only Italians. When Tiernan complained that Sinnott was preaching in English as well as Italian and using English religious instruction, Curley replied that he was doing so on the bishop's advice. On the other hand, the bishop corrected Sinnott for providing marriage and funeral services for non-parishioners.

SLOVAKS MAKE PROGRESS

Things were even less peaceful in the Slovak parishes. Father Joseph Martincek, pastor of Sts. Cyril and Methodius in Binghamton, succeeded in reducing the parish debt of $38,000, when he arrived in 1917, to approximately $20,000 in 1923, while making more than $35,000 in improvements on the parish buildings. He angered some parishoners, however, by inviting Father Killett of St. Patrick's to assist with Masses on Sunday and preach an English sermon each week. When neighboring English speaking Catholics attended the church, the Slovaks felt their presence undermined the national character of their congregation. They equally resented the drift of more Americanized members toward the English speaking parishes. In 1923, faced with "serious trouble," the bishop asked the Franciscans to take over the parish. Already serving Slovak parishes in other sections of the northeast, the community agreed and sent Father Cyril Orendac to Binghamton. Born in New Jersey and educated in Austria, Father Cyril was 45 and already something of a troubleshooter, having brought order out of "chaos" in a similar parish in Indianapolis. Martincek did not take the change easily. Proud of what he had accomplished in Binghamton, he worried that

the transfer would cast a shadow over his reputation and give loyal Catholics reason to believe he was being driven out by the opposition, whom he characterized as "the bolshevik element." Martincek went to Indianapolis to warn Father Orendac. Unfortunately, this trip was read as insubordination, and the bishop forced Martincek to submit his resignation.

Curley had reason to be pleased with the Binghamton decision because it brought to the diocese a Franciscan who would prove invaluable in the years ahead. Orendac showed his skill quickly, investigating the alleged demand for a new Slovak parish in the Downsville section and submitting a detailed, balanced report to the bishop. These Slovaks wanted a new parish because the Sts. Cyril and Methodius congregation "make fun of their dialect." Orendac wisely added that he suspected that the continuous quarrels undoubtedly made them hope that "in a place of their own there would be peace." However, there were already Polish and Lithuanian churches nearby, so at least a new site should be chosen in an area of the community where there were many unchurched Slovaks. For the time being, he recommended setting up a mission at the present site, for the purchase of which many families had mortgaged their homes. A year later, this had been done and Orendac persuaded them to deed the property over to the bishop. Faced with competition from a nearby Polish National church and a schismatic Czecho-Slovak church, the bishop recognized the new mission, St. Anne's. A barn was renovated with the help of the parishioners and two priests moved into the farmhouse turned rectory. In 1934, the parish was incorporated and Joseph Osip was appointed pastor, a post he would hold for 30 years.

Every Slovak parish, it seemed, had problems. In August 1928, parishioners at St. Joseph's in Endicott asked the bishop to remove their pastor, Father John J. Pochilly. Apparently, the bishop agreed because a short time later he sent Father Florian Billy to the parish. He first had to straighten out some unusual financial arrangements. In the process, he aroused considerable opposition. Trouble reached a boiling point in 1934. The 115 members of the St. Anthony Lodge of the Slovak Catholic Union complained that Billy refused to confess them as a group as they prepared for their patron's feast day and denied them use of the hall and the reservation of front row pews. After characterizing the signers as weak personalities, lax Catholics or people with "selfish grievances," Billy explained that behind the protests was tension in the parish between Slovaks and Moravians. The parish was a "national boiling pot." A Slovak himself, he had made no discriminatory remarks and was trying his "level best to be a Catholic priest and to get this parish in line with the regular and customary ways of running parishes in our diocese." Toward this end, he had abolished the "so-called annual meetings which, as you know, have been the ruin of many otherwise good parishes."

The bishop was satisfied with Billy's response, but conflict continued and shortly after, the bishop once again called upon the Franciscans for help. They agreed to take over the parish, and Father Julian Hubal quickly won the love of a large group of mothers in the parish. However, his nerves were shattered and he was removed by his superiors. Sending another pastor, Father Urban Koval, the provincial added some comments on the nature of the problem at St. Joseph's and other Slovak parishes. Once again, it was lay determination to control church finances:

This is the season of the year when in these parishes the so called annual meetings are insisted upon by certain elements for the election of lay trust-

ees, ushers, sextons, organists etc. These meetings have afforded agitators the opportunity to agitate and trouble makers the opportunity to make trouble. At these meetings the frequent routine is to vent ill seasoned opinions on administering the parish and to find fault with priest, bishop, and pope. It is a form of laicization. The pastors of our community respectfully request a statement of your excellency to the effect that Slovak parishes, like every parish, must be administered in the canonical-legal manner prescribed, namely by the bishop, vicar-general, the pastor and two lay trustees as the board of trustees, and by this board only, and that the two lay trustees are elected by the bishop, the vicar-general and the pastor, and that the so-called annual meetings are out of order and have no competency in the matter, and that only such meetings may be called as are called by the pastor and then only for the purpose, for instance preparation for a bazaar or social, for which they were called.

More than a statement of episcopal authority would be needed. On March 9, 1935, 250 parishioners staged a public demonstration against the pastor, demanding "representation in financial matters and the appointment of officers" and the return of Father Julian. Thirty police were called to the scene to disperse the crowd, and the experience calmed the situation temporarily. Once again Father Cyril, now in Schenectedy, was summoned. He met with the various factions, but failed to resolve the dispute. Faced with a boycott of contributions, Duffy was prepared to let Father Julian return and to allow the parishioners to name four possible trustees, from whom he would select two, a major concession. The dissidents, however, insisted on electing their own trustees to be "confirmed in office by the bishop," to elect the sexton, collectors and ushers, to count the money with the pastor, to sign all checks, to have a veto over the purchase and sale of property, and to report to an annual parish meeting, as had been done in the past.

Father Cyril Orendac was a good man in a crisis. He visited house-to-house, finding that the support of the lay leaders was broad but shallow. Only approximately 10 percent were refusing to contribute until the leaders told them to. Sixty percent were waiting to see what would happen. Cyril understood that time was on the bishop's side, but he also apparently liked the people. Even when discussing the most difficult lay opponents, he was always calm, detached and, at times, compassionate. "These people can say the meanest things and hurt you to the quick, still, in spite of all that, they are not bad at heart." Several things were at stake in this fight. As the mothers indicated, there was a matter of pride. They felt they had been "ruled with intimidation, terrorism and tyranny" prior to Father Julian's coming. His removal was "un-Catholic, un-Christian and unjust." "We Catholic Slovaks," the mothers wrote, "the bishop cannot tolerate no (sic) longer since we have been taken too much for granted."

There also was some class feeling. Defending the parish meeting, one group said it was Slovak tradition "to take heed of the poor as well as the wealthy members of the congregation." They and others mentioned the number of church members transferring to Protestant and schismatic churches. Perhaps most important, however, was the simple recurrence of the "trustee impulse." The laymen were used to holding their parish meetings, they had shared the financial power, and, like so many before them, they saw no reason why those who paid the bills should not have some power over parish affairs. At no time did they demand the right to appoint or remove priests. Though they did demand the return of Father Julian, they did so only on an *ad hoc* basis, convinced there had been no good reason for his removal.

Bishop Duffy granted the point, and Father Julian returned. The climax came in the early weeks of 1937, when the parish selected four names and then, on a second ballot, selected two and ordered that only those two names should be submitted to the bishop. Father Julian warned them that this procedure would prove unacceptable to the bishop, but he sent the names along. The bishop responded that, under no circumstances, would he abide by that choice and proceeded to take the other two members nominated. By this time, with Father Julian back, the dissidents faced declining enthusiasm among their supporters. By 1940, Julian could report that four names had been selected and approved peacefully. The process resulted in an incomplete victory for the bishop and his designated pastors, the Franciscans. The steady, patient approach of Father Cyril, offering acceptable parish services, while talking constantly with all factions among the laity, gradually wore down the opposition. Despite the clear opposition of the Franciscans even to holding parish meetings, the meetings indeed continued. On the other hand, despite the bishop's desire to choose trustees as in other parishes, Duffy and later Bishop Foery proved remarkably flexible, granting the concession of returning Father Julian and allowing the parish to nominate a slate of candidates. Firmness and flexibility at the top, and patience and careful negotiation from the pastor, combined with the simple factor of exhaustion to win the day for the diocese. The Franciscans and the bishops undoubtedly trusted the truth of a statement by Father Billy at the start of the fight that the children were altogether different from their elders. Less passionate about nationality, at least in Church affairs, and more susceptible to the embarrassment of highly public Church disputes, the younger generation could be trusted to abide by the American form of Church government, at least as long as the basic goals of pastors and people were the same, and as long as basic pastoral services were provided satisfactorily.

MORE POLISH PARISHES

The days of Polish parish formation were not over. In Endicott, a small Polish community had been served by priests from Binghamton since 1910. Most of the families were unskilled laborers at the Endicott Johnson Shoe Company or farmers from the surrounding area. The group hoped to purchase the former Slovak church of St. Joseph when the new church was completed, but the land was sold before they could bid on it. However, the new congregation did succeed in dismantling the building and using the materials. Although weekly collections were only $15, they succeeded in raising almost $2,300 through subscriptions by 1930, when they purchased four lots. The men of the parish, with the help of Father Holocinski of St. Stanislaus, excavated the site and laid the foundation. One family donated a team of horses and George F. Johnson gave $1,000 to purchase pews. The new church was attached as a mission to St. Stanislaus until the first resident pastor, Father John A. Kociela, was appointed in 1936. St. Casimir's was one of the few Polish churches without a school, but sisters from Binghamton provided instruction in religion and Polish language to 120 children each week.

Another Polish community took shape in Fulton. Polish people worked in the woolen mills and worshiped at Immaculate Conception church, traveling occasionally for confession or for feasts to Sacred Heart in Syracuse or later to St. Stephen's in Oswego. In 1908, Father Stephen Plaza had organized the latter parish, and the following year he helped the Poles in Fulton establish the St. Michael's Society to plan for an eventual church. His successor, Father Simon Pniak, continued to celebrate Mass for the group in the basement of Immaculate Conception for 10 years. Pniak also used the money collected by the St. Michael's Society to purchase lots, but when he neglected the community after 1920, building plans faltered. In 1925, Father Piejda arrived to revitalize the Oswego congregation. He offered Mass in public halls in Fulton as well. As many parishioners opposed the site selected earlier, Piejda sold it and acquired a new site whose house was converted into a church and rectory. In 1930, the community received its first resident priest and, in 1931, three Felician sisters were assigned to St. Michael's to assist with religious and Polish language instruction.

At St. Stanislaus in Binghamton, there was an unusual outcome to a fight. A dissident faction proved victorious.

Complaints reached the chancery in late 1925 that the pastor had kept parish accounts secret and recently had announced a parish indebtedness far beyond what previously had been mentioned. Because the lay committee brought the matter secretly to the bishop, and because the chancery already had grown suspicious about the annual reports, the bishop was receptive. The pastor was instructed to have a thorough audit of the books, and to meet regularly with the trustees to pay bills, count money and balance the books, all of which he agreed to do. When the audit was completed and new trustees chosen, the chancellor probed several items while the lay leaders raised new questions. The pastor's explanations were unconvincing and the bishop transferred him and told the trustees that half the acknowledged debt to the parish would be paid within 10 days, the rest within three months.

In Syracuse, Transfiguration parish's problems persisted into the 1920s. A lay group which had been meeting in the church since 1919 decided to build its own clubhouse, independent of the parish. The pastor tried to persuade the group to postpone these plans in order to help with raising money for yet another addition to the school. The club attempted to foster Polish customs and traditions and, at the same time, promote Americanization by helping people get their citizenship papers, learn English and register to vote. When the hall opened in 1925, a Mass was celebrated and the building was offered for use of parish societies free of charge.

That same year, an addition was built onto the school at a cost of $25,000, but the pastor, worn out by the debt, was increasingly detached and unavailable. People grew angry, many transferred to the neighboring parish of St. Vincent de Paul and those who remained were taunted as "cousins of the pastor." Although working-class parishioners were earning $28 a week, revenue fell disastrously. Lay teachers were dropped from the school and the sisters struggled with classes of 60 or more. When the depression hit, only continued borrowing prevented foreclosure of mortgages. However, the pastor refused parish demands to examine the books as a step toward improving conditions. Finally, the pastor resigned in 1933 and was replaced by George Guzewicz. He had been raised at Sacred Heart, educated at St. Bernard's and served for a short time as assistant at Holy Trinity in Utica. He abolished the parish meetings and annual election of trustees, but embarked on a vigorous program of fundraising activities which drew families back to the church. Bazaars, picnics, dances, raffles, bake sales, plays and school pageants all helped improve the situation to the extent that he could install a new heating system in 1937 and bring the parish rolls up to 300 families before leaving for a new assignment in

Binghamton in 1939.

All was far from peaceful at the other St. Stanislaus, organized in 1911 for Polish people on the east side of Utica.

During the war, the parish succeeded in erecting a combination school and church. In 1926, Italian-born Father Dutkiewicz took charge, finding growing divisions and dissent within the congregation. As a result of an earlier dispute, parishioners had been electing two trustees to oversee accounts. They became angry when Dutkiewicz, backed by the bishop, ended this arrangement. In June 1928, the now-appointed lay trustees informed the bishop that conditions in the parish had deteriorated. Only one-fourth of the people were attending Mass, receipts had dropped by half and the trustees were being kept in the dark regarding expenditures. After conducting his own investigation, the bishop exonerated the priest, and urged the trustees and people to cooperate. Privately, the bishop believed the dissidents were "communists." Bishop Curley explained to the apostolic delegate that he intended to end the annual meetings and elections, which he had tolerated "for the sake of peace." Writing to the parishioners, Curley admitted that Dutkiewicz may have made some mistakes, but he judged they were not serious enough to justify "disloyalty and dissatisfaction." He asked the dissidents to reconsider:

How would you feel, if you were a pastor serving to the best of your ability the interests of your parishioners, while some of them were questioning your methods and endeavoring to undermine your influence? A pastor in the United States, even with the sympathetic support and encouragement of his parishioners, frequently has many periods of worry and anxiety in meeting the financial obligations of the parish. Therefore let the trustees and their friends put aside all past and present grievances and make a new start, determined to do their part in supporting their church and do nothing to add to their pastor's perplexities and anxieties. If they do this, I pray that God will bless them and their families and give them the grace to persevere to the end.

It was not to be. In February 1929, the pastor and a newly named trustee formally demanded the return of the parish books and documents from the former trustees, who in turn, had their lawyer inform the vicar general they would not do so. The trustees relied upon their supposed right to nominate men to be named trustees, a right not found in the diocesan statutes. Furthermore, the trustees' argument that only paying parishioners could be considered members of the Church was unsupported in Church or civil law. As a result, the trustees were ordered by the courts to return the papers, which they did. This description of the struggle at Holy Trinity sounds mild enough, but along the way police were called and, if one priest is to be believed, one woman threw mustard in the pastor's face. In any event, here as in a few other cases, episcopal control had to accommodate longstanding custom and overcome suspicion of the clergy's competence, if not honesty. Only time, the arrival of a new generation less interested in parish affairs, along with more effective pastoral service, would heal the wounds of these fights, which were bitter and left scars for those who took part.

Other Polish parishes were more peaceful and experienced steady growth during the postwar years. Sacred Heart's huge church and school in Syracuse prospered under Father Rusin and later Father Piejda. Holy Trinity in Utica was by now an almost equally large parish. In 1921, Bishop Grimes con-

firmed 591 young people there. In 1926, Curley confirmed 705. In 1924, Holy Trinity's school enrollment peaked at 1,400 students in eight grades. It was a stable, prosperous parish under Michael Dzialuk, a Polish-born priest with a doctorate from Rome who, according to the proud authors of the parish's history, could converse easily in "15 or 16 languages."

Transfiguration in Rome also grew steadily. In 1923, the Felician sisters taught more than 250 children in the parish school and, in the 1930s, it served a parish of 1,700 people. It is hard to imagine a Polish parish without a school. In Central New York it is hard to imagine Polish schools without Felician sisters, a Franciscan community driven out of their native Poland by the Russian government after 1864. The first emigrants went to Polonia, Wisconsin, to assist the pioneer Polish priest, Joseph Dombrowski. From there, the expanding community sent a group to serve in Buffalo in 1900. It was from the Buffalo province that the first sisters came to Sacred Heart in Syracuse and, after that, they were courted by every new Polish parish. Eventually, they staffed not only Sacred Heart, but Transfiguration in Syracuse, St. Mary's in New York Mills, St. Stanislaus in Binghamton, St. Casimir's Lithuanian church in Endicott, St. Stephen's in Oswego, Transfiguration in Rome and St. Stanislaus in Utica.

EASTERN RITE CATHOLICS

If there was one large lesson out of the experience of ethnic pluralism, it was that not all Catholics need be the same. Determined to build a united Catholic Church in the United States, the bishops gained control over Church property and the appointment of clergy. But they recognized, however reluctantly, the need for national, foreign-language parishes, and they worked hard to recruit priests to serve in them. By World War I, in the cities of the Syracuse diocese, there were German, Italian, Polish, Slovak, French and Lithuanian parishes, each with their church

buildings, sometimes within blocks of each other. From the outside, the American Catholic Church may have appeared hopelessly

CATHOLICS OF THE EASTERN RITES

In the early days of Christianity, missionaries went out from Palestine — to Rome where Catholics began to worship in what came to be known as the Latin or Roman rite; to people in Greek lands who developed the Byzantine rite; to other parts of the Middle East and Africa, where Catholics began to worship in various rites. All of these various faith communities were part of the same Catholic Church, each with their own bishops and patriarchs in communion with each other and with the Western patriarch in Rome, the pope.

After the empire divided, the communion among the bishops was split — the pope and the Latin bishops, other patriarchs and bishops of the East. This split remains today between the Roman Catholic and the Eastern Orthodox Churches.

Gradually over the centuries, there was some reconciliation as several of the eastern groups resumed unity between themselves and Catholics in the West. These are the Eastern rites of the Church — fully Roman Catholic in faith and in their unity with the pope, yet retaining their ancient liturgies, separate diocesan jurisdictions, and their own practices and customs.

Several parishes of these Eastern rites exist within the boundaries of the Latin-rite diocese of Syracuse:

MELKITE: The Melkite Church is part of the Byzantine (Greek Catholic) rite, serving Catholics from Greece and the Middle East in communion with the patriarch of Antioch. The local Melkite diocese is based in Newton, Massachusetts. One local parish exists — St. Basil Melkite church in Utica.

RUTHENIAN: The Ruthenian Church is a part of the Byzantine rite serving Catholics of Czechoslovak, Hungarian, and Russian background. The Ruthenian Church in this area is served by the diocese of Passaic, New Jersey. Two parishes exist locally — Holy Spirit Ruthenian church in Binghamton, and Sts. Peter and Paul Ruthenian church in Endicott.

UKRAINIAN: A third member of the Byzantine rite, the Ukrainian Church, serves Catholics with roots in the Ukraine. The local diocese is based at Stamford, Connecticut. Four area parishes include Sacred Heart Ukrainian church in Johnson City, St. Michael Ukrainian church in Rome, St. John the Baptist Ukrainian church in Syracuse, and St. Volodymyr the Great Ukrainian church in Utica.

MARONITE: The Maronite Church, part of the Antiochene rite, has been united with the Holy See since St. Maron founded it in the fourth century in the Middle East. The Church includes Catholics of Lebanese heritage in communion with the patriarch of Antioch. The local Maronite diocese is based in Brooklyn. The single area parish is St. Louis Gonzaga Maronite church in Utica.

divided. In fact, the members of these churches had much in common. If they sometimes made much of their different customs and devotions, they shared the same faith, the same basic doctrines and a similar approach to morality. Different in their nationality, they had in common the immigration experience itself, a sense of distance from the major institutions of the community and a tenacious determination to be American, while holding fast to their traditions. If some priests and bishops saw national parishes as a temporary expedient, and some parishioners were not reconciled to America's episcopal and clerical domination of parish affairs, all were worshiping in the Latin tongue and following the same basic sacramental rituals.

Not quite all. There were Eastern Rite Catholics who belonged at home to ancient Churches that had developed their own liturgy. When the eastern and western Churches split, they refused to follow the Orthodox into schism. Remaining loyal to Rome, they also remained faithful to their traditions. This meant that they often celebrated their liturgies not in Latin, but in their native tongue, their clergy married and they looked to the leadership of patriarchs.

The patriarchs were bishops of major sees who ruled the national Churches while remaining in communion with the Holy See. When immigrants from Lebanon, Syria, Armenia and the polyglot lands of the Balkans arrived in the United States, some were Catholics but of different rites than the dominant Latin rite of the bishops and most parishioners. They posed unique problems for the American bishops because their needs could not be met by ordinary parish clergy. Their distinctive liturgy required the services of priests of their own rite. In most cases, their Churches allowed the clergy to marry. This latter practice particularly disturbed American bishops, who, in 1890, petitioned Rome to prohibit Eastern Rite clergy who

were married from serving in this country, and to prohibit priests trained here from marrying.

Rome went along with the American bishops on this last point, at least for a time, but otherwise made few concessions to the American bishops. The Vatican's Congregation on Oriental Churches protected Eastern Rite Catholics against discrimination and regularly warned American bishops to respect their ancient customs and discipline. On marriage cases in particular, the American bishops were told to scrupulously respect the jurisdiction of the Oriental Churches over the groom and his children. Even when the man in question wished to change rites, Roman permission was required and it was rarely granted.

In the 1920s, when these groups had their own American hierarchy, these rules were enforced even more strictly. In 1924, for example, Joseph Osip wished to become a Roman Catholic priest. Osip was raised in Austria. His mother was a Roman Catholic; his father a Ruthenian Catholic. Osip was baptized and confirmed in his father's Church before the family emigrated after World War I. In Binghamton, the family attended a Latin Rite Slovak church. When Joseph expressed the wish to enter the diocesan priesthood, his father was warmly supportive. Nevertheless, Bishop Curley had to seek permission from the Greek Catholic bishop to receive Osip as a candidate. The bishop told Curley he was opposed to such changes of rite, in principle. He would make an exception in Osip's case, but only if he became a priest. Should he leave the seminary, the change of rite would be null and void.

At first, many of the Eastern Rite immigrants were as confused by American pluralism as their fellow Catholics were by the appearance of Catholics so different from themselves. Some found a temporary place of worship in Polish or Slovak Catholic churches

An Eastern flavor extends to the architecture and decoration at St. Louis Gonzaga church for Maronite Catholics in Utica. (Photo: St. Louis Gonzaga church)

or, as in Utica, in an English-language parish like St. John's which went out of its way to serve their needs by inviting priests of their rite in Pennsylvania or Ohio to visit occasionally. Sometimes, however, they found a home in a Russian or Greek Orthodox church, with its similar liturgy and language, in some cases, it seems, without recognizing the difference.

Nevertheless, several Eastern Rite churches were solidly established before World War I. In Syracuse, Catholics of the Ukranian Rite, many from the Austro-Hungarian Empire, worshiped for a time at Sacred Heart.

However, they worried about the erosion of traditional loyalty because Orthodox and anti-clericals seemed more equipped to preserve their language and customs. A lay committee was organized in 1896. It purchased a building the following year and found a resident pastor for St. John the Baptist Ukranian Catholic church. By 1913, the small community had a beautiful permanent church. In Utica, Maronite Rite Catholics from Syria and Lebanon met at St. John's, where they were visited by priests from New York City and Scranton. In 1907, Father Louis Lotzif arrived and St. Louis Gonzaga parish was organized with 500 members. Three years later, they had their own church, complete with a rectory located in room above the church. As the first Maronite parish between Albany and Buffalo, it rallied Syrians and Lebanese Catholics throughout Central New York. Yet, not all from these countries were Maronites. Some Syrians were Melkites, as were a scattering of immigrants from other countries of southeastern Europe and the Middle East. In 1918, they too opened a church in Utica, St. Basil's.

In Broome County, Byzantine and Ukranian Rite Catholics called themselves Greek Catholics. St. Michael's in Binghamton, composed mostly of immigrants from Czechoslovakia, some of whom had been meeting with the Russian Orthodox, opened in 1906. By 1915, the parish had a spacious church of its own. In Endicott, a community composed of Slovak or Russian speaking immigrants found a home in Sts. Peter and Paul, organized in 1905. They too rallied to the cause of providing a church which, with the help of George F. Johnson, opened in 1919. All these developments took place largely through lay leadership, as communities sought to provide through their church the means of preserving family and communal traditions and ensuring that the century-old struggle to prevent slippage into Eastern Orthodoxy or irreligion was not lost in the United States. While Bishops Ludden and Grimes did not actively assist these efforts because their energies were directed elsewhere, they knew that Rome was watching and offered at least their moral support. For ecclesiastical backing, however, the lay leaders had to turn to priests of their own rite, first to visit, then to help them find a resident pastor. Even more than Polish, Slovak and Lithuanian churches, these tiny, apparently somewhat exotic, congregations bore witness to the tenacity with which immigrant peoples held

fast to their ancestral faith and the sense of community associated with it.

The conflicts which rocked Slovak parishes were confusing. Issues of national rivalries, both within congregations and between parishioners and the hierarchy, often were mixed up with conflicting perceptions of lay responsibility, democratic values and religious loyalties. This was even more true in some Eastern Rite churches. At Sts. Peter and Paul in Endicott, schismatic priests used the American prohibition of clerical celibacy to agitate the congregation in the 1920s. For a time, the dissidents gained control over the parish. Conflicts arising from the problem of control over church funds divided St. Michael's in Binghamton. There, the dissidents refused to accept the authority of the Greek Catholic hierarchy, took control of their church and won a court battle over the property. The loyal Catholics withdrew and founded Holy Spirit church under the Greek Catholic exarch, or patriarch. Other Eastern Rite churches, especially the Maronite church of St. Louis Gonzaga, were more stable. Under Francis Lahoud, a remarkably energetic pastor who arrived in 1933, St. Louis overcame internal battles over control of Church funds and erected a new church with the backing of Bishop Duffy. It moved to the forefront of Maronite congregations in the country.

Yet, with exceptions like St. Louis, these Eastern Rite parishes were at the fringes of diocesan life. In 1926, when Rome asked for the number of "Russian" Catholics and "schismatics" or Orthodox in the diocese, Curley sought information from local pastors. Their answers were sketchy at best, referring to tiny congregations but, with little information on membership. A similar questionnaire in 1931 on Melkite and Maronite Catholics brought a similar response. These Eastern Rite Catholics, most by now subject to their own hierarchy, were only partially the bishop's

At St. John the Baptist Ukrainian church in Syracuse, Father Philip Bumbar (left) and Monsignor Basil Seredowych hold a tapestry used in services. (Photo: The Catholic Sun)

responsibility. They were, instead, as one parishioner put it, "the stepchildren of the diocese." Yet this did not prevent the bishop from urging Rome, in the strongest possible terms, to override the protests of Ruthenian Rite priests and continue the ban on married priests in the United States. The Eastern Rite clergy regarded this ban as a violation of their historic rights within the Roman Catholic Church.

In the years between the wars, the Syracuse diocese became an even more organized and disciplined Church. Few voices of dissent were heard, as the bishops attempted to express in organization the vision of the Church as "the happiest and most peaceful society." Integration of Catholics into a unified and secure subculture, knit together by a common faith and bonds of association was the goal, one which was coming closer to fulfillment. The biggest obstacle remained the Church's internal cultural diversity because many newer immigrants had not yet become "practicing Catholics" and even those who had did not yet fully accept "American" ways of dealing with Church affairs. At times, bishops and priests grew impatient and attempted to compel obedience, but more often they recognized that persuasion, through patience and good pastoral care, were far more effective. Room was being made in the one house of the Catholic Church. Gradually these Catholics were moving in.

PAROCHIAL TREASURE

PARISH LIFE IN THE YEARS BETWEEN THE WARS
1920s-1940s

In the United States, religious denominations have as their major function providing services and support to local congregations. The Catholic Church carried out that task in the period between the wars by providing priests, taking on a growing number of responsibilities in charities and education that could not be handled by individual parishes, attempting to keep the Church united both in faith and discipline, and ensuring a sufficient degree of uniformity to limit inter-parish competition and conflict. For most Catholics, however, the diocese was distant, known to them almost exclusively through the person of the bishop. In some cases, as when they were dissatisfied with their pastor, they experienced the diocese as an institution. A small number active in Holy Name, the Catholic Women's Club and a few other activities had a more positive experience of participation in the diocese. But for most people, the diocese was the bishop. He gave them a sense of unity as Catholics. He connected them to that vast history they dimly knew through their catechism class and the symbols in their churches. He also connected them to that world-wide Church centered on the pope and known to them through their contributions to the missions, their awareness of problems in their old world homelands, or press reports of Church conflicts with governments abroad. Catholicism as sacrament, doctrine, morality and way of life they knew largely in their parish. In practice they were parochial in their religious life. Scholars regularly insist that in American society, with its freedom, pluralism and dependence on the voluntary action of people, Christians are always to some degree congregational. They make practical decisions in terms of their congregation or parish. Bishops and priests knew that, for most people most of the time, the parish was the Church. The major responsibility of the diocese therefore, had been and remained the strengthening of parish life. In these years, parishes were thriving beyond the expectations of even the most optimistic of the earlier generation. The history of parish life was a remarkably successful story. In these thriving churches, schools, convents, rectories, and in the people whose lives moved around them in varying orbits, lay what one bishop would call "parochial treasure." He added that this "treasure" had been accumulating through the sacrifices of generations, with each called to redeem that legacy in the quality of their faith and the witness of their lives.

RAPID EXPANSION

In the diocese of Syracuse, there were two periods of extraordinary expansion in the twentieth century. The first came after the First World War and lasted until the onset of the Great Depression. The second would begin after the next war and last almost 20 years. The diocese had 101 parishes before World War I. By 1930 that number had grown to 130, yet even that did not keep up with the growth of population. The average size of the parish in 1917 was 1,381 persons. By 1930 it had risen to 1,454 despite 29 new parishes. The building boom was fueled by increased income, as ordinary parish revenues, apart from special drives for new construction, rose 150 percent, from slightly more than $1,000,000 in 1917 to $2,600,000 in 1930. This almost doubled the ordinary income of the average parish. Even when the factor of inflation considered, parish revenues still doubled, a growth which reflected an increasing prosperity among Catholic factory workers and lower middle class shopkeepers, teachers, civil servants and clerks. Together, these improving conditions created and sustained the optimism and self-reliance so characteristic of Bishops Grimes and Curley. They encouraged the diocese to allow a dramatic increase in parish debt, which rose from $1,300,000 dollars in 1917 to $4,500,000 in 1930. Again, considering the rise in prices, the increase was still dramatic, as the debt in 1930 was almost $3,500,000 in constant 1917 dollars.

The raw information about parish construction was no more revealing in the 1920s than a century earlier. What gave meaning and spirit to the process was the involvement of ordinary people, for whom the growth of the parish was a matter of commitment and pride. A good example is found in a brief history of Blessed Sacrament Parish in Syracuse, written by a parishioner in 1937, 16 years after the parish was established. The document reflects the pride of the people and the way in which the story of a parish could take on almost mythical dimensions. Eastwood was a neighborhood on Syracuse's eastern boundary with the town of Dewitt. Catholics in that area attended St. Matthew's church in East Syracuse. But after the war, it became clear that this sparsely populated section was to become an area of rapid growth. Richard J. Shanahan, for 18 years assistant to Michael Clune at St. John the Evangelist, took up the task of establishing a new parish. He approached Eastwood village authorities for permission to say Mass temporarily in the town hall. For a weekly fee of $15, they agreed. With the help of two parishioners, and with materials borrowed from St. John's, the hall was prepared for the first Mass on September 18, 1921. The anonymous historian records this happy event which, "not withstanding the inclement weather and unchurchlike set up," was attended by 125 "mostly Irish" parishioners:

It was a dull, dreary morning, the sky was heavily overcast, a cold wind swept through the village, the dust stirred by the revellers of the night before had scarcely subsided in the hall; the fire horses on the first floor below gave evidence of great nervousness and stamped their iron shod feet heavily in their stalls. In all it was little better than the crib at Bethlehem and yet such as might warrant the same momentous results that grew out of Bethlehem.... It was a humble beginning but destined to succeed because it was the work of God and God's church has never failed.

The next step was to purchase property. In February 1922, the parish acquired for $22,000 a six-acre site of 36 building lots on both sides of James Street. It was a large tract, and an expensive one. The historian's explanation mirrors the expansive hopes of this generation:

The future was to be considered and that alone warranted its purchase...it made it possible to adopt one style of architecture for every church unit; it made it possible to avoid the crowding of buildings close together, thus destroying their beauty; above all, it offered opportunities for development for future years — play grounds for the little children, fields for baseball, football and tennis and all the other sports that boys and girls love so much.

Not the least of its attractions were a house, soon a 14-room rectory and a barn converted into a temporary chapel. To prepare the barn, the men of the parish came in "after their own harvest day's toil." When they had done what they could, a builder put on the finishing touches for a price of $9,000, and Blessed Sacrament had its own place of worship.

In the previous century, Catholics had been deeply conscious of their status as newcomers in Protestant communities. Catholics of Eastwood in the 1920s were still not fully at home. As the parish chronicler noted, the beginnings were not accomplished "without much attendant worry and grave fears." The Ku Klux Klan "was then at the peak of its power and the height of its determination to destroy the the Catholic Church and its progress in America." Three fiery crosses were burned on the eastern hills of the village "attracting villagers to the scene (while) the pastor sat silently by and prayed that this demented un-American group" would miraculously come to realize what the "scripture meant when it spoke of the Fatherhood of God and the brotherhood of man." Yet, outside of these incidents, non-Catholics were courteous. Many even contributed to the Catholic cause. When the pastor went to vote for the first time in the village, a well known Protestant politician approached him and said he had told "these Protestant people, brothers of mine" that "it took a Catholic priest to come out here and practically steal the best piece of property in Eastwood." He loudly predicted that, within a decade, they would see a beautiful convent, school, church and rectory on the property.

Unlike his nineteenth century pioneer forebears, Father Shanahan was not alone. A retired naval chaplain helped out with Masses until 1922, when an assistant was appointed. Ten years later a second assistant was added. By then six Masses were being said, straining the capacity of the chapel. In 1925 it was renovated to double its size. It was a mark of the times that the next building was not a new church, but a school. Plans were drawn up, contracts bid, and the school and a convent erected for slightly more than $200,000. Built in Gothic style with variegated red brick, litholite stone trimming and slate roofs, the school had nine classrooms, an auditorium, library, and basement recreation rooms, club rooms, cafeteria and showers.

Two churches preceded today's impressive Blessed Sacrament parish complex in Syracuse's Eastwood neighborhood. The first church was the Town Hall, where Sunday morning Mass followed a Saturday night neighborhood dance in the same rooms. The second church was a small parish building dedicated in 1922. (Photo: Chancery Archives)

The pastor, an admirer of the Sisters of St. Joseph from his days at St. John the Evangelist, had the job of persuading them to staff his school. Hat in hand, he visited their motherhouse and returned with the promise of four sisters. The school opened with four grades in the fall of 1930, an event with which the anonymous historian closed the history, quoting from the reminiscences of one of the sisters:

> When the school opened on the feast of Our Lady's nativity, September 8, 1931, 168 pupils were present to register for its first four grades. High Mass was celebrated by Father Shanahan and at the conclusion a procession of priests, teachers, parents and pupils was formed. Led by cross-bearer and acolytes, the group, which presented a picture which will long remain in the memory of those who witnessed it, proceeded to the school, where the children were seated in their respective rooms. The building was blessed and the work of educating youth in a truly Catholic manner was begun. The sisters readily won the confidence, love and respect of their little charges.

If the earlier generations of priests loved to build churches, as Father Lowery had admitted, their successors in the 1920s took equal pleasure in building schools. In Cortland, even before the long planned St. Mary's church was finished, Father Patrick Donohoe was planning a school, using the bricks of the St. Mary's of the Vale church as part of the foundation. Completed by the end of 1927, the school was a "New Years gift to the pastor," as one enthusiastic parishioner put it, helped along with a donation of $80,000 from a Mrs. Duffy, who was a direct descendant of original parishioners, and another $10,000 from her sister, who had married a local

industrialist.

A similar commitment to parochial school education was evident at Our Lady of Lourdes in Utica. In 1913, St. John's bought land and a house for a Sunday school in the western reaches of the mother parish. In November 1917, a small group of Catholics in the neighborhood voted to turn the house into a chapel and a new parish began under Father James Collins. Five years later, with the help of a "big, old fashioned picnic," the 676 members raised $15,000 to pay off the mortgage. The next year they purchased a prime piece of property a few blocks away, where they planned first a school, then a new church. With the help of a parish men's club, the pastor launched a $100,000 drive, "directed toward the building of a parochial school as the first unit of that impressive Catholic establishment which we all visualize in the future as a fitting ornament to ours, the most beautiful section of the city, a source of pride to our people and a lasting monument to our faith and zeal." Plans were drawn up for a large school equipped with wide corridors, fireproof material, a modern ventilating system, an auditorium to accommodate 1,200 people, a gymnasium to "afford our boys and girls every gymnastic indulgence and development," bowling alleys, billiard rooms and shuffleboard courts. In addition the auditorium would serve as a place for Mass because their tiny church now was badly overcrowded.

The men's club asked a pledge of five dollars a month for 20 months from each of 500 families. Their plea was followed by a personal appeal from the pastor, then a door-to-door canvas. There was bitter disappointment when the drive fell short of its goal, but the lay leaders demanded a recanvas. Once again Collins wrote to his people, describing the determination which had marked that meeting. The fair name of the parish "must not be sullied by defeat," he wrote. "Failure at this time would mean a disgrace that would be hard for you and me to bear." When the returns were in, the parish had $125,000. The bishop and consultors granted permission to borrow up to $300,000. Eventually their debt reached $225,000, a serious matter when the depression began almost immediately after the school opened with 275 children in the fall of 1929. Fortunately, Collins had contacts with the national office of the Knights of Columbus, which took over the mortgage in 1931 without any additional payment of interest.

Not all the energy of these years was poured into schools. At St. Mary's in Oswego, Father Joseph A. Hopkins, begged, pleaded and shamed his people into raising enormous amounts of money with which to build one of the most beautiful churches in the diocese. In a little more than a week in 1920, he raised $100,000 in pledges. Parishioners hauled stones from the field, helped raze the old church and dig the foundation for the new one, and did much of the heavy construction and stone work until the building was completed and furnished in 1925. The dedication was among the most impressive ever held in the diocese, with bishops attending from around the country. The parish took enormous pride in what it had achieved. When Hopkins died in 1928, the parish placed a plaque in the entry way to the church, on which were inscribed the following words:

Father Joseph A. Hopkins (Photo: Chancery Archives)

IN MEMORY OF
JOSEPH A HOPKINS
PASTOR 1902-1928
Our church has been built and con-
secrated. Many minds and hearts have
conspired to finish this noble work. Its
very stones are from our fields. Its
every gift is a Thanksgiving to the
Almighty. May He regard everyone
who has labored in the task. May he
bless all who kneel here to worship.

Oswego Catholics sometimes felt they were on the outskirts of the diocese, but they lacked for nothing in their two major parishes. At St. Paul's, Father Timothy Howard had succeeded the redoubtable Dean Barry in 1915, warned by the bishop to go slow in placing the parish on "modern foundations." He did, but soon had the church redecorated and its finances stabilized. A man of excellent education and refined taste, Howard poured his creative powers into the rectory, which became one of the wonders of the diocese. He hired Syracuse architect Ward Wellington Ward, one of the leaders in

240

the arts and crafts movement in the United States, to remodel the priests' residence. Ward hired a local carpenter to provide a beautiful oak staircase carved to match the intricate wood paneling. There were three fireplaces, each with a distinct design of pictorial tiles known as Moravian. One illustrated the four seasons, another the four evangelists and the third, eight medieval musicians. Stained glass from the Keck studios in Syracuse was installed, while the dining room had a 12-foot ceiling with ornamental shields and plaster archways. The furnishings were superb antiques, dominated by a specially designed dining room table reminiscent of the Arthurian legend of the Knights of the Round Table.

As these examples indicate, pastoral work was still heavily oriented to building and fundraising. At St. Paul's in Binghamton, Father Joseph Bustin called himself part of the "laboring class" of the diocesan priesthood. He became pastor in 1924 and found a massive parish plant valued at $500,000 and a debt of more than $135,000. In 12 years, spanning the worst years of the depression, he reduced the debt to $7,500 while paying almost $38,000 in interest, contributing more than $22,000 to Lourdes hospital, and making improvements valued at $105,000, a remarkable record. Martin Hughes began his priestly life first as Barry's neighbor in Oswego, then as Hourigan's in Binghamton. He spent his last years straightening out yet another parish, St. John the Baptist in Syracuse. Facing a massive parish debt, he cut expenses to the bone, stripped the church of any unnecessary or expensive decorations, took the collection himself with a wire basket, so the the sounds of coins would rattle but the sounds of bills would not. He launched a parish school and challenged his parishioners to pay their pew rents. At the same time, this sturdy veteran of parish construction resented the increasingly intru-

sive interventions of the chancery. He responded testily to an inquiry from Bishop Curley that, yes, he had paid the sisters the extra salary that was due them. "If your compliments were not so much intertwined with your unkind and unjust criticisms," he added, "the hard road of life might be made safer for some of us."

As Hughes irritation indicated, the bishops were supervising parish affairs more closely than in the days of independent pastors like Barry and Hourigan. The parish remained the center of Catholic life, and its financial and pastoral problems were the bishop's major preoccupation. Personnel problems had eased a bit, because priests now were coming forth from the seminaries in greater numbers. But finances remained crucial. The financial and pastoral problems were interrelated to such a degree that priests and bishops spoke of them in one breath. Where the financial support was solid and dependable, the bishop believed, people were attending church and were satisfied with its pastoral services. Conversely, effective pastoral services brought forth the revenue needed to sustain them. Still, people needed to be reminded of their responsibilities. On the occasion of parish visitations, the bishops almost always reminded parishioners of their obligation to support their Church. Bishop Curley put it clearly at one church dedication:

So, dearly beloved, you have here now, in parochial treasure, valuable and attractive land that may not be encroached upon by interests of another nature. You have splendid parochial equipment, you have a beautiful, a most attractive church in which to give, I trust, even greater service and glory to God. I need not tell you that you have, also, an additional parochial debt. However, you would not have encouraged your

242

pastor to assume it unless you were ready to support him in its responsibilities, unless you were prepared to return to God, in willing sacrifice a generous measure of earthly goods that he has permitted and will allow you, in good health, to acquire.

Curley's frequent denunciations of pride sat side by side with equally frequent appeals to it. Again and again he spoke of the progress of the Church and the worldly blessings which Catholics enjoyed. One eye may have been turned toward that better world, but another was clearly on this one, where congregations and pastors were doing well. "God has favored you in very many ways," he told an audience at the opeing of a new school. "There are millions of human beings in the world living in squalor, poverty and distress; you are enjoying at least some of the comforts of civilization and enlightened progress." In comparison with souls living in darkness, his listeners could "see God in the light of true faith" and enjoy the "countless spiritual consolations and supports he has provided through his holy Church." Between their membership in that Church and their enjoyment of some of the benefits of civilization, there was an evident but unstated connection.

Obviously a bishop like Curley also insisted on maintaining some controls over parish finances, but in the prosperous 1920s he favored expansion. Between June and December 1925, Curley and his consultors approved mortgages and loans of $354,000, ranging from $900 for the purchase of a lot at St. Mary of the Snow in Otter Lake, to a $96,000 mortgage taken by St. John the Baptist in Syracuse. Borrowing continued at an even greater rate through the later 1920s, acquired from local banks or from insurance companies known for their interest in church loans. A small but growing number of loans were granted on a short term basis from one parish to another, or from diocesan reserves like the bishop's charities fund. All these transactions required the approval of the bishop and his consultors. The latter body was gradually emerging as a financial and construction committee, examining and re-

With help from his secretary Father (later Bishop) David Cunningham, Bishop Curley led the diocese into an era of parish expansion. The pair are shown here in 1931 at a funeral Mass in Syracuse. (Photos: Chancery Archives)

viewing notes and mortgages, making recommendations to financially troubled parishes, and examining building plans and contracts. Parish proposals for new churches and schools brought full reports. Pastors were summoned before the board to defend their proposals, as when Grimes' friend Father Mahon persuaded the board to approve a $260,000 proposal to complete Most Holy Rosary church in 1927.

Curley was also alert to future needs, especially in providing land for anticipated expansion of parishes, schools and charities. Consultors meetings often were taken up with proposals by parishes or by the bishop himself to buy land which eventually might prove useful to a parish or might serve a population constantly on the move in search of single family homes. By this time the automobile was rapidly changing patterns of settlement. Leading clerics in every region were quick to let the bishop know where people were moving, what eventual needs might develop and what parcels of land for sale might be expected to appreciate in value. At one meeting in February 1930, for example, the consultors considered parcels for two possible parishes, and for a future home for Catholic Charities and educational offices, deciding before the day was over to purchase real estate at a cost of $100,000. To strengthen the bishop's hand in dealing with national parishes, Curley made it one of his first orders of business to clarify existing legislation regarding parish finances. By-laws for each parish corporation were signed by the pastors and trustees, with a copy inserted in the front of the minute book and another returned to the chancery office. These detailed by-laws provided that the corporate powers of the parish would be exercised under Church law, that the parish would receive the pastor selected by the bishop, and that the trustees would be "practical Catholics and members in good standing of the parish." These by-laws legally strengthened the bishop's hand by requiring a four-fifths vote in financial matters, ensuring that he and his vicar general exercised a de facto veto over any major parish transaction. In fact, while Curley and Duffy recommended that pastors consult parish leaders on all financial plans, and while effective pastors used their trustees to help enlist lay support for major projects, the trustees were becoming more and more a rubber stamp, often meeting only to fulfill legal requirements. Only in the few ethnic parishes, which continued the annual parish meeting in which trustees dealt with an active lay constituency, did they exercise serious power in Church decision making.

THE GREAT DEPRESSION

In an era of rapid expansion, difficulties could arise when centralized procedures were not followed. At St. Joseph's Slovak church in Endicott, for example, Father Florian Billy found that the parish was paying $2,000 annually in life insurance premiums on certain laymen of the parish. The arrangement had been made by the previous pastor and trustees with the Security Mutual Life Insurance Company as a condition for that company granting a mortgage on their new church. When Billy informed the chancellor, Father McEvoy, the latter responded that it had not been approved by the diocese. In almost all cases, banks were anxious to take mortgages on church property, McEvoy argued, so that there had been no need to accept such costly conditions. McEvoy wrote the company representative that the arrangements were contrary to diocesan policy and that they were not binding without the bishop's signature. The earlier pastor and trustees had taken those steps "as individuals, not as parish officials." A company officer replied, describing the previous pastor as "your representative;" he could not believe that such a large loan was negotiated without the bishop's knowledge, and he pointed out that the first year's insurance premium had been paid with a parish check. After some further correspondence, McEvoy met with company officials and an agreement was worked out.

The heavy debts acquired through the expansive 1920s posed problems when the economy slowed down. In Syracuse, at least, the depression did not begin in 1929. In a report in January 1928, Father McEvoy wrote of massive layoffs at a number of area manufacturers. All were hoping for a resump-

tion of business, but "some authorities on labor tell us that conditions are the worst since 1904." He warned against extravagant spending, noting that "the produce man looks to the ultimate consumer; we must look to the ultimate giver." McEvoy had no idea how bad it would get. Beginning with the stock market crash in the fall of 1929, the economy sank into a serious depression. After a brief movement toward recovery in 1931, the collapse of the world wide banking system sent the United States into the worst economic crisis in its history. By March 1933, one of every four Americans was out of work, farm prices were at the lowest levels ever and banks of entire states were closing their doors. Despite the energetic efforts of the federal government under Franklin Roosevelt, "hard times" would continue for six years.

The depression caught some parishes in the midst of ambitious plans. Many were undaunted. At St. Vincent's in Syracuse, parishioners voted to continue construction of a parish high school, with unemployed men joining in the work in order to cut costs. While this impressive recommitment was taking place, the pastor, Father Dougherty, was collecting cards identifying the unemployed, and mobilizing what resources he could to help. He promised to keep any aid "a matter of confidence between you and the pastor, a matter of trust that we hold sacred and will not violate." In 1931 he organized a parish employment bureau to help find part time work for unemployed parishioners.

Completion of the high school increased an already substantial parish debt, and payment of annual interest of $3,197 on a total debt of $136,000 preoccupied the parish throughout the decade. With the help of an elected "committee of 100," the parish kept up a drumbeat of appeals. Envelopes were introduced in 1935, with one side for the rectory and church, the other for the school and convent. Annual lists of donations were printed. Special collections helped meet emergencies, while parishioners organized a seemingly endless series of card parties, bazaars and fairs. Exhausted by these in 1934, they began a new "interest fund," with families pledging $10 a year solely to meet interest payments. Each Sunday the names of those meeting their pledges were announced. The system proved remarkably successful and led eventually to the reduction and elimination of the entire debt. But this was only after years of struggle.

Parish after parish labored under such interest payments. The story is told of one pastor who asked the banker who held his mortgage, "Did you ever own a school?" "Why no," the banker replied. "You do now," responded the grim-faced priest. In Binghamton the banks collapsed and one bank defaulted on several million dollars. This all but eliminated the money set aside for Lourdes Hospital. Bishop Curley told Cardinal Hayes the diocese had lost $70,000. In the Church, as elsewhere, the banking crisis forced a close examination of accounts. The Syracuse diocese remained remarkably free from scandal, although one parish did lose its reserves of more than $75,000. In July 1932, the governing board heard an appeal from Father Howard McDowell who had succeeded Father George Mahon at Most Holy Rosary in Syracuse. The parish had $200,000 in short term notes, $291,000 in mortgages and another $21,000 of floating debt, a total of more than $500,000. At first the members discussed asking banks for a temporary lowering of the parish's interest to four percent. But after reflection, the board decided to ask this of all banks with loans to any parish in the diocese. The banks were considering this appeal when Bishop Curley died.

When Duffy took office, McEvoy gave him a list of 47 parishes, not including Most Holy Rosary, with six percent notes totaling

$971,777.56. Two Utica parishes had more than $100,000 each at this rate of interest. Duffy met this situation head on, winning agreement to lower interest rates in the more desperate cases and then moving to secure uniformity in handling parish obligations. New regulations were prepared, ordering all parishes to use one note form, to transfer all demand notes to time notes, preferably for 90-day periods, and to ensure that all contained the signature of both the pastor and the bishop or vicar general. No notes otherwise taken would be honored. Copies of these new regulations were sent not only to parishes, but to banks in the diocese as well. Duffy then approached the banks again with the request that interest be lowered from six to five percent as a number of banks already had done, using the now uniform regulations to build his case that these obligations were guaranteed. The banks responded positively, and the parishes were secured for the moment. Later William T. McCaffrey, president of the Lincoln National Bank and Trust, wrote an insurance company executive and described the impression the bishop made:

We have found Bishop Duffy to be a very competent administrator. When Bishop Duffy arrived I was president of the Syracuse clearing house and I had certain suggestions which I wished to make. Before I could make the suggestions, Bishop Duffy outlined his plan of procedure and there was nothing left for me to say. Bishop Duffy is a young man, not yet fifty, and in vigorous health. He has not only the cooperation of every banker in the diocese but also their admiration of and confidence in his ability.

By the later 1930s, relations with banks were so good that the chancery's intervention could dramatically assist a local parish. In 1938, for example, the Oneida National Bank and Trust

Company agreed with the pastor and parishioners of St. George's church to reduce temporarily the interest rate on their mortgage from six to four percent. It was a sign of the intimate relationship that now existed. A bank official privately informed the bishop of this agreement and suggested that the parishioners were disturbed by a mysterious $900 note dating from the administration of the previous pastor. Diocesan takeover of that small amount might "strengthen their morale considerable and bring about a greater effort to carry on."

The depression certainly slowed the rate of expansion in Catholic parishes, but the increase in the Catholic population slowed as well. Although only six new parishes were founded in the 1930s, as compared to 29 founded in the previous period, average parish size rose only from 1,454 to 1,538. Parish ordinary receipts also dropped from $2,600,000 to $2,100,000, an average loss of 20 percent in each parish, although the deflation of prices during the period meant that real income remained almost the same. The tremendous expansion of parish debt, which had fueled the enormous expansion of new churches and schools in the 1920s was reversed. Total parish indebtedness dropped from $4,500,000 to $4,000,000, and average parish debt from $34,684 to $29,439. Once again, when the debt is translated into constant 1917 dollars, the real indebtedness of the parishes rose slightly. The financial picture of the 1930s, however, was one of stabilization as expansion slowed, debts were consolidated and refinanced, and people hurt by the unemployment of the period concentrated on preserving what they had built, at home and at church. The experience left the lay people, pastors and bishops with a new sense of caution on financial matters. It was a caution that would persist even through the years of prosperity and renewed growth that followed World War II.

CATHOLIC FAMILY LIFE

Parishes were, of course, far more than business enterprises. By now the religious life of most parishes, including most national parishes, was centered almost entirely upon the sacraments. Reverence for the Eucharist and emphasis on the central role of the Mass in Catholic life was the product of almost a century-long effort to make casual Catholics practicing Catholics. Since the earliest days of the diocese, pastors had arranged monthly communions for distinctive groups. Indulgences attached to prayers, devotions or practices like church visitation almost always carried as a condition reception of the sacraments of penance and communion. Devotion to the Blessed Sacrament, from the older practice of Forty Hours and benediction, to the newer novenas and perpetual adoration societies, all reflected a distinctively sacramental approach to religious life. In 1940 there were 36 parish societies devoted to a patron saint, less than half the number of 1920. Of course, the scriptures were read at Mass and families were encouraged to have a Bible in the home and to pray individually and as families. But, without question, these were secondary and generally regarded as additional devout practices resting upon the foundation of the far more serious and efficacious practice of attending Mass and receiving communion.

Despite the emphasis on problems of sexuality in contemporary moral teaching, there were few programs or activities in the parishes which directly related to family life. The whole life of the parish, from sacraments through social events to the parish school, supplemented family activities and supported parents in their effort to raise their children. It affirmed marriage and family life and thus enhanced Catholic morale. Yet the Church devoted surprisingly little attention to married couples as couples, and hardly noticed when the depression brought a startling decrease in

The Church long has affirmed marriage and family, with persistent encouragement for Catholics to marry in the presence of a priest, as in this photo of a 1950 wedding at St. Matthew church in East Syracuse. (Photo: Virginia Millert)

the number of people getting married. From a high of more than 2,600 marriages celebrated in 1929, the number of marriages in the diocese dropped to 1,657 in 1932, rising slowly thereafter to a new high of 2,825 in 1937, then dropping sharply the next year. Perhaps this was a result of the recession which lasted through 1938. The revival of the economy resulting from the rearmament associated with the war in Europe brought a dramatic increase to 3,277 marriages in 1940 and 3,765 in 1941, the latter statistic almost 33 percent higher than any earlier recorded figure. Given the almost weekly lamentations about sexual promiscuity and declining re-

spect for marriage which issued from Church leaders during the period, it is very surprising that there is no record of any Church leader in the diocese noting this relationship between economic hard times and declining marriage rates, or showing concern about young men and women forced to delay marriage because of the poor economic prospects.

Three family problems drew direct attention — divorce, which was condemned regularly; preparation for marriage; and mixed marriages. The latter were a special problem because bishops and priests instinctively believed what later studies would show to be true, that mixed marriages contributed to reduced religious practice and disaffiliation from the Church. This was a major reason for building Catholic schools, especially high schools. At St. Anthony's in Syracuse, for example, more than 1,100 students attended the school, and there were weekly dances and a variety of social affairs designed in the pastor's words, "to keep the young people parish-minded and enable them to work and play together." No wonder a contemporary observer commented that St. Anthony's was a parish noted for its young people "marrying their own." Certainly one test of the success of the Catholic subculture was the rate of intermarriage. By that test Syracuse did better than one would expect in retrospect, though less well than Catholics suspected at the time. Earlier in the century, diocesan officials had calculated that mixed marriages accounted for between 23 percent and 26 percent of all marriages celebrated before a priest between 1896 and 1912. Italian, Polish and Slovak Catholics rarely asked the priest to perform such marriages, so that Bishop Grimes feared that the proportion of mixed marriages in English speaking parishes may have been more than 40 percent. Figures like these made Grimes and many others conclude that assimilation led to the declining loyalty reflected in mixed marriages. This in turn, led them to a greater understanding of the value of national parishes, a stronger emphasis on religious differences with Protestants, and more important, a more intense commitment to Catholic schools. However, that strategy had only mixed success. On the basis of a 1941 questionnaire, diocesan leaders calculated that out of 48,000 Catholic families in the diocese, 8,000 or approximately 16 percent, were in mixed marriages. Yet the same study demonstrated that for the years 1931 to 1941, the percentage of marriages contracted between Catholics and non-Catholics held fairly steady between 26 and 30 percent. Thus the mixed marriage phe-

nomenon was widespread even at the peak of the Catholic subculture, although some were beginning to wonder whether "conversion" of the non-Catholic party might balance off the "perversion" of the Catholic.

Certainly the Church did all it could to discourage mixed marriages. All such couples had to marry in front of a priest. They promised that their children would be raised as Catholics, with the non-Catholic party solemnly promising not to interfere with that process. Despite such rules, pastors often had to be a bit more flexible, especially when faced with a situation where a couple indicated that they would be married before another minister or public officer if denied access to the Catholic ceremony. As a pastor told the chancellor in one case, the only grounds on which he would seek permission to bless a mixed marriage, was that the non-Catholic party, despite taking instruction, refused to become a Catholic and the priest judged that the couple would proceed with the marriage in any case. Those who did marry elsewhere had to seek reconciliation because they were excommunicated. The priest approached by such persons had to apply to the chancery to absolve them from excommunication if married before a minister, and from heresy if they had worshiped in a non-Catholic church.

Marriage instruction was a major clerical responsibility to which Curley admonished his priests to give more serious attention. It was a chance for a "heart to heart talk" and a "wonderful opportunity for shaping the destinies of that young couple and the progeny," the bishop said. Priests were told to emphasize the need for patience, loyalty to each other, intolerance of interference from family or friends and, most importantly, the "sacral character of the marriage tie as a sacrament." They should introduce the "divine injunctions" regarding indissolubility, abortion and birth control. They should be prepared especially well on the latter subject, said Curley. Many young Catholics had read the propaganda of the "minions of Satan" and the priests could "readily understand how they would read it with avidity and how their minds would be possessed accordingly." Priests should be prepared to meet their arguments or be "woefully embarrassed." He admitted that these were subjects which the priest, because of his "sacredotal character...dreads to approach and above all to discuss with the laity." Nevertheless, "despite this very proper reluctance," Curley thought it was imperative for priests to address the topic, as St. Paul considered it necessary to admonish "his converts who were living under similar conditions and who were becoming impregnated with similar pagan practices."

TEACHING THE FAITH

Marriage instruction was only one aspect of the priest's role as teacher. From the earliest days, one of the priest's most important responsibilities was to instruct his people, few of whom had received any religious education in the basic doctrines and moral teachings of the Church. Curley, Grimes and later, Bishop Walter Foery agreed that the priest's role as teacher remained central to his vocation. Where they did not "lead in this regard," Curley argued, "little advance is made by the Catholic Church." Obviously, the most frequent and effective instruction took place from the pulpit. There are few surviving sermons written by parish priests, so it is hard to know the character of local preaching. However, beginning in the 1920s, the hierarchy began providing an annual series of sermon outlines to ensure that, everywhere in the diocese, the same topic was discussed on a given Sunday. In the nineteenth century Church, the reiteration, in simple terms, of basic Church teaching was part of the overall

effort to make "practical Catholics." In the between the wars years, in contrast, almost every sermon had a moral rather than dogmatic theme. Even sermons on Marian dogma ended with discussion of the special relevance of devotion to Mary in a time of pride, human selfishness, materialism and sexual permissiveness. As Cardinal Hayes told New York priests when he gave them the same outline, "in an age so fatally individualistic, with moral principles often swept away in a flood of carnal pleasure, we must bulwark the souls of our people against the peril of a wrack and ruin to their faith."

In Syracuse, the sermon outlines followed a four-year cycle. First came the Creed, with Sunday sermons covering the existence and attributes of God, creation, original sin, the life, death and Resurrection of Jesus, and the authority and marks of the Church. The second year dealt with mortal and venial sins, the Ten Commandments and the commandments of the Church. Next came the "Means of Grace" as the priest explained each sacrament, the doctrines of grace and various devotions. Finally, in the fourth year, sermons developed "the Christian way of life," with the topics covered including the Lord's Prayer, the rosary, devotions to Mary, theological and cardinal virtues, the family and various "modern fallacies." Each year, provision was made for annual sermons, often on days of special collections. These included the Legion of Decency, vocations, missions, Catholic reading, religious education, the Holy See and, on the first Sunday of Lent, fasting and the need for penance. Only in the early 1960s were substantial revisions made in these outlines in an effort to ensure correspondence between the homily and the scripture readings of the day.

One of the few priests who left behind written texts and outlines of his own sermons was Father William Sheehan. Father Sheehan was a talented, popular priest who served as pastor of Immaculate Conception in Fulton and St Patrick's in Binghamton before his death in 1940. An intense, scholarly man, Sheehan interspersed his sermons with literary references and informed scientific commentary. His complex arguments about topics like divine creation, the authority of scripture and the evidence for the Resurrection may have puzzled some listeners. Yet he managed to punctuate his lecture-like homilies with timely references to exploitative employers who paid low wages, the sin of anti-Semitism or the scandal of a local "joint" kept open through political corruption. He could wax eloquent on sexual sins, birth control and the supposed hedonism of modern culture. But he also attacked "spineless" Catholics who seemed to leave their conscience in Church when they "got up a bit in the world." Such "religious slackers," proud of their success, never would point out the "prejudice and hatred" that kept "whole groups of people" from opportunities for advancement. Sheehan was one of those people, rare but prominent in the 1930s, who were conservative in their religious views, but honest in applying Church teaching to troublesome questions. "The whole world knows that every Catholic is expected to be as uncompromising in all questions of faith and morals, at all times, and under all circumstances, as is the very Church of which he is a member," Sheehan said. It was a high, if rigid, standard. He expected much from his people and said so.

At the same time, his faith and preaching were very Jesus-centered. Almost every topic led to Jesus, and always the Lord was described in terms of love and mercy. He and his people were certain and at times, self-righteous, but they were also in the hands of a loving God. So were the world and its people, among whom they lived. Priests like Sheehan were churchmen, profoundly devoted to the Church and committed to its service. Even the best of them were also products of a

Father William F. Sheehan
(Photo: Chancery Archives)

Catholic subculture, whose angle of vision on the world was shaped by the occasionally near-paranoid defensiveness of the modern Church. Yet they were also pastors who liked their people and cared deeply about their welfare. This pastoral concern, and the networks of families and friendships that knit people together, tempered the harsher tones and sharper edges of Catholic consciousness. If, in fact, the Church was not yet the Kingdom of God, and even if Curley's vision of "the happiest and most peaceful society" was exaggerated, it was in fact a community where love, compassion and generosity combined high ideals with fully human hopes and expectations. Like the risen Jesus, it indeed pointed toward a newer and better world. It asked people to bear witness to this and, at the same time, bound up wounds, eased anxieties, and shared a portion of that love which, if not yet full, was real, tangible and present.

The symbol of this dedication to the Church, of aspirations for the next life and of permanence and fidelity in this one, was the church building itself. It was, as Bishop Duffy told a confirmation congregation, the result of the cooperative effort of pastor and parishioners: "When the things of the soul dominate, men will leave after them footprints on the sands of time." In concluding a history of buildings and improvements at St. John the Evangelist in Pulaski in 1936, Father Michael Lyons wrote:

> The church property as it appears today is a tribute to both the priests and people who during the last 48 years have sacrificed themselves a great deal to achieve its present condition, a sacrifice rewardable, if not in this life, most certainly in the next. Its exterior simple elegance is an incentive to enter and pray. Its interior splendor is an invitation to reverence and love of God. Indeed, in spending themselves, the parishioners evidence the fruit of earnest pastors who have instilled into their minds the disposition not only to know God but to do His will.

To do God's will was to join in the parish's spiritual, sacramental and social activities. A parish historian of St. John's in Utica described the five-year pastorate of Father Robert J. Bogan from 1920 to 1925 as "characterized by constant emphasis on the importance of personal consecration to the way of life taught by the church." His successor, Monsignor David Dooling, described that way of life clearly:

> Jesus Christ was the greatest teacher the world has ever known. This is his schoolhouse. You will learn here no new doctrines. We bring no new religion, but the ancient faith taught to the disciples.
> Here you will be taught the ten commandments, love of truth, love of neighbor, respect for the rights and property of neighbors, justice and mercy, and other creeds. Your teachers will be no experimenters but anointed priests of God. More than ever before, the teachings of Christ are needed. Vice is rampant, disregard of order prevalent, the charm of worldly pleasure great. As the years come and go, as sorrows and disappointments come, you will learn more and more to regard this church as a haven and rest, an anchor to hold you fast to things of truth. You will hold it dear because it will be rich in treasured memories. The altar rail and confessional will be as spiritual flowers blossoming for your soul. Here may you receive courage to bear your cross, your griefs and disappointments that none can escape. At life's close, God's church earthly will be be transformed into God's church eternal.

It was a glorious picture, confirmed by heavily attended Masses and occasional parades, processions and Holy Name conventions.

NEW MISSIONARY APPROACHES

The sheer busyness of most Catholic parishes obscured the fact, evident to the most thoughtful parish leaders, that many people were really involved very little in the Church. As early as 1885, Father Clune had lamented that the same few people always seemed to do all the work in the parish. More recently, Italian parishes were famous for the yawning chasm between the massive numbers of people in the neighborhood and the few who attended church and the even fewer who contributed to its support. But even in more developed congregations, there was a large gap between the ideal of unity in faith and community and the reality that many did not attend Mass regularly, many more did not contribute to the church and, in fact, a fairly small number took part in parish activities other than the sacraments. Indeed, under the outward appearance of prosperity, unity and power of many urban parishes, there was a foundation often pockmarked by indifference, disaffection and apathy, more often than not correlated with poverty and family problems. This reality only became universally evident in the 1960s, when the urban crisis shattered the complacency of much Catholic life. However, there had been signs evident to those who looked closely.

One parish which did take a close look was the cathedral parish of the Immaculate Conception, which conducted a full-scale parish census and prepared a detailed report in 1941.

The report contained an alphabetical listing of parish members, a street directory and an inventory of outstanding pastoral problems, including an intensive examination of the 44 "colored people" who were members of the parish. The report found that there were 2,311 Catholic families and 6,172 individuals within the parish boundaries. Of these, only 170 rented pews and another 623 used envelopes, now the major source of income. Twenty-five percent or 1,521 people said they attended other churches with varying degrees of regularity. Even more interesting were the pastoral problems: 1,076 had "neglected their Easter duty," 225 marriages were "irregular," and 171 had delayed first communion, 256

confirmation and 225 baptism. There were 1,313 "lax Catholics" who rarely, if ever, attended church. The street directory examined these problems by district, seemingly demonstrating a correlation between poverty and disaffection. Adams Street for example, in one of the poorer sections, listed 48 families and 127 Catholics, of whom 61 were lax, 39 failed to perform their Easter duty and 10 whose marriages needed attention. Unfortunately, the outbreak of the war and lack of personnel prevented any response to this information.

What everyone who thought about it knew was that this response would have to be the same as that of the early missionaries. The Church would have to go out to the people. One of the most effective pastoral innovations of the period came with the arrival in the diocese of the Parish Visitors of Mary Immaculate. This community was approached in 1935. After a visit with Father Joseph Panesi, pastor of St. John the Baptist in Rome, and his assistant, Father Edward D. O'Connell, seven sisters arrived in July. They immediately launched a parish census and summer school of religion. The latter was so popular that the sisters were persuaded to continue a "story hour" when the school ended, until regular religion classes began in the fall. At the request of the Utica Catholic Charities office, they received a young woman into their home who had recently been released from a reformatory. In the fall, they launched religion classes for public school children at three centers located near the schools. There they began first communion and confirmation classes, calling at the homes of families whose children did not enroll. At the same time, they launched a series of confraternities and sodalities for children of all ages. By the end of the school year, 200 children were attending released time classes and another 500 were going to Sunday school programs. Young men and women were trained by the sisters to assist in teaching the younger children. During their second summer school, two sisters worked with lay volunteers, while the other sisters continued parish visits among the Italians and began similar visits among the Polish families of Transfiguration church. On Pentecost, 250 children received first communion. On Corpus Christi, the children helped decorate the church and joined in a massive procession through the streets around the church. An old woman, noting the increase of young people at Mass, commented that they were "nice and clean and all dressed up."

The sisters organized picnics and trips to the shrine at Auriesville. The young people were provided packets of religious articles and candy to bring with them on visits to shut-ins and older people in their homes or neighboring institutions. Under arrangements with the local welfare office, free milk was delivered to the convent for distribution to the children. Meanwhile, the sisters aided young people having trouble with the police and helped Father O'Connell mobilize the parish youth for the diocesan-wide battle against immoral literature. No area of need missed their attention. In July 1936, sisters were visiting Polish and Italian migrant laborers in the camps outside Rome, distributing religious articles and arranging for a field Mass, which 65 people attended. This remarkable record caught the attention of others and two sisters were sent to conduct a parish census at St. Patrick's in Syracuse.

In 1938 Catholic Charities in Rome petitioned for community chest funds to support some of the social work of parish visitors. The request was denied at first, but was granted after the city's four pastors attended a meeting and pleaded on their behalf. The Rome *Sentinel* reported that, during the previous year, the sisters had assisted 889 families with meals, clothing and shoes. They had assisted 14 delinquent boys on probation

and 70 others whose cases did not get to court, while caring for two unmarried mothers and providing free lunches to 150 poor children. Courts began referring young men to their charge for probation, as did local hospitals who came upon troubled youngsters. They helped find employment or eased the process of return to school, while doing casework with needy families. A number of adult committees assisted in the work, further strengthening the parish.

All the while, the sisters continued their work in the parish, launching Boy Scout and Cub Scout programs, increasing their attention to high school age children, and using these programs to gain the attention, respect and eventual return to the Church of parents and other adults. In this they experienced some success. In 1938 they reported to their mother general that, on their arrival in 1935, they had noted a decidedly anti-clerical tone in the Italian community. This was changing gradually. One sign of the change was the fact that the local CIO unions, heavily Italian and Polish, had invited Father O'Connell to address them at their meetings, where he introduced them to the social encyclicals of the Church. "The young people's reverential attitude toward the priests is having its effect on the older parishioners," the sisters concluded happily. Gradually the sisters accepted invitations to conduct parish censuses in other areas of the diocese. There could be little doubt of their enormous impact, which would find its climax in the flourishing growth of Italian parishes in the years after World War II.

Another innovation was Assisi House, established from 1938 to 1941 in connection with St. Bartholomew's church in Norwich. Staffed by the Sisters of Christian Doctrine in a house donated by the non-Catholic mayor of the community, it was a social service and catechetical center. Welcomed by the Dominican sisters who staffed St. Paul's school, the new sisters began with parish visitation. They noted the needs of families, invited children to catechism and urged people to attend church. Their visits provided the pastor with a

GOING ON ERRANDS FOR GOD

Julia Teresa Tallon grew up the seventh of eight children born into an Irish farm family at Waterville. Her faith was nurtured at St. Bernard's mission church and later at St. John's in Utica, where she worked in a mill and, in her spare time, helped care for orphans.

In 1886, she became the second daughter of St. Bernard's parish to choose religious life, when, at the age of 19, she entered the Daughters of Charity. Julia Teresa returned home after a few months. But with guidance from a priest at St. John's, she soon joined the Sisters of the Holy Cross. Thirty-three years later, she heard a new call — to leave the security of her convent and school and go out into the homes and streets to seek out "strayed and fallen-away souls of men and women, in order to bring them back to God and to His Church."

On Assumption day 1920, Julia Tallon, now aged 53, founded a new religious order, the Parish Visitors of Mary Immaculate.

At a time when other sisters remained close to their convents and to the schools and hospitals they staffed, Mother Teresa had broken out of the cloister. Her parish visitors set aside their veils and wore hats and coats into the streets to conduct door-to-door missionary efforts. Such a parish census, Mother Teresa told a national Church meeting in 1934, is "not only a systematic study of parish conditions but a veritable missionary crusade of Catholic Action.... The wayward are instructed and reclaimed to the Church; faithful Catholics are exhorted to become fervent and apostolic ... (and) all are urged to contribute personal interest and service to the upbuilding of the Catholic Cause." The sisters also visited hospitals, jails, orphanages and asylums — "God's messengers, going on errands for Him," said Mother Teresa.

In many ways, Mother Teresa Tallon was ahead of her time. Besides founding an active community of home missionaries, she also encouraged her sisters to adopt a spirituality that was both contemplative and active. "Contemplation for the street," she called it.

Julia Teresa Tallon of Waterville, before her entrance into religious life. (Photo: PVMI Archives)

254

profile of the Italian community and its needs. They prepared children for the sacraments, organized a Corpus Christi procession, and held a party to honor graduates of the public

"When we meet a person we shall have to see the image of God; no matter if he is dirty and drunken and rough...." This spirituality came to be shared by many — by another religious mother named Teresa, and by uncounted numbers of clergy, religious and lay persons involved in spreading the Word of God and sharing an active love among the homeless, the abused and others in whom they see the face of Christ.

Mother Teresa Tallon's spirituality led her to rise above the older Catholic practice of seeing evangelization as the province of priests and sisters. She was an outspoken advocate of the ministry of what she called "lay apostles."

"Opportunities occur far more frequently for the laity to exercise zeal in conversing with a neighbor than for the priest, no matter how apostolic he is," she said 40 years ago. To equip the lay apostles for evangelization, parish visitors sought opportunities for the laity to grow in prayer, learn and meditate on scriptures, and study theology and Church teachings.

Mother Teresa also had a special message for Catholic women, who in those days were seldom seen as agents for evangelization. "Women have proved very efficient messengers — an evangelizer is a messenger carrying the Good News of Jesus Christ. Their sympathetic understanding, and tactful ministrations have worked wonders in the sphere of saving souls. Mary Magdalen was commissioned by Christ himself to announce to the apostles the tidings of Christ's resurrection. It is true that the apostles did not believe her, because *she was a woman*. We should not become discouraged, therefore, by rebuffs or by a lack of appreciation."

Though her community of parish visitors remained small, Mother Teresa's vision was echoed by the Second Vatican Council. Her twin themes of taking the Church to the people and involving the laity in Christian ministry today are hallmarks of the Catholic Church.

elementary school and the school of Christian doctrine. They also assisted the pastor in organizing a Legion of Mary and a St. Cecilia's Music Guild. At Christmas time, the sisters helped the parishioners organize a float, filled with young people singing carols, which visited the shut-ins of the parish, and ended at an outdoor crib where the Brownies and Girl Scouts presented a pageant of the Christmas scene.

Irish Catholics might have been forgiven for thinking this was rather primitive work, like that done by the missionary priests of an earlier generation, yet another sign of the failure of the Italians to catch up. The irony of the situation would be evident only years later, though it was already there in the cathedral study. From the viewpoint of a parish like St. Lucy's in Syracuse in the 1970s, questions might arise about the nature of success and the signs of progress in the Church. The possibility might suggest itself that the Parish Visitors in Rome and the Sisters of Christian Doctrine in Norwich, like the early Franciscans in Utica and the pioneering missionaries in canal and railroad camps, were somehow the standard against which all else must be measured.

For the moment, such questions were muted. Energy and enthusiasm lay elsewhere. Catholic life in Syracuse parishes was rich and variegated during the period between the wars. Aside from the impressive missionary work done among the Italians by these remarkable sisters and the continuing relief work of Catholic Charities and parish St. Vincent de Paul societies, there was no dramatic rush into social action with the onset of the Great Depression. Undoubtedly, in Central New York as elsewhere, the reforms of the New Deal and the rise of the industrial unions drew a positive response from working-class Catholics. Duffy was supportive of the New Deal and brought to his diocese the program of the Catholic Conference on Industrial Problems to familiarize interested clergy and lay people with Catholic social teaching. But the energy and resources of the Church were directed to maintaining parishes and schools, and, when looking outward, to defending traditional values of marriage and family life against real or mythical enemies. It was a Church which reflected the experience of success. Against long odds and some considerable resistance, Catholics had built lives for themselves in America and in the 1930s the preservation of those gains was an all consuming activity. There were still unmet religious and human needs, but parish Catholics, for the most part, were not ready to be summoned to action, save in the relative safe channels provided by the Holy Name Society and the Legion of Decency. When they marched out of Church to do battle, it would be once again not at the call of the Gospel, but at the summons of the state. War was in the offing. Catholics in the 1940s, like their ancestors two decades before, had their doubts, but they would spring to the nation's call when the moment came.

REACH EVERY CHILD

COMMITMENT TO CATHOLIC EDUCATION
1930s-1950s

During the 1930s, the diocese of Syracuse did not match larger dioceses either in internal modernization or in the promotion of social action. The local Church remained a highly decentralized organization, with most of its energy and resources committed at the parish level. Mobilization of the diocese for charity had stalled. The finances remained largely under the pastors' control, though with increasingly close scrutiny from the diocese, and education was still largely a parish affair. The Holy Name Society and the Legion of Decency manifested concern with public morality, but the diocese experienced few of the movements for social reform which sprang up in other parts of the country. No Catholic Worker house appeared in the diocese, the liturgical movement drew little attention, the rural life and interracial apostolates were all but unknown, and there was little interest in the labor movement. While a few priests spoke out in support of the New Deal or in opposition to communism, Catholicism remained largely a private affair, focused on the family and the parish.

In well established parishes, the parochial school required a considerable investment of money and personnel, but efforts also were made to attract public school children to religious instruction. As the Catholic population became more Americanized, the danger arose that barriers between Catholics and others might weaken and religious indifference, or at least declining enthusiasm and Church support, might result. For years, thoughtful churchmen had argued that only Catholic schools, or at least solid religious instruction, could ensure the continued strength of the Church once Catholics were at home in the United States. Not surprisingly, by the late 1930s, this idea was enjoying new popularity in Syracuse. The result was a concerted effort to make Catholic education universally available. When prosperity returned after World War II, Catholic education became the centerpiece of diocesan work. Bishop Walter Foery set the challenge early in his administration: the Church must do all it could to "reach every child."

Shortly after Christmas 1936, Bishop Duffy left for a Florida vacation. He had hardly settled in when a telegram arrived informing him he had been named bishop of Buffalo. Duffy was genuinely surprised. "I had not thought when we parted at Christmas that it meant the end of so pleasant an association," the bishop wrote Father Cunningham. The telegram had been "a real bolt from the blue." Five months later, another "bolt" struck in Rochester, when Walter Foery, pastor of Holy Rosary parish and diocesan director of Catholic Charities, was named to succeed Duffy as bishop of Syracuse.

Only 47 years old, Foery was a lifelong Rochester resident. Born of German and Irish extraction in 1890, he attended parochial schools, the preparatory seminary of St. Andrew's and St. Bernard's Seminary. After ordination in 1916 he served at Mount Carmel, a predominately Italian parish, becoming pastor only four years later. There he established large catechism classes for children and adults, taught in both Italian and English. An excellent baseball player as a young man and a lifelong fan of the New York Yankees, he achieved early popularity by establishing parish athletic teams. As a young priest, his theology was quite conventional and his sermons reflected the energetic and practical spirit that marked American Catholic culture. Foery filled the church and hall with an endless round of social, educational, athletic and religious programs. Once a year, all activities ceased and a parish mission took place. This allowed time for the spiritual priorities of the community to become re-established, to be followed once again by entertainments, bazaars, fairs and basketball games.

In 1930, Foery became director of Catholic Charities for the Rochester diocese and two years later was made pastor of Holy Rosary parish, while retaining his Catholic Charities leadership. He genuinely enjoyed parish work, but, with the diligence and discipline that marked his personality, he taught himself the primary methods of social work and became a competent administrator of the increasingly complex programs of a modern Catholic Charities office. He built a local and national reputation as a leader in social services, serving as a delegate to an international conference on social welfare in London in 1935 and becoming prominent in Associated Charities, Rochester's version of the Community Chest.

An intimate friend of Bishop Edward Mooney, a bishop with strong national influence, Foery must have known that his name was on lists of priests being considered for promotion to the episcopate. Nevertheless, he genuinely seemed shocked when informed that Rome intended to appoint him bishop of Syracuse. In a message to the people of his new diocese, Foery spoke from experience of the increased scope of Church activities: "The Church has multiplied her interests in behalf of her children." On August 18, he was consecrated in St. Patrick's cathedral in Rochester. On August 31, he arrived in Syracuse, greeted by a large crowd. The following morning, September 1, he was installed by Bishop Conroy of Ogdensburg. It would be a long reign.

FOERY AND SOCIAL JUSTICE

In Foery, Syracuse had an experienced administrator, very much in touch with modern forms of organization. Like Curley before him, he had a broad vision of the diocesan Church providing services, not only in parishes, but in educational and charitable institutions.

The day had long passed, he said shortly after his arrival, when "we may limit our Catholic interest and Catholic activity to the spiritual well being of the individual and the material up-building of the parish." A wide array of human needs, made evident during the depression, required the bishop to ask his people for their personal and financial support. Rather than rely on a "small willing group," he preferred "to turn to the diocese effectively organized."

Naturally, given his background, Foery's major interest was in organizing social services. He greatly admired the profession of social work, with its combination of personal concern, efficient forms of organization and support for social reform. In 1938, he told a convention of social workers to continue their balanced commitment to both social justice and individual freedom. He said they should reject those on the right who were "willing to yield only the minimum they consider necessary for social safety," and those on the left who turned to class conflict or to the state as the sole custodian of the general welfare. Foery's position reflected his strong support of Catholic social teaching. He was one of 16 bishops who signed the far-reaching 1940 statement "The Church and the Social Order," a progressive defense of the welfare state, strong trade union organization and government regulation.

In Syracuse, however, there was little evidence of Catholic support for union organization or social reform. While Bishop Duffy had invited Dorothy Day to visit Syracuse in 1935, there was no Catholic Worker community in the diocese. Area Catholics had supported the campaigns of Alfred E. Smith and voted Democratic in the 1932 and 1936 elections, but there was little of the sense of social crisis which filled other cities. The social encyclicals, frequently referred to by Bishop Duffy and promoted by a small number of individual priests, usually in letters to the editor, were not known or used widely as the basis of significant action, either in the parishes or in Catholic Charities.

In the early days of his leadership in Syracuse, Foery demonstrated his deep con-

Father Walter Andrew Foery, a pastor and Catholic Charities director in Rochester, was 47 when he began what would become a 33-year tenure as the fifth bishop of Syracuse. (Photo: The Catholic Sun)

cern for the poor. "How amusing it is at times to hear people say 'if we only could lift the poor to our own level, if we could improve their conditions so that they would have better opportunities for culture and education,'" Foery told one group of well-off donors. "How much more correct it would be to say 'if we could only be lifted to the level of the poor. If we had the heroism of those who live in the slums of our cities. If we had the courage to face difficulties of a hard existence that is so beautifully exemplified in the lives of the poor.'" He was even stronger in his conclusion: "It is our strict duty in conscience to share our goods and, in so doing, let us hope they would share with us their courage and Christian resignation." In another talk to diocesan women, he referred to a statement he had heard regarding a black man, that he had "no strength of character" and "could not stand up under adversity."

I wonder if I would stand up under these adverse circumstances. How many of you women would care to test the strength of your character under the stress and strain of adverse circumstances. What would be the result? Possibly, very possibly, we would fail the test.

In the depression years, he argued, the problem of the poor was rarely one of character, but was more frequently one of social conditions, particularly unemployment. The first contribution Catholics could make to society was to strive for the improvement of social conditions, "with our votes and our voices" and by joining "organizations to further this end." Catholics should make a sincere personal commitment. "What right have I to apply remedies to the social condition of my community, if by my own life and my own example, I contribute to these conditions?" Foery asked. People also needed education to understand the nature of the problems and evaluate the means of dealing with them. As a teacher concerned with the moral law, Foery thought it his responsibility to address these question, not posing concrete solutions, but insisting on the moral dimension and the obligation of action. He was planning a pastoral letter on social justice when the United States entered the Second World War.

Before the war, Foery thus showed a great interest in social problems, and his speeches and papers place him among the more progressive members of the American hierarchy. While almost all bishops supported social reform and trade union development

during the depression years, few were as clear as Foery on the need to understand the problems facing poor people, to examine one's own social and political responsibilities, and develop an educated, sophisticated grasp of the sources of social problems. These views, formed early in his priestly career and deepened by his participation in Catholic Charities work, stayed with him, but his public positions became more conservative after 1940. Part of the reason was simply that social reform became less popular during the war and during the prosperous Cold War years that followed.

Furthermore, the Catholic population almost doubled between the end of the war and the opening of the Second Vatican Council in 1962, so that the day-to-day pressures of providing pastoral, educational and charitable services overwhelmed other considerations. Finally, the poor whom Bishop Foery knew in his pastoral work were, for the most part, Catholics, and when he spoke of the struggles and dignity of the poor, priests and people alike thought of the unemployed Irish, Italian, Polish and Slavic parishioners they knew so well. After the war, many in these groups would experience new prosperity, seen in the building projects in ethnic parishes and the end of the bitter disputes which had marked their relationship with the diocese. The new poor would be from other racial groups and heavily non-Catholic. As Bishop Foery's reference to prejudice against blacks indicated, he was well aware of the needs of such people. However, social justice and reform would be on the back burner for Foery, as for most Americans. Yet his appreciation of these problems would surface again in the 1960s, when poverty, racial discrimination and human rights returned to the top of the national agenda and posed new challenges.

Foery did find an expanding Catholic Charities program when he arrived in Syracuse in 1937. Stalled by the priests' reaction

Bishop Foery was a strong supporter of activities for young people, such as Catholic Charities' Camp Morning Star Manor at Little York Lake near Tully. (Photo: CYO)

against Curley and Hopkins a decade earlier, Catholic Charities experienced renewed growth when the problems posed by the depression overwhelmed parish resources. Community Chest programs expanded dramatically, and the state and federal government actively became involved, first in direct relief, then in a broad array of social programs. In Syracuse, Utica, Rome and, after 1937, in Binghamton, local Catholic Charities offices received substantial grants from Community Chest for relief, child care, family assistance and youth programs.

Foery threw his support behind these efforts, giving particular attention to youth. As far back as Hopkins' 1924 report, there had been concern in the diocese about youth work. Yet, in 1936, an inquiry by Bishop Duffy showed little interest in developing Catholic Boy and Girl Scout troops or other youth programs except camping. When Foery came to Syracuse, he pushed for increased youth work, but met considerable resistance.

At a clerical conference in 1940, Father Shields Dwyer presented a plan for parish and diocesan youth councils. Foery gently lent his support, telling the priests that the increase of mixed marriages, the "general decline of Catholic interest and zeal," the increasing rate of juvenile delinquency and the aggressive expansion of youth work by the YMCA and YWCA all provided reasons for action. Father Dwyer's proposal drew little response, but he was appointed youth director for Catholic Charities. A study of youth work in the city of Syracuse focused attention on the need for a youth center in the heavily populated North side of the city, an Italian and German section covering five parishes. Foery referred to the proposed center as "an extension of the home, the church and the school" whose aim was "to develop good citizenship through the medium of proper leisure time activities." In January 1944, a former furniture store on North Salina Street was purchased and the North Side CYO began, assisted by $15,000 from the Community Chest. Dances proved most popular, but a variety of recreational, vocational and cultural programs sprang up, and the center became a major institution in the neighborhood. With this success in front of them, and with increased resources available after the war, parishes expanded youth work dramatically, coordinated through the vigorous youth office of Catholic Charities.

RELIGIOUS EDUCATION

Another area which drew Foery's immediate attention when he came to Syracuse was religious education. Under pressure from Rome to provide better religious instruction for children in public schools, the diocese already had mapped plans for a major effort. Its origins went back to 1924, when a committee of ministers petitioned the board of education for permission to survey public school children. The children would be asked to complete a card indicating the church to which they belonged and whether or not they were attending Sunday schools. The ministers solicited Catholic support and Bishop Curley asked McEvoy's advice. The latter responded negatively, in part because the survey might place Catholics in "an unfavorable light." At the cathedral, for example, a congregation of 7,000 had only 350 children in Sunday school. The survey would provide useful information, but practically pastors could do little with it. One poor parish had at least 3,000 children who should receive religious instruction. To reach them all, the pastor would have to instruct 500 children every day of the week. If this was known, McEvoy warned, ".our non-Catholic brethren would be glad to help him out." The project died, but the incident indicated that there was, in fact, a major problem.

Syracuse had hardly ignored catechetics since the days when John Devereux gathered children in his home for Bible study. Still, heavy immigration had strained parish resources, while the emphasis after 1910 on parochial schools lowered the place of religious instruction of public school children. In parishes with schools, school parents tended to be among the most active parishioners. They, with the priests, naturally regarded parents whose children were in public schools as members of dubious loyalty with no great claim on parish resources. Parishes

without schools were normally poorer, with larger numbers of less active parishioners. As a result, the problem grew. A survey in February 1929 showed that 15,000 children were not attending Catholic schools. The bishop urged pastors to develop a "system" to provide "equal opportunity for religious education," but recognized it could not be "developed nor put into practical operation in a day."

The large number of Catholic children in public schools drew the attention of higher Church officials. The Holy See received regular reports on religious instruction and told the American bishops to "add to the number of *volunteer catechists* who repair to the country districts on Sundays and feast days to teach the Catechism." In 1935, the Vatican ordered every diocese to set up a catechetical office to promote Christian education and to establish the Confraternity of Christian Doctrine (CCD) in every parish. Some steps were taken to meet this demand, but not until Bishop Foery took charge was the full weight of diocesan leadership thrown behind efforts to instruct these children. Under the motto "Reach Every Child," Foery ordered pastors to mark September 18, 1938, as Catechetical Day, when they would preach on the subject and attempt to enroll new members in the parish confraternity. "The instructional work of the diocese has not been developed to its fullest," Foery admitted. "Many children (are) not being reached by the facilities now provided and many others are inadequately instructed." Studies had been made to determine the causes of "leakage from the Church," Foery wrote, "but pastors need no study to convince them that many defections from the faith are the result of insufficient religious instruction." If the self-interest of the Church were not enough, there was the battle against evils plaguing Church and society. "During these days of free expression and unrestrained freedom when our people are being innoculated by evil reading, questionable movies, bad companionship, with all their baneful effects, more than ever we must renew our spirit for the fight against the world and its influences."

The confraternity aimed "to have every youth in the parish come under its influence, and to have every adult where possible receive its benefits." The parish organization was supposed to "take precedence over all other parish sodalities and societies." Its members included teachers, home visitors who tried to persuade parents to send their children to class ("theirs is the work of salesmanship"), "helpers" who assisted with transportation, classroom preparation, attendance and safety, leaders of discussion groups and parent educator groups, and associates who raised funds and prayed for the work. The program of CCD involved four "units of work." The largest and most important was the instruction of elementary school children through religious vacation schools or year-round classes. Second was instruction of high school age children "through suitable discussion clubs or other successful means." The third area was "religious discussion clubs" for adults, "meetings of ordinary individuals, in groups of about ten, to discuss religion on a planned basis, in which carefully prepared outlines are followed." Finally, there should be parent education programs.

Foery and his superintendent of schools and director of religious education, David Gildea, planned to implement this complete program of religious education. In a speech to a national CCD conference, Foery outlined the diocesan program, headed by the well-established summer schools of religion, which had begun in the 1920s. By 1939, 50 priests, 100 sisters, 13 seminarians and 89 lay people taught in these schools, which were attended by slightly more than 5,000 children. The diocesan program received a big boost in April 1940, when Governor Herbert Lehman

signed a law which implemented earlier court rulings. These rulings permitted "absence for religious observance and education" from public schools for one hour a week upon written request from the parents. Clergy conferences were devoted entirely to developing programs of catechetical instruction to take advantage of the law, and by the fall, 85 percent of the parishes had done so.

At first, in many areas, classes were held in public school buildings. As late as 1944, 96 parishes enjoyed this benefit. Pastors had to develop programs, children had to be identified and their parents' consent obtained, local school authorities had to be persuaded to implement the permissive legislation, and Church officials had to be responsible for the transportation and safety of the children. All of this had to be done according to school districts, which did not always correspond to parish boundaries, so that inter-parish cooperation was necessary. Providing teachers was no small matter. Most sisters who had been offering summer or Sunday school instruction were parochial school teachers unavailable during school hours, while lay men and women who were working also were unavailable, so a new cadre of mothers had to be recruited and trained. Furthermore, the program forced Church officials to take a new approach to public schools and to other churches. Foery told the priests to cooperate with public school officials and to "avoid friction" by refusing to allow non-Catholics to attend "our classes....You must be fair and use honorable methods."

One result of the increased interest in religious education was that new figures became available which showed earlier ones to have been overly optimistic, allowing many public school Catholics to pass uncounted. A comprehensive survey of diocesan education in 1940 found that, of the 41,000 elementary age school children in the diocese 15,355, or 37.5 percent, were in Catholic schools. Of

October 9, 1939 — the first time when Catholic children attending Syracuse's Washington Irving School were allowed to leave their school during the day for religious education at the cathedral. With clergy, religious, and volunteer lay teachers, similar "released time" instruction was offered throughout the diocese. (Photo: Chancery Archives)

slightly less than 17,000 high school age children, 3,356, or 19.8 percent, were in Catholic schools. Of the remainder, 22.6 percent of the elementary age children in public schools and 33 percent of the public high school students still were receiving no religious instruction in released time, Sunday school or religious vacation school. Nevertheless, considerable progress had been made. Summer vacation schools served 5,138 students, while 3,248 adults were enrolled in 174 discussion groups in 73 parishes, and numerous parishes without schools had established religious education centers staffed by

sisters. At Immaculate Conception in Fayetteville, for example, the Third Order Franciscans served 675 pupils from four parishes and a mission. Even more impressive was the St. Cecilia's Catechetical Guild in Solvay, staffed by the Missionary Franciscans, which was serving 1,300 elementary and high school students. Similar centers were functioning at St. Anthony's in Utica, St. Mary's in Baldwinsville, Assumption in Utica, St. James in Syracuse, St. John's in Binghamton and St. Joseph's in Boonville.

As the school year opened in the fall of 1941, Foery addressed a pastoral letter to the people of the diocese reminding them of their obligation to provide for the religious education of their children. Out of a desire "to safeguard the welfare of your children," the Church built schools and worked tirelessly for the instruction of children in the public schools, he told them, but too often "parents are inclined to shift their responsibility to others." He pleaded for their "cooperation with Pastors in this important work." As for the pastors, Foery was very much in earnest, regularly reminding them that, according to canon law, "it is a proper and most serious office, especially of pastors of souls, to provide for the catechetical instruction of the Christian people." Gildea prepared detailed annual reports providing information on the number of public school children receiving no religious instruction in each parish. On the basis of these reports, the bishop kept constant pressure on pastors to fulfill their responsibilities.

To this point almost every activity in the diocese had depended upon the support of the pastors. No bishop had challenged their almost absolute control over the quantity and quality of services available at parish level. Even the mandating of CCD, which arose from papal orders, carried few sanctions. Pastors might well have expected that the formal establishment of the programs would be enough, as it had been with other mandates like the Curley order to establish the Holy Childhood Confraternity. Foery, however, was very much in earnest, and he was assisted by priests like Gildea and David Cunningham, whose priestly careers centered on diocesan administration and who were determined to bring greater unity and efficiency to diocesan work. Not unexpectedly, pastors, especially those who had long experience in the diocese, resented the implied criticism and the interference in their parochial affairs. In 1943 Father McPeak of the cathedral, for example, claimed that Gildea's

surveys were unreliable because of the high level of mobility of inner city residents. Father Charles McEvoy, himself once superintendent of schools and now pastor of St. Anthony's, also challenged the statistics. The bishop replied to McEvoy that baptismal figures over the last 10 years indicated a steady growth among the school age population. He repeated his challenge: "May I ask what solution you have to offer?" McEvoy was furious, responding to Foery's "interesting letter" by defending his own statistics: "Of a mathematical turn of mind, I have made a study of many such things." During his 18 years as pastor, McEvoy claimed, the children of his parish had been well instructed. He made this statement not as "a novice or as a member of a 'junior braintrust' but as an educator with wider experience than most priests of the diocese." McEvoy concluded with a ringing defense:

I have lived under five Rt. Rev. and Most Rev. Bishops, as a student I was obedient to the first—Ludden. I lived and worked with two—Grimes and Curley; and I have been somewhat active under the other two: Duffy and your excellency. And whatever anyone may have told you, I have rendered obedience and absolute loyalty to them all.

Apparently Foery took strong action, because McEvoy apologized quickly for any discourtesy contained in this letter, and withdrew his remarks about a "junior braintrust." Never again would Foery's authority be challenged by his priests.

The advent of released time, pressure from Rome to instruct children in public schools, and Foery's own conviction that the religious instruction of the young was crucial to the survival of the Church, along with the financial constraints which inhibited the expansion of Catholic schools, led to a dramatic extension of religious education through CCD. The practical problems of launching these programs, however, limited attention to such other CCD objectives as adult and parent education. Only in a few parishes, like St. Cecelia's in Solvay, did many adult discussion clubs take shape. There was somewhat more interest in early childhood education, expressed through visits to new parents and leaflets with ideas about home religious practice, usually carried out by parish Mothers Clubs. Such programs depended upon priests, sisters and a growing, but still poorly trained, group of lay volunteers. Nevertheless, the energetic attention to CCD from 1937 to 1945 represented a major step toward the goal of universally available Catholic education.

If the 1950s were in a special way "the age of the Catholic school," the religious education of children in public schools was not neglected. In fact, with the help of the released time program and Gildea's highly developed CCD system, the diocese claimed to come close to Foery's original goal, reaching more than 90 percent of the elementary school children and 80 percent of those in high school. In the school year 1948-1949, approximately 28,000 of 30,000 children in elementary school and 10,200 of 12,400 high school children were being served by a network of parish and released time programs. These programs were taught by 335 lay people, 643 religious and 498 priests. Thirty elementary and 22 high school programs were offered in the public school buildings themselves. Sixty two units (parishes or catechetical centers) reported 100 percent coverage of Catholic high school students and 84 reported 100 percent coverage of elementary age children. From the beginning, CCD had called for lay involvement in educational work. In the 1950s, the number of lay catechists gradually increased and along with

it, the need for new and better training. In 1959, there were 432 lay teachers and teacher training programs were being held at three centers throughout the diocese.

Despite these impressive figures, there were problems, some of them serious. Pastors and sisters agreed that the released time programs were far from ideal. The time required to transport students, take attendance and get things organized limited instruction severely, some claimed to as little as 20 minutes. The high figures for high school attendance began to drop in the late 1950s, reaching a low of 74 percent in 1958-1959. This gave rise to a suggestion from the religious education office that consideration be given to establishing catechetical centers near public high school buildings. This would enable students to participate on a more flexible basis, reflecting changes in their schedules. Many of those connected with the program also worried about the quality of instruction, especially that provided by lay teachers whose training was minimal at best. Most of all, there was the powerful set of ideas supporting Catholic school education. These ideas could not help but make these programs seem far from ideal and limit the amount of support provided by parents of Catholic school children or parishes with heavy school budgets.

CATHOLIC SCHOOLS

When Foery arrived in Syracuse, he found a strong Catholic school system which had made steady improvement for two decades under the leadership of Charles McEvoy, but still faced enormous problems. McEvoy's notes of school visitations in 1931 provide a window into Catholic schools of the period. Occasionally he was deeply impressed, as with one teacher during a first grade arithmetic class at St. Stanislaus in Binghamton:

One of the best baby teachers I have ever seen; excellent work; loads of motivation; fine example work; cards and extra work for brighter children. Fine personality; fine results; yet sister says she has a slow group this year.

Or, in another arithmetic class:

A game was in progress. Aisles are named after Saints; there is keen competition. Children greatly interested and were anxious to learn. It was a fine demonstration of teaching.

But the problems were enormous. Teachers talked too much or too little, with soft voices and no control, or with little apparent grasp of their subject, especially in the upper grades. He noted that, in some schools, "dull" students stayed in the same class year after year. He thought they should be moved along to "divide up the burden." Some classes spent too much of their time on such students, while others ignored them in favor of the brighter children. In schools where two grades were taught together, he traced discipline problems to the failure of the teacher to assign work to those in their seats, while others were at the board. In another, he was irritated that all teachers used "clickers," instead of their voices, to give directions. In one class, he thought a student who called out "S't'r" should have been corrected. However, he noted in another, where student response had been slow and uncertain, that he had heard the teacher berating the students before he entered. "Perhaps that action explains a lot," he wrote. In his recommendations, he urged the use of plan books, state attendance records, the Palmer method of penmanship and the use of the diocesan-mandated texts. He made suggestions about keeping buildings cleaner, improving light and ventilation, making more adequate use of space and improving classroom methods, especially by involving the students and using more question-and-answer and recitation methods.

Father Charles McEvoy was the energetic school superintendent who on one occasion argued, without success, against St. Anthony's school in Syracuse adding a high school while its grade school was overcrowded and understaffed. Ironically, McEvoy later became pastor of St. Anthony's. (Photo: Chancery Archives)

269

By far the biggest problem was overcrowding. At St. Louis in Oswego, for example, the seven students in the first grade were taught in the same room as the much larger eighth grade. At St. Patrick's in Oneida, 15 high school students, spread over four years, took the services of four teachers, while two teachers taught the first four grades with 127 pupils. At St. Mary's in New York Mills, there were 74 children in the third grade and 80 in the fifth. State tests showed the students at St. Mary's were two years behind expected grade performance, a result McEvoy thought reflected a test bias which placed those who spoke Polish or Italian at home at a clear disadvantage. At St. Anthony's school in Syracuse, eight Sisters of St. Joseph and two lay teachers taught eight grades, 515 students, in classes ranging from 43 to 70 pupils. Five of the school's 15 rooms were unused because the pastor would allow no more lay teachers and additional sisters were unavailable. To the superintendent's dismay, the parish was, nevertheless, in the process of beginning a high school. To make matters worse, more than 300 children from the parish were in public schools. The superintendent's comments were sharp.

> *A pastor's duty, as we see it, is to work for the Christian education of all the children in his parish. This education is best provided for in the parochial school; and where a parish has a parochial school, all the children of that parish should if possible be enrolled.*

Lack of equipment and a library, overcrowded elementary school conditions, straightened financial circumstances and inability to meet standards for New York State certification, all seemed to indicate that there was "only one logical solution." This solution was to abandon the high school and concentrate on meeting the needs of elementary age children. Unfortunately, the superintendent had no power to impose this recommenda-

tion, and it was ignored.

The depression had an impact on Catholic schools, though by 1933 no elementary schools had closed. Indeed, one had opened during the previous year. However, at least one high school did not make it. The troubled history of Assumption Academy in Utica came to an end as parishes reneged on their assessments. By 1936 the school was closed and it was leased to the city of Utica for use as the local headquarters of the Works Progress Administration. In Syracuse, Christian Brothers Academy (CBA), a private school with relatively heavy tuition, also found it difficult to attract students and came to the brink of disaster. In August, the bishop wrote the priests of the diocese, urging them to identify students who would be qualified to attend the school if tuition assistance could be found. He requested them to seek out CBA alumni in their area who might be persuaded to provide that assistance.

Enrollment in diocesan schools expanded during the 1920s, from 13,252 in 1917, to approximately 19,000 in 1930. Elementary school class size declined as more teachers became available. In 1917, classes averaged 43 pupils, with classes in some of the larger urban schools almost staggering. Mount Carmel in Utica and St. Cyril in Binghamton averaged 71 students a class. By 1930, the average remained more than 40, but only a few schools averaged more than 50. The highest was Sacred Heart in Syracuse with 61. During the 1930s, under the weight of the depression, school enrollment actually dropped to less than 15,000 in elementary schools, down from more than 17,000 in 1930. Conversely, high school enrollment increased from 1,800 to almost 3,000. As a result, elementary school class size dropped dramatically to a diocesan average of 34. The drop in elementary enrollment in the period was alarming, but, with finances still hampered by hard times and with schools making steady improvement in instruction, there was little evident desire to take concerted action.

Nevertheless, as the depression eased, Monsignor Gildea brought to the school office a new level of professionalism. His papers were filled with reports and articles dealing with educational methods, public policy issues, and even the amount of sleep and number of calories needed by growing children. In his reports on school visits, he gave careful attention to materials and methods, emphasized positive encouragement rather than strict discipline and complained about the still large classes in some schools. He insisted on careful records, in accord with local and state laws, and made regular recommendations about standards of performance expected at each grade level. In 1940, he launched a newsletter for teachers, "In School Circles," with new ideas, a survey of publications, and information about meetings and conferences. He was as unsympathetic as his predecessor with parish high schools. Often undersupervised, understaffed and unequipped, they overburdened parish resources and did not provide the child with as good an education as the public schools. He felt this was a condition which canceled out the parents' obligation to send the children to Catholic schools.

The items listed in Gildea's visitation reports may have indicated a certain utopian idealism of freedom, order, motivation and content, but they surely called into question any contention that the Catholic school system relied solely on brute memorization or was conducted by men and women with no familiarity with the best educational theories. Gildea's visitation notes in the early 1940s included such perceptive comments as "work books prove wretched crutches," "make libraries available to pupils; classroom libraries to be encouraged," "attention to art in ALL GRADES," "give help to enable students to study alone," "display work; brighten up rooms with colored borders," "individu-

alize instruction," "best work achieved when work is a challenge to the pupil," as well as the more characteristically Catholic "call leading groups by name, e.g. St. Jos., St. Mary's, St. Pat's." He also commented on problems posed as always by limited budgets: "Weakness in reading allowed to develop after 2nd grade—no books one cause."

The diocese had decided years before to work toward a uniform curriculum, and to do so within the framework of New York State Regents exams. Shifts in state examinations could require the diocese to change texts and curriculum, a process for which the diocesan office was responsible. However, it was a responsibility that hardly could be carried out without the cooperation of the sisters who would do the teaching and the pastors who would pay for the books. In 1937, for example, when the state adopted a new syllabus in arithmetic, a new series was needed to prepare eighth grade students for the Regent's examination. Gildea obtained materials from 14 publishers and with the help of more than 50 sister teachers, began a two-stage evaluation process. While in theory, every school should adopt the texts selected, decisions in fact had to be made at the school level, where the pastor controlled the purse. But this process, repeated again and again, gradually led the schools toward greater uniformity and strengthened the bonds between the diocesan office and the teaching staff, thus reducing the power of the pastor.

Gildea paid close attention as well to changes in public policy. In 1939, the state authorized the extension of transportation, health and safety programs to non-public school children. Based on the theory that these services were for the child, not the school, and that all children deserved equal access to such services, these changes again required interaction of parochial school officials with local school boards and committees. Pastors were advised to guide their parents throughout the process of applying for such services, noting that they could expect them only where they were already available to public school students. In 1939, under a New York state law aimed at overcoming illiteracy and lack of English-language instruction among immigrants, an Emergency Adult Education Program authorized holding classes for adults in parish buildings. Gildea informed pastors that the field of possible instruction were very wide, including homemaking, ceramics, music and art, and that they should call on the local official in charge to begin such courses in their parishes. In 1938, New York state voters were to pass judgment on nine amendments to the state constitution. These amendments included provisions for exemption of Church property from taxation, and the right of children to school transportation, health and welfare services. Father Gildea wrote school principals urging their active support for these provisions.

Bishop Foery was deeply committed to Catholic schools and did not rest easily with the declining enrollments he faced when he arrived in the diocese. He kept as close an eye on such figures as he did on CCD coverage. He had little tolerance for the argument that parish programs for public school children made parents believe what one pastor called "a new heresy," namely "that it is no longer as important or necessary to send children to the Catholic parochial school." This priest used the argument to place the blame for the decline of his own school on the parents and, by implication, on the bishop, who had not reminded the people of their "grave responsibility" to send their children to Catholic schools. The bishop was not put off, ordering the pastor to visit the homes of parishioners to urge them to send their children to his school. He also ordered the principal to work with the diocese school office to improve its program because its weaknesses had been

Monsignor David Gildea (Photo: Chancery Archives)

cited by parents as their reason for preferring the public school.

In June 1945, with the war ending, the pressure on pastors to expand parochial school enrollments intensified. The bishop noted that, between 1930 and 1943, the number of children enrolled in Catholic schools declined from 20,360 to 17,967, while Catholics in public schools rose from 23,373 to 38,756. As a result, the bishop called the attention of a number of pastors to their canonical responsibility to provide the opportunity for quality Catholic education to every child. He told Monsignor Piejda of Sacred Heart, for example, that while he might never again reach the peak of 1,538 children enrolled in 1928, much could be done to increase the number of children in his school. He placed the burden directly on the pastor: "Priestly contacts with families in which there

272

are children of school age will do much to attract to your classrooms those who have formerly been enrolled in the public schools." An almost identical letter was sent to Father William Morris at St. Paul's in Binghamton. When enrollment increased in the fall, the bishop praised his efforts, noting that "it would be fatal...if we did not continue...to preach consistently the obligation of our parents." In a letter to Father Joseph Canfield of St. Charles in Syracuse, which did not have a school, the bishop noted that three reasons ordinarily prevented provision of a school — lack of children, money or teachers. St. Charles already had shown it had the children and the financial resources. The bishop was convinced that, "in due time," sisters would be available, and he told the pastor to begin planning to build. To the pastor at St. Mary's in Baldwinsville, he was even more direct:

During the past several years the parish has been able to set aside a sizeable sum of money. This money has been given with the idea that the parish would further expand its facilities and, particularly, make greater provision for the training and religious instruction of the children. It is our opinion that this can be best accomplished through the building of a parochial school. The Bishop, the pastor and the parents are bound by a most serious obligation to provide to the best of their ability for the religious and moral education of their children. (Can. 1113).

Most pastors with schools were anxious to maintain and increase enrollment as Foery urged. At St. Vincent in Syracuse the aging Father Dougherty let few occasions pass without referring to the obligation of the parents to fill the school. In August 1941, for example, he appealed to parents of small children entering school for the first time to come to St. Vincent's: "They need us and we need them." He asked parents to approach high school age children from neighboring parishes and invite them to attend their school. There would be no charge of any kind except for books. "We also call the attention of children and parents alike to the necessity, the absolute necessity, of Catholic education in grade and high school in these particular times; and of the conscientious responsibility and obligation of children and parents particularly to take advantage of it." Four years later, the message was the same: "Send your children where they belong, to a Catholic school." To make the case as strong as possible, and to combat the "new heresy," the line between Catholic and non-Catholic schools had to be drawn as sharply as ever:

The schools of America do not educate, they do not lead forth the hidden powers of souls their pupils possess. How could they, since they omit God?....Even Catholic teachers in public schools ("ask them") dare not mention God in his personal dealings with man. So non-Catholic schools simply are not capable of educating Catholics and this is true at all levels of grammar, high school, and college. That's why you are foolish to send children to non-Catholic schools. Why waste your money and their time? They might teach mental and physical skills that will enable your children to make a living. But education should teach pupils not how to make a living but how to live. They may make social and business contacts at school. That can be done more quickly, with less expense, and with scarcely half the spiritual danger, outside school. Make no mistake. There is genuine danger for Catholic children in our public schools. No, not because they'll 'lose their faith.' Maybe they won't. Yes, because they'll emerge anemic, stunted, below-par spiritually.

The bishop clearly agreed. He told teaching sisters that they had reason to be proud, because the war proved that "our Catholic schools have been successful" and their graduates proved themselves "great soldiers, great men and great Americans." After the war, patriotic considerations remained paramount. "It is our ambition," Foery argued, "to turn out a manhood and a womanhood in whose hands the destiny of the nation will be safe," and this required that students "have in their souls the habits upon which citizenship is constructed," which included "(One) the habit of obedience to authority" and "(Second)...the habit of sacrifice for the common good."

During the dedication of a school in 1953, the bishop said that, because the role of the Church was "to lead souls to God and to teach the ways of salvation," education was a matter of paramount importance. CCD was inadequate, because schools *alone* can unfold the meaning and implications of Christian faith." The divorce of religious and moral instruction in tax-supported schools was bearing fruit after several generations of "purely secular" education. Catholic schools, in contrast, helped solve social problems by training moral individuals. "Create good individuals and you create a good world," Foery argued. "Make good citizens and you make a nation and when nations are good, yes, you have a good world, a world of peace, of security, of justice and of charity." The Church, Foery claimed, could solve the world's problems, if "only you give it the youth." Catholics, therefore, should provide schools as their religious and civic duty: "Your post office and your armory are built by your government," Foery said, "but your school will be built by you."

In a variety of forums, the bishop thus indicated that Catholic education was his top priority. He insisted that the school was crucial to the survival of the Church. Recognizing the degree to which Church affiliation was becoming a matter of self-conscious decision, he insisted that only education in a Catholic atmosphere could protect the Church against the snares of indifference and laxity. Even his theology of Church leadership rested on an educational foundation. "The bishop of the Roman Catholic Diocese of Syracuse has many obligations, but I believe they can be reduced to one: namely the teaching and preserving of the faith," Foery said. "There are many ways and many means which he can use to discharge this obligation, but these also can be reduced to one: namely the instruction of our people." In 1958, he told the priests that schools were the "problem of the day" for the American Church and, if they were not interested in the schools, they were not interested in the Church.

The bishop's exhortations and pressure had their effect because parochial school enrollment expanded rapidly after the war. It reached almost 20,000 in 1947-48, and then increased 50 percent in the next six years. By 1960, there were 31,408 students in elementary school, compared to 14,903 in 1940, and there were 5,369 in Catholic high schools, compared to 2,940 two decades earlier. This rapid expansion was the major problem the clergy faced in the postwar years. "All Catholics must be made to understand they have a serious responsibility to finance and support Catholic education," the consultors said in a 1950 report. Collections for parochial schools were to be "arranged in such a way that the support of the school is maintained by the parish and not merely by those parishioners who send their children to the school, nor was anyone to be excluded from the benefits of Catholic education on the ground she could not pay for it." To bring the obligation home, the diocese recommended a special school collection each month in every parish.

Providing teachers was another serious problem. The educational work of the Church was succeeding in Syracuse, Foery said, but the "harvest has outgrown us" because there were not enough laborers for schools and catechetical centers. In 1947-48, there were only 10 lay people among the 578 teachers in Catholic schools. Most pastors and people agreed with Foery's statement 10 years earlier that Catholic schools could fulfill their "purpose" only if "the entire teaching staff" was composed of priests or religious. Yet, this insistence had to be modified as the demand for Catholic schools, fueled by the strong language of the bishop and most pastors, outran available religious personnel. The Sisters of St. Joseph told Foery in 1951 that they could staff more schools if they could have one or two lay teachers in each. Foery seemed sympathetic, although he told the provincial superior that priests and people were not ready for such a move: "It may be that the idea will take hold after some time, but at present tradition is against it." Five years later, it was clear that the need for teachers would require tradition to give way. In their 1956 report, the diocesan consultors concluded reluctantly that "both priests and parents must be made to realize that the employment of lay teachers in the parochial school is a necessity and additional lay teachers must be obtained to help solve the crisis in Catholic education." Finding suitable lay teachers and paying their salaries was "a problem that will unfortunately harass our pastors for many years to come."

Foery could pressure pastors to provide education and he could urge parishioners to support local programs, but the parish remained responsible for its school. The one page of diocesan educational regulations of a half century earlier had become, by the 1950s,

a 47-page booklet. That booklet contained administrative procedures, curriculum, records, health and safety programs, testing, discipline and extracurricular activities. The handbook stated that the goal of Catholic education was "to encourage the child to develop good work habits and to capitalize on his special aptitudes and interests; to foster a respect for the Christian dignity of labor and to promote zeal for social justice," and to pursue cultural development and "moral and spiritual perfection." These goals required the cooperation of the home, Church, community at large, and in most cases, the parish. While the high standards set by the superintendent may not always have been met, there was in fact a great deal of cooperation between the diocese and the parish, school, parents and classroom teachers. Most parishes with schools devoted more than half their normal receipts to school purposes in the 1950s. Parish members did not pay tuition. Students from neighboring parishes did. The bishop encouraged the parish which sent children to a neighboring school to pay that charge. However, some pastors felt that the parents should pay, and the question was disputed frequently. Otherwise, the only charge on a student's family was for books. At St. Mary's in Oswego, for example, students paid $12.50 each, reduced when a family had more than two children in the school. Parents were "required" to attend four parent meetings a year, while many served as volunteers, room mothers, traffic guides and served meals or supervised recess. There was sometimes a weekly charge for milk, and a variety of parent and student fundraising efforts, with candy drives being the most popular. The parish, too, spent enormous energy in raising money for the school. In the 1950s, bingo began to appear, causing criticism from non-Catholics.

Expansion of elementary enrollment meant that the pressure for new high schools would grow as the bulge of increased numbers passed through the lower grades. Since the establishment of the diocesan education office, successive superintendents had looked unfavorably upon the establishment of parochial high schools. With elementary classes too large and facilities inadequate, they argued that opening high schools simply spread already strained resources too thin. Yet pastors had the final word and such high schools did open. By the 1950s, high school education had become as much a part of the accepted landscape of American life as the grammar school. The drive for Catholic schools, pushed so hard by the bishop during and after the war, together with the demographic changes of the period, created a popular desire and a logical necessity for extended opportunities for Catholic high school education. Bishop Foery and Monsignor Gildea recognized and approved this development, but they were even more convinced that the need could not be satisfied on a parochial basis.

Other dioceses in New York State had prohibited the further development of parochial high schools in favor of regional schools under diocesan sponsorship and control. Foery hoped one day to do the same. He told the pastor of St. John's in Binghamton, for example, that parochial high schools were "too restricted in their personnel, too limited in their number of students, and above all, they are not able to give the courses which can be had in the central High School." He looked forward to the building of a fully equipped central Catholic high school in Binghamton. Yet, at the time Foery was writing these words, Monsignor D. Francis Curtin, pastor of St. Patrick's, told the press no new Catholic high school was needed in the city, where his own parish and St. Paul's had parish high schools. But the bishop was insistent. On March 11, 1957, he had a statement incorporated into the minutes of a meeting of diocesan consultors:

> *I want it clearly understood that the bishop of the diocese fully and thoroughly recognizes the need for the expansion and building of more high schools in every part of the diocese. While some progress has been made in the circle of secondary education, by no means has it been adequate (because) too many of us are interested in our own parochial high school.*

In Rome, as early as 1951, Foery told local pastors they should either make better use of the present facilities or begin plans for a central Catholic high school, which "may be the solution." But it was in Oswego that the plan was launched. In January 1953, after consultation with the city's pastors, the bishop announced that a central Catholic high school would open in the fall on the site of the former St. Francis Home. It would open after a capital campaign of $300,000 to renovate the buildings and construct a combination auditorium and gymnasium. With a diocesan priest as principal and a sister as vice-principal, the school would be coeducational and offer a full academic program. Launched with a $5,000 gift from the bishop, the campaign eventually topped $370,000 and the school opened in September with two classes and 110 students. The bishop thought this "historic event" was one of the most "glorious chapters" in the history of the diocese because, as the first central Catholic high school, Foery felt it would be "working out the methods and developing the plans which we hope and pray will soon be realized in every community in the diocese."

In Endicott, when the bishop granted permission to Father Hopkins at St. Ambrose to open a high school in 1953, it was with the understanding that it would become eventually a central school for the community. After some resistance, this plan went into effect in 1955, with the name of the school changed to Seton High School. In 1960, the school was expanded at a cost of $600,000, two-thirds of which was borne by St. Ambrose. Utica Catholic Academy, long associated with St. John's, also became the responsibility of all the parishes of that city in 1958. A major fundraising effort to improve the building and facilities was held a year later. Another major fund drive led, in 1960, to the opening of Utica's Notre Dame High School, staffed by the Xaverian brothers.

Binghamton, with its intense ethnic loyalties, and Syracuse, with many small parish high schools, proved hard to crack with the new plan. Only after long and not always harmonious negotiations with pastors did Foery judge the time was ripe. In the early 1960s, in Onondaga County, a $4,000,000 drive was held to build two Catholic high schools. Bishop Ludden High School opened in 1963 and Bishop Grimes High School two years later. Also in 1963, Rome Catholic High School finally opened.

Almost simultaneously, a drive for $1,500,000 was held in the Binghamton-Johnson City area for a school to accommodate 1,000 students to be built on the site of the former St. Mary's Home.

PUBLIC EDUCATION

"Reach Every Child" never implied seeking to improve public education. Indeed, concern about the quality of public school education was almost never discussed, except when high standards were seen in terms of competition with Catholic schools. Discussion of education, in fact, seemed at times almost entirely self-interested. Yet, there was a clear need to explain how Catholic schools contributed to the public good. There was, for example, emphasis on the savings to the local community. In Binghamton, when the drive for a central high school was launched, campaign literature estimated the savings to the city as

the same amount as the goal of the drive, $1,500,000. Gildea regularly came up with such estimates, including replacement costs for school buildings and per capita costs for the students if they were shifted suddenly to the public schools. In greater Syracuse in 1956, there were 12,109 students in 22 elementary and 12 high schools, staffed by 274 religious and 14 lay teachers, saving the taxpayers $4,365,899.95 annually. To replace the Catholic facilities would cost $8,640,000. Estimating that $2,800,000 would be returned to Syracuse in state aid, the total savings were $10,205,731.95.

On the other hand, the Church needed public school cooperation in released time, so the rhetoric about "Godless" schools and the injustice of "dual taxation" had to be blended with a more cooperative approach. When local authorities banned the use of public school facilities for religious instruction in Chadwicks, the pastor of St. Anthony's responded by demanding payment for the use of his parish parking lot for recreational purposes by the neighboring public school. Some parishioners, including a member of the school board, objected. The bishop wrote immediately, rescinding the pastor's action as an "error in judgement" and stating his own commitment to cooperation between parochial and public school leadership. In 1958, Father Michael L. Dacey became embroiled in a heated controversy with officials of the Union Endicott school district. The dispute focused on alleged efforts to force a Catholic public school teacher to withdraw his children from a parochial school and resign as head of that school's parent organization. The controversy also was highlighted by the alleged withdrawal of an invitation to Dacey to address a public school PTA by a principal who charged that Dacey was opposed to the public schools. Dacey pushed hard for vindication, but diocesan officials insisted that Dacey was acting as an individual "priest and citizen."

They regarded public and parochial schools as "partners in education." Partners, perhaps, but the rhetoric connecting secular education with immorality, corruption and communism, and the almost total preoccupation of the Church with its own children, made the Church a somewhat questionable participant in public discussions of education. This was unfortunate because there was much to be learned from the success of Catholic schools.

The growth of Catholic education was the result of a correlation between parent and school objectives. Immigrants had built and maintained schools primarily to ensure that their children's education did not disrupt the continuity of national and religious traditions and thereby create family conflict and alienation across the generations. Church leaders understood all this and developed an educational approach which blended family, Church and school into a mutually supportive subculture. This subculture defined and affirmed identity, while encouraging development of the skills needed for successful life projects. Because there was a broad consensus among parents, teachers and clergy, the school could concentrate on education and leave other life adjustment and socialization processes to the family and parish. In the postwar suburbs, as in the prewar urban neighborhoods, people in the midst of rapid social change, which promised a better life but challenged traditional identity, found in their churches the basis for maintaining continuity and identity, while pursuing the elusive ideal of happiness.

Father Gildea, the most thoughtful exponent of Catholic education in the diocese, had a firm grasp on all this. He clearly expressed the twin emphasis on parental responsibility and Church control which so bewildered outsiders. On the one hand, Gildea argued, the education of children belonged to parents, and schools were their agents to assist, not to supplant. No system should ever strip parents of their authority and responsibility. On the other hand, formal education had its limits. When schools attempted to launch into social welfare, or when they set overly ambituous educational aims, they overstepped not only their authority but their competence and ended up weakening themselves for the work that they could do. What he presented as a Catholic philosophy of education, then, was not an ideal for the school alone, but for a blended fabric of home, school and Church:

> *The sum total of those social, intellectual, moral and religious changes that take place in the life of an individual from birth to that point in life when he is capable of proceeding alone, is called education. These educational changes parallel in a sense the child's physical growth from infancy to maturity. Life's educational processes are patterned according to the purposes of life possessed by those directing the child's education. In other words, our philosophy of life dictates our educational philosophy. Consequently ... the Catholic philosophy of education includes not only the preparation for life in the practice of a profession or trade, but the voluntary constriction of that living within the framework of religion and the moral law.... The Catholic philosophy of education considers the whole person, body and soul, mind and will, in relation to his temporal and eternal life.*

When Catholic schools expressed that "voluntary constriction," while affirming the goals of social acceptance and economic advancement of most parents, they were remarkably successful. But the possibility that Church and parent expectations might someday differ was increased by the old problem of lay participation. Even at their best, Catholic schools restricted the role of parents and lay parishioners to financial, spiritual and moral support. Priests, bishops and most religious assumed that their goals and those of the parents were the same, so that open dialogue about policies and programs was unnecessary. The result too often was that parents saw themselves as recipients of the benefits of Catholic education, rather than as active participants in the process. Foery regularly complained that parents tended to pass off their responsibility for education to the school and the parish, rarely noticing that the very structure of the educational system encouraged that result. Catholic leaders consistently saw parents in terms of their children, not as mature and responsible participants in the Church and the school.

Equally important, Catholic education, like Catholic religious life, remained essentially private. Recognizing the need for, and the benefits of, training for citizenship, the diocese mentioned social responsibility in most statements of purpose. However, the central themes remained loyalty to the Church, establishment of "objective guides for conduct," and laying a "basis for the sanctity of the home." Religion, for youth, should lead the soul to God. For adults, it should "steady the soul's contacts with the world" and "convince the soul that earthly cares and possessions are not everything in life." Foery argued against a philosophy of education that did not allow the Church to "direct people in their family lives, in their actions in the market place, the factory and the home," but he stated the alternative as a Church that "watches over and guides men as they live so that they can be properly directed to their last end—an eternal destiny of happiness." The bishop wanted the Church to teach people how "to live a complete life as an individual, as a member of a family, as a citizen of the state, as a member of the church and child of God." Yet, the preoccupation with incorporating child and adult into a Catholic subculture based on the home, on the practice of the faith and clearly defined moral rules, all oriented toward an other-worldly salvation, made Catholic education almost obsessively private. Yet these critical comments should not obscure the magnificent achievement represented by Catholic education. While sharp limitations existed on the religious education of public school children, expanded youth work and active family involvement in the parish could offset them. The schools themselves helped thousands upon thousands of working-class Americans begin the process of social and economic advancement. The schools of the post-war years provided an education at least the equal of that available in most public schools. If they turned Catholics and their Church in upon themselves, they also provided an environment which gave clear direction and purpose to life and instilled a sense of personal moral responsibility. In a nation whose commitment to universal education was perhaps its most radical democratic experiment, Catholic schools helped make that experiment at least a partial success. In the process, they ensured that the Church and its institutions remained available to a later generation. And that generation might have the material resources and social opportunities to make new choices about private and public life, and perhaps contribute in its own way to the task of making its Church a living embodiment of Christ's presence in the world of Central New York. That generation would come to question the value or the practicality of Catholic school education, but, as the diocese began its second century, it had found no alternative form of education as effective as that pursued by Bishop Foery and the Catholics of his generation.

THE ANSWER
TO THE WORLD'S
WOES

THE PUBLIC LIFE OF AN AMERICAN CATHOLIC CHURCH
1940s-1950s

Among the many paradoxes which surround twentieth century American Catholicism, perhaps none is more confusing than the Church's vigorous criticism of the surrounding culture and its simultaneous expression of a proud, even aggressive, patriotism. In the 1930s, powerful sermons on subjects like birth control suggested the American Church was as alienated from prevailing institutions as was the Church in Europe. Outsiders could be forgiven for thinking that American Catholics might harbor some of the same feelings toward democracy evident among Franco's forces in Spain or the opposition to the Third Republic in France. When Catholics prevented an advocate of birth control from speaking or attempted to use their political clout to censor films or magazines, some non-Catholics worried that the Church might someday throw its weight behind an attempt to overthrow American institutions. When they heard bishops and priests, in their enthusiasm for Catholic schools, condemn public education as "Godless," anti-Christian and un-American, non-Catholics well might have wondered if they felt the same way about other public institutions which similarly excluded Christianity.

Yet, if they listened closely, they also would hear that American Catholics were deeply patriotic, and they interpreted the teachings of their Church in terms of fundamental human rights. They also would hear that Catholics supported as strongly as any group in American society, labor's right to organize and the government's responsibility to alleviate the suffering of the poor. Far from feeling alien and estranged, American Catholics felt increasingly at home in American society. Few were aware that the papacy had condemned Church-state separation and regarded religious liberty as a compromise still, acceptable only where the Church was a minority. Fewer were aware that the papacy felt Church-state separation should be changed, where possible, to a close cooperation, even union, of

Church and state which would place sharp restrictions on the freedom of non-Catholics to worship and evangelize. An even smaller number were aware that the papacy and local Church leaders in Italy, Austria, Spain, Portugal and Germany were sympathetic to extreme right-wing political movements. For all their ambiguous rhetoric, American Catholics loved their country, and appreciated the freedom and opportunity they enjoyed. They also loved their Church so strongly, in part, because they sincerely believed its teaching supported American democratic values. At the same time, their Church was no longer on the outside and they were grateful. In 1944, Bishop Foery told Rome: "No civil laws impede episcopal jurisdiction or infringe on the church's dignity. On the contrary, every honor is shown to the episcopal office by public officials and all citizens."

The key to the paradox of Church's effort to be solidly patriotic while strongly criticizing many aspects of American life lay in the conviction, grown to an unquestioned assumption in the years between the wars, that loyal Catholicism was good Americanism and good Americanism was loyal Catholicism. Whether the issue was dirty movies, "sexy" magazines, divorce, birth control, capitalism or communism, Catholic speakers, including the Syracuse bishops, invariably argued that the Church supported authentic American values of personal dignity and voluntary sacrifice for the common good. And indeed supported those values more thoroughly and intelligently than any other institution in American society. What was needed was an opportunity to demonstrate the depth of this conviction that, in Bishop Foery's words, the Church "had the answer to the world's woes." The opportunity came with the Second World War and the Cold War that followed, when the long combination of loyal Catholicism and patriotic Americanism came to its climax. The Church now showed itself a most loyal supporter of the nation, and the nation now was clearly seen as God's agent for the preservation of Christian civilization. If once Catholics had thought themselves a minority, looked down upon and excluded, they now found their Church the valued ally of their government and their faith enlisted in the national cause.

Bishop Foery, when he came to the diocese, warmly supported social reform. At the same time, like his predecessors, he valued a united and disciplined Church. The fights carried on by the campaign against indecent literature seemed to express a consensus: there was no hint of opposition from Catholic sources. On the other hand, such public policy issues as the debates over isolationism and internationalism, which raged after the outbreak of war in Europe in 1939, found no such Catholic agreement. Nationally, many bishops championed isolationism, but Bishop Foery had few comments to make, and there were few echoes of these controversies in Syracuse. One of the few centers of serious intellectual life, the Catholic Women's Club, brought to Syracuse famous lecturers like Monsignor Fulton Sheen, Frank Sheed, Anne O'Hare McCormick and Alfred Lund. When McCormick proposed speaking about the European War in 1941, the chairperson responded that the subject "sounds as if it might be a controversial one. The series is given in a public auditorium and so a controversial subject must be avoided. Maybe you attack the question from a strictly neutral point. Maybe that is the topic we should have if the mind of the church plays a leading part in your discussion." This caution reflected well the atmosphere of Syracuse Catholicism.

WORLD WAR II

On December 7, 1941, however, the war became uncontroversial. Bishop Foery spoke quickly:

> *In this hour of great national crisis it is imperative that we lift our hearts in confident prayer to Almighty God. It is indeed fitting that we beg His blessing upon the President of these United States, so that, with wisdom and justice, he may guide our nation in these distressing days. It is our serious obligation to ask Almighty God to extend his protecting hand over the armed forces of our beloved America.*

As for the Church, it once again stood ready to play its part: "We place our resources at the disposal of our country and we ask our people to pray that God will grant us victory." Two days after the attack on Pearl Harbor, Foery used an address to a local American Legion post to urge everyone to rally behind the government. On December 15, he wrote the priests of the diocese of the need for chaplains. Already, before Pearl Harbor, four Syracuse priests had volunteered. The first, Father Joseph B. Delahunt, eventually received a Purple Heart for wounds suffered in action.

Before the war was over, 32 Syracuse priests had enlisted. Large numbers of military personnel also filled local colleges, turned into training facilities, and priests serving the campuses were hard-pressed to meet their needs. Parishes saw young men and women go off to war. Their names were posted in the church and prayers were requested, as the fears and anxieties of war became part of the experience of almost every family. By diocesan count 26,032 Catholic young men served in the Army, 9,361 in the Navy and 2,735 in the Marines, while 288 women served in the armed forces. Slowly, another list also appeared on parish rolls. Before the war ended, 1,030 young Catholics would die in battle.

Once again, as in the earlier world war, the separatist tone of Catholic leadership gave way immediately to full-scale cooperation with other churches to unify the nation. The President declared Sunday, May 17, 1941, "I am an American" Day and Foery responded enthusiastically. "The President calls upon us to rededicate ourselves to the principles of the Republic and it is indeed fitting that this rededication should be identified with the day of the week when we publicly consecrate ourselves to God." The bishop had noted as a young priest during the First World War that national crises seemed to draw people together in a healthy sense of dependence on God and a willingness to sacrifice for others. The Church, of course, welcomed the opportunity and the responsibility. Catholics were encouraged to support Red Cross drives, buy saving stamps and bonds, limit their con-

Father Michael J. Lyons was one of 32 Syracuse diocesan priests to serve as military chaplains during the Second World War. Lyons, the first chaplain in New Guinea, attained the rank of full colonel. He received the Legion of Merit award. After the war, he became pastor of Holy Family parish in Syracuse's Fairmount neighborhood. (Photo: Chancery Archives)

sumption of needed commodities and participate in a variety of civic activities. The Church had its own campaigns. Even before the United States entered the war, the first collection for the relief of victims of war raised $35,000, the largest special collection in diocesan history. Many Catholics were still close to their immigrant roots and felt special

pain as their homelands were devastated. None were more generous than Polish Catholics who raised money for refugees, looking forward prayerfully to the rebuilding of their native country after the war. In April 1944, Foery wrote to Father Piejda of Sacred Heart, which had more than 1,700 young men serving in the armed forces, praising Polish relief efforts as "a glorious page in the history of Catholic Syracuse."

The United States government's policy toward refugees, however, was not unambiguously humane. By rigid enforcement of the quota system governing immigration, Jews largely were excluded from the country and so were many others displaced by the war. In 1944, the president bent a bit and created the War Refugee Board with authority to transfer some European refugees to temporary havens in the United States. In June, Fort Ontario near Oswego was designated as a center for 1,000 refugees. There was some concern about how they would be received in the town, but Oswego proved generous and hospitable, thanks in part to the town's national parishes and an advisory committee on which Father James Shanahan served as vice-chairman, and which included Father Jeremiah Davern.

The routine of Church life continued largely unchanged during the war. Parishes had regular prayers for peace and for the welfare of people in the service. Trustees requested permission to invest parish funds in war bonds, and a variety of special collections took place. However, the sacraments still were celebrated with regularity and parish activities intensified as pastors still struggled to pay the bills. From top to bottom, the Church carried on. The diocese promulgated new regulations governing the work of missionaries begging for funds, Catholic press month was promoted in terms of public problems to which the Church thought it had answers, and the Legion of Decency pledge seemed even more of a patriotic act. At St. Vincent's in Syracuse, the pastor wrote in his announcement book for December 14, 1941, the Sunday after Pearl Harbor: "These are *days* and *times* of *Catholic action,* prayer and confession and holy communion. Be *loyal* to God and country - *do not fail - both need us.*" The following week, the bishop's letter was read, and the pastor again appealed for prayer and Catholic action. After that, however, there was little to suggest there was a war going on aside from an occasional request that families drop off the names and addresses of boys in the service. Later, in 1944, there was a strong appeal for support to the United War Fund and Community Chest campaigns, but the great events of the war were not remarked upon.

Perhaps no problem posed by the war concerned the diocese more than the trend, through family or national necessity, for women to join the workforce. In his *ad limina* report to the Holy See in 1944, Bishop Foery noted the grave dangers posed to marriages by an absent husband and a wife in the workplace, and the threat of a long-range trend toward working mothers and empty homes. In October 1942, the diocesan school department prepared a report which showed that 20.1 percent of the mothers of Catholic school children were working full or part-time. Of the 1,854 working mothers almost 1,400 worked day shifts and approximately 60 percent of these had another adult, in most cases a grandmother, at home to care for the children. More than 500 families did not have an adult available, and of those, two-thirds had paid baby-sitters. In submitting this report to the Onondaga War Council, Father Gildea and Father Joseph Toomey, director of Catholic Charities, recommended adoption of "the Block Mother Plan" which would designate a woman in the neighborhood to oversee the children. They also submitted the results of their survey to the State War

Council, including similar recommendations spelled out in greater detail. The program should be recognized as an emergency one. It should not be construed to mean that the state "approves the concept of mothers installed in industry, since the fundamental concepts of American democracy may be preserved best by having mothers retain their prime responsibility as housemakers and not as wartime producers, and that certainly the mothers of young children should be taken into employment only when all other sources of personnel have been exhausted." The "block mother" plan was not adopted state-wide. Surprisingly, there is no indication that parishes attempted to implement it on their own, though several parishes already had day care centers and several others were set up during the war. Unfortunately, despite the creative and responsible tone of the report, there was a tendency to moralize the issue. The report ignored the widespread employment of Irish, Polish and Italian mothers in the past and worried that high wartime wages might, as Foery put it in 1949, "cause some to become greedy for the material things of life and to become discontented with the simplicity of the home."

The Vatican's Holy Office, in the midst of war threatened Rome in 1943, sent out to the Churches of the world guidelines for confessors on the sixth commandment, warning in particular against unintended familiarities between priests and women. In the same manner, Bishop Foery, in 1944, discussed quite dispassionately in his report to the Holy See the traditional concern that Catholics might become corrupted by the "pagan" society in which they lived. He assured the Vatican that in his diocese every effort was made to "avert the dangers of mixed marriages...The best fruits against this evil," he pointed out, "came from the formation in parishes of societies of youth where, under proper supervision, friendships are formed among Catholic young men and women." Only one marriage in a hundred ended in divorce, though here again he feared that "the attitude, truly pagan and Unchristian, toward marriage on the part of most non-Catholic citizens is a danger and a threat to the right morals of our own people." So too was the prevailing attitude toward birth control, "the worst and most frequent vice among our people against the sanctity of marriage." He admitted this growing practice might have been encouraged in part by the poverty of the depression, but it was most encouraged by the "desire for material comfort and pleasure on the part of husbands and wives." Abortion, however, was rare, though in 1943, 41 persons had sought reconciliation with the Church for that sin.

Such problems remained peculiarly important to Church leaders. So did their disdain for non-Catholic morality, although their new public role required that such attitudes be kept private. Publicly, Catholic clergy championed civic harmony and consensus. For Bishop Foery, as for most Americans, the principle at stake in the war was that of human rights, on which Catholic and American ideals were identical, so that participation in the war was a religious, as well as a patriotic, act. As he told the Catholic Womens Club in 1943, the war was one of ideas: "In this conflict, the important thing for you and for me to understand, the idea that we as Christians and Americans must have firmly fixed in our hearts, is the dignity and value and worth of every individual, whether the individual be on the far flung battle lines of the world, or some old man who looks out the window of a home for the aged waiting for the call of God to come to him." If the Church had a special place, he claimed rather self-righteously, it was because Christianity, unlike most modern ideologies, upheld the idea that the dignity of the individual was based on God's creation.

The Churches of the rest of the world and the Vatican now looked to the American Church for help. Bishop Foery expressed the new maturity of his Church in his appeal for contributions to the Society for the Propagation of the Faith in 1941. Foery noted that the American Church was built by missionaries from Europe, many of whom had received financial support from that same society, now elevated to "Our Holy Father's Community Chest for Missions." With Europe prostrated by the war, the now prosperous and free American Church had a special obligation to assist struggling churches in "the field afar." This was not merely picking up the slack, but a bold new venture of this young, healthy vigorous Church on the world's stage. Catholics "should avoid the notion that we are merely defending Christianity; that we are holding off our enemies," Foery wrote. On the contrary, American Catholics were fulfilling the Lord's commandment to increase and multiply and demonstrate that "the answer to the world's woes lies in the Christian way of life."

Foery shared the relief all felt when the war ended in 1945. Thanksgiving services took place throughout the diocese. "This is a day of great joy and jubilation for all Americans," he said. During the years of long and bitter struggle, "we have petitioned Almighty God for his blessing and benediction upon our cause.... All our military strength and ingenuity would have failed if He had not been on our side." On the other hand, the end of the war brought great responsibility. "We must assume the task which in military victory God has placed in our hands." The death of so many Americans left a heavy burden on those who remained. They must have a firm grasp on the ideals for which they died, and must defend and extend those ideals to build a future of "peace with justice... A broken world must be mended, enslaved peoples must be made free, the smaller nations, the littler people of the earth must have their God given rights fostered and protected." The high sounding words of the war must turn out to be more than "pretty phrases with no accomplishment intended."

ANTI-COMMUNISM

Of course, the war did not end easily. Refugees needed to be assisted and the bishops' wartime relief collections continued, with a new emphasis on food and clothing. People were asked to conserve food and to exercise restraint, while the nation carried through the difficult transition from war-time mobilization to "normalcy." Most important, the conflicts among the allies eroded dreams of peace. In asking prayers for the United Nations during its founding conference, Foery warned against pessimism and urged renewed dedication to the work of building a peaceful world. But, too quickly, such pleas became linked to the struggle against Russia and communism, as the spectre of Soviet domination spread over eastern Europe and threatened to move west. Father Oley at St. Vincent's in Syracuse, appealing to his people for the 1948 relief collection, put the confusion and anguish clearly:

Though victory came more than two years ago, the wounds of the most devastating war in history still fester angrily. Today Europe and the countries of the far east stand at the threshold of the greatest crisis in history. Christian civilization itself is at stake.

The threat of communism was nothing new to the Catholic Church, which had been warning of the danger for years. The Church had denounced the ideology even more strongly than it had criticized Fascism throughout the 1930s. In the United States, concern about communism had grown in the 1930s. However, aside from a few almost ritual denunciations, little of this concern was felt among Syracuse area Catholics. But when the war started, the American bishops and the Vatican were deeply concerned about the Soviet Union. In preparing his report to Rome in 1944, Foery refered to a questionnaire from the Holy See which contained inquiries about the communist danger in his diocese. He responded with information about the tiny votes received in recent elections by socialist and communist candidates. In early 1945, he received another "confidential questionnaire," this time from the National Catholic Welfare Conference in Washington, asking him to list any known communists in the area. His answer included 13 names obtained, the report said, with the help of two local police officials. Foery noted that there were perhaps 100 party members in Syracuse and 50 in Utica. Their followers were few and there was "no appreciable communist influence on labor." Although there had been some communist activity in Syracuse unions, the CIO was predominately Catholic and, like the AFL, was "generally sound." Charges of communism levelled against the labor movement and President Roosevelt in the previous election were "political Propaganda," the bishop thought; public opinion in the diocese was "antagonistic to communism" and marked by "feelings of disgust" at "Communist political maneuvering in Europe." The bishop thought the "local picture" did not require a "positive counterprogram." However, he did hope to develop a labor school in the diocese to assist local union members to resist communist penetration, should it develop. A short time after this report was filed, Foery named several priests to serve on a "vigilance committee" to report on "subversive activities against the church." It seems to have been a paper committee, its inactivity reflecting the conviction of local Catholic leaders that such subversion was not a real or immediate danger.

Communism, however, was a very real danger to world peace, and the bishop and his priests lost no opportunity to associate the national cause with the Church in the years following the war.

Bishop Foery regularly called upon the people of his diocese to contribute to the Bishop's Relief Campaign for the Victims of War and to the Propagation of the Faith. If once the appeal to missions had been largely evangelical, it now became laced with political meaning. In October 1948, Foery described the "army of missioners" as "the world's finest patriots" engaged in a "bloodless war" between "the spiritual conception of life and the pagan one." The issue of the Cold War was clear:

> *The world cannot go on indefinitely half spiritual and half pagan. Sooner or later, the one will overcome the other.... It took a mighty effort to win the recent global war and the victory has resulted in disillusionment for us all, for so far, it has been merely a material victory. How much more important is this universal war that is being fought by the church and the Son of God on the one side, and the forces of evil, materialism and apathy on the other....*

Sunday, September 17, 1950, was designated as Crusade for Freedom Sunday and the bishop asked priests to persuade their people to sign the "declaration of fredom," a summary of human rights and their divine source. He also informed them that committees would be visiting homes inviting donations for a free radio network to be established in Europe. Such support for citizenship campaigns remained constant throughout the 1950s, expressing, in Foery's words, "our determination to join with all our fellow citizens ... in our eloquent expression

Monsignor Robert Dillon (left), the diocesan chancellor, and Father William Shannon of the cathedral were featured in this press photo supporting the 1954 appeal for the Bishop's Relief Fund for Victims of War. The advent campaign sought $5,000,000 nationally to help refugees in Korea, Southeast Asia, and the Middle East, which then were the areas of most need. (Photo: The Catholic Sun)

of our belief in God, the giver of human rights, and in the capacity of our form of government to preserve those rights."

The Cold War, then, was a struggle between good and evil, and the Church had no hesitation throwing its weight behind the nation's cause.

Even in the world wars, Catholics had not made so intimate an association between their nation's cause and God's. This polarized vision of the world struggle now became part of the rhetoric of not only public appeals for assistance to suffering people, but of the Church's religious life as well. Marian devotions, prayers for the conversion of Russia, and demonstrations of Catholic piety in public parades and conventions all featured stirring appeals for peace placed within the context of a war to the death between God's people and God's enemies. It was powerful language,

For Catholics in the 1940s and '50s, devotion to the Blessed Virgin Mary often was linked to the cause of peace and opposition to communism. At events like this May crowning at St. Peter's church in Rome, Mary was honored for her example of personal holiness and family devotion — and for her Fatima message of world peace and the conversion of Russia. The theme was repeated throughout the diocese. Father William Shannon in 1951 called his times "The Age of Mary," because the Blessed Mother had risen up to lead Catholics against what he called "the diabolical threats to world peace." More moderately, Father A. Robert Casey contrasted communist hate with Christian love, suggesting that Mary did not call on Catholics to destroy communists but rather to pray for any of the human family which suffers for justice's sake. In Utica, Church demonstrations blended religious and patriotic themes. And Bishop Foery wrote to each priest and sister in the diocese, calling for "a secret crusade of prayer" to spread devotion to Mary as the best way to defeat the philosophy of communism. (Photo: St. Peter's church, Rome)

which fused Catholic and American loyalties and made even religious activity like worship and prayer a contribution to the cause of democracy, freedom and America.

May 1 was a day of special prayers for the Russian people, with noon-time services in the cathedral and other centrally located church-

es. When the American Legion launched a "Back to God" movement in 1953 to encourage increased attendance at religious services, Foery endorsed the movement "wholeheartedly." A memo prepared in the chancery described this program as responding to the "general moral breakdown" in the country. "The imminent threat to our country comes from irreligious social decay," the memo declared. For people who lacked "religious belief, nothing in the end is likely to be sacred, nothing worth preserving." Religion should "permeate every part of our national life, moral, political, economic, industrial, educational, social and cultural."

When Hungary's Cardinal Mindzenty was arrested in 1948, Foery joined the American bishops in a barrage of protests, writing persistently to the press, the state department, congressmen and senators. Pamphlets and comic books were distributed widely and priests were invited to a special showing of a film, "Guilty of Treason," as Foery joined a nationwide effort to arouse public opinion against the arrest. When a letter writer in Binghamton claimed the arrest was met with "hysteria," Father William Shannon charged that the writer had been duped by local communist sympathizers, adding comments about the "pretty pink phrases" of Eleanor Roosevelt. The letter in question and several others raised questions about Mindzenty's pre-war and wartime politics. No Catholic response dealt with these questions, but instead all denounced the letter writers as communist sympathizers and enemies of the Church. On February 6, 1949, Foery preached on the matter in the cathedral. Comparing Mindzenty to the Founding Fathers, he claimed that he was arrested because of his defense of religious freedom, one of the freedoms for which Americans had suffered and died during the war. His sermon once again collapsed all distinctions:

The history of the church is, to a large extent, the history of the priesthood. Where priests have failed, the church has failed. Where priests have been successful, the church has triumphed. Hence it is that the very first act of the tyrant against the church is against

the priesthood. To destroy the faith, to annul the divine command of Christ, the priesthood must be destroyed.

To weaken the faith of the people, to disperse the flock, the shepherd must be destroyed or eliminated. This is the basic reason for the imprisonment of the Cardinal of Hungary. He is accused of treason because he demanded for his people and himself the God given rights which all Americans give their blood and lives for. If he is guilty of treason, so were the founding fathers.

One source of this passion was deep concern for the plight of Catholics in communist countries. In 1951, the last Sunday of the year was set aside as a day of prayer for the afflicted millions behind the Iron Curtain. Special appeals for Catholics in Poland, Hungary, Lithuania and China were made throughout the 1950s. In 1948, Italian Americans played an important role in sending money and support to families in Italy, urging them to vote against the communists in that year's national elections. So successful was this that, in May 1953, Archbishop Karl Alter, chairman of the administrative committee of the National Catholic Welfare Council, urged bishops to organize another such campaign for that year's elections. Foery sent this memorandum to the priests of the diocese, asking them to keep it confidential and emphasizing Alter's suggestion that the matter be brought to the attention of Catholics of Italian descent "prudently," stressing the latter word "in order to avoid further attacks against the Church in Italy." Letters to relatives and friends should warn of the dangers of communism and give assurance of "sympathetic understanding and aid on the part of America."

When war came again in Korea in July 1950, Foery urged prayers for the success of

290

the United Nations cause, and asked reserve chaplains if they wished to return to active duty. Priests ordained between three and 10 years were asked to consider volunteering. He warned that the pressing need for chaplains might require sacrifice, specifically suggesting that parishes with two assistants would have to anticipate a reduction. He further asked the priests to cooperate with civil defense planning.

After the Korean War, Monsignor Richard Clark was appointed the chief Catholic civil defense chaplain in the Onondaga area. The purposes of the chaplains were to assist, in case of a nuclear attack, in the "maintenance of firm resolution and composure of the people through preaching and worship; through pastoral care of families and individuals, creation of a sense of responsibility and spiritual security among the people to meet the possible exigencies of attack on a scale never experienced before in the United States; maintenance of courage and spiritual well-being among children through regular programs for religious instruction." In the "post-attack phase," the "clergy should be of great help in sustaining and restoring morale." In November 1953, civil defense preparations were tested in a full-scale alert. Plans were based upon the preservation of churches and hospitals in outlying areas, adequate transportation and communication facilities, and a relatively short period of response. The chaplains' role in the post-attack phase was reflected in the last items in the schedule of events, in which the chaplains were to announce the availability of services in surviving churches and thank volunteers for their heroic assistance. The diocese extended permission to use schools for defense welfare centers, fallout shelters and evacuation centers. Clark asked priests to enroll as chaplains with their local civil defense office, so that they could receive proper identification and be covered under insurance provisions of the

state. Enrollment involved fingerprinting, signing a loyalty oath and issuing of a photo identification. By May 1953, 118 priests had enrolled and been issued civil defense identification numbers. The consistency of the diocese's patriotic support was reflected in Bishop Foery's letter to the local director for inclusion in the office's newsletter:

The defense of our beloved country is the duty of every citizen; the protection of our lives and those of our neighbors, is a necessary precaution if we are properly to care for these gifts of God. It should be the prayerful and watchful concern, in all matters that pertain to the interests of our Nation, to see that we are prepared for any eventuality.

This concern deals naturally with strengthening our moral standards and our political institutions of our Nation so that we might prevent the undermining of our democratic principles. However, in the event an enemy would be so blind as to direct an armed attack against us, the Civil Defense Organization would be of essential and paramount importance to us on the 'home front' to protect the young, the old, the sick and infirm, from the ravages of the atomic or hydrogen bomb.

Chaplains also were appointed for National Guard and reserve units, and the diocese observed Armed Forces Day with appropriate prayers and ceremonies. When a local armory was dedicated to war hero James B. McConnell, who had been raised at the House of Providence, Foery took the occasion to clarify the relationship between the Church and national defense. He told the audience that he did not have to emphasize the need for an armory or for the army reserve program, which, he was certain, was "obvious to you all.... I do not believe that any American questions the need for well trained men to carry out our defense programs," Foery said. Of course, all hoped that the men trained in the armory would never have to enter battle, but this "prayerful hope" was "not enough....We must be certain, as far as we possibly can, that if the need for battle ever arises, we will be defended by men who know their business and who, in defending themselves, will understand they are defending the country."

Anti-communism did not exhaust the bishop's interest in public affairs. Foery consistently supported the United Nations, urging prayers for its success after the war, lending full support to UN Day and UN Week, and defending the organization against increasing American hostility in the 1950s. While the bishop was cautious about dealing with civic organizations until he was assured they were "sound," he never expressed sympathy with McCarthyism. He told a LeMoyne graduating class that congressional investigating committees had discovered "some of the weaknesses of our democracy," but failed to indicate "our strengths." By going too far, he added, they raised the danger that "good men, so desperately needed" might refuse to serve in government. In addition, Foery consistently supported organized labor, endorsing the right to form unions, strike and maintain a union shop, and evenhandedly called for a just resolution of local strikes. Each year on Labor Day, he preached at the cathedral on labor-management cooperation and the need for a just distribution of economic goods. In 1949, the bishop agreed to allow his name to be placed among those on a statewide citizens committee supporting a state referendum for a large bond issue to be used for public housing. In 1955 and 1960 he issued strong statements against the opening of stores on Sunday. Perhaps his most energetic intervention in

political affairs came in the period 1948-1950 when he joined other American bishops in organizing opposition among Catholics to the Barden bill. This legislation provided federal aid to education, and sparked a battle which led to a public exchange between Eleanor Roosevelt and Cardinal Spellman. Foery called the bill "unAmerican and discriminatory" for failing to include Catholic schools in its provisions, and he called on his priests in a confidential letter to arouse their people to action to prevent its passage. Later, when another aid to education bill was before congress, Foery warned that, by excluding Catholic schools, the legislation threatened to establish a "monolithic" public school system which would be "the first step toward totalitarianism."

MORAL BATTLEGROUNDS

The old battle against indecent films and publications was not forgotten, but the tide of the battle was turning. The Legion of Decency had been perhaps the most successful Catholic action program in national history. Pressure on the movie industry had resulted in establishment of an office to monitor films and, by the forties, few films violating legion standards were appearing. Throughout the war, the annual pledge was renewed regularly, but there was rising concern at the increased number of partially objectionable films. In 1947, Foery told a local woman that, by simply portraying moral evils like murder, suicide and divorce, many movies were detrimental to the moral health of the community. Already, legion leaders were worried about a reaction. One priest called for a "quiet campaign" against one film "because publicity would only defeat our purpose." Despite protests and promises of support from local police, the Church failed to prevent the showing of the condemned movie, "The Outlaw," in 1946. This was the

292

first crack in the dike. In 1955 Foery appealed to the people to boycott theaters which consistently violated legion standards. "The owners of these theaters understand only one language," he wrote. "They seemingly lack the moral sense but they would reap financial profit to the ruin and degradation of their patrons." But there was little response. In 1956, the legion entered its last major fight against the movie "Baby Doll." The Syracuse *Post Standard* at first refused to advertise the film, drawing a protest from 30 Protestant ministers who thought freedom was endangered by "the power and ability of any organized minority pressure group to impose it's own standards on the community." The paper responded editorially that, while it was aware of the strong criticism of the bishop, it had been concerned about the "growing breakdown of morality in literature and art for more than three years" and had taken action independently. The *Herald Journal* reported that at least one pastor advocated a boycott of the film, and one theater turned it down after receiving a call from officials of the Knights of Columbus. Finally, another theater agreed to show the film, and the *Post Standard* carried an ad. "If there is any time that the Legion is being severely tested, it is the action of Warner Brothers on this picture," the bishop wrote a priest. "If it turns out to be successful and becomes a money maker, future action on our part will be extremely difficult." Controversy over "Baby Doll" continued in local papers for two years, but the showing of the movie and its relative success marked the ebb of legion power. When the local American Legion asked Foery to join in a protest against the movie "Advice and Consent" on political grounds in 1962, Foery showed a new caution:

We judge it would be imprudent to make a public statement condemning

the film . . . You know what happened in the past when this was done, viz. many people who had no information about the film and had no intention of seeing it would go to the theater just out of curiosity, thus defeating the purpose of the announcement. We therefore judge it prudent to have our priests make mention of it in our parish societies, and other groups, when a fuller explanation can be made, and thus accomplish more than a public announcement.

The pledge continued to be mailed to parishes, with homily suggestions. In 1964, the Legion of Decency revised the pledge to give it a more positive tone, promising to promote films that were artistically and morally commendable, as well as to discourage indecent pictures. By 1967, the bishop's cover letter to priests noted that many parishes no longer administered the pledge during Mass, but the material might be helpful if the pastor chose to present it to his people.

A similar decline hit the campaign against indecent literature. Earlier concerns had fallen into the background after the war, but were revived in the late 1950s. In September 1960, when the bishop wrote the priests reaffirming his commitment to the fight, several lay groups were putting pressure on the post office department. The bishop asked the priests to call attention to their meetings, but the public climate was unsympathetic. The battle against birth control was growing more heated, but found the Church almost equally unsuccessful. In 1958, Bishop Cunningham checked Planned Parenthood's plans to participate in the New York State Fair held in Syracuse. Informed of these plans by William F. Baker, director of the fair, Cunningham told him that Planned Parenthood's program was "essentially immoral" and the Church would oppose its participation "with every means at our command." Lobbying succeeded in excluding Planned Parenthood that year, but it appeared at the fair in 1959 when Catholic officials received no advanced warning. Privately, Cunningham was pessimistic, telling Bishop Scully of Albany that eventually he thought "we are going to lose this battle which has so successfully been waged by our local Catholic community for so many years." The following year, Monsignor Daniel Lawler of Catholic Charities received advance information from Catholics in the state bureaucracy, but the decision on Planned Parenthood's application was "kicked upstairs" to the governor's office. Planned Parenthood was denied admission on the excuse that space was not available. As a basis for excluding Planned Parenthood, state officials suggested that the Knights of Columbus, which had a booth at the fair, also should be barred in 1961, along with all religious groups. This suggestion was not received well. The battle was, as Cunningham anticipated, all but lost.

Locally, the Church's fight with Planned Parenthood reached another fever point in 1959. The Church withdrew in protest from the Metropolitan Health Council of Onondaga County when Planned Parenthood was admitted to membership. Monsignor Lawler, then a member of the MHC board of directors, stated that the issue was not one of "religious controversy but of community concern." He believed his position coincided with "the traditional American view regarding artificial birth control." Because birth control was a violation of natural law, it attacked the integrity of marriage and the health of family life, and many local citizens regarded it as "a perilous threat to the happiness, health and security of the community, the nation and the human race." Moreover, Planned Parenthood was not a health organization, it supported abortion and its membership would jeopardize local support for the Community Chest

which funded the MHC. If the MHC accepted Planned Parenthoods' application, he would resign, call upon Catholic hospitals to do the same and urge other agencies to reconsider their membership. The bishop supported Lawler, and when the MHC accepted Planned Parenthood, Foery ordered Catholic hospitals and charities agencies to withdraw.

A NEW ISOLATION

The fights against indecent films and magazines and against birth control found Catholics increasingly isolated during the post-war years. If these positions were to be upheld, it seemed, it would have to be by a united body of the Catholic faithful. On some matters, that unity seemed to be in danger. In 1953, the bishop called the priests' attention to a national study showing that only 51 percent of Catholics agreed with the Church on birth control and divorce. So too, the old concern about mixed marriages grew more intense as Catholics, moving to the suburbs from their old neighborhoods, mixed with those of other religions, raising the danger that many would marry outside the Church. In fact, the number of mixed marriages, which had risen to a high of 30 percent, dropped off after the war. However, Foery and others remained convinced that Church-related activities, which helped Catholic boys and girls form friendships with one another, were the best defense against this problem.

The corollary of support for Catholic organizations was avoidance of non-Catholic ones. In the 1950s, for example, membership in the Young Men's Christian Association was again a nationwide problem. Some bishops thought a common policy should be adopted. Foery agreed, but wanted it kept secret to avoid the controversy of a public statement. In Syracuse, he thought that approximately 15 percent of the total membership of the

YMCA and Young Women's Christian Association were Catholics, but one layman told him the figure was 50 percent. The bishop knew of no one who had lost the faith through these contacts, but he did know several who had grown indifferent. Locally, the chancery refused permission to a layman to serve on the YMCA board in 1954 on the grounds that, despite changes in its constitution, the YMCA still was a religious organization. While priests could address Y groups and he offered no objection to mere membership, Foery did feel that public identification with the organization was prohibited by canon law, papal decision and the religious purposes of the Y. In 1962, when a Syracuse resident wrote the pope that he was planning a career in YMCA work, the chancellor told the young man that the Y was a "religious organization" and, therefore, "obviously it is not for Catholics." The following year, an Oswego pastor was denied permission to sit in on a meeting of the fundraising committee of the local Y.

Many other inter-faith organizations were under even more vigorous assault for alleged communist sympathies. In 1954, for example, Thomas E. Harney sent Foery a large pile of documents professing to prove that communists were using the National Conference of Christians and Jews to infiltrate "red" material into classrooms, especially during Brotherhood Week. Rome, too, was placing a damper on ecumenical or inter-religious activity. In December 1950, the apostolic delegate forwarded a secret memo from the Holy Office regarding the International Council of Christians and Jews. The memo charged the council with promoting equality of all religions, citing with particular disfavor a statement at one of their congresses calling for an attitude of "absolute indifference in regard to nationality, race and religion." Catholics could not take part in such groups or their meetings without specific permission, the

Vatican reminded the bishop. These regulations were to be observed with particular in regard to conventions known as "ecumenical" which "Catholics, either lay or clerical, are by no means to join without the previous consent of the Holy See." The bishop could authorize Catholics to attend such gatherings, but only as observers. They should not be persons prominent in Catholic life and, by no means, should such events be held on Catholic premises.

Syracuse Catholics needed few such reminders. The Church remained wary of any form of religious cooperation. Under the banner of civil welfare, common religious observances might suggest Catholic acceptance of a type of cooperation which minimized religious differences. The diocese did join with the Council of Churches and the Jewish Welfare Federation to sponsor a forum on civil and religious rights in 1947. However, the diocese threatened to withdraw from ceremonies marking the dedication of the city's war memorial when the sponsoring committee agreed to include an evangelistic service as part of the week-long program.

Warnings against the mixing of religious activity were even more common at the parish level. In 1951, Bishop Cunningham advised a Catholic musician not to present a concert in a Methodist church. In 1953, an organist was warned against playing in a Protestant service, even for pay. In that same year, a talented Catholic singer was told that there had been complaints against his singing for pay at non-Catholic services. Even though he was paid, and stayed for only part of the service, his participation contributed to "the success of the religious service" and therefore constituted a form of cooperation which was not allowed.

Several issues arose in the post-war period to arouse non-Catholic suspicions and revive interreligious disputes. These included the continuation of President Franklin D. Roosevelt's practice of maintaining a Catholic ambassador to the Vatican and the revival of Catholic agitation for aid to parochial schools. In 1950, Protestant pastors meeting in Syracuse expressed concern about censorship and Catholic power, occasioning charges by the *Catholic Sun* of a revival of "the unburied spirits of the KKK." A chapter of Protestants and Other Americans United for the Separation of Church and State (POAU) was formed in Syracuse and its meetings and public lectures angered Syracuse area Catholics. The organization for its part protested a commencement address at LeMoyne College in which the speaker pilloried Paul Blanshard, whose book, *American Freedom and Catholic Power,* was a *cause celebre.* On the other hand, when Syracuse University had as a commencement speaker G. Bronly Oxnam, a POAU stalwart accused of communist sympathies by Senator McCarthy, Catholics were equally upset. When the head of the Los Angeles POAU chapter lectured in Syracuse and Binghamton, local papers were filled with Catholic protests.

Perhaps the most striking examples of continued Catholic separatism, and the persistence of intergroup tensions came in an area long neglected in the diocese—higher education. Foery's first post-war project was one of the most ambitious in the history of the diocese, the launching of a Jesuit college. There is some evidence that such an institution was discussed as early as 1904. However, serious discussion with the Jesuits began only with Foery's arrival and especially with his formal invitation to the Jesuits, extended in 1941. Planning went on throughout the war and, in May 1945, the Jesuits purchased a 103-acre site on Salt Springs Road. Soon materials began flooding the diocese for a $1,000,000 drive directed by a professional firm from New York City. Launched with Foery's personal contribution of $5,000, the drive reached all parishes, with their fixed quotas, as well as the local community. The

bishop argued that the new school would provide a Catholic educational alternative in Central New York, it would enable the community to meet the needs of Catholic students who could not afford to go elsewhere, and it would provide a Catholic school for the servicemen who would be going to college under the GI Bill of Rights. In addition, Foery believed it would bring benefits to the diocese by providing training and continuing education for Catholic school teachers.

His strongest arguments for the school, however, demonstrated the militant Catholic Americanism of the period. Foery argued that the college would be "dedicated to the concept of Americanism." He contended that LeMoyne would educate leaders who would "obey the law of the land and respect the wishes of the employer," practice sound business ethics, respect the sanctity of marriage and help their neighbors. Most important:

> *It will provide for the city a truly American school with religion and morality as the foundation stones. It will, therefore, be a religious school, and not a secular institution, for secularism eventually begets paganism. Its philosophy will be diametrically opposed to communism, the straightjacket of humanity inducing eventual slavery and the elimination of the upper class. It will train men in the basic truths of America which are admittedly Christian; in mental alertness through classes in logic; in ability to evaluate, analyze and make proper judgments.*

While the drive was a huge success, with 75,000 people pledging $1,500,000, trouble developed at the start. The bishop had worked closely with the Jesuits throughout the planning process and had announced to the

The first buildings are constructed at LeMoyne College in Syracuse. (Photo: LeMoyne College)

public that the school would open in the fall of 1947. However, when he visited the site in December 1946, he found that, despite his constant urging, construction had not begun yet. Not only had he made promises to the public based on Jesuit commitments, but he worried that many GIs had postponed beginning college in 1946 in order to enter LeMoyne in the fall of 1947. Exasperated, he wrote the Jesuit provincial that "I have decided for my own peace of mind and for my own prestige I should no longer be associated publicly with LeMoyne." He had promised himself that the "disappointments" and "pain" had been so great he would remain away from the construction site and would refer all inquiries to the Jesuits. "The bishop is not in a good position when he is

obliged continually to attempt to save face by saying that we got away to a poor start on construction but we hope that part of our experience is now over." Coming so soon after the drive, the bishop's withdrawal could prove disastrous. Perhaps not coincidentally, in March 1947, Father William Schlaerth was appointed president and plans were made to open in downtown rental quarters in the fall.

Schlaerth and Foery got along, work was begun and finally, in September 1948, the buildings were ready for dedication. In a letter to the president intended for publication, Foery placed the college in the context of the contemporary mission of the Church:

In these days of distress and confusion, when many of God's creatures dare to flaunt his law, when individuals deny even the existence of God, when world ideas in general are being tainted more and more by pagan philosophy, it is heartening to find another Catholic college, with its philosophy and traditions firmly rooted in 2000 years of Christianity, raising the Cross of Christ with all that it connotes, to counteract the current evils among individuals and among nations. Indeed, it is becoming more obvious day by day that Western Civilization must be saved by its ideas rather than by the might of its arms. It is in Catholic colleges such as LeMoyne that these weapons will be forged.

The Church-related character of the college was clear. Despite the presence of many veterans among its students, LeMoyne banned alcoholic beverages on campus, limited the number of dances and parties and prohibited them during Lent, and imposed a dress code that required coats and ties for men and banned "ultra-masculine modes of dress" for women. Faculty members wore academic gown, and in 1950, this was compulsory for seniors as well. Classes began with prayer, and attendance at the annual Mass of the Holy Spirit was mandatory. Church regulations touched academic matters as well. Permission to read books on the Index had to be applied for from the bishop in each individual instance by a priest who would promise to "guide and direct the reader." This was required for both faculty and students. Regular requests to read such works as *The Communist Manifesto* and writers like Goethe, Zola and many others filled the correspondence of the diocesan chancellor.

LeMoyne developed a solid program, and its graduates became prominent in local affairs, but it did not become the creative

element in diocesan life that Foery had anticipated. Not that it had no impact. In 1946, Father Gerald C. Treacy launched a school of industrial relations which was one of a network of Jesuit-sponsored "labor schools." It enrolled numerous local labor leaders, young workers, businessmen and priests in a number of programs. These programs were aimed at developing familiarity with Catholic social teaching, helping union members to become more effective in opposing communism and building democratic unions, and opening up the community both to the right of labor to organize and the need for just and peaceful labor management relations. But the anticipated benefits for Catholic teachers and adult education never materialized fully.

In 1958, Father Robert Grewen, the president, wrote the bishop, explaining that the number of students from within the diocese was decreasing. Grewen suggested the bishop write a pastoral letter emphasizing the benefits of education at LeMoyne, noting especially the "great danger to the faith and morals of young men and women attending non-Catholic colleges." This danger was increasing, Grewen thought, "because of the number of professors in these schools who have no respect for religion of any sort, proclaiming themselves to be atheists and agnostics, and in their contact with students who are religious treat them with a contemptuous and almost sneering attitude." Grewen also asked the bishop to tell local Catholics that it was their duty to support LeMoyne. Even though the tuition had risen, it had, through the sacrifice of the Jesuits, remained lower than most neighboring institutions. On the financial parts of this recommendation, Foery probably had few problems, though he had some. At about the same time, he complained to other bishops that Catholic colleges like LeMoyne did not do a good job establishing their own networks of lay supporters, and depended too much on Church support to generate students and donations. On the other parts of Grewen's proposed message, Foery was in full agreement because he shared the conviction that non-Catholic institutions of higher education were dangerous for Catholics and probably subversive of national well being as well.

This was evident in his lifelong attitude toward Syracuse University, where his controversial chaplain, who exemplified the militant Catholicism of the post-war years, generated controversy and publicity beyond any other priest in the diocese. A Catholic chaplaincy was established in 1934 at Syracuse University under Father Gannon Ryan. In 1937, there were almost 1,000 Catholic students among the 5,219 at the university. In 1938, at the initiative of some Catholic alumni and local laymen, the Thomas More Foundation was organized. Its board, composed of several local priests and lay leaders, raised money so that Ryan could be independent of the university. One of 11 charter members of the National Newman Club Federation, the Syracuse chaplaincy offered a full range of courses in Christian doctrine and apologetics, study clubs for graduate, law and medical students, counseling services, novenas and retreats, as well as Masses. In 1939, the foundation held a fundraising drive to provide a building with chapel and classrooms. This was endorsed by the bishop, who agreed that, if people became estranged from the Church after attending the university, it was because their religious growth did not keep pace with their intellectual training. However, when a layman in Utica questioned his support for a Catholic presence at this traditionally Methodist university, Foery responded that he regretted that Catholic parents sent their children to non-Catholic colleges. It was the duty of clergy and laity to hold the number of such students to a minimum. Nevertheless, the foundation had been organized by laymen to meet the pastoral needs of students

Father Robert Grewen (Photo: LeMoyne College)

299

attending the university. They wished to provide a building that would not be shared by other sects and "this has met with my approval," though he would do all he could to correct any false impression that Syracuse University provided a substitute for Catholic education.

During the war, Ryan's work changed dramatically as Syracuse became a center for training military personnel. Large numbers of the men and women were Catholics and there was a heavy demand on his time.

In August 1943, the bishop assured Ryan of his "appreciation" for his "splendid work," but suggested things would change with the advent of a new Jesuit college at the end of the war. Syracuse University was "definitely a

Methodist institution," Foery thought;

> It seems to me that it would, therefore, be unwise to make their schools more attractive to our Catholic people. We would give to our Catholic people an official approval of these schools and they would find in this act of ours a release from their own obligation to provide Catholic education for their children.

The bishop was sincere in his suspicion of the university. In 1944, the university wanted to give him an honorary degree, but the bishop, while he appreciated the courtesy, refused the honor. "I feel I can do a greater service to my church in these controversial areas at Syracuse University if I do not accept this honor," Foery said, "I have a conviction that no man should accept an honorary degree from an institution of learning unless he can give full loyalty to that school and its principles." Yet the number of Catholic students at Syracuse grew dramatically after the war, with no noticeable effect on LeMoyne. Ryan continued to deplore this trend. "I liken the situation to prisons," he told the bishop, "where Catholics get themselves occasionally, much to the dishonor of the Catholic name. Nevertheless the Church sends Catholic priests to look after them.... This is a cruel comparison for pious Syracuse ears," he admitted, but "it has been my Charitable expression." In 1947, there were more than 3,000 Catholic students on the main campus. With the help of an assistant, Ryan busily provided religious services, special devotions, retreats, novenas, classes and discussion clubs, often drawing huge crowds. The new Protestant chaplain, Charles C. Noble, was cooperative, helping arrange for rooms and offering to share in planning calendars. Nevertheless, given the increase in the number of Catholic students and the near total absence of Catholic faculty, trouble was

predictable. In the 1950s, many college professors and students were reading and discussing Blanshard's *American Freedom and Catholic Power.* This book appealed to a rather fashionable anti-Catholicism. It was exacerbated by the widely held belief that churchmen strongly supported the anti-communist crusade of Senator McCarthy, and by long-standing conflicts over birth control. In January 1951, Ryan got word of a strong attack on the Church delivered in a class. He wrote the vice-chancellor of the university, Finlay Crawford, that it was his "keenest desire to avoid a public controversy," but his silence should not be interpreted as weakness. University officials apologized, but Ryan was not satisfied. Alert to further slights, he found one when the student newspaper criticized Cardinal Spellman's attack upon the condemned movie, "The Miracle." On Sunday, January 21, Ryan told his congregation that, in many university classrooms, Blanshard's book had surpassed the Bible in popularity, and academic freedom was interpreted as license to lay every sort of sinister purpose at the door of the Catholic church. "Offended Hebrews complain about the unfairness of 'The Merchant of Venice' and its miserable Shylock, a classic of the English language is withdrawn, and no one objects," Ryan complained. "Crusading Protestant ministers denounce gambling at horse races ... and no one raises objections." But when "a Cardinal of the Catholic Church voices his protest because a sacred truth of Christian faith is blasphemed sacrilegiously ... a hue and cry goes over the vale of Onondaga shouting 'censorship,' 'fascism,' 'authoritarianism,' 'thought control'." The "hour glass" of Catholic patience was running out, Ryan warned.

Dean Noble attempted to improve interfaith relations, suggesting that Protestants, Catholics and Jews dine together during Brotherhood Week. For two years, the event was held without incident. But in 1951, Noble recommended as speaker Professor Kirkley Mather of Harvard. Shortly after the event was announced, a local engineer approached Ryan with charges that Mather was a member of many communist-front organizations. Ryan directed the man to university authorities and, when contacted by Noble, insisted that Mather deny or repudiate the associations. Otherwise, he would not be able to continue as a banquet sponsor. Noble then proposed that a new speaker be found, but that Mather speak at Protestant services the same day. When this became known, Ryan was denounced. Charges of McCarthyism and clerical censorship filled the local press and reached the national wire services. Mather defended himself, and when he spoke in the chapel, the audience was four times as large as usual. After Mather's speech, Ryan told the press that "this man lacks any concept whatever of the evil forces which are engulfing the world and bringing suffering and death to tens of thousands of American kids in Korea." Unfortunately, Ryan told the press, "tripartite religious cooperation on this campus has been dealt a mortal blow." When "the practical gauntlet of brotherhood was laid down, many revealed ... that brotherhood was to them a word." In his 1962 report, he stated that the Mather incident had severed all relationships with the Protestant chaplain. Unfortunately, his resistance to efforts by Dean Noble to revive cooperation were interpreted by many Catholic students as reactionary. They become "rebellious" because the Church "will not tailor its regulations to meet their social and political ambitions." What was happening on campus in this regard reflected wider currents, Ryan thought. "We see much of this semi-schismatic tendency today, throughout the country," he wrote. "Even personally pious Catholics grumble because the church is not more 'democratic' or more 'American.'"

Monsignor Gannon F. Ryan (Photo: The Catholic Sun)

301

For all his hostility to the university, Foery did provide pastoral services and Ryan was, by all reports, an excellent priest, his program one of the best in the country. Syracuse was not the only non-Catholic school served. As early as 1940, Father Raymond P. Lawrence was serving the Catholic students at Hamilton College. After the war, attendance at colleges and universities skyrocketed, even as the new Catholic college was opening in Syracuse. The bishop took the initiative to meet the needs of Catholic students at public and private institutions. In October 1946 he told the pastor of Our Lady of Lourdes in Utica to have his assistant call upon authorities at the new Mohawk College and see what could be done to solve the religious problems on that new campus. "You will recall," he wrote, "that the Holy Father, while He condemns attendance at neutral or nonsectarian schools, obliges us to provide religious care for those that do attend."

The public stance of the Church, then, was militant and self-confident in the post war years. Anti-communism and the Cold War set a new context for the Church to define its relationship to American culture and society. Sexual morality as a focus of intergroup conflict persisted, but popular support for moral crusades eroded. In their place was a strong affirmation of the identity of Catholic and American values and loyalties, a set of ideas defended by Church leaders and embodied in popular support for Catholic institutions, and powerful patriotic emotions which left little room for self-criticism. The voices of modest inquiry heard elsewhere, for example, John Courtney Murray, who was arguing on behalf of a more disinterested engagement with public concerns, or John Tracy Ellis, who launched a nationwide debate over Catholic intellectual life, hardly dented the self-assurance of Syracuse Catholicism. Like Catholics everywhere, those in area churches welcomed the election of John F. Kennedy in 1960, took enormous pleasure in the respect he won by his graceful and energetic conduct in office, and mourned with particular anguish when he was killed. However much they may have disagreed with his politics, they and all Catholics saw President Kennedy as one of their own. In many ways, his death marked the end of an era in American Catholic history because, as he was laid to rest, the Vatican Council was meeting in Rome. At home, the civil rights movement, to which he had only begun to respond, was moving toward a more powerful challenge to national complacency. But, at that moment, few could anticipate what lay ahead, so full were they of the sadness of a life taken from them which was so full of promise. His election marked their acceptance as Americans. His message had begun to pull them out of themselves to the pursuit of national ideals. When he died, it may have been that a certain kind of Catholic possibility died with him.

At such moments, Catholics have great resources of prayer, compassion and solidarity to fall back on. Typical of the moving sermons preached on the Sunday following the president's assassination was that of Father Joseph Champlin in the diocesan cathedral. Champlin began by noting that this prosperous Church perhaps had forgotten that "to be a Christian means to follow the cross." He then sketched the various crosses that had afflicted the Kennedy family, and noted the parallel between the Christian call to love and the president's call to sacrifice for the public good. Admitting that Kennedy had faults and that many disagreed with his policies, Champlin argued that he had done much for the Church as the first Catholic president. If he had opposed the Church's call for aid to private education, he had lived a Catholic life and the public was informed about that life, from the baptism of his son John, through his attendance at Sunday Mass and the comforting of his family by the ceremonies of his death. Listening to services from St. Patrick's cathedral following the tragedy, Champlin told of a non-Catholic who told a reporter she simply wanted "to pray for the President in the Church where he worshiped." Finally he was a "family man" who tried with his wife to be a good parent. Champlin asked if anyone could look at the photographs of him playing with his small son or holding his children's hands as they came from an airplane without a lump in the throat, or watch his wife take the ring from her finger, place it in her dead husband's hand and kiss it, without being moved. He closed by asking the congregation to kneel in prayer:

> Let us pray. Almighty God, grant that the noble soul of our martyred president may be delivered from the pains of purgatory and soon join his son Patrick who this very day enjoys the glories of heaven. Grant that his wife and family may have comfort in this hour of sorrow and assistance in the difficult and lonely years ahead. And grant that our new president may be given wisdom and strength to guide our great country. We ask these things through Jesus Christ, our Lord and Savior, who lives and reigns forever and ever, world without end.
> Amen.

A FLOURISHING PLANT

GROWTH AND CONSOLIDATION IN THE POST-WAR CHURCH
1940s-1950s

The diocese of Syracuse, under the leadership of Bishop Walter Foery, was one of the best organized in the country. Catholics of Central New York had been remarkably successful in building and consolidating their local Church. Only an understanding of the strength of organization and the meaning it had for Catholics of the period can explain the problems which arose after the Vatican Council which opened in 1962. Then the bishops of the world placed the institutional aspects of the Church in the context of its community life and its mission of service to all humankind. That emphasis on community and mission did not abolish or even minimize authority or organization, but it did place them in a different perspective. This was problem enough for a Church which had made organization the center of its life and work for almost a century. Yet, it was precisely the strength of that organization, its leadership, its institutions, and its sense of solidarity across linguistic, economic, social and racial barriers, which enabled the Church to look to the future with confidence.

The diocese as an organization was designed to do what parishes could not do for themselves. The bishop, who embodied the diocese, had to maintain its unity, ensure its orthodoxy, make its finances secure and supervise its personnel. Among his most important tasks was to encourage vocations, provide seminary education, and build the competence, morale and spiritual health of the clergy. Just as the bishop attempted to find priests to staff parishes, he helped parishes find sisters to teach in the schools. He also recruited sisters, brothers and religious order priests to staff institutions which the diocese required, for example, LeMoyne College, the hospitals and orphanages, and special works like retreats. This combination of unifying the parishes and overseeing their work, while expanding activities directly under diocesan control, created a growing diocesan bureaucracy with an increasingly professional approach to administration. All the while, the bishop served as the main pastor and teacher, speaking out on matters of moral concern, clarifying and reinforcing the teachings of the Church, and occasionally calling to the attention of Catholics and non-Catholics problems not normally noticed or addressed. Under Walter Foery, the diocese of Syracuse did all this very well by contemporary standards, more than justifying the comment of the apostolic delegate in 1954, when he told the bishop his diocese was "a flourishing plant in the vineyard of the Lord."

Despite the vigorous activity which marked his first years in Syracuse, Bishop Walter Foery did not move easily into episcopal leadership. He took his responsibilities very seriously and was a little overwhelmed by his new office. Forty years later, he told an interviewer he had been "too young for the job" and was "frightened to death." In July 1938, he wrote his friend, Archbishop Mooney, that he felt "in need of a 'let down,'" adding, "I did not find the physical effort too much, but the parades, the speeches, and the dinners have made me cry 'enough.'" The new bishop fainted on several occasions, causing considerable concern to his staff, who arranged for Foery to spend some time resting at a country cottage. Later, his staff purchased a vacation home for him on Lake Skaneateles. Yet Foery told one priest years later, "I hate vacations"; invariably he would rest for a couple of days, then conduct a full round of business at the lake. During the year, he disliked breaks, preferring the routine of the office to the enforced leisure of holidays and weekends. While the bishop was rarely sick, his friends and advisors were unusually concerned about his health, perhaps as a result of the emotional strain evident in his early years in the diocese. He recruited an able team of advisors, led by David F. Cunningham, who became auxiliary bishop in 1950. Cunningham supervised most of the

diocesan offices, assisted later by Father John T. McGraw, while Robert Dillon and Richard Clark served as Foery's aides. Once he had this trusted, competent staff in place, Foery left them in office for more than two decades. Even after each had became pastor of a parish, they retained their chancery assignments. In addition to making Syracuse a well organized, financially sound and stable diocese, they diverted criticism from Bishop Foery so that the bishop was extremely popular with both priests and people.

Many refer to Foery as a "priests' bishop" and there can be no question that, even during the years of controversy which followed the Vatican Council, he enjoyed the affection and loyalty of his priests, which he returned in generous measure. He cared deeply about them, was immensely attentive to their needs, sensitive to their personal problems and always available. They appreciated his compassion when a family member died, or when ill health or a personal problem brought sadness and depression. Few report conversations with Foery about theology or spirituality, nor did he discuss diocesan business candidly with any but trusted insiders. He was a shy man, with a good deal of German reserve, but the bishop and the diocese had a degree of clerical solidarity unusual even in those days, when few priests challenged episcopal authority or criticized

Church practices. This sense of trust and mutual support would cause some problems when demands for change exploded after Vatican II. Then many would feel a pressure toward conformity which made their suggestions seem divisive of the tight clerical family. However, that same quality meant that Syracuse experienced little of the bitter public conflict between priests and bishops which rocked many dioceses in the 1960s.

Bishop Foery disliked conflict and hated to be taken by surprise. A methodical, systematic man, he studied issues, made decisions and stuck by them. There are few examples of his responding thoughtfully to criticism, even fewer of his changing his mind. He could not be pressured to act quickly in difficult situations. Callers made appointments, were greeted by the secretary, stated their business and were kept waiting, perhaps just a few minutes, while the secretary announced their presence. Always, if a difficult matter was to be discussed, Foery wanted to be prepared. His passion for order and predictability produced some legendary qualities. If he was to visit a school, parish or religious house for a ceremony, the schedule was established precisely ahead of time, and it was kept. He insisted that affairs start at exactly the announced moment. If confirmation was at 10 o'clock, that did not mean the procession started from the rectory at 10, but that the bishop was at the altar, turning to greet the people at exactly 10 o'clock. If a banquet was at six, that meant that at precisely six the master of ceremonies rose to announce grace. On such occasions, when the schedule was not followed, the person in charge could expect a rebuke later, if not an embarrassing expression of the bishop's dissatisfaction on the spot. There are stories of Bishop Foery leaving events which started late or at which the speaker spoke too long. One of the local papers picked up clerical banter when it referred to three methods of keeping time —

standard time, daylight savings time and "Foery time."

Syracuse, then, was an extremely well organized diocese. Its orderliness, clear lines of authority, and established procedures for making decisions and resolving disputes all reflected the personality of the ordinary. At Bishop Ludden's consecration, the homilist referred to the bishop as the captain of the ship, subject only to the admiral, the pope. During Bishop Foery's administration, it was a tight ship, run with great efficiency and in no danger of sinking. There were no loose cannons on the deck, few mavericks who ventured to the frontiers of ministry or did not fit easily into the diocesan organizational chart. Syracuse was a mature American Church, fulfilling its basic historic objectives of preserving the faith of the children of the immigrants and securing its respected place on the local and national scene. It was the local version of post-war American Catholicism. which in the 1950s experienced the fulfillment of many of its dreams.

POST-WAR PROSPERITY

Certainly the outstanding accomplishment of Foery's long leadership of the diocese was the expansion of the physical facilities of the Church of Syracuse. Crucial to this success was the work of the diocesan building commission, chaired for many years by Cunningham and run by his close friend, Monsignor David C. Gildea. In 1962, on the 25th anniversary of Foery's appointment, the commission prepared a detailed report which showed a quarter century of "amazing population growth," from 202,000 to 369,000 Catholics, and "equally incredible" physical development through an expansion program of $85,870,981. This expansion was concentrated in the 15 year period after 1947. The first 10 years of Foery's leadership had been marked by consolidation following the diffi-

Bishops Foery and Cunningham participate in the dedication of Immaculate Heart of Mary parish at Liverpool in 1951 during a time of expansion among Catholic parishes. Two decades later, declining populations would mean that few new parishes would be established. (Photo: Chancery Archives)

culties of the great depression and the shortages occasioned by the war.

The report classified this expansion under two headings, diocesan and parochial. Diocesan physical expansion ranged from 35 camp cabins at $2,000 each, to three new diocesan high schools totalling $6,000.000. Altogether, 93 new buildings cost $36,652,690.67. Included were a new chanc-

ery building and the Pius X Home for retired priests built for $931,000; motherhouses, novitiates and retreat houses for $6,300,000; hospital expansion, including schools of nursing, for more than $10,000,000; and 28 diocesan educational facilities for $18,700,000. This last category included new buildings at LeMoyne College and Christian Brothers Academy, and central high schools in Oswego, Binghamton, Utica, Endicott, Rome and Syracuse. Another $790,000 was spent on new Catholic Charities offices in three cities, and development of three diocesan sponsored camps. Also, 224 new parish buildings were erected during this period, ranging from a $15,000 rectory at Holy Rosary in Hannibal to a $900,000 church at Sts. Cyril and Methodius in Binghamton. Fifty three new churches were built and 13 others renovated at a cost of almost $20,000,000. There were 49 new rectories costing almost $4,500,000, and an equal number of new convents at $6,000,000. An incredible 35 new parish schools were constructed at a cost of $14,600,000, and another 25 social, recreational or catechetical centers at $4,400,000. The total of more than $85,000,000, the report concluded, would build 4,290 homes at a cost of $20,000 each. If five persons lived in each one, there would be a city the size of Oswego.

Some of the accomplishments of individual parishes during the period were astonishing. St. Vincent's, where the church burned to the ground, spent a total of $1,646,000 on church, rectory, convent and school. Sacred Heart of Syracuse spent $1,400,000 renovating the church and adding a $585,000 combination gym, catechetical center and auditorium. St. Cyril's, in addition to the new church, built a $195,000 convent and a $65,000 auditorium-gymnasium. Perhaps most interesting of all, in the listing of parish construction, only 13 parishes were marked "no construction reported."

Since the creation of the diocese, there had been some clear rules regarding building. The first synod had legislated that no new church could be erected or old church renovated without the plans, estimated costs and contracts being approved by the bishop. No building commission was established formally until the 1914 synod, so the application of these rules was sporadic at best. At the 1942

synod, the original rules were reaffirmed and made more specific. After that date, the building commission was extremely thorough in carrying out its tasks for the bishop. As a result, Cunningham and Gildea exercised enormous power. More than anyone else, they determined who could build, when they could build, what they could spend and what they could borrow. This was far more than a "dollars and cents matter." The building commission was, in a variety of ways, a diocesan planning office, making judgments about where new parishes were needed, whether a new convent should precede or follow a new school, and where catechetical centers might be preferred to schools. Personnel matters also came into the commission's purview because, as Gildea pointed out in an annual report at the height of the building boom, it was not the lack of available capital that most often led to hesitation about approving new projects, but "lack of personnel to staff the new projects." Aesthetic judgements were common. Gildea told one pastor his plans were rejected because of their "very unusual character." Instead, the commission suggested "a conservative type of church architecture in keeping with sound tradition and within the feelings and experience of Catholic people generally." Even relatively minor projects needed commission approval. New stations of the cross, a repaved parking lot, an addition to the convent, any project that involved more than $1,000 had to go through the commission. If a parish was having trouble paying its debts, if its building projects suffered lengthy delayes or if it had to borrow money for relatively small jobs, the pastor could expect questions from the commission and *de facto* supervision of his affairs.

Cunningham's attention to detail was legendary. In one parish, he carefully inspected the tile floor, noted several tiles improperly laid and insisted that they be replaced before the bill was paid. At his own church, St. John the Baptist in Syracuse, parishoners recalled his lengthy inspection of new pews and his satisfaction when he discovered that faulty screws had been used in a number of them. Once again, the carpenter was summoned to complete the job properly. Gildea was his match, studying plans carefully, making suggestions, and meeting with the architects and planners. When one parish was adding a gymnasium to its school in 1952, Gildea suggested changes regarding the location of administrative offices, health rooms and reception areas. In effect he provided a new design in place of the three alternatives submitted, and offered to meet with the architect to show him how it could be done.

The volume of work after the war was enormous. In his 1959 report, Gildea noted 71 projects had "come across the bishops desk" that year. Of those 31 were completed, including 22 new buildings, 18 still were under construction and 22 were in the planning stage. Finally, in 1960, the number of projects began to decrease. As Gildea noted, the tremendous building growth of the diocese could not continue indefinitely. While the number of religious vocations had increased, it had not kept pace with the demand for new educational facilities, contributing to the drop-off in new school construction. Similarly, the bishop could not create new parishes when there were not enough priests to staff them. The liturgical changes inaugurated by the Vatican Council brought a new round of church construction and renovation in the later sixties, but the age of school construction was ending, as was the expansion of Catholic parishes.

Most of the money for these projects was raised by parishes or religious communities, but diocesan resources also were expanding. Since the 1930s, the diocese conducted an annual diocesan needs collection. This was used to cover deficits on Loretto Rest and

other diocesan institutions, and to pay the cost of Catholic Charities offices, the education office, membership in state and local Catholic organizations, legal services and general chancery expenses. In 1940, the bishop asked each parishoner to give two dollars annually, and this amount rose with the years until the needs assessment reached $220,000 in 1960. It was the only collection to provide the bishop with money to run the diocese, but income also was generated by a variety of trusts and burses, most of which were restricted to a specific purpose, for example, seminary education. In 1955, the diocesan needs collection was supplemented by a special diocesan development campaign aimed at raising $750,000 for a retired priests' home and a new diocesan office building. In promoting the drive, the bishop emphasized that it was the first capital campaign since 1924. The diocese, he reminded people, was not a "natural phenomenon. It does not just grow. It is not like the post office. The grim truth is that a diocese is built by people, by people who love the faith." However, local campaigns and recent campaigns for religious order projects seemed to limit the response. The goal was not reached.

In January 1954, the apostolic delegate, Amelto Cicognani, a friend of Foery, praised the diocese as "indeed a flourishing plant in the vineyard of the Lord." He had reason to be grateful because the Syracuse diocese made major contributions to Rome and to larger Church projects. In 1953, for example, the diocese contributed $146,000 to the National Shrine of the Immaculate Conception in Washington, D.C. A steady flow of money for various permissions flowed to Rome through the delegate's office, as did a sharply increased annual Peter's Pence collection and large contributions to the Holy See during the bishop's ad limina visits. In addition, the diocese seemed bent on making many priests monsignors. Each appointment brought a bill for $180 to $225. On Pope John XXIII's 80th birthday, the diocese forwarded two checks, $15,000 from the laity and $10,000 from the bishops and priests.

For all the achievements in the diocese, one persistent problem, the *Catholic Sun,* was not solved. The *Sun* was graced by the poetry and reflective essays of Father John Lynch, perhaps the best writer the diocesan clergy ever produced. Foery and his fellow priests greatly admired Lynch, but most were critical of the *Sun* and resentful of the pressure exerted on pastors to subsidize its publication. Foery complained about typographical errors, too much advertising and "not enough news," the latter particularly deplorable given the excellent materials available through the National Catholic News Service. In 1956, Foery told priests and people that the paper needed a professionally trained priest-editor. Such a person did not appear, and the diocese explored other arrangements, all without success. In the 1970s the bishop promised to increase circulation to 50,000 by forcing parishes to subscribe for 50 percent of their parishioners. However, there was resistance, with some priests expressing objections to the content of the paper in the strongest possible fashion. Later, changes were made in the format of the paper, and the problem eased a bit, but as late as 1980, 45 percent of the parishes were under their 50 percent quota.

By the late 1940s, the Church also was making extensive use of the radio. In addition to the broadcast of national Catholic programs, the diocese had its own Catholic Hour under Father Martin J. Watley. In 1942, Father Lynch began weekly broadcasts under *Sun* sponsorship, using local clergy. That same year, priests in Rome and Utica began similar broadcasts, while several local stations carried a daily rosary which became popular after the war. In 1949, the first diocesan television broadcast featured an interview with Monsignor Cunningham on the arrest of Hungarian Cardinal Joseph Mindszenty. Regular television broadcasts began in 1954. By then, Father William J. Shannon had been appointed diocesan director of radio and television.

ROLE OF THE LAITY

As Bishop Foery's reference to a "priest-editor" of the *Sun* indicated, Syracuse was not a center of the lay apostolate or Catholic action. The diocesan Holy Name Federation declined after the war, while there had never been a diocesan council of Catholic women. The lynch pin of women's activities was the Catholic Women's Club, organized as a cathedral parish group in 1919, and, after 1926, headquartered in its own building on East Onondaga Street. The club sponsored retreats and devotions, regular visits to hospitals, orphanages, sanitariums and Loretto Rest, and provision of Christmas baskets for the poor. Perhaps its most notable activities were cultural, as the club provided a reading room and lending library and sponsored lecture programs featuring Maisie Ward, Fulton Sheen, Clarence Manion and other well known Catholic intellectuals. While these were invariably well attended, they and the club gradually declined in the post-war years.

Lay movements which prospered elsewhere occasionally appeared in the diocese. In 1949, an Albany layman proposed door-to-door visits by lay people to the homes of non-Catholics to inform them of the teachings of the Church. However, Monsignor Dillon responded that the programs of the Confraternity of Christian Doctrine and the Propagation of the Faith were succeeding and a new program would be unnecessary. He answered, in a similar vein, a proposal to establish a Catholic Evidence League, a group which did street reaching and defense of the Church. Somewhat more successful were efforts to begin Cana Conferences for married couples. The first group of 35 couples met at

Blessed Sacrament in Utica in 1949, but it remained for a time limited to this parish. When another pastor in Binghamton applied for faculties for a visiting priest to conduct a Cana Conference Day in 1950, Dillon showed typical diocesan caution, reminding him that a priest must conduct the conference, or at least be present "to guide the one who is to give such a talk so that the presentation will be properly done." Another Cana group got under way at Our Lady of Lourdes in Utica in 1951. Gradually, under careful direction, Cana expanded by 1960 to 13 parishes. In addition, Catholic Charities, which took charge of family programs, actively encouraged pre-cana programs for engaged couples. In 1960, more than 1,200 couples participated The more independent Christian Family Movement (CFM) made less progress. Founded in Chicago in the late forties, this movement featured small group meetings with prayer, Bible study and a regular program of action. The action program usually focused on a local problem, for example, racial relations, care for the poor, or hospitality for foreign students. The program not only proved a good vehicle for assisting families, but encouraged adult knowledge of the faith and more open dialogue between lay people and their chaplains. However, CFM actively championed new ideas regarding the role of the laity in the Church, and thus was regarded with suspicion by many priests and bishops. This was true in Syracuse, although the chancery placed no obstacles before pastors who wished to inaugurate and take responsibility for the program. In the few parishes where it appeared, CFM had great impact. Several prominent Catholic political and civic leaders were inspired by the program, and many priests testified to its influence, but its numbers remained small and restricted to the few parishes with venturesome pastors.

While extremely cautious about lay organizations, the diocese was alert to the spiritual needs of lay Catholics. One area of rapid growth was lay retreats. Father Joseph L. May was director of the Layman's Retreat Association for the diocese and reported as early as 1942 great interest whenever closed retreats for the laity were available. Impressed, and anxious to provide retreat facilities for priests, the bishop invited the Jesuits to take up retreat work in the diocese. Jesuit Father Robert Grewen, working closely with the bishop, purchased property in Syracuse for a retreat house and the Jesuits began offering programs for laymen and priests, while conducting parish retreats and Lenten programs as well. Women also were interested in retreats, but not until the mid-1950s was a house available for any considerable number. At that time, the Sisters of St. Francis opened Stella Maris in Skaneateles as a summer villa for the sisters and a retreat house for lay women the rest of the year. Earlier, they had offered small group retreats at their convent in Syracuse, while days of recollection and spiritual direction were also available at the Dominican monastery in the city.

While the diocese was not noted for vigorous programs of Catholic action, there were some isolated examples. In Utica, a group of laymen took up the work of the Narbeth movement, headed by F. Karl Rogers from Pennsylvania. The Catholic Information Society of Utica mailed materials on the Church to non-Catholics and promoted the printing of Roger's newspaper column in a variety of outlets in the Utica and Binghamton areas. Lay activists also found some support from individual priests. In Syracuse, some gathered around Father Charles Brady in his Don Bosco and Dominic Savio groups of youthful volunteers working with inner city black children. Another interesting group was a "Professional Sodality" formed in 1957 after a study week at LeMoyne under the direction of Father Daniel Berrigan. Through daily Mass, reading of scripture and prayer, they attempted to pursue spiritual growth, while participating in the lay apostolate. They organized an institute on housing at which Berrigan spoke on the moral issues of exploiting the poor. Some, including Delores Morgan, attended a convention of the sodality in New York in 1959. That year, Berrigan and one of the lay people invited the bishop to attend the installation of new members, but the bishop did not encourage a closer relationship with the diocese. The sodality hoped to become a center of the lay apostolate in the community, offering adult education, spiritual direction, and opportunities for evangelization, street preaching and community service, but the chancery responded that such needs were already being met.

The skeptical, cautious approach to lay initiative reflected a strongly institutional, organizational view of the Church. In a talk to LeMoyne students in 1951, Auxiliary Bishop Cunningham said that the Church, since the Reformation, had placed too great an emphasis on the distinction between clergy and laity. Together they should share responsibility for the Church's mission in the world. A short time later, he told another audience that the fight against trusteeism unfortunately had limited the laity's role to financial support. Yet, while Cunningham understood the problem, his solution tended to perpetuate it because he limited the laity's mission to defending the Church against attack and giving good example through "temperate and sober habits in practical living." Being Catholic was still a matter of accepting one's place within the organization because, as Cunningham concluded one of these talks, "obedience to the Church is the distinctive badge of the Catholic." Foery was even less open. In turning down the sodality's offer to open an apostolic center, the bishop told its members he nevertheless supported the lay apostolate "because of the patient assistance it gives to

our parish priests."

The Legion of Mary, which was parish-based, completely under clerical control and devoted to helping the pastors, was Foery's ideal form of lay activity. The minutes of a 1952 clergy conference summarized the bishop's remarks on the lay apostolate. "The bishop pointed out the willingness of our laity to assist the priests and encouraged the priests to make use of this assistance." Although the diocese had few lay-oriented programs and almost none independent of clerical directions, Foery nevertheless felt compelled to warn the priests against possible "abuses," reminding them that, to qualify as Catholic action, any group must have a specific mandate from the bishop.

Foery's attitude toward the laity, and Cunningham's before Vatican II, can be characterized best as maternal. In addition to envisioning the lay role in terms of helping the parish priests, both regarded the laity as "sheep" to be shepherded by protecting them against a secular world in which their eternal salvation was endangered. Foery expressed those attitudes as a young priest when he told his Rochester parishioners that the Church was "wise mother." He said the Church was like that mother who understood that it was not enough to tell her children what they were forbidden to do; she also had to "give them a substitute" and "furnish them with some activity they may do." This was important for young people, of course, but also for adults, who would face in the future greater leisure time and, as with children, there would be a tendency of their "impulses" to develop along "unwholesome lines" unless directed elsewhere. "Play is a great building force in the child's life," he noted, while "the play of the adult seems to make up for the wear and tear of daily work and to offset the strain of responsibility." It was for this reason, as he put it later, that the Church was "multiplying its interests on behalf of her children.'' Rarely has the self-assurance and protective elitism of the Church been expressed more clearly than in a talk Foery gave to the National Council of Catholic Women while still in Rochester:

The church is often called by us 'our holy mother, the Church' and she is so called because of her motherly interest in us. There are times when our earthly mother scolds us (or) corrects us. Then again, she encourages us, praises us. By her liturgy and ceremonies and feasts she lifts us up and fills us with the spirit of triumph and victory. There are other times when she makes us face hard facts of life, turns us back upon ourselves to make us humble, contrite. All this done because she is our mother. Now the church, our mother, understands human nature, understands it thoroughly. She knows our weakness, our inclinations, the temptations which we must conquer or which will conquer us. She looks upon us as a mother looks upon her children, with watchful and anxious eyes.

CONTRIBUTIONS OF RELIGIOUS

The diocese had many needs beyond the parish level, and even in the parishes there was work, especially in education, which could not be done by priests alone. The diocese relied for this work not on lay people, but on religious. Historically, the diocese of Syracuse made little use of religious orders of men other than Franciscans. In 1944, there were in the diocese only 31 religious order priests, 23 of them Franciscans, and 14 Christian Brothers. The former still staffed several German parishes. The latter staffed their own high school, Christian Brothers Academy, which conducted a major fundrais-

ing campaign in 1960. That same year, the diocese welcomed the Stigmatine Fathers, who purchased an estate in Waterville to be used as a novitiate. While concentrating on their own men, the priests occasionally assisted in neighboring parishes.

The Marianists also conducted a novitiate in the diocese. In 1965, with Foery's permission, they established the Gabriel Richard Institute to promote lay leadership. In 1970, they began opening their doors to a variety of spiritual and apostolic renewal movements, especially Marriage Encounter. The center became known as Bergamo East and offered family enrichment programs, retreats and study days for Church personnel. Overwhelmed by staff and financial problems, the center closed in 1981.

For many years, the diocese had relied heavily on the service of religious women in its charities and schools. In contrast to the relatively small number of religious men in the diocese, there were, in 1940, 803 sisters from 15 different orders, led by 240 Sisters of St. Joseph, 179 Franciscans and 123 Daughters of Charity. While each Syracuse bishop upheld a model of the Church with the priest as its center, in fact a great deal of its essential work was carried on by these women. Most of the time, relations between religious and clergy were cooperative, if not close, but there was always some strain under the surface. Two examples gave some hint of tensions that would take place later. One came at Syracuse University, whose fine arts departments attracted a small number of sisters, especially during summer school. As a courtesy, their superiors invariably wrote to the bishop, who responded that he and his staff did not regard the university as a suitable place for study for any Catholic, much less a religious. Some sisters withdrew, but a growing number explained patiently why they must take the program offered there. Eventually, the bishop gave in, granting them permission, but insist-

NUNS FROM OUR PARISH

"How blessed, Lord, are those who dwell in thy house!
They will be ever praising thee."

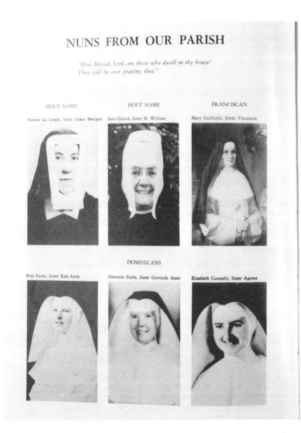

HOLY NAME — Norma La Londe, Sister Grace Benigna

HOLY NAME — Sara Church, Sister M. William

FRANCISCAN — Mary Guilfoyle, Sister Vincentia

DOMINICANS — Rita Fuchs, Sister Rita Anne; Gertrude Fuchs, Sister Gertrude Anne; Elizabeth Connelly, Sister Agnese

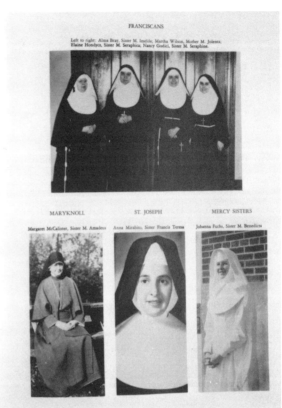

FRANCISCANS

Left to right: Alma Bray, Sister M. Imelda; Martha Wilson, Mother M. Jolenta; Elaine Hondyca, Sister M. Seraphica; Nancy Godici, Sister M. Seraphine.

MARYKNOLL — Margaret McCalister, Sister M. Amadeus

ST. JOSEPH — Anna Mirabito, Sister Francis Teresa

MERCY SISTERS — Johanna Fuchs, Sister M. Benedicta

315

The Syracuse diocese has been blessed with sisters of many different religious communities serving in parishes, schools and Church institutions since the earliest days of its oldest parishes. Often their dedication went unrecognized. But when Fulton's Immaculate Conception parish observed its centennial in 1954, the anniversary book celebrated these native daughters in religious life. (Photo: Chancery Archives)

ing that they take housing with a religious community off campus. At the University, these nuns encountered Gannon Ryan, the Catholic chaplain, who was incensed particularly by the presence of nuns on the campus. In July 1938, he met Sister Esther, a founder of the Catholic College Art Association and a faculty member at St. Mary's of the Woods College in Indiana. Apparently the two had a heated argument about her plans to study art because she wrote him apologizing for her "ungracious attitude" during their visit. She explained that, some years before, she and others had inquired where in the United States they could study Christian art and had been told that there was no school with the necessary program. Instead, they had to immerse themselves in Catholic philosophy and study art in one of the country's better art schools, making the integration themselves. "Having done these things," she told the priest sharply, "I am now told, by implication, that I have dishonored my sacred profession, and this by one who has not known the dangers and uncertainties of pioneering in uncharted ways." Sister Esther was not finished. She supposed Ryan knew that it was impossible to do advanced work in the professional art schools "without the courses of which we spoke," presumably courses in anatomy and drawing from nude models. This fact had impeded the study of art and caused it to be neglected in Catholic schools, "with the result now sadly evident in the uncultivated tastes of our people" who "accept whatever sentimental and gaudy products manufacturers and dealers choose to foist upon their ignorance in the name of religious art." Now, because some had surmounted these difficulties, a struggle "which you deplore as an evil" there was a trained group of religious teachers capable of educating Catholics without exposing them to the "unpleasant circumstances with which they were confronted." They had formed the Catholic College Art Association to foster programs in Christian art. Voices like this were a missing ingredient in the life of the diocese of Syracuse, where few any longer "knew the dangers and uncertainties of pioneering in unchartered paths." A price would be paid for this absence in years to come.

The second incident came in 1942, when Monsignor Carson, pastor of St. Peter's in Rome, wrote the chancery agreeing with a description of conditions in his sister's convent described in an enclosed report. The basement was damp; the kitchen was, in fact, a small porch with no basement under it, cold at all times. There was no closet space in the entire building. The sisters hung their clothes on hooks in the hallways. The first floor was used for religious instruction classes because the church hall was too cold, so the sisters lived on the second floor, eight sisters in three rooms. Guests used a cot in the pantry. It was "a poor excuse for a convent." The chancellor thanked the pastor for his "fine report" and expressed the bishop's "hopes that in some way the conditions can be changed," but, in any case, "he values your suggestions highly." In fact, Carson had made no "suggestions."

Behind the attitude of Ryan, Carson and others lay the seeds of serious problems.

The large number of sisters working in the diocese meant that Foery was called upon to speak at many ceremonies marking the major events in the lives of religious. His notes for these talks indicate that he had a highly idealized view of the life of religious women. Always they were described as living lives marked by dedication, sacrifice, a yearning after spiritual perfection and constant service to the Church. Convent life appeared to him an island of serenity in a world filled with conflict and change. Those who thought life there was drab or uninteresting were simply wrong, he stated confidently. Convent life was "attractive, interesting and all absorbing." It brought with it a readiness to live boldly and dangerously and a joy and satisfaction that came from living for things which were eternal. "The nuns are very precious today," he told a teachers convention in 1954. "The demand for their services is beyond any reasonble hope of meeting it. Yet we must continue to hope and believe that, since our work is the Lord's work, God will in some way provide the means." Nuns, people and Church all lived in a rapidly changing world, he admitted, but each must hold firm. Like their students, the sisters "must have a firm grasp of eternal truths and resist the pressure of this constant change."

One of the two largest communities, and the only community with its motherhouse in the diocese, was the Third Order Franciscans. In 1953, there were 454 sisters on mission, up from 319 in 1945 and almost double the 226 of 1934. Of those, a little more than half worked at schools, catechetical centers, hospitals and Loretto Rest in the diocese of Syracuse, about the same proportion as two decades earlier. The operation of the Franciscans was no small matter. In 1941 they owned $2,800,000 worth of property at St. Joseph's and St. Elizabeth's Hospitals and St.

Bishop Foery addressed most of the teaching sisters in the diocese in a 1963 conference held at the War Memorial auditorium in Syracuse. At that time, most of the Catholic school teachers were sisters, but within a few years many of these religious women would branch out into additional apostolates in social service or parish ministry, and lay teachers would become a regular feature of Catholic education. (Photo: The Catholic Sun)

Francis Home, together with the motherhouse, novitiate and convent school in Syracuse. They had only $200,000 in debts and annual income was more than $500,000. Their mission now extended across many parts of the United States and Hawaii. In all, they served almost 5,000 grammar school and 400 high school students, 334 student nurses, 2,571 children in catechism classes and almost 27,000 patients in their hospitals. In 1957, they launched a campaign for new buildings at the motherhouse, the total cost of which eventually would exceed $2,500,000. The goal of the campaign was $750,000 and, of the $1,100,000 eventually raised, $764,000 came from the Syracuse diocese, most from parishes where the sisters served.

The Sisters of St. Joseph, with the Franciscans the largest community in the diocese, also experienced rapid growth in the post-war years. In 1960, they had 253 sisters staffing 23 parochial schools in the diocese. A $5,500,000 program of new buildings for their motherhouse near Albany was launched in 1961, and the bishop and his consultors granted permission for fundraising in the 22 parishes of the Syracuse diocese served by that community. The Sisters of the Holy Names of Jesus and Mary served Holy Names Academy in Rome. They also had a novitiate there. In 1961, they had a new novitiate and college. The lack of personnel forced them to withdraw, a decision made easier by the formation of a new central high school in the city. They left several sisters at St. Joseph's school in Liverpool until 1970. In 1958, there were 43 Sister Servants of the Immaculate Heart of Mary serving at Most Holy Rosary in Syracuse, St. Patrick's in Oneida and St. John the Evangelist in Binghamton, where they taught students in three elementary and one secondary school, while teaching catechism to another 1,213. The Sisters of St. Francis of Allegheny served at three parishes, St. Mary's in Cortland and Rome and Blessed Sacrament in Utica.

CHANGES IN CHARITIES

By the 1940s, Catholic Charities was established solidly in the diocese. However, its development reflected the tensions of a Church whose language was separatist, as in supporting parochial schools and resisting cooperation with other churches, but whose charitable and social programs required cooperation with non-Catholic agencies and with the government. Problems with Community Chest came to a head in 1944. The new Northside Catholic Youth Organization (CYO) had not yet been adopted formally as a Community Chest agency, although it was featured in some Chest publicity releases. The diocese had also dropped its subsidy from the Loretto Rest budget, turning to the Chest for support. In addition, Foery thought that support for Catholic institutions had not grown since the advent of the Chest and that the annual diocesan needs collection was not supported as it should be because of the Church's identification with community-wide fund raising. When a list of chest agencies published at the end of August did not include the Northside CYO, Foery acted quickly. In ominous terms, he warned officials that if the CYO were not accepted before a scheduled meeting with Syracuse area clergy, he would discuss with them the possibility of withdrawal from the campaign. At the same time, he told the priests that they should consider a new diocesan drive to enlarge the

diocesan needs collection to include the CYO and fill the gap that would be left by withdrawal from the chest. In an emergency meeting the chest accepted the CYO, but the priests nevertheless discussed the bishop's suggestion. Some supported a separate drive, which would identify the people more directly with their Catholic agencies. On the other hand, they did not want to cause problems during the war. Foery concluded that it would be unwise to withdraw from the chest at present, but the question would be considered more fully when the war ended.

In the post-war years, however, the Church became more, rather than less, involved with the Community Chest. Foery considered the Community Chest "the city and county organized in working together to solve problems that are common to us all." As such, it made a substantial contribution to Catholic charitable work. In 1948, for example, the Utica charities office received $18,000 of its $25,000 budget from the chest; St. John's Home $33,500 of its $97,900 budget, and St. Joseph's Infant Home $23,250 of its $112,000.

In Binghamton in 1949, the Community Chest provided $20,000 of the local Charities budget of $41,000, and also provided an additional emergency grant of $3,000. Although the Oswego charities office did not become a participating agency until 1952, by 1961, it was the largest affiliated agency, receiving $14,750 of the chest's total budget of $98,837. These local offices gave emergency relief and usually offered various child care programs, while its staff counseled needy persons and helped them find assistance from other agencies, sometimes through home visitation and case work. Parish aid programs were declining in these years. St. Vincent de Paul Societies, in particular, gradually faded in many parishes, which instead referred emergency cases to local charities offices. The advantage was that the needy family received a full range of services. The disadvantage was that it became increasingly expensive to provide direct emergency assistance. In Binghamton, for example, the local office in 1949 spent $15,800 on salaries, $7,800 on administration and $17,332 on relief and child care. In 1962, Monsignor Lawler placed the figure of total funds allotted to Catholic agencies from local drives at $528,000. Of that $329,000 came in Onondaga County, $72,000 in Utica, $70,000 in Broome County, $27,000 in Rome and the rest scattered between Fulton, Clinton and Oswego.

Yet, the lack of enthusiasm among the diocesan clergy and the bishop's warnings against thinking chest contributions fulfilled one's responsibilities reflected the wider problem of loss of identification of Catholic pastors and people with the institutions their forebears had built but which now relied so heavily on government and Community Chest support and third party insurance payments. In 1961, Lawler, who had become director of Catholic Charities, told Foery that many Catholic laymen working on the United Fund, which by now had replaced Community Chest, regularly expressed hope for "more vigorous support" by the priests. He urged the bishop to offer a personal word of encouragement to the clergy at their fall conferences, but the argument he used reflected the problem. The United Fund was the *"sole support"* of most Catholic Charities agencies, he wrote with considerable exaggeration; "without it, the diocese could not carry on its works of charity for orphans, the aged, our youth, the sick, our needy families and children." If this were in fact true, then lack of clerical support at a time of rapid building expansion and heavy financial demands was at least understandable, because these matters could easily seem community, not church, responsibilities.

For all their problems, some diocesan charitable institutions thrived. Loretto Rest, once a financial headache, now was a stable

and even profitable institution. In 1960, it had $100,000 on loan to three parishes. In 1960, the institution served 189 persons. Per diem expenses were low because of the services provided by the Sisters of St. Francis, while old-age assistance, Community Chest and various insurance programs covered much of the costs of residence. Catholic hospitals also were solidly established semi-public institutions. Our Lady of Lourdes, St. Elizabeth's and St. Joseph's conducted major fundraising drives after the war, St. Joseph's raising $1,500,000 for a new building. On the other hand, local committees were working to coordinate health services and, in Syracuse, the university was developing a medical center, and proposals to affiliate or coordinate services threatened the autonomy of St. Joseph's. Refusal to cooperate might cost the hospital the services of doctors anxious to use the facilities of the new center and risk charges that St. Joseph's was being "obstructive, non-progressive, hidebound and reactionary." The bishop considered it a "plain statement of my duty" that "no teachings or practices contrary to the Catholic faith are taught or permitted in the hospital." He urged the sisters and the board to go slow, cooperate to the extent possible, but preserve an escape clause which would allow withdrawal if that became necessary.

Another continuing problem was the relationship between religious orders and the diocesan charities office. The bishop regarded the director of Catholic Charities as his delegate, and he wanted charitable institutions integrated with other social services and coordinated more closely with diocesan policy. In 1943, for example, the bishop asked the superintendent of St. John's Home, Sister Rose, to discuss a recent report from the state Department of Social Welfare with the Utica charities office headed by Father Joseph G. May, who already had a copy. One recommendation dealt with improving the educational program of the students by sending them to school outside the institution. The bishop and Father May, without Sister Rose, agreed to urge local officials to continue to pay the teachers at the home. Failing that, they would ask neighboring pastors to take the children into their parochial schools. The sisters, ignored in this decision, were upset.

Tension between the Daughters of Charity and the diocese intensified because such incidents multiplied in the post-war period. In 1947, Vincentian Father Francis J. Dodd, on behalf of the sisters, suggested turning over to the diocese the four institutions the sisters staffed — St. John's Home and St. Joseph's Infant Home in Utica, and the House of Providence and St. Vincent's Asylum in Syracuse. The bishop, undoubtedly worried that such a step would signal the sisters' withdrawal from the work, resisted this suggestion. At Father Dodd's suggestion, a survey was taken of child care in 1951. St. Joseph's and St. John's decided to merge and, with Catholic Charities, develop an intensive system of foster care. In 1955, the sisters again asked that the property, badly in need of repair, be transferred to diocesan ownership. The diocese acted quickly and the property was conveyed to the board, now headed by Father May and composed of the two bishops and seven diocesan clergy. At the time of the transfer, there were no outstanding debts, the Community Chest picked up the bulk of the operating deficit and volunteer groups generated some revenue for repairs. The population of the school was dropping, largely a result of changes in child care policy, which now emphasized adoption and foster care. In 1958, the child population dropped to 50, far too few for the large building, while paradoxically, the school's financial situation improved with some large bequests which were placed out as loans to area parishes. The choices were difficult. One option was to use the property for a residential care facility for

50 children. The other, arising from the prospect of 2,000 high school-age children emerging from the post-war baby boom, was to spend $900,000 converting the property for use as a high school. This was the policy followed, and on January 1, 1960, the historic home closed its doors.

A similar pattern emerged in other parts of the diocese. St. Francis Home in Oswego was closed in 1952 after consultation between the diocese, Community Chest and the Sisters of St. Francis. In Binghamton, St. Mary's was not part of the Community Chest, so there was no outside agency to pick up the deficit. In 1953, the bishop told the sister superior that "children's institutions are passing through a new phase." While he believed the need for such institutions eventually would arise again, there seemed little hope for the immediate future. A secret decision to close the school was made in 1953, with the land to be used for a Catholic central high school. The Sisters of St. Joseph were asked to keep the school open for a year, with a limited staff. In 1954, however, plans for the new school were abandoned temporarily and the bishop asked them to continue the child care institution until other arrangements could be made. Confusion reigned as different signals about the home's future reached area pastors. In 1959, Foery correctly told a sister that foster care and adoption were replacing orphanages, but he went along with a plan of the board to raise funds in the parishes for repairs. When the drive topped its goal by a comfortable figure, he told local charities officials he had no plans other than to maintain the institution as long as it met community needs. In 1959, faced with new building needs, the board applied for membership in local United Fund, but before the decision could be finalized, the old plans for a central high school were resurrected. In February of that year the bishop told Lawler that any repairs to the building should be minimal. He said it was now "our conviction that the home should be closed, first because of the lack of a child care population, second because the buildings are unfit and third because we need the property for a Catholic High School." In April, the diocese offered to purchase the property from the sisters for $100,000. The last child was placed on August 4 and the home formally closed its doors a week later.

Conflicts between sisters and Catholic Charities were most intense at the Syracuse orphanages. St. Vincent's and the House of Providence merged in 1952. By that time, the physical plant was in the hands of the independent board dominated by Catholic Charities.

Tension existed almost from the beginning. When there was public discussion in the press of the use of some of the institution's property for a public park, the Daughters of Charity protested that they had not been consulted. They had agreed to continue to staff the home after turning over the property, but as Father Dodd told the bishop, "you will understand that there could be conditions under which we would not ask the sisters to work." By early 1958, such conditions had arisen. In January, Foery met several times with Sister Angela, superintendent of the house, concerning problems between herself and Catholic Charities. The conflict arose from the agreement of Catholic Charities, working with the Community Chest, to provide a full time social worker at the orphanage. The social worker had responsibility for coordinating relations with public agencies and overseeing the process of returning children to their families or to other forms of care. Monsignor Joseph Toomey, diocesan director of Catholic Charities, told the bishop that Sister Angela thought the provision of a social worker was "nonsense," but he hoped to persuade her to "understand our interests." The job of the social worker was to make sure

every child was known to Catholic Charities, to represent the sisters at case work conferences and to coordinate agency services in the interest of the child. The sisters argued in response that the social worker made decisions about admission and removal without consulting the sisters, that she did not allow the sisters to talk with parents or other social workers, and that she interfered with the affairs of the house. The bishop told Sister Angela that the sisters were to have the care of the children only "while they are in the House of Providence." They were prohibited from any direct discussion of discharge with anyone other than the social worker. Thus the Catholic Charities director, through the social worker, would retain full control over every case. Faced with this policy, the sisters consulted with the administrators of the House of Providence. On December 12, 1957, they informed the bishop that they would withdraw from the home by next June. This decision was based on "a very objective study" and arose from differences so "fundamental that a compromise would be highly unsatisfactory to both parties." Over the next three months, there were innumerable conversations with the charities staff and the bishop. The bishop reported that he told Sister Angela that "what she wants...she will have." Nevertheless, in March, the sisters reaffirmed the decision. Foery was very upset, writing that he had made every effort to remove "irritations." The sister superior, Sister Isabel, responded that, if their relationship had been "more with your excellency," there "would not have been any serious difficulty." However, contacts had been largely with Catholic Charities and from that agency they had "much to suffer, especially since the diocese accepted ownership of the physical properties." To illustrate the problem, she quoted from a letter from a Catholic Charities official in 1953: "I furthermore told Sister Justine two things: first, that when matters of policy and usage of the property were to be established, they were the prerogative of the corporation and that, as an employee of the corporation I did not want her taking singular and exceptional steps." Sister Isabel commented: "That word employee speaks volumes and suggests the thinking that has been the cause of all the trouble." Subsequent meetings and letters demonstrated clearly that "the sisters had no responsibility beyond the spiritual and physical care of the children and must take no part in the all important social work." When the sisters protested to the bishop, they received a response from the director of Catholic Charities, the last paragraph of which stated that he could not possibly treat "all the subjective thinking that must have motivated your letter to Bishop Foery." On the contrary, Sister Isabel stated, her thinking had been "objective." They did not wish to dictate the policies of Catholic Charities, but simply could not be expected to work under such policies.

Eventually, the Sisters of Social Service replaced the Daughters of Charity in September 1958. This transfer was carried out amicably. Foery thanked the Daughters and gave them a check for $500 to help on their new missions. The sisters and the children sent him a box of homemade fudge. On September 7, the Syracuse *Herald Journal* reported that the sisters were leaving because of a decision to concentrate their energies on teaching. The bishop issued a statement noting that this was incorrect. Their decision was made because "the social service work of the institution was placed in the hands of lay people" which made "an intolerable situation for the sisters" and caused them to withdraw after "many years of devoted and zealous service." The bishop's reference to lay people of course was misleading. The fact that the social worker involved was a lay person never entered into the discussion. Charities officials

believed the sisters were refusing to accept the professionalism needed in the new era of complex interaction of social agencies and casework approaches to social problems. The sisters obviously rejected that charge and contended in response that they could not work in an institution in which the basic decisions about the children were taken out of their hands.

Perhaps most revealing was a Pontifical Mass held in Utica at the end of 1959 to mark the conclusion of 125 years of service of the sisters in caring for the orphans of that city. The event had a prophetic character, forecasting problems that would be repeated in years to come. There was the reluctant bishop, telling the lay volunteers that he shared their "sorrow that the decision ... was necessary." There were the volunteers, whose anguished letters of the past year expressed incomprehension at why Catholics no longer could care for the needy in their own community. There were the sisters, gratified that needs once left to the uncertainty of private charity now were to be met through public responsibility. They were determined to use their spiritual and personal resources to meet new needs where the Spirit led them. The decision was there too, hovering over the ceremony. The give-and-take had gone on behind closed doors, few lay persons were consulted, Church officials and sisters had not been very candid with each other and the decision was made finally by ordained members of the Church, honestly seeking to do the right thing for the children, Church and community. Bishop, priest, and lay people undoubtedly wondered whether perhaps they had taken the sisters for granted too long.

Bishop Foery, sincere and generous as ever, could have spoken for many Catholics when he wrote Sister Ann Maria of St. Mary's in Binghamton in January 1958. In the letter he noted that the budget had been balanced the previous year solely because the sisters took no salaries for their work, a situation that had been true for many years. The bishop revealed more than he realized when he concluded: "I doubt that there are very many who really understand this and recognize it. I know that it escaped my attention for a number of years."

BLACK CATHOLICS

Sisters were not the only group whose presence had escaped attention for many years. The first evidence of black Catholics in the diocese came in 1893 when the Syracuse Catholic Union listed "one colored member," William Murdock. Two years later, Daniel A. Rudd, the black editor of the *American Catholic Tribune,* lectured under Bishop Ludden's sponsorship in Rome, Utica, Oswego and Syracuse. According to the *Catholic Sun,* "several of the leading Catholic colored citizens" met following Rudd's talk to plan an organization, but nothing more was heard of it. In 1928, in response to an inquiry from Father Louis B. Pastorelli of the Josephite Fathers, Bishop Curley reported that there were 44 "colored Catholics" in the diocese. In 1940, when Pastorelli again inquired, Cunningham listed 98 Negroes in the diocese, 48 adults and 50 children, of whom two adults and 21 children were in orphanages or institutions. While specific pastoral work was not reported, there was in fact a pocket of action, and the diocese was well informed. On May 1, 1940, Dorothy Hayes told Cunningham of an interracial forum at the Plymouth Congregational Church at which a number of speakers had described racial prejudice in the city. She described the Protestant participants, including a minister who urged students to agitate their churches on the question of racial justice. She noted also a "young colored speaker" who was a Catholic. Introduced to several of the Catholic women, the speaker mentioned three other

black Catholic families in the city. Hayes made this report without comment, but others were determined to join the interracial apostolate. While its origins are unclear, by 1941, there was a Catholic Interracial Guild in the city, probably started by the Catholic women present at the Plymouth church meeting. On May 15, the bishop congratulated Miss Anna E. Thompson for the work the group was doing for "the Catholic Negroes of the city," particularly a local census which had uncovered 45 black Catholic households in Syracuse. He appointed Father Norcott of St. Joseph's French church to act as moderator and placed the group under the patronage of St. Peter Claver. While assuring them of his deep interest in the work and his desire to do all in his power to help, he advised them to go slow:

I must caution you that the work of the church moves slowly. And if at times this procedure irritates us, I believe that you will eventually discover that the experience of mother church has taught her that haste makes waste and may destroy the very objective we have in mind.

It was advice Bishop Foery rarely forgot.

The Church might move slowly, but events did not. Dorothy Hayes was familiar with a number of black families in the city and, in 1941, heard several stories of young blacks being refused admission to Catholic schools. An inquiry to Monsignor McPeak led to an unpleasant conversation, so she decided on her own to prove to the young black mothers that, whatever may have been true in the past, there was no longer discrimination. Offering to pay the tuition herself, she persuaded one woman to enroll her daughters in Catholic schools. After a year, she reported that the one child enrolled at St. Anthony's had a satisfactory year but the one at Cathedral had not. The child's mother reported that her daughter was singled out and humiliated by her teacher. The mother investigated and, after a sympathetic conversation with the principal, met the teacher, who charged that her daughter was impudent because she refused to attend services at the Cathedral. When the mother reported that they regularly attended St. Joseph's French church, the teacher attacked that church and its priests. The teacher charged that when she scolded the girl, she just stared at her. Angry, the sister admitted she may have said some things she should not have. In any event, the girl decided not to return to Cathedral school. Apparently this information was communicated to Julian J. Reiss of the New York State Commission Against Discrimination, who met with Foery and welcomed the bishop's promise to discuss the principles involved with the priests.

In such discreet ways, the diocese first confronted the question of racism. Cathedral school was not alone. In December 1945, Foery received a strange letter from Thomas J. McDonnell of the national office of the Society for the Propagation of the Faith. The president of Manhattan College said that the college had received an application for admission for a black student submitted by Miss Isabella Lanigan, chairman of the scholarship committee of the Catholic Interracial Guild of Syracuse. Somehow, this application was considered by the board of trustees of the college, who referred it to McDonnell to determine whether the Propogation of the Faith was in favor of its receiving consideration. McDonnell wanted to know from the bishop the status of the guild: "You can appreciate how careful the colleges must be in considering the applications of this nature, so only worthy students will be accepted." The bishop apparently found nothing unusual in this, because he replied that the guild had his approval and had "accomplished many worthwhile things for

our Negro population." However, he added rather gratuitously:

There are in the group several overzealous individuals who sometimes fail to show good judgment. These individuals are apt to find difficulty where none exists and to claim discrimination where there is no ground for such a complaint.

Here matters stood when Father Charles Brady appeared on the scene. The 13th of 15 children, Brady was educated at St. Bonaventure University and Christ the King Seminary and ordained in 1930. He served first at St. John's in Utica, then at Most Holy Rosary in Syracuse, where he became immensely popular, known for his gentleness, warmth and especially for his visits to the sick. In 1941, Brady volunteered for chaplain duty and served in the Pacific. There he became attached to a heavily black unit, an experience of which he did not talk often, but which apparently deeply influenced his priesthood. When he returned to Syracuse, he received permission to work among the minority population of the city. Appointed "city missionary," an old Protestant term, he lived at first with his friend Father David Norcott, pastor of St. Joseph's French church which had the largest or at least the most visible black congregation in the city. With the help of friendly lay supporters, many from Most Holy Rosary, the Foery Foundation was established to finance his work and a house was purchased on Forman Street. There Brady served people, meeting and befriending blacks, persuading their children to enter Catholic schools, and responding to the daily problems of finding shelter, food and clothing. He attended baptisms, weddings and funerals, and practiced a ministry almost unique for a priest in the diocese of Syracuse. He did not expect to build a church, he had no interest in organizing black people for

With supporters functioning as the Foery Foundation, Monsignor Charles Brady took his special ministry into the streets and homes of Syracuse's city neighbors, where he showed a special care for black persons. In this photo on the steps of the foundation's center, Brady chats with several children from his neighborhood — (left to right), Joseph, William and Dawn Morgan, and Fred and Thomas Rhodes. (Photo: Bishop Foery Foundation Corporate Board)

social action, though when that happened he was delighted, nor did he want to establish an office or agency in Catholic Charities. Nor was he a social worker. Most of all, Brady's work was a matter of presence, of being with people and not for them, of being a servant and not a leader. In the process, he was, for a number of people, a revolution, perhaps a revelation. One black Catholic layman, William Chiles, recalled years later meeting Brady and returning home to tell his wife, "I've found him," at last a priest who cared for black people.

Brady's work was radical in its simplicity. He wished to be among people, witnessing to the care of Jesus and the Church, helping them with their problems when he could, encouraging them in their struggle to make a decent life and hopefully bringing some of them into the Church. Perhaps no individual

has been as influential in the history of the diocese, yet it remains difficult to describe exactly what Brady did. As Dolores Morgan, one of Brady's closest friends, recalls, no one was too sure what the new priest at the French church was up to, but "strange little things began to happen." People began to find baskets of food on their porch, and sick people received bouquets of flowers. People began to gather at the Foery Foundation in the 15th ward. Some came to receive help, some to give it. Business and professional men told each other of this priest and his work and, before they knew it, they were drawn in. LeMoyne students and former students, members of the Interracial Council and people Brady met began dropping by to sort clothes, teach in classes, supervise recreational programs for the children, or follow Brady's request to attend a wake or visit a sick person in the hospital. They were, as many recall, "hooked," not by any particular theological message, but by this simple, warm priest who was doing good and made them feel good when they helped. Everyone recalls that, among Brady's many qualities, was that he treated everyone the same, rich or poor, black or white. In his peculiar mode of speech, he called them "St. Carl" or "St. Charles." He would meet people on the street with phrases like "my dear" or "my gorgeous," and they were not embarrassed, but invariably felt better about themselves. Yet, while he treated everyone alike, his special care and his special work was with black people. They were his people. His gentle tolerant good nature broke occasionally into bursts of anger, even violent language, and invariably that happened when black people were mistreated in language or in fact.

Working among black people in the 15th ward of Syracuse, as the population grew and the housing stock deteriorated, Brady was keenly aware of discrimination, poverty, inadequate housing and sanitation, and all the

325

other problems facing poor and black people in the city. Such facts excited in him something more than "concern." He would seek out prominent local citizens with influence in real estate or politics and personally take them on tours of the area. He would return from meetings with city officials tired and upset, but he did not stop pushing. In the late 1950s, the federal government began pouring money into cities for urban renewal projects and slum clearance began in Syracuse in the 15th ward, with little provision made for the displaced residents. On the one hand, Brady and his supporters pushed for relocation programs. On the other, they joined with black groups to encourage open housing, hoping that instead of relocating the ghetto, black families could move peacefully into white neighborhoods and integration could take place. This of course brought the beginning of what would become massive conflict in Syracuse and elsewhere. Foery strongly supported neighborhood integration, but few Catholics and fewer priests signed the open housing petitions. At one point in the late 1950s, Brady appeared at a hearing dealing with a proposed public housing project to be located in his old parish, Most Holy Rosary. When he stood to speak on its behalf, residents booed him. It was a shocking experience, not only for Brady, but for many in the parish who loved him and for many of his priest friends. It would get worse.

Foery's relationship with Brady was complex. On the one hand, he admired Brady, recognized his dedications and gave him his affection, which Brady always returned. He loved Foery and always praised his compassion and understanding. Foery, however, was a cautious man, and a churchman. He never could admit failure in his Church. For Foery and for the diocese of Syracuse, Brady was the first challenge on their homeground. There has been no Catholic Worker house and no highly visible Catholic lay apostolate

Father Brady organized the Don Bosco Club and Dominic Savio Society to organize adult volunteers to teach religion, supervise recreation, and provide role models for children affiliated with the Catholic Interracial Council. (Photo: Bishop Foery Foundation Corporate Board)

groups, no labor priests or vigorous social action leaders. Brady represented the challenge such groups presented, a challenge to be more open, more honest and more attentive to the hard demands of the Gospel.

While Foery remained conservative, he had no doubts about the principles and no lack of personal compassion for black people. In August 1946, Foery issued a statement deploring violence against minorities. In March 1947, he told an interracial gathering at the Convent school that, as a teacher, he intended to reiterate some old principles drawn from the Christian creed, principles that contradicted the practice of injustice and discrimination. He agreed with those who said that prejudice was a national problem, he deplored claims about black intellectual inferiority, and he denounced as hypocrisy a national policy which urged free elections in Poland, while allowing the state of Georgia to deny the vote to one third of its citizens. In February 1949 at the Foery Foundation's biannual dinner, he praised Brady and his work and denounced two particular expressions of race prejudice, misinterpretation of the Noah story in the Bible and claims that low IQ scores demonstrated Negro inferiority. He appealed to Negroes to follow the example of Job, to remain patient and retain their confidence in the eternal justice of God.

In 1947, the Catholic Interracial Guild became the Catholic Interracial Council, affiliated with a network of such groups around the country organized by the Jesuit pioneer John LaFarge and his lay associate, George Hunston. The council met at the Foery Foundation building and its members were warmly supportive of Brady's work and received his advice in return. However, the council and foundation were distinct entities with somewhat different purposes, which became blurred in later years when racial issues moved to the forefront of Syracuse life. Brady was concerned primarily with bringing the Catholic faith to black people. The council was interested in promoting awareness of the problem of race among white Catholics and turning the spotlight to examples of

prejudice and injustice. Their programs drew increasing attention as they brought well known speakers to town, worked for revision of school texts and began to join civil rights groups in the struggle against discrimination.

By the early 1960s, Brady had become, through the force of personal example and the witness of his life, a major force in the diocese and in the city. The 5,000 blacks in post-war Syracuse had become 12,000 and the 27 practicing Catholics were now more than 400. There were 59 black children in 10 Catholic schools and the foundation building was a heavily used facility. There, the Catholic Interracial Council with its 180 members held its meetings and 240 children took classes in religion, music and crafts, watched movies, and organized plays and picnics, all under the supervision of 28 young men and women organized by Brady into the Don Bosco and Dominic Savio societies. At least 500 people attended the biannual dinners and were considered members of the foundation, while there were 200 women in an auxiliary of the foundation. There was now in the diocese a man, a group and a cause which would offer a somewhat different example of the Church, the presence of Christ, in Central New York.

Syracuse Catholicism was on the verge of a new era. So was the American Church. In 1960, John F. Kennedy was elected the first Catholic president of the United States. His election marked a milestone in American Catholic history. Once a tiny minority, later looked upon as a Church of foreigners whose teachings contradicted American democratic ideals, the Catholic Church was now an accepted and influential presence in the United States and in the towns and cities of Central New York. Now one of the Church's own was the president, admired for his youthful energy and idealism. John XXIII was the pope, and his warmth and openness already had signaled a new day. The American press and even Protestant church leaders seemed genuinely moved by the warm pope's smile, openness and goodwill. The pope and the president made Catholics feel proud. It seemed that the hard struggle of generations for freedom, prosperity, acceptance — all to be achieved while preserving the integrity of faith — had now somehow reached its climax.

The Church in Syracuse could share in that sense of accomplishment. Its churches and schools were everywhere, it seemed, sparkling in the sunshine, with the fresh bricks and soaring steeples uniting the old and the new, the most ancient of Christian faiths and the most modern of religious, educational and charitable facilities. The bishop and his priests were competent, respected and very much united to one another. The finances were solid, there were many vocations to the priesthood and the religious life, and prospects for the future seemed unlimited. And there were few loose ends. John Hughes' advice of long ago had been followed. The lines were drawn very tight. There were no dissident theologians, no passionate activists and almost no critical voices inside the Church. Here and there a priest attending liturgical conferences or working with the Christian Family Movement might have had some questions, and, at the Bishop Foery Foundation, the first shades of doubt fell across the hearts of a few committed people when fellow Catholics resisted the appeal for open housing. But by and large it was a very tight ship, firmly in the grasp of the captain. The old fights were over. The new ones had yet to begin.

NO LONGER
A PIONEER CHURCH

UNITY AND SOLIDARITY IN AN AGE OF EXPANSION
1940s-1950s

I n reporting to Rome in 1944 on the condition of his diocese, Bishop Foery wrote:

The morals of the people generally are good, founded in faith and religion. This is true of both private life in families as well as public morals in the towns and cities. At the present time we are deeply concerned about maintaining and deepening the religious bonds of private family life. We have pointed out repeatedly the sacred character of family life and its divine institution as the foundation of all well organized society—we have recalled the primary duty of parents in the care of their children and we feel that our efforts have been blessed with much fruit. The priests of the diocese have faithfully and strongly supported our efforts in these things. The faithful are founded in the true life of the spirit in all parts of the diocese—external pomp is very modest. The people manifest a deep reverence and frequently a holy affection for the clergy. They are most respectful, reverential and considerate toward the Bishop. We are deeply gratified with their devotion and love of our Holy Father.

Even granting the hyperbolic language which characterized such reports, Foery had every reason to feel gratified. The diocese of Syracuse had emerged from the depression with its finances under control, with a solid, united and well disciplined clergy, and with talented, loyal leadership. There were many things missing, of course. There was no Catholic college yet, no centers of the liturgical movement, no groups interested in what was coming to be called the "lay apostolate" and little social action. The absence of movements of that sort perhaps exaggerated the image of the Church as a "happy and peaceful society." So did the preoccupation of the Church with "private family life." The strong rhetoric about dangers to American democracy of the last decade was suspended in midair, never translated into significant pastoral action. Instead, religious life centered on schools, parishes and priests, and on organized Catholicism, at which the Syracuse diocese excelled.

Well organized as it was, the diocese was equipped to deal with the major facts of the post-war years — the rapid rise in population, especially of children, and the economic improvement and the opportunities for higher education for veterans which began to transform the Catholic population. Increased earning power and education also meant physical mobility, out of center cities and to the suburbs, where the children and grandchildren of the immigrants now required pastoral services. For the first time, the Church was there ahead of them. Rather than groups of lay people gathering for services, raising money and building churches, then begging for clergy, the diocese anticipated population growth, moved quickly to establish new parishes, and provided not only churches, but schools for its new middle class Americanized constituency. As Bishop Foery put it when launching a drive to renovate the cathedral in 1958, Syracuse was "no longer a pioneer diocese." The 1950s were the apex of American Catholic history, when church attendance reached all time highs and Catholicism demonstrated its capability of retaining the faith and loyalty of the new generation in an organized Church clearly and distinctively Catholic and now fully American as well.

The Catholic population of the diocese grew from 189,087 in 1940 to almost 350,000 in 1960 and the number of parishes from 136 in 1940, to 151 in 1950 and then to 162 in 1960. The trend was to larger parishes served by two or more priests in order to provide a sufficient base for parish schools. As a result average parish size rose steadily from 1,538 in 1940, to 1,770 in 1950, to 2,155 in 1960, the latter figure the highest ever recorded in the diocese. The overwhelming majority of this increase took place in territorial (rather than ethnic) parishes, which had accounted for only 58 percent of the Catholics in 1940, but in 1960, covered 72 percent.

In 1940, 61 percent of the children in parish schools were in territorial parishes, but by 1960 that figure had risen to 80 percent. German parishes, which had provided 18 percent of the diocesan population when it was founded in 1886, now accounted for only three percent. Polish parishes had accounted for 14 percent of the Catholics in 1917 but, although their numbers increased 30 percent between 1940 and 1960, their proportion of the diocesan population dropped to seven percent in 1960. Even the Italian parishes, which experienced vast improvement in the post-war years, had accounted for 23 percent of the Catholic population of the diocese in 1940. By 1960, that percentage dropped to 14 percent.

The parishes had never been better off financially. During the immediate post-war years, old debts maintained through the depression years were paid as the Church cut its ties to banks and outside lending agencies. With the return of prosperity, an enormous expansion took place. Total parish indebtedness of $1,200,000 in 1950 jumped to $6,700,000 in 1960. However, that debt was well secured. When Foery took over, two-

CHURCH RESOURCES			
	1917	1940	1960
Catholics	139,540	209,177	349,164
Parishes	101	136	162
Average parish size	1,381	1,538	2,155
Average parish debt	$12,783	$29,439	$41,393
Average parish receipts	$10,600	$16,000	$96,000

thirds of the parish debt was held by banks, insurance companies and other outside lending agencies. The Church succeeded in the 1950s in freeing itself from this dependence and financed its expansion with internal funds. Of the almost $3,500,000 in parish debt in 1957, only $357,000 came from outside; $1,500,000 came from other parishes, $763,000 from the three cemeteries of St. Mary's and St. Agnes' in Syracuse and Calvary in Utica, and $110,000 from Loretto Rest. In addition, the diocese itself had loaned parishes almost $700,000 from burses, the seminary fund, the diocesan needs collection, the House of Providence account and a variety of chancery accounts including the Grimes Foundation. In 1954, the chancery prepared a list of parishes with money to loan, some on a short-term basis because of their own future building plans. Those reserves totaled $1,687,000. Some parishes had large amounts of money available. Assumption of Binghamton topped the list with $180,000 while Sacred Heart of Syracuse followed with $121,000.

The truly startling increase came in donations to the Church. Total parish revenues were $2,187,000 in 1940. By 1950, they had risen to more than $5,500,000. Total parish income for 1955 was $8,600,000, of which a little more than $4,500,000 was ordinary income, with another $3,200,000 in extraor-

dinary income from building drives and special campaigns and approximately $860,000 in diocesan collections. In 1960, parish revenues reached $15,640,777, an increase over 20 years of 600 percent. Even when the figures are held in constant dollars, allowing for inflation, parish revenues increased three and one-half times. Average parish receipts, exclusive of special campaigns, were slightly more than $16,000 per parish in 1940. By 1960, they reached $96,548. In 1940, according to the figures supplied by the parishes to the chancery, diocesan rates of giving were $10.46 per capita. In 1950, they had reached $20.99. In 1960, per capita giving, exclusive of special drives and campaigns, was $44.79. Italian giving still lagged behind the diocese as a whole, but, between 1940 and 1960, per capita donations for regular church collections in Italian parishes rose from $3.56 to $25.57, a rate of increase considerably larger than the diocese as a whole. Eastern European parishes were even more astonishing. In the 10 Polish parishes of the diocese in 1960, per capita offerings were $54.61. In the two Lithuanian parishes, the average parishoner gave $71. Most remarkable were Slovak parishes, whose rate of giving in 1940 was already more than double the rate of the diocese. In 1960, the four Slovak parishes received slightly less than a million dollars in ordinary receipts from 8,108 parishioners, a per capita rate of $119.95.

All of this reflected the prosperity of the country and the region, and even more the rapid transformation of the Catholic people. Once a working class population who filled the blue-collar jobs in American industry, Catholics were enjoying a rapid ascent into the middle class. With the help of the G.I. Bill, young Catholics were attending college in ever larger numbers. Upon graduation, they began moving into managerial and professional positions, settling in new, suburban housing developments, and proceeding to have large families. By the 1960s, studies would begin to prove that Catholics had arrived. They were as likely to attend college as anyone else and some Catholic groups had surpassed even the mainline Protestants in income. Italians and Eastern European Catholics still lagged a bit behind the Irish and Germans in income and occupational status, but by the sixties they too were moving rapidly ahead. Even those who remained in blue collar, factory jobs participated in the prosperity of the period as the new unions, built in the 1930s, delivered ever improving wages and benefits. By the time John F. Kennedy was elected president in 1960, symbolically completing the Americanization of Catholics, the Catholic people while not exclusively middle class, had come to resemble in their class composition the society around them. Ethnic loyalty and working class status no longer made Catholics different. Increasingly, only religion did that.

One good example of these developments came in the suburbs of Binghamton. Shortly after the war, Monsignor Cunningham stated that this would be an area of more rapid growth than others, with IBM expanding production and purchasing land for home construction. He was right. In 1949, the new parish of Christ the King was established in Endwell, with Charles F. Aylesworth as pastor and its 700 parishioners drawn from St. Ambrose in Endicott. By 1956, Aylesworth

was begging for an assistant because he now had 2,000 parishioners and was saying three Masses each Sunday. At two of those Masses, chairs had to be set up in the choir and the sacristy. Even then, many were attending neighboring parishes. These parishoners were well off, too, and the pastor's financial reports drew praise from the bishop as evidence of the "generosity of your people." The praise was deserved. In 1950, the first full year of the parish, ordinary parish income was $6,600. By 1960, it passed $16,000. Even more dramatic was extraordinary income, most of which came from pledge drives. In 1950, this income was just short of $13,000. It rose to $20,000 in 1955, when Aylesworth's 2,000 parishioners, men women and children, contributed to all collections, parish and diocesan, an average of $200 per person. Contributions continued to rise, reaching $40,000 by 1959 and a whopping $64,000 in 1961. A $42,000 loan from St. Ambrose to begin the parish was paid off in 1955, and between 1956 and 1961, the parish added $210,000 to its own building fund. Money from the parish reserve fund was loaned to other parishes and some was made available for work on Seton High School in Endicott. In 1962, the parish announced plans for a $400,000 parochial school and convent. As the newspapers reported, this was further evidence of growth in the area. In addition to the older schools of St. Ambrose and St. Joseph's in Endicott, Good Counsel in West Endicott had opened a school a year earlier, St. Anthony of Padua recently had broken ground for a school and Our Lady of Sorrows in Vestal was beginning its plans to build one. The story was similar in Johnson City and in the major Syracuse suburbs like Liverpool.

Bishop Foery kept a close eye on these developments. He regularly praised pastors like Aylesworth whose performance was particularly outstanding, telling one, for example, that his annual report had given "this episcopal heart great joy." A report which showed a still large debt, in contrast, "staggered my courage and very definitely destroyed my appetite and sleep." He told one pastor:

It is my hope and prayer that [your people] they will help you immediately to obtain more funds so as not to be obliged to increase your debt further. I am writing this letter reluctantly as I do not like to cause anybody concern or worry. It is, however, true, that we will have more worry if we do not face the facts.

As Father Robert Driscoll once quoted Foery, a priest "cannot build without putting something of himself into it."

As these words indicate, money was a central preoccupation and often a measure of success and failure. Growth was so rapid, and the need for churches, schools and personnel to staff them so great that the role of lay people could easily, almost unconsciously, be defined in terms of "helping Father," largely by giving money. "PARTICIPATION," the pastor of St.Vincent's in Syracuse wrote in his announcement book in May 1947, then added:

To administer a parish is serious business. Indeed to look after all the interests of the parish often requires a business executive, theologian, and the canniness of a financier rolled into one. Generally your priests have willing hands to help in their parish duties and in no sense can they be more willing or more welcome than in a generous, steady financial support. To help in parish business is to participate in the divine mission of the church.

A period of prosperity, with its ever escalating demands, brought to such priests, on whose shoulders so much responsibility

rested, anxiety in many ways as intense as that of the depression years. Facing the budget for his school for the coming year, one pastor told the bishop, "it scares me truthfully." Apparently the bishop encouraged him to set the problems directly before his people. In a very long letter to his people, the pastor explained in great detail the problems of the parish and school, attributing them to rising costs and giving habits which remained the same as 20 or 30 years before. Of the 296 families with children in the school, 22 did not have envelopes, another 15 did not use them and 185 did not contribute enough to cover the cost of their child's education, which the previous year had been $153.49 and would rise the following year to $185.95. Only 47 couples exceeded that amount. In a typical week, 14 gave $10 3-$19, 1-$8, 5-$7, 4-$6, 47-$5, 15- $4, 162-$2, 95- $1.50, 705-$1, 89-$.75, 456-$.50, 15- $.35, 106-$.25, and 145 gave less than $.25. Apparently his appeal worked, but other parishes abandoned such pleading and hired professional firms who conducted campaigns which successfully doubled or tripled weekly giving. The spirit of such drives was captured in a box prominently featured on page one of a leaflet handed to parishioners during a door to door appeal:

Must I be giving again and again forever? 'Oh, no', said the Angel—and his glance pierced me through—'Just give till the Master stops giving to you'.

Even Bishop Foery was not immune. When he joined the people of Blessed Sacrament in Utica for a "Thank You" celebration at the end of a fundraising drive for a new church in 1954, Forey told the people the parish was "really the whole church in miniature." To be complete, it needed three elements, and Foery stated them in order. First, "there must be a school where we are taught the doctrine of the Savior, where the law is made known and emphasized, where we are alerted to our spiritual wants and necessities." Second, there had to be a the priest, a dispenser of the mercy of God who applied the grace of the redeemer and worked for the salvation of souls. Finally, "in the parish there must be a church," with the altar and tabernacle. Schools, priests and churches, it seemed, made a parish, and they all cost money. Providing that money in what the bishop called "constant activity" was closely connected to the life of faith.

When pastors were too cautious, Foery told them that building and renovation could "deepen the devotion and increase the generosity of parishioners." In contrast, when parishes were too eager, Foery told them too large a debt could have the opposite effect. "We are not concerned about building monuments," he wrote in one case. "To build a church that would be beyond the capacity of the people would add nothing to religion. It would destroy it." Perhaps realizing that his own concern with financial stability might contribute to a confusion of means and ends, Foery told one pastor: "We are not expected to construct buildings that last for eternity, but we are expected to build the faith in people for eternity."

THE PERSISTENCE OF PLURALISM

Burned by the embarrassing conflicts with ethnic parishes during the years between the war years, the diocese anticipated problems as the national parishes moved into a new generation. As in the past, the direction of Church policy was to phase out these parishes by encouraging English speaking children to attend territorial churches. At clergy conferences in 1944, Monsignor Cunningham explained that the territorial parish was the "ideal." National parishes for immigrants

were provided "until these people should become adapted to the customs and ways of their new country." Children had the right, however, to join a territorial parish. The only question was how. So the bishop promulgated procedures by which a person formally could affiliate with the parish in the neighborhood by submitting a card, after which the pastor was to notify the pastor of the national parish the person had attended previously. The attention to this matter indicated a desire on the part of the diocese to encourage English speaking children to affiliate with the territorial parish, although as yet no further moves were made to push such movement.

Another possibility, given the rapid increase in population, was to change the status of some national parishes to territorial. In 1948, the bishop read an article which claimed that bishops could allow people other than Germans to become members of German national parishes. He wrote the rector of St. Bernard's to inquire whether this was true. The question was important in Syracuse, he said, because there were three or four national parishes which should become territorial "if they are to get the most good from their parish plants" and serve their people efficiently, although "the territorial pastors are decidedly opposed to any change in the present arrangements." Perhaps for that reason, no direct steps were taken in this direction.

As in the past, prosperity eased interparish rivalries, as the growing sea of donations at least temporarily raised all the ships. Despite the Americanization of their people and the attitude of diocesan leaders, ethnic diversity flourished in post-war America. Perhaps the most startling of all post-war developments was the vigor of Eastern Rite churches. Father Lahoud of St. Louis Gonzaga achieved a spectacular success when he persuaded Cardinal Eugene Tisserant, the Maronite head of the Vatican Congregation for the Eastern Churches, to visit Utica for the ceremonial

Cardinal Eugene Tisserant, head of the Vatican Congregation for the Eastern Churches, was close to the hearts of Maronite Catholics at St. Louis Gonzaga parish in Utica. In 1954, he sent this Christmas photo to the parish, with an inscription written in French, "To my dear Monsignor Francis Lahoud, asking God to bless you and all your parishioners, the faithful Maronites of Utica." Cardinal Tisserant later visited the Utica parish. (Photo: St. Louis Gonzaga parish)

burning of the parish's mortgage in 1947. Despite Bishop Foery's reservations, St. Basil's Melkite parish finally built a new church. In Johnson City, Sacred Heart Ukrainian Rite church worked for 30 years to raise money for a lovely cedar church, beautifully decorated and furnished, which opened at last in 1977. Foery, like his predecessors, disliked the vigilance of the Eastern Rite clergy, especially

when they insisted on the strict interpretation of marriage laws requiring the couple to follow the groom's rite. "We have, as yet, found no way of preventing our Latin boys and girls from falling in love with the boys and girls of other rites," the bishop told the New York vicar general in 1957. "Nor do we have any way of prevailing upon them, in all instances, to have their marriages performed in the rite of the groom. I am hoping that some day Holy Mother the Church will permit the parties to make their own choice." Yet the bishop must have admired the vigor and determination of these parishes, preserving the loyalty and dedication of so many even as they became more and more Americanized. One proud Ukrainian priest, interviewed at the dedication of Sacred Heart's new church, spoke for generations of ethnic Catholics. "Every church we build in America is another sign that we are not giving up," he said. "We are like the anvil and the hammer."

Other groups might have said the same. For Polish Catholics, the war was an experience of struggle which touched their national roots and did not end in 1945, as their homeland fell under Soviet domination. Between 1943 and 1950, Syracuse Polish Catholics raised large amounts of money for the Catholic League for Religious Aid to Poland, ranking the diocese 13 among 83 dioceses in the county which participated. The Church by now clearly had won the struggle for influence in the local Polish community. In 1954, Monsignor Piejda of Sacred Heart reported to the bishop that there were only five tiny congregations of the schismatic Polish National Catholic Church in the diocese, with from 35 to 60 families each. In contrast, Sacred Heart in Syracuse had 1,800 families; St. Stanislaus in Binghamton, 700 families; Transfiguration, Rome, 600; Holy Trinity in Utica, 1,800; St. Stanislaus in Utica, 350; and St. Mary's in New York Mills, 700.

In 1939, Piejda had succeeded Francis

Rusin as pastor at Sacred Heart. After quickly paying off the large parish debt, he made expensive renovations of $150,000, and in 1953 opened the $380,000 Sacred Heart Academy, the first Polish parish high school in the state and the only parish high school opened in the city after the war. Similar prosperity was evident elsewhere. When John Kociela became pastor of Transfiguration in Syracuse, he rejuvenated the parish societies, formed a Polish American Catholic Club and began a harvest festival similar to that celebrated by the people of Poland. In November 1945, parishioners burned the mortgage on their old church and almost immediately began planning a new one. With the help of the harvest festival, bingo, bake sales and other fundraising events, they completed a new $650,000 church in 1956. The debt was paid within six years. Transfiguration in Rome grew to 3,000 parishoners, built a convent, opened a summer camp, Camp Polonia, and enlarged the church and rectory. In 1958, the parish purchased the former Rome trade school for $25,000, and, in a "do it yourself project," transformed the building into a sparkling new elementary school. Holy Trinity in Utica also showed few signs of decline. Plans for a new school started in the spring of 1959. An impressive facility was provided, which with its furnishings eventually cost more than $500,000 dollars. Enrollment never again approached the level of the 1930s, when it had more than 1,000 students, but the school remained strong, with smaller classes and much improved facilities. An active Legion of Mary group visited the sick, underprivileged and homebound, while a variety of sodalities raised money for the parish and missions.

The post-war years were even more exciting for Italian parishes. More than any other group, the Italians had been slow to develop parishes and schools. Much progress was made during the thirties, but expansion of

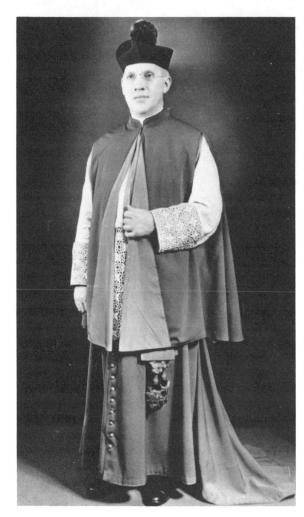

Monsignor Casimir S. Piedja, pastor of Sacred Heart parish in Syracuse, was a recognized leader among Catholics of Polish heritage throughout the diocese. (Photo: The Catholic Sun)

parish facilities was limited by the depression, which had a severe impact on the heavily working-class Italian population. St. Mary of Mount Carmel in Utica was serving 3,000 families in the 1940s, making it perhaps the largest parish in the diocese. Long marked by energetic and innovative pastoral outreach, the parish faced new problems with the war, when many men were in the service and their wives entered war-time jobs. In September 1943, the parish opened a day care center staffed by Franciscan sisters, assisted by lay volunteers, to provide care for the pre-school children of working mothers. After the war, Mount Carmel, like all Italian parishes, found the young veterans and their families more prosperous, and more enthusiastic about the Church, than their parents. There and elsewhere, long-delayed plans for churches, schools and parish centers finally came to fruition. At St. Joseph's in Oswego, Monsignor Jeremiah Davern purchased land for a parish house from the Masonic Lodge. However, when Bishop Foery visited the parish in 1949 for confirmation, he told the new pastor, Francis J. Furfaro, that they should consider not a parish house, but a new church. In 1951, the parish had $110,000 in its building fund and the time seemed ripe.

Plans were drawn up for a 600-seat church and the parishoners agreed to a drive for $125,000, launched at the end of May. A total of $210,000 in pledges was received, and the building opened in 1958. In Cortland, the people of St. Anthony's had been worshiping in their former spaghetti factory since 1917. Throughout the thirties, the parish worked to raise money to continually improve the church, but after the war it was clear that it was too small. The old structure was demolished. The parish worshiped in the county court house until a new building was ready

A MONUMENT TO SACRIFICE

When St. Stanislaus Kostka parish in Binghamton gathered to commemorate their new church in 1954, a banquet booklet contained the following tribute:

"Our parishioners are proud of their new church, and rightly so. It is indeed, a monument to their efforts over the years. The parish has made great strides spiritually, and has amassed much valuable property. It is a tribute to the impelling forces of love of God and love of freedom which inspired the early parishioners to make sacrifices, in order to express their allegiance to God, and to express the beauty of their souls. To sacrifice something, such as a donation or an offering, means to deny oneself something necessary or something legitimate, and to offer it to God through one's church. To sacrifice something means to give till and when it hurts. That is real love of God, or of country. So, as much as it is desirable, it is most difficult to enumerate names of all who labored and sacrificed, to have a parish church, rectory, school, and convent, at last, in St. Stanislaus Kostka parish in Binghamton.

"Sacred with us all is the memory of parishioners who departed, many of whom have yearned to see the new church. Let us keep their example of fortitude in mind. Likewise, it is fitting to show due respect to the living organizers of the parish. For the parishioners of the future, it is well to keep in mind that our fathers built this parish to provide for us a house of worship and a place for education. They were not selfish. They sacrificed because they loved God, and they loved their children. Now, it is the duty and obligation of parishioners to maintain all the church property, and to support the parish in a proper manner, and to assist in parish undertakings when asked to do so, so that in that way we shall be faithful to the memory of our fathers who did such great things for us.

"May Almighty God reward and bless every one who sacrificed and offered something to make the new church a reality. Only in this manner could it have been built. And, hope your happiness and joy to-night are complete!"

for its dedication, appropriately on St. Anthony's day, June 13, 1951.

Perhaps the most dramatic changes came at St. John the Baptist in Rome. In 1925, the parish financial report showed receipts of $6,800. Two decades later, during the war, that figure was still only $13,700. In addition to a small church, there was the center where the Parish Visitors provided religious instruction for 1,600 children. In 1940, Father Edward O'Connell, assistant to Father Panesi, who served as pastor from 1917 to 1944, began organizing the parish young people into a Catholic Youth Organization. The CYO sponsored highly successful dances, picnics, athletic teams and concerts by well known artists like Louis Armstrong and Glen Gray. After the war, as these youth activities continued, the graduates became active members of the Catholic War Veterans, the Mothers Club and Holy Name Society, and the parish sprang to life. Under a new pastor, Father Victor Ciciarelli, receipts rose to $44,000 in 1945, and the next year a building drive for a new church was launched. Even now it was not easy, and Ciciarelli could use the old lash of national embarrassment. "The Italians of Rome are all talk and no action," one letter from the pastor and building committee read. "You've been talking about building a new church for the last three years and what have you done about it? You've pledged $150,000 and paid only half the amount. All talk and no action." But action there was, with the carrots of dances, fairs, festivals, CYO concerts and fireworks displays and the stick of shame, as when the pastor said he would not sign the membership cards for the Knights of Columbus men who did not attend church. The goal of $400,000 was reached, and the new church opened in May 1954, when six Masses drew more than 5,000 people.

The struggle of the Church to gain control over Italian religious life was all but complete.

In 1944, the Cosmos and Damian Society of St. Anthony's in Endicott complained to the bishop that the pastor would not allow them, on the saints' feast day, to remove the statues from their place of honor in the church to one where they would be exposed to veneration by the people, in other words, to allow the traditional procession to take place. "After God, we love and venerate our patron saints with all our hearts," they wrote. Foery was unmoved, responding with full support for the pastor. The important thing was not the veneration of the saints, Foery wrote, "but the imitation of their virtues and our submission to the authorities of the church." A similar problem at St. Anthony's in Utica led a group of laymen to write the apostolic delegate. When queried by the bishop, the pastor explained that, once the people understood that the proceeds did not go to the church, they had withdrawn their support from the Cosmos and Damian society and "come to the church," and the observance of the feast was "now completely in the field of religion." Still, even Foery thought some pastors went too far. When a new church was built at St. Anthony's in Cortland, some statues were removed. After talking with an angry parishioner, the bishop recommended that the pastor explain that he understood "how dear these statues are to them." While it was not "in accord with the architecture" to have them in the new church, they should be kept carefully in the basement and brought out on their respective feast days.

American Catholicism before the Second Vatican Council was changing dramatically, In the new suburban parishes in Liverpool or Johnson City, Irish, Italian, Polish and Slovak names showed up indiscriminately on the parish rolls. Leaving behind the old neighborhood and the nationality-shaped parish, these people were building new communities that were definitely Catholic and very American, but no longer "ethnic" as well. Yet the old national parishes were far from dead. Some flourished in stable neighborhoods, others retained the loyalty even of a more dispersed population by gradually changing in style and priorities, accommodating new needs and interests. Holding fast to tradition, these parishes provided a continuing identity, a special and unique way of being American and Catholic. In an anniversary volume prepared for their Golden Jubilee in 1960, the Polish parishoners of Our Lady of Chestochowa, St. Mary's, of New York Mills described their parish as one where sermons now were said in English at two Masses each Sunday but Polish language remained and Polish customs and traditions were observed. The parish included many who still did not have sufficient command of English to benefit fully from services in other parishes. But there were also Catholics of Polish descent who spoke English quite well, but preferred to pray, sing, listen to sermons and make their confession in Polish. Justly proud of their thousand-year heritage, they did not want to deprive themselves or their children of "those great treasures." Instead, they "wanted to create in their own souls a harmony of their Catholic, American and Polish spiritual heritage." In the words of Pope Pius XII, they knew that their peculiar blend of Catholicism and nationality was "not a breaking of Catholic unity but a sharing of peculiar gifts." The role of national parishes in the past, and of their Americanizing descendants, could not have been stated better:

A man of three cultures may better reflect the infinite fullness of God's perfection than a man with only one. There is no one culture, no one rite, no one language, no one work of art, no one saint, no one form of Catholicism, whether Italian, French, Irish or Polish, that could adequately represent

God's immense riches of wisdom and beauty. Each of them reflects only one aspect of his infinity.

It was a statement of the value of diversity which would have to be re-learned, in new situations, in the years ahead.

BUSY PARISHES

In all parishes, national and territorial, the basic routines of parish life were those which had taken clear shape by the end of World War I. At St. John the Evangelist in January 1941, for example, there were five Sunday morning Masses, beginning at eight o'clock. Benediction of the Blessed Sacrament took place at three o'clock on Sunday afternoon. In many places, it was held in the evening. Vespers had all but disappeared. Baptisms were performed at four o'clock; confessions were heard from four o'clock to 5:30 and 7:30 to nine o'clock on Saturdays and the days before Holy Days of Obligation and First Fridays. Sunday school classes were held after the nine o'clock Mass, while religious instruction for public elementary school children was offered Tuesday at 2:30. Junior and senior high attended released time classes. At St. Vincent's, a similar routine was supplemented by a continuing series of dances and card parties, raffles and food sales. The three or four priests who served under Monsignor McPeak at the cathedral referred to that parish as a "religious supermarket," with the usual numerous Sunday services, three morning, one noon time and one evening Mass daily, a host of novenas and devotions, visiting responsibilities at the two Catholic hospitals and calls at the non-Catholic hospitals in the city, a parochial school and released time programs for downtown high school and elementary schools. Cathedral priests also could be asked to serve as chaplains to police and fire departments, and National Guard units, and to deliver invocations at almost daily civic events and service club programs.

One parish, St. John's in Oswego, described the activities of a typical busy parish in the 1950s. The "regular religious activities" included, besides Masses, confessions, baptisms, marriages and funerals, "Christmas Midnight Masses," Forty Hours devotions, missions and mission projects, Lenten services, confirmations and May crownings. The altar guild held monthly meetings, communion breakfasts, Christmas parties, covered dish suppers, banquets, bake sales, clothing drives and fall festivals. The Legion of Mary sponsored prayer and rosary devotions, visited the sick and needy, and assisted junior organizations for girls and young women. The school auxiliary sold cookbooks, held rummage sales, Christmas parties, pantry parties, an annual Silver Tea Benefit for the sisters, and altar boy and choir banquets. The Holy Name sponsored parish parties, communion breakfasts, father-son banquets and helped paint, shingle and otherwise maintain the church, school, convent and rectory. The men worked hard at the regular fund drives as well. During the period, St. John's continually worked to improve its physical facilities. One report gave a three year summary:

Mention should be made of the many improvements to the church, rectory, school and the Convent. A list would include the following: New gas boiler for the church, gas conversion in school boiler, new gas water heater in the school and rectory; plumbing, such as, lavatories in the vestibule of the church, renovation of plumbing in the rectory, school and Convent; electrical, such as, rewiring of the church with a new control panel installed, school rewired with added fluorescent light; repairs, such as, pointing steeples, caulking, new roof, new glass doors in the vestibule of the church, chain

fence, enlarging of the garage, also a passage way through it connecting the rectory and the church; in the school, setting up of smoke barriers, including fire resistant materials, automatic fire detection system, a new kitchen and renovation of the hall at a cost of $9,500, classrooms painted, floors refinished.

All this supported the sacramental life of the parish. Nationally, Mass attendance reached all-time highs, and similar devotion was evident in the diocese. In 1960, Father Harold Quinn of St. John's found that, of his 1,242 parishioners, "good, bad and indifferent," 90 percent had made their Easter duty, while 79 percent attended Sunday Mass weekly and 26 percent received communion every month, the latter considered quite an acceptable figure in the days before the Vatican Council. Quinn was an excellent pastor, and he knew well that these figures revealed only "one aspect of the spiritual condition of the parish." It indicated little of the "spirituality," which "may be lax, superficial, deep or shallow." After all, he warned, "when things seem too good, the devil is usually very active."

The Eucharist was far and away the most important element of parish life. Reception of communion was a major measure of piety. Benediction, forty hours and a variety of novenas centered on the Divine Presence. When the tabernacle containing the hosts and the sacred vessels were stolen from St. Anthony's in Endicott in 1943, people filled the church at Masses of reparation for the desecration of the sacred hosts. Out of the tragedy, according to the pastor, came "a great increase in awareness of the presence of Christ in our churches and a great renewal of devotion." Given this devotion to the Eucharist, pastors expected not only attendance, but decorum, at Mass. The pastor of St.

AN ACTIVE PARISH

Parishes are centers of much activity for Catholics — building friendships, deepening faith, helping others. Consider, for example, St. Patrick's in Binghamton. In the 1960s it had a full schedule of activities for its 3,000 members served by a pastor, two associates, and another priest in residence.

Each Sunday was a time for five Masses. Daily there were two morning Masses, another at noon, and a final one in the later afternoon, with extra Masses on First Fridays. Confessions were held Saturday afternoon and evening and on the eve of holydays. A regular novena of the Miraculous Medal was held Monday evening, with Exposition of the Blessed Sacrament on First Friday and First Saturday. Baptism, confirmation, marriages, and funerals were arranged regularly, and priests frequently visited hospitalized or shut-in parishioners.

Parish societies provided for a full range of activity — adult choir, Altar and Rosary Society, altar boys, Catholic Youth Organization, athletic teams, dances, picnics, and excursions. There also was a Holy Name Society for men, a Golden Age Club, parents guild, Nocturnal Adoration Society, parish senate, and ushers club.

A most important parish organization was the Confraternity of Christian Doctrine, with several groupings:

—Teachers division for the parish school of religion;

—Parent Educators division to promote Christian home life, prepare Cana conferences, and help parents participate in the religious education of their children;

—Helpers division to provide clerical assistance, transportation, babysitting, and other aid to the religious education program;

—Fishers division as parish ambassadors to visit newcomers, seek out alienated or lapsed Catholics, help with the parish census, and promote attendance at religious instruction or adult faith programs;

—Apostles of Good Will division to invite non-Catholics to open houses and religious services and to organize small dialogue groups in the neighborhoods.

Monsignor Frank Harrison, the pastor, wrote in an outline of parish services: "We are very happy to have you as a member of our Parish family. We have a varied program of spiritual, educational, cultural and social activities that are available to you. By joining in these activities, you will become better parishioners. These are times which demand of us an unmistaken loyalty to what we believe.... You will make new friends, and we can all work together for the glory of God and the salvation of our own souls. The time you spend with the parish family will be an unforgettable experience of your Catholic faith."

Vincent's in Syracuse, Father Oley, had a particular problem with people who left before Mass was over. "Spiritual yokels" he called them in 1945. "The assumption is they have to go early to feed the ducks." A year later he was equally incensed about people who arrived late. "HEY, YOU'RE LATE" he wrote in large letters in his announcement book for September 8, 1946. Mass "begins with the prayers at the foot of the altar and it ends when the priest leaves the sanctuary," he explained more calmly. Missing any part of the Mass "can be sinful, mortal or venial," depending on whether one missed the minor or major parts of the Mass. "To miss all the prayers before the offertory, or all after communion," was a mortal sin. Yet "our rush order Catholics do that many a Sunday. Do they return for another mass?" It was a rhetorical question.

For years, diocesan leaders had sought to improve the devotional life of the diocese by improving the quality of church music. Foery did not slacken in his predecessors' determination to produce first rate church music. Father Gerard Horan was diocesan director of music and head of the priests' choir when Foery arrived, but he resigned for health reasons within a few years. Foery then sent Father James Callaghan to study liturgical music at Manhattanville College and, in 1942, named him music director for the diocese. When Callaghan resigned 11 years later, the bishop applauded the "rapid progress" in church music during his leadership. Foery described the directives of Pius X as a call not to sing at Mass, but to "sing the Mass." Congregational singing was to "be encouraged as much as possible," a goal pursued in the energetic music education program in diocesan schools. Yet, although Syracuse enjoyed a national reputation for its efforts to improve the quality of authorized church music, the result was not entirely satisfactory. Father William Shannon, who directed the music commission after Callaghan, regularly worried about the lack of male voices for choirs, the loss of interested men at the age when their voices changed, and the general indifference of pastors and people to congregational participation. In a candid moment, Foery noted in 1953: "It must be admitted that our church music has not developed over

the years in parallel with our church buildings and furniture. Little has been done to make the music of the Liturgy more beautiful and Catholic."

If eucharistic devotion, especially at Mass, was at the heart of Catholic life, devotion to Mary had become almost as important. In 1946 the Holy See was considering the formal proclamation of the bodily assumption of the Blessed Virgin as a doctrine of the Church. Inquiries were sent to the bishops of the world asking about the state of Marian devotion. Rome need not have worried about devotion to Mary in the diocese of Syracuse. The month of May was celebrated in the parishes with considerable enthusiasm, while the praying of the rosary during October and throughout the year was enormously popular. At the cathedral the annual May Day service was well attended. Marian societies were active in parishes, and in Utica, the alumnae of the College of St. Rose sponsored an annual May Day parade in which 20,000 to 30,000 people joined. It was followed by a large prayer service in a local stadium which regularly received front page coverage in the local press. Throughout the 1950s, the bishop gave this event his unequivocal support, despite a ban on processions applied to the popular devotion of Italian Catholics.

Perhaps most impressive was the growth of the Legion of Mary, which the bishop called "the most important form of Catholic Action" in the diocese. It had begun locally in Binghamton in 1945 and was established formally in the diocese in 1949. The legion was built on parish units, called praesidia, and diocesan units, called curia. Members were dedicated to personal sanctification and active cooperation "in Mary's and the Church's work of crushing the head of the serpent and advancing the reign of Christ." The first annual report listed among their parish works taking the parish census, visiting homes to encourage "lax Catholics" to return to

Church and to recruit children for religious education, visits to hospitals, institutions and shut ins, supervision of the whole range of youth activities from nurseries during Sunday Mass through parish youth councils, encouragement of parish devotions and home devotions like the "block rosary," teaching Sunday School, recruiting members for parish societies, distributing Catholic literature, maintaining pamphlet racks, and helping with the care of the altar and parish records. Through the 1950s, more and more parish praesidia were organized, and Foery gave the legion his strongest blessing. In 1958, he told a legion group that it was the "orderly and ordered battle array of the church militant," an appropriate military metaphor for a Church which saw itself as the surest support of American ideals and Christian values. It also reflected accurately the diocesan approach to the lay apostolate, solidly located in the parishes, helping the priests.

PRIESTS AT THE CENTER

Bishop Foery, as we have seen, had a high view of the priesthood, almost identifying it with the Church, leaving little room for laity or religious. Addressing the Franciscans on the centennial of their establishment in Syracuse, he said:

The history of the Catholic Church is essentially the history of the priesthood, since priests are the living instruments through whose ministry Christ's mystical presence abides in the church until the end of time. The priest is accredited teacher of the word of God. He is the dispenser of the mysteries of God. He is the witness of Christ. Where the spirit of priestly life flourishes, there the church flourishes. Where it grows cold, lifeless and indifferent, there the church suffers tremendous loss. Destroy the pri-

esthood and the bond between heaven and earth is broken.... The history of the priesthood, fascinating and unique as it is, is the history of the church.

These were strong words, placing great responsibility on the priests of the diocese and the bishop, whose care for his local Church began with his supervision of the clergy on whom it all depended.

Foery delegated many of his responsibilities to subordinates, but he took personal charge of the clergy. He examined parish reports closely and did not hesitate to send along comments. The building commission kept watch over any expenditure of more than $1,000. If a pastor wished to install a new heating system or paint a building, he needed permission. Foery was a man of detail, and his advisers were masters of such matters. During the bishop's parish visits, usually at confirmation, diocesan officials examined the parish accounts and the parish property.

One pastor was told to purchase a new tabernacle veil, another to replace the worn carpets in the church. Painting, roof repairs, paving of driveways and parking lots, all were matters for resolution after the bishop's visit. In addition the pastor needed numerous permissions for dispensations, from reading the marriage bans for three weeks, for any form of mixed marriage, for celebrating Mass in a private home, for exemptions from fasting regulations. Placing an altar or stations of the cross in a convent, and celebrating a wedding on Sunday, all had to be cleared. Even the inventory of the pastor's possessions, submitted on taking charge of a parish, might draw a comment. When one pastor's list covered three single-spaced, typed pages, and included cordial glasses, and silver salt and pepper shakers, a diocesan official suggested that some of it be given away or be purchased by the parish.

Clerical dress and behavior was also the

subject of strict regulation. Priests were required to wear the cassock and the biretta. "The posture of the priest in the sanctuary should be as dignified when sitting as when he kneels, avoiding in particular the crossing of knees, or slouching, as if in an easy chair," Monsignor Dillon told a clergy conference in 1952. "The minister of Christ, in the presence of his God, should evidence his faith by his posture as well as by his words." They were expected to wear black suits on the street and required at all times to wear the Roman collar. The "preservation of clerical dignity, as evident in clerical attire, was a matter of serious obligation," according to Dillon. The priest was a source of scandal to the laity and to non-Catholics when he appeared in public "without the Roman collar or even lacking any semblance of clerical attire." Dillon particularly criticized "those who imitate the college student by dispensing with the hat and those who smoke on the street."

The public life of the priest also was circumscribed. No priest from outside the diocese could speak within it without the bishop's permission, and none within it could speak publicly without prior approval. Nor could any priest accept "any temporal office in a secular organization," nor become a member of any "so-called fraternal organization, except those which are established under Catholic auspices." On ordination, the priest was presumed to have voluntarily surrendered the right of free speech. "Without prejudicing in any way the civil rights of the priest, we forbid any priest of the diocese to enroll as a member of any society which is merely political; nor shall any priest give a public address on political matters without first having consulted the Bishop."

Bishop Foery was attentive to his priests' continuing education, especially through the semi-annual clergy conferences, which he attended and made mandatory for priests. Ordinarily, one session each year dealt with a

344

As chancellor and later as vicar general, Monsignor Robert E. Dillon tried to encourage priests with a view of the Catholic Church beyond the diocese's seven counties. (Photo: The Catholic Sun)

theological problem and one with a pastoral question. In 1949, for example, the subjects were papal infallibility and canonical penalties against communists. In an address at a 1952 clergy conference, Monsignor Robert Dillon emphasized the need for priests, like lawyers or doctors, to keep abreast of the ecclesiastical sciences which they were applying.

Yet these clerical conferences evidenced an understanding of priestly learning which reflected the certainty and confidence of the post-war church. However, these conferences hardly introduced the priests to theological speculation or to the underlying conflicts in scripture studies, historical theology or ecclesiology which would burst into the open at Vatican II and challenge the intellectual as well as the pastoral capacity of the local priesthood. Monsignor Dillon's 1951 paper of Pope Pius XII's new encyclical, *Humani Generis,* for example, admirably summarized that document's warning against modern theological and philosophical errors. However, few Syracuse priests were familiar with modern scripture studies, the "new theology," existentialism or process philosophy which had occasioned the encyclical. Dillon closed by expressing gratitude to the Holy Father for steering the straight path through the errors of modern thought. "Our theology is like the mile posts which mark the highway and which we seldom even look at when we know the road, yet it is a source of confidence to know that they are there when we become confused," he concluded. Unfortunately, few became "confused" and felt a need to "look" at the "mile posts," much less at the holes in the road.

For all the limitations of this clerical culture, there can be little doubt of the high quality of diocesan pastoral work. The Syracuse clergy in the diocese were almost exclusively involved in parish life. Of the 308 priests of the diocese in 1943, only 27, less than 10 percent, were religious, and, of those, 21 were involved in parish work. If the 20 chaplains and sick, retired and absent priests are excluded, a whopping 227 of 246, or 90 percent, of diocesan clergy was either pastors or assistants. Moreover, Syracuse priests were now home-grown. Ninety-two percent of the 358 priests in the diocese in 1950 were born in the United States. Sixty percent were born in the diocese. They were also older. The average age rose from 39 in 1940, to 45 in 1960. Only 33 percent were less than 40, compared to 50 percent two decades earlier. More and more had a similar educational experience as well. In 1940, approximaely one-half of the diocesan priests had been educated at St. Bernard's in Rochester. By 1950, that figure had risen to 55 percent and, by 1960, to 64 percent. They enjoyed the admiration of the community at large, and the respect and affection of their people, largely because they were excellent pastors. Years later, Bishop Cunningham, who was so much a part of this generation of priests, described the heart of priestly ministry in terms of presence and care at moments of marriage, birth, family crisis and death.

Most of all, the priesthood was a total, lifelong celibate commitment. The realities of Church life in the fifties were filled with buildings and budgets, mortgages and contracts, heavily attended Masses, constantly increasing demand for a variety of sacramental, devotional, educational and social services, and an overreaching conviction that the Church stood as the most solid defender of American values and the strongest bulwark against communism. The bishop insisted however, that the commitment of the priest and his ability to persevere in that commitment rested upon the spiritual life, on prayer, meditation and spiritual reading. At a 1958 clergy conference he warned the priests against reading what would tempt them to sins of the flesh, and against hobbies and recreation which would make their priestly duties secondary. Despite the pressures of the organization and the constituency to become successful through growth, administrative ability or popularity, the bishop warned: "Do not make the externals the occupation, do not become absorbed in the social problems of the day (because) these can destroy the proper perspective of the priest. Always

In the 1940s and 1950s, an average of eight or nine priests were ordained each year for the Syracuse diocese. But expanding needs and a focus on an almost exclusively clerical leadership caused worries of too-few priests for the diocese. (Photo: Chancery Archives)

remember there is an altar, a confessional." There is no way to measure the inner spiritual life of the priests, but they served diligently and competently at the altar and in the confessional, they persevered in their commitment and, if their people were the judge, they met their responsibilities superbly.

The Syracuse clergy were good at their job, but there was never enough of them. Between 1941 and 1960, 173 priests were ordained for the diocese. Yet the bishop and his staff constantly complained that the number of clergy was not adequate. The sense of urgency seemed most strong in the early fifties. During the war years, 45 men were ordained to the priesthood, an average of nine a year. A sharp drop-off occurred after the war. Between 1946 and 1953, only 38 men were ordained. In the three years of 1951 to 1953, only 10 were ordained. In 1949 and again in 1954, Bishop Foery took the extraordinary step of requesting permission from Rome to ordain some seminarians before they finished their studies. Then, as the results of the post-war revival of religion began to be felt, ordinations jumped dramatically. Two years after the 1952 low point of one ordination, Bishop Foery ordained 19 men to his diocesan priesthood. In 1955, 16 were ordained and in 1956, 18, dropping then to 13 in 1959 and 11 in 1960. In the six years from 1954 to 1959, a total of 95 ordinations took place, an average of nearly 16 a year, far beyond any previous figure in diocesan history.

Nevertheless, expanding needs and the weight of contemporary understanding of clerical leadership made the shortages of clergy a neverending problem. Foery continually urged his priests to work for vocations. The frequency with which he spoke to them on the subject indicates he was not satisfied they were doing their best. Foery also hoped to take up a project long considered in the diocese, to begin its own seminary. As late as 1965, he responded to a request for funds from Catholic Charities that "the building of a diocesan seminary" had "the first claim on my support." However, the plan was not brought to fulfillment until after Vatican II when Aquinas House was established for college-level candidates.

At Foery's request in 1962, Father Joseph Champlin diocesan director of vocations, conducted a detailed study and proposed a vastly expanded vocations program. It would designate certain priests to give vocation talks to both Catholic and public school youngsters on a continuing basis. By assigning them to specific parishes and schools, and providing them with written materials, they could follow up these talks with visits and counseling.

Champlin suggested that these talks include the opportunity for students to express an interest, and that those doing so be contacted and put on the mailing list for a regular vocations newsletter. In addition, he urged the bishop to forbid the practice of confining altar boy service to students from Catholic schools because statistics indicated that 90% of the local priests once had served on the altar. He also thought the diocese should encourage formation of a chapter of Serra International, a men's service club dedicated to promoting vocations, a project Foery preferred to postpone until their program was functioning smoothly. He did take up some of Champlin's other suggestions, and organized a club for interested young men, but by that time new forces were at work which would transform the problem before the end of the decade.

SIGNS OF CHANGE

There were signs of change on the horizons, some coming from Rome, but neither Bishop Foery nor his priests were yet alert to them. This complacency became evident in 1958, when a parishioner, Arthur Meehan of Deansboro, wrote to the bishop, reporting that he had moved recently to the town from Cincinnati where he had been active in a progressive parish. He told the bishop he was concerned about the absence of a school in the parish of St. Mary's in Clinton. In addition, he urged the bishop to promote the dialogue Mass. Citing the experience in his previous parish, he argued that the dialogue Mass, with active community participation, impressed non-Catholics, discouraged praying the rosary and other devotions never intended for use during Mass, increased the number of communions and built the proper "Christian community spirit." As was usually done the bishop sent the letter to the pastor, Father Raymond P. Lawrence, with whom Meehan had discussed these matters. Lawrence, a convert from the Episcopal church, began and ended his letter with comments on Meehan. He called Meehan "a difficult person inclined to take over" and representative of "the layman who wants to tell, not only his pastor, but even his bishop, what to do." As for the dialogue Mass, Lawrence had numerous problems:

Personally, I have always felt that the liberty enjoyed by the worshiper to follow his own inclinations in participating in the Mass was a fine thing. I shrink from the thought of marshaling everyone and dragooning them into doing the same thing and saying the same prayers in concert with everyone else. I had an experience of that in my Episcopalian days and enjoyed the freedom of the Catholic— once I had experienced it....Also, I think many of the older people today would be greatly disturbed by an effort to force the Dialogue Mass upon them. They would feel that they had been robbed of the Mass as they had always known it.

The bishop told Lawrence, "I agree with the attitude which you have taken," but he could not "take any official position on the Dialogue Mass" because the Church permits it if requested by the pastor or someone in charge of a school. Fortunately, Foery noted, only one parish did.

The bishop may have shared Lawrence's attitude, but both were in for some shocks. There had already been some major changes sent out from Rome, including dispensation from fasting on national holidays, reduction in 1957 of the fasting time before communion from three hours to one, and encouragement of more active congregational participation in Holy Week services. In January 1959, the bishop sent his priests directives from Rome which moved the dialogue Mass from the optional to the mandatory, so that all parishes now had to begin a program of congregational participation because "obedience to the Holy See demands that we do so." The bishop suggested a step-by-step approach, beginning with the simple responses like "Et cum spiritu tuo," insisting that the people be taught to pronounce the words correctly and "of course taught its meaning." Then they would move to the Orations, Kyrie, Sanctus and Agnus Dei. He noted that some parishes already had made great progress in bringing about this participation, but now "all of our parishes *must* make the same progress." Apparently, as Lawrence had feared, the "liberty" of parish devotions was to be challenged. The pope and the bishop were "dragooning" people into "doing the same thing and saying the same prayers with everyone else."

To assist pastors with these reforms, with their yet unseen implications for community, priesthood and ministry, the bishop appointed a diocesan commission on the liturgical apostolate. Monsignor John P. Phelan was chairman and included in its members was Champlin, a newly ordained priest familiar with the liturgical movement. In those days, Roman decrees were law. At St. John the Baptist in Syracuse on April 12, 1959, the pastor reminded his people of the changes in fasting regulations and Holy Week observances. Then he said, "Direct order from the Holy Father for all to take an active part in offering Mass." A microphone had been placed on the altar so that they could hear him. The following Sunday they would find cards in their seats with "easy to learn" responses. One of the priests would be in the pulpit to direct them, beginning with the simplest responses.

In May 1961, the diocese found that the simplest responses were being given in 81 percent of the parishes. The Our Father was being recited in 69 percent of the parishes, were employing a layman to serve as lector and lead the congregation. Pastors in approximately 10 percent of the parishes thought that about one quarter of their people took part, while 33 percent thought they enjoyed 100 percent participation. Fifty six percent thought their parishes were improving. Forty one percent thought they stayed about the same. Surprisingly, 72 percent of the pastors thought the people favored some use of vernacular in the Mass. Sixty-nine percent of the pastors themselves were in favor, while 31 percent opposed. Comparable figures for the assistants were 76 percent and 24 percent.

Things were changing, and there were signs that it was only the beginning. At a fall clergy conference in 1961 Champlin informed the priests that Pope Pius XII had brought about "numerous and significant reforms" and there were "more and deeper revisions to come." It was a "period of transition for the Liturgy" and change would come gradually, through experimentation. Champlin noted that American priests, who liked things "cut and dry," would find this process "slow and unpleasant." He asked for patience and understanding as they tried to apply the "liturgical wishes of the Holy See to our own diocese." He noted that at least 80 percent of the parishes had responded to the bishop's decree of 1959 on congregational participation and his comments forecast the future:

Many priests do indicate the obstacle presented by the Latin language for an intelligent and practical response by the people to the Mass prayers. Some have found this so great as to make extensive participation impossible; others, while achieving almost full response from the people, still feel that the laity do not have their heart in the program because of lack of understanding of the words. Over 70% of the priests in our diocese feel some

In Syracuse, and later in Washington with the National Conference of Catholic Bishops, Monsignor Joseph M. Champlin was a forerunner in liturgical renewal. Champlin told priests that the liturgical reforms of the early 1960s were the first of such developments they could expect in the only coming years. (Photo: The Catholic Sun)

parts of the ordinary of the Mass in 43 percent and the congregation joined in the responses made by the altar boy in 52 percent of the parishes. Fifty-six percent had the Gospel and Epistle read in English while recited in Latin by the priest. Twelve percent *vernacular in the Mass would be of distinct pastoral value for the souls in their care.*

These results had been communicated to Rome. In the meantime he reminded them that the 1958 Instruction did permit "indirect participation," using an English paraphrase of the Latin, for example, with the people reciting the Apostles Creed in English as the priest recites the Nicene Creed in Latin.

Champlin, as a seminarian and young priest, regularly attended the annual national liturgical conferences where these matters were discussed. This was unusual for a Syracuse priest because the diocese was

peculiarly parochial. Only a few Syracuse clergy had gone away to Washington or Rome for advanced studies. Neither seminary education nor local clerical culture encouraged theological study beyond reading formal Church statements. Foery himself had resisted the efforts of a lay friend to interest him in the moderately liberal, lay-edited *Commonweal* magazine because he thought it occasionally marred by a subtle anti-clericalism. Oral history testimony suggests that the few intellectually inclined priests were rather independent and isolated. Moreover, Foery did not encourage his priests to attend national meetings or join national organizations, and few did.

When the decrees regarding liturgical changes came, few, including the bishop, understood the theological foundations of those reforms. They particularly did not understand the theology of the Mystical Body of Christ which would call the Church to become a more cooperative, intimate community of the faithful and perhaps enlarge the area of lay leadership and responsibility. Nor, despite the long struggle to increase congregational singing, did many see the contradiction present in Lawrence's argument. Despite the appearance of solidarity and unity communicated by the Latin Mass, many worshipers were engaged in private, personal devotions, just as, despite the apparent submission of the laity to Foery's almost exclusively clerical definition of the Church, most Catholics had little sense of a common mission in the world beyond "private family life." The modest liturgical reforms of the last years of the pre-conciliar era found the Syracuse Church orderly and obedient, and uncovered a surprising degree of support for the vernacular language because pastors saw the possibilities of more vigorous community life present in a revitalized worship. But few anticipated what lay ahead. The ideas surrounding the liturgical movement would burst forth in unexpected ways in an ecumenical Council, which Pope John XXIII summoned to meet in Rome in the fall of 1962.

TOWARD
THE ETERNAL KINGDOM

VATICAN COUNCIL II AND THE SYRACUSE CHURCH
1960s-1970s

In 1950, Monsignor David F. Cunningham, who had served on the chancery staff since 1930, was named auxiliary bishop. Twelve years later, he traveled with Bishop Foery to Rome for the Second Vatican Council. They got along well, these two men. Between them, they shared many of the qualities common among American bishops. Foery's personal reserve and dedication to his job sometimes obscured his powerful convictions, which no one could doubt when they heard his strong voice and clear diction convey a passionate love for the Church and total confidence in its teachings. He was also like many American bishops because of the mutual respect and affection he enjoyed with his priests. Cunningham complemented Foery with other qualities notable among American bishops, particularly his administrative ability, attention to detail and somewhat hard nosed approach to discipline. The atmosphere in the diocese was not marked by deep intellectual concern, but both men were highly intelligent and quick to learn. It was Cunningham, the second-in-command and administrator, who stayed for the council. Foery was excused early in the first session and never returned. Cunningham sat doggedly through the debates of all four sessions. On each trip, he went and returned with a bulging briefcase and his speeches and notes indicated that he read the material and grasped the issues. During the 1960s, he took more and more responsibility for diocesan leadership, though he would not become bishop in his own right until 1971. When he did take command, he was a considerably different man than he had appeared before the council. He may not have understood fully the momentous theological transformation which had taken place, but he grasped some of the central truths which informed the council's deliberations. He knew that the Church was called to a spiritual renewal which would make it more a community of love, and that all the rest, including buildings, would have to serve that end. He knew, too, that the mission of the Church extended beyond its own members to embrace the whole of humanity in the love of Christ. And he had caught a sense of what it meant to distinguish between the Church, human, fallible and struggling, and the Kingdom of God.

By the time Cunningham became bishop, he probably could not have referred to the Church as "the happiest and most peaceful society." For one thing, many Catholics by that time were no longer either happy or peaceful. But there was something more, a sense that he captured in Rome that the Church stood always in the light of Christ in the scripture and the Kingdom yet to come. As such he sensed that the Church had little to boast of and much to do, much more than could be accomplished without the grace of God operating through His people. This meant more humble bishops, and more trust in God and in the ordinary men and women who made up His church. At times Cunningham stumbled and old attitudes reappeared. And at times the simple weight of the organization he had helped construct would get in the way of the new dream. But he had caught that dream, more and more of his people came to share it, and the Church in Syracuse, now moving "toward the Eternal Kingdom," would never be the same again.

Bishops Foery and Cunningham had no idea of the revolution the Vatican Council would bring, but they were excited about the prospect of attending. In mid-July 1962, Foery wrote a pastoral letter and ordered a novena for the success of the council to be held in every parish and religious house between October 3 and October 10, the scheduled opening day. Monsignors Richard Clark and John McGraw traveled with the bishops, sailing from New York on the USS Constitution in the company of 36 bishops and a host of priests. It was a rough voyage at first, with little sunshine and heavy seas. Once the weather cleared, the trip was leisurely, with stops in Casablanca, Gibralter and Palermo. Cunningham was an enthusiastic traveler. Moslem Casablanca was a unique experience. He was struck by "the contrasts between modern office buildings and open bazaars and each with its own specialty, from food, rugs, sandals, fezzes to camel saddles and perfumes." Fascinated by Moslem customs, the Syracuse priests were still

incurably American. "Most of the women wore a veil over their faces to their eyes," Cunningham wrote good-naturedly. "We wondered about it being a help to our girls, the lipstick that would be saved, the rouge and powder not necessary, and the added time that could be given to study." But it was a passing fancy. "We agreed we would prefer our fine young girls as they are, rather than hiding behind unsanitary face covers." The last and deepest impression was less happy, because they departed from the city in "a rather sad frame of mind, that the poverty is so great that we felt deeply for the poor people and the hungry ill-clad children."

By October, they were in Rome beginning to experience the vigorous discussions in coffee shops and recreation rooms where bishops and theologians gathered.

Those accustomed to the authority and prestige of the bishop at home would find it hard to appreciate the awe and reverence which the council caused in the bishops themselves. The sweep of renewal stemmed in part from their profound sense of the universality of the Church. It also came from the responsibility that rested on them, not as local bishops but as participants in a collegial hierarchy united around the pope. For Cunningham in particular, the council was a moving event. His excitement was evident in his report on the opening ceremony:

Well, yesterday was the big day, historic, marvelous in its setting, moving in the picture of over 2000 bishops with Pope John opening the Council. The bishops alternated with the choir in the "Veni Creator," sung all the responses, recited the Gloria, Credo, Sanctus and Agnus Dei with the celebrant, Cardinal Tisserant. Bishop Foery and I stuck together and we had perfect places.

Both bishops were stirred by the spectacle: "You saw for the first time Bishops of every continent of the world. They were young and old, black, yellow and white; some wore peculiar vestments, others were dressed like Americans." Above all, there was Pope John XXIII, who seemed to touch something deep inside Bishop Cunningham. After the opening ceremony, he saw the pope address a throng in St. Peter's square. "He talked for thirty five minutes," Cunningham reported. "What a man!" When the American bishops met the Holy Father in a reception at the North American College, Cunningham again was moved. Throughout the session, the Syracuse delegation had a boylike sense that the pope was always in the background, with the welfare of the whole Church at heart. Monsignor Clark reported that "the Holy Father has a loud speaker in his room that brings him all the proceedings. They say it is impossible to pull him away from it."

Then came the hard work of the council, with long sessions in the council chambers and meetings of the American bishops to consider matters before it. Foery and Cunningham were conservative Churchmen, but they had never conducted chancery meetings in Latin. All council business was. "Some of the talks are in classical, long sentence style, others in clear, simple form that helps us," Cunningham wrote. "It is interesting to hear, even if one doesn't grasp all the details." Foery was tiring. Within a few weeks he was given permission to return home, which he did, accompanied by Clark. Interviewed back in Syracuse, Foery described his sense that the Holy Spirit was truly present in the council's deliberations. Privately, he was surprised at the progressive tone of the discussion. As he indicated to one priest, no one could really tell the outcome: "What will happen, nobody knows."

Bishop Foery's departure from the council and his failure to return for the later sessions is a mystery. Attendance was considered a serious episcopal responsibility. One had to receive permission from the Holy Father to be absent and by no means was this granted easily. There is no surviving record of his dealing with the Vatican for permission. Nor is there an indication of serious ill health. Aides worried about him but that was normal, because they always were unusually protective. Perhaps the nervous condition which manifested itself early in his administration was more serious than anyone suggested. Combined with the fact that Foery's pro forma resignation at age 75 was not accepted by Rome, the decision leaves a major question mark. The fact that he did not attend even the crucial moments of the first session, much less the great debates of the next three, was of considerable significance for the diocese of Syracuse. Bishop Foery carried out renewal according to Vatican directives, and he remained a pastorally sensitive person, but there was something missing. In sharp contrast to Bishop Cunningham, he seemed more worried than excited by the changes, more

354

Bishop David Cunningham and Bishop Walter Foery attended the first session of the Second Vatican Council in 1962. Later Foery returned to Syracuse, while Cunningham participated in the council, became even more enthusiastic about Pope John XXIII, and seemed to absorb the spirit of renewal which fed Vatican II. (Photo: Chancery Archives)

concerned about extremes than about the benefits which would come. One wonders what might have happened if he had stayed and caught a bit of the hopeful vision that his colleague did.

Cunningham and McGraw remained as the weather turned cold and rainy. Cunningham, always a Churchman, could not admit publicly that there were disagreements among the leaders. However, privately, he noted that the French and German bishops were well organized. That is "fine with me," he added, "because I think they think as we do on many things." The "we" were the American bishops who were going to school, meeting together to discuss the council documents with their own experts. Cunningham shared their surprising sense of nationalism. At one session, scripture

Bishop Foery was pleased to meet Pope John XXIII at the opening of the Second Vatican Council. But for unknown reasons, he did not participate in the council beyond the opening session. (Photo: Chancery Archives)

scholar Barnabas Ahearn analyzed the document on revelation. In the discussion which followed, he was challenged by the apostolic delegate, but answered the objections forcefully. Cunningham was delighted because, as he reported, the American bishops were not too happy that the Italian archbishop insisted on attending their meetings. In the sessions which followed, Cunningham showed a growing identification with his brother bishops from the United States and the issues they made their own, particularly the text on religious liberty.

There was little in Cunningham's numerous letters to indicate he understood the theological issues churning below the surface of the first session. However, he clearly sympathized with the "progressive" desire to make sure that curial officials did not control the council and that it developed its own voice. His growing sense of the dignity of the hierarchy

and the idea that these bishops, united with this remarkable pope, constituted the leadership of the Church, led Cunningham to side with the progressives during the first session. A decisive moment came in November, when the majority of bishops wished to send many of the documents back to commissions to which they would elect new members. Cunningham described the battle and its outcome for his friend, Monsignor Gildea:

> Yesterday a vote was taken on the document on Revelation to continue discussion or to interrupt (send back for revision) which would simply mean an entirely new schema on the subject. The entrenched curia people on the matter, especially Ottaviani and Ruffini, had excluded all scholars except their own from the commission.... So a real fight went on for about a week and the vote to strip required 2/3 or about 1450. The dubium was cleverly fixed. We (the American Bishops) were against the present schema but it failed the 2/3 by about 100. Pope John had listened to it all and last night had a meeting to say that the Council was not going to be run by only a little better than 1/3 — so today all were startled, most delighted, to receive the message that he was appointing a new commission for a new schema.... You can imagine how crushed Cardinal Ottaviani and company are! What a Pope!

By the time Cunningham returned to Rome for the second session, he was aligned solidly with those determined to ensure the independence of the council and overcome the conservatism seen to characterize actions of the Roman officials. In November, Cunningham reported behind-the-scenes efforts to bring matters into the open by "getting the intransigent attitude of the curia more and more on the Council floor, so that in the light of day obstructionist tactics may be neutralized." Later he told Gildea that the curia "was taking a bad banging on the schema on bishop's rule of their diocese. Bishops don't want anything standing between them and the Pope." Cunningham thought limiting curial control of local affairs would bring about "better diocesan administration." However, he did not translate local independence into isolation, because he strongly supported proposals for stronger national conferences of bishops, a proposal opposed by conservative prelates in New York and Los Angeles but supported by the midwestern bishops. "The coasts are not controlling the tides of episcopal opinion," he wrote. Cardinal McIntyre of Los Angeles thought "the curia is okay," but Cardinal Meyer in Chicago was closer to the majority in backing national episcopal conferences with judicial "force." In short, Cunningham took collegiality seriously, a collegiality expressed in the fraternal cooperation of brother bishops with one another and with the pope, exemplified in practice in the council itself. The doctrine of collegiality "extends the horizons of individual bishops beyond the confines of particular dioceses to the dimensions of the church universal," Cunningham said. With the pope, the bishops now felt "a responsibility for the care of the entire church." Cunningham, whose career was centered so heavily on local diocesan administration, was experiencing a new vision of the Church and its mission, and he was excited.

Monsignor John McGraw (left) and Monsignor David Gildea (right) accompanied Bishop Cunningham to the second session of the Vatican Council in 1963. (Photo: Chancery Archives)

FIRST FRUITS OF THE COUNCIL

Cunningham was well aware of the controversies that had begun. When he returned to Syracuse at the end of the council in 1965, he told reporters that, besides the liturgical reforms already underway, he expected there would be further mitigation of fasting regulations, closer ecumenical contacts, development of parish councils and greater leadership from the American bishops in the nation's religious affairs. On the most difficult question among Catholics, birth control, he also anticipated that change was not over. There was now a deeper understanding of Christian marriage, "a change...in which great emphasis is placed upon love between the husband and wife and less emphasis upon the procreational function of the married state," Cunningham said. However, he insisted that there had been no change as yet in the Church's position forbidding the practice of artificial contraception, which was under study by a papal commission. On this and other aspects of renewal, he urged Catholics to remain open to the call of the Holy Spirit and "keep the spirit of acceptance" with which they always had treated Church authority.

By now, the auxiliary bishop was well versed in the theology that informed the council documents. In talks delivered around the diocese, he emphasized the sacramentality of the Church and the rich variety of images used to capture its mysterious life. He gave special attention to the "Mystical Body of Christ" and the "People of God," stressing the manner in which all members of the Church were called to holinesss and each shared in the priesthood of Christ. Cunningham attempted to help people capture the force and power of the council's call to center faith on Christ and focus the Church on the sacramental presence of Christ in his people bound together by baptism, by eucharistic sharing in Christ's life, and by ministry to the pain and suffering of the world. The Church was "not merely a hierarchical structure, a collection of juridical ordinances, a massive complex of buildings, organizations and societies," he said, "but ... a community of all men who believe in God and Christ and who walk through this life ... toward the eternal Kingdom of heaven." This was shocking talk in the heretofore self-assured, rather complacent Syracuse Church.

For Cunningham, the Dogmatic Constitution on the Church, with its emphasis upon the whole community of believers as "the people of God," was the most important text of the council. It found its practical expression, he believed, in the liturgical reforms which got underway almost immediately after the first two sessions. He hoped that Syracuse Catholics would learn the value of common prayer, so that the Mass would not be looked upon as an "interruption of their private recollections, prayers and meditations." He urged people to "a patient docile acceptance of the new liturgy as the will of God expressed by the Holy Spirit through the Council." He said the new liturgy would "soon bring to them and to all many new graces, joys and consolations of our Catholic faith." He understood that it would be hard to leave behind the liturgy people had long known. "Although they did not understand the language of the Mass and were inactively present only, they felt secure in the familiar ceremonies and rituals," he told one audience. The "wonderment" of the laity at change in the Mass thus arose from "a lack of knowledge that all baptized and confirmed members of Christ's body, the Church, share in some way in the priesthood of Christ, and therefore should not be only onlookers, merely hearing Mass, passive and inert," but actively joining in offering the Eucharist as an event of the Church and a sacrament of the entire community.

Liturgical renewal was to bring about "fuller participation of the people in the ceremonies and worship of the Church," so that the Mass expressed the bond among parishioners and between them and "every other Christian in the world."

For, as you kneel with your neighbor here on Sunday morning, as you join your voices in hymns of joyous praise, as you offer with them and the priest at the altar all of your common sacrifices, you are expressing in a concrete manner your faithfulness to Christ's command to love one another. Gathering together at the altar and praying together as a group is the external manifestation of what your everyday lives are and should be, that is, lives filled with charity, sympathy, kindness and generosity for your brothers and sisters in Christ.

Liturgical renewal was, therefore, "the very first fruit" of the council. It reflected all its "fundamental concepts," such as "the universal call to unity, the stress on the oneness of the People of God, the clarification of our duties to our fellow men, and the bond of charity which must be exercised in our daily lives and extended far beyond our parish, our community and our country to all."

As indicated earlier, many liturgical changes came before Vatican II. In 1959, priests were instructed to bring about participation in the Mass, both through music and recitation of some Latin responses. In 1960, Rome ended the common practice of distributing communion before or after Mass or during a sermon. Champlin's "indirect participation," with a lay lector reading the epistle and gospel in English and the people reciting in English some of the prayers of the Mass, was permitted in 1962. These were minor compared to the changes coming from the council. The first was Mass facing the people. In 1964, priests received permission to erect a temporary altar for this purpose, but, within a few months, Bishop Foery temporarily suspended these permissions. In September 1965, new guidelines were issued which involved not only the altar itself, but the visibility of the celebrant and the arrangement of the sanctuary. The directives associated with this first major liturgical innovation expressed well the organized character of the diocese. Gildea's building commission provided detailed rules for physical arrangements, including the location of "low candle holders and thick, stubby candles" and arrangement of altar cloths. While there were "no detailed rubrics for Mass facing the people," the liturgical commission found a few. The prayers at the foot of the altar should be said facing the altar to "indicate clearly that these prayers belong to the celebrant and his ministers alone and in no way concern the people." At the final blessing, the priest was told to place "his left hand (palm down) on the altar instead of on his breast." This caution reflected well Bishop Foery's own reservations. As he told one pastor:

We are always encouraged to be careful about our gestures, our signs of the cross and our movements at Mass. It is especially emphasized that we be

The "very first fruit" of the council was liturgical renewal. With traditional architecture stemming from a time when lay people were spectators at Mass, churches like Holy Trinity in Syracuse could at first do little more than place a temporary altar for Mass facing the people. Later when new churches were built or when older churches could be renovated, many ways were found to shape a worship environment in which people could more actively participate in the celebration of Mass. (Photo: The Catholic Sun)

very watchful and careful of these when we are facing the people. You are aware, as I am, that saying Mass every day can be done with great devotion and reverence and at the same time we can develop some 'non-liturgical' habits which are not necessarily inspiring. May I suggest, there-

fore, that whoever says Mass facing the people be exact in all the gestures which are required and, particularly, on the signs of the cross that are made during Mass.

Use of English was even more challenging. Despite earlier indications of wide support for this change, many priests were worried. Father Lawrence, the former Episcopalian, reminded his fellow priests that his old church was not filling its pews, although its English prayers and liturgy were quite beautiful. Father Harold Quinn, more sympathetic than most to liturgical innovation, thought that the changes would be hard, even though "our people...want to be led." Foery agreed, telling Quinn, "it is going to be difficult for us all." Yet, most pastors found the people surprisingly receptive when the vernacular was introduced in Advent 1964. Father Daniel O'Brien of Holy Cross parish in Dewitt reported to Foery that "the participation, after the first two Sundays of curiosity, became complete, tremendous, and wonderful to behold."

Another pastor reported approaching a group of older women and asking if they could live with the change. They surprised him when one responded, "Thank God we lived to see this day" and the others nodded in agreement.

No sooner was English introduced than more changes came in Lent 1965, including omission of the last gospel and the prayers after Mass. These small changes took two single spaced pages to list. They amounted to a shift in the spirit of the Mass, again designed to elicit community participation. In 1966, permission was granted to invite the congregation to gather around the altar for the liturgy of the Eucharist. In January 1967 guidelines were issued for concelebrated Masses and for the reception of communion under both species on special occasions, for

example, at ordinations, weddings or reception of newly baptized converts into the Church. While in some parishes people already were receiving communion while standing, Foery was opposed to this practice, which was not permitted formally until 1971.

In 1968, diocesan officials informed authorities in Washington that liturgical reform had been quite successful. Use of the vernacular and Mass facing the people were received well, lectors and commentators were well trained, communion reception had increased, and there was greater participation and a greater sense of community. The only negative notes were the music, the feeling of some older parishoners "that these changes mean changes in essentials" and a widespread judgement that the Mass "terminates too abruptly after Holy Communion." In October, the bishop wrote the pastors in a tone which suggested his reservations had been overcome.

One of the joys of the new liturgy for both priests and people is the mass facing the congregation. It aids priests and bishops to be more reverent in action. It stimulates us to communicate clearly and audibly the dignity and sacredness of the liturgy. For the people it brings a sense of identification with the priests offering and with Christ's presence in the sacrifice.

In that same document, he ordered pastors to make use of lectors, recommended use of song leaders and melodies with guitar accompaniment, and introduced a new funeral rite. Home masses were described as "an excellent occasion for instruction in the liturgy and can help build a sense of community within a parish."

In 1970, the liturgical renewal reached its climax when the changes were consolidated into a new and simplified format, the Rite of Paul VI. The greeting, the revised Confiteor, the new form of ending the Lord's prayer and a variety of new short prayers were introduced, as was a three year cycle of scripture readings and optional periods of silence and meditation. The new law provided that the host should look more like bread, that vestments could be of synthetics instead of silk, and that ceramic vessels could replace the gold and silver of the past. Announcements had to wait until just before the blessing at the end of Mass, while the detailed instructions of the old ordo, which had prescribed every detail of the priests actions down to the donning of the vestments, were modified dramatically. Change was not over. In 1971, the diocese adopted the policy of anticipated Masses on Saturdays and the days before holy days.

There were three elements to liturgical renewal in the diocese, as there were to most of the other changes coming about as a result of the council. One was the crucial role of the bishops. Foery and Cunningham were both conservative men because they were Churchmen first of all. They accepted change, but insisted that it be carried out in accord with Vatican guidelines and the collective policies adopted by the American bishops. Foery's emphasis was on control. "As you know," he told Father Champlin, "the temptation to experiment with the liturgy is one many find very hard to resist. We are trying in accord with our responsibilities to control unauthorized experimentation." On several occasions, he indicated his concern that change was tending to undermine respect for the Eucharist. Like other older priests, he worried that, in changing the forms of the Mass, something essential and important might be lost. Foery also was moved by pastoral concern. "These are trying times," he told one priest. "We know we have an obligation to protect the Faith with which we have lived and to which we have dedicated our lives." When he warned against using the pulpit to

discuss speculative developments in theology, he was less concerned about orthodoxy, which was challenged rarely, than with encouraging his priests to be sensitive to people. "It is confusing to the people when we do not distinguish between opinions and doctrine," he wrote. "Our people have a right to be aware of some of the present day opinions, but our preaching should always be given in a sensitive and pastoral approach."

The second factor was the pace of change. Directives and guidelines came regularly from Rome and Washington, a flood of books and articles poured from the presses, priests and sisters were attending workshops and seminars, and students and adults active in renewal movements were experiencing new forms of liturgy apart from the parish church. Newly ordained priests were learning theories about the liturgy quite different from those learned by their elders, while more and more people in home Masses were experiencing community celebration in new ways. Liturgical reform had begun at the top, but soon the pressure for additional change from the bottom was very great, and suggested the need to relax control and to provide space for some diversity. Foery told one priest that, while official directives had to be adapted to particular parish situations, individual experimentation would not be allowed. But of course, this was the problem. Pastoral responsibility might suggest the need for change to respond to one group, for example, the use of guitar music with youth, yet that change might not meet the needs of all. Pastoral considerations pointed toward diversity, at the same time that they placed limits upon it.

The third factor was the rising importance of the liturgical commission. With the pace of change in theory and practice intensifying, the bishop naturally had to rely more and more on those who kept current with the legislation and were informed about what was going on in other dioceses. In addition, each change required some training of priests, lay lectors and others, so that the new forms could be done properly. In 1966, the diocesan commission asked to have the privilege of sharing in the promulgation of the bishop's decisions, so that there could be greater coordination and avoidance of the stop-start experience which had taken place with Mass facing the people. In addition, they launched a newsletter to keep pastors and others informed of changes. Most important, they held workshops and clergy conferences which helped priests and lay leaders to implement the decisions which had been made. The music commission, under Father William Shannon, later with the help of talented newcomers like Father John Zeigler, Father Adam Smalley and its first lay director, Duane Sutton, played a similar role.

RESERVATIONS ON RENEWAL

At first, the liturgical commission had a top down approach. Noting the directives from Rome and Washington, and experience elsewhere, it recommended changes and suggested ways in which they could be carried out. Workshops were held to train people, not to consult them on what should be done. Later, as conflicts arose among priests and people, local Church leaders learned that reform from the top would not work without support at the bottom, so that greater consultation was needed before and not after changes had been decided upon. The experience of reform, mediating between the need to initiate changes coming from Rome and to exert some control from the top, and the demands for change and the resistance to change at the bottom, was a learning experience for those who served on the commission, an experience which would be valuable in the years ahead.

The complex interaction of these factors was evident in many areas. For example, the Syracuse diocese had worked hard to promote the use of approved musical texts, to train organists and choirs, and to promote use of Gregorian Chant, but the majority of parishoners had never responded fully. Renewal pushed aside these older policies which had little popular support. Naturally, the bishop sympathized with parishioners and musicians who had supported the diocesan program for so long. Particularly anguishing was a letter from a woman who had served as organist in two large churches for almost 15 years and was fired on the argument that an organist was "no longer needed." She was incensed by the folk, or "hootenany Mass," as she called it. On all scores, Foery was sympathetic. He told her that the need for organists and choirs was insisted upon in all official documents, while her statement on the folk Mass agreed with his own experience:

While they are tentatively permitted for adolescents, I hope, with you, that they will not become part of our church's worship. This of course does not depend upon the Bishop but upon the Liturgical Commission and the people as a whole.

As his words indicated, the bishop now had to place his own preferences in the context of new Church requirements and changing pastoral needs.

Monsignor Shannon, head of the Music Commission, was won over to the folk Mass by one he witnessed at Christian Brothers Academy. He introduced it to the cathedral with the help of Father John Ziegler. The folk Mass, they believed, allowed young people to praise God in "their own idiom." Foery rather reluctantly agreed to allow such Masses, and soon new forms of music were multiplying. Cathedral concerts, choirs and special event Masses served to introduce and popularize new music, while the commission also provided pastors and musicians with approved forms of hymnals and popular songs. The changes were not universally popular, but generated enough support to override Bishop Foery's reservations.

Another problem arose with Mass in the home. Foery had no trouble with this when there was serious reason, the pastors permission was obtained, the surroundings were fitting, and there was no identification between the Mass and any refreshments that might be served, but he had two basic reservations about the spread of this practice. First, it would introduce a distinction between those who wanted Mass in their home and "those who do not feel they are in a position to do so because of poor housing conditions or lack of funds to undertake such a venture." Secondly, he worried that such a practice would be detrimental to the parish church as a center of worship. Yet some pastors argued for permission on pastoral grounds. It was appropriate, for example, that one of the first parishes to offer home Masses was St. John the Baptist in Rome. The pastor thought it would be particularly helpful in reaching deteriorating neighborhoods, housing projects, homes for the elderly, or rural areas falling between the cracks of neighboring parishes. Once again, pastoral considerations backed by the liturgy commission justified the extension of policies which initially made the bishop nervous.

Nevertheless, as these examples suggest, what was pastorally beneficial for some might not be for others. Cunningham was right to argue that reform was needed because the people should "not be only onlookers, merely hearing Mass, passive and inert." However, Foery was equally right to insist that change should be managed to ensure that what was "essential" to the Mass was not lost. As this line between continuity and change was not drawn clearly, conflict was bound to arise. In only a few cases did this involve all-out resistance to change. At St. Anne's in Binghamton, for example, Father Ferdinand

Hattala, with the support of a conservative lay group, Una Voce, held fast to the Tridentine Mass. A small network of traditionalists persisted, causing some anxiety for diocesan officials throughout the post-conciliar period, but they were generally isolated. More typical were divisions in a parish over the pace and style rather than the substance of liturgical change. In 1972, for example, Bishop Cunningham appointed to one parish a pastor who turned out to be "a confirmed conservative," causing complaints from a large body of parishioners. When the bishop moved him to a more conservative parish, his supporters charged the move had been made in response to a "small clique" of "new Catholics ... power seekers ... a band of destroyers ... vicious people."

Their tempers were not cooled when his replacement began innovative liturgies, especially for children. Banners proclaiming "love" and "happiness" worried one woman, who wondered how those could be achieved "without devotion to the Sacred Heart and the Blessed Virgin Mary." Others thought authentic liturgy could not take place amid the distractions of contemporary music, balloons, and "singing, slides and guitar homilies."

The bishop asked Father Champlin to respond. He explained that the new liturgical directives were "officially flexible," providing a "definite structure and texts," but leaving room for "much adaptation on the local level." Contemporary art, banners, balloons and films were permitted, even encouraged, if they enhanced a "prayerful, faith filled celebration of the liturgy." To another parishoner upset by contemporary liturgies, Father Champlin tried to explain why they had come about. "Your pain and confusion is understandable," he wrote:

For decades the congregation's role in Catholic worship had been a relatively

GOING BACK TO "THE ORIGINAL MASS"

As the diocese implemented liturgical reforms following the Second Vatican Council, pastors tried to explain the changes to their congregations. A priest at St. Vincent de Paul parish in Syracuse used the following explanation:

"One thing we always used to hear about the Catholic Church was that it could not change. Well, if you have that idea in your head, KEEP IT THERE! IT IS TRUE! And yet, on the other hand, we have seen a lot of changes in the Mass in recent times, and we will soon see some more. Now, how can the supposedly unchangeable Church be changing so much? The explanation lies in the fact that the Church remains the same *always* in essentials and changes only in incidentals. Some people easily confuse the incidentals with the essentials, but there is a real difference between them....

When we were conceived, we were but one single tiny cell. But look how that cell divided and multiplied and then we were born. Immediately we began to grow and develop so that today we are quite different from what we were when we were born and vastly different from what we were at conception. But, through all those incidental and significant changes, we each remain the same person. There is something about a person that makes him who he is, and it is that essential something that cannot change....

"Now the same is true of the Church and the Mass.... The Mass was born, as you know, almost two thousand years ago on Holy Thursday night when Christ said the first Mass. Over the centuries the Mass has grown and developed just as a human being does. Before Vatican II most of us had the idea that the Mass we knew was the Mass as it always had been. In fact, we thought, no matter where we went in the world, the Mass would be the same both in the ceremonies and the language used, Latin. But this was not true. By the time of the Vatican Council, the Mass had been celebrated in several languages and in many different ways. But despite the differences, one fact remained: The Mass celebrated was the Eucharist commanded by Christ.

"For the next three weeks we will try to explain the new changes, the WHY of them, and show that it is but an attempt to return to the original Mass."

363

silent one. We have identified reverence and prayerfulness with a quiet and hushed atmosphere in church. In that perspective, singing, slides, guitar homilies and balloons at Mass must indeed seem bizarre, to say the least, and surely irreverent. However, the church has officially, for over 50 years, urged, even commanded, active participation by word, deed, silence and singing. Implementation, as we might expect, has been uneven, depending largely upon the interest, efforts and talents of the parish priests.

Where there was disagreement, there had to be openness and mutual give-and-take on both sides, Champlin argued, and a willingness of both sides to try "to catch and foster the spirit of prayerfulness and faith which should saturate these liturgies." If agreement proved impossible, the bishop now allowed freedom "to seek out another parish," with services more in line with one's "own personal preference." This all made good sense on paper, except that one woman made the understandable response that it sounded as if she and her family were to be pushed out of the parish in which they and their parents had worshiped for years. Achieving agreement among diverse groups within a parish was difficult, particularly if neither side was prepared to bend, with the parishoners allowing some diversity in the liturgy and the priest making a sincere effort to meet the needs of those with which he disagreed. In most parishes in the diocese of Syracuse, in fact, that sort of agreement was reached. The relative moderation of most lay Catholics, the loyalty of the priests to their bishop, the great pastoral skill of most pastors and a growing willingness to consult parishioners meant that, in most cases, with some pain and no little argument, directives were followed, options were allowed, and people accepted the fact that there would be some things with which they did not agree. While all this was going on, it should be remembered that the Church and its people did not live in a vacuum. As the first changes of the Vatican Council were introduced, John Kennedy was killed. Before they were consolidated in 1971, Martin Luther King and Robert Kennedy had followed. During the same period, a terrible war had dragged on in Vietnam, and many American cities were stirred by racial conflict and violence. No wonder that, for some, there seemed little to rely upon. Consequently, to experience change even in the beloved rituals of the Church could shake the very depths of one's sense of identity and arouse passions not easy to contain.

Finally, there was a certain pathos and humor in the whole process. In the parish mentioned earlier, the minority of conservatives, disappointed when their rather traditional pastor was changed, might have been excused for thinking things had gone too far.

One woman who wrote the bishop was upset by the priest's informal greeting, his playing of the guitar during the homily and the unusual readings with which he introduced meditation after communion. At Pentecost 1973, she exploded:

The trite banner [which] hung high from the portico of (the) church June 1 and 2 read 'Happy Birthday To Us'. The balloons strung from crepe paper at the end of the Sanctuary were blown up. Unfortunately, the candles on the altar table where 11:30 Mass was celebrated June 2 were blown out. 'Happy Birthday to You' groaned the organ as the gifts were taken up. My Church has gone from sublime to ridiculous.

Perhaps the most obvious public impact of the renewal of the liturgy were the changes in public space first and then in the buildings themselves. The area's churches simply had not been built to accommodate Mass facing the people. Introducing even the temporary altar was no small matter, especially if the purpose of unifying celebrant and congregation was to be realized. Yet the altar was only the start. The decrees from Rome suggested many other things, such as the reduction of the number and visibility of large statues, which might distract attention from the central event of the Mass. The decrees also suggested movement away from elaborate decoration toward more simple painting and furnishing, and the drastic rearrangement of the sanctuary. At St. Joseph's in Boonville, for example, a smaller altar built for celebration facing the people was installed. A large picture of St. Joseph and the Child Jesus gave way to a large wooden crucifix placed over a red velvet backdrop. Large statues of St. Joseph and the Blessed Mother were replaced by smaller ones, located to the right of the altar, while chairs for the celebrant and altar boys were placed at the center of the sanctuary, with a baptismal font to the right and free standing candles located next to the altar. An altar of repose for the Blessed Sacrament was removed from behind the altar to a new space to the side. In some other parishes, the Blessed Sacrament was placed outside the main church altogether. In one suburban parish, the pastor decided to move the repository to a small chapel set up for daily Mass. Some parishioners protested to Bishop Foery, who opposed this practice. "The church without the Blessed Sacrament," he wrote, "takes on the atmosphere of a Protestant assembly place." The pastor reluctantly returned the Blessed Sacrament to the church.

Despite such problems, in Syracuse as elsewhere, liturgical reforms were widely accepted and generally popular. National studies throughout the period showed overwhelming approval of the reforms, and what discontent existed, focused on problems which predated and transcended these reforms, most notably, preaching and music. In a growing number of parishes, as liturgy committees worked with the priest, as lectors and musicians received more and better training, the quality of worship improved, so did popular support for it. In a 1976 diocesan survey by a committee of the Priests' Senate, liturgy received high praise, but continued efforts at improvement ranked second among the priority needs of the diocese. The work of the liturgical commission was appreciated, but the committee noted that many pastors did not have active liturgical committees or liturgical teams composed of various ministries because they did not know how to use them. By that time, bottom up approaches with extensive lay participation had replaced the top down style of the early years of renewal. Liturgical reform now was located solidly with a wide effort to revitalize parish life as a whole. Cunningham's goal of building

a more united community, "the People of God," was not yet realized in full, but the process of renewal was well advanced.

ECUMENISM

While Cunningham's understanding of the theology of the Council documents and his openness to change undoubtedly surprised many local priests, Foery's sympathy with the problems all this posed was more predictable. Yet the difference should not be exaggerated. Both supported renewal, and both believed it should be carried out within the structure of the Church, which should be protected carefully. If each man was at times ambivalent, this reflected the fact that the council was at most a half-way revolution. The new emphasis on episcopal collegiality, for example, did not challenge directly the centralization and infallibility of the pope defined at Vatican I. After the council, it was still true that the pope's decision was final and other deliberations were advisory in nature. However, it was also true that the bishops could claim the right to be consulted and to insist that the pope's authority operated within, and not apart from, the college of bishops. This ambivalence could and did filter down, to become reflected in relations between priests and bishops, and even between pastors and the new parish councils.

Similarly, the council used a new language to describe the relationship between the Catholic Church and other Christian denominations. It invited non-Catholic Christians to dialogue, accepted a share of the responsibility for disunity and, pledged to work for better understanding and eventual fulfillment of the Lord's plea that "they all may be one." Ecumenism was publicized highly and of course of great interest to non-Catholic Americans. To many, it seemed a reversal of long standing Catholic attitudes and policies. Yet earlier laws and regulations remained in force, so that initiatives in the ecumenical area could remain highly circumscribed. American bishops, sympathetic with the ecumenical movement and anxious to respond to new themes of dialogue and friendship, worried that such actions might be misunderstood and undercut the loyalty and obedience of Catholics. Thus, after the second session of the council, the hierarchy issued some warnings and reminders to their priests. In a letter marked "confidential, not for publication—not for public discussion—for your own private use," Bishop Foery told his priests that, without question, priests and people were "confused about the ecumenical movement in the church." The letter said the confusion arose from the work of "writers and speakers" who used ecumenism to express their personal opinions and predict what the council might do.

To help ease the alleged "confusion," the American bishops reminded priests of earlier laws and the 1949 Instruction. Both strictly limited contact with non-Catholics and upheld the bishops' responsibility to "carefully watch publications by Catholics and see that censures and prohibitions were honored." Foery spelled out what this meant. The bishop must be assured that "no priest-writer or priest or lay speaker in our Diocese gives the impression that we are about to compromise our doctrine or that we are seeking union with our separated brothers by the giving up of our essential dogmatic and moral teaching." As always, the thing to be avoided was the "indifferentism to which compromise leads." Anyone invited to address a mixed assembly should notify the bishop and make clear the "procedure you wish to take." Yet Foery then ended the letter by quoting Paul VI's call to clergy and laity to:

Continue with calm and reverence to draw closer to our separated brethren,

not turning down some opportunities for calm and friendly conversation and, being more concerned for their welfare *rather than* our honor, *they may seek together the means for recomposing brotherhood, based on the identity of the faith and mutual charity which was desired by Christ for his Church.*

Monsignor John McGraw, who accompanied Bishop Cunningham at the council, was active in ecumenism. As the first secretary for the ecumenical commission, McGraw visited Protestant churches throughout the diocese, sharing with them his insights into the Decree on Ecumenism. He also conducted workshops for diocesan priests to acquaint them with the spirit and message of the decree.

Few areas of Church life were more supervised and controlled than relations with other churches. Generally, participation in any form of service in a non-Catholic church was forbidden, although in special cases the diocese might grant a dispensation to participate in a wedding or baptism. Permission was required, not just for explicitly religious events, but for clerical participation in civic gatherings or ministerial meetings as well. Nevertheless, the council's invitation to dialogue legitimated new openings throughout the Church. In 1964, Foery granted permission to the priests at St. John's in Binghamton to attend a luncheon at Ross Memorial Church. Foery told them that no attempt should be made to conceal the fact that differences existed, but these did not preclude working together for the good of the community and development of "a friendly spirit which could and should exist among all Christians." In the cities of the diocese, the social problems arising from urban renewal and racial discrimination accelerated the trend toward cooperation.

Monsignor William J. Shannan, rector of the cathedral, joined most other priests in taking up the cause of ecumenism and Church unity, in the years following the Second Vatican Council. (Photo: The Catholic Sun)

much had been done to break down misunderstandings.

While such formal exchanges moved forward, popular participation could not be avoided, if for no other reason than the intense publicity which had been given to the council's ecumenical efforts and to the dramatic steps taken by priests and people in other dioceses. Father Shannon of the cathedral organized a prayer service for Christian unity on Sunday, January 23, 1966. All priests from the diocese were invited to attend, as were Syracuse area ministers and their congregations. Episcopal, Methodist, Congregational, Lutheran, Baptist and Presbyterian ministers took part with the priests in offering prayers, scripture readings and hymns, while Shannon's sermon emphasized the call of Pope John and Bishop Foery for attentiveness to those things that united Christians one with another. While this event was taking place at the cathedral, similar services were being held to mark Church Unity Week in other parts of the diocese, and not all in Catholic churches.

In a religious culture dominated by concern about boundaries between churches and loyalty to one's own, the impact of these experiences would be dramatic. Mary O'Connor of St. Mary's church in Cleveland attended one service in a local Episcopal church. "We knew the event to take place would be history, the first of its kind since the founding of the village of Cleveland," she recalled. "Never before had an invitation of this kind been extended or accepted." On a "strange and marvelous" winter night, she and her Catholic friends entered the church and saw a Methodist couple on their left, and an Episcopalian couple on their right. Methodist, Episcopalian and Catholic clergy offered prayers and read from scripture, and together the congregation recited the Apostles Creed. "We were brought together by the essence of the ecumenical movement, to be

In September 1965, the diocese joined with the Council of Churches to establish guidelines for formal dialogue between priests and ministers. Monthly meetings were held, rotating among the churches, with the host clergyman serving as chairman for that meeting. By year's end, the priests agreed that joined to God in a spirit of good will, charity and well being," O'Connor recalled. "It was something exciting, never before experienced."

In 1966, a formal diocesan Commission for Ecumenism, chaired by Monsignor Frank Harrison and with Father John McGraw as secretary, prepared "interim directives governing ecumenical exchanges." The document encouraged informal discussions among clergy and laity, participation in jointly planned ecumenical services and collaboration in community service. While the Church was not yet to join local councils of churches, priests could accept invitations to serve as observers. Participation by Catholics in non-Catholic worship services was limited and intercommunion strictly forbidden. Care was to be taken to avoid indiscriminate use of conditional baptism of converts, but only Catholics could serve as sponsors at Baptism and Confirmation. Catholics could act as witnesses at non-Catholic marriages and the reverse privilege also was granted. Banns could be announced and a nuptial Mass celebrated at a mixed marriage and the non-Catholic's clergyman could offer prayers and remarks after the ceremony. Parishes were encouraged to exchange open houses and to join, under the direction of the clergy, in interfaith dialogue aimed at clearer understanding and clarification of points of unity and difference. It was a modest document, carefully restricting the door that was opening slowly, designed as much to create a system of control as to facilitate interaction that already was moving speedily ahead.

But control was not always possible. In January 1970, Sister Connie Murray, a Holy Child sister and graduate student at Syracuse University, shared the pulpit of Plymouth Congregational church. "Had anyone told me ten years ago I would be wearing a suit and standing in the pulpit of a Congregational church, I would not have believed it," she

said. The changes initiated by the Council had drawn Catholics to the scripture and its call to love and to service, she argued, a call which posed challenges for both the churches. There was a fear that things "were going too far" and some hoped "all this will settle down and we'll be rigid and stultify again." For her part, "if you don't have faith in the working of the Spirit, then it is frightening because we do not know where we are going; this to me is exciting." It was a time, she concluded, for "trying to get along with each other in the spirit of our Lord Jesus Christ."

Carefully structured theological dialogue among clergymen and prayer services aimed at and reflecting "good will" and "well being" were one thing, serious commitment to unity and fellowship was something else. Tensions were bound to arise between the long felt need of the Church for its own distinctiveness and integrity, and the call to look to those things which united Catholics and other Christians. Foery and Cunningham, like many bishops, presented a positive public face, but had reservations. These were evident in confidential discussions among the American bishops about the dramatic moves taking place in seminary education, where students were being encouraged to study with non-Catholic teachers and to interact with seminarians of other churches. Foery told a bishops' committee that such steps could lead to opportunities for dialogue, and this was good. However, study with non-Catholic teachers should be confined to the more "mature" seminary students, and even then, "Catholic scholars should have the opportunity to clarify any concepts which are at variance with the truths of our faith." Cunningham likewise thought that many benefits could arise from contact among seminarians, but he was even more worried about their impact. "In our troubled times for the faith, our seminarians could well be fortified in an attitude against the authority of

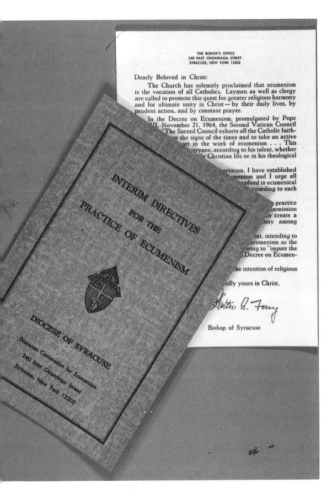

Christian ministers. Seminarians were "young and impressionable," Cunningham wrote, "anxious to present a sympathetic face to Protestant students. I fear danger in too much mingling with Protestant seminarians, married or looking forward to marriage. It could be harmful to their dedication to celibacy as a prime requisite for the priesthood."

Yet the bishop's public face was one of great sympathy with ecumenical efforts. From March of 1965, when Foery addressed an ecumenical dinner in Binghamton, to the mid-1970s, the bishops could be seen at innumerable interfaith events throughout the diocese, affirming dialogue and discussion. They also often pointing toward what, at one point, Bishop Foery called a "new ecumenism," one which he said "could even be called secular" and which would focus on practical projects aimed at assisting the underprivileged and improving American democracy.

A second stage of ecumenical development took place around 1970. In religious terms, it led away from interfaith services to exchanges aimed at generating appreciation for each church's distinctive forms of worship. In Binghamton, the local First Presbyterian church and St. Mary's exchanged pulpits and, in 1973, Father Stephen Litz of Utica asked permission for such exchanges among Utica churches during unity services the following January. In January 1974, Cunningham accepted the plan, cautioning Litz that "I would expect that the ministers who would be invited to preach in our churches will be carefully screened so that we would have no question about their presentations as fitting for our beliefs and as being acceptable to our people." Litz responded gratefully, noting that such local exchanges corresponded with Vatican guidelines and represented a significant step forward beyond "ecumenical services" which had "outlived their usefulness" and toward acceptance of the "legitimate diversity

Monsignor Frank Harrison chaired the diocesan Commission for Ecumenism which encouraged ecumenical dialogue, joint worship services, and cooperation in community service. Some restrictions remained; but the Second Vatican Council finally had broken the Church free from centuries of religious isolation and distrust, and the Church in the Syracuse diocese was ready for a new relationship with other Christians. (Photo: Chancery Archives)

the hierarchy, or even the Supreme Pontiff," he wrote. "Might there not be the sowing of seeds for internal danger to the faith by the immoderate mingling of seminarians?" Equally problematic were the divergent life-styles of of our own worship.... We are aware of the need to have discrete screenings of all clergy involved," he added. "We also have clergy who ought not have a greater audience."

The other step taken in the early 1970 was to create new bodies to replace the Councils of Churches, thus allowing Catholic participation. In Utica, priests were appointed to the Greater Utica Ecumenical Commission. Its purpose, the bishop told them, was to create "a climate of cooperation among the faith groups of the Utica area." In 1971, the Syracuse Council of Churches gave way to a new Metropolitan Church Board. Cunningham's speech at the inaugural meeting demonstrated the distance traveled in a few short years. The bishop praised the council for its school of religion, its chaplaincies and court work, and its ecumenical witness, which left a debt of gratitude as the local Christian community sought "new ways to be effective instruments of God's grace." The new body, he hoped, would preserve the spirit and many of the programs of the council, but, with a broader base, move into new areas and allow the whole Christian church to be more effective.

A decade of ecumenical development raised havoc with long-standing requirements of Church policy and canon law, as an increasing flood of requests for dispensation from rules regarding baptism, marriage and funerals poured in on the chancery office. In 1976, the ecumenical commission presented the bishop with a revised set of guidelines. These new rules reflected enormous changes in the attitudes of Catholics and relations among Christians. No longer were there to be indiscriminate rebaptisms of infants or adults. If they had been baptized in a Christian church in accord with that church's rite, the baptism was to be considered valid. When baptized Christians sought admission to the Church, they were not required to abjure heresy and to receive absolution from excom-

munication, ending a process normal in the United States for more than a century. Instead, only a simple profession of faith was expected now. The new Rite of Christian Initiation of Adults was recommended as a process for parishes to use in accepting new members into the Church, while the formal moment of reception should come during Mass and confirmation should be administered at that time. Only Catholics should act as sponsors at a Catholic baptism, though members of other churches could serve as witnesses, as could Catholics in non-Catholic churches. With the Orthodox, the reciprocal right of serving as a godparent was affirmed. In general, intercommunion was not allowed, though there was a whole range of exceptions "when the gaining of grace on some occasions demands it." These included danger of death, imprisonment, persecution or other "grave necessity," when it was impossible to obtain a non-Catholic minister, there was a spontaneous request for the Eucharist and a faith in harmony with that of the Catholic Church. The bishop could grant a dispensation as well for marriages, funerals and times of special need in an ecumenical family, such as the illness of a child. Once again, relations with the Orthodox were more intimate because, in principle, Catholics could participate fully in Orthodox ceremonies and fulfill their Sunday obligation, and the reverse was true as well. Similar regulations made easier funerals of Catholics and non-Catholics in ecumenical families. Non-Catholic ministers could participate in the service, read prayers at the graveside, or, in special cases and with the bishop's permission, perform the ceremony in a Protestant church.

Most dramatic were the changes in regulations regarding marriages between Catholics and Christians of other churches. The diocesan guidelines established "ecumenical marriage" as the proper term to replace "mixed marriage." The change was more than words:

In preparing a couple for marriage, the priest should stress the positive aspect of this union as a sign of the Christian unity we are seeking. For such a marriage, with a strong bond of love and loyalty which crosses the barriers of a divided church, could be a real sign to all of the triumph of a holy love over the divisions of the churches. The priest should advise the Catholic party to acquire some knowledge of the other's religious convictions and to share occasionally in his or her worship services. Given the increasing number of ecumenical marriages in our society, it is imperative that these couples receive pastoral care, not only in the preparation and celebration of their marriage, but afterwards, throughout their life together. This care should be supplied jointly by both Catholic and other Christian clergymen.

Catholic partners still were required to practice their faith and do all in their power to raise their children in the Catholic Church, but promises from the non-Catholic partner were eliminated. Dispensations to marry Orthodox Christians before an Orthodox priest were granted regularly, but dispensations to marry in a Protestant church would be granted only for serious reasons, including avoidance of family alienation, winning parental consent, recognition of the significant claims of relationship or friendship with a non-Catholic minister. In such cases, the Catholic party should include in the wedding invitation a card indicating that such permission had been granted by the bishop. Catholics and non-Catholics could serve as witnesses at marriages in each other's churches, while priests were encouraged, when invited, to attend ceremonies in non-Catholic churches and to invite ministers of the non-Catholic party to participate in the Catholic ceremony. In Catholic-Jewish weddings, neither party should be asked to surrender their religious convictions. The bishop would consider requests for such marriages to be held in a neutral place or to be presided over by a rabbi.

371

Syracuse Catholicism always had been moderate and moderate it would remain. There were very few lay people or priests who wished to move rapidly ahead with liturgical experimentation or to unite with Protestants, nor were there many who wished to stand pat. The local Church would implement conciliar reforms, but carefully, and the bishops hoped, without unduly disturbing the order they had established in the local Church, an order they thought reflected the order Christ intended for his Church. They would keep a close eye on what other American bishops were doing, hoping to "be "neither first nor last" to implement a reform. As Foery put it in distributing to his priests copies of the Roman decree on implementing council reforms:

There has been and unquestionably will be much confusion resulting from many of the private interpretations about these Decrees of the Council. Many of these interpretations have not met with the approval of the Church nor will they necessarily be acceptable to the American bishops. We must bear in mind, therefore, that we are priests of the Church who recognize the duty and the right of the Holy Father to direct and to guide us. With this basic principle in mind, it is my prayer that confusion will disappear and acceptance of the Church's teaching will be the rule.

Foery, Cunningham and even Frank Harrison, who became bishop in 1977, were not in the forefront of reform, and they wished to keep things as much as possible within the orderly structure of the diocesan Church. On the one hand, they had a responsibility for the life of the Church in the diocese and were not shy about fulfilling that responsibility. On the other hand, with increasing personal commitment, they believed in the words of the council documents and their own speeches, that the Spirit was at work in the events around them. They were permissive, allowing loyal priests and religious to explore new avenues of dialogue and new areas of ministry, and they welcomed with growing conviction the introduction of new procedures for developing congregational participation in the liturgy. None of them were theologians so they did not have an abstract approach to issues like ecumenical relationships. Rather, they welcomed concrete, practical steps to build better relationships and to work together on problems of common concern. Beyond that, they neither pushed hard toward ecumenical cooperation, nor did they hold back. Like most of the American Church, ecumenism had become, by the end of the 1970s, a matter of "wait and see." There were other problems to occupy attention, internal matters of Church reform and new relationships between the hierarchy and clergy on one side and lay people and religious on the other, and external matters of social justice, human rights and world peace. On these changing matters, too, the Syracuse Church would be not first and not last.

ADJUSTMENTS IN CATHOLIC EDUCATION

SHAPING NEW APPROACHES TOWARD LEARNING
1960s-1980s

Among the works of the American Catholic Church, none absorbed more energy and money than education. From the earliest days, Sunday schools, parochial schools, academies and colleges dotted the landscape. In the United States, with its religious pluralism and constant mobility, immigrant parents knew their children could learn of the traditional faith, and thus learn about the sources of their parents' lives and hopes, only if they were consciously instructed. Later American parents learned that their children, increasingly at home in America, would have to be given knowledge of their faith if they were to make informed religious and moral choices. Priests and parents came to believe that schools were the best means to do all this. In Syracuse at least, the religious education of public school children was not neglected, especially after the advent of released time. Bishop Foery's goal, "to reach every child," came close to fulfillment in the 1950s, through schools and religious education programs bought with enormous financial sacrifices.

After Vatican II profound problems hit Catholic education. Declining enrollments, mounting costs and fewer religious vocations brought crisis to the schools, while difficult questions arose about the relationship between schools and parish religious education. At the same time, changes emerging from the council, intersecting with changes in the Church's own internal composition and the challenges raised by social and political crises in the country, called into question the content, character and purpose of all educational work within the Church. As Monsignor Charles Eckermann put it, "adjustments" were taking place in Catholic education, and the process was far from complete. As pastors long had known, education was a vital element of parish life and one of the foundations of Church membership and morale. At stake in debates about schools and religious education was far more than budgets or priorities. In many ways, education, especially schools, had held parishes together; people's investment in the Church, personal and financial, was motivated in part by their commitment to their families and their sense of responsibility toward their children. Long excluded from policy-making and given to believe that the Church was fully competent to educate their children, people had little basis on which to evaluate changes proposed from the top, and little experience to bring a positive response when told that education was a matter of their personal responsibility. Around issues of education, clustered larger questions about the content of faith, the purpose of the Church and the relationship between the people and those who served them in the Church's ministries. Painful educational conflicts demonstrate many diverse strands of contemporary American Catholicism and left large questions for resolution by future generations.

THE SCHOOL CRISIS

As the 1960s began, optimism about Catholic education had never been greater. In 1961 Catholics in Onondaga County pledged over $4,000,000 to build two 840-student high schools to be named after Bishops Ludden and Grimes. At the same time, in Binghamton and Johnson City, the Church raised $2,500,000 for a central high school to be built on the grounds of the old St. Mary's Home. Utica and Rome also were opening new diocesan high schools. There were 41,840 students in Catholic elementary and high schools schools in 1963, up from 36,305 five years earlier. In 1962 the schools had thrown open their doors for the general public as part of a national campaign to win support for including Catholic schools in the benefits of a federal aid to education bill before Congress.

The glow from all this hardly had dimmed before some large problems appeared. Ludden High School opened on schedule, but Grimes was delayed by building costs and Bishop Foery's second thoughts about the need for another diocesan high school in Onondaga County. As Ludden prepared to graduate its first class in June 1966, costs had risen sharply. In 1967 and 1968 deficits at Utica Catholic Academy were apportioned among the city's parishes. Some pastors were

dissatisfied with their assessments; all were upset by the additional burden on the parish budgets.

Increasing costs, along with population shifts, were posing new problems for parish schools as well. Declining Catholic population in urban neighborhoods threatened the existence of some schools, and the need for tuition charges at all levels raised the danger of limiting the advantages of Catholic education to those who could afford it. In January 1963, Foery reminded the priests that every child, regardless of financial status, had the right to receive a Catholic education. Tuition adjustments should be made when more than one child attended a school, and pastors were to use funds from the recently established monthly collection for Catholic education to assist parents with genuine financial need. If that amount was not enough, they were to use general parish funds. Yet Foery had to repeat the reminder, a sign that not everyone agreed that parishes, not parents, were responsible for the costs of Catholic education.

In 1964 Foery noted that local Catholics had always been generous in responding to appeals to build schools, but "the response to appeals for operating costs has not always been so encouraging." While parents had to help pay for education, Foery insisted that

"Catholic schooling, like public schooling, is the responsibility of all. All Catholics should share the cost."

One obvious target for this increasing financial pressure was the parish high school, which some felt had been rendered obsolete by the new central high schools. In 1968, St. John the Evangelist High School in Syracuse closed, leaving some angry parents and parishioners. The bishop, ordinarily present at graduation, told the pastor it might be best if he did not attend that year. This was a significant event. During Foery's administration, diocesan offices and agencies had always been seen as supportive of parish growth and development. Now, with the pressure of numbers and costs, the centralized planning and control Foery thought necessary for the high schools brought parishes and the diocese into conflict. Decisions about parish schools no longer could be made by individual parishes alone, and some of the bishop's decisions, even though they were made in the best interests of the Catholic children, would run counter to the loyalty and sacrifice so many had made for a particular parish school. One result was a sense of distance between the diocesan bureaucracy and the parishes, and even between the bishop and the parishioners. In the context of all the other changes taking place, especially in liturgy and social actions, it was bound to be a difficult time.

One solution, obvious on the surface but directly opposed to powerful traditions, was cooperation among neighboring schools. Problems of declining numbers of sisters, for example, could not be handled on a parish-by-parish basis without forcing the sisters to make choices of priorities best made by the parishes themselves. Declining numbers of sisters and increasing education costs suggested a sharing of resources. But carrying such changes into practice required considerable tact. Statements about "the common good" could easily be interpreted by loyal parishioners as suggesting that they were narrow or selfish, even bigoted. After a meeting on these problems at St. Stanislaus in Utica, for example, one parishioner told the school superintendent, Father Thomas Costello, that parishioners would resist a cooperative plan, even if it meant closing their schools.

Similar problems arose at Sacred Heart in Syracuse, once the most crowded school in the diocese. Enrollment was declining, as it was at St. Patrick's and St. Lucy's on the west side. In the fall of 1972 when committees in each parish were asked to study the situation, the parishioners' suspicions were aroused, despite Bishop Cunningham's assurances that he had no "pre-formed plan" for consolidation. He assured one mother that he understood how important all these schools were to those who supported them: "If we can maintain them as they are, so be it, but all the work of last winter and spring questions our ability to do so." Nevertheless the head of the 500-member Mothers' Club at Sacred Heart wrote to Costello, challenging the whole idea on the basis of long-standing assumptions of parental and parish responsibility:

Our rights under the Bill of Rights are being infringed upon. We have the right to worship as we please, and also the right to choose the school for our children. You must realize that Sacred Heart was founded as a Polish Roman Catholic Parish. We are proud of our heritage. This strong ethnic feeling would be lost in any merger attempt, and also lost would be the financial support of the large number of Polish suburban families who would no longer see any reason to bus their children into the city.... Without the people you have no financial support and no school of any kind, merged or otherwise.

In pleading for her school, this mother expressed the close association of family, church and school which in fact had made Catholic schools unique:

Sacred Heart school and parish is a way of life for its families. It is the spiritual core so desperately needed in this day and age of drugs and moral decay. We trust our children to the Felician sisters, and we have confidence in the dedication and watchful eye of our clergy. We strongly believe that it is our duty to preserve the school for the benefit of our children and those of future generations.

Education might be a collective diocesan responsibility, as Foery claimed, but the parish school was also "a way of life," which knit families and church together. Consolidations, and even more, school closings, could seem to mean an unraveling of the bonds of faith, friendship and common purpose, a jolting experience, however necessary.

If at times the diocese seemed uncertain about particular decisions, the bishop did not back away from the commitment to Catholic schools. Cunningham encouraged parents to send their children to Catholic schools as "the most effective means we have for religious education." Far from having outlived their usefulness, the bishop was convinced that "never before has the Catholic school been more important to the Catholic Church and to society." In 1973, appealing for support and setting policy on tuition, the bishop repeated that financial need should be no barrier to Catholic education, nor should race, creed or nationality bar the door. Where a child had no particular parish, the cost of his or her education would have to be borne by

The 1970s were hard times for Catholic schools, but throughout the diocese educators, pastors, and parents continued their efforts to maintain the strong heritage of these schools. Here, enthusiastic teachers greet children eager to learn at St. Thomas Aquinas school in Binghamton. (Photo: The Catholic Sun)

the individual school; assistance to Catholic students would have to come from their parishes.

Because the schools assisted the Church as a whole in the pursuit of its mission, they were the work of the entire community. Perhaps they were, but parishes and people had other responsibilities as well.

The situation could be illustrated by a parish council meeting at St. John the Baptist church in March 1973. Council members were angry because after nine months of discussion a plan for consolidation of schools on the north side was scuttled. While their own school was adequately staffed and funded for one more year, this meant that they were facing grave difficulties, compounded by their

$100,000 contribution to the building fund for Ludden and Grimes, and their $10,000 annual subsidy for the Catholic central schools. The council members agreed that their primary responsibility was for their own school. One member even moved that they remove the school from the parish and diocese altogether, establishing it as an independent school eligible for state aid. He withdrew his motion, but the council unanimously decided that no more money would be paid by the parish for support of diocesan schools. When the pastor communicated this to the bishop, he referred to studies being made, making it an inappropriate time for drastic decisions, and said he rejected the parish council decision.

In Endwell, students from Our Lady of the Angels parish attended Christ the King school. Diocesan policy was that their tuition was the responsibility of the whole parish, though pastors were free to request parents to pay this charge if they could afford it. The pastor sometimes sent the parents a personal envelope to remind them of their obligation, while charges to the parish bothered the parish council. In the summer of 1968, Costello visited the parish and suggested that the envelope might appear a bit like "dunning." He suggested instead a broad-based discussion of Catholic education from the pulpit. In the spring 1973, the parish council was told that the following year there would be 124 parish children in the first eight grades, costing the parish $39,000 — 35 percent of parish income. Assessment for the Catholic high school took another $15,000. So the overall school program, serving at most 200 children, consumed more that 50% of the parish's total budget. Meanwhile, religious education was seeking $17,500, 15 percent of the budget, for 850 students. At Our Lady of the Angels and many other parishes the obvious questions were asked: Was this a fair allocation of resources? What would happen if the proportions were reversed? How could parents be brought to greater involvement in the training of their children? Many professionals thought adult education was a priority, but learned the hard way that the seed had to be planted before the desire for more knowledge of the faith could grow. This suggested parish spiritual renewal. On the other hand, one parishioner argued that the introduction of new programs of first penance and first eucharist, which required parent participation, were seen by some parents as blackmail. Overall, the council's discussions ended with a desire to enhance Christian community to bring about more vigorous participation so a foundation could be laid for dealing with the questions of goals, priorities and distribution of resources. In the fall of 1973, discussion of such renewal efforts, aimed at getting a fuller picture of parish needs as defined by the parishioners themselves, was increasingly common.

The most successful early effort at consolidation came in the parishes of Broome County through an intensive process of planning involving parishes in Endwell, Endicott, Binghamton and Johnson City. Naturally, people were distressed at media reports which suggested that their parish school might not survive the process, but the bishop attempted to ease these concerns, emphasizing the need for cooperation and continuing effort to maintain quality. As he wrote to one worried parishioner:

> *You may rest assured that any plan that is adopted for consolidating the schools in Western Broome will accommodate all the children of the area who wish a Catholic education, and this without doing violence to the teacher-student ratio. We are committed to providing quality Catholic schooling to all the children whose parents desire it for them. No child*

presently in attendance at a Catholic school, and no child who seeks admission, will be denied entry.

The climax of consolidation conflicts came when the diocese announced the closing of Seton High of Endicott and its consolidation with the Catholic Central High School of Binghamton, now to be called Seton Catholic Central High School of Broome County. "In order to avoid an uncontrolled collapse of the school system, the direction of effort is to guide the system to stability and permanence by consolidation," Cunningham explained. "In some instances, unfortunately, it does become necessary to lose schools." Schools existed, he insisted, to supplement the work of the parish, the parish "does not exist for the school." Cunningham was extremely upset that some parents became so emotional as to give the appearance of threatening sabotage against the system by threatening to withhold parish offerings in order to "intimidate me in my decisions." He said harassing telephone calls to his office reflected "immaturity and childishness." He would not reverse the decision about Seton High's closing despite a vigorous "Save Our Seton" campaign and resignations of 4 of the 7 lay members of the area school board.

Similar mergers took place elsewhere. In Utica, three high schools were consolidated into one in the fall of 1976. In Rome, three elementary schools were restructured with two K-6 programs and a junior high. In Syracuse, four parish high schools closed, and studies were underway which would lead to closing two more. In Oswego, one high school served the area.

By the end of the 1970s, there were several distinct constituencies contending over school policy. A series of regional school boards had been established to make studies and recommendations. On different occasions their recommendations had been opposed by parents, teachers, religious communities, even the bishops, while the bishop often found himself caught in the middle between two or more of the parties. In addition, religious communities, so crucial to staffing the schools, long had had their own planning bodies, and their communication with the diocesan schools frequently was confused as they dealt with the bishop, individual pastors, the school department or school boards. Lay teachers were now a majority of the teaching staff, yet their opportunities for participation in decision making were limited. In the late 1970s they began to discuss unionization. Meanwhile, in the wake of diocesan reorganization, the vicar for education, Richard Lawless, and the school office, now headed by Father James O'Brien, were working with the various groups to develop more coherent organization and better communications. The result was the Catholic School Covenant, adopted in 1981, which set forth a philosophy of the diocesan school program which argued that the school constituted a faith community carrying out the teaching mission of the Church, with administrators and teachers comprising a "team" that shared in an educational "ministry." The convenant clarified the role of regional school boards and provided for organization of teachers and administrators. The hope was that this system would improve communication, create a sense of shared responsibility for the educational mission of the Church and its schools, ease the process of consultation in making policy decisions, and insure greater support when decisions were to be carried out. By this means, some of the problems of teacher unionization might also be avoided, as diocesan officials made clear their desire for a more collaborative approach than unions offered. Tension among parishes, the school office, parents, teachers, and administrators might remain, but the diocese was better prepared than ever before for planning,

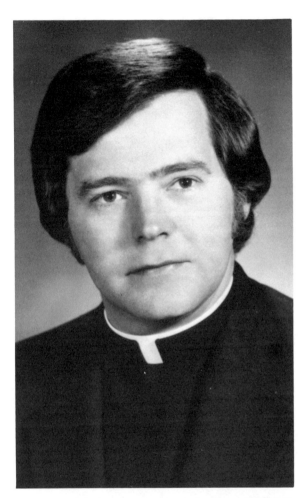

Diocesan administrative reorganization resulted in Dr. Richard Lawless (right) serving as vicar for education and Father James O'Brien (left) as superintendent of schools. Together, they worked with teachers, principals, parents, and pastors to build strong "teams" concerned about Catholic schools. In 1981 their work resulted in the Catholic School Covenant which set forth principles of shared responsibility in the educational mission of the Church. (Photos: The Catholic Sun)

shaping priorities and making difficult decisions.

The school question had become a matter of numbers, for the tremendous expansion of the post-war years had been reversed in the 1960s; with a declining student population came the pressure of fixed costs. The total number of students in Catholic elementary schools in the 1980s was actually greater than in 1950. But they went to larger schools, as the number of schools had dropped from 65 to 49. The tremendous expansion of population was seen in kindergarten enrollment, which skyrocketed in the late 1950s and early 1960s, then dropped rapidly in the 1970s, reaching the 1950 level again. High school

CATHOLIC SCHOOLS 1950-1980

	1950	1960	1970	1980
Students:				
Kindergarten	1,654	2,673	1,512	1,614
Elementary (1-8), parish	15,589	28,735	24,133	13,242
Elementary, private	—	137	61	178
High (9-12), parish/diocesan	2,351	5,369	8,221	4,410
High, private	646	539	963	685
Total	20,240	37,453	34,890	20,129
Teachers	564	1,297	1,275	1,346
Schools:				
Elementary	49	71	77	65
High	13	18	19	9

380

enrollment thus dropped later than did grammar school enrollment, because the former continued to increase in the 1960s as elementary enrollments were dropping. Smaller class size, more specialized instruction and rising expectations about the quality of education kept the number of teachers stable. This meant rising payroll costs as lay teachers replaced sisters in the classroom. By 1980 parish high schools had disappeared; those high schools which remained were under diocesan control, with policy established by local and regional school boards. Elementary schools remained largely parish based. With consolidation and area-wide planning, many now were financed by a combination of tuition and parish subsidies. In addition, parishes paid another subsidy to the high schools.

Collective responsibility for parish elementary schools was even harder to bring about. This was so both because support was rooted in parish pride and tradition and because it was difficult to gain support from people without children in the schools. Nevertheless, by the mid-1980s the diocese had moved toward wider sharing of responsibility for both junior high and elementary school education. Enrollments had stabilized, but several high schools and elementary schools remained in jeopardy.

In 1982 Bishop Harrison appointed four regional task forces to give substance to his pledge of an "efficient" Catholic school system. He gave these task forces four goals to be achieved by 1987, including organization of the elementary schools into regional systems, complemented where feasible by central high schools; sharing of financial support among participants through tuition and among the larger community through parish subsidies; strengthening the tuition assistance program for low-income families; and efficient administration and allocation of resources. In September 1984 the task force reports were published. They described the economic problems faced by the schools: the sharp drop in enrollment, rising costs associated with hiring more lay teachers, increasing fixed costs and the growth in tuition over the last five years, and the need for increased parish subsidies. In the northern region, attention centered on Bishop Cunningham High School where the bishop had promised to keep the school open if supporters could develop enrollment to 170 with $1,000 tuition, a process that was still being pursued. Most controversial were the recommendations for the Syracuse area and Onondaga county, where parishes were to be clustered and would share the costs of running the junior high school in their district. Because of the broad consultation and sharing of responsibility, prospects for implementing the task force's decisions were better than ever before.

There was another point of view, one heard little to date but with powerful support from Monsignor Charles Eckermann, who served as principal of Ludden High, as pastor of St. John the Baptist and as a member and president of the Syracuse Board of Education. In an interview published in the *Catholic Sun* in August 1984, Eckermann noted that the declining numbers of religious and increasing costs had made Catholic schools, which were the "best vehicle we have devised for transmitting our Catholic values from one generation to the next," less and less available to Catholic families. Like it or not, this decline would continue and the same trend toward fewer, consolidated and centralized schools would take place at the elementary level as had already taken place in high schools. The flip side of the coin was that the majority of Catholic children would attend public schools, and it was these children who should enjoy priority consideration. Taking issue with the bishop's emphasis on Catholic schools, Eckermann was blunt: "If we look at the situation a bit more realistically we have to admit that, although the Catholic schools are good, they are no longer a priority, and we ought to get more seriously involved in the public school system."

A study prepared in 1983 showed a steady decline in enrollment in Catholic schools, larger in the cities than in the suburbs, but substantial overall. In the previous five years there was an overall annual rate of decline of 3.2 percent and that decline was expected to continue for the next five years, based on population data. Between 1978 and 1982 the proportion of religious on school faculties had declined from 40 to 30 percent. In only one parish in the diocese was tuition covering more than half the cost of running the school. In most, tuition covered between 30 and 40 percent, the rest was met by subsidy from the parish receipts. In many urban schools, the subsidy for the school took between 30 and 40 percent of parish income. Eckermann concluded:

If you really look at it, there's what I would call adjustments that are taking place in Catholic education and although they may hurt us, because it is a change in our basic tradition, it is not all bad. If we will accompany the movement of more and more of our youngsters to public schools, with more and more interest on our part and more and more effort on the part of our teachers, parents and administrators, by what we say and how we live, by our interest, then we will make those schools more responsive to our needs.

RELIGIOUS EDUCATION

While support for Catholic schools became increasingly difficult to maintain, and while public school education was not at the forefront of the Church's attention, there had been great progress in parish religious education. But once again, progress was marked by the growing pains of renewal, and like so much of the rapidly changing Church of the post-Vatican II period, change was taking place without coordination with other areas of Church life. 1963 was one of the years Bishop Foery had to submit a report to Rome on

CHILDREN LEAD THE WAY

—→·✠·←—

Many times throughout the life of the Catholic Church in Central New York and the Southern Tier, children and their need for religious education were the impetus for beginning new parishes. The concern for passing on the faith from one generation to the next extends from the early settlement days through the years following the Second Vatican Council.

In the 1960s, in the tiny village of Leonardsville in the southeastern corner of rural Madison County, Catholics had to be mobile. Some attended St. Theresa's church in New Berlin, 14 miles down the Unadilla River; others traveled to St. Joseph's church in West Winfield, across the border into the Albany diocese.

In the fall of 1968, the pastor at New Berlin, Father Richard O'Neill, began holding religion classes in Catholic homes in Leonardsville for children attending the local elementary school. Later these released-time classes were held in the Leonardsville American Legion building.

When Father Vincent Mirabito became pastor the following year, he purchased a schoolhouse trailer and parked it on donated property. This CCD center quickly became a gathering place for the 94 Catholics who lived around Leonardsville, and soon they asked Father Mirabito to celebrate Mass in the trailer.

Bishop Cunningham gave his permission, and the first Mass was celebrated there on April 4, 1970. First Communion for seven children followed the next month, and on June 12 a parish council was elected. On June 15, Bishop Cunningham created a mission for Leonardsville, with the trailer church-school dedicated to Our Lady of the Valley.

catechetics, and it was a proud statement. Of the 75,610 children in public schools, the diocese claimed that 92.2 percent were receiving religious instruction.

This work was carried out by 349 priests, 810 religious and 772 lay catechists, the latter figure representing a huge increase over the 432 involved four years earlier. The report pointed with pride to new religious education centers, training programs for lay teachers and support from parishioners and parents.

The rosy picture painted in the 1963 report to Rome obscured serious problems that had plagued religious education from the beginning and would intensify amid the changes brought by the Vatican Council. Foery was at pains again and again to remind parishioners of their responsibilities for the religious

education of their children and to remind pastors of their canonical responsibilities to provide for that religious education. The need for these reminders suggests something less than full support for Foery's long-standing goal of quality religious education for every child. In one talk, for example, he insisted that religious education confined to Sunday worship and perhaps a brief Sunday School program was not enough, for it gave "the growing child the impression that religion belongs to Sunday and may be put aside during other days of the week." Moreover, the provision for formal education was imperative, because in many cases, "if we are to touch the lives of some children we must overcome bad home influences." In letters to priests he insisted on their responsibility for

In the 1960s, diocesan leaders realized that more needed to be done to provide Catholic education for children in public schools. Father John S. Russell (above) and later Fathers Norbert C. Henry and Michael Meagher as diocesan directors of religious education helped parishes implement professional and energetic programs to help all youngsters learn Catholic faith and morals. (Photo: The Catholic Sun)

school to pay for. The bishop rarely noted that his own policy on schools encouraged this practice, as did the obvious allocation of diocesan and parish resources.

In 1965, for example, he again told priests that, while the Catholic school was "the ideal" they were obligated by their position as pastors to provide schools of religion for public school students with "the best facilities, staff and teaching aids within our power." In a statement sincerely meant but belied by long-standing priorities, he insisted that "these children must not be treated as inferior in any way to the children fortunate enough to attend our parochial schools." Secondly, he was concerned that priests emphasize that parents were the primary religious educators of their children and that they make every effort to help parents fulfill their "sacred function." Thus there was need for adult education. He therefore announced a major reorganization of the CCD program, with a priest advisory board to assist the diocesan director and a lay board to advise the priests.

In April, Father John Russell was appointed diocesan director. Russell found the situation worse than he had expected. Two years later he estimated that, in sharp contrast to the 1963 figures, there were at least 27,000 youngsters receiving no religious instruction. In released time programs there were many parishes with no or poor records of attendance; where figures were available, there was evidence of marked absenteeism and a sharp drop off in attendance after the fifth grade. Many parishes had yet to establish CCD boards and at least half the parishes had no substantial CCD program, whatever might appear in parish reports. Twenty-five thousand children in CCD had no classrooms or were being instructed in inadequate locations. Forty thousand were in classes where the student teacher ratio was over 40-to-1. The average class time was 30 minutes, in many

public school children, undoubtedly reflecting a widespread tendency under the pressure of parish life to subordinate that program, particularly if the parish had an expensive cases much less. Of the lay teachers, 50 to 60 percent had received no catechetical training. Less than 15 percent of the parishes held faculty meetings; 40 percent gave no progress reports to students or parents, sixty thousand students were without benefit of ordinary visual aids; and forty thousand were instructed in rooms without a blackboard. Russell proposed steps to deal with these problems and asked for a budget. For a long time his request went unanswered.

He finally received approval of a $35,000 budget, the amount indicative of the continuing imbalance between the diocese's professed goals and its actual priorities. Still, with this support and the help of innumerable volunteers, Russell began to address the problems. In the fall of 1966 five teacher formation centers began around the diocese.

Russell was a professional, elected president of a new organization of diocesan directors of religious education in 1966. He and others like him were determined to bring systematic organization and teaching by training professionals for parish service, improving facilities by the development of parish religious education centers, extending parent and volunteer involvement through adult education programs and adequate teacher training programs, and providing appropriate support with regional centers, professionally staffed, where teachers could be trained, materials distributed, and audio visual and other instructional aids made available for parish and school use. What they wanted, in short, was what Foery promised in 1969 — that catechetics for public school children should at last move out of its status as the "stepchild" of Catholic education.

By the end of 1969, a number of these reforms had been introduced under Russell and his successor, Norbert C. Henry.

In December of that year, a full-time coordinator was hired for the Utica area to work on teacher training; there were two full-time people working in Binghamton and five out of the Syracuse office. There were also five regional resource centers, and diocesan and regional committees had been established. The bishop designated that year's CCD Sunday as Adult Religious Education Sunday, and the following year's program carried through this theme. By 1970, 22 parishes had appointed religious education coordinators; 80 parishes now had CCD boards. Budgets had risen dramatically with the addition of professional staff. Tension with schools developed as religious communities, which were cutting back on school service, made personnel available for religious education work, particularly in poorer parishes. Parishes cooperated in opening or extending religious education centers and sharing staff, while the relationship between staff and parish was becoming more professional, complete with formal contracts, job descriptions and specification of responsibilities.

In the early seventies new efforts were made to reach older children. One important step was to push back the date of confirmation from grade five or six to grade eight, thereby encouraging continued attendance of junior high school students. Despite the establishment of two faith centers near public high schools, high school CCD attendance remained low, allegedly because of poor parental support, scheduling problems and lack of publicity. Gradually the problem broadened out. In 1976 a committee produced a study of the relationship of young people to the Church, noting the decline of participation not only in high school religious education, but in CYO and other youth programs as well. To draw young people to the Church, it was necessary that parents have a positive attitude toward the Church and a concern for the religious life of their youngsters, and that parish priests have an open and flexible approach to youth. The committee recommended concentration in each par-

New efforts were made in the seventies and eighties to expand religious education. Parishes and Catholic schools gave new focus to young children, and Sister Jane Bourne of the Syracuse Franciscan Sisters opened the Gingerbread House pre-school in Syracuse (left). Meanwhile, Jean Hill (right) coordinated religious education of children and adults in rural Chenango County. (Photos: The Catholic Sun)

ish on a broad-based program of what would soon be called youth ministry, to develop coordinated social, recreational, spiritual and educational activities. This study focused on high school age students; almost nothing was said about the 18 to 25-years-olds who were neither married nor in college. Cunningham urged priests to support more efforts with young adults, but few concrete proposals were made.

By 1980 volunteer teachers were providing religious instruction for 91,000 public school children. The budget for the Religious Education Office in 1979-80 was $248,971. During the year, 550 people attended workshops held to familiarize teachers with the National Catechetical Directory. Sixty-seven of the parishes had the services of a certified religious education director and the diocese began using cable television as form of adult education. A variety of adult education and teacher formation programs were helping to improve the quality of instruction, while 880 mentally handicapped students were served at 24 catechetical centers throughout the diocese. There were eight resource centers serving catechetical programs and six faith centers serving public high schools. This work developed under a mission statement which defined the role of the Religious Education office as one of "supporting and assisting the local church with its delegated catechetical tasks, helping form competent catechists and facilitating unity while respecting the authentic diversity among our people."

CONFLICT IN EDUCATION

The introduction of these reforms in religious education was generally welcomed and supported, as the dramatic increase in lay volunteers and parish budget and staff indicate. But the development of religious education involved more conflict than the liturgical reforms. Almost without exception, diocesan religious education staff and local religious education coordinators, professionally trained in education and theology, held with considerable commitment to a vision of the post-Vatican II Church which emphasized community, participation, shared responsibility and respect for the individual. Educationally this meant that parents were called to share their faith with their children. Pastorally it meant that the Church should move more and more to become a community marked by the equality of all Christians in baptism and the call to holiness, and by a theology of gifts in which the Holy Spirit calls from the community those with the charisms needed to fulfill its responsibilities. The word ministry covered many aspects of this approach, because it incorporated ideas of community, shared responsibility and equality. Thus, beneath complaints about the need to become involved in the educational process, was a deeper theological problem which went beyond questions of authority to issues of the nature of doctrine and the responsibilities of ordained ministers in teaching.

Foery and Cunningham gave Russell and Henry their full support for religious education, while attempting to ease the anxieties of those upset by new programs. To parents worried about their new found responsibility as teachers, Foery wrote that classroom instruction would continue and that their task was to encourage their children by "their example of prayerfulness." To others concerned about classroom presentations of other religious beliefs, he responded that the children had a right to this information but such teaching "in no way neglects the fundamental truth that our Church is the one and only one established by Christ." Com-

plaints did not always come from individuals. In 1969 one parish CCD board wrote the bishop of their concern with "the confusion which exists in the Catholic Church today." Describing themselves as "a middle of the road group with perhaps Traditionalist leanings," they argued that the press, the CCD programs and the Church generally were biased towards "Reformists" and denied the traditionalist point of view a fair hearing.

Foery and Cunningham were not entirely unsympathetic with some of the complaints generated by religious education. Bishops for the most part regard themselves primarily as pastors and shepherds, and they care deeply about the unity of the Church and the good will of the community. Divisions are more than an administrative problem, especially when they arise from deeply felt religious concern. Obviously they appreciated the faith, commitment and generosity of teachers and staff; but they also understood the faith and loyalty which informed many who complained, and felt their pain over the confusion and conflicts occasioned by rapid change. The bishops, therefore, insisted that the Vatican's catechetical directory and the American bishops' own National Catechetical Directory guide all programs and be available in every office. To remove, or at least soften the acrimony which at times entered into the debate about religious education, they told teachers to use the catechism as a reference book. All this was designed to overcome what Cunningham called the "fuzzy presentation of doctrine" which so disturbed parents and to ensure that the responsibility to "teach what the Church teaches" was in fact the goal of all programs.

An event foreshadowing later Roman intervention into American Church affairs, took place in 1972 when an active parishioner and CCD teacher wrote to Cardinal John Wright in Rome complaining of the presentation made at an adult education program by a sister on the diocesan CCD staff. Normally, the apostolic delegate or Roman officials sent such letters to the bishop, but to the bishop's surprise, Wright responded directly and sympathetically to the parishioner. He wrote that if what she had said was true, she should approach the sister and "tell her to see these people in the following order: 1) her confessor, 2) her psychologist, and 3) her bishop, and ask him to relieve her of her duty as a teacher of children." The letter writer, delighted, sent copies to the bishop and to the teacher's religious superior. The superior wrote Wright a very strong letter threatening to bring charges against him for violating canonical procedure.

The sister was devastated, but defended herself strongly with the backing of Father Henry. Cunningham was furious. He wrote Wright expressing astonishment at his letter, a "radical departure from past procedure," assuring him that the sister in question was "dedicated, highly qualified and completely faithful to the teaching of the magisterium." Most important, he said, "not only has the teacher been unjustly accused and hurt but your letter had given the impression that our CCD office may not be doctrinally sound. I am sure that you will understand how this can adversely affect our hard working staffs as well as the effectiveness of their efforts." Wright responded that he had so many letters of this sort he had attempted to find a new way of dealing with them by appealing to the writer's conscience by using the words "if the statements quoted are true." Nevertheless Wright's attitude was clear. "We are living in troublesome and troubled times.... The letters pouring in show that we are becoming a community of hatred rather than of charity and love."

As Wright's words indicated, there was an atmosphere of crisis throughout the Church. Pope Paul VI publicly anguished over departures from the active ministry, theological speculation which seemed to threaten long-standing doctrines and a divisiveness marked by defections from the left and the right. The United States experienced a long series of shocks from the assassination of John Kennedy through the urban riots which seemed to punctuate every summer and the murders in 1968 of Martin Luther King and Robert Kennedy, to the continuing violence in Vietnam and intensifying rebelliousness among the young. For Catholics, these all intersected with changes in their own community as authority and taken-for-grantedness seemed to collapse.

In Syracuse these pent up emotions seemed to burst in the winter of 1968-69 on the superintendent of schools, Thomas Costello. The issue was a sex education program for the diocesan schools. A local committee, concerned by confusion and uncertainty among young people and the evident rise in early sexual activity, had chosen a program used earlier in Rochester and cleared it with diocesan authorities.

Teachers were summoned to a series of meetings to familiarize them with the material; and a group of conservative Catholics attended the last of these workshops, part of which dealt with advice on dealing with extreme sexual behavior. Shocked, they contacted the local newspaper. A reporter looked at the material and wrote a sensational series of articles, citing passages out of context and giving them the most sordid interpretations. Rarely had a religious issue excited so much local interest. Letters poured in to the bishop, radio talk shows and television news programs spread the controversy; within a few days, the program was withdrawn.

The opposition mirrored the anxiety stirred not only by change in the Church but by the wrenching changes taking place in the larger society. One theme, by far the most reasonable, was that the program represented a series of attacks on parental authority. "Sex education is the prerogative and responsibility of the parent, who is best able to judge his own child's degree of emotional maturity and readiness to accept the various stages of information," one woman wrote. "When given in the privacy of the home, in an atmosphere of love and belief in and dependence upon God's will, I believe a deeper and healthier understanding of the life process will result." She was not alone, though her calm, thoughtful tone was unusual.

A second, far more common theme was an overwhelming sense of moral collapse. Letter after letter mentioned sex education in the same sentence as hedonism, promiscuity, drugs, music, long hair and a whole range of symbols of youthful rebellion against prevailing cultural standards. Two women characteristically referred to the program's materials as "smut" and "pornography" but they quickly added that they knew they would not be listened to because they were "neither red, black, brown, yellow skinned nor a misused underpaid welfare recipient, an unwashed parasite or a hairy student protesting being alive." Another well-educated parishioner referred to the program as "one of the most insidious and diabolical encroachments on the minds and souls of our children that one could imagine." In all such arguments, people pictured themselves as isolated and lonely, abandoned by the Church amid a sea of immorality. Even Foery told one letter writer, "Sometimes I feel like I'm standing alone on this very important matter."

A third theme was that this program revealed the dangers present in the effort to change the Church. The whole project of renewal seemed to some an adaptation to prevailing cultural standards, which people had long been taught were bad. One writer attacked the program and connected it with talk about the Legion of Decency in which she claimed the priest argued that children should be allowed to form their own con-

A public outcry arose in the late 1960s when Monsignor Thomas J. Costello, as superintendent of schools, led Catholic schools in implementing guidelines by the American bishops for sex education. The sensationalized outcry eventually subsided, but it would be another decade before Catholic schools throughout the diocese adopted a full program of family life education, including sex education, as a component of religion and biology classes and spanning from early elementary grades through high school. (Photo: The Catholic Sun)

science regarding what movies they would see. Many made similar associations between the program and the behavior of priests and sisters. The Church seemed to be infiltrated by enemies. Again Foery shared some of this attitude. Writing a Rochester acquaintance he said, "I agree with you that the Church is in crisis at the present time and that we have many within its ranks who contribute to its difficulties.''

By this time, Foery obviously shared some of the feelings of Pope Paul VI. If he had been a strong advocate of liturgical renewal and open-minded on social issues, he had little sympathy with the new theories of moral development reflected in the sex education program. He wrote few responses to favorable letters, save one to a layman who found the program valuable; Foery simply stated he did not agree. To many of the protesters he responded that the program had not received diocesan approval. To a woman who did not want her daughter subjected to a text on love which she described as ''pure filth,'' he insisted she could take her daughter out of the class. To the lady concerned about the priest speaking about children and movies he wrote: ''My reaction is exactly the same as yours. In fact I am considered to be too conservative in many of our rectories, convents and homes.''

Angered by the newspapers' treatment of the program, the public reaction which it excited and the bishop's disclaimer of responsibility, Costello wrote a 3,000-word letter to the editor of the *Herald Journal.* Costello explained that he and many other school officials had believed there was a state mandate for such a program; there was such a mandate in the American Catholic bishops' pastoral letter ''Human Life in Our Day.'' Boys and girls were taught together in order to reflect the notion that sex is ''sacred not secret,'' and to encourage boys and girls to respect one another.

What the newspaper called the ''mating habits of animals'' in grade one included such items as observation of plant life, baby animals with their mothers, care for the young and the hatching of a fertilized egg. Similar sensationalism had been used to describe the curriculum of other grades, the worst when

the paper described a fourth grade program as ''sharing family experience of sex activity,'' when in fact it encouraged examination of family life, including prayer, helping the sick, eating and playing together and sharing family experiences. Far from supplanting parents, general school meetings on the program were scheduled, as were meetings by individual grades so parents could be discussing the same concepts as were dealt with in class. Comments at meetings held before the program was withdrawn were favorable. In Rochester, parents in five schools were polled and 94 percent favored the program.

Although the editor offered to print the letter if requested by the bishop, it did not appear, and the impression made by the original articles lingered.

In 1973 Syracuse University's College of Human Development sponsored a conference on ''Enhancing the Role of Parents as Sex Educators of Their Own Children.'' It was not sponsored by the diocese, but Sister Marguerite Tierney of the Family Life Divison of Catholic Charities and her superior, Father Charles Fahey, were consulted, as it was intended to be an interfaith gathering. As Sister Marguerite understood it, the principles of the conference corresponded to those of the Church: Parents have primary responsibility for the sex education of their children and churches have a role to play in assisting parents, especially in regard to the moral dimension of sexuality. Accordingly, she gave the college the CCD mailing list to send out announcements. The problem arose when that material went out. Sol Gordon, a controversial advocate of relatively liberal views on sex education, had been added to the program without the diocese's knowledge. The announcement contained a flier which Sister Marguerite found to be ''a thoroughly distasteful and repugnant periodical representing views and approaches entirely foreign to our values.'' Again, protests poured in. ''Santanic forces from all sides imperil our homes, schools and yes even our churches." One person wrote: "Our Catholic Church is floundering in waves of immorality." Bishop Cunningham's form response to these letters was apologetic, explaining that Sister Marguerite and Father Fahey had been given to understand it would be solely an interfaith conference addressed only by clergy representatives. The bishop was "shocked and upset" and he assured the people that Gordon's principles were "directly opposed to what the Church teaches and can accept."

When the diocese had calmed down a bit, Bishop Cunningham was able to develop a reasonable policy and set it before the people, quoting the pastoral letter of the American bishops on education:

> *The aim is not to supplant parents but to help them fulfill their obligation. They have a right to be informed about the content of such programs and be assured that diocesan approved textbooks...meet the requirement of propriety. But when these reasonable conditions have been met, parents should not allow continued anxiety to be translated into indiscriminate opposition to all forms of classroom education in sexuality. Such opposition would be contrary to the teaching of Vatican Council II and the pastoral policy of the American bishops.*

Cunningham recognized the anxieties parents felt, and the diocese had set three guidelines for family life and sex education programs — the primary responsibility belongs to parents; sex education should be given in the context of moral values; and parents have the right to have their child excused without adverse consequences for the child.

The sex education controversies found few heroes. Bishop Foery showed that his loyalty to his subordinates had limits, even when they had followed all the proper procedures. For once he was closed to alternative positions, and his inability to question his own decisions and attitudes prevented any response to his staff and to those who thought the program valuable and worthwhile. The CCD and school personnel who developed the program stumbled over their by now characteristic procedure of making important decisions before consulting lay people or parish personnel. Many of the latter, in turn, failed to defend either the program or the basic concept, at least publicly, though many of them were well-aware of the need for more positive and effective sex education in parishes and schools. Newspaper reporting of religious affairs was at its worst, distorting the program and misinterpreting motives. The content and character of the letters of the more passionate opponents demonstrated that the cultural context in which Catholicism is embedded is more complex and in need of more intelligent attention than those in favor of renewal understood. Nothing was more badly needed in the concrete circumstances of contemporary Catholic life than a positive approach to love, marriage and sexuality. This incident suggested that achieving that approach would require more trust and mutual concern than was possible in the highly charged atmosphere of the period.

ORGANIZED OPPOSITION

The religious education reforms of the post-conciliar period uncovered real divisions in basic issues of doctrine, authority and community in the Church. Where these reforms were carried out in a positive atmosphere, it was possible to grow through the tensions of change. But increasingly there were individuals and groups who felt that the whole Church around them was departing from the true spirit of Catholicism, and some were prepared to do all they could to expose what they saw as the heresies and aberrations around them. In the process, self-righteous passion could disrupt the delicate balance of Church life and cause enormous pain to good people. This was what happened at St. James in Cazenovia in 1971. A group of lay parishioners, headed by Charles Pulver, challenged the religious education program of the pastor, Monsignor A. Robert Casey, and his staff. Beginning in the summer of 1971, Pulver began to question the orthodoxy of Sister Catherine Millington's presentations in adult education, teacher training and the CCD program. He and his supporters argued that she violated the National Catechetical Directory and refused to allow teachers to use the Baltimore Catechism. They also opposed the invitation to a local public school teacher to work as a consultant in the CCD program because, they charged, he had expressed doubts about specific doctrines taught by the Church. Other incidents added to their anger, including presentation of a rock music production in the sanctuary of the church. In January they formed a local chapter of Catholics United for the Faith to study Church doctrine, announcing that step in the *Catholic Sun.* They charged that Casey denied them meeting space in the church and that, after meeting with him and Sister Catherine, Pulver was "fired" as a CCD teacher.

At the start the dispute was civil, as Pulver and Casey seemed to have a good relationship. But problems intensified, in part because Pulver was adamant on the need for what he took to be sound doctrine. The controversial CCD teacher, for example, was a practicing Catholic, a superb high school teacher and the leading force in the local drug prevention program.

Pulver agreed with all of this, referring to him in the friendliest terms, but thought this irrelevant to the basic point that the man was "unsound" in his doctrine and would commu-

391

Monsignor A. Robert Casey, vicar general of the diocese and pastor of St. James parish in Cazenovia, was the brunt of a campaign by the conservative group, Catholics United for the Faith, which was upset by religious education and many other changes in the Church following the Second Vatican Council. The campaign failed to generate much interest among lay Catholics, largely because of its attacks against a priest like Casey, who enjoyed enormous respect among the clergy and the laity. (Photo: Chancery Archives)

nicate error and doubt to the youngsters. This led to some difficult exchanges among the principals. Pulver accused Casey of valuing his friendships "above the interests of orthodoxy in the faith" and seemed genuinely puzzled when such charges made people angry. Pulver and his associates finally took their case to the bishop, who asked for Father Casey's response. By this time Casey admitted being upset at the time the dispute was taking from his parish duties, but even more at the "slander" on the names of good people and the distortions and half-truths which filled the letters and publications of his critics. He demonstrated these distortions in persuasive detail, defending the teacher in question and his CCD program. Having listened to both sides, Bishop Cunningham wrote Casey a letter to be read to the parish council assuring the priests, Sister Catherine and the staff of his "full approval." Pulver's next step was to propose an alternative CCD program to be taught by members of his group. He took this idea to Cunningham, who wrote him expressing his approval. This letter caused an immediate storm, appearing to give credibility to a group which had been bitterly attacking the parish leadership. A long dispute followed in which CUF demanded use of the parish facilities, and the bishop insisted that their program must be under the CCD office and supplement the parish program, for which the pastor and parish council had responsibility. When the parish council ruled that the children must attend CCD in addition to CUF classes, Pulver argued that the bishop had insisted that parents had the right to attend to their children's education and were free to not choose attend CCD. On March 12, after a stormy meeting, the parish council voted to deny CUF the parish facilities because its proposal did not meet the goals of the parish program and was not truly supplemental as required by the bishop. The whole controversy had received national attention through Pulver's account in the conservative paper, *The Wanderer,* which portrayed Casey and Cunningham as vaguely loose on orthodoxy

and persecuting the CUF group.

Casey and Sister Catherine received enormous support from many parishioners. Casey was clearly a superb pastor and the CCD program was well-attended, with competent, well-trained teachers and enthusiastic participation by both elementary and high school children. Parishioners were particularly upset when Casey was forced to take an extended vacation for his health.

The bishop was angry at the tone and spirit of the CUF group. In response to an inquiry from the apostolic delegate, the bishop wrote: "It is truly amazing to me and to the parishioners of Cazenovia that a small group...can hurt so many people and be so determined to obstruct the excellent catechetical program." Pulver, who was supported by from three to six families, "feels called upon to defend the faith against all who do not agree with him." People in the parish were less upset by the desire for an alternative program than by "the tactics of half-truths, amplifications and distortions used in trying to destroy the program and by their animosity toward the pastor and religious education coordinator." There was simply no question that Pulver was wrong about the CCD program at St. James. In speaking of CUF Cunningham wrote:

> One of the things that has not been achieved is what Pope John said about the Council, that it is a Pastoral Council, and the teaching of the Church must be interpreted to the period in which we live, with new knowledge of signs, new knowledge of theology and new depths of philosophy. We have to interpret the things that God has revealed in the light of all these new helps that we have. And so he said that the truth of the deposit of faith is one thing, sacred; their interpretation is another. The inter-

392

pretation that I understand is being taught there...by our CCD and probably throughout the world are the new interpretations the Council expected and requested and Pope John said must be done.

On June 9, 1973 Bishop Cunningham came to Cazenovia and preached at a Pentecost Mass in tribute to the teachers in the parish school of religion. His words were a direct rebuke to CUF and its local supporters. "Unhappily there are some who find it difficult to accept development of doctrine within the Church," Cunningham told the congregation. "Even Pope John met opposition as he was preparing for the Council" from those the pope referred to as "prophets of doom."

The Cazenovia fight was over, but CUF was far from dead and would cause Cunningham, his successor and, in its national form, all the bishops, a host of headaches in the years to come. But in Syracuse it would remain marginal, registering its negative protest against every diocesan initiative and more than one pastor or sister, but never gaining widespread support, even from clergy, religious and laity who may well have sympathized with their basic convictions about doctrine. One reason was simply that they had chosen, by the accidents of Pulver's residence in Cazenovia, the wrong target. Casey was one of the most respected and well-liked priests in the diocese. Just as he was praised by his parishioners for his understanding and moderation, so he was respected by conservative older pastors and energetic younger priests. He was a man of maturity, strength of character, openness and intelligence, and he was a caring pastor and dedicated priest. That he would be unorthodox was, for most diocesan priests, laughable; that he was pastorally insensitive was incredible; that he should be subjected to public abuse and

private attack was almost unforgivable. The incident made it all but impossible for CUF to mobilize any but negligible support among the clergy and, lacking clerical backing, much support among the laity. If they were to win their struggle for orthodoxy, they would need to circumvent the local Church and go through the press and internal Church politics to higher authority. That, in fact, is what the organization eventually did, and not without success.

Yet there was a problem. Doctrinal pluralism is a fact in the Church, as is the necessity for some limits to that pluralism if there is to be integrity in the Church's witness. Maintaining the unity of the Church at a time when this sort of pluralism appears is a pastoral, not theological, task. It requires an ability to see beyond ideas to people, as Pope John suggested when he argued, in commenting on dialogue with Marxists, that ideas are one thing, the people who hold them are something else. One can and should contend with false ideas; one can and must respect the fundamental dignity of the people who hold those ideas. On that basis the Church seeks a loving, not crusading, presence in the world, and in that spirit it seeks to enter into dialogue and ultimately into communion with those who share faith in the Risen Christ. CUF, on this occasion, lost sight of the people, as Casey never did. The resolution, proved so often in the history of the diocese when people worked out their differences, was to focus on the people.

One of the most bitterly contested issues in religious education, and the least expected, was the question of receiving first communion before first penance. In the United States the order had long been penance first, then communion, but catechists and religious education experts had always been unsure about "the age of reason," the traditional criterion for reception of the sacraments. Even more, they questioned whether the order itself was proper, suggesting as it did communication of the reality of sin and the need for forgiveness before adequate appreciation of the presence of a loving God and the gift of his presence in the Eucharist. While experts discussed these issues, change came gradually at first. A sister catechist wrote to the bishop in 1968, asking whether children could receive communion first, and delay penance until the fourth grade. Through his secretary, the bishop said he had no objection, provided the practice met with the approval of the pastor involved. He recognized individual differences whereby some children might "develop a sense of sin and be prepared to receive the Sacrament of Penance much earlier than others." This made it seem unwise to establish a "cut and dry policy," though he also recognized the problems that might arise in attempting to offer catechesis on an individual basis. Personally he thought fourth grade "as delaying a bit too long," but he was prepared to leave that judgment to the pastor involved.

In 1971, after clergy conferences in which many agreed that sacramental preparation was an excellent way to involve adults in religious education, the bishop sent out interim guidelines which emphasized the primary role and responsibility of parents preparing their children and "deciding the time and manner" of reception of these sacraments. In addition, the guidelines stated that the two sacraments should be separated in time sufficient to "emphasize the distinctiveness and individual dignity of both" and "to erase the still prevalent notion that confession must precede the reception of the Eucharist." Children were to receive communion by the end of second grade and were to have the option of family or group reception. First penance, on the other hand, "need not be prior to first communion but should be received by the end of the third or fourth grade." The document containing these guidelines offered a long list of theological, psychological and historical facts regarding this practice. Parents were to be made familiar with these facts "so that they do not impose an obligation to confess where none exists and that they do not encourage their children to confess too early." The practice of receiving penance first was less than 50 years old, so the departure from the practice was "actually the more traditional order."

Despite the fact that these guidelines and their supporting information did not actually forbid penance first, they clearly aimed at changing the order of sacramental reception and postponing penance until a later date. This arose from the combination of scholarship, filtered to the diocese through the professional training of religious educators, and pastoral practice involving parents, in which the emphasis on the benefits and truths of the Eucharist seemed more appropriate to the needs of children and families. Nevertheless, parents played an ambiguous role. As the cover letter indicated, there was desire on the part of diocesan educational leadership to involve parents not simply because it was their right but because their desire to have their children receive the sacraments made it a good moment "to involve adults in religious education." So, while parents had the "primary role," they had to be informed of their responsibility, be prepared for the task and cooperate with the parish in carrying it out. Parents were not consulted about these changes, and might have reason to doubt the sincerity of a claim that they had primary responsibility when they had no role in shaping the policy they were to implement.

Trouble arose in July 1973, when Cunningham wrote the priests enclosing an official letter indicating that the experiment approved by the Holy See of allowing first communion before penance "is now ended." Cathechetical programs in Syracuse, as in 100 other dioceses, would have to be rearranged.

Religious education leaders took this to mean that parents had the option of penance first, but that penance first was not mandatory. In December 1977, after Cunningham's retirement, Bishop Harrison told the priests that children had a right to receive the sacraments at the age of discretion; there must be adequate catechesis; a substantial period of time must elapse between reception of the two sacraments; parents had the primary role in preparing their children and this must be made fully known to them; and parents must participate in formal preparation for reception of the sacraments. Children had the right to receive penance before communion, provided they were properly prepared and disposed, but the traditional obligation of receiving the sacrament only when in a state of serious sin was also recognized. Pastors should have available a program for those parents who might choose to have their children receive penance at a later date.

Pulver was immediately back into the fray, charging in *The Wanderer* that, while the bishop stressed the agreement between diocesan guidelines and Vatican directives that confession come first, there remained subtle differences, for the bishop clearly expected that most would choose to delay confession and "keep studying about it." One bishop wrote Harrison asking for copies of his guidelines and noting that some priests in Rome went "beyond the Birchites" in their demand that confession first be enforced and he quoted another American bishop to the effect that "it had to be done by drilling them just like the old days." Harrison responded that in the Syracuse diocese the child could choose to go to confession first, but "what we don't do is drag them over to church as a class and say that now everyone must go to confession." Yet he thought things were not so different than in the past. "What we are doing is not too much different than in the old days. If a first communicant came into

confession and said 'I have nothing to tell,' you merely gave such a one your blessing and sent him on his way. I think they are making a mountain out of a molehill."

In March 1981 the diocese issued new guidelines on the reception of the sacraments. These emphasized the collective decision of parents, catechists and priests in determining when the child was ready for reception of these sacraments. Harrison made it clear that these two sacraments should not be confused.

He assured his people that each child would have the opportunity to receive the sacrament of reconciliation first if the parents so desired and the child manifested an understanding of and desire for the sacrament, but no child would be forced to receive that sacrament before communion, or dissuaded from doing so. The diocesan policy therefore remained intact, and religious educators reported that the majority of parents still opted for the later reception of the sacrament of reconciliation, as it was by now called. Director Michael Meagher put it clearly in 1980:

Our diocesan guidelines for First Eucharist and First Penance recognize the right of the child to receive both sacraments and also recognize there will be cases when a child is ready to receive Eucharist, but not of sufficient growth to receive the Sacrament of Reconciliation before Eucharist. Our diocesan guidelines very much respect the right and freedom of the individual child. We also insist that catechesis for the Sacrament of Reconciliation proceed First Eucharist. In this way, an intelligent decision about the readiness of the candidate for Reconciliation is able to be made by the parents, pastor, catechist and candidate. I am not aware of any priest that insists on First Eucharist before First Penance. I

Monsignor Eugene Yennock and Bishop Costello celebrate a Teacher Appreciation Mass in the Southern region of the diocese, part of the growing Church consciousness to affirm Catholic educators. (Photo: The Catholic Sun)

believe that all pastors and religious educators are concerned that the option for receiving the sacrament of Reconciliation be given to the candidate.

AN AMBIGUOUS LEGACY

When the Senate Committee on the conditions and needs of the diocese issued its report in 1976, education occupied a central place. The need for adult education was the number one priority listed among the needs of the diocese. "Development of viable solutions to the problem of Catholic educational work at all levels" ranked third, and youth ministry tied with two other items as a fourth priority. The Priests' Senate added a concern for public high schools. The committee emphasized the need for greater coordination of schools and religious education.

Three years earlier, after wide consultation, Monsignor Costello and Father J. D. Kane had submitted a controversial report citing an "overemphasis on the school question to the detriment of other educational apostolates, to say nothing of the greater mission of the Church as a whole." They recommended creation of a diocesan board of education, staffed by a vicar and composed of represent-atives (including parents and other lay people) from schools, religious education, adult educa-tion, continuing education of priests and campus ministry, along with liaisons from the Priests' Senate, the sisters' organization and Catholic higher education. In the end, internal conflicts stymied reform. But the problems posed by change and the need for more adequate planning remained.

In 1893, in the midst of the school controversy stirred by Archbishop John Ireland's attempt to develop a compromise with the public schools, Bishop Patrick Ludden of Syracuse told Rome that Catholic education was "an absolute necessity." Lud-den thought Ireland's proposal for coopera-tion was impossible given the nature of American church-state separation and re-ligious pluralism. In addition, like the option of Sunday schools, it was clearly inadequate, for "who does not see that one hour weekly instruction is insufficient to instill the faith." Moreover, Ludden added realistically, "youth must have free time for recreation and for parents or pastors to force on them religious instruction in their free time would make religion odious and boring." While he agreed in principle with the Vatican's emphasis on the responsibilities of parents, he once again added a note of realism. "Most of our children come from working class families," he wrote. "These parents are fully occupied with earning their daily bread and have neither the time nor talent to give religious instruction to their children." There were only 8,000,000 Catholics in a country of 63,000,000 people; the nation was for the most part "without religion and quasi-pagan." Thus, Ludden felt there was no hope of safeguard-ing the faith if Catholic schools are destroyed or their efficacy is notably diminished." Yet, two years later, Ludden noted pessimistically that, given the lack of popular support and inadequate financial resources, there was little chance of expanding Catholic schools in his diocese.

In many ways the Syracuse Church, and the Church in the United States, had come full circle by the 1980s. Accepting the force of Ludden's argument, Catholic leaders had strongly supported parochial schools. Even when released time became possible, many noted that the brief time available was not adequate to provide religious instruction and moral guidance. Older children and teenagers did indeed resist encroachments on their free time, and many parents, still busy "earning their daily bread," lacked the interest, ability or confidence to carry out the educational task alone. Catholic school covenants sought to "teach Catholic doctrine, build community in faith and foster a spirit of service to others," while catechetical programs estab-lished equally comprehensive and lofty objec-tives. Vast improvement was made in reaching those goals with children who became fully involved and whose parents were supportive, but no one could be satisfied that the "absolute necessity" of religious education was being met.

397

The future was uncertain at best, but some clues could be found in the past. Catholic schools had flourished when the purposes of the Church were clear and challenging and arose out of the experience of faith and friendship of ordinary men and women. People wished to enable their children to become successful Americans while also becoming men and women of integrity, with religious and moral principles that would enable them to overcome the dangers of materialism and indifference and remain honest, decent and faithful to their own community. To a remarkable degree, the schools worked. Perhaps only when the Church recaptures a clear sense of purpose — with goals arising out of the hopes and aspirations of its people, grounded in communities of friendship where people of like faith find the affirmation and support to pursue those goals with integrity — will the educational enterprise recapture both enthusiasm and effectiveness. For that to happen, the Church will have to translate the covenant's words about mutuality, shared responsibility and common faith into concrete experiences of dignity, equality and freedom — not only in schools but in the wider educational apostolate. If it can do so, the Church might make an important contribution not only to itself but to the common educational work of local communities and the nation. In the end, education, like the Church, is not for itself, but for the world, for all men and women called to the Kingdom of God and the realization of their full humanity.

NEW WINE,
OLD WINESKINS

THE CHALLENGE OF CHURCH RENEWAL
1960s-1970s

After Vatican II, bishops submitted their resignations at age 75. For unknown reasons, Bishop Foery's was not accepted and he remained on as the ordinary of the diocese until 1971, when he was succeeded by his long-time associate, David Cunningham. Rarely has a bishop been as well prepared to preside over a diocese, for Cunningham had been auxiliary and coadjutor bishop for 20 years. Energetic, and like Foery a man almost entirely oriented toward work, he had served through much of that period as pastor of St. John the Baptist parish. Best known in the diocese for his work with the building commission and his careful surveillance of construction projects during the building boom of the Foery years, he was regarded by his parishioners as a good preacher and a kindly man, especially caring at times of family crisis and death. He was deeply moved and intellectually awakened by the Second Vatican Council. To everyone's surprise, he was more open and positive than Foery in dealing with liturgical renewal, reforms in church structures, such as the Priests' Senate and parish councils, and with the renewal of religious education. When he became bishop of the diocese, Cunningham showed the same love for hard work and concern with detail that always had been his strongest characteristics. Earlier he had shown little interest in social problems, but as bishop he took leadership on controversial issues like racial integration, poverty and amnesty for Vietnam war exiles. Many believed he was a better bishop than they had anticipated. If he never achieved the intimate relationship with his priests Foery enjoyed, he clearly had their respect and loyalty. During his administration, conflicts stirred by renewal continued as the Church attempted to pour the "new wine" of spiritual renewal into the "old wineskins" of the parishes and diocesan organizations. Tension was unavoidable, but the experienced Cunningham skillfully maintained the unity of the local Church, assuring it a firm foundation as it approached the end of its first century.

399

One of the ironies of Cunningham's administration was that construction of new buildings almost ended. Between the end of the first session of Vatican II when the first liturgical reforms were introduced, and 1980, 38 churches were built or substantially renovated. Diocesan regulations remained strict, but pastors' complaints and the deeper involvement of parish councils brought some loosening of controls over design, if not over finances. The admitted conservatism of Gildea and Cunningham gave way to more flexible approaches, seen in the great variety of architectural designs and use of internal space in buildings erected during these years. Most of this construction came before Cunningham took charge. Between 1963 and 1971 new projects totaled $27,500,000; $11,000,000 was for new churches and over $6,000,000 for new schools. The rest was for gyms, rectories, convents and catechetical centers. Most striking was the slowdown in construction of new schools. Only six were built, all of them approved before the end of 1965. No plans for new schools were approved between 1965 and 1972. There were nine school additions and four remodeling projects, all but one approved before the end of 1965. Put another way, school plans approved in 1963 totaled just under $6,000,000; in 1964 the total was slightly over $2,000,000, and about the same total in 1965, when the $1,700,000 Grimes project was approved. No school building, improvements or additions were approved thereafter, save for a $128,000 project at St. Cecilia's in Solvay in 1967.

There was less activity, then, in areas for which Cunningham was prepared, and more activity in reforms, in which the bishop and the diocese had less experience. One difficult area was implementation of conciliar ideals of collegiality and shared responsibility. After years spent bringing priests and lay people under control, the diocese was now called upon to move away from episcopal and clerical domination and toward forms of community, participation and sharing of responsibility, for which there were few precedents. In 1965, for example, Bishop Foery mandated the establishment of parish councils. "The apostolate of the whole Church is the common concern of clergy, religious and laity," the decree stated. "Each member has the right and the duty to use the gifts the Holy Spirit gives him for building up the Church, not merely as individuals but in union with others, especially his priests, who in turn are collaborators with the bishop." In this initial stage, the parish councils were strictly advisory and included the elected president of each parish society, the president of the senior praesidium of the Legion of Mary, the parish president of the CCD executive board and the two lay trustees. The pastor served as ex officio member and could appoint other members; it was recommended that these amount to no more than six. By 1972, the chancellor could report that every parish had a council and the diocese was pleased with their work to date.

Still, there was room for improvement, and in February 1972, Bishop Cunningham sent pastors and members of parish councils new guidelines developed from his reading of council minutes. He still emphasized their advisory role, as they provided the pastor with "valuable information and indispensable assistance for the enlightened decision-making which is demanded of spiritual leadership today." Cunningham insisted that council members should state their views openly and honestly. The old form of appointed membership was replaced with a combination of directly elected members, appointees and representatives of parish committees, along with the parish priests. Finally, Cunningham stressed the responsibility of parishioners to strongly support diocesan policy: "It is expected that no parish council would ever assume a position in opposition to the

THE RISE AND FALL OF A MISSION

In the 1830s, southeastern Oswego County became a haven for French Canadians seeking a new start in a new land. These were a people who held tight to their Catholic faith. As the community known as Little France grew, its residents decided to begin a church.

They began by meeting each Sunday in each other's homes — praying the rosary and reading Mass prayers from the missal. Occasionally a priest celebrated Mass in one of the homes. In 1842, 11 families built a small wooden church which they called St. Mary's. Soon priests were coming more regularly, and by 1855 the little community was being served by Franciscan priests from Syracuse. Perhaps not coincidentally, it was around this time that Little France renamed its church in honor of St. Francis of Assisi.

When the Syracuse diocese was established in 1886, the 300 families at St. Francis church were served by a nearby mission of St. Anne at Colosse, a German-French-Irish settlement. In 1914, St. Mary's parish was established in Mexico, responsible for the smaller settlements in southeastern Oswego county.

At that time, Little France counted about 150 persons, with the usual parish activities of Sunday School, Holy Name, and Altar-Rosary society. One young man had gone off to join the Franciscan friars. Two decades later, membership at St. Francis mission continued to drop, slipping to only 41 persons. As other areas of the diocese were growing and forming new parishes, Little France had seen most of its residents move away.

By 1951, Mass no longer was celebrated each Sunday at St. Francis mission. The few remaining parishioners complained to the bishop, who asked the pastor at Mexico to be more regular in serving the mission church. A few years later, more complaints reached the bishop; 52 people had signed a petition, but the pastor said only 10 adults and six children could be counted as members of St. Francis mission. Meanwhile a new mission had been started several years earlier at Parish, less than six miles from Little France. The new mission was serving 125 people, including some families from Little France. The number of worshipers at Parish was growing each Sunday, the pastor told the bishop; the priest felt the Little France petitioners were sentimentally trying to hold on to a historic mission church that was no longer serving its purpose.

The bishop gave the Mexico trustees permission to discontinue winter Masses at St. Francis mission in 1964, and nine years later the mission was permanently closed. Its people now are served by St. Anne's church at Parish, which has become a hub of the growing rural Catholic community in southeastern Oswego County, where the Church still traces its origins to the faith of the settlers who 150 years ago came to Colosse and Little France.

Bishop's diocesan wide programs."

FORCED MERGER

As these modest steps indicated, the Church was not yet ready for a full sharing of responsibility, or even of information. In 1967 a bitter fight broke out in Binghamton which demonstrated that despite the call for participation and use of the phrase "the people of God" the Church in Syracuse still had the lines held tight. During the 1950s, St. Mary's in Binghamton suffered a steady decline of population and income. Irish and other English speaking Catholics left the city for the suburbs; their places were taken by a growing black and later Hispanic population. Assumption of the Blessed Virgin Mary just a block away, in contrast, was finally experiencing financial prosperity. Many Italians who left the neighborhood remained loyal to the parish and the long-standing financial problem disappeared. Income at Assumption rose from $5,500 in 1941, when founding pastor Father Matthew Pellegrini was still struggling to maintain his parish, to $18,000 in 1944. After World War II income increased dramatically as a series of fund-raising efforts appealed to a new sense of confidence and pride among the growing number of college-educated parishioners. Indeed, among parishes with money to lend in 1955, Assumption topped the list. Like many Italian parishes, Assumption had never built a school, but Italian children began to fill the vacant desks of St. Mary's, leading to problems between the two pastors.

Father Pellegrini had long looked forward to building a new church and challenged his people to work toward this objective after the war. In 1951 he returned to Italy and was succeeded by his assistant, Father John Conway. In 1964 Conway approached the diocese for permission to build a church, a catechetical center and a rectory. At the same time, St. Mary's financial problems were becoming acute. At the bishop's initiative, trustees and pastors discussed a possible merger of the two parishes, but both sides agreed that such a step would cause innumerable problems. Nor did Assumption show interest in the bishop's suggestion of possibly relocating the parish. St. Mary's, hurt by urban renewal and highway construction, continued to decline and had to borrow $6,000 from the diocese to meet its assessment for Catholic Central High School. In this context, Assumption received permission to erect a catechetical center, but not a new church. Many parishioners were disappointed by this decision, but the building committee explained that social events in the center would help raise money. Conway, launching the $250,000 campaign, called it "the first step toward building a new church." In April 1966 the catechetical center was ready. That fall, the school problem was resolved as the two pastors agreed to share in its management and cost and to establish an interparish planning committee. Thus, after a series of discussions between pastors, occasionally including trustees, discussion of merger was dropped in 1964 and considerable progress had taken place on the school issue.

Father Lawrence Daley of St. Mary's retired in April 1967. On April 30, the trustees of Assumption were invited to the rectory after Mass and Conway told them the bishop had decided to merge the two parishes. Less than a week later, the trustees met, to be informed that a new parish corporation would be set up, to be called St. Mary of the Assumption. June 4 would be the opening day for this new parish; it would be housed in the old St. Mary's church and the pastor would be Father Conway from the Italian parish. Bishop Foery wrote a letter to be read at Mass, describing the problems faced by parishes in urban areas which forced such decisions for the "spiritual welfare" of the people. He was hopeful that "this new parish, taking its strength from parishes that are old in tradition and foundation, will continue to be young in spirit and will continue to keep alive and active the church and the neighborhood." He knew the change would be hard, especially for the older people; when some wrote him, he responded that he understood their sentiments and the sacrifices they had made. He had reached his decision only after long study and much prayer, and he was confident that every provision would be made for the Italian people. He told Conway that when he himself had been appointed pastor at Mount Carmel in Rochester so many years before there was disappointment "because I was an American," but it soon disappeared and he won the parishioners' cooperation. Later the bishop lost confidence in Conway, but he consistently saw the dispute in terms of Italian separatism within the Church, setting forth the long-standing argument that national sentiments must give way for the greater good of the Church. This was the same argument used in fights with Italians, Germans, Slovaks and Poles for almost a century. As he righteously wrote one protesting parishioner early in the battle:

You are aware that no national group is excluded from any parish in our diocese. It makes no difference whether a parish consists of the Polish people, Slovak, Irish and so forth. You are aware also that there had been a friendly relationship between the national groups in America. This is because we are not Irish, German or Italian, but we are American-Italian, American-Irish or American-German. We err if we expect the rights and privileges of our country and at the same time overemphasize our national origin. This does not mean that we are ashamed of our origin but that we are

proud of our present American citizenship.

Italian-American Catholics of Assumption who opposed the merger could be forgiven if they thought their bishop was charging them with being both bad Catholics and un-American.

Thus began one of the most bitter and lengthy disputes in the history of the diocese. The decision had been made with little or no consultation. Monsignor Frank Harrison, dean for Broome County, was not informed, and most likely Father Conway was as surprised as he claimed to be. Many parishioners of Assumption, told for years that they must sacrifice for a new church, were hurt and puzzled.

After long years of neglect, their parish had become strong and vibrant. Now, as they saw it, Assumption was being submerged into a declining parish, bringing its financial resources to save its neighbor, all without being asked. About 150 parishioners formed a Committee of Concern under the leadership of Frank Filleto. The leaders of the opposition were far from inexperienced immigrants, and they had considerable support. One petition had 1,643 names, of whom only 150-200 were children. They knew the power of publicity and used it skillfully to demonstrate the gap between consensual values of democracy and participation and the arbitrary power of the pastor and bishop.

Soon they learned that the property of the old parish, which they had planned to use as a parking lot, was to be turned over to Catholic Charities for use by neighborhood residents. The dissidents urged people to withhold contributions to the Church. Conway decided that their dissent had gone too far. He told the firm which printed parish envelopes to drop the names of the dissenters from the parish roles:

Making this personal, these paesans

403

are giving me a hard time. The bishop had given permission to demolish the old church and rectory but, after finding out that homestart [sic] from Catholic Charities was using the latter, his excellency figured that it was better than merely tearing it down for a few cars for bingo once a week. Result— they are teed off and telling people not to use envelopes. Gave them a sermon Sunday they won't forget for a long time.

These and other arbitrary actions of the pastor, such as excluding his opponents from the parish center, drove moderate parishioners into the dissident camp.

The bishop agreed that Conway had indeed been imprudent, but he urged parishioners to work with him to restore peace. At the same time he gently rebuked Conway, telling him that he did not have the right to exclude people from the parish. In August, the priest and dissident leaders met with the two bishops and an agreement was reached regarding the church property. Unfortunately, the lay people felt the pastor violated the agreement by continuing to exclude people from the parish center. One further effort at a settlement was made a year later when the bishop agreed to allow the old parishioners to worship as "Assumption Church" in the center, to have their own priest and to have a full accounting of the funds, with future arrangements to be negotiated. Because the diocesan counsultors rejected it, this compromise also failed. Cunningham again told the dissidents that they must reconcile themselves with Father Conway. Perhaps one reason for the failure of the diocese to back down was hinted at in Cunningham's reference to the testimony of "area priests" to Conway's good work — clerical authority was at stake.

The diocese had been clever in its approach to the merger. Rather than transfer the property of one church to another, which would cause severe canonical and legal problems, they created a new corporation to which both churches transferred their property by vote of the corporation. The parishioners of Assumption, nevertheless, perceived the move as a merger of their church into the territorial parish, with the loss of autonomy and pride which a distinctive Italian institution had given them. Older parishioners recalled Father Pellegrini's embarrassing reception in Binghamton so many years before, when he had been turned away from St. Mary's rectory and forced to stay in a hotel. They also remembered the years when the Italians had worshiped in the basement of St. Mary's. They remembered their founding pastor's lifetime of service against enormous odds and his constant appeal to the Italians to match other groups in providing proper facilities for their religious and social needs. Now, when they finally had responded, they were denied their own property, deprived of their old church, forbidden to build a new one and even turned out of the catechetical and recreational center. Their reaction was not helped by the attitude displayed by Conway and other local and diocesan Church leaders, who, for example, privately attributed much of the opposition to racial animosity toward the blacks who were increasingly dominating the neighborhood.

Years before, Assumption had squeezed black property holders from their block, but that action had nothing to do with this episode, nor was there any evidence that prejudice influenced their opposition to the diocese turning over their property to Catholic Charities.

Stymied at home by their failure to organize a financial boycott, the rebels had two avenues of action in law. First, they brought a civil suit against the diocese, which eventually reached the state's highest courts. The suit was buoyed at first by the state requirement

Father John J. Conway is shown here in 1959 with altar boys at Assumption of the Blessed Virgin Mary church in Binghamton. A decade later the priest was embroiled in a bitter dispute which began when, without consultation, Bishop Foery decided to merge this Italian parish with the nearby Irish parish of St. Mary's. The Irish church was to be used for worship, with Conway named as pastor of the new parish, St. Mary of the Assumption. (Photo: Chancery Archives)

to hold hearings prior to church mergers, but the dissidents lost because the action was not technically a merger but a transfer of property to a new entity. Numbers did not matter, because the parish corporations, composed of the bishop, vicar general, pastor and two lay trustees, had voted for the transfer. As Bishop Foery put it boldly: "There is no relationship between the members of the parish and the corporation." Second, the dissidents turned to Church courts. They appealed to Rome and were for a time more successful, as the congregation responsible for migrants took an interest in their case. But eventually, in 1972, they lost there as well, largely through the intervention of Cardinal John Wright on the side of the diocese.

The conflict gradually receded from the headlines, though remnants of the committee remained. As late as 1984 the pastor reported that once in a while a note in the collection basket reminded him that the dissidents were still in the congregation. The conflict, which came at a time of tremendous turmoil in the Church, the nation and the innercity did not show the diocese at its best. The bishop and his advisers remembered the hard struggle to establish clerical and episcopal authority. Yet they forgot the equally hard won lesson of so many national disputes. The lesson was that, whatever the Church and civil law might say, people would be brought into Church discipline by actions that respect their traditions and acknowledge their pride, not by arbitrary imposition of the will of the leader. The dissidents remembered the many actions which had demonstrated contempt or disrespect toward Italians, but they forgot the many years when lay people had not supported their church and Italian priests and sisters had relied upon outsiders for support. Conway, local Church officials and the chancery demonstrated from time to time that traditional prejudice toward Italians was far from dead. Clerical leaders occasionally suggested that the parish would be better off without the dissidents; they invariably attributed base motives to the leaders and they rarely questioned their own actions or motives. Neither side demonstrated strong elements of tolerance, mutual understanding or sensitivity, much less a concern for the welfare of the Church, but the diocese, with its resources, was most at fault. Outsiders, faced with charges and countercharges in the press, fights about control of the bingo game, and inattention to the poverty in the neighborhood, might well have wondered what the long history of Catholic growth in the area had been all about.

It was to avoid such problems and better express the mutual commitments of priests and people that parish councils were established. Since the earliest days when trustees controlled Church property, parishioners had fought to retain pastors they liked and get rid of pastors they did not like. What changed in the 1970s was not this problem, but the mechanics through which such decision were made. The Binghamton fight was almost the last example of completely arbitrary action by the diocese. At the local level arbitrary action was being replaced by the contributions of parish councils, ordinarily composed of men and women who felt a real sense of responsibility for the welfare of the parish. Wider public discussion of parish welfare, and

new bodies for dialogue and consultation, meant that the Church's business was more public, and personnel decisions could not be carried out in secret.

These changes were evident, to take but one example, when news got out that the popular Father Robert Hall might leave St. Mary's in Oswego where he had served for more than 20 years, to become pastor of another large parish in Utica. The decision was reached after informal discussion between Hall, a number of prominent diocesan officials, the new diocesan personnel committee and the bishop. Unfortunately, parishioners were not consulted about the decision and the reasons for it, and a short but heated public controversy arose, with a different outcome than at Assumption. Petitions poured in from Catholics and non-Catholics alike, an ad hoc committee won support by door-to-door solicitation, and the parish council was placed under great pressure to take action. Bishop Cunningham, who "loved St. Mary's more than any parish in the diocese," as he had grown up there, was caught in the middle — wanting to act in the best interests of the parish while respecting the wishes of the pastor and the advice of the personnel board. Only after considerable confusion did the bishop reluctantly ask Hall to stay, bringing an end to the crisis — an end result due in large part to the responsible action of parish council leaders. The episode showed the value of consultative bodies. Informal consultation among the clergy, perhaps acceptable and practical in the past, would no longer work.

A NEW ROLE FOR PRIESTS

Personnel problems had always been central to the life of the diocese. In its early days, the church grew in part through the pastoral dedication and skill of remarkable missionary priests scattered across upstate New York. Bishops, desperate for priests, relied heavily on the few who were available. The priests in turn grew used to their independence. The most obvious lesson of the Church's early history was that successful parish work depended heavily upon good pastoral service, which meant the priest's provision of the sacraments, personal care for people at moments of crisis, and his near total identification with the life of the people he served. As the Church grew larger and more complex, bishops became first and foremost pastors of the pastors. They knew that all the Church's projects in charity, education and evangelization depended on strong parishes, which in turn depended upon sensitive, skilled and loyal priests. Building a cadre of home grown priests, carefully attending to their personal needs, supporting their work with diocesan resources, and forming personal bonds of friendship and loyalty with the priests became the bishop's number one job.

In handling these problems, in the post-conciliar period, the diocese began with many advantages, most notably the great trust between Foery and his priests. The fact that Cunningham and his successor, Bishop Frank Harrison, were local men, for whom these priests were friends as well as pastoral colleagues, meant that retirement was a more honorable option. It also meant that priests were treated with greater respect and dignity than was often the case in other dioceses. In addition, the diocese had a retirement fund and living accommodations for retired priests at the Pius X home, which Foery built in the 1950s. Medical costs were borne by the diocese, and a variety of opportunities could be provided to continue pastoral work on a part-time basis. Another area of concern was alcoholism. In 1973, after consultation with the clergy, Cunningham announced a set of policies and procedures for dealing with this problem. These included a request to confront other priests who exhibited problems, a panel of clerical and professional advisers to

assist in the process of recovery, a pledge to assist priests, and a promise of future assignments within the diocese for recovered priests.

Gradually, changes were made as well in priests' compensation. In many parishes the Christmas and Easter collections, long for the support of priests, had risen above $2,500. Some priests were concerned about the propriety of this policy, but there was no consensus. In 1973 the diocese adopted a new policy, which represented a series of compromises. The Easter collection became the income of the parish. The Christmas collection was divided — one-fourth to the clerical fund society, the remainder to the priests of the parish. Stole fees went to the parish, but priests retained the income from Mass stipends, which averaged $1,500 a year. In 1978 salaries were $2,100 for pastors and $1,800 for associates. Each priest received an $1,800 car allowance, $100 for a study week and $75 for an annual retreat. That year the annual payment of $200 for health insurance was replaced by a diocesan wide plan paid for by the parish or diocese.

More important was the extension of collegiality in the diocese. In 1966 Bishop Foery asked the priests to report on their sense of the needs of the diocese. The reports covered a tremendous spectrum of problems, ranging from local living conditions to the foreign missions, but the need for a Priests' Senate topped the list. The bishop acted quickly on these recommendations. A committee drew up a constitution for a senate; it was discussed in deanery meetings and adopted in the fall of 1967. Designed to improve communications and provide advice to the bishop, the senate was not a legislative body. Separate senate bodies were organized in each of three deaneries, with priests elected according to a variety of categories. They met regularly, received proposals from the bishop and initiated proposals to him. Once a year, the three deanery senates convened as a full diocesan senate, but the tripartite system was clearly an effort to minimize the pressure for greater sharing of responsibility. As with parish councils in their initial stage, the senate reflected the bishop's desire to fulfill the mandate of the council while keeping renewal within the boundaries of established structures.

In 1969 a survey of diocesan priests showed an impressive degree of satisfaction with their work and their assignments. Slightly more than half the priests surveyed returned the form. The response group was well-distributed by age and function. Only 16 priests responded "no" to the question "Do you feel your present assignments meets your ability, experience and preference?" and only 16 answered "yes" to the question of whether they desired a change of assignment at the present time. As the senate committee concluded: "Ours is substantially a happy body of priests." The senate took up problems of compensation, insurance, continuing education and personnel policy like pastoral appointments and transfers. Foery was generally pleased with the results. Cunningham thought that Syracuse, in contrast to other dioceses, found its clergy and bishops avoiding confrontation as in a "boxing ring" but working together in service to their people.

Still, the process of improving communications was not without pain, even in Syracuse. Foery was hurt by the suggestion that reform was needed:

> It is unfortunate that there is an impression among a few that the doors of the Chancery are not open to our priests. My policy has been to make myself available to my priests who wish to see me. Only one condition is placed on this and that by necessity. It is advisable, though not necessary, to make an appointment so that you may

Bishop Foery fulfilled the requirements of the Second Vatican Council to establish a Priests' Senate in the diocese. But he organized them separately in three geographic areas, minimizing their involvement in diocesan administration. (Photo: The Catholic Sun)

> be certain that I will be available on that particular day.

In the early 1970s, in addition to continuing work on personnel policy, the senate became more deeply involved in public issues: supporting the United Farm Workers, endorsing efforts to extend social justice programs, backing the bishop in his support for amnesty for Vietnam War conscientious objectors and working for a constitutional amendment on abortion. The senate also anticipated future work on projects all of which eventually bore fruit, including development of a Diocesan Pastoral Council, use of professional managers for the clerical fund society, development of team ministry, implementation of the permanent diaconate, and development of a diocesan self-insurance plan.

Perhaps the most painful, and surely the most dramatic expression of the problems of renewal in the priesthood was the departure of some prominent Syracuse priests. At least 40 Syracuse priests left the active ministry between 1965 and 1980. Bishop Foery took note of this problem even before the council, but his deep commitment to his priests made it particularly difficult for him to understand this phenomenon. Yet, as with so many problems, attitudes changed when a person's own life was deeply touched. In 1974 a priest particularly close to the bishop left without warning. The bishop was shocked, but responded with sincere personal concern for the priest and his family. Eventually the priest applied for and received dispensation. The two men awkwardly regained contact with each other, and an important friendship was preserved.

Such personal ties forced everyone to look beyond their own shock and disappointment when such departures took place. By the 1970s a more humane and pastoral approach had replaced the previous tendency to suppress news about such events, to cover the name of the man in question with a vague stigma of disgrace, and to force him to relocate away from the diocese, his family and friends.

In 1971 Bishop Cunningham approved the formation of a fund, to be administered by the priestly formation committee, to assist priests leaving the active ministry. While not condoning the actions of these men, he wrote, "we can sympathize with them in the difficulties they have encountered and assist them with genuine love." This attitude persisted and diocesan priests contributed generously to the fund. Later in the decade, however, it became difficult to obtain dispensation from priestly vows, so priests were placed in the difficult position of having to refuse to preside over the marriage ceremonies or even attend the weddings of friends. They and their bishop had to struggle with their respect for each person's personal decision and their responsibility to uphold the discipline of the Church and the integrity of the sacraments of holy orders and marriage. The complexity of these matters reflected deeper problems of priestly ministry which had become central to the life of the Church by the end of the diocese's first century of life.

Both Foery and Cunningham were deeply interested in enabling their priests to become better pastors, and both were surprisingly open to new methods of meeting pastoral problems. In the years after Vatican II, the bishops supported a strong program of continuing education for priests which supplemented the traditional clergy conferences. In 1967 and 1968, in response to an initiative from Father John Madden of Utica, Foery brought to Syracuse a psychologist who specialized in training priests in pastoral counseling. Foery recalled that before becoming bishop he had attended many seminars around the country on psychology and psychiatry, at which he and others learned better methods to assist people in difficulty. In the years that followed, programs in theology, scripture and ministry were regularly available to Syracuse area priests. In 1977, for example, there was a study day on pastoral ministry featuring outstanding scripture scholars and theologians and a talk by Bishop

Albert Ottenweiller of Toledo, who had pushed the American bishops toward a more positive approach to parish renewal. Later that same year, a continuing education program on family ministry was held, followed by workshops on team ministry.

Yet priests remained for the most part preoccupied with their own parishes, and a cooperative understanding of priestly ministry proved difficult to develop. Implementation of conciliar reforms regarding liturgy, parish governance and religious education required a high degree of uniformity across parish lines. Too great a gap between neighboring parishes could encourage lay people to unite behind priests upholding different approaches and thus divide the diocese. This accounted for Bishop Foery's dislike of experimentation and his insistence on following Vatican directives. The ideal of collegiality and the council's mandate for the formation of priests' councils to cooperate with the bishop coincided with the practical need for communication among priests and cooperation in carrying out common policies. Finally, the issues of racism, poverty and resistance to the Vietnam war all stirred passions and aroused conflicts in local communities. These were problems which could not be avoided in parish life and often required neighborhood and city wide cooperation. This encouraged the ecumenical movement and at the same time highlighted the need for greater cooperation and sharing of resources among parishes and parish clergy.

One example was in Oswego, where the racial crisis led local pastors to issue a statement on implementing the American bishops' pastoral letter of 1968. Oswego itself had few black residents, but there was a considerable movement of minorities into the area as migrant workers. Equally important, while the city's economy was relatively stable, the county was near the bottom of the state in per capita income. Priests decided to collect clothing and food for distribution among the

poor. They requested funds from the poverty collection, bought a truck and hired a driver, and planned for several distribution centers. All this was done through a new, informal grouping, the Oswego Priests' Council. Once launched, this organization, which was really nothing more than a regular gathering of area clergy to discuss common problems and explore areas of cooperation, could not help but branch out into other areas of common interest. By 1970 the group was discussing establishment of a "meals on wheels" program, participation in radio and newspaper work, sharing CCD resources and cooperation with the local ministerial association. Inevitably the most difficult interparish problem was brought before the group when the bishop wrote urging them to give more enthusiastic support to Oswego Catholic High School. Enrollment had dropped from 599 in 1962 to 368 in 1970, and many people believed this was due in part to "the insufficient promotion of the high school, on the part of the priests." Foery urged each priest to become a "salesman for the high school." Furthermore, he challenged them to establish a committee to explore consolidation of local Catholic elementary schools. Perhaps the school question proved too controversial, or perhaps the easing of racial conflict removed one of the major motivations for cooperation, but in any case, meetings grew less frequent. In 1978, with the building of a second nuclear power plant in the area, there was a brief revival of interest, but by the end of the decade the Oswego Priests' Council had passed from the scene. While the diocesan senate remained an important vehicle for clerical deliberation, the ideal of closer interparish cooperation remained unfulfilled. Priests, like lay people, remained parish oriented, and the work of building a stronger sense of diocesan consciousness, vital to the mission of the Church, was still before the local clergy.

The introduction of the permanent diaco-

The first permanent deacons were ordained for the Syracuse diocese in 1978. The following year Bishop Harrison, assisted by Deacon Wesley Brush, Father Robert Yeazel, and Deacon Thomas Crossett, ordained three men in the Southern region of the diocese — (left to right, kneeling) John Sims, Dominic Rossi, and James Gallagher. (Photo: The Catholic Sun)

although he had no objections to the use of deacons in other dioceses. Impressed by the success of the permanent diaconate elsewhere, Syracuse finally decided to launch a program in 1975. The announcement indicated that deacons would preach and assist at the Eucharist, but their "most characteristic ministry" would be "the public service for individuals in the name of the Church," exercised most notably in working with the sick, the aged, those in prison, the poor and rejected and any others who "stand in need of the care of Christ." It was also expected that they would be involved in their own communities, not only with the parish council but with neighborhood and community organizations. Priests in parishes and officials in diocesan agencies were recruited to help with training, through which the deacon was introduced to a variety of ministries.

The diaconate represented one expression of a dramatic shift taking place among Church personnel — a change reflected in the use of the word "ministry" which, in its broadest definition, meant service to the Church and its mission.

nate was vigorously debated among the American bishops in the late 1960s. Some felt it could provide invaluable assistance in areas where clergy were scarce or unavailable. Others worried that its introduction might hamper vocations to the priesthood or limit enthusiasm about the development of lay ministry. Foery thought the work assigned to deacons could be done by "qualified laymen,"

RENEWAL AMONG THE LAITY

Bishop Cunningham, like Foery before him, thought the parish was the only real center of Catholic life. In each parish, as in the Church as a whole, the mission was to proclaim the Gospel in word and sacrament, offering its community life in living witness to its beliefs and extending the reign of God in its service to all. Worship, evangelization, religious education, promotion of human rights, protection of the unborn, elimination of poverty, care for the elderly and for young people, rebuilding neighborhoods, renewing integrity and honesty in business and government — these all required the cooperation and mutual support of each member of the parish. This went far beyond Bishop Forey's earlier definition of the parish as school, priest and church; it required full lay participation and active engagement with problems beyond the parish. Now, however, there was a new self-consciousness in which ethnic parishes and those organized around the needs of groups of people had given way to the "voluntary parish" composed of men and women who made a personal decision to join in the parish ministry.

This new self-consciousness made it a difficult time to be bishop. In addition to persuading priests to implement liturgical changes and establish priests' councils, Cunningham had to respond to a seemingly never-ending series of complaints. Some lay people thought the informal approach of the younger clergy was irreverent; others found the traditionalism of older priests equally intolerable. When a priest preached on civil rights or peace, he was condemned for expounding a "social gospel"; priests who rarely preached on such matters were accused of ignoring the teachings of the Vatican Council and the American bishops. One parishioner complained about the Mass being said in English; she said when she was young she was far more impressed with what she could understand only dimly. She noted that teachers discussed sex in CCD class, but the statue of a saint who died in defense of her purity was removed from the Church. Parishes whose youth groups performed "Jesus Christ Superstar" found some parishioners were appalled, perhaps remembering the diocese's earlier efforts to purge the Church of secular music. Others missed the sermons about the evils of communism; one even inquired to the apostolic delegate whether the Church had repealed its opposition to communism.

As for the priests, the new emphasis on community could be frustrating; "the latest ulcer-maker" is a "sensitivity session," one wrote. And it all still took money. When collections dropped off in one parish, the council asked the pastor to speak to the people. He did so, warning that he would begin publishing the names of all those who had given only a dollar a week. The tactic worked, as collections jumped 25 percent, but the move brought a rash of angry letters to the bishop. Even relatively prosperous parishes resented the apparently endless demands of the diocese. At Holy Family in Fulton, parishioners contributed generously to a building fund for their new church, the pastor reported, but every time they were ready for a final drive a new diocesan project intervened. In less stable parishes, like St. Vincent de Paul or St. Anthony's in Syracuse, efforts to reach out to the neighborhood angered some parishioners and reluctance to do so irritated others.

Conflicting expectations were unavoidable and could only be managed by widespread consultation and closer cooperation among parishes and pastors, but such collaboration in the diocesan Church was slow in coming. One of the unanticipated consequences of renewal was the revival of personal piety and, most dramatically, the appearance of a tremendous interest in personal and group prayer, especially prayer which expressed personal experience of God's presence. The most dramatic example of this was charismatic renewal which began in 1966 in Pittsburgh, and rapidly spread across the United States and eventually to other parts of the world. This "Catholic Pentecostalism," expressed in such "gifts" as spontaneous prayer, praying in tongues, prophecy and healing, was late arriving in Syracuse. When the National Conference of Catholic Bishops inquired about the matter in 1972, priests who were asked had only sketchy information. But several priests were interested. Later that year the bishop began receiving letters from individuals testifying to the impact of charismatic renewal on their lives. Large meetings were being held in Binghamton, Utica and

Syracuse.

Father James Fallon established the Emmaus House of Prayer at Christ the King convent in Endwell. A core community lived at the center, which provided space for prayer, spiritual direction, Bible study and other forms of adult education and spiritual enrichment. Fallon eventually was allowed to devote all his time to the house and served as the bishop's contact with the growing pentecostal movement. The House of Prayer served as the center of the charismatic movement in the Southern Tier, and as time went on it became more and more committed to traditional virtues of poverty, chastity, obedience and fidelity to the call of the Holy Spirit. They had few illusions about the cost:

> By living the radical Gospel we proclaim the Lordship of Jesus Christ. This type of "radical Christian living" will not "prosper you" or win over many friends. It is not practical, or even rational, but it is our calling as disciples of Jesus of Nazareth. We have been promised by Christ that if we live this way we will be persecuted. It cannot be avoided. If we wish to join Jesus in His resurrection, we must go with Him through Calvary. To do so will set us free from the fears that hold people captive and bring us a sustaining joy that no one can ever take from us.

There also was a strong charismatic presence in the Liverpool area. Father Carlo Stirpe was the link among local prayer groups. When he was transferred in 1978, there was a tremendous outpouring of concern. The bishop met with local lay leaders who then organized a board composed of pastoral teams drawn from a dozen local groups.

A similar board was formed in Syracuse, and a spiritual renewal center established. Later a service board for prayer groups in the diocese was also established. Gently the bishop guided these communities wherever possible into an affiliation with a parish, using the help of sympathetic and understanding clergy. At the same time more and more people were drawn to participate in prayer groups; as time went on, most were non-charismatic. By responding pastorally, without the suspicion and warnings that marked the diocese's response to so many earlier lay movements, the local Church gained enormously from charismatic renewal.

Another area of rapid, even dramatic, development was the diocesan Marriage Tribunal. Canon law always provided avenues for Catholics to seek annulments of their marriages; this was indeed defined as a right available to all in the Church. Yet in practice few knew about these opportunities and even fewer could afford the expense involved or knew how to deal with the complexities of the Church's legal procedures. In addition, the tribunal was seriously understaffed until 1957 when Father John McGraw became its full-time secretary. After the council, the American bishops won temporary approval of a set of procedural norms to simplify and speed up the annulment process. Pastorally, as priests became more sensitive to the needs of people in troubled marriages, use of the diocesan tribunal expanded rapidly. In less than a decade, under the leadership of Father Edward Hayes, the tribunal office grew from one full-time priest to four, from processing five cases a year to a caseload of 199 in 1973 and to more than 600 a year in the 1980s. From a few small offices on the first floor of the chancery building, the tribunal now occupied almost the entire fourth floor. As Cunningham told his priests in 1974, the problem was staggering. One report showed that in the diocese there were 7,851 couples married outside the church, 2,645 Catholic spouses separated and 2,937 Catholics divorced. In 1970 the civil courts granted 3,805 divorces in the diocese; if Catholics were 35 percent of the population, this could mean 1,000 or more Catholic couples were involved in divorce that year. In the law of the Church, each couple that asked for an annulment had the right to have its case heard by the tribunal. "This decision cannot be made at the parish level," the bishop wrote. "To refuse to submit a case to the tribunal, to place unnecessary stumbling blocks for its submission based on one's own personal judgment, is either to require a person to live a life of celibacy, an extreme requirement which Church law might not so require, or, for those who cannot live a celibate life, to marry or to remain unmarried outside the Church." So there were profound pastoral reasons for the expansion of tribunal work and for efforts, not only to facilitate the annulment process, but to strengthen diocesan programs of marriage preparation and marriage support:

414

> *As parish priests, we should have a pastoral concern for those who have gone through the painful and often traumatic experience of the breakup of their marriage. How often we have told such persons prior to their marriage...to quote the words of the old marriage ritual,"no greater happiness can come to you in this earthly life." But instead of fulfillment, these persons have found heartbreak. Instead of a hopeful future for themselves and their children, they now face a most uncertain one.... Indeed their preparation for marriage may not have been sufficient. Indeed, they may have been unwise in the selection of their marital partner. Indeed, they may have humanly failed in their efforts to make a success of their marriage. But even if they have, we must "not break the bruised reed or quench the smoldering*

As society brought increasing pressure on married couples and general acceptance of divorce, the Church responded to support couples planning marriage, couples already married, and couples experiencing marital difficulties. As part of the educational support, a variety of books became available to help couples strengthen their marriages. (Photo: The Catholic Sun)

> *wick." They have already experienced too much rejection in their marriage to have this reinforced by any rejection on our part. If Christ the Good Shepherd can speak of leaving the ninety nine and going after the one that strayed and then placing it on his shoulders, rejoicing, we who are called to be shepherds must endeavor to do likewise for those whose marriages have failed and who often feel themselves estranged from the Church.*

As divorced Catholics became more visible

and articulate about their experience, pastoral care of the divorced and separated moved from the fringe to the mainstream of Church life. In 1976 a ministry to such persons was launched in the Utica-Rome area; the next year a budget for the group was approved. In 1978 Bishop Harrison presided at a liturgy at St. Patrick's in Binghamton, held in conjunction with the annual meeting of the New York State Conference of Separated and Divorced Catholics. The following year he told Bishop Hickey of Rochester that he had established a diocesan committee to examine the problem, and in 1983 he wrote his priests urging their support for this ministry, now coordinated by the diocesan Family Life Education Office.

One result of this pastoral attitude toward broken marriages was a growing concern about the preparation of couples for marriage. Christian Family Movements had become established in some sections of the diocese even before the council, though they did not enjoy strong diocesan support. In the late 1960s Catholic Charities established a Family Life office. Diocesan regulations grew more specific on the time needed between approaching the parish priest and celebrating the marriage, priests attended workshops on preparation and a variety of forms of marriage preparation were made available. Diocesan guidelines were developed for dealing with particular problems, such as early marriages.

But specific programs of support for married couples, beyond the ordinary services of the parish, were slower to develop. The appearance and growth of the Marriage Encounter movement in the 1970s, like the Christian Family Movement of the previous generation, reflected a certain vacuum in Church life created by the lack of specific pastoral attention to growth within marriage itself.

Marriage Encounter first appeared in the United States under the auspices of the Christian Family Movement. It differed from that movement in that it centered its attention on the couple, rather than on the family or the larger community. Just as the Church had come to recognize the significance of the decision to marry and had introduced procedures to insure that that decision was made with reflection and awareness of the responsibilities and commitment involved, so Marriage Encounter spoke to the reality that the commitment to permanent and faithful marriage was not made all at once but needed to be regularly reaffirmed, particularly in the context of the pressures experienced by nuclear families in an age of rapid mobility. By 1973, Marriage Encounter had come to Syracuse. In February of that year the director of the Family Life division reported that the movement was spreading rapidly in the diocese and needed attention "lest we have a real problem on our hands."

She thought that all family life programs should be under diocesan supervision. Worried about the inclusion of non-Catholic couples on weekends and the charge that the movement was "soft" on birth control, she suggested that the family life advisory board become the "guardian of the program." Movement leaders resisted such control, while diocesan efforts to maintain dialogue with them only had mixed results. By the late 1970s Marriage Encounter began to level off in popularity, but the failure to develop a closer relationship with it left the diocese without a solid program of marriage enrichment.

In dealing with charismatic renewal, the marriage tribunal, Marriage Encounter and issues like first penance, Cunningham took a more positive approach then Foery. While both were concerned to keep renewal within traditional organizational structures, Cunningham was more flexible, less given to warnings and more impressed with pastoral needs and popular enthusiasm. He showed a similar willingness to explore new forms of ministry.

SISTERS FACE RENEWAL

Renewal following the Vatican Council had been encouraged for priests, and quickly lay people began to actively participate in the Church's ministry within their own parishes. But of all the groups undertaking renewal within the Church, religious communities of women embraced it most fully.

In February 1969, representatives of 16 religious communities serving in the diocese began formulating plans for a Sisters' Council, later to become the Council of Religious. The sisters set a large agenda aimed at improving communication among religious communities and between them and the bishop, promoting the renewal of spiritual life, and supporting Catholic education. In addition, almost from the start the Sisters' Council showed considerable interest in problems of social justice. The group developed a counseling service for religious and strongly supported the formation of houses of prayer for retreats and spiritual direction. Despite the sisters' work, tension between the diocese and individual religious communities arose from diocesan failure to consult religious and from the failure of some communities to cooperate with the diocese.

In 1972, for example, the Broome County School Board was considering a variety of plans for school consolidation. The Sisters of Sts. Cyril and Methodius informed the bishop that if St. Joseph's school closed, they would withdraw from the system.

A similar experience took place in Syracuse, when a committee decided to merge schools on the North Side. The parishes involved were on the verge of implementing this decision when Mother Viola of the Franciscans announced that no change would be made at Assumption. She had not been consulted and insisted that her community,

which staffed the school, would make such decisions. Moreover, she made it clear that their responsibility was to the particular parish and school, not to the diocesan educational enterprise as a whole, however much they might sympathize with other parishes and with the bishop. Such episodes showed the independence and determination of religious leadership and the advent of a new day in relations between religious communities and bishops. But they also demonstrated a lack of communication as educational decisions were made without serious consultation with the religious communities who, more than any other group, had made the expansion and success of schools possible.

But the biggest changes were taking place within individual communities. For years the cloistered Dominicans at the Syracuse monastery were forbidden to step outside its walls at any time. Many felt that the possibility of an occasional walk in the countryside would be of benefit, but relaxation of the firm rule required a good deal of consideration — and then a good deal of red tape. On problems like this, Foery and his advisers trusted the judgment of the sisters. The chancery was less sympathetic with the community's desire to build a new monastery. Uncertainty about vocations was one reason; another was the still incomplete process of renewal which, by changing the rules of enclosure, might require building renovation. Moreover, the bishop was reluctant to have the community leave the city for the suburbs, although the rural setting might at first glance seem more appropriate to the contemplative life. As a result, the monastery's large building fund continued to grow. The community made occasional generous donations to the diocese, but as social problems became urgent Bishop Cunningham asked them to assist more generously the Church's work among the poor. The sisters, still anxious for a new home, resisted this

416

appeal, though they did make regular contributions to specific projects.

By 1979 the monastery was down to 12 members, but morale was high. The grill which had long separated the sisters from the sanctuary in the chapel had been replaced by glass windows. Sisters were allowed to leave the enclosure to visit sick parents or sisters who were hospitalized and to vote. The rosary was no longer said around the clock, but the psalms were chanted at seven intervals throughout the day, and the sisters made rosary beads and other religious articles for sale. Sister Mary Augustine, the prioress, told the press the sisters considered themselves "liberated women because they had chosen the contemplative life." They sought silence and solitude not to escape from the world or to flee its ills but "to heal them by lifting the world and all its ills to the Father in prayer." Eventually, the community would also have its new building, not in the country but at its Syracuse location, committing itself to the witness of the contemplative life into the diocese's second century.

Among the religious communities serving the diocese, only the Franciscans had their headquarters in the diocese.

After Vatican II, the winds of renewal swept through what had been a quite conservative community. When Mother Viola informed the bishop in the summer of 1967 of the departure of five sisters, the bishop was sympathetic. "It is unfortunate for Superiors that apparently the Vatican Council has created some confusion among some of our priests, religious and laity," he wrote. "I use the word 'apparently' because it is not the Council that has caused the confusion. It is these wild interpreters and speculative theologians who are failing to make the distinction between personal opinion and the teaching of Holy Mother Church." In Mother Viola the bishop had a sympathetic listener.

In 1966, a number of changes were

introduced in the community on an experimental basis. Local superiors had more authority, sisters were allowed an at-home vacation of one week and a day each week when they could fulfill their spiritual and house responsibilities on their own. The habit was made a bit shorter, and daily schedules were changed to allow for informal recreation, personal spiritual reading, talking at table during meals and attendance at some evening functions outside the convent. Letters were no longer opened, and the chapter of faults was changed to a personal examination of conscience and a short talk.

But Mother Viola still had serious reservations about renewal. In 1971 she attended the founding meeting of the conservative Consortium Perfectae Caritatis. As she informed the vicar for religious, the group accepted all the Vatican II and post-conciliar documents coming from the Holy See, but subscribed to several "essentials" of religious life. These essentials included: the "pursuit of holiness as the basic essential in the practice of the evangelical counsels"; support of the Holy See and its right to interpret the norms of religious life; a permanent ecclesiastical commitment by vow to a corporate apostolate under the guidance of the hierarchy; responsiveness "to the Roman Pontiff and his authority" as exercised through the Vatican congregations; witness through a distinctive religious habit; and emphasis on community life and communal prayer. While all of these sounded sensible, they stood in some contrast to the emphasis of other communities on individual apostolates, smaller and more decentralized community life and shared responsibility. Furthermore, Mother Viola shared some of the theological views of opponents of renewal.

Internally, she resisted calls for further reform and despite pleas from the bishop, refused to call a chapter for renewal as mandated by the council. The problem was

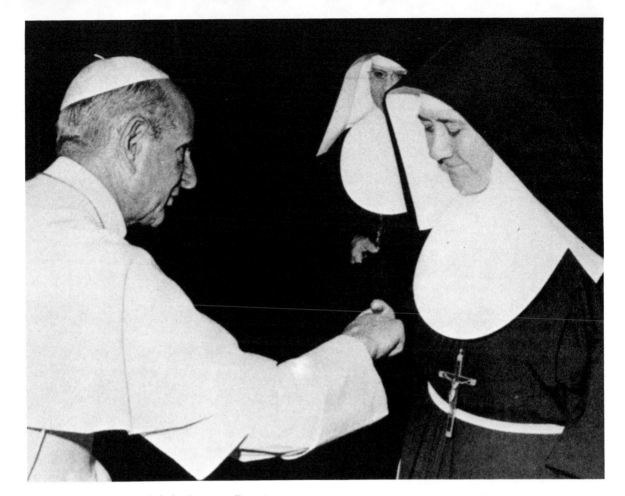

Mother Viola Kiernan led the Syracuse Franciscan Sisters following the Second Vatican Council, but she had strong reservations about the renewal of religious life. The Syracuse Franciscans had long been known as a conservative community, and Mother Viola sought to keep her sisters that way. (Above) Mother Viola greets Pope Paul VI on a visit to Rome. (Photos: The Catholic Sun)

evident in one letter to her sisters denouncing deviations from community rules and accusing sisters who wore secular clothing of having a "teenage mentality and worldly vanity." By 1968 several sisters had left because of the alleged failure of the community to engage in the process of renewal. Mother Viola claimed they "had fallen victims to emotionalism, irrationalism and a very immature attitude." She argued that renewal meant a "humble submission to the Church and a balanced acceptance of the difficulties of life." "Submission to the Church" apparently did not extend to the local bishop. The vicar for

religious reported to Foery in September 1968, that there was considerable unrest in the community. Foery wrote inquiring when a chapter for renewal would be held. Mother Viola responded that the Chapter of Election scheduled for 1971 would follow on a process of spiritual renewal and community reflection begun in 1969. When the Chapter of Election finally met, she told the community they were meeting "at one of the most troubled periods in the history of the Catholic Church, one in which religious life is in grave danger." Pleas from some sisters for renewal based on the needs of the Church, Father Francis' spirit, and the community's "healthy tradition" were overridden, and Mother Viola was re-elected superior general.

In 1974 new leadership came to the Franciscans and many responded to Bishop Cunningham's pleas to become more involved in the social apostolate. Noting the enormous contribution religious had made to the Church's work among the poor, he emphasized that there was a personal responsibility of every religious, whatever her work, to implement the demands for justice. "Accepting the personal responsibility to minister to the needs of the Church, each sister must seek to arouse the conscience of Christians who may think that religion consists in worship alone and in the discharge of certain moral obligations," he told the sisters. "They must be taught they cannot plunge themselves into earthly affairs in such a way as to imply that these are completely divorced from the religious life. All must answer to Christ, how much do we really want justice? Do we want it as much as a starving man wants food and as much as a man dying of thirst wants water?" By this time the internal conflicts had been resolved, and, while their numbers were declining and their apostolates changing, the Franciscans were as vital to diocesan life as ever.

Other communities experienced less dra-matic conflicts as the process of renewal was taken to the depths of individual self-examination and re-commitment. The Sisters of St. Joseph lost many members and at times had to face criticism for cutting back on their teaching commitments and for insisting on more lay teachers and on a greater role in decision making in the schools in which they served. With their headquarters located outside the diocese, their internal problems were not of such immediate concern to local bishops. Relations with the diocese were warm and the bishops appreciated the sisters' willingness to serve inner city schools and to assume new ministries. Communities which were forced to abandon their institutional commitments to schools often left individual sisters behind — teaching, doing social work or, increasingly, engaged in pastoral ministry. Old institutions closed, like St. Mary's Hospital where the Little Company of Mary had replaced the Sisters of Charity in 1956, and new communities arrived. In 1976 two women appeared in Syracuse seeking to establish a monastic Benedictine Foundation. They stayed for a while at the house of prayer at the Dominican Monastery and eventually found land in Windsor, where their tiny community offered retreats, engaged in handicraft production and offered their services in various ways. The Benedictine group grew and showed every sign of becoming a permanent element of the diocesan community.

In May 1970 the Sisters' Council, responding to reports of a national convention in Cleveland, voted to affiliate with the National Assembly of Women Religious. Speakers at the conference, it was noted, had stressed "the need for greater personal freedom within structures of religion so all may, as religious women, bear the witness needed in the world today." In this spirit, the Sisters' Council discussed personnel policy, including the options of "open placement" with sisters applying for positions and "self-placement" in which her choice of apostalate was limited by the the existing commitments of her religious order. The minutes report the theological principles governing the discussion:

> *1. To be fully a woman, a spiritual woman involved with others.*
> *2. The woman religious belongs to the whole Christian community.*
> *3. The woman religious belongs to the whole religious community.*
> *4. The woman religious is and remains a member of the people of God.*
> *5. A sister is a woman first and a religious second. If sisters are to be women of hope in the world today, they must let the people of God know that they are part of them and of the world also.*

In June 1972, representatives reported on the NAWR national convention, which had passed resolutions calling upon the bishops to support acceptance of women into the permanent diaconate and "to full participation in the priesthood." As the Church moved through the seventies, the minutes of these meetings demonstrated an increasing consciousness of the women's movement and women's concerns as central to the work and witness of sisters. In supporting unionizing efforts of California farm workers and Louisiana cane cutters, the council noted the particular impact of poverty on women. It also supported developments of shelters for homeless women and passage of the Equal Rights Amendment.

The rapid evolution of women religious brought many challenges to the Syracuse Church. Ironically, the sisters, whose contribution had so often passed unnoticed as Bishop Foery admitted at the closing of St. John's Orphanage, became by the 1970s the very heart of renewal in the local Church. Nowhere were the dilemmas posed by renewal more evident. As numerous commentators have argued, Vatican II was at best a "half-way" revolution, which pointed toward a new vision of the Church as a community in service to the needs of the human family without in any way abandoning an older understanding of the Church as a hierarchical institution oriented toward eternal salvation. What happened in Syracuse took place all over the world, as bishops and other Church leaders attempted to pour the "new wine" of spiritual renewal, ecclesiastical reform and social responsibility into the "old wineskins" of parish and diocesan organizations centered on the clergy and hierarchy. The council's call to all for widespread participation and shared responsibility did not fit easily into these older forms of organization. The increasing self-consciousness and articulate intelligence of women religious determined to serve the church precisely by drinking in the "new wine" offered enormous possibilities of new life, even while threatening to burst the "old wineskins."

Pursuit of these twin goals — full participation in the ministry of the Church, and service to the poor and oppressed — could be understood more personally and passionately through the shared experiences of women. Taken together, they pointed toward a fuller and richer life for the Church, with women taking roles of leadership and responsibility. At the same time, they promised to bring women, and their Church, into conflict with those who might feel that things were going too far, fearing that the new possibilities awakened by renewal could jeopardize the unity, integrity and fidelity of the Church. From such conflicts, choices for individuals and churches would emerge in the last years of the first century of the diocese of Syracuse.

COUNTED
AND JUDGED

PAROCHIALISM YIELDS TO INVOLVEMENT IN SOCIAL ISSUES
1960s-1970s

T he Syracuse bishops were strong supporters of the renewal ushered in by
Vatican II, but they were cautious about the pace of reform and anxious
to "keep the lines tight," at least as tight as possible. Like their brother
bishops, they believed the American Church had much to be proud of —
its vibrant parishes where people came to Mass in numbers surpassing any nation on
earth, a network of schools from kindergarten through college that was unique in
Christian history, a system of charitable agencies and institutions that was the
country's largest private system providing for human needs, an organized Church of
over 40,000,000 members united in their faith, generous in their financial support,
and deeply loyal to their clergy and bishops. This truly amazing Church had been
built in a country which provided no direct assistance to religion and where many
citizens looked upon Catholics with fear and mistrust. It was built by a people whose
history was marked with poverty and immigrant status. Now many of its members
had succeeded in realizing the dreams of their parents and grandparents — attending
college, winning positions of respect in their communities, owning their own homes
and providing comfortably for their families. The "American dream" had drawn
many immigrants to these shores and sustained them through depressions and wars;
for many American Catholics, that dream had been fulfilled. For their Church there
had been a similar dream — a vision of a loyal, united, believing people, committed
to the practice of the faith and maintaining beautiful churches, high quality schools
and compassionate and effective charities. That dream, too, had been achieved to a
degree which surpassed the hopes of even the most optimistic of earlier generations.
Vatican II did not end all that, but it did introduce some alternative bases on which
to assess success and failure. Pope John raised the question at the start of the council
of whether the Church was seen by others in a way that attracted them to Jesus and
to the Gospel. Was the Church, this Church, really like Christ — able to attract
people as He did, to minister as He did, to be faithful to the will of the Father as
He was faithful? New images poured forth from the council — the image of the
People of God, raising questions about power and status in the Church and

suggesting equality and mutuality as the dominant characteristics of diocese and parish; the image of the Servant Church notable less for its prestige and influence than for its love and compassion for those who suffered, even those, perhaps especially those, who were outside its boundaries; the image of the Pilgrim Church, ready to throw off the heavy baggage of the past if it inhibited the ongoing journey toward the Kingdom of God. Each of the images suggested challenging standards against which the Church and each of its members would be measured. For the Church in Syracuse, it was a troubling experience. It might have been a matter for calm, quiet discussion if the council was the only source of such questions. But the discussion did not remain calm, and the clash of symbols and the accompanying questions did not remain a matter for study guides and clergy conferences. While parishes were experiencing changes in the liturgy, while Bishop Foery was worrying about "confusion," while the senate of priests was working to build a new relationship between priests and bishops, no one lived in a vacuum. In the spring of 1968, Bishop Walter Foery told his priests, "We are now being counted and judged." The context of that statement was not a new directive from Rome or a new evaluation of renewal, but a new set of issues — race and war. God was speaking from another source. The words were occasioned by the assassination of the Reverend Martin Luther King Jr.

CONFRONTING SEGREGATION

In 1956, the Catholic Interracial Council sponsored a speech by Jesuit George Dunne on "The Sin of Segregation." The speech was distributed in pamphlet form with an accompanying letter from Bishop Foery, who asked his people to recall their own history. Without surrendering their national or religious traditions, Catholics had fought for and achieved equality. Could they not encourage black people to do the same? It was not a rhetorical question. The growth of the black population and the rebuilding of the center city was causing an exodus of minority families from their old neighborhoods, some into white communities. Father Brady had been booed by his former Most Holy Rosary parishioners

when he spoke in favor of a nearby housing project, and the few priests who signed a petition favoring "open housing" were surprised to find themselves in a small minority among the clergy. Nevertheless, influenced by the gentle persuasion of Brady and the small but growing number of black Catholics, Foery took his stand on the side of integration. "We cannot expect people to develop the best that is in them if we keep them in the worst environments," the bishop said in 1960. Self-interest as well as religious idealism required deliberate action to ease the process of social change. "Our concern as bishop and priests is not only to recognize the change but to do all in our power to maintain the value of our properties and the properties of our neigh-

Monsignor Charles Brady gently guided Bishop Foery and other priests to a stronger vision of racial justice. Brady's name became synonymous with the Church's growing recognition that the Gospel called for friendship and fairness among people of all races. (Photo: Bishop Foery Foundation Corporate Board)

borhood," Foery told the clergy. "We can do this by taking part in the relocation of displaced families and encouraging them by word and example in the upkeep of the physical, material and spiritual values which we prize so highly and which must be maintained if we are to preserve our neighboorhoods." Rather than complain about the problems and "do nothing about them," Foery told the priests to help by serving on neighborhood committees and by cooperating with urban renewal programs. No priest could "stand aloof from this very pressing and important problem," Foery insisted. The moral teaching on equal rights "binds each and every one of us in conscience" and "to fail to do our duty in this matter is to fail in our priestly mission."

Therefore, there was no question of the Catholic position on the principles involved, and Foery spoke out strongly and frequently on behalf of civil rights. He met regularly with Brady and with William Chiles, a leading black Catholic layman who became the city's relocation director in 1959. His friendship with Chiles helped the bishop understand the human dynamics of the situation and the feelings of responsible black leaders. After one long Friday night conversation, Chiles wrote Foery:

425

When one is involved in a desperate struggle to achieve a goal as important or in some respects more important than life itself, and is confronted continuously with what appear to be insurmountable obstacles, it is difficult when the walls of opposition begin to crack not to become even more impatient and, like Joshua, want them to come tumbling down. I have lived with the process of progressive erosion all my life and now at last the pace has accelerated. I am, therefore, disappointed whenever the acceleration fails to move at an even pace across the total front of race relations.

Foery's pastoral instincts were touched by such experiences, and by the plight of poor families struggling under the double burden of poverty and racism. Yet those same pastoral concerns helped him understand the fears of people in changing neighborhoods, and he tried to encourage gradual change which would take those anxieties into account:

Americans have been proud of their

*homes. They have taken great interest
in their neighborhoods. They have
been anxious that their neighbors in
no way contribute to the down-grading
of their private property. This is
commendable and should be encouraged. However, the upgrading of
people does not necessarily mean the
downgrading of a neighborhood. This
must be avoided if we do not wish to
make our cities one vast slum. It can
be avoided if we cease to treat some of
our people as second-class citizens and
if we give them the opportunity to live
in the dignity and decency that
becomes the children of God.*

The Church had to lead on this issue, Foery
believed; to do otherwise would be untrue to
its trust. This meant support for "open
occupancy."

*This does not mean that we are
expected to open our neighborhoods to
everyone. It does not mean that we
must surrender our moral standards or
even our economic status. It does
mean, however, that we will not
exclude a family of good moral
character from renting or purchasing a
home in our neighborhood because it
differs from us in color or nationality.*

Moderate as this position was, it projected
Foery into the leadership of the local religious
community as the civil rights movement
pushed ahead. In early 1963 Brady and Chiles
attended a national conference on religion and
race in Chicago. On their return, they urged
Foery to organize local religious leaders into a
permanent body to make clear the position of
the churches and synagogues and to take
practical steps to achieve integration. Guided
by Chiles, Foery summoned a meeting, which
was well-attended and led to the formation of
the Syracuse Council on Religion and Race. It

was an ecumenical breakthrough; as Vatican
II's discussion of ecumenism filtered back to
Syracuse, the bishops seemed relatively unin-
terested in theological dialogue but regularly
emphasized joint work on social concerns.
The conditions of the times meant that this
did not remain talk but found its way to
practical expression as Catholic, Protestant
and Jewish clergy struggled to respond to the
call for civil rights. Moreover, the bishop by
his silence allowed local priests to join a large
Syracuse delegation to the March on Washington led by Martin Luther King in August
1963, and thereafter he consistently supported
federal civil rights legislation. Still, as late as
the summer of 1963 Foery told Washington
officials that racial tensions in the diocese
were "minor" and well addressed by the
Foery Foundation, the Catholic Interracial
Council and the new ecumenical committee.

Such complacency proved short-lived
however as the civil rights movement, backed
by a growing network of committed Catholics,
gathered momentum in Syracuse. After considerable agitation, the Catholic Schools office
and the Catholic Interracial Council held a
workshop for 500 teachers in the spring of
1964 to begin examining school policies,
curriculum and texts. At the same time, the
council was calling attention to discriminatory
hiring policies in local Catholic hospitals, and
housing issues were becoming even more
heated as new federal programs accelerated
the process of clearing slums and providing of
public housing for the poor. In 1960 Foery
had told Broome County pastors that efforts
to integrate housing should remain voluntary,
but neighborhood resistance suggested that
something more than moral exhortation was
needed. In 1964 Foery asked a committee
headed by vice-chancellor John T. McGraw to
come up with a program to engage the entire
Catholic community in the fight for racial
integration; the result was the Catholic
Neighbor Training Program. This effort was

launched in Onondaga County, where 50 parishes sent over 600 delegates to a series of eight meetings to discuss Church teaching as it affected housing, employment and neighborhood development. At the opening session, Foery argued somewhat defensively that the clergy had not been "moral cowards" in dealing with segregation, which was not just a Church problem but one which "belongs to the community." In his keynote address, however, Father Edward J. Hayes was more critical, charging that while Syracuse did not have "a Jim Crow section on [its] buses and public facilities" it did have "Jim Crow sections when it comes to housing, job opportunities and...education opportunity."

The purpose of the program was to establish parish committees to join "moral leadership" to local community efforts for overcoming segregation, improving housing conditions and stimulating neighborhood development. Organizers found the parish delegates fully supportive of the basic principles but less clear on their "application to local problems." Nevertheless, by the time the training phase ended, 60 percent of the parishes had local committees organized.

In some parishes the committee worked hard to bring local housing issues into the open, but it was not easy. A clergy-laity committee in Skaneateles, for example, organized on an ecumenical basis with the local Episcopal church. Through several meetings they wrestled with racial problems from the point of view of a largely white village, where few black families could afford to live. As in most parishes, the Skaneateles committee pointed to the need for further education and gradually faded away. In a few urban parishes, the committees remained in existence with concerned people participating in various community projects over the next few years; but overall the program had little direct impact on parish life. There was little diocesan follow-up to assist local committees.

Most clergy still saw the problem as one requiring lay initiative, and even where there was concern, it was difficult to identify local projects in which parishioners could become involved, especially in parishes outside the center city. While the long-range impact of the Catholic Neighbor program on parishes may have been less than hoped for, it did help to clarify and institutionalize the moral position of the Church. Most Catholic clergy now knew where they stood on the moral issues, although these convictions had not yet created a sense of moral responsibility as strong as was felt around marriage and sexuality. Still, after the Neighbor program, there was a more deeply felt understanding that something must be done to bring about a greater measure of fair treatment and equal opportunity for black Americans.

Despite the good will of the bishop and diocesan staff, the Catholic Neighbor program faltered because no plan was developed to support parish committees. In dealing with the black Catholic community, a similar lack of coherence led to another setback. The small but growing black Catholic population was spread among several city parishes, but the largest number worshiped St. Joseph's, the French national parish located near the cathedral in the heart of what became the urban renewal district. A small but lovely church, St. Joseph's was Father Brady's home when he embarked upon his ministry in the black community; its pastor, Father Norcott, was one of the few priests other than Brady with a following among blacks. When Mayor William Walsh inquired about the parish in 1962 when urban renewal was changing the face of the surrounding neighborhood, Bishop Foery responded that the parish "makes a tremendous contribution to our work among the Negroes." The bishop added that in the future a change might have to be made, presumably because the French national basis of its existence had eroded, but at the moment St. Joseph's was "fulfilling a need and assisting us in the work of the Church."

Yet, just a few months later, the diocese decided to close St. Joseph's. Parishioners were angry. "People build shrines today for the most materialistic things," one wrote, "but that little church was so alive and ... has been a picture for everyone, besides such a peaceful place of prayer." One non-Catholic asked a friend how a church with no serious financial problem could be closed against the will of its people. He was told that there was "absolutely nothing" that could be done, for in the Church, "like it or not, there is no democracy, even in temporal matters that have nothing to do with dogma." Foery told Father Norcott there was no canonical reason to justify the parish's continuation. With its national basis gone, St. Joseph's "in the present circumstances trespasses upon the territorial parish which in this instance is the Cathedral." To avoid the requirement to get Vatican approval to close a national parish, the diocese merged St. Joseph's and its considerable financial reserves with St. Bridget's. The furniture of the church and rectory was distributed between St. Bridget's and the new parish of Christ the King in Bayberry. Black Catholics were dismayed by the decision. Years later many would contend that it was one of two decisions which dampened the possibility of realizing Brady's dream of a significant conversion of blacks to the Catholic Church. The other was the failure to ordain a black priest for the diocese. At one point a young black man was studying for the Syracuse priesthood but, for unexplained reasons, he transferred to the diocese of Brooklyn. Some years later he returned to the city to preach a mission, but his appearance underlined yet another disappointment.

Yet clearly the Church had come a long way. Foery's statements, the work of Brady, Chiles and the Catholic Interracial Council,

By the 1960s, St. Joseph's French church in Syracuse had lost its French base; but it had become the hub of a growing ministry among black Catholics. So the diocese's decision to close the church disheartened many, adding a stumbling block to those trying to build up the Church in the black community. (Photo: Chancery Archives)

the sincere if limited effort of the Catholic Neighbor program, the revision of texts and curriculum in Catholic schools, and the bishop's leadership in forming the Committee on Religion and Race gave the Church a more favorable profile in the black community than it probably deserved. In addition, as the national civil rights struggle heated up in 1965, there was a committed Catholic network of support in Syracuse. While Martin Luther King was marching for voting rights in Selma, Alabama, Catholic priests helped organize rallies in Binghamton, Utica and Syracuse. Later, a delegation of 44 Catholic clergy, religious and laity left for Selma to join King on the march to Montgomery. Included were Brady, Fathers Thomas Costello, Edward Hayes, J. Murray Elwood, Walter Donero, Charles Eckermann and Charles

Fahey, together with Sister John Joseph of St. Joseph's Hospital and Sister Robert Joseph of St. Anthony's school. Costello, the superintendent of schools, Fahey, director of Catholic Charities, and Robert McAuliffe, a layman active in Catholic Charities, played important roles in the Crusade for Opportunity, the umbrella organization for Syracuse participation in the national War on Poverty. At the same time, Syracuse University organized the Syracuse Community Development Association to stimulate community organizing; Costello served on its board and a young priest, Frank Woolever, entered the local training program.

Inability to find housing for minority families, even in public housing projects, brought about a growing sense of injustice and a rising militance in the Catholic Interracial Council, which backed efforts to organize tenants and residents of poor neighborhoods. Brady, whose temperament shrank from confrontation, nevertheless believed deeply in the rights of black people to speak and act for themselves. His willingness to support goals set by the community, even if he had reservations about the approach, caused some distance to develop between himself and other priests, who worried that such organized protests spawned and accentuated rather than reduced conflict. Brady, for example, was willing to allow the Foery Foundation to be used by tenant and neighborhood groups seeking to develop their own capacity to act, a stance which led to a painful break with some of his oldest supporters. Things got even more tense in 1965, when the CIC lent strong support to a struggle against the employment policies of Niagara Mohawk, the region's major utility company. The CIC board unanimously adopted a resolution which stated that the company exemplified the "moral guilt of industrial and commercial institutions in Syracuse regarding the hiring of Negroes." In

April the CIC planned a Holy Saturday march in support of the protest. Local pastors decided not to participate, but Brady joined the march. His life commitment to working with, not for, the people and his determination to be present on the side of those whose rights were denied required this of him. Only one priest, Father Donald Bauer, joined him. Brady never criticized other priests, but it was a painful moment. It was also painful for a number of younger priests, placed under pressure not to take part. A wedge was driven into the body of the clergy, a new experience for the Syracuse diocese.

As the racial struggle heated up, Foery maintained his earlier stand on principle, and he defended the right of people to demonstrate. He denied that the civil rights movement was under communist influence and insisted that the entire community had a responsibility to its poorer members, especially to those whose poverty was the result of discrimination and neglect. He favored efforts to enable the poor to speak for themselves and take a full part in the life of the community, and he lent moral support to local projects of the national War on Poverty.

In September 1965, Foery joined Episcopalian and Methodist church leaders to endorse an integration plan for the Syracuse public schools. They argued that the school authorities were seeking to give every child the fullest educational opportunity and that children in more advantaged areas would benefit from association with children from cultures different from their own. The next summer, the CIC suggested that some form of cooperation between Catholic and public schools on the south side might be appropriate, even if it meant closing Catholic schools. Foery was not about to close the schools of the area, but he did support integration at Croton school, which he called "the last *de facto* segregated school in the community." He urged Catholics to support another voluntary busing plan which would bring white children into the school and black children to other neighborhoods. Foery also supported a proposal from the Catholic Schools office to stop transfers into the Catholic schools from the public schools. He declared that "the Catholic school will not become a haven for those fleeing desegregation and integration." Integrated education was better education, he insisted, and he praised the city for adding new facilities to the inner-city school. Part of the process of education, he wrote, was "learning how to live and work with people. We have much to learn from one another, particularly when our cultural backgrounds are not identical."

Throughout the development of the racial issues in Syracuse, housing was the most pressing problem with which the church became involved. Several parishes, like St. John the Evangelist, eventually launched their own housing programs under federal legislation which eased the process by which non-profit corporations could obtain low-interest loans to rehabilitate existing structures or to build new ones. In 1962 the bishop wrote a letter of endorsement to the Federal Housing Administration on behalf of the Mount St. James Corporation, organized by a group of local graduates of Holy Cross College to provide integrated, low-income housing for the elderly as part of the Near East Side Urban Renewal Project. Later, management of this housing was assumed by the Christopher Community which eventually became the housing arm of Catholic Charities. The diocese also consistently supported public housing. As conflicts between local housing officials and low-income residents intensified, the bishop, guided by Chiles, Brady and Catholic Charities professionals, developed a fairly clear position on housing issues, which he used as a basis for nudging the public and private sectors to provide adequate housing while supporting tenant, neighborhood and

other forms of organization which could enable the poor to become something more than passive spectators in the process. In a private letter to the mayor in August 1965, Foery stated his admiration for the city's efforts to bring federal programs to bear on local housing problems, but he expressed concern about displacement of residents by the construction of a new state mental health facility on University Hill. Instead, Foery consistently championed "scattered site" housing which attempted to avoid the massive public housing projects of the past, as well as to promote racial integration, by providing housing for the poor throughout the community through smaller units, renovation of existing buildings, and later, use of rent subsidies. Furthermore, Foery told the mayor he thought that there should be more constructive procedures for dealing with tenant grievances in public housing; that every effort should be made to allow the residents to participate in the decision-making process; and that new construction should not move forward until there was sound evidence that decent, affordable housing would be available for those displaced. These were controversial views, especially the scattered site approach and endorsement of tenant self-determination.

The Church did more than advocate the cause of the poor and advise public officials. Parish programs continued and the Religion and Race Committee formed the Syracuse Area Improvement Corporation in 1965. With Chiles and several priests on its board, the new agency began purchasing and rehabilitating buildings. By the fall of 1968 the corporation owned 20 houses, 10 purchased with federal assistance and 10 bought on the open market. A directly Catholic entry into the housing field came in 1969 with the formation of Better Syracuse Living, a nonprofit housing corporation launched with a low-interest loan from the diocese and backed financially and organizationally by St. Lucy's

Father Brady and Auxiliary Bishop Cunningham enjoyed the advice and friendship of some of the diocese's leading lay Catholics — (left to right, standing) Eugene T. Waters, Dolores Morgan, and William Chiles. Laypeople such as these helped the Church address some of the racial and housing issues facing Syracuse during the 1960s and 1970s. (Photo: Bishop Foery Foundation Corporate Board)

parish. The group aimed to support self-help projects which would enable low-income residents to own their own property. By the plan, families were assisted to make the initial down payment on an FHA mortgage; then, with their own labor and volunteer help, they rehabilitated the property until its improved value equaled the down payment. BSL then transferred ownership to the family under its own mortgage. By the end of 1969, eight families were in BSL homes and there were 24 planned for the coming year.

The diocese walked a tightrope on housing policy. On the one hand it wished to do all it could to support the legitimate aspiration of the poor and minority groups to decent housing, a right supported in Catholic social teaching as a necessary basis for family life and the personal growth needed to take advantage of educational and employment opportunities. Moreover, Catholic priests and social workers were close to the scene and recognized the injustice of dismantling slum neighborhoods without making provision for their residents and saw the failure of concentrated and segregated low-income housing. On the other hand, as Foery had indicated in his early statements on racial integration, maintenance of property values and stable neighborhoods was also a pastoral and practical concern. Responding to a critic in 1970, Monsignor Fahey asked for patience, as the Church and other institutions struggled to find ways to provide decent housing while minimizing dangers to neighborhood stability. But housing was linked to racial integration, and Fahey was clear that the support provided by the Church, modest as it was, for black people and their aspiration for equal rights and opportunity, not only was grounded in Church teaching but in the experience of American Catholics as well.

431

Although it may seem distasteful to some, the fact of life is that we live in a community of different ethnic make ups. There is no place in America where we can remove ourselves from this situation. The history of Syracuse is replete with the immigration of low income people, first living in the ghettos, then moving to other parts of the community. This is equally true of Italians, Irish, Germans, Polish and French. Our national parishes throughout the city stand in evidence of the ghettos of earlier times. It was not without considerable prejudice that

Italians, Irish and Polish have moved into Eastwood, or into the Valley or into Westvale.... The Church has a long memory in terms of its role in assisting these folks, who were its own, in a very special way to become part of the broader community. It is a history it cannot forget. Fundamentally, our interest in low income housing comes from the words of our Blessed Lord who said very clearly that our salvation is predicated upon our acceptance of those who are in need. This is a good time to test whether or not we are truly Christians.

Race, housing, and poverty provided many points of testing; many people were meeting that test, but Catholic efforts seemed uncoordinated. In 1967, Catholic Charities established the Office of Inner City Development under Father Frank Woolever to provide a vehicle to organize the diocesan response to inner-city problems. The origin of the office went back to a 1967 memo in which Monsignor Daniel Lawler urged establishment of an urban division in the Catholic Welfare Office. This division was to extend and coordinate parish programs of service to the poor; make casework and counseling assistance available in the neighborhoods; and establish a network of neighborhood centers with such services as clinics, centers for the handicapped, reading rooms and senior citizens clubs. The new office would also relate to the Crusade for Opportunity, the Organization of Organizations, the Human Rights Commission and other local programs and agencies. Most interesting was Lawler's suggestion that efforts be made to revive the St. Vincent de Paul Society in as many parishes as possible to provide immediate services and to stimulate urban and suburban parishes to respond to the needs of the inner city. He

emphasized that existing agencies were doing "heroic work" but were hampered by "the institutional framework of our units," while the new office "would break out of that pattern and bring our services of charity directly to the people who need them, most of whom do not know how to reach out to them."

The new office was funded largely by St. Andrew's parish, whose members voted to donate 10 percent of each Sunday's collection for Woolever's work. Priests, sisters and lay people working in the city served as an inner-city board, cooperating with other local groups, challenging the diocese on the use of its resources and providing small grants for local and neighborhood projects. A task force of inner-city activists, known as Opus Justitiae, also was organized, drawing in social action leaders from other parts of the diocese. The first meeting of this latter group in November 1968 set an extensive agenda, exploring issues of Church policy like the assignment of inner-city clergy, the relationship between pastors and assistants and between priests and social workers, the need for more sermons on justice, and the recruitment of priests and seminarians to work in the Spanish apostolate and in parish housing projects. A newsletter, *Link,* reported on inner-city work in which many parishes in Utica, Rome, Binghamton and Syracuse were now heavily involved.

Woolever was a dynamo, second only to Brady in his range of contacts and credibility in the minority community. When it appeared he would be leaving to serve as chaplain for an activated national guard unit, Monsignor Fahey listed 26 different activities with which he was involved. Apparently Fahey's panic and prayers proved availing, as Woolever remained and the inner-city board met regularly, exploring problems, investigating disputes and creating a presence with the school department and city officials. The board participated in hearings on discrimination in the building trades, coordinated volunteers working with local neighborhood centers, helped these centers and other local groups apply for grants, supported a citywide coalition for quality education, lobbied for improved facilities in the city's schools, issued public statements, such as one opposing welfare cuts, and provided a vehicle for Catholic participation in ecumenical programs like the Interfaith Urban Fund and the Joint Strategy and Action Committee.

At the same time, the most active clergy and religious were questioning the Church's overall response to social needs, a problem made concrete by the demands made on priests and sisters by the day-to-day work of their parishes, religious communities and schools. One participant noted that the clergy's time was consumed with parish maintenance, office work, school problems and athletic programs, all areas that could be covered by a lay person. They suggested that some priests be appointed as "neighborhood coordinators," resident in a parish but working with a variety of neighborhood agencies and groups. Meeting with Bishop Cunningham, they designated 12 Syracuse neighborhoods as areas of special need; most cut across existing parish boundaries. Each might have a priest assigned to it who would work under the Office of Inner City Development and attempt to coordinate Church services and stimulate further parish response to immediate local needs. In presenting this proposal to local pastors, Fahey and Woolever argued that:

While the priesthood remains always the same, it must always be responsive to the challenges of a particular social context. We share the conviction that the role of the priest in the inner city, and especially in poverty and in working with minority groups, has yet

to be defined clearly. It is therefore the responsibility of all of us working together to share our collective wisdom on the subject.

Response was limited, and the proposal never went further, but it reflected the extent to which events had shaken the confidence of diocesan leadership in the once taken-for-granted approach to priestly ministry.

During 1967 and 1968 as attention in Syracuse focused on social services and housing, racial tension eased somewhat. But the tragic assassination of Martin Luther King in April 1968 brought the race problem back to the fore. At an emergency meeting, Catholic and Protestant clergy decided to seek support in their churches for an allocation of 10 percent of church budgets for programs for the poor. Shortly thereafter, a series of clergy conferences was held throughout the diocese, reviewing the steps taken since the formation of the Catholic Interracial Council in 1941. Sermons on two Sundays in June were devoted to racism and to "the call of Christ from the hearts of the poor." "The tragic events in our nation over the past few months have emphasized cleavage and divisions which today embitter many American," Foery wrote. "We who are called to be instruments of reconciliation between God and man must become instruments of reconciliation between men of all races." Some thought that the road to reconciliation did not lie through the older methods of better understanding but through new forms of organization and action aimed at redressing inequalities, so that the relationships among people might become more equal and just. If there had once been doubt where the bishop stood, either on the principles involved or on the participation of his priests in action organizations, he ended it:

Having received several letters regarding the race question, and in particular

FIGHTING THE SIN OF RACISM

The mid-1960s was a time of racial tension throughout the nation, and the Church response often was led by Catholics in social ministry. In Binghamton, that focus was provided by Father Ronald Bill, assistant director of Catholic Charities. He was a "street priest" — often at block meetings with black residents, other times helping blacks through the legal system, sometimes in local marches and other civil rights activities.

In 1968, Bill was a Binghamton delegate to a national meeting aimed at helping communities reduce racial tension. When he returned, Bill told a public forum that "perhaps some good has come from race riots, because they make us more sensitive to the issue of race." When the local press implied that the priest was endorsing rioting and violence, Bill's relationship with the police became strained. For a while he was seen as an enemy of law and order, and he once was briefly jailed following a racial scuffle in the city.

Eventually Father Bill was able to help create some positive responses to the race issue. Catholic Charities began sponsoring sensitivity sessions with black and white high school students; it helped a community group establish a co-op store in a black neighborhood. Bill helped organize an education program for police to improve their understanding of blacks; he also organized chaplains to ride with police on night calls to help prevent or ease hostilities which could erupt. Bill later was elected president of the Binghamton chapter of the Urban League, an unusual leadership role for a priest and a platform to continue bringing to the public such Catholic concerns as justice, equality and respect for individuals.

When he later reviewed Church involvement in civil rights, Father Bill found three reasons to "feel good." "It showed our black brothers and sisters that the Catholic Church kept faith with them. It showed that we were not afraid to take our lumps by being identified with their struggle for freedom, even at the risk of personal danger. And it gave us credibility as a Church because we were part of their struggle."

The Church emerged from the 1960s needing to continue responding to the struggle for civil rights. But events such as Father Bill's advocacy and activism in Binghamton helped Catholics understand and act on the teaching, which was taking root throughout the Church, that racism is a sin.

434

the involvement of our priests in it, I wish to advise you that each priest under my jurisdiction is free to make his own choice as to what degree he wishes to involve himself in this moral question confronting us today.... We must make every effort to solve it. We are now, every one of us, being counted and judged by our attitudes on discrimination.... To discriminate against a man solely because of his race or color is immoral and a sin against our Father in heaven. The Catholic Church has taken a stand on this question. The American bishops have taken a stand; I have taken a stand. What particular position my priests take, beyond their obligatory support of the Negro and his fight against discrimination, depends upon their individual consciences. There exists no canonical grounds on which I can deprive my priests of their obligation and right to support this cause. Were violence to result from their actions, that would be another matter. But I can not, and will not, interfere with their peaceful participation.

The bishop appointed a staff subcommittee on race and minority questions to develop a program for the diocese which would emphasize the responsibility of every person and every parish to work to overcome poverty and racism. The committee called for establishment of urban task forces in each region, parish housing committees, affirmative action hiring programs, subsidies to inner-city schools and, most important, financial grants without strings to local self-help organizations. Foery did not adopt all these recommendations, but he joined other community leaders in efforts to prevent further racial polarization and keep from Syracuse the violent disorders that hit many other cities. In the summer of 1968, pastors were asked to help find summer jobs for young people and Foery joined other religious leaders in planning joint action, including an "inter-faith urban fund." In addition, Foery decided to launch a diocesan poverty collection.

Unlike earlier appeals for charitable assistance, the bishop now emphasized the role of parishes and people as "enablers," providing resources and moral support to poor people so that they could solve their problems through their own efforts. The Church would try "to offer help unselfishly, without conditions or restrictions" to community development projects because, the bishop argued, "it is only in the exercise of responsibility and

power that one learns responsibility and the proper exercise of power." The goal was to achieve the same kind of participation which earlier groups had achieved. As the bishop put it in urging parishioners to share in the poverty drive, "it is only through the attainment of effective control over one's own life that frustration, which breeds violence and despair, can be conquered." In 1970 the American bishops launched the Campaign for Human Development, a nationwide effort based on similar principles, to raise money to be used for self-help and organizing work among the nation's poor. Of the collection, taken in November, 25 percent remained in the diocese, and the rest was allocated nationally. Thus the diocese had two sources of funds for its own "war on poverty," the spring collection and the local portion of the fall CHD campaign. A local Human Development Task Force decided on grants to parishes, neighborhood centers and self-help projects throughout the diocese.

While Church agencies were working to assist poor and minority people through outreach programs, neighborhood centers and various forms of community organization, the leadership of the Church remained convinced that action against injustice and oppression must involve the whole Church, and particularly the parishes. Many urban parishes were already deeply involved with the inescapable problems of their neighborhoods. On the northeast side, Monsignor Lawler, now pastor of St. John the Evangelist, helped develop a neighborhood center under ecumenical sponsorship, with seed money from Catholic Charities and the Council of Churches.

At Transfiguration in Rome, located in yet another deteriorating neighborhood, Father Matthew Luczycki, angered by the direction of renovation of downtown shopping areas, formed the South Rome Improvement Association and sought funding for four Felician

Sisters to do a census of the area and lay the foundation for an organizing effort. In Utica Cornhill People United, with funding from the Church's Campaign for Human Development and an ecumenical urban task force, organized people in the deteriorating Cornhill neighborhood, an area of lovely old homes which had been subdivided or abandoned. Eleven churches participated, along with an equal number of community groups, forcing the city to demolish abandoned buildings, obtaining more police protection, street and playground improvement and transportation, tax re-evaluation and pressuring landlords to care for their property. Father John Schopfer and Sister Barbara Ginter were particularly active in this broad-based organizing effort. St. Lucy's in Syracuse supported Vincent House, a neighborhood recreational social service center located at the former rectory of the lamented St. Joseph's German church.

Sister social workers on the St. Lucy's parish staff worked closely with families and expressed the parish's commitment to the neighborhood, but the sisters and priests knew they were "merely scratching the surface," as they put it. Poor housing, unemployment, family conflicts, youth problems and lack of spiritual direction or moral guidance presented an alarming picture of human suffering, giving rise to recurrent requests for more personnel. At the same time, the parish was declining in numbers and support. For many, the school had been the focal point of the parish community; those who still had children of school age were deeply upset by the prospect of its closing. In 1973 when a proposal was made to merge with St. Patrick's, conflict arose; those concerned about neighborhood problems suggested that the group concerned about the school was acting in a less-than-Christian manner. Members of the parish staff at one point agreed that "in the modern world the spirit of sacrifice (going without all the

luxuries and nonessentials) has become a characteristic almost exclusively found in the lower brackets." These were painful words when heard by a parishioner of moderate income struggling to meet the large tuition payments. In fact the elementary grades remained open while the high school merged with St. Patrick's. St. Lucy's became a model of an inner-city parish serving the needs of its neighborhood; but the process of turning outward, there and elsewhere, was painful.

St. Andrew the Apostle church in Syracuse was another active parish, sponsoring educational programs, joining in zoning and code enforcement projects and, in 1967, becoming one of 50 groups associated with the Organization of Organizations, the major community organizing effort among poor and black residents in the middle sixties. The parish also provided the major financial backing for Father Woolever's work in Catholic Charities.

St. John the Evangelist, another active city parish, assisted PEACE, an area community organization which rented the former parish convent. Another neighborhood center, Hickory Corner, was served by the sisters and priests while the parish paid its utility and insurance costs. The parish housing committee rehabilitated properties and made them available to low-income families.

Perhaps no parish changed as dramatically as St. Anthony of Padua. Under the leadership of Father Charles McEvoy, the parish had a wide variety of programs for all ages, along with a full parish school which in the thirties had more than 1,100 students. After the war, two new parishes were erected within St. Anthony's former boundaries and school enrollment dropped gradually. In 1960 Monsignor David Gildea moved over from St. Vincent's to become pastor, bringing his interest in construction and fund-raising. He began a long series of renovation projects, totaling over $500,000 between 1960 and 1965. At the same time the capacity of the congregation was changing; in 1967 Gildea pointed out that, while monthly expenses has risen almost $1,600, donations were down almost $1,000 a month from the previous year. He urged his people to adopt a system of "Fair Share Giving" of five percent of their income, and seemingly took little notice of changes in the neighborhood, where by 1965 there were severe tensions between black and white youths. Gildea contended that, while parish concern extended to all, "nothing special" was done for "Negroes as such." By 1968, many parishioners had sold their homes and moved to the suburbs; among the black families filling the neighborhood, there were few Catholics. In 1970 John Costello became pastor and began to renew the parish in response to its changed environment. Bingo became a means of supporting the school, with its declining enrollment and ever mounting expenses. The school launched a number of community oriented programs while the church became more involved in neighborhood community organizations. In addition to sports, dramatic and other recreational programs for the young, there was now a thrift store, a food pantry, and services for the elderly and for those addicted to drugs and alcohol. By 1973 school enrollment was down to 591 and the high school was closed. The parish was paying $11,000 for high school assessment, while charging $150 for parishioners and $250 for non-parishioners in the elementary school; 40 percent of the students came from outside the parish. That same year an Urban Ministry program was organized among nine Catholic inner-city parishes, with its director, Holy Cross Father Thomas Hooley, in residence at St. Anthony's. The parish, while struggling financially, was working to become a living expression of the Gospel message.

While the response of inner-city parishes to the problems of the 1960s was impressive, these efforts did not touch the majority of Catholics who lived in areas which were better off and at some distance from the scene of urban conflicts. The neighborhood program had stumbled over lack of follow-up and the inability of parish committees to discover an approach which could capture the attention and support of their fellow Church members. In some parishes, concerned Catholics were deeply frustrated by what they took to be the indifference of their pastor and fellow Catholics. For example, on April 7, 1968, the Sunday following the assassination of Martin Luther King, a parishioner wrote Bishop Foery:

It is an officially declared national day of mourning. Racial violence and its attendant hatreds are spreading through some of our major cities. And what mention is made of it by our parish spiritual leaders? What spiritual guidance are we given? With what is the time of the homily at Mass concerned? With announcements and reminders of schedule changes designed 'to avoid having the rectory bothered by unnecessary telephone inquiries.' I find this absolutely incredible. Is our Christian obligation really fulfilled by mentioning Dr. King's name, in the list of people to be prayed for and by announcing that someone else *will be holding a memorial service downtown?....By your own actions you confirm the arguments of those who claim that the church is irrelevant in the modern world.*

This was unfair, of course, for the diocese and many of its parishes were actively engaged in the fight against poverty and discrimination, but the parishioner's anger reflected the fact that much of this work was confined to inner-city parishes, neighborhood centers and sisters and priests involved in

437

specialized ministries. The majority of Catholics remained relatively untouched. While most were undoubtedly sympathetic and contributions to poverty collections showed considerable generosity, the new emphasis on the social mission of the Church had not yet found expression in most parishes, where traditional problems of worship, community life and education were demanding attention as school costs rose and renewal brought a series of sometimes disturbing reforms. As the commitment of the Church's leaders to social justice and equal rights deepened, the gap between their understanding of Church responsibility and that of many priests and parishioners would become a serious problem for the diocese, as it was for the national Church.

VIETNAM

By 1968 another issue had arisen, the Vietnam war, which shook even more severely the self-assurance of Syracuse Catholic leaders and posed more pastoral problems. In discussions of race and poverty, Foery and others drew as readily on American values of equality and human rights as on Gospel values or Church teaching. The problems posed by modern war, in contrast, forced many Church leaders to take a stand on specifically Christian moral standards, in at least apparent opposition not only to national policy but even such cherished values as patriotism and civic loyalty.

In previous wars and during the Cold War, the diocese had few reservations about the justice of America's cause or the Church's responsibility to contribute to the war effort with chaplains, prayers for victory, support for men and women in the service, and strenuous efforts to sustain civilian morale. Elsewhere, amid pockets of reflective Catholics, doubts arose with the advent of atomic weapons. Some theologians wondered aloud if

the use of such weapons could ever be justified, and a handful of Catholic pacifists protested against the escalating arms race, though few of those reservations penetrated the Syracuse Church. The issues were hotly debated at Vatican II, where the council condemned the use of weapons of indiscriminate destructive effect and endorsed the right of Catholics to affirm the peaceful witness of the Gospel by refusing to bear arms. Partly as the result of intense lobbying by American bishops, however, the council balanced these statements with reaffirmation of traditional teaching regarding the right of self-defense, the legitimacy of deterrence, and the acceptability, even praiseworthiness, of military service. Foery expressed the mood of most American bishops when he told Syracuse friends that they had been "delighted" with President Kennedy's "show of strength" during the Cuban missile crisis, which took place during the first session of the Vatican Council.

By the time the council ended in 1965, the mood was changing, for the United States government had launched into a full-scale war in Vietnam. Problems of the morality of that war and its conduct were before the American Church, pressed by a growing Catholic peace movement among whose leaders were two brother priests from Syracuse, Daniel and Philip Berrigan. The Berrigans' hard working father, Thomas, had been a strong union man; in 1944 he defended the union shop in a letter to the *Herald* calling the labor movement "the hand maid of Christianity and Americanism." His brother, Edmund, became a priest late in life, after the death of his wife, and served for many years as pastor of St. Stephen's church in Phoenix, where his nephews often came to assist during vacations. Their brother, Jerome, a school teacher, was a leader in the Catholic Interracial Council's work on housing, employment and education. The two Berrigan brothers entered religious

Father Daniel Berrigan was a product of the Irish-Catholic neighborhoods of Syracuse who became a nationally known advocate of social justice and racial integration. But it was as a symbol of nonviolent protest against the Vietnam that Berrigan was best recognized, as he helped spark a national Catholic peace movement. (Photo: The Catholic Sun)

orders and left the area for their training. Daniel became friendly with Father Brady and later was assigned to teach at LeMoyne, where he organized the Professional Sodality and a residence, International House, for students preparing for voluntary service in Latin America. A nationally known poet, Daniel Berrigan was an outspoken advocate of racial integration and social justice in Syracuse. As early as 1958 he denounced slum conditions in the 15th ward; that year the Sodality joined actively in working for better housing. He and his brother wrote a moving letter to the local press following the 1963 march on Washington, urging Syracuse Negroes "to continue to disturb our cowardice." In 1965 they joined Protestant and Jewish leaders in organizing Clergy and Laity Concerned about Vietnam. That same year one of Berrigan's former LeMoyne students, David Miller, a Catholic Worker, was the first American to publicly burn his draft card. Jesuit officials, under urging by New York's Cardinal Spellman, banished Daniel Berrigan to Latin America, sparking a national protest. When he returned, he and his brother participated in a series of actions against the war, including the destruction of Selective Service records in Catonsville, Maryland, in 1968, for which they were sentenced to jail. Assisted by members of the now very visible Catholic peace movement, Daniel Berrigan spent months in hiding before being led off to prison. By then "the Berrigans" had become symbols of a large and surprising Catholic opposition to the war. Their actions were known in their hometown — appreciated by some, bitterly denounced by others.

At first the diocesan response to Vietnam was confined to the usual prayers for military personnel and for peace. But it was soon evident that this war would be different. The conciliar teachings on peace, Pope John's encyclical *Pacem in Terris,* and the nonviolent witness of Martin Luther King had created a more challenging climate for the churches. No longer would prayers for victory or moralistic denunciations of the enemy pass unnoticed; more than ever before, war itself was at least as great an enemy as the other side. Asked in January 1969 by a Binghamton reporter what was the greatest problem facing the Church, Foery replied without hesitation, "world peace."

Perhaps the sharpest problem posed was conscientious objection. Before the council, most Catholic moralists upheld the traditional teachings on the just war, arising from the principle that states, like individuals, have the right to self-defense and to the use of force, governed by principles of morality, to safeguard their rights. Pius XII had criticized, if not condemned, pacifism, but the council argued that Catholics could legitimately renounce the use of force and states should make provision for such conscientious objection. Thus Catholics began to seek conscientious objector status, and the American bishops endorsed their right to do so. At the same time, many bishops continued to question the legitimacy of pacifism. In a letter to priests occasioned by Pope Paul VI's designation of January 5, 1969 as World Day of Peace, Bishop Foery endorsed the council's teaching but distinguished between "true peace" based on "the highest and most universal values of life, justice, freedom and love" and "pacifism" which often was "intended...to smother in men's minds the meaning of justice, of duty and of sacrifice." As for Vietnam, Foery agreed with the American bishops that it was a just war, but he also reflected the changed climate by quoting a recent statement of the national bishops that the issues involved in the war had to be kept under constant moral scrutiny. It was a sign of the times that the bishop concluded by telling the priests that his letter was intended for their guidance and was not to be read from the pulpit. His public letter to the laity was far shorter, confined to a general appeal for prayers for peace, although the suggested sermon notes prepared by the USCC and included with the letter contained much sharper quotes from Vatican II than those used by the bishop.

Bishop Foery's secrecy about his own judgment reflected the strong feelings that surrounded the war. To those who wrote to inquire about conscientious objection, the bishop responded with a letter which simply cited the conciliar documents and accepted the availability of the conscientious objection alternative. Copies of pamphlets prepared by the national bishops' conference were distributed in the diocese, but only in 1971 did Catholic Social Services begin working with other local groups to make draft counseling services available at the Bishop Foery Foundation offices. Eventually, working closely with the American Friends Service Committee, the office trained 20 counselors and conducted workshops throughout the diocese, not only in parishes and schools but in outreach centers aimed at high school dropouts and minorities. In 1972 the office suggested an innovative peace education program to bring Church teaching into the parishes, but it was not implemented.

Much earlier, the passions stirred by the war were felt in Syracuse. Across the street from the chancery, anti-war protesters distributed leaflets and marched with signs denouncing the war almost daily. On March 19, 1969, a young man from Auburn soaked himself with gasoline and set himself afire. Passersby and chancery priests intervened, but the youth was badly burned. Local priests, sisters and lay people wrote regularly to Foery and Cunningham, asking that they do more to register a moral protest against the war. Gradually their response grew more sympathetic, as sentiment against the war grew within the Church and among their brother bishops. When a representative of the Syracuse Peace Council inquired in 1970, Bishop Cunningham expressed sympathy with the group's work, although he noted somewhat apologetically that they could not expect him to identify with non-payment of taxes, defeat of political candidates or abandonment of military installations. By this time many priests in the diocese were active against the war,

440

joining peaceful demonstrations and supporting protests, especially among students on area campuses.

When campuses across the country exploded in May 1970 following the invasion of Cambodia, students at the Newman Community at Utica College wrote asking to meet with the bishop because of the "silence" of the Church on the moral issues of the war. This time it was Bishop Cunningham who wrote, reflecting the moral ambiguity which so disturbed anti-war Catholics. He insisted that the American "bishops have spoken out on these questions," noting phrases like "this hour of supreme crises" and the bishops' warning that "our moral posture and deportment" would be "judged by history and by God." He then went on to discuss the moral issues involved in a very general way, concluding that each person would have to make up his or her own mind. He insisted on the right of conscientious objection, denounced the use of violence both by those who opposed the war and those who "must uphold law and secure justice," and insisted that prayers for peace were not enough, for peace "must be built up every day by the works of peace." Both sides, of course, thought they were doing that; Cunningham recognized the division, in the community and in the Church, and called for "dialogue and civility," but he left his own position unclear:

So I urge our clergy and laity not to close your hearts to those whose views differ from yours. Rather, strive to listen to one another, to work together to provide a forum where honest, conscientious differences can be rationally discussed and evaluated, where we can all learn from one another. In this manner we can become more sensitive, as we all must, to the moral aspects involved in these issues. Hopefully, this might urge us

all to a better work in a cooperative way in our mutual search for peace, a peace for which we all yearn.

This was a new experience for the Syracuse Church; on a pressing moral issue, their leader refrained from taking a stand and invited them to share in the process of moral decision making while, even more remarkably, respecting those who disagreed. As his letter indicated, Cunningham had by no means accepted the principles of nonviolence but continued to adhere strongly to the traditional teachings regarding the just war, teachings which themselves admitted of the possibility of conscientious objection and civil disobedience. The fullest expression of his personal views came in response to a letter challenging a program of junior naval ROTC at his parish high school, St. John the Baptist. The bishop had little patience with the critic:

Unfortunately, you seem to be of the mind that every person in uniform is an agent of war, while, on the contrary, they are to be defenders of peace against aggressive powers.

He then cited those sections of the conciliar documents which made the case for legitimate self-defense and military service. Perhaps a bit defensive, the bishop went on to discuss patriotism, which he thought was an expression of each person's duty to care for the human community. Love could not be confined to home and family, he argued; properly understood, love opened one to patriotism, "a special form of piety binding a person to his historical and cultural sources." Patriotism made practical demands — loyalty to the nation, collaboration in its political order and "the will to seek the moral perfection of (one's) people." This teaching informed the obligations of citizenship and admitted "no concessions from political expediency to violations of justice." Civil disobedience,

441

Bishop Cunningham chats with a mother and her child after Mass at Quantico, Virginia, in 1972 when the bishop visited Father Angelo Libera, a diocesan priest serving as a military chaplain. (Photo: The Catholic Sun)

therefore, might be "the patriot's deepest expression of love, when other actions would only pass over or strengthen a process of injustice corroding the community." For, in the end,

> *Patriotism is love and love wills the good of the other.... The axiom 'My country right or wrong, but still my country' can be in conflict with the church's teaching and morally offensive. If it means the upholding of a wrong by one's country, it fails in the moral obligation of undoing the wrong and condemning the actions of his country when they violate justice and charity. As I said above, this is a patriot's best expression of his love. This was the tragic failure of Germany under Hitler.*

Thus Cunningham, like Foery, admitted the possibility of dissent and active opposition, but left the application of moral principles to the conscience of each person. Some who obviously felt the war was justified rejected, as

Cunningham did, the identification of Christianity with nonviolence and wanted the bishop to correct those who were arguing against the war on the basis of Church teaching. LeMoyne professor Anthony Bouscaren, for example, was incensed by the literature available in churches, much of it from the USCC, which failed to explain traditional just war teaching. As he saw it, the growing opposition to the war was based on insubstantial or incorrect information about the war itself and on principles of pacifism which enjoyed at best only marginal support in Church teaching. On the other hand, a growing number of priests, sisters and lay people could not accept a war which seemed in conflict not only with the peace-making imperatives of the Gospel but with such long-standing just war principles as proportionality and discrimination, which limited the use of armed force to military targets and to a level reasonably proportionate to the goal of the war.

For some, the war was both a matter of personal conscience and pastoral responsibility. One example was Father J. Murray Elwood, chaplain at Oswego State College. Elwood had done graduate study and was principal at Rome Catholic High School before coming to the college in 1966. During the civil rights movement, he had been active, joining the Syracuse group that went south to march with Martin Luther King in 1965. In the early stages of the Vietnam war, he had ambivalent feelings. On the one hand, he heard the Church's call to peacemaking set forth by John XXIII and Vatican II; on the other, he was reluctant to express a judgment about Vietnam, especially from the pulpit, because he believed that reasonable people could disagree in their application of Christian principles to the complex situation in Southeast Asia. Later he could recall a personal turning point — a photograph of the My Lai massacre, which led him finally to share with his congregation his own judgment against the war. When campus activists, including some of his Protestant colleagues, organized a march in 1967, he declined to participate. After the bitter events of the 1968 massacre, however, he felt a responsibility to join them, and this sense of responsibility became more intense as anti-war sentiment mounted among the student body. He worked with a moratorium march in 1969 and, when the campuses erupted in May 1970, he joined students, faculty and other clergy in demonstrations and protests. The shooting of students at Kent State University made feelings extremely volatile on all campuses, and Elwood worked hard to keep lines of communication open between campus activists and the police, and to channel student frustration into constructive action in the local community. He helped train students to go, two-by-two, through the community talking with people about the war; the experience was valuable, people were responsive and potential conflict was eased. Years later, Elwood could look back on the experience with some pride, noting mistakes that had been made but convinced that there were moments of crisis when "one has to say more than words...and take positive stands." That he did so with his people, and always with the deepest concern for their welfare as they struggled with the issues, showed pastoral sensitivity, but it also left its mark in a sense of distance from others in the Church, as the convictions formed by the experience did not easily fit into the available patterns of ministry.

Bishop Foery sympathized with priests like Elwood, whose activism was rooted in pastoral responsibility. Moreover, he was a Churchman, quite prepared to criticize public morals or public policy if his ecclesiastical responsibilities required that of him. What was far harder for him and others was the suggestion made by some that the Church itself was part of the problem. At LeMoyne's commencement in June 1968 just a few days after the assassination of Robert Kennedy, William H. Lazareth, dean of the Lutheran Theological Seminary in Philadelphia, offered a ringing denunciation of the Christian Church for its isolation from the pain and suffering of the world. Many looked upon the Church as "phony" and Christians as hypocrites, he argued. "There is so little passion in our preaching, so little urgency in our sense of mission, so little empathy with the suffering....We want to get along by going along." What was needed, he contended in the language of the "secular theology" so strong in the period, was a church which would "replace religious talk about a religious 'God' with worldly talk about wordly Christ." Foery, present at the commencement, was incensed, to put it mildly. Refused permission to answer the speaker, he told the president of the college he was cutting all his own and diocesan ties to LeMoyne because of the president's failure to respond "when the Church was maligned, college education degraded, and the Jesuits called phonies." Later, the split was smoothed over, but the episode showed how the events of the time, stirring passions and challenging the Church, could open deep divisions in the community and leave real wounds which would be hard to heal.

A final controversy arose in January 1973, only days before the signing of the Paris agreements which brought an end to American participation in the Vietnam conflict. The dispute centered around St. Andrew's church, where the pastor and many of the parishioners had long opposed the war actively. On January 6, Father Francis Pierson, secretary to the retired Bishop Foery, preached at St. Andrew's, reviewing Church teaching and emphasizing the 1971 statement of the American bishops that the war could no longer be justified and that the "speedy ending of the war is a moral imperative of the highest priority." He urged people to make their views known to their senators and congressman and to write the bishop, asking the diocese to contribute medical supplies for those injured during the December 1972 bombing of North Vietnam. This latter suggestion arose from a letter written by the pastor and six parishioners to Bishop Cunningham a few days earlier in which they took note of the bishop's request for medical supplies for victims of the recent earthquake in Nicaragua. The earthquake was "a tragic accident, inescapable fate," they argued, but the bombing in December was "a calculated destruction of life" made in the name of the American people. They urged that the bishop and the diocese "take a new stand against the killing," that all make reparation by prayer and fasting, and that all act as citizens to insure that such bombing did not happen again. The parish had decided to add another collection to that for the earthquake victims, one for medical supplies for North Vietnam to be sent through the American Friends Service Committee; they urged the bishop to suggest that all pastors do the same.

Cunningham responded with assurance of his "horror at the bombing, as well as the whole war in Indochina" and of his sense of responsibility to share in alleviating the pain and suffering of the people of Vietnam. Unfortunately, he argued, efforts by the Church to channel humanitarian aid to the North had consistently been stymied by the North Vietnamese government's refusal "to accept conditioned or controlled donations." Accordingly, he thought such a collection inappropriate. Yet he insisted he would do everything he could to encourage the government to work toward a reduction of suffering and, when hostilities ended, would attempt to afford opportunities for the people of the diocese to assist in relieving the suffering caused by war. He regretted that so many issues were presented by the news media as one more example of "decision making by confrontation" for neither "the cause of peace nor of Christian community" was served by such an atmosphere.

Race, poverty, and war, the wrenching issues of the 1960s, had combined with the dramatic changes occasioned by the Vatican Council to transform the face of Syracuse Catholicism. Parishes in urban areas were turning outward toward their neighborhoods in new ways, using many of the techniques of the past under new forms to assist people in building community institutions capable of easing the suffering of poverty and discrimination and laying a foundation for democratic participation and social progress. The sharply defined moral issues of racism and war had challenged the complacency of the local Church and brought deep divisions into the Catholic community itself. The bishops, first Foery, then Cunningham, beset daily by the internal problems posed by renewal and by the sharp declines and rising costs in Catholic schools, were forced at the same time to provide moral guidance to their own people and to share in the public task of helping the whole community deal with its deepening divisions and agonizing conflicts. They were not alone in feeling that, through the force of historic events around them, they and their Church were being "counted and judged." The call of the council to set out in new directions was made concrete and immediate by the unexpected and seemingly insoluble dilemmas posed by change in American society and culture. Few realized in 1970 that the pace of change was about to slow down a bit, but that these conflicts of the 1960s would leave scars that could not easily be healed, and that internal conflict within the community had in fact only begun.

445

THE
REAL WORLD

PUBLIC RESPONSIBILITY IN AN AGE OF RENEWAL
1960s-1970s

A s the diocese of Syracuse passed from the sixties to the seventies, and from the leadership of Bishop Foery to that of Bishop Cunningham, the internal renewal ushered in by the Second Vatican Council intersected with the call to social responsibility spurred by the problems of the nation and the local community. Bishop Cunningham had emphasized that renewal was intended to make the Church a more compelling witness to the Gospel and to inspire its members to better serve the human community. Authentic renewal could not take place without serious confrontation with injustice, violence and war. But that confrontation could not be an authentic expression of the life of the Church unless it involved the whole community and reflected its shared faith. In their relationship with the larger society, Catholics had to face the demands of the Gospel, to which all must respond, while learning to engage in dialogue about the application of those demands to the concrete situations in which the Church found itself.

Within the church there was a new voluntarism, "do it yourself Catholicism," as Father Andrew Greeley called it. At the same time, many Catholics felt an increasingly urgent sense of responsibility for the fate of the human family. Mediating between a prophetic emphasis on the demands of the Gospel and a pastoral tendency to seek the least common denominator was "the real world," as Catholic Charities official Harry Honan called it — the world in which the Church and its people lived every day. That world required both idealism and realism. When Catholics were complacent, the bishop challenged them to action; when they acted with passion and commitment, the diocese noted the need for organization, accountability, and cooperation. At times, the diocese refused to act, and was challenged on the basis of its teaching; at other times, when the bishop spoke and acted decisively, he was criticized for dividing the community or for trespassing in areas beyond his competence as a religious leader. Only gradually did it become clear that — with many people, many needs and many responsibilities — the local Church would require some time to work out new forms of dialogue, consultation and shared responsibility if it was to strike the proper balance between the pastoral and public responsibilities which it faced.

Bishop Cunningham had been prudent and cautious during the Vietnam war. He had not taken a strong stand and generally followed the position of the American bishops, finally agreeing with them in 1971 that the ending of the war had become a "moral imperative." Ironically, the most bitter controversy with which he became personally involved arose from the end, not the conduct of the war. In a Lenten pastoral letter in April, 1973, he applied the Holy Week themes of discipleship and forgiveness to the conditions left by the war. "The people of Vietnam, both North and South, whose villages and cities were bombed, the natural growth of their sustenance defoliated, their children and parents burned with napalm, have a claim upon us at least in Christian charity for aid during their reconstruction days," he wrote. By emphasizing charity rather than justice, the bishop clearly wished to avoid problems of war guilt and reparations, but he also was gently siding with the generous compassion of the parish of St. Andrew's a few months earlier.

The bishop then called attention to "young men who in sincere conscience fled the country rather than participate in what to them was an immoral war." Conscience was a "sacred and personal matter ... particularly when it involved those who refuse to have any part in taking the life of another," Cunningham argued, quoting at length from a resolution of the American bishops; "all possible consideration" should be given "to those young men who, because of sincere, conscientious belief, refused to participate in the war." While this was hardly an endorse-

ment of general amnesty for "deserters, draft dodgers and resisters" as critics soon charged, it was a clear call to heal the wounds created by the war and create a spirit of reconciliation in the country.

But the passions of war were still high. Headlines announced the bishop's calls for "amnesty," a word not used in the letter, and for aid to North Vietnam. Long-time opponents of the war praised the bishop, but local newspapers were almost uniformly critical and even many senior priests seemed angry. Cunningham insisted that his appeal for "limited amnesty" applied only to those who were "sincerely troubled in conscience and can give evidence of such and are ready to perform some service to the community." He also expressed concern about prisoners of war and those missing in action. Still it was difficult to respond to letter writers whose children had served or been killed in Vietnam. The bishop told them he offered no brief for "draft dodgers or deserters," but he insisted that there were many who had "sincerely objected to what they believed was an immoral war." American draft laws made provision only for those who refused to serve in all wars, he explained. Church teaching allowed for objection in conscience to particular wars based on the principles of the just war theory. It was for young men who had refused service on these grounds that he spoke.

More serious than opposition to Cunningham's support for "limited amnesty" was a widespread conviction that the bishop had no right to address such issues at all. One

Bishop David Cunningham took seriously his role as "the official Catholic teacher in the diocese," as he addressed moral aspects of issues like war, racism, and abortion. (Photo: The Catholic Sun)

endless circle of hate and revenge towards all people, even our enemies. This is not to be interpreted as unilateral disarmament, but does require international agreement to end the insane arms race that could trigger the destruction of humanity itself. My effort is to help our people to reflect on what is required to change the climate of relationships.... This is the Way of Life taught by Jesus Christ in His precept of charity. "You have learned how it was said: You must love your neighbor and hate your enemy. But I say this to you: Love your enemies and pray for those who persecute you; in this way you will be sons of your Father in heaven (Matthew 5:43-44).

angry Catholic told Cunningham: "we are tired of clergy wandering and drifting in and out of their sworn vocations, from one 'moral crisis' to another, having no direction to their own lives, attempting to direct ours on matters that belong to Caesar." Cunningham answered that he was "the official Catholic teacher for the diocese." War, like all human activity, "must always be measured in terms of morality." He had offered his reflections to contribute to reconciliation and to building a more stable peace. Troubled, the bishop told a sister who supported his stand that many failed to see the responsibility of Christians "to forgive as we are forgiven" and "use our resources to build back what we have destroyed." More generally, as he told another writer:

We have obligations to open up the

THE RIGHT TO LIFE

It seemed strange at the time that Bishop Cunningham, who had never indicated strong moral opposition to the Vietnam war, would become the center of such controversy after the war and express, as he did, such a strong personal commitment to the rights of conscience. One reason was that what the race question and the war had done for others, the issue of abortion was doing for Cunningham, causing him to ask hard questions about his country and about the moral integrity of his Church. Indeed he had begun to link the two problems of war and abortion as early as his sermon at a Mass of Thanksgiving for the end of hostilities in Vietnam in January 1973, only a few weeks after the Supreme Court decision overturning almost all legislation banning or limiting abortion:

It is ironical as we all rejoice that the killing, the destruction of human life is ended by the cease fire, our Supreme Court has established that abortion on request is a public policy of the nation.

We seek to save lives by ending the war, and at the same time condemn to death hundreds of thousands of unborn children.... As the bishop of Syracuse I urge our people not to accept the court's judgment or its reasoning.

Foery and Cunningham had been concerned about abortion for several years, especially as they worked with other bishops on political problems.

After a 1966 state constitutional convention, New York State bishops provided funds and open support for the Research Institute on Catholic Education in a campaign to win aid for parochial schools. At the same time they formed a state Catholic Conference and a New York State Catholic Committee to replace the old Welfare Committee. The conference dealt only with specifically Church related matters, while the committee was concerned with housing legislation, welfare assistance, capital punishment, criminal justice and other social issues.

However, the problem which caused the most heated debate was abortion; pressure built in the 1960s to amend New York State's restrictive laws. In January 1967, Bishop Foery set forth the basic Church position. "The unborn child has a right to life," he wrote. "The convenience, social circumstances, or the wish of the parent can never take away this basic right of the child." The state was obliged to "protect the rights of the innocent and the vulnerable" and "must not abdicate its responsibility." He urged citizens to write the governor, senate and assembly majority leaders, and their own senators and assembly representatives. Later, as the battle in the legislature heated up, he again urged pastors to do all they could to encourage their people to write. That fight was successful, but the bishops anticipated that the war was far from won. Attention focused particularly on

Catholics. At a meeting in March 1968 the bishops expressed concern "that the Catholic mind does not understand the issue." A secret statewide poll showed that three-quarters of the state's Catholics favored access to abortion in cases of rape, incest or danger to the mother's or child's health. Even among those describing themselves as involved in their Church, 63 percent favored such a change, in spite of the fact that 91 percent knew that the Church was opposed. As Bishop Donnellan of Ogdensburg put it, the people accepted the Church's teaching on the moral issue, but many resented any effort "to impose our will on the electorate."

Despite the efforts of the Church, the state law legalized abortions.

Bishop Cunningham told his priests: "Many Catholics have yet to realize the gravity of the problem." He reminded them to take every opportunity to expound the Church's reverence for life. Individuals, particularly in health care, were going to face difficult decisions. Priests should be aware of the "consciences of others who differ with us," but encourage Catholics to "stand firm in witnessing their respect for life and the highest ideals of the medical profession."

Cunningham described the decisive Supreme Court action striking down the nation's remaining abortion legislation in January 1973 as "heartbreaking." The decision was, he said, one more sign of a growing "callousness" in the United States toward life itself. "May God have mercy on us for our selfishness, our violence and our cruelty." He praised the emerging prolife groups and pledged his help to reverse the court ruling. He urged doctors and other medical professionals not to succumb to social pressure and perform abortions, and he told his people that in the case of a conflict between God's law and the laws of the state, they were to obey the law of God. October was set as Respect for Life month, with sermons, educational programs

450

and a Respect Life collection, the proceeds of which would be used to help provide alternatives for women with problem pregnancies. Later the New York State Right to Life Committee was allowed to take up collections outside churches.

The situation led to an unprecedented leap into politics. In January 1974, on the first anniversary of the Supreme Court decision, Cunningham told his people that a constitutional amendment was needed to establish the unborn child as a person in the eyes of the law. Parishioners were asked to develop public information programs, petition the state legislature, and write their congressmen and senators. "Our system of government requires citizen participation; in this case there is a moral imperative of the highest order for such activity." The day this letter was read, many took part in a march in downtown Syracuse and bells of area churches were rung at noon. The following year, parishes were instructed to organize Human Life Councils to work for a constitutinal amendment by letter-writing, personal contact, voter registration, and public education. Lists of congressmen sponsoring amendments or opposing them were distributed. The line between Catholic prolife groups and politically oriented right to life committees was blurred; in many places the personnel were in fact the same.

Cunningham's commitment to oppose abortion and work for a constitutional amendment was clear and unequivocal. It led him to sharp exchanges with other religious leaders and to an uncharacteristic political activism. He emphasized the primacy of the moral law, allowed no dissent from Church teaching, bombarded priests and people with reminders to be vigilant, and sought to overcome Catholic ignorance or deviation by regular and persistent affirmations. In addition he unhesitatingly urged involvement in the policy arena through parish groups focused almost entirely on techniques of political pressure. In 1977, he insisted in a pastoral letter that "the only realistic way to deal with the problem is to amend the Constitution so as to provide clear and unquestioned protection for unborn children." The contrast between all this and earlier work for racial integration, social justice and peace in Vietnam could not have been greater. On race, the diocese had taken clear moral leadership but had done little after the failure of the Neighbor program to push local parishes to action; after 1970, attention to race questions clearly went on the back burner. On poverty, the Church had supported efforts to raise money to assist the poor, and backed legislation to that effect, but had made few efforts to educate or organize Catholics. On the war in Vietnam, both Bishop Foery and Bishop Cunningham had stated the general principles and left it to individuals to make the application of those principles to the problems raised by the war. Beyond the draft counselling work of Catholic Social Services little active effort was made to broaden Church participation in public activity for peace. But the abortion issue was clearly defined from the beginning; the bishops knew where they stood. Far from being inhibited by lay resistance evident in polls, the hierarchy moved quickly to launch an all out educational campaign, not only to make the principles better known but to win support for their application to the problem and lend support to political groups working to achieve that policy objective. At the same time, Bishop Cunningham's enthusiastic and deeply felt articulation of prolife principles led him to a stronger position on other matters, evident in his stand on amnesty and soon in even stronger positions on peace, social justice and human rights. Given all this, it is startling that his most serious challenge on abortion came not from the left, from peace and social justice activists urging him to give the same energy and dedication to their cause that he did to abortion, but from a minority of conservative Catholics who surprisingly thought their bishop soft on abortion.

From the start Syracuse was far ahead of most other dioceses in following out the pastoral implications of its strong prolife position. The bishop emphasized the need to assist women with unwanted pregnancies and to "lift the stigma" from women and children in such situations. On November 19, 1971, Sister Marguerite Tierney of the family life office of Catholic Charities told Bishop Cunningham of a local program called Birthright, which offered assistance to such women. Shortly after, Birthright became affiliated with Catholic Charities and relocated its office at the Chancery.

Birthright was also the name of a an international movement of assistance to unwed mothers originating in Toronto. In the spring of 1973, its officials wrote Bishop Cunningham, concerned with rumors that the Syracuse program would "refer girls for abortions if the girl insists that she wants one." Cunningham explained that the local agency received "warm encouragement and some financial assistance" from the diocese, but was non-sectarian and had its own board. He defended Birthright:

> While our Catholic Charities activities have been extensive in dealing with unwed mothers ... Birthright has performed thoroughly admirable service in the community. I have been close to its operations and watched with great edification the way in which they have worked with girls. I personally am very proud of the way they function and know that their activity is done thoroughly within the context of solid traditional Catholic teaching.

Cunningham was upset. "All of us," he added, "have enough enemies from without;

let us who share common ideals be of support to one another." Birthright leaders in Syracuse and nationally may well have agreed, but the local agency decided to change its name to Support to avoid complications. The larger organization seemed satisfied, but those who had aroused their attention in the first place were not.

In late 1973 the bishop began to receive letters from the local Right to Life leaders expressing concern about Support's executive director, Cheryl Riggs, a non-Catholic who had once been associated with Planned Parenthood. Her experience had confirmed her prolife convictions, and the bishop thought this made her well qualified:

> Certainly the fact that someone has come to be pro-life through her own life experience, and therefore more deeply committed to the movement, should not be a reason for withholding support, but rather should be a comfort in that we have leadership from a person who has dealt with the subject not from afar and theoretically but has developed convictions within the context of her own life situation.

Opponents disagreed. Most vocal was Charles Pulver, now a regular correspondent for The Wanderer. The bishop assured Pulver that he again had looked into the work of Support and found that it was providing hundreds of young women with alternatives to abortion. Naturally some made the "tragic decision" not to carry their child to term, and the board and staff attempted to be supportive of such persons. The bishop added his strong personal endorsement of this approach:

> While not condoning immoral practices they remain supportive of individuals. It would seem to me this is entirely in accord with the teaching and example of our Blessed Lord.... I

must admit that it is with a degree of satisfaction that I see so many people from all walks of life come into our chancery with such heartbreaking situations and find therein persons who will work with them and love them and provide skillful, professional service in the most difficult moments in their lives. As you know, Support is not part of the diocesan structure, but I am convinced they are offering a most Christian service worthy of our assistance. Our firm efforts to modify the tragic Supreme Court decisions should not be confused with a callousness toward individuals who are in need of the ministry of the Church. A loving concern toward individuals is not weakness but rather following the command of Christ.

The bishop's reinvestigation had been occasioned by the remark of a Common Council candidate and a member of Support's board that Support was not an anti-abortion organization; later she clarified her statement by explaining that it was a nondenominational organization with a strong respect for human life and for the unborn but was "a nonjudgmental service agency." This bothered some Catholics. In May a parishioner and her son picketed Mrs. Riggs' appearance for a talk at the Christian Brothers Academy and later in the month the newpapers reported that a group calling themselves "Concerned Catholics" were to meet with the bishop to demand that Support be removed from its offices in the chancery. At issue were continuing charges that referrals were made for birth control and abortion, but the bishop and Catholic Charities reaffirmed their commitment, insisting that no person was assisted to obtain an abortion. On June 16, 1976, about 50 people picketed the chancery building and the story received wide publicity throughout

the diocese and in The *Wanderer.* The picketing continued for nine weeks.

The bishop praised the picketers for their interest and agreed to meet with them. At those meetings, in conversation with leaders of the Committee of Concerned Catholics, and in letters to the press, the bishop held fast to a strong anti-abortion policy, but insisted that the organization could not be faulted if some of its clients resisted their anti-abortion advice. Support was also uniquely successful; one report said the group had recently counselled 138 women and 126 decided not to get abortions, a truly remarkable record. But their open, non-judgemental approach which helped the woman make her own decision did not coincide with their opponents' view that an agency backed by the Church should unequivocally enforce Church teaching. Concerned Catholics hit at Support from a number of sides. Members called the office, claiming they had a particularly difficult pregnancy and asking for names of doctors who would perform abortion. The receptionist said they did not give out that information; when pressed she suggested the caller contact Planned Parenthood. The committee also explored the funding of the organization. The City and County Youth Board, for example, provided small grants, and expected a nondenominational, open-minded approach, including provision of birth control information.

Support was dominated by professionals, many with counselling background and skills. Unlike national Birthright, which took a directive, anti-abortion approach to the counselling of pregnant women, Support took a more professional, non-directive approach, in accord with its conviction that many who came to it for help were unclear on their own values and frequently caught in a range of life problems. Focusing on the person, Support attempted to help her deal with her problems and respected the decisions she made. On the surface the problem was abortion but, as the bishop knew, Support had been established precisely to provide an alternative to abortion in a setting different from those available at Planned Parenthood and the Upstate Medical Center; there was a bias against abortion and this was made clear to all clients.

The big weakness was not abortion, but birth control. Many of the women were involved in sexual relationships while unwilling or unable to become mothers; some insisted that the relationship would continue and they sought information regarding conception control. As Fahey explained to the bishop, public funding agencies often required that information regarding family planning be made available to clients. At Support, the staff made clear their opposition to extra-marital sexual activity, and told clients the agency did not give contraceptive information; those who persisted were told they could seek it from their physician, a neighborhood health clinic or Planned Parenthood. Fahey admitted that things were "generally done in this way at our hospitals and at our social service agencies." If such actions were not allowed, the Church would simply be forced to withdraw from many areas of social service.

In the past, the diocesan response to such situations had been inconsistent, even with Planned Parenthood. In 1970 Cunningham, then coadjutor bishop had denounced the "crime" of birth control and promised that the Church would remain the "enemy" of the "birth control movement." The diocese had fought to prevent Planned Parenthood from presenting an exhibit at the State Fair. Also the diocese had withdrawn from the Metropolitan Health Council when Planned Parenthood became a member. Yet, in Binghamton, where small Community Chest grants went to Planned Parenthood, Catholic Charities continued to participate and supported the annual campaign. When criticized, Foery

For decades, the Syracuse diocese has been active in championing the Church's pro-life position — not only against abortion, but for helping pregnant women and single parents and, more recently, in extending the pro-life ethic to support service projects for the poor, an end to capital punishment, freedom from nuclear build-up, and the decrease of U.S. military activity in Central America. (Photo: The Catholic Sun)

responded that withdrawal would not sharpen public perception of the Church's already clear stand but probably would create sympathy with Planned Parenthood. There, he said, Planned Parenthood sincerely tried to respect the conscience of those who sought its services and in the bishop's judgement its contribution to abortion was minimal. Situations like this showed the imperfection of the world, Foery wrote. God tolerated evil, though was not pleased with it; "in some instances, we must too." From a pastoral point of view, he concluded, "it is our judgement that the evil resulting is so minimal that it has to be tolerated in the face of a greater evil should another course be followed."

However, after 1968, this moderate position

454

was no longer tenable, as birth control had become a test case of loyalty for bishops and priests. When the Vatican Council was considering the question, Foery thought there should be a study of the rhythm method, and he worried that a number of physicians would not recommend it because they found "its use was doubtful and uncertain." Like many other bishops, he wanted "a statement by the Holy See to clear up this ever widening confusion." In 1968, overriding the advice of a special papal commission, Pope Paul VI confirmed the long standing teaching that every act of intercourse must be open to life. Bishops Foery and Cunningham had no difficulty accepting the teaching and were shocked by the critical reaction of many priests and theologians across the country. On the question of authority, Cunningham was clear and determined. As far as the diocese was concerned, Pope Paul's *Humanae Vitae* was a positive, authoritative and "obligatory statement" which set forth "without ambiguity, doubt or hesitation the authentic teaching of the Church concerning the objective evil of contraception." While compassion, understanding and kindness should operate in the confessional, the clear public teaching of the Church removed any confusion that may have existed and, as a bishop, he was responsible to teach what the Church teaches. In the end, birth control broke the Church connection with Support. The bishop found it impossible to defend Support's policy of making referrals, even for information, to Planned Parenthood. Support's board and staff on the other hand, could not in conscience refuse to explain to clients the availability of birth control.

On September 13, 1976 Bishop Cunningham sent a memorandum to the board of Support explaining that he had "no difficulty" regarding their "attitude and counselling on abortion" but, because of the "referrals by the agency to Planned Parenthood," he would no longer be able to defend their work or allow them to receive diocesan funds.

Two weeks later Harry Honan, regional director of Catholic Charities, told the Respect Life committee that, while many might "dissent" from the bishop's decisions, they had to live in the "real world," avoid endangering other programs, and find other means to assist women experiencing unplanned pregnancies. He pointed out the range of services the diocese had developed, including financial assistance through Catholic Social Services, natural family planning through the Family Life bureau, and programs to help the mother keep her baby and develop parenting skills. The bishop explained to the priests his decision was based "not on public pressure" but on his "office as teacher." Artificial contraception was not a solution satisfactory to the Church, so he could not fund an agency that made referrals "to assist young, unmarried women in an immoral relationship, and to give instruction of a safe operation in their activity."

One of Concerned Catholics' non-negotiable demands was that the diocese provide financial backing for a new chapter of Birthright in the city. In the fall a group of local Catholics did in fact launch such a group, and the bishop sent Mary McGann, it executive director, a letter of congratulations. The Respect Life committee, which already was funding other assistance programs, refused to provide funds for Birthright, in part because the latter would not accept the terms of affiliation with Catholic Charities. For months the committee and Birthright argued, with Bishop Cunningham, now nearing the end of his term, caught in the middle. When Bishop Frank Harrison succeeded Cunningham, he and the Charities staff decided that a more professional counselling service providing an alternative to abortion was still needed in the community. Discussion between Support, Charities and the bishop proceeded through 1977, when a Catholic replaced Mrs. Riggs as executive director. The Committee of Concerned Catholics complained to Rome. When the apostolic delegate again inquired, Harrison told him the committee was "an extremely self-righteous group" who were "simply obstructive of everything we try to do." Harrison's irritation was clear: "I am a bishop who has taken an oath of fidelity to the Holy Father and to uphold the magisterium. You can be certain that I will keep that oath, and that I will safeguard my people."

At the end of May 1978, Support issued a policy statement which explained that it did "not make referrals for abortions or contraceptives," while it did pursue the nondirective approach which it had followed previously.

After consultation, Harrison concluded that if Support operated within these policies it was entitled to affiliate with Catholic Charities.

Coming in the wake of many bitter controversies and at the end of his administrations, the Support battle must have been particularly frustrating for Bishop Cunningham. He was known among the priests as a man who was unflappable and said at the worst moments that, somehow, "we will muddle through." At times during this episode he became angry, justifiably so, when his own integrity was called into question. The papal decision to reaffirm the ban on artificial birth control, however, placed the bishop in an untenable situation. It must have been especially painful because he was so impressed by Support's work, and so appalled by the behavior of Concerned Catholics. As Fahey pointed out, if the Church simply refused to associate with agencies which provided birth control information, it would have to pull back from many of the social services it offered. The Church cooperated with many groups and agencies with which it

disagreed; this had never been a purist church. Yet association with an agency which provided the information on where birth control information could be obtained was not possible, however admirable and effective its efforts to prevent abortions. To have made another decision would have required candor and courage, and might well have divided the local Church. But the problem of integrity and credibility would not go away, as birth control and abortion would continue to pose difficult questions for years to come.

CATHOLIC CHARITIES

Harry Honan, Syracuse area director of Catholic Charities, wrote in his 1976 annual report that the issue of Support "more than any other tested our new organizational style and policies, proving them to be weak where strength was required." The Charities staff had learned from the experience and "realized more than ever that Catholic Charities must soon determine its long-range role, especially as it attempts to be community based and still reflective of the Catholic Church." Honan's remarks reflected major changes in diocesan charitable work, changes which not only involved reorganization but opened up new questions about the relationship between Charities, the diocese, and the Catholic community.

One element of the story of Syracuse Catholicism was its development as a modern American institution, utilizing techniques spawned by a rapidly advancing industrial society. Its bishops were great organizers who placed its pastoral, educational and charitable activities on a solid financial foundation, developed procedures for control and accountability, utilized modern methods of fund raising and administration, and gradually introduced more highly trained, professional personnel. Nowhere was this process of modernization carried out more dramatically

When the new Catholic Charities building was dedicated in Utica in October 1967, clergy active in social services throughout the diocese were present, including (seated, left to right), Monsignor Daniel E. Lawler, Bishop Foery, and Monsignor Joseph May, and (standing, left to right), Father John McCrea (diocesan Charities director), Father John Madden, Father Charles Fahey, Monsignor Robert Davern, Father Frank Woolever, Monsignor Francis Willenburg (Utica Charities director), and Father James Quinn. (Photo: Chancery Archives)

than in Charities, where the Church gradually become more and more integrated with other agencies and institutions into a modern "system" of social services. Church teaching clearly upheld the responsibility of the state to provide for the basic need of its citizens. As early as 1919 the American bishops had called for public insurance against sickness, accident, and unemployment and for a national system of old age pensions. Catholic hospitals and charitable institutions were often the first developed in American cities, but from the start many people regarded the provision of these services as a public, not a Church, responsibility. The Church did not insist on total independence of its charitable institutions as it did in education, but instead cooperated, first with community wide fund raising in Community Chest, later with governmental agencies.

Faced with the challenges of new needs and broadening definitions of human rights in the 1960s, Catholic Charities was pulled in two directions. As an established and responsible institution in the community, Catholic Charities was part of the system that was being challenged. As a community of faith, present with and among those in need, the Church was called to speak on behalf of human dignity, especially for the poorest and most neglected members of society. Tension between public responsibility and Gospel values was felt within the offices of Catholic Charities, which was at one and the same time a set of institutions and agencies sharing with others responsibility for meeting human needs and part of a Church which felt an increasingly direct responsibility to take its stand with and on behalf of the poor. It was an uncomfortable position.

The Church in Syracuse was fortunate to find during this period some remarkable leadership in this area. Monsignors Daniel Lawler and Robert Davern were experienced Charities priest-professionals respected in the community and enjoying the trust of the bishop. Davern brought remarkable energy and imagination to the parishes he served in Syracuse and Binghamton, while Lawler helped local parishes develop new forms of outreach into the community. Lawler brought into Catholic Charities Father Frank Woolever, who had been trained in the anti-establishment activism of community organization, to head up the innovative Office of Inner City Development. During the sixties, Lawler set a new agenda before the local Church; but it was his successor, Charles Fahey, who enabled the Church to act on that agenda.

As a young priest, Fahey caught Lawler's attention. He was sent off for further studies and returned as a trained social worker. He played a key role in the Catholic Neighbor program, then turned to his professional

interest, care for the aged, which was becoming a major area for public investment. Loretto Rest soon became the hub of Loretto Geriatric Center, a multifaceted set of programs serving the varied needs of the elderly. Two major responses to those needs were St. Camillus Nursing Home and Bernardin Apartments. Later additions at Loretto Rest included more apartments for both ill and ambulatory residents and extended care for those with special needs. Catholic Charities also helped local groups launch elderly housing projects in Norwich, Manlius and Pulaski and build nursing homes in several locations, including St. Luke's in Oswego, and St. Joseph's in Utica. The Church played an initiating and supporting role in these projects, but independent boards owned and managed the institutions. In a 1973 report, Fahey told the bishop that on six construction projects the diocese, with a contribution of less than $1,000,000, had stimulated buildings costing more than $32,000,000. In 1970 a nutrition program, Keener Seniors, was launched in numerous locations in the Syracuse area. Meals for the elderly often led to recreational and social programs, some in parish centers, others in neighborhood centers sponsored by community groups. The patterns developed in elderly care and repeated in medical and child-care work — which saw Catholic Charities providing leadership and technical services to broad based community groups to develop plans, win public funding, and provide services under independent, non-profit corporations — represented a creative response to new sources of funding both state and federal. They also gradually withdrew the Church from being the formal provider of these services. Fahey also developed an innovative "affiliation" process, used with Support, which allowed independent agencies to receive technical assistance, some financial support, and a structure of accountability without surrendering their independence or

AN ADVOCATE FOR DECENT HOUSING

For the last three decades, Catholic Charities in Binghamton has been finding innovative and effective ways to realize the church's long-felt need to help people find decent places to live.

Under Monsignor Davern in the 1960s, Charities joined with other groups and agencies to advocate for better housing. Davern was a leader of the Binghamton Housing Authority and helped found Metro-Interfaith, an ecumenical group concerned about housing. From these positions he could help the Church become an effective advocate for the housing needs of Broome County residents.

In the 1970s, Monsignor Ronald Bill not only continued the advocacy stance of his predecessor, but he also moved Charities into providing housing for hundreds of residents. Charities became the local sponsor for the federal "Sweat Equity" home ownership program, through which families were helped to rehabilitate and purchase older homes. Bill also organized an affiliate agency that built senior-citizen housing in Endwell and Great Bend, Pa.

When Bill moved on to become diocesan vicar for community services, Binghamton Catholic Charities passed to the leadership of his assistant, Joseph Slavik. He picked up on one of Bill's final projects — to provide housing for the mentally handicapped. In 1978, New York State had decided to de-institutionalize people living in mental hospitals. Under the plan, local agencies — including Catholic Charities in both Binghamton and Utica — were designated to provide housing, transportation, recreational, and case management services for the former mental patients. Slavik developed a series of group homes in Binghamton — two houses for 28 mentally ill and emotionally disturbed persons in a supervised setting; three more homes for 12 people who were a bit more independent; and four apartments for 12 people who could live independently with some outside support. Charities also opened a group home for 12 emotionally disturbed teenage girls. Meanwhile plans continued for another housing unit for the elderly in Johnson City, with plans for a similar unit in northern Broome County. Catholic Charities, Our Lady of Lourdes Hospital, and SEPP (the Charities housing affiliate) began talking about a retirement village somewhere in the county as a project for the 1990s.

Elsewhere around the diocese, Catholic Charities offices likewise were providing housing — elderly units in Onondaga and Oswego counties, housing for the mentally handicapped in Oneida County. But Broome County became the model of how the Church, sometimes on its own and other times by cooperating with public and other private agencies, could provide housing for many people — the elderly, poor families, and the handicapped. It was model that worked well. With such experience and early leadership, and aided by the diocese's own housing management agency, Charities has made possible housing for elderly and handicapped people not only throughout the Syracuse diocese but in the dioceses of Albany, Ogdensburg, Rochester, and Buffalo as well — 25 buildings with 1,500 apartments throughout upstate New York administered by the Syracuse diocese.

their eligibility for other sources of funding.

Day care had long been of interest to the Church, first among immigrants such as the Italian community in Rome where the Parish Visitors provided assistance for working mothers, then again during the war when local Church officials spearheaded a drive to provide care for women drawn to employment by wartime conditions. The urban crisis of the 1960s exposed the existence of many female-headed households caught in a cycle of poverty. If such families were to be assisted to become self-sustaining through job training and employment, adequate child care would have to be provided. Fahey told the bishop in August 1968 that provision of such services was one of the most pressing needs of the diocese. "While affirming strongly the traditional conviction of the Church that it is preferable for mothers to remain in their homes, we recognize that there are individual instances where the mothers must work or de facto they are working," he wrote. Responding to a community need and attempting to provide leadership on the issue, Charities organized the De Paul Day Care Corporation to stimulate "sound day care" in the community. One such program began at the CYO center in Fulton, another was planned for the Tremont Street area of Syracuse and a cooperative day care center was set up at the House of Providence.

The centralization and professionalism of social services, together with the increasing involvement in nondenominational programs with federal support, tended to create a distance between Catholic Charities and the parishes. Throughout the country as Charities professionals reflected on their work in light of the council, concern developed to recreate ties between the service of Catholic Charities and parish life, for example by decentralizing emergency social service delivery. The National Conference of Catholic Charities sponsored a national program of "parish outreach"

460

Youth programs long have been supported by the Syracuse diocese. Monsignor Ronald C. Bill served for more than 10 years as summer-camp chaplain for Binghamton Boy Scouts, for which he received the St. George scouting award in 1974. (Photo: Catholic Charities)

designed to assist parishes to once again become involved with the human needs of their neighborhood and community. In the Syracuse diocese this took a number of forms. One was to strenghthen the relationship between parishes and neighborhood centers, especially in urban areas. Later rural parishes were assisted to work together to reach out to pockets of rural poverty. In the late sixties Father John McCrea, as director of Catholic Social Services, attempted to return direct emergency relief services to parish centers. Assisted by small grants from the Campaign for Human Development, several such centers opened and Catholic Charities staff continued to encourage parishes to broaden their ministry to human needs in their neighborhood. Before long, this program had become one of encouraging the formation of distinct Human Development committees in the parishes, with local Catholic charities personnel training the members. While most parishes eventually established these committees, only a few were active, and the problem of bringing parishes to a constructive role in the social mission of the Church persisted.

By the time Fahey took charge of Catholic Charities in 1969, it was clear that organizational reforms were needed. Catholic Charities had become through the half century of its existence a wide ranging network of 72 organizations, agencies and programs. It was far from a neat, tightly organized institution. Charities and chancery funds were mixed, there was a complex array of bank accounts, investment portfolios and trusts, all in the hands of the bishop and the diocesan corporation. Fahey carried forward changes begun by Lawler, using new lay advisory boards, professional leadership, involvement of staff in decision making, and decentralizing administration away from Syracuse to the regional offices in Utica, Binghamton, Fulton, Cortland and elsewhere, each under committees of priests, religious, and lay people. Most important, Catholic charities became a corporation separate from the diocese, though still directed by the bishop.

Harry Honan then carried out a study of internal operations which led to further reorganization of the programs into four distinct divisions. The family division included social services, residential services such as group homes, and Alliance program for abused children. The neighborhood division took in neighborhood centers, Keener Seniors, human development and parish CYO. An administrative division provided the management and accounting services formerly provided by Christopher Community, while the latter became the housing affiliate of

Catholic Charities. Finally a special services division was responsible for public relations and development work. In 1977, a parish services division was created, to coordinate the Parish CYO program and the Human Development committees.

Reorganization provided a way of brokering the variety of pressures to which the Church tried to respond. Neighborhood centers continued to be tremendously affected by shifts in public funding for programs for pre-school children, families, parents and senior citizens. Northside CYO expanded its services to senior citizens with the help of public funds while a variety of group homes for juveniles, emotionally and mentally handicapped youngsters and others were similarly dependent upon public assistance. Adoption, foster care and family and emergency assistance programs drew more heavily on Church and community support and interlocked Catholic Charities with other local community groups. Even the Catholic Charities building reflected the complex interaction of Catholic, local community and public activities; in 1976 it housed meetings of a host of organizations including, in the words of one report, "prayer groups, youth ministry, Engaged and Marriage Encounter Groups, confirmation classes, Junior League, City-County Youth Board, community institutions and others."

Internally Charities had clarified its organizational structure and achieved the clear public accountability for funds required by its public role, but its relationship to the Church as an organization and to the Catholic community as a whole remained ambiguous. If it was far from a house divided, it surely was one with many rooms, not clearly a single family home, a set of cooperative apartments, or a hotel. In its uncertainty, and in its vigor and responsiveness to changing currents of human needs and public policies, it reflected the uniquely American, if complex and often inefficient, realities of pluralism, federalism,

461

and the never quite separate separation of Church and state. Unable to depend solely on private resources any longer to meet the needs spawned by advanced industrial society, neither did Americans want to hand them all over to the state. While public and private sectors struggled toward a new relationship, and while each was torn by debates about its role and resources, those basic human realities and human needs remained. Catholic Charities' problems reflected its virtues, for it sought to combine the compassion and generosity of its religious and cultural tradition with the efficiency, accountability and shared responsibility that are the marks of democratic government at its best.

462

As in so many other areas of modern Catholic life, Charities faced dilemmas which did not allow for unambigious choices. The Concerned Catholics, and other groups who regarded the Church's collaboration with outsiders as carrying too high a cost in integrity, demanded that the Church sever its ties to government and its association with other private-sector agencies in order to maintain a clear and unambigious witness to its doctrines. In doing so, they exposed the manner in which those associations had forced agencies to adopt standards and procedures which had no direct reference either to the Gospel or to specificly Catholic teaching. To go in either direction, back to Church or out to the public with no ties to the Church, would mean that there would be clarity but a price would be paid by those in need; the Church did not have the resources, and the state did not have the compassion, understanding and respect for the independence and integrity of "clients" to meet the needs of the needy without demeaning them. The struggle of Catholic Charities, then, mirrored the larger struggle of a Church come of age — a church called upon to play both religious and public roles. In its own way the Church was little different from the newly

successful Catholic business executive, labor leader, or government official sometimes finding that reconciling the religious values with public responsibilities was no mean trick. If in the sixties it seemed that what was needed was to persuade Catholics to follow the teachings of the Church on race, poverty and peace, by the 1980s it had become a question of acknowledging that the translation of Gospel values into effective action was a complex process requiring the full participation of all Catholics in formulating Church priorities and sharing with others responsibility for constructing a more just and peaceful world. Here, as elsewhere, what began as an organizational problem became a pastoral one, for the most important link between the community of faith and the wider society was the individual lay Catholic.

BEYOND THE ORGANIZATION

One dramatic result of the upheavals of the 1960s was a growing awareness of the gap between the proclamation of the Good News in Jesus and the realities of life in the "real world," including the Church. The bishops at Vatican II had been inspired by a renewed

Father Raymond McVey (left) was the guiding force behind Unity Acres, a residential project to aid homeless men. (Photos: The Catholic Sun)

vision of the Church experienced in Pope John and in the council. Others came to share something of that vision. As they tried to put that vision into practice in their parish, in Marriage Encounter or charismatic renewal, at the Foery Foundation or in the Catholic Interracial Council, they sometimes found themselves in conflict with their Church, with the bishop or their pastor, with Catholic Charities or the school office. Tension between the demands of the organized Church and those of the Gospel was inevitable; it could be the source of growth, as individuals were called by the Church to share responsibility for its common life, and as Church institutions were challenged to greater integrity by the witness of prophetic individuals like Father Brady, the Berrigans, or another remarkable priest, Raymond McVey.

In 1968 McVey, then a young curate at St. Lucy's in Syracuse, felt the need, as he put it later, "to get out of this institutional environment and get closer to the neighborhood and closer to the needs, so that perhaps I could do something for a man and his total life, rather than just bandaiding the situation." Strongly influenced by commitment to Gospel poverty of Dorothy Day and Catherine

deHueck Doherty, McVey began a neighborhood center at the corner of Seymour and West Streets, soon after moving from the rectory to a small home on Chester Street which he made a refuge for homeless men. Within a year and a half, larger quarters were needed and he moved to Huron Street; at about the same time he raised money to purchase land in Pulaski for a home for alcholics and others in need. The Syracuse house, now Unity Kitchen, offered soup and shelter on the model of the Catholic Worker houses. Volunteers organized by Anne O'Connor helped find food, clothing and money for the house. McVey became more and more involved at Unity Acres, the country place where men from the city could prepare for renewed entry into society, so that Father Richard Keough became the key figure at the city house, joined by two sisters, three former students, and an energetic Mexican-American layman, all of whom now lived in a staff house in the model cities neighborhood, which soon shifted to an abandoned factory on West Adams Street. It was, as Keogh put it, "a catch all facility acting as a portal to the greater society for its most down and out members." In addition to food, clothing and shelter, the community offered referrals to medical, legal and social services, and to Unity Acres. They offered help finding jobs and arranging transportation; they published a newsletter, visited prisons and helped former prisoners, all the while attempting to build a sense of Chrisitan community and to support efforts for world peace and social justice.

McVey and his friends believed in a radical commitment to Christ and viewed the poor as "Christ among us." They were to be treated as guests. Formal efforts at rehabilitation were foreign to this spirit, as was the bureaucratic approach which followed upon incorporation, tax exemption and receipt of government funds. Instead McVey and his friends depended upon the grace of God and the

463

support of the community. The group was admired by many priests and by Bishop Cunningham, but the Church was a highly organized and responsible institution, and at times found it difficult to respond to the unorthodox methods but altogether Christian concerns and methods of Unity Acres and its supporters.

McVey and others had participated in nonviolent civil disobedience and presented an organized challenge to the institutional Church's monopoly on Catholic action in Syracuse, a monopoly previously questioned only indirectly by groups like the Catholic Interracial Council and Daniel Berrigan's Professional Sodality. They were asking very hard questions. "Christianity is not a law and order club, but a goad and barb to the world," McVey wrote in 1970. "What about our parochial schools, our big churches, our comfortable communities—they are full of dead men's bones." This challenge was coming from inside, not outside, the Church; a few months later a top ranking chancery official asked that the ordination of the new auxiliary bishop, Frank Harrison, be conducted with simplicity and the money saved be used for the poor, so that the Church's deeds not contradict its statements. As another priest put it, McVey was teaching them "some new lessons about Gospel and Church."

By 1972 Unity Acres property in Pulaski, a former tuberculosis sanatorium, was bursting at the seams. Another, larger property became available in Sackets Harbor near Watertown. An abandoned military installation, it had a number of buildings thought suitable to the group's plans to organize small businesses, and McVey and his supporters were anxious to purchase the property. One problem was that local residents were alarmed, and their fears were not eased when McVey explained that they did not attempt to rehabilitate the addicts, former prisoners and down and out

men they served, who were free to come and go as they pleased. Community opposition was not the only problem. The bishop originally agreed to co-sign a note which the group would take to purchase the property, but he was overruled by his consultors. Shocked by this decision McVey, joined by a number of priests and lay supporters, conducted a prayer service at the chancery. Cunningham agreed to find some way to assist the group, but early efforts proved unsuccessful as the lay Catholics approached doubted the stability and long range prospects of the enterprise. In June 1972, a fire swept the Pulaski property; in this crisis the community rallied to McVey's support. McVey suddenly decided to concentrate on rebuilding and expanding the Pulaski property. Unity Acres agreed to incorporate and establish a board, donations were solicited with the bishop's support, and Unity Acres not only continued but thrived. But the tension between its radical, personalist approach and the bureaucratic realism of Catholic Charities persisted.

Yet the diocesan Church was enriched by the presence of Unity Acres, Unity Kitchen, and a variety of other small, prophetic communities which sprang up to meet the needs of the poor, express a Christian witness to peace and nonviolence, and to provide a setting conducive to living the Christian life beyond what was expected, or perhaps was possible, in most parishes or most vocations. It was a hard lesson to learn, for the history of American Catholicism left a strong legacy of concern for unity, loyalty, and organizational coherence. Bishops naturally preferred that "Catholic" activities take place within official Catholic institutions. But institutions have their own virtues and limitations and are rarely if ever able to fully embody the demands of the Gospel. In 1973, when Father Brady's health was failing and the building which housed the Foery Foundation was no longer adequate, a decision had to be made about the future of his very special ministry to black people. Brady's most loyal followers hoped that his ministry could continue under independent auspices, perhaps in one of the parishes around which black Catholics were congregating. Catholic Charities leaders, on the other hand, felt that the services could best be provided by trained social workers in the new Southwest Community Center, which had the facilities and funds needed. At a climatic meeting, the Charities people won out, and the Foery Foundation was relocated to the publicly funded neighborhood center. There, the situation no longer allowed religious services, but social workers and volunteers continued to provide a variety of services for families and children. Brady was honored there, but he was not comfortable. He did not complain, but friends felt he was hurt. His witness continued in many places and among many people, including those at the Foery Foundation, but what he and Father McVey represented could not find full expression within what the professionals defined as "the real world."

While attempting to help parishes become more involved in relieving human needs, the diocese also continued to wrestle with the need to help the poor obtain justice and, in the words of the Campaign for Human Development "break out of the poverty system through their own doing." The Human Development Council continued to distribute funds from the CHD and local poverty collection to a variety of groups such as food cooperatives, neighborhood centers, and tenant organization. The earlier Office of Inner City Development died in the early 1970s, but sisters and priests continued working in the inner city. In 1976 they drew together once again to form the Board of Urban Ministry, composed of pastors and representatives from nine downtown parishes. Cunningham was pleased with the new

group's emphasis on the parish. "One particularly appealing aspect of your plan is the strengthening of the role of the parish in urban life," he wrote.

By the plan, nine parishes would be represented on the board and would relate to the vicar general of the diocese. Each would contribute $1,000 to the budget and additional outside funding would be sought. Father Thomas Hooley, a community organizer, was hired as executive director. He and the board put together a grant from the Campaign for Human Development and another from the Comprehensive Education and Training Act (CETA) program to hire a team of organizers. In the spring and summer of 1977, working with Syracuse United Neighbors, which also began with help from CHD, Urban Ministry took a leading role in opposing the location of a solid waste disposal facility in a predominately black neighborhood. Aided by Monsignor McGraw's preaching in the cathedral, a letter from Bishop Harrison and a demonstration in which Auxiliary Bishop Thomas Costello took part, the decision was reversed. Hooley continued to work on organizing around redlining, insurance discrimination, and once again housing, causing considerable tension with local officials and agencies.

The confrontational approach of community organizing was not the only problem. The Urban Ministry Board also challenged what they took to be an effort by Catholic Charities to end the Human Development Committee and bring CHD under the control of their office. By that time Hooley had left, but SUN and several other urban groups served on the Urban Ministry Board and some organizing staff remained working under the its umbrella. In addition, a new initiative was taken when Father John Shopfer was appointed Southwest Urban Missioner, an appointment designed to enable him to play a role similar to that of Brady in earlier years. In the early 1980s under Sister Alethea Connelly, Urban Ministry continued to support parish based organizing work and helped create the Office of Black Ministry under Sister Clementine Lynch.

In the midst of the urban crisis, as attention was drawn to poverty and discrimination, the diocese began to recognize the growth of another group plagued by these problems, the Spanish speaking. In major urban areas, the presence of a large Hispanic population had already drawn considerable attention, but in Syracuse the growth of this community was slow, confined for years to migrant labor camps in the agricultural regions of the diocese. In 1960 the growth of the Hispanic community in Utica led to a survey of community needs by the Legion of Mary and active efforts, with the help of the Legion, to draw Puerto Rican families into parish life. By 1969 there were at least 5,000 Spanish speaking Catholics in the diocese and that year the first Spanish Apostolate office was established with a layman, Milton Valladare of Rochester, as director. The project grew out of the work of Catholic Charities and several parishes with migrant workers. Father Woolever arranged for a Spanish Mass at St. Lucy's and a surprisingly large group appeared. Father Robert Chryst was studying Spanish in Puerto Rico at the time, and on his return he was assigned to St. Lucy's. The new apostolate was beseiged by problems.

Valladare spent most of his time in the Utica area and in 1971 Chryst took over, funded by the Poverty Collection with an extra grant from the bishop. By 1972 Chryst was serving 2,500 residents of Onondaga county and consulting with parishes and agencies throughout the diocese, attempting on a shoestring to assist with social problems and provide religious and catechetical services. Later controversy developed as to where to locate the apostolate, which in many ways came to resemble the traditional immigrant parish, but without a single church to rally

By the end of the 1960s there were an estimated 5,000 Hispanic Catholics in the diocese. The Church responded with a variety of pastoral, social, and educational services, such as this Spanish-language religious education program at St. John's church in Utica. (Photo: The Catholic Sun)

the community. Eventually, Chryst continued with a focus on Syracuse, with Father John Flanagan serving Hispanic Uticans out of St. John's parish, and Fathers John Zeder and Paul Keebler ministering to Spanish speaking residents of Broome County.

TOWARD A NEW REALISM

If the relationship between Catholic Charities and non-Catholic agencies mirrored the tensions of the Church in the years following the Vatican Council, so did the continuing struggle to serve the poor. The race crisis, the war on poverty, and Vietnam broke open the long standing isolation of

Syracuse Catholicism just as the effort to implement Vatican II was breaking down its historic parochialism. Foery, and even more Cunningham, took seriously the leadership of the American bishops on public issues; they well knew that local work for racial and social justice and world peace depended on the national, even international work of the Church. They followed the leadership of the American hierarchy on civil rights, federal support for low-income housing, welfare reform, and amnesty for Vietnam-era conscientious objectors. Bishop Foery also followed the lead of the American bishops in lending public support to the organizing efforts of the United Farm Workers led by Caesar Chavez.

He joined with other religious leaders of the community in endorsing the UFW's boycott of California grapes. Later Foery and Cunningham gave similar public support to the strike and boycott conducted by Mexican American workers at the Farah pants factories in Texas, personally contacting some of the stores involved. Father Donald Bauer was allowed to work in this campaign nationally. Foery noted that the diocese was not remiss in advocating causes of social justice:

The people of the Diocese have had a long history of participation in various important social causes. Many of our religious have actively demonstrated their views in a variety of ways in the public forum. I have positively supported their right to do so (even in some instances where I have disagreed with a particular position).

To a layman who questioned the bishop's support for the farmworkers, Cunningham explained the teaching of the Church on trade unionism and the results of the national bishops' examination of the California situation, concluding that, for the bishops, "to walk away from the struggle" would be to "violate their own principles of justice and charity." The Church's insistence on the right to organize and to participate freely in union activity, without fear of reprisal, aimed at a more just and democratic approach to economic life:

Through this sort of orderly participation, joined with an ongoing formation in economic and social matters, all will grow day by day in the awareness of their function and responsibility. Thus they will be brought to feel that according to their proper capacities and aptitudes they are associates in the whole task of economic and social development and in the attainment of the universal common good.

On this and other matters the American Church and the Church Universal were calling Syracuse Catholics to a more vigorous missionary responsibility to the poor and those deprived of their human rights around the world, and to participate in building a more just and humane world. Generous and compassionate, they responded quickly to appeals for help.

In April 1975, Bishop Cunningham wrote a letter to be read at Masses which was unusual in that it was not another appeal but a note of thanks for the response to his earlier appeals on behalf of the poor. Returns for the previous year included $55,000 for the Respect Life Collection, $130,000 for the Propogation of the Faith, $72,000 for the Campaign for Human Development, $70,000 for Catholic Relief Services and $74,000 in a special emergency collection for refugees in Cambodia and Vietnam. In addition there were innumberable fasts and fund raising events in local communities in response to the world hunger crisis. It was, as the bishop indicated, a "magnificent record of Christian charity."

On the other hand, Cunningham could expect considerable criticism when he followed the American bishops in calling attention to unjust social structures or government policies. In 1974, after he had publicly questioned repressive policies in Chile and the Philippines, several Catholic critized his alleged support for "revolutionaries." Cunningham responded that in those situations many were being imprisoned, tortured, put to death and exiled. "In light of oppression of the poor, would you keep silent?" he asked his correspondent. "Do you wish the bishops to turn their heads and be silent? Or would you have them speak for justice for the poor, the oppressed and for those who are fighting for their dignity as human beings?"

By the time Bishop Frank Harrison took charge of the diocese in 1977, those questions were pulsing through the Church of Syracuse. The challenges of the 1960s left in their wake a small but vigorous peace movement working for the most part outside parish and diocesan structure, a series of communities working more or less independently to serve the poor and witness to the Gospel, most visible in places like Unity Acres, Unity Kitchen, Vera House, Dorothy Day House and a variety of soup kitchens and store fronts. Meanwhile Church leadership was alert to the Christian option for the poor and the human and Catholic responsibility to make peace and work for justice. While some chose to pursue these goals through intense personal commitment on a full-time basis, most Catholic lay people still lived and worked in that "real world," and so did their Church leaders. In that world they felt the compelling call both to witness to the Gospel and to fulfill the responsibilities of what used to be called their "state in life." One might admire the courageous work of Father McVey, the anti-war protestors who continued to challenge the arms race, and the nuns and priests at work in the inner city. But the cutting edge of

renewal, the "testing" point for the Syracuse Church lay elsewhere, with those from bishops to parishioners who struggled to understand how that call of the Gospel to faithful worship, friendship with other Christians, care for all God's people and for the world God had made, could be brought to life in the midst of daily responsibilities. Each individual, every community, the whole Church it now seemed, had little assurance and less complacency, heavy responsibilities and few clear answers. But one thing at least was clear: None could do it alone.

The leaders of the Church in Syacuse were always realists. The great pastors of the nineteenth century, whatever their personal theology, loved the Church and knew that, to secure their Church in the rapidly changing world of the United States, they had to build parishes and schools, and that meant they had to raise money. And they did. Bishops Ludden, Grimes, Curley and Duffy would have liked all their people to follow in the footsteps of the Irish and Germans by building their churches, supporting their pastors, and putting aside the supposedly superstitious practices of the past in favor of the "American way" of respectable behavior, church attendance and financial support. Bishop Foery came to the diocese with a well thought out understanding of the social mission of the church, but he put concern for social justice aside when the more immediate demands of the war and then of his rapidly expanding Church brought forth other priorities. Nowhere was this Catholic realism better revealed than in Bishop Foery's early statements on race problems, when he recognizeed that property values and neighborhood stability had to be considered if human rights were to be securely achieved. This realism was not merely an accomodation of the moral demands of Christianity to the practical requirements of an institutional church, though that was part of it. It was far more a

A FRIEND OF 'WOMEN IN CRISIS'

The story of the Church in Central New York is peppered with "second career" men and women who make great contributions later in life. One such person is Sister Mary Vera Blank, a Sister of St. Joseph who has given Christian service in a concrete way to homeless women.

After years of teaching, Sister Vera became a social worker. She was superintendent of St. Mary's Home for Children in Binghamton and a similar orphanage near Albany, later a college sociology professor, and since 1965 a social worker for St. Lucy's. In the inner-city neighborhoods around St. Lucy's, Sister Vera rediscovered a problem she had seen too often before — too many women with no place to live.

"It might be the case of an abused woman, a transient one, or perhaps for other reasons that she would be asking for shelter for the night," recalled Sister Vera. "I was deeply concerned about this problem because the number of these women seemed to be on the increase."

At an age when most people have been settled into retirement, Sister Vera found the resolve and energy to help. She interested others in a shelter for women in crisis. Soon donations and grants were received, and a friend donated a three-family dwelling which the city helped renovate.

On July 19, 1977, Vera House received its first guest, the first of more than 1,500 women and children needing temporary help. Seven years later, the shelter was relocated to an unoccupied convent to provide more room for pregnant and unwed teens, widows evicted from their apartments, homeless wives undergoing divorce, and especially women who had been beaten or abused by their husbands or boyfriends.

Today Vera House has a professional staff and volunteers, but Sister Vera remains a permanent member of its board of directors, helping maintain her guiding philosophy "to offer a woman in crisis the opportunity to stay in warm, supportive surroundings while she is resolving her immediate problems and planning for the future (and) to help the woman overcome what often is a poor self-image."

Sister Mary Vera Blank (Photo: The Catholic Sun)

469

compassionate understanding of human needs and human limitations, grounded in the pastoral foundation of the American Church. Foery and his priests well understood that their people had worked and struggled to win the security and respectability evident in their strong parishes and stable neighborhoods. This had been the experience of liberation for earlier generations of poor and oppressed people, who had found in the faith of their Church and the friendships of their parishes the resources they needed to support their quest for a better life. That quest was as much a response to the call of the Spirit and as flawed by human limitations and fears, as any other movement for liberation. The bishop hoped that the memory of that experience would help his people understand and affirm the similar quest of their black neighbors, but he suspected that would not happen if his "good people" were treated as enemies.

Realism gave Bishop Foery and his predecessors some sensitivity about the way the more established classes in society often attempted to assist the poor by methods which exploited the working and lower middle classes, a realism evident in Ludden's disdain for "organized charity" and Foery's moderation on open housing. When Church leaders spoke of the "real world," they were not trying to undercut the moral witness of those who challenged Catholic complacency in the name of the poor or the victims of injustice, though that was sometimes their unintended effect. What they were trying to do was remind others of what they knew from experience — that in the real world lived real people; that in the name of doing good, harm could sometimes be done; that in addition to the danger of doing nothing, there was the danger of doing the unintelligent or the ineffective. At their best, they asked who bore the burden and who reaped the benefits of social change. They did not always explore that question to its fullest extent. They often shied away from the conflicts with other institutions and their own better-off members which that question might occasion. And they too frequently made rhetorical affirmations of justice a substitute for action. But they did uphold the principles, they cared about people and they nurtured the surest foundation for the Church's public witness to the Gospel message, its pastoral presence as a community of faith. In the tension between such realism and the prophetic Gospel-based witness, the Syracuse Church was finding new ways to follow an old vision — to be the Body of Christ and do the work of the Lord in Central New York.

WE ARE
THE CHURCH

UNITY, RENEWAL AND MISSION
1970s-1980s

In 1976, to celebrate the American bicentennial, the bishops of the United States organized a national convention, the Call to Action conference, which met in October in Detroit. Nearly 2,500 delegates representing almost every diocese and national Catholic organization studied the results of two years of parish discussions and regional hearings and drew up a set of recommendations. Originally intended to focus on the application of Catholic social teaching to American problems, the program's open dialogue spilled over into problems of parish life, education, ministry and church government. Some of the recommendations aroused opposition, but the conference was a significant experiment in open discussion and shared responsibility. Cardinal John Dearden, who had been the first president of the National Conference of Catholic Bishops, was the moving spirit behind the conference. As the host bishop, he presided over its deliberations. In his opening address, Dearden stated that Vatican II had summoned the Church to become ever more fully a "community of faith and friendship." What had been learned through a decade of renewal, he thought, was that Catholics — bishops, priests, religious and laity — wanted to respond to that call but were not always sure how to do so. "All of us are committed to the Gospel of Jesus," Dearden said. "The tough part is translating all that into action." Both "the pastoral task of building the Church" and "the public task of serving the world" required "concrete and specific choices about how to spend our money, allocate our resources, direct our personal and collective time, energy and talents." To make those choices, he suggested, Catholics needed "to meet, debate and make some decisions." The convention represented a step toward such shared responsibility, so that the Church could become ever more fully the Church, not for its own sake but for the sake of the whole human community which it hoped to serve. "That is what we are trying to do here," Dearden concluded. "We are trying to begin a new way of doing the work of the Church in America.

Dearden's words may well have sparked a note of recognition among delegates from the diocese of Syracuse. There as elsewhere the combination of religious renewal and social upheaval of the 1960s left most Catholics shaken. Common faith and networks of friendship extending through families, neighborhoods, schools, ethnic groups, apostolic movements and parishes still held the Church together.

Conservatives who opposed to the whole process of renewal, and radicals who would jetison the institutional church had few followers in the diocese. Syracuse Catholics were little inclined to stand in judgment on others, even less to demand the Church's total transformation. Yet neither were most Catholics satisfied to muddle through. Faith, friendship and love demanded at the very least that the Catholic people share in the task of making the local Church a more convincing witness to the presence of Christ. How to do that was the issue, in Syracuse as in Detroit. Like Dearden, local leaders knew that there were no easy answers. Decisions about the community's life and mission would have to be made together. Like it or not, Syracuse Catholics too would have to find a "new way of doing the work of the Church." When the new bishop of Syracuse, Frank Harrison, declared "We are the Church," he was summoning his diocesan Church to deepen its faith and extend its bonds of friendship in order to reach out in love to a suffering humanity. The Call to Action, rooted in the Gospel and made compelling by the needs of people, had brought those delegates to Detroit; the same call was heard in Syracuse and in Binghamton, Utica, Rome and Oswego. Learning how to respond, how to make those personal and collective decisions, provided the central theme of the Syracuse Church as it moved towards its second century.

In 1971, 58-year-old Frank J. Harrison, pastor of St. Patrick's in Binghamton, dean for Broome and Cortland counties, consultor, and vicar for religious, was named auxiliary bishop to Bishop Cunningham. Born in 1912 in Syracuse, Harrison's grandparents had been Irish immigrants. He grew up in St. Lucy's parish, where he attended school and served as an altar boy. His father, a railroad worker, gave him a love of baseball and the son became an outstanding athlete, playing for St. Lucy's and later for Notre Dame University. He prepared for the priesthood at St. Bernard's and was ordained in 1937, on the same day news was made public that Bishop

Foery had been appointed to Syracuse. Next came two short stays at Mount Carmel in Utica and St. Mary's in Binghamton, then 16 years at the cathedral where Harrison taught school, coached teams, preached, visited the sick and served as the popular chaplain of the Syracuse Fire Department. In 1956 he became the first pastor of St. Andrew's, previously a mission of St. Anthony's. After providing vigorous leadership to the drive for new high schools, he was appointed pastor of St. Patrick's in 1963. That same year he was made a monsignor. Known for his ability to mediate disputes, he was a popular priest, enthusiastic about renewal but generally re-

472

garded as a moderate.

In 1976, as Bishop Cunningham's retirement drew near, the Priests' Senate established a committee under Monsignor Joseph Champlin to survey the condition of the diocese, evaluate its long range needs, and develop a profile of the next ordinary. After extensive consultation, the committee listed as major needs — adult education, liturgical renewal, solutions for the problems of Catholic education, development of youth ministry, parish spiritual renewal and expansion of Catholic social services. The committee opposed division of the diocese; it recommended that lay people become more involved in decision making, and urged that women be encouraged to take a greater role in the life of the Church. As for the new bishop, the committee suggested that he should be relatively young, have pastoral experience, be deeply familiar with Scripture, Tradition and Church teaching, be prayerful, be able to communicate easily, and be a man of vision with a clear sense of direction. On all criteria except age, Frank Harrison fit the description quite well. Rome must have agreed because, with Cunningham's backing, Harrison was selected to become the seventh bishop of Syracuse.

On February 6, 1977, at a massive celebration in the Syracuse War Memorial with his two predecessors looking on, Harrison was installed by Cardinal Terence Cooke of New York City

More than 8,000 people attended the ceremony, and few were unmoved. Newspaperman Mario Rossi caught the day best:

What existed in the War Memorial on that unforgettable afternoon was a certain, almost indefinable element, maybe best described as a reaching out between laity and clergy — the establishment, as it were, of a rare line of communication, a dialogue that articulated the need for love and understanding and even more importantly, the willingness to transmit these things. It was a language universal. And it was a message that went beyond the confines of the hall and transcended religious separatism and touched all who would listen.

One reason for that mood was that Harrison, putting aside the tone of triumphalism which usually marked such events, shared his personal faith and invited everyone to join him in bringing that faith to deeper life:

And now, as your new shepherd, may I share with you my faith. I believe in the Word of God. I believe that the Word can bring light into the darkness of man's questioning, doubt and confusion. I believe that the Word reminds us that we are all the beloved of God and that this truth calls each one of us to be free.

I believe that the Word calls us to live together as a community of faith; it summons us to reach out in loving service to one another—calling us to support and help those less fortunate than we. It bids us to accept one another as brothers and sisters in the Lord. It commands us to be forgiving—it has the power to strike down the barriers that divide us. I believe that in the Word we are the new city of God—we are and can become the heavenly Jerusalem where all people can live together in the presence of the Lord—one in faith, one in peace and one in love. I believe that this is the mission that the Word of God is calling me to—but it is a task that I cannot do alone. Together we are the church—the mission of Christ, of the

Church, is our mission. Bishop, priests, religious, laity—together we are called first to experience this power of God's Word in our own lives, then to bring the powerful Word to others—to the poor, the oppressed, those in need, to one another.

Yes, this is a formidable task—it is a challenge—it is a dream. But I firmly believe that it is and that it can continue to become even more a reality. As we set out on this mission, may we together find strength—find hope in the promise that God had made to you and to me when he said, "I am with you always; I will never forget you; I hold you in the palm of my hand."

474

For a decade and a half the Syracuse Church had attempted to sort out what it could take along on the journey to a new future represented by the call of Vatican II. If once the task had been to build the pioneer Church, and later to maintain and extend that Church to encompass ever more diverse nationalities and a rapidly Americanizing middle class, Harrison made clear that the heart of the new era would be to move out in loving service to all people.

The dilemma of renewal was to retain the sense of being one Church, emerging from a common history, sharing a common faith and recognizing a bond in the Spirit, while attempting to transform the world into the Kingdom of God, the kingdom of justice, freedom, peace and love. Harrison, in his inaugural sermon and his early statements, made clear that he fully embraced the past, with its concern for the unity of the Church and the integrity of its teaching, but that his face and the face of the Church was turned ahead, toward the Kingdom of God, and outward, toward women and men in need of the saving Word of God.

The link between past and present, between the internal preoccupations of the past and the challenging mission of the future, was community, the bonds of faith and friendship. In Advent 1978, Bishop Harrison published a short, eloquent pastoral letter, "We Are the Church," intended to serve as a "mission statement" for the diocese, in light of which "all efforts at determining priorities, plans and goals" should be carried on. Its message was simple and echoed the themes of the installation. The Church was a "unique family" in which those who were "one in their belief in Jesus Christ and in their common struggle to make His message, His mission and His presence alive and well today in the midst of humankind" experienced "the fullness of life as it has been shared with us by God himself." Pastoral renewal, strengthening the community life of the Church in its parishes and uniting all its people into a single diocesan Church, was inseparable from the mission of service to the world. Catholics were called "to hear that Word and to make the truth, the power and the reality of that message credibly present to those who yearn to hear it." People looked to the Church to hear "the story of Jesus" and to find "in the authenticity of its life" the "meaning of Jesus' message." The Church was thus called "to be community" for the lonely, abandoned and alienated. Those searching for the presence of God, for "compassionate solidarity," "loving respect," "unconditional assistance" should have their needs met in the Church. In a world of freedom and diversity, Harrison understood, people would respond to messages whose credibility is demonstrated in life, so that the witness of contemporary Christians was the means of evangelization. Catholics were called to be what they professed, to witness to their faith as "lights to the world" by an "authenticity of lifestyle" that would provide "living proof of the possibility of the Gospel message":

Frank J. Harrison in 1977 became the seventh bishop of Syracuse, the first native son to preside over the diocese, which was nearing its 100th year. One of his first actions was to publish an eloquent and prayerful pastoral letter, "We Are the Church," outlining the mission he saw for himself and his seven-county diocese. (Photo: The Catholic Sun)

This then is the mission of God's family today. Be it in sanctuaries, in our families, our neighborhoods, our churches; be it in the societies of our cities, our nations, our world; be it in the halls of our schools, our campuses, our hospitals, our centers of government; be it on the streets of our ghettoes, our marketplaces, our countrysides, the work of the Church is the work of the Lord—a work proclaimed by his Word, enlivened by his spirit, sustained by his promise.

The center of the Church's attention was not the people who were already members of the Church, though their care for one another was a crucial sign of their commitment to Christ and their dedication to his Kingdom. Rather the people who were most the object of the Church's concern were:

Those searching for meaning, value and direction ... those whose lives have been drained of joy and enthusiasm ... those confused by contemporary value systems and the claims of false prophets ... those imprisoned by the internal chains of guilt, of poor self-esteem, and of human respect ... those imprisoned by the external bonds of social structures, consumerism, bureaucracies ... those whose radical aloneness has become a painful loneliness, whose unanswered pleas for acceptance have generated feelings of abandonment ... those who feel alienated by differences of belief, origins or lifestyles ... those driven by a spiritual hunger ... those whose experience of life is impaired by circumstances beyond their control ... the poor, the hungry and the unemployed, the sick, the infirmed, and the forgotten elderly ... those, both young and old who experience doubt and question why ... those for whom the human thirst for knowledge goes unquenched... those for whom the limitations of past answers are the difficulties of today's explanations.

To reach out like this was no easy matter, as long experience demonstrated. Community requires time and treasure and talent for the nourishment of its own life. Christian community requires more, liturgy and prayer, knowledge of Scripture and Tradition, attentiveness to the forms and structures of the Church's own life. For a bishop, the successor of the Apostles, too great emphasis on those in need could risk the charge of ignoring the needs of the Church, just as too great emphasis on the needs of the Church could risk the charge of hypocrisy when faced with the gap between the image of Jesus' own ministry and the realities of administration, fund raising, personnel management and all the other activities of bishops and pastors. Harrison was too much the pastor to ignore his own people, too much a priest of that ever so organized Church of Syracuse to ignore the many responsibilities which came with his episcopal office. But more than anything else, he wanted to nudge and lead and persuade and inspire his people to look up from their preoccupation with the daily tasks of life to the greatness of their call from God, and to put aside their own differences in order to help each other respond to that call.

From this arose his vision of "the diocesan Church," what Vatican II called the local Church — bishop, clergy, religious and lay people working together to fulfill God's will. "You may not believe it," Harrison told one critic, "but I am most interested in getting the people of the diocese involved in working together to care for all our needs." He explained without embarrassment his "dream" of God's people of the diocese of Syracuse: "Working together in all areas of the mission that has been given by Christ, to feed the hungry, to take care of the elderly, to bring the young to Christ, to do whatever we must do to witness the presence of the Lord Jesus with us." For all the talk of "shared responsibility" since the council, he believed that sharing had not yet taken root.

> *We've got to get together if we want to reach out to many of these problems. You know, as well as I, that there are an awful lot of people out there who are suffering and they need healing. They need help. We are trying to do whatever we can to help, simply show them that we care.*

The time had come to find that "new way of doing the work of the Church" so that "our parishes become what they should be, true communions of faith and love."

REORGANIZING THE DIOCESE

Harrison's "dream" of the Church working together to fulfill its mission implied that, as much as possible, diocesan resources should be directed toward shared objectives. In 1977, Harrison asked Father John Ziegler to conduct a research project on diocesan organization and pastoral planning. The result was a full-scale reorganization, dividing the diocese into four administrative regions and grouping ministries under six administrative headings. Episcopal vicars who presided over the four regions, Rome-Utica, Binghamton, Oswego-Fulton and Syracuse, had authority to carry out numerous episcopal responsibilities, such as canonical visitations, installing new pastors, consulting parish councils, ironing out disputes within and between parishes, and insuring coordination between parishes and administrative offices. The six administrative vicars were assigned responsibility for education, community service, parish life and worship, personnel, planning and research, and administration. The exclusively clerical domination of diocesan life changed as Richard Lawless, a layman, was appointed vicar for education and Sister Barbara Garland was appointed vicar for personnel. The final aspect of diocesan reorganization was the formation of clusters of eight to ten parishes, which in turn chose representatives to regional assemblies to advise the regional vicars and their cabinets. Plans were laid for the formation of a Diocesan Pastoral Council to be composed of elected representatives from these area assemblies. The bishop, auxiliary bishop and regional vicars would be ex-officio members of the council, along with representatives of school boards, religious education, Catholic Charities and priests' and sisters' councils, with additional appointed members to represent minority groups and "special ministries."

The regional and administrative vicars met regularly with the bishop and auxiliary bishop as a diocesan cabinet, providing the bishop with advice and working for better coordination of diocesan policies and programs. Over the next several years, the diocese worked hard to make the new structure work, both by directing pastoral services toward parishes and by insuring a high level of consultation before major decisions on diocesan policy were made. The diocesan pastoral council, which would embody most fully Harrison's vision of the diocesan church, was slower to develop, as the leadership struggled to take into account local, regional and diocesan concerns and balance broad based participation with the responsibilities of the bishop. At times the structure seemed cumbersome, and some of its elements needed revision on the basis of experience, but the diocese was well situated to act in a united fashion as its members grew in a sense of themselves as a local Church united around the bishop, as an essential element of their Catholic identity and responsibility.

Bishop Harrison's second major effort to implement his vision of the diocesan Church was the Hope Appeal. The diocese had long resisted public financial accountability. Bishop Cunningham opened up a bit, publishing the first diocesan financial report in the *Catholic Sun* in 1972. Although that report showed a large deficit in the diocesan school office, there was no major effort to increase assessments on parishes during his administration. Harrison found the diocese relatively free from debt but, he told the priests in December of his first year in office, diocesan receipts of $200,000 a year had remained relatively stable for years while expenses had risen to more than $400,000. The difference was made from the diocese's own sources of income. These included restricted endow-

ments, such as seminary burses used to educate young men for the priesthood, and unrestricted endowments totalling $4,500,000, the income from which covered the annual gap between income and expenses. Use of this income for operating expenses, however, meant that diocesan resources were static and left little room for expansion. If diocesan programs, such as tuition assistance to needy students in parochial school, were to grow, then diocesan income simply had to be increased.

The diocese had already achieved some impressive gains in its financing. By 1970, both insurance and workmen's compensation disability funds had been set up, so that the diocese could handle these expenses internally, with substantial savings. Plans were underway to formalize a diocesan financial pool which would centralize the process of parishes loaning money to one another. In 1978 total parish indebtedness was $6,200,000, of which half was owed to cemeteries and the remainder in almost equal amounts to other parishes and to the diocese itself. Thus, parishes had already experienced the benefits of working together. Harrison hoped that more and more Catholics would see how they could by the same route better pursue the mission of the Church, especially in charities, social action and education.

Rather than increase the needs assessment, Harrison decided to attempt a wholly different method of funding; as it was "our first diocesan effort together," he asked the priests for their full cooperation. The basis of the Hope Appeal, as it was called, was the theme set at Harrison's installation, the diocesan Church and its people:

One of our hopes is that we might be able to raise the consciousness of our people to the theological reality of our diocesan Church, or as the documents of Vatican II refer to it, the "local church." We do so little together as the local Church that maybe this effort together in Christ might help them to see that the local Church is the bishop, his priests and his people. The message we want to bring to the people is simply this: together we are the Church and these are our needs, to *help the poor, to assist our disadvantaged, to care for our sick and our elderly, to instruct our children.*

In launching the drive, Harrison pointed out that during the previous year more than 185,000 persons had been recipients of some service of the diocese. CCD, faith centers,

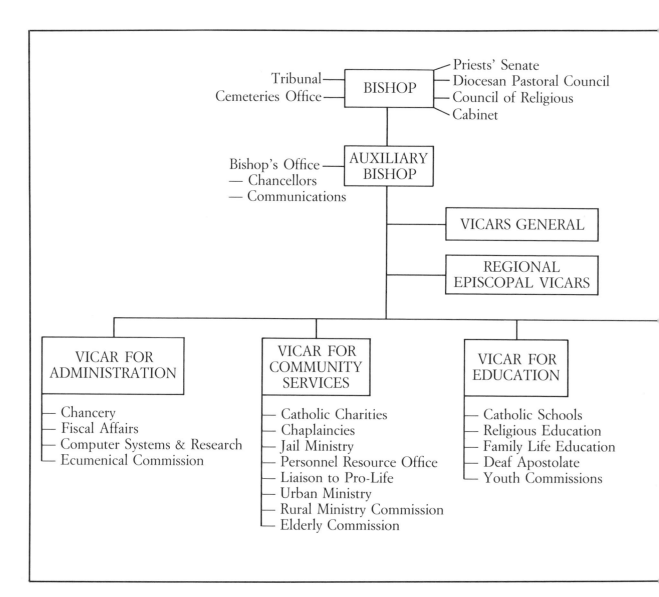

marriage preparation, religious education for exceptional children, teen age programs, campus ministry, Catholic Charities all received their share of attention, while 2,290 children in Catholic schools received some form of financial assistance. Beyond the figures, Harrison claimed that door-to-door visits by parish teams were as important as the fund raising, for they would provide opportunities to "dialogue about the Church" and its needs and how each person could help. "We want desperately to develop that sense of Church that all participate in the ministry of Christ," he argued.

Not everyone was convinced. The old resentment of diocesan intrusion into parish

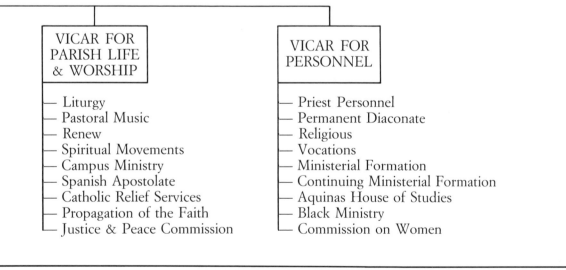

DIOCESAN ADMINISTRATION

(Based on 1977 reorganization, with modifications made through 1986)

VICAR FOR PARISH LIFE & WORSHIP

— Liturgy
— Pastoral Music
— Renew
— Spiritual Movements
— Campus Ministry
— Spanish Apostolate
— Catholic Relief Services
— Propagation of the Faith
— Justice & Peace Commission

VICAR FOR PERSONNEL

— Priest Personnel
— Permanent Diaconate
— Religious
— Vocations
— Ministerial Formation
— Continuing Ministerial Formation
— Aquinas House of Studies
— Black Ministry
— Commission on Women

life which had plagued Bishop Curley half century earlier was still present. Some priests quite candidly told the bishop they had real reservations about backing the diocesan bureaucracy. Then there were some upset by renewal and by the new priorities of the Church. One parishioner promised a large donation if the bishop would restore respect for the liturgy by abolishing the handshake of peace, ending communion in the hand and stopping deacons from speaking in church. Another threatened a boycott because he believed the bishop gave funds to radical organizations. Others were concerned about Church support for the peace movement. To all such critics the bishop responded patiently, explaining what the diocese did, and why it did it. Despite such apparent reservations, the Hope Appeal was a big success. In 1980 the goal was $1,600,000 and total pledges came to $1,900,000. That year diocesan costs were $2,100,000, of which $527,000 went to the administrative service vicariate, $436,000 to the community services, $780,000 to education, $171,000 to parish life and worship, $179,000 to personnel, $32,000 to planning and research and $44,000 to the regional vicariates. The following year the goal was $1,800,000 and receipts topped $2,000,000 dollars.

With administrative reorganization completed and the Hope Appeal firmly established, Harrison began a process to establish priorities for diocesan development. The Cabinet, the Priests' Senate and the Diocesan Pastoral Council all were asked to list in order what they considered to be the major needs of the diocese. The results showed some gaps between administrators, clergy and laity. All shared a concern for parish renewal. The cabinet ranked improvement of the liturgy first, adult spiritual formation fifth, and parish council development seventh. The senate placed diocesan, regional and parish spiritual development at the top of its list, while the

The Hope Appeal was started not only to raise needed money but also to give people a better understanding that the diocese, more than the parish, is the Catholic focus of the local Church. Father Richard Kopp, vicar for administration, was given the task of overseeing the annual campaign, which consistently exceeded its growing annual goal. (Photo: Sister Barbara Garland)

pastoral council made "parish development through spiritual renewal" its number one priority. All groups also favored improved social ministry in the parishes, with ministry to the sick and elderly ranked second by the pastoral council, sixth by the cabinet and ninth by the senate. The pastoral council also listed parish-based programs of social service fourth. On the other hand the senate ranked parochial schools fourth, the cabinet placed them ninth, but they did not make the ten priorities of the pastoral council; religious education of public school children ranked third for the pastoral council and sixth for the senate, but did not appear on the cabinet's list. The cabinet placed development of lay ministry fourth, but it did not feature on either of the other two lists. All agreed on the need to pursue social justice and world peace; however, this was the second ranked concern of the senate, third with the cabinet, but ninth with the pastoral council.

With this sometime conflicting advice in hand, Bishop Harrison proclaimed six priorities for the diocese for the period 1982 to 1987, the latter the year scheduled for his retirement. First came parish renewal:

> *Within the next five years, we the Church of Syracuse, will share the vision of parish as community—what it ought to be—a community seeking out the learning of our faith and the ways of living it—a community of love—caring for those afflicted by human misery, the poor and the suffering—to do all in our power to relieve their need and in them to serve Christ.*

Under this heading the bishop included the spiritual formation of clergy and non-ordained ministers, the renewal of liturgical life, and evangelization of those outside the Church. "Like charity, I think evangelization has to begin at home," he wrote. "Only after we have renewed (evangelized) ourselves, only after we have developed a sense of genuine community in all our parishes and institutions, thereby creating a warm, welcoming atmosphere, will we be prepared for an outreach program to the unchurched, the alienated and non-believers."

Second the bishop placed a pledge to eliminate injustice and discrimination within the diocesan community and then to act for "peace and justice, locally, nationally and globally." Third was a pledge to develop an efficient organization of the Catholic school system, with particular concern for the education of poor and minority group children. Fourth came the improvement of religious education of public school children, along with adult faith formation and parent participation in preparation for the sacraments. Fifth was ministry to families as well as to "persons in other life situations" and sixth was ministry to the sick and elderly. In an addendum, the bishop promised to continue existing programs of social service, vocations, parish council development and youth ministry, but he insisted that resources and energy would be directed toward these six goals.

RENEWAL IN THE PARISHES

While working to improve diocesan management and to broaden participation in decision making, Harrison recognized that the "local Church" rested upon a parish base. As his approach to the Hope Appeal suggested, he knew that participation in parish life was still the major way in which Catholics shared in the life and ministry of the Church. He believed that there, too, shared responsibility was crucial to the realization of his dream. Accordingly, the vicariate for parish life and worship prepared new guidelines for parish councils, emphasizing Harrison's themes of community and shared responsibility. The council was "a coordinating and unifying structure within the parish community" which should bring about "full participation of the whole parish in its mission." It should reflect the various elements of parish life and should seek to build consensus on major matters of policy. The pastor as the "bishop's representative and the spiritual leader to the parish" bore "ultimate responsibility for and authority in the parish community." However, priests and deacons were rooted in the community; their ordination did not separate them from but committed them to the community, so that they were not above but were "in partnership with the Council." As the constitution of Our Lady of the Angels in Endwell put it, the pastor and the council work together "in planning and implementing the affairs of the parish." "The ultimate responsibility is the pastor's, and his decisions are final," but council members should "pursue their own ideas according to their sincere convictions." The pastor and staff normally implemented the decisions of the council but, in extraordinary circumstances, they might act contrary to the council's judgment. If parishioners felt "frustrated by rejection" they could appeal to the bishop.

As these words indicated, parishes were pursuing a bottom up process of learning to work together. For example, when Monsignor Charles Sewall became pastor of Our Lady of Lourdes in Utica, he divided the parish into 32 neighborhood groups and met in living rooms with more than 500 parishioners. The problems he found were simple, like the sound system of the church or a vague feeling that the parish was too large and impersonal; or they were unavoidable, like the drain of school expenses on the parish, which had a flourishing elementary school and more than 60 percent of its high school age students in Catholic schools. In response, some changes were made in the sound system, the priests began greeting people outside church after Sunday Mass and training lay people to serve as greeters, and some new programs were developed to assist the elderly and to reach out to pockets of poverty within the parish. Before long there seemed to be new enthusiasm in the parish, and plenty of lay volunteers for new ministries. In retrospect, Sewall thought what made a difference was less the changes than the neighborhood meetings themselves, at which people got to know the pastor and one another, to air some of their often unspoken discontent, and to discover

that despite their problems they still had much in common.

Parish renewal was often a matter of building from such foundations, identifying or forming smaller groups of parishioners to share their faith and work together and, in the process, become the building blocks of the larger parish community. In some cases this meant identifying groups with particular problems, bringing them together, and assisting them to share their experience, reflect on it in light of their faith, and perhaps find ways by working together to better deal with their problems. The elderly, young adults, divorced and separated Catholics, all became areas of special ministry, enabling community to form and Church to grow. In other cases it was a matter of neighborhood or blocks, people living close together who, by praying and working together, began to overcome some of the anonymity of modern life, to experience Church together and perhaps work together to meet needs from educating their children in the faith to coping with drugs on the street corner.

Experiences like Monsignor Sewall's confirmed the idea that renewal best took place not from the top down, with programs and directives coming from the chancery office to be implemented in local parishes, but from the bottom up, with people finding in a renewed appreciation of their faith and the friendship and support of their fellow Catholics the inspiration and power to be the Church. When the diocese set parish renewal as its number one priority, its approach reflected this commitment to grass roots work. The Church wished to bring the Gospel to those outside its membership, but could best undertake that work only "after we have renewed ourselves" and created "a warm and welcoming atmosphere," Bishop Harrison said. Noting that such a division was to some extent artificial, the bishop nevertheless established a top level committee on evangelization to work with the vicariate of parish life and worship. The committee reviewed the evangelization and parish renewal experience of other dioceses and the work of the national bishops' Parish Renewal Project. Members concluded that the diocese should lend its support to a deliberate program of parish renewal and chose for that purpose Renew, a program which originated in Newark, New Jersey, and enjoyed growing popularity around the country. At the same time, the education vicariate was working to introduce into parishes the Rite of Christian Initiation of Adults, a process for instructing and welcoming converts which emphasized shared faith and the participation of the parish community. These recommendations were discussed by various diocesan bodies and adopted. All of 1983 was spent in planning and training leadership for Renew's three-year program built around small home groups, reflecting on themes drawn from scripture and aimed at bringing about both personal spiritual renewal and the revitalization of parish community. During each season liturgical and homiletic materials were integrated with the reading and themes of the discussion, while in Syracuse television materials were prepared and workshops held to integrate the RCIA with the Renew program. Meanwhile, priests were preparing themselves to promote spiritual renewal in their parishes. For more than a year, clergy conferences and other diocesan activities were suspended as priests throughout the diocese participated in the Emmaus process of spiritual renewal. In June 1983, a year of retreats, small gatherings for priests to share their personal faith with each other, and opportunities for personal reflection on Christian service and priestly ministry ended with a two-day convocation of all the priests of the diocese. The convocation featured a procession of more than 340 priests in downtown Syracuse to a special Mass at the cathedral.

Renew was launched in the fall of 1984, and the widespread support it received indicated that the notions of shared responsibility and community were now more than words but were providing the foundation for liturgy, parish councils, religious education and social service.

Yet, this commitment to parish renewal carried a price. Sometimes Church leaders underestimated the significance of community formation and apostolic service outside parish boundaries. Syracuse had never had strong movements, and diocesan response to the Professional Sodality, Marriage Encounter and charismatic renewal indicated a determination to keep Catholic action within clearly defined parish boundaries. The leveling off of these movements, and the renewed attention to the spiritual and apostolic tasks of parishes reinforced this general attitude. One interesting alternative community, for example, was the "Covenant Community" in Utica, which grew out of the activist movements of the sixties. The spiritual and liturgical experience of its members made their participation in normal parish life difficult. Instead they developed a routine of meeting in local high schools and in homes, worshiping and praying together and developing their own programs of religious education and apostolic service. When Harrison was reorganizing the diocese in 1978, they hoped for some form of recognition, but they were disappointed. When they asked to be placed on the chancery mailing list, they were told that the bishop's "main thrust is the parish and (he) would certainly want information to filter to various groups through the parish rather than directly."

Similarly, when Bishop Harrison announced that the charismatic House of Prayer was closing, he said that the shortage of priests made the step necessary, but his real reason was his determination to bring such efforts more securely within the framework of the parishes. As he told Father Phelan:

My primary concern is that we bring the people of God to a new awareness of the Gospel message by inviting them into closer experiences with the sacramentality of the body of Christ in their parishes.

Aiming at a unified diocesan Church, Harrison hoped to channel the energy of spiritual renewal through the parishes. This was commendable, but when made exclusive, neglected the flexibility which new forms of pluralism required, and risked alienating, or leaving unsupported, many whose zeal and dedication left them uncomfortable or unwelcome in their parish.

By the 1980s, the bottom up approach was also redefining personnel policy. No longer did the bishop make parish assignments alone. Instead, when a pastoral vacancy occurred, people and priests alike became involved in an elaborate process of decision making. Representatives from the diocesan personnel committee visited the parish council to explain the process by which a new pastor would be chosen. The council then assessed the needs of the parish and described the qualities they desired in a new pastor. In 1979, for example, the parish council at St. Mary's in Cortland attributed their parish's growth as a "spiritual community" to the previous pastor's "intense spiritual leadership," his "openness to lay involvement and his support of various renewal efforts." They noted the special importance of the parish's religious education programs, its "neighborhood coordination program (a mini parish concept) aimed at building christian community," its excellent liturgies and "very active, devoted and talented music ministry." They listed the characteristics they thought important in a pastor for their parish: strong spirituality, mature judgment, administrative experience, commitment to parochial schools,

and enthusiasm about lay participation, particularly in the council, youth ministry and the new ministries of lector, extraordinary minister of the Eucharist and catechist.

Once the council completed its work, priests were then invited to apply for the vacant position. The letter of invitation listed parishes with vacancies and offered a full description of each. In November 1978, for example, the description of an opening at St. Margaret's in Mattydale gave the size of the parish, number of envelopes, annual income, debts and assets, pastoral and support staff, statistics of marriages, funerals and baptisms for the previous year, the size of the school and CCD program. The estimated time demands were given: sacramental ministry 29 percent, teaching 15 percent, hospital and shut in visits 8 percent, home visits 3 percent, advising and counseling 12 percent, meetings 28 percent, and maintenance function 5 percent. The "significant needs" of the parish were listed as "adult religious education, community outreach and growth in prayer." Similar information was provided for Our Lady of Angels in Endwell, where the "most significant need" was again adult religious education but the distribution of time estimate was quite different, with 73 percent given to sacraments and teaching and only 4 percent each to meetings and counseling.

Applicants for these positions were asked to provide detailed information about their talents and abilities. If they were applying for a co-pastorate they had to attend a "team ministry workshop" and understand and follow the guidelines for co-pastorates approved by the senate. Pastor applicants then were interviewed by the personnel committee, which made recommendations to the bishop. Applicants for associate pastor positions were interviewed by the pastor of the parish with the vacancy; the committee reviewed pastors' lists of acceptable candidates, and candidates lists of acceptable parishes, and once again recommendations were made to the bishop.

Some priests had worried that the new parish council guidelines, by emphasizing the role of the priest within the community, deemphasized his authority over parish life. Similar problems were present but not yet fully clarified in these new, bottom up approaches to parish renewal and personnel decisions. These programs were built upon an image of the Church as a community of men and women equal in their baptism, sharing their gifts with one another. Liturgy committees now helped plan the worship services; religious education committees helped manage the CCD program, hired and evaluated professional staff and encouraged lay catechists to share in program development and decisions; finance committees shared responsibility for drawing up parish budgets. In all of this the priest was still crucial, of course, and the quality of his pastoral leadership almost always determined the vitality of the parish. Yet his role was blurred as community took precedence over hierarchy, and prayer, spiritual growth and shared responsibility took precedence over doctrine and discipline. The priest was still, in the words of the parish council guidelines, the "bishop's representative"; he was ordained to an office which carried with it power and authority, quite apart from the personal qualities or leadership ability of the man who occupied it. There was thus an ambivalence between the communitarian emphasis of renewal and the hierarchical organization of that community, an ambivalence that could become serious when a priest with more traditional views replaced one who encouraged and affirmed lay leadership and responsibility, as the parish council profiles of desired pastors indicated. In Syracuse for the most part these problems were avoided, as more and more priests shared the vision and commitment of bottom up renewal, but here and there hard experience occasionally led lay people to wonder

how long the new invitations to community and responsibility would be issued.

NEW FORMS OF MINISTRY

One thing more than any other seemed to guarantee that the new style was here to stay. This was the problem of vocations, with the prospects of fewer priests to serve parishes with ever increasing needs. When one priest who had been active in a house of prayer was reassigned to full time parish work, Harrison told a couple who expressed their dismay that "six or seven parishes" were in need of associate pastors and he had none available: "If we don't have strong parishes, we don't have anything. If our shortage of priests continues, and it seems as though it will, all priests in special work will have to be put back in parishes." Some parishes, formerly served by two priests, were cut back to one. In Skaneateles, the parish of St. Mary of the Lake was forced to close its mission, St. Bridget's in Skaneateles Falls. At the same time development of lay participation made heavy demands on the clergy. At first glance, new parish programs aimed at developing lay leadership were supposed to lift some of the burdens of work off the pastor, but in fact these programs were labor intensive, requiring the priests to attend innumerable meetings of parish committees, to become closer to enthusiastic lay volunteers, and to coordinate the work of a growing variety of parish programs and services. In many parishes, at the same time, the traditional work remained, raising and administering money, supervising the parish school, presiding at sacramental services, preaching, and perhaps continuing to serve as chaplain of the local fire department and offer the opening or closing prayer at innumerable civic events.

Sister Barbara Garland in the personnel vicariate made the study of these problems her first priority. One conclusion was that in

485

addition to using lay volunteers, the diocese had to develop authentic lay leadership, capable of organizing and directing parish programs. Detailed examination of the growing role of lay people in the the diocese resulted in establishment of a formal program of training. This Formation for Ministry program began in the fall of 1980 with 77 candidates representing 47 parishes and two institutions. The bishop warmly endorsed this program, which soon became a central element in diocesan life, assisting lay persons not only to become more skilled as catechists, but to work in emerging areas of social, youth, liturgical, family and out-reach ministry. People who wished to enter this program spent two years in scriptural, theological and other studies, while receiving practical training in the area of ministry with which they were engaged. They then were formally commissioned by the bishop and took on roles of leadership in their parishes or, in some cases, in special ministries. At a commissioning ceremony for 32 men and 43 women, Harrison said that "the Holy Spirit calls forth the gifts and talents of these people to benefit the Church's ministry." Among the group was a woman who worked with the deaf apostolate, another who did youth ministry at the Utica Faith Center, a man who worked in the diocesan religious education office, another with the Spanish apostolate in the Oswego-Fulton area, a religious education coordinator from the Griffiss Air Force base parish of St. Thomas More, a woman active in jail ministry, the founder of Widows and Widowers of Oswego County, as well as many engaged in pastoral, catechetical and social service ministries in parishes. By 1985 there were 221 of these commissioned lay ministers in the diocese.

This development of lay ministry raised questions about the diaconate program. A coordinating committee recommended that new candidates for the diaconate enter the

two year formation for ministry program, and spend an additional year in service in one or another ministry before going on for ordination. The bishop adopted this recommendation in 1980, but asked Sister Barbara to set up a new committee to examine the diaconate. A year later he informed the committee that permanent deacons would be considered only where there was a precise need, so that in the future an individualized formation program would likely be used.

In 1977 the diocese also initiated a series of workshops on team ministry; priests applying to serve as co-pastors of parishes were required to take part in one of them. As the chancellor explained, team ministry involved "the voluntary sharing of authority and responsibility by priests assigned to a parish." He admitted this was a "very narrow definition of the term" and had reference to co-pastorates rather than to "the broader Vatican II concept of working together as a team of all concerned with ministry in a parish." That was, in fact, the long range goal of the personnel committee, and the present policy was designed to be "a beginning, a mustard seed" which might eventually bring "total involvement of all who minister to the Church." What all this pointed toward was what one report called "new models of collaborative ministry" involving clergy, religious and lay people working together to continue the work of the Church in the traditional areas of worship, prayer, counseling, education, and outreach to the poor and needy, to explore new areas of human need, spiritual and material, and new frontiers of mission in work for peace and justice.

With the new spirit of shared responsibility, and the emergence of many lay people willing to share in the work of the Church, the diocese could face the prospect of fewer priests without fear. By January 1984, 319 diocesan priests active in the diocese (162 pastors, 86 associates, and 71 in special

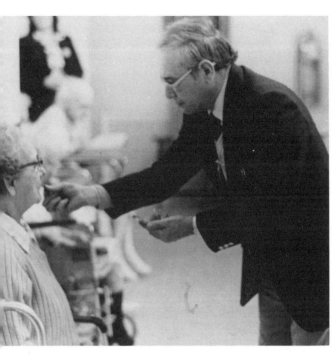

As the diocese began feeling the effects of Church renewal, other ministers joined the priests in offering spiritual care and leadership. One new group of ministers were permanent deacons, who most often provided parish and pastoral care assistance. (Photo: The Catholic Sun)

could bring new problems. A survey of 400 lay ministers brought 229 responses; 73 percent were volunteers, 14.8 percent part time salaried and 12.2 percent full time salaried. The overwhelming majority, 64.4%, were women, while 63 percent were between the ages of 36 and 55. Use of lay ministers would find middle-aged women of considerable education as the largest talent pool, while attention would have to be given to attracting men, young people and older, retired persons. Many would require salaries, while the use of deacons as full time ministers would bring even heavier financial burdens, as they indicated high salary needs when surveyed. The rise of lay ministry, then, raised questions of the role of women in the Church and posed problems of financing, neither of which would be easily resolved.

ministries) represented a 20 percent decline in associate pastors in five years — a trend that would continue. The total of retired priests had risen from 38 to 45. The proportion of priests under age 45 had dropped from 50 percent in 1974, to 42 percent in 1979 to 35.6 percent in 1983; those over 60 had risen from 26 to 37 percent during the same period. Another study indicated continued decline in the number of priests, while their average age would rise to 52. Thirty-six were ordained between 1974 to 1979, 20 between 1979 and 1983 and a projected 17 between 1983 and 1987.

The answer to this problem must be a greater role for lay ministers, but this solution

AUTHORITY AND ORTHODOXY

There were many perils in the bottom up approach, to be sure. As the participants in Utica Covenant Community and the Endwell House of Prayer learned, the bishop was by no means letting things entirely "hang loose," allowing community to form and Church to develop as the spirit moved people. He was well aware of his own responsibility to insure doctrinal orthodoxy and ecclesiastical discipline, but he had learned that the best way to do those things was by building bonds of faith and friendship throughout the Church. The bishop and the local Church were likely to be misunderstood by conservatives and radical alike; the former saw the Church as dangerously vague on doctrine, the latter complained that hard issues of justice and peace moved slowly through a Church bent upon maintaining its unity.

In Syracuse at least, problems came far more often from the right than the left. When Charles Pulver established the regional chapter of Catholic United for the Faith in 1972, he told Bishop Cunningham they intended merely to study their faith and "support, defend and enthusiastically advance the efforts of the teaching church." Their sole concern, he told the bishop, was "orthodoxy in the faith." They were as good as their word. When distinguished biblical scholar Raymond Brown lectured at the invitation of the priestly formation committee and the Sisters' Council, Pulver used the pages of the *Catholic Sun* and the *Wanderer* to call the talk "one of the worst attacks on the magisterium in recent memory." Outraged, Cunningham rejected the charges as "absolutely untrue" and praised Father Brown for "his scholarship, his balance and his complete loyalty to the Church." CUF was even more unhappy with Cunningham's successor, Bishop Harrison. In March 1977, the Concerned Catholic Committee left over from the Support fight picketed the chancery to protest the "anti-god and anti-American positions taken by the new bishop." They were still chasing Support, they wanted Harrison to publicly disassociate the diocese from the controversial stands taken by the Call to Action conference, and they charged that he did nothing to oppose abortion or to challenge the "satanic forces" at work in society. In a letter to priests they included a pamphlet containing birth control information which they charged had been distributed at a pre-Cana conference.

They also told their own followers to do "everything in our power" to "frustrate" the Hope Appeal. In 1977 they protested a week-long institute on moral theology which featured moral theologian Father Charles Curran among the speakers.

The diocesan response was swift and unwavering. Father Lavin, diocesan public information officer, defended Curran as a distinguished theologian and a priest in good standing and argued that the diocese had a responsibility to make available to its personnel the insights of theologians of Curran's stature:

> *We deeply regret and deplore the fact that Father Curran's name has apparently been added to the list of religious figures, including Bishop Frank J. Harrison and retired Bishop David F. Cunningham, who have been made targets of scandalous innuendo, villification and character assassination by a group shamelessly professing love for the Church and adherence to Gospel values.*

Harrison, like Cunningham, was fully aware of the problems posed by theological pluralism, but he was determined to face those problems directly rather than resort to what he called "witch hunting." When a local priest raised sincere questions about Curran's views, Harrison responded that he was aware of the problems but pointed out that Curran was a member of the faculty of Catholic University, that his views were common among moral theologians, that he would be speaking as one of four theologians engaged in dialogue and mutual correction, and that diocesan Catholics could be trusted:

> *I recognize that in the area of theological issues, we must respect both the right of academic freedom and the responsibility to be faithful to the traditions of the Church. I firmly believe in the ability of our priests, religious and laity who would attend such a program to listen, reflect in the light of the official teaching of the Church and form their own judgments. If a person chooses to agree or disagree with a professional theologian, I strongly prefer that they do so on an informed basis rather than on the basis of a reputation which oftentimes today is created for an individual.*

Here as elsewhere Harrison trusted his

While extremist critics attacked Bishop Harrison for being unfaithful to Catholic teaching, the bishop maintained close allegiance with Pope John Paul II and with his fellow bishops in the United States. (Photo: The Catholic Sun)

priests and people. Indeed trust was the cement which held the rapidly changing Church together, and the bishop knew that the questioning of motives and the charges of disloyalty and heresy could create a climate of suspicion which could easily divide the Church and destroy all the hard won gains of the past. Like Foery and Cunningham before him, he was inclined to regard even those who disagreed with him as motivated by

honest concern for the Church and sincere faith in God, so he approached controversy with a marked pastoral concern which allowed for dialogue and kept open the possibility of reconciliation and cooperation.

WOMEN IN THE CHURCH

After the formation of the Sisters' Council in 1969, women religious moved rapidly into roles of leadership in the diocese. Indeed, the sisters seemed more enthusiastic about renewal than any other group. Many sought theological updating at LeMoyne and in the burgeoning summer programs in theology and ministry around the country. At the same time lay women were also taking leadership in their parishes. Women were elected to serve on parish councils, women professionals appeared more regularly among the leaders of Catholic Charities and attained visibility in their front line service in urban neighborhoods. The very language of renewal, with its emphasis on the people of God, the dignity of the human person, and the attainment of human rights, all supported and legitimated the movement of women into more active roles in the Church and toward inevitable challenges to long accepted practices. In the process, tension developed between the pastoral experience at the local Church and the requirements of the Church Universal.

A good example of change through inadvertence was the rapid decline of the practice of women covering their heads when entering church. Indeed, someone who left the Church in the 1963 and returned seven years later would have been startled on entering church to see the majority of women without hats or handkerchiefs pinned in their hair. This change was not decreed by the council nor ordered by the bishop nor studied by a diocesan commission. It just happened. Perhaps it had been a practice which had long outlived its justification so that once questioned, it sank from view; or perhaps, as some conservatives claimed, it was a sign, like receiving communion standing, of a declining sense of the majesty of God and the sinfulness of human beings. Whatever the reason, it happened, and when someone asked about it, the response was simply confusion. In 1969 someone did ask the chancery whether the diocese had granted permission for women to attend Mass with their heads uncovered. Assistant Chancellor Father Pierson responded by quoting St. Paul: "but every women praying or prophesying with her head uncovered disgraces her head" (I Corinthians 11:5) and canon law: "women should assist in modest dress and with heads covered, especially when approaching the table of the Lord." This practice, incorporated into law, still had force, Pierson argued. On the other hand, he noted weakly, custom had always to be considered in interpreting the law, and the Code of Canon Law was in fact in the process of revision. So, he concluded, "I would stress the positive aspects of assisting at Mass and not exaggerate this particular point."

Conservative Catholics found another departure from church discipline in the diocese in the use of altar girls. When complaints came in about this practice in one parish in June 1974, Bishop Cunningham told the pastor that it was not allowed, a decision which led to a protest letter from several women in the parish. The chancellor responded by explaining that it was not a personal decision on the bishop's part; "quite the contrary, Bishop Cunningham is very pleased when children choose to participate actively in worship. Unfortunately, however, the traditional Liturgical Norms of the Roman Catholic Church prohibit women, young girls, or women religious from serving the priest at the altar." It was thus a question of "obedience to the laws of the church," not of "women's rights" or "the worthiness of the female sex." Apparently, the word had not reached everywhere, because in December Charles Pulver complained about altar girls in yet another parish, pointing out that Bishop Head of Buffalo and the apostolic delegate had both stated it was not allowed. "It was very clear from their response that girls may never serve Mass," Pulver wrote. "They are forbidden to do so by the third instruction on the liturgy." Again, the bishop was forced to agree. The pastor in question was sent a letter similar to the earlier one, with the secretary adding that he personally felt badly that the situation had arisen. The bishop then sent a brief memo to all priests reminding them "that girls and women serving at the altar other than in the capacity of lectors is not allowed."

The problem of women's ordination was even harder to handle. In 1976 the Congregation on the Doctrine of the Faith attempted to put a stop to discussion of ordaining women with a statement which insisted that the Church had no authority to do so. Bishop Cunningham echoed the words of the declaration that "the rejection of ordination of women to priesthood is based on the attitude of Christ who chose only men for his priesthood, excluding even His Mother, who far excelled the Apostles in holiness." Cunningham expressed sympathy with those who would be disappointed, but asked for their prayerful consideration of the declaration, hoping it would not be seen "as a discrimination for male superiority." The Church had spoken out against sex discrimination in the secular orders and had called women to new ministerial and decision making roles in the Church, he pointed out, and "such roles become even more urgent in light of this Declaration."

Bishop Harrison was particularly close to these problems, both because of his local work as vicar for religious and his membership on the national bishops' liaison committee with the Leadership Conference of Women Religious.

In his work at the national level, Harrison tried to increase dialogue between the bishops and religious women. In 1978, for example, he told Sister Mary Daniel Turner that conservative organizations were making inroads on the LCWR's support because the conference was not making enough effort to enlist the support of the grass roots religious,

many of whom were unaware of its work. Equally important, he told her, many bishops felt that the religious were constantly telling the bishops what they needed from the hierarchy, but rarely asked the bishops what they wanted and needed. Finally he advised them to drop their emphasis on ordination to the priesthood, a subject on which the Holy Father had spoken and which made the Vatican Congregation very nervous. Instead he advised a broader approach to reform: "At present it would appear better to simply pursue a more general approach of women in ministry in the Church. Eventually it may lead to the diaconate and who knows where else."

Harrison deeply appreciated the service of women religious in the diocese, and his openness to their greater role in ministry reflected the pastoral needs to which the diocese was trying to respond. But, as with priests, the contributions of individuals could not obscure the difficulties posed by declining numbers. In 1984 a study of women religious showed that two communities, the Sisters of St. Joseph with 38 percent and the Franciscans of Syracuse with 30 percent, provided more than two-thirds of the Sisters active in the diocese. The median age of those two communities respectively was 51 and 55. More disturbing, the Sisters of St. Joseph projected that the 229 sisters at work in the diocese would drop to 222 by 1987, while the median age would rise significantly. The Syracuse Franciscans projected a drop from 227 to 203 and an increase of the median age to 58 1/2. Among the 374 sisters responding to the survey, one fourth were over 65, less than 15 percent under the age of 40. In 1982 just under 60 percent were still involved in education, a drop of only 10 percent since 1978.

Interestingly, the number of sisters in community service and social work had risen only from 3.67 to 4.8 percent, but those in parish ministry now constituted more than 20 percent. More important 35 percent listed pastoral work, spiritual counseling, liturgy, youth ministry and religious education, all parish ministries, as those they were most interested in, while only 17 percent listed school education. Asked what ministries would be needed most in the future, only 7 percent listed elementary and secondary education and only 8 percent thought this work would have to be developed and strengthened in the diocese. In contrast 39 percent thought parish ministries would be most needed, and 42 percent thought they would have priority in future diocesan plans. The diocese could be well pleased with the attitude of sisters working there, for 92 percent felt the diocese was trying to include sisters in the decision making process, 90 percent thought sisters were trying to share in diocesan activities, and 91 percent felt the work of sisters was appreciated.

In early 1980 the *Post Standard* carried a series of articles on modern day sisters which illustrated some of the more dramatic changes which had taken place and the massive shift in attitudes among women religious. Sister Barbara Garland, a Sister of Charity from New Jersey, as vicar for personnel was the highest ranking sister in the diocese. The newspaper took some delight in calling her the "boss" of priests, sisters, seminarians and deacons. Sister Patricia Geary, a Sister of St. Joseph, was pastoral assistant with special responsibility for the elderly at St. Vincent de Paul parish. Sister Barbara Ginter was organizing support locally for the boycott of J. P. Stevens products in support of a unionization drive. Sister Mary Ann Rodgers was diocesan associate vocations director, president of the Sisters' Council, and part of a pastoral team at the Upstate Medical Center. Asked if she thought women would eventually be ordained, Rodgers responded affirmatively, but said that before it happened, "the model of priesthood will have to change."

Sister of Charity Barbara Garland became the highest ranking woman in diocesan leadership when she joined Bishop Harrison's cabinet in 1979. As vicar for personnel, she helped the bishop address the ministerial needs of priests, deacons, sisters, seminarians, lay ministers, and diocesan lay employees. (Photo: The Catholic Sun)

The sisters had always played a major role in the diocese, but so had lay women. Yet only a few of these achieved sufficient recognition to leave "their footprints in the sands of time." Most often they were taken for granted, as was noted by the woman who told a priest critical of females joining mutual benefit societies that he had no objections when they worked on the parish fair. Or they were patronized, as was the Catholic Women's Club, the only major non-parish organization of lay women. In 1968 some efforts were made to organize a Catholic women's council from the declining Women's Club, the Catholic Daughters of America and several smaller groups, but nothing came of it. Some of these earlier groups did not survive the process of renewal. The Ladies Catholic Benevolent Association did, but it was far less visible than in the past, with no local chapters active in parishes. Another mainstay of women was gone, as the Catholic Women's Club passed from the scene in 1971. When it closed its doors after 51 years, the leaders hoped it would survive as an organization, and it did, though on a small scale, offering scholarships to needy children, holding parties at the Veterans Home and visiting shut-ins. In August 1982 they held a "nostalgic silver tea" in the old building, decorating the walls with pictures of more prosperous days and filling the tables with scrapbooks. For the event, ladies pulled from their trunks the clothes of other days, described by Arlene LaRue of the *Herald Journal:* "middy blouses with pleated skirts, gym bloomers, striped jackets, shawls, capes and skimmer hats."

The charming nostalgia of this scene contrasted with the seriousness of the problem of women in the Church. Even before the American bishops decided to write a pastoral letter on women, Bishop Harrison established a Commission on Women in Church and Society which began holding hearings throughout the seven-county diocese in the winter of 1983-1984. The commission of ten women and two men, chaired by Suzanne LaLonde, solicited written comments and researched issues women named as important.

In a preliminary report, they noted three major areas of concern within the Church. People were concerned about broadening the role of women in ministry and in decision making, eliminating sex-exclusive language, and addressing more adequately such problems as sexuality in marriage, problem pregnancies and domestic violence. Second, people were concerned with the role of women in society, including such issues as sexist language, lack of strong female role models, insensitivity to the problems of single parents, and the diminishing value placed on the role of the mother. Finally, they were concerned with poverty and the need for adequate day care, child support, employment opportunities and wage equality. The commission directed attention to problems of all women, not just religious, and thus promised to change the context and focus of the Catholic discussion. Most of all, the commission was effectively demonstrating the fact that discontent was widespread; continuing discrimination against women no longer would claim legitimacy.

EMPHASIS ON SOCIAL MINISTRY

If these problems challenged the Syracuse Church, Harrison could take satisfaction in the support given by women, especially women religious, to his leadership on matters of social justice and world peace. Leaders of religious communities working in the diocese regularly praised the bishop for his strong stands on racism, poverty, nuclear weapons, and Central American policy. Harrison's commitment to social justice was reinforced after 1978 by his new auxiliary bishop, Thomas Costello. Born in Camden, Costello grew up in Rome, attended Niagara University and St. Bernard's Seminary and was ordained in 1954. He later studied education and canon law at the Catholic University of America and in 1960 took over the diocesan school office, guiding the system through the period of its greatest challenges. He joined Father Brady in Selma in 1965 and later participated in demonstrations in support of racial justice. He had long championed strong leadership from the diocese, and an orientation toward the mission of the Church in service to the world. Echoing Harrison's own pronouncements, Costello said: "I see developing a new concept of the diocesan Church, something broader than just the parish church, and I am delighted to be a part of that developing concept."

The commitment of the diocesan leadership to those in need was clear. So was the generosity of local Catholics, evident not only in their contributions to fund raising appeals and their support of social service projects but also in assisting Vietnamese refugees. Responding to national appeals, Syracuse Catholic Charities was given responsibility to coordinate local resettlement efforts. Several local foundations provided financial assistance, and LeMoyne College provided support. Conservative Anthony Bouscaren, who had consistently supported the war, was very active in the resettlement program, as were many others who had been equally strong in opposition. Individually or in cooperation with other Catholic and Protestant churches, parishes took responsibility for sponsoring Vietnamese families, providing them with food, clothing, and shelter on their arrival, assisting them to find homes and employment, getting their children started in school and locating the assistance they needed from public and private agencies. By February 1976, Bishop Cunningham expressed profound satisfaction with the work of the diocese in settling 259 Vietnamese refugees. However, the numbers in need of help remained high and in July 1979 Bishop Harrison called on pastors to continue their efforts.

Between 1979 and 1984 the diocese helped another 238 families involving more than 500 Indochinese people resettle in the area. At the same time assistance was given to 150 Polish families, not just by predominately Polish but by other parishes as well. Throughout, the goal was to assist the family to achieve self sufficiency, and this goal was accomplished in almost all cases. The resettlement program was evidence of the continuing vitality of parish life and the enormous potential of the local Church when its energies were mobilized around concrete tasks.

Refugee assistance was no easy matter, but there were echoes of history in the problems that arose, and signs of new life in the assistance a more prosperous and connected parish could offer the newcomers, help unavailable in years gone by. The newcomers from Southeast Asia rarely had relatives or friends from the old country to greet them, as was so often the case for the European immigrants. To take one example, a Laotian family arrived in Syracuse, headed by a couple aged 20 and 21, with one child, two young sisters and a young brother; after their arrival, their sponsoring relatives left the community. St. Anthony's parish, one of the city's poorest, intervened. A housing committee located a rent-free apartment and mobilized a team to clean, paint and decorate it. A medical committee arranged appointments for the four children and saw to it they got the shots and medicine they needed. The food committee not only brought in meals but helped the young couple learn to compare prices, choose nutritious food and handle the problems posed by language. The clothing committee did similar things while the education committee not only helped the children settle in school but arranged for an English program for the whole family. The public assistance committee helped the father, who had already gotten employment with the help of Catholic Charities, arrange employment for his younger brothers and sister. Finally a transportation

Catholic Charities has been active throughout the diocese in helping refugees from other nations — Cuban children, Southeastern Asia immigrants and Polish refugees such as these, who learn English with the help of a volunteer from Syracuse's Sacred Heart parish. (Photo: The Catholic Sun)

committee helped get the children to their appointments and the father to work on days the bus did not run. As the chairperson of the committee reported, this family was a victim of war, the parishioners had a responsibility to help, and the benefits were theirs: it has been "a marvelous experience."

Another group who received renewed attention were Native Americans. When Father James Carey became pastor of St. Lucy's in 1978 he found perhaps 1,500 Indians residing on the west side of the city; many were fallen away Catholics, some of whom had been attracted to the revival of Longhouse religion in recent years, as the bishop told Cardinal Cooke in seeking his support for a grant from the Bureau of Indian Missions for Carey's work. This grant of $20,000 was eventually received, and Carey worked hard with a group of Catholic Iroquois to make his parish an attractive and hospitable community. The Indian members of the parish were invited to redecorate the daily Mass chapel. With volunteer labor and donated materials from area Indian artists, a lovely chapel was constructed which became a kind of spiritual home for this community, whose leaders hoped to develop skills and knowledge for outreach and evangelization among their fellow Indians, many of whom were extremely poor and in need of social services and community support.

In August 1985, 3,000 Catholic Indians from all over the United States attended a five-day Tekawitha Conference at LeMoyne, the first of these annual conferences held east of the Mississippi. Native costume and ritual, liturgical ceremonies, discussion of problems and possibilities for Catholic Indians marked the conference, whose highlight was a caravan to the major centers marking the life of Blessed Kateri Tekawitha, the first lay person of the North American Church to be beatified. The affirmation of Catholic faith, together with the recovery of native traditions, marked another step toward reconciliation with the one of the darkest features of local Church history, a record of imperialism, long neglect, and not inconsiderable discrimination. As one participant put it:

I went to a Catholic school and they always used to tell us not to [celebrate Mass] in the Indian way because they thought we were praying to a different God, and that was wrong. But it's one God. They tried to separate the Church and the Indian way, but they're really not separate. The Indian way and the Catholic way are one.

As Simon LeMoyne had said, "God is everywhere."

Following the early 1970s, black Catholics had received less attention in the diocese. St. Anthony's was a parish for many of these families, and its programs kept alive the possibility of an authentic black Catholic experience in the diocese. Father John Schopfer, the missionary to the Southeast side of the city, hoped to keep alive something of the Brady spirit at the Brady Faith Center, a drop-in center located across from the Southwest Community Center. In 1980 the diocese endorsed establishment of an office of black ministry with funds raised by black Catholics, staffed by Sister Clementine Lynch, and

495

Native American Catholics gathered at LeMoyne College in 1985 for their national Tekakwitha Conference, celebrating their blend of Catholic faith and Native American culture. (Photo: The Catholic Sun)

housed at St. Anthony's. This office attempted to assist programs in the black community and in 1984 established the Sister Mary Theodore Williams scholarship for a black student going to college. The Brady Research Committee, composed of friends of the late city missioner, held an annual Brady Mass attended by the bishops and many priests and lay people, as well as leaders of other black churches. Still, racism was not at the top of the local agenda, and only in 1984 did the continuing reality of discrimination once again receive widespread attention. At a press conference called by local black Catholics to announce that discussion of the newly published pastoral letter of the nation's black bishops would begin in the diocese, Dolores Morgan charged that the diocese had "put racism on the back burner" in recent years. Bishop Costello agreed with her statement that racism was "alive and well" in the diocese. "There's racism in the church. I don't think we can deny it," Costello said.

Earlier in the week, Costello had apologized for the fact that no black persons served on the Onondaga County task force studying Catholic schools. Morgan added that the Bishop Foery Foundation had seven directors,

Despite what Bishop Costello identified as persistent and subtle racism remaining within the Church, black Catholics such as these members of the St. Martin de Porres gospel choir in Syracuse could celebrate their heritage both as black people and as Catholics. (Photo: The Catholic Sun)

OK to be black and OK to be Catholic and darned important to be both." Asked how the diocese could lessen racism, Costello responded candidly: "If I knew I'd be a genius," adding in Brady-like language, "its a very delicate thing. All we can offer is to walk the way with them."

Nor had the Spanish Apostolate expanded greatly. In 1977 it submitted the results of a study of the growing Hispanic population in the diocese, estimated at 7,000, with substantial communities in Syracuse and Utica and scattered families elsewhere. The overwhelming majority were from Puerto Rico and were experiencing the process of adjustment in ways not dissimilar from those of earlier immigrant groups. For the most part, Spanish speaking people came to the area with little education, entered marginal, often seasonal employment, and suffered from low income, inadequate housing and considerable discrimination. According to the staff, they had received little "religious indoctrination" at home, and traditional folk religion remained strong. Indeed, the description could well have been given for many earlier immigrant groups, largely uninstructed in their faith, anxious for the Church to baptize their children but otherwise given to forms of devotion that were family centered and had little to do with organized Church practice. The migration experience, as with earlier groups, gave rise to severe problems of family breakdown, dependency, and a sense of exclusion. "Cultural values are maintained through super human effort in the face of a society which frequently equates being different with being inferior, or, worse, views groups through stereotypic or myopic caricatures," the report stated. In this situation, pentecostal and fundamentalist churches were making inroads into the community. The report noted their religious emotionalism and, perhaps forgetting Bishop Ludden's homilies, accused them of promoting a "puritanical

497

all white. There were 500 black Catholics in Syracuse, but only one black sister and one black Franciscan Brother. While there were 770 minority children among the 5,879 students in Onondaga County Catholic schools, there was only one black elementary teacher among 700 throughout the diocese. Costello and Morgan welcomed the letter of the black bishops, which encouraged black Catholics to express themselves and take their rightful role in the church. As Morgan put it: "This is the first time someone has said its disdain for dancing, 'worldly pleasures and vices.'"

The apostolate had one full-time priest working in Syracuse who offered weekly Mass, sacramental preparation, counselling and advocacy through a community center on Seymour Street. In Utica two priests from St. John's offered a weekly Mass and assisted local community programs as best they could while working full time in their own parish. In Broome County there was one priest who offered services in Spanish. The report concluded that more personnel was needed, including five-full time priests, seven deacons and two sisters to work as teams throughout the diocese, while even more priests should learn the language and receive pastoral training. While there was some response, no major effort in Spanish ministry was undertaken. In 1980 when the bishop surveyed consultative bodies on the priorities of the diocese, outreach to minority groups was mentioned only by the senate, ranking seventh among its priorities.

One area in which the diocese did undertake a major effort was among the handicapped. While Catholic parishes were always available to handicapped people and priests visited shut-ins, the Church and other institutions only recently had explored ways in which normal facilities could be made more accesable to people with severe physical handicaps. The American bishops published a pastoral letter on the subject in 1978, advocating changes designed to allow handicapped people to have as full a measure of their rights as possible. One area the Church promised to explore was access to church buildings. When Bishop Harrison announced such plans, there was a warm response from handicapped people, one of whom described in moving terms the loneliness she had long felt when unable to negotiate the steep steps at her church. Within a few years, parishes, schools, church halls, even the chancery

office, were outfitted with ramps and more important, priests and people were alerted to the presence and the feelings of disabled people.

The second priority established in 1982 pledged the diocese to "identify and remedy any injustice" within the Church and then "to act boldly for peace and justice in the community, the nation and the world." Harrison was as good as his word and put Sister Barbara Garland, vicar for personnel, to work on the first element of this pledge. She held hearings throughout the diocese and talked with diocesan offices, agencies and consultative bodies. After extended negotiation, in which diocesan policy towards unions, wage and benefit schedules and relations between paid and volunteer workers were fully discussed, the bishop issued a policy document and guidelines for implementation on Labor Day 1983. "The Church as Employer: Renewal in Our Working Relationships" broke the mold of "neither first nor last." Printed in national publications, the document drew praise from many quarters. It drew from Church teaching two basic principles: the dignity of the human person and the need to act for the common good. The bishop mandated that all involved in an area should participate either directly or through representatives in policy development and review. Discrimination on the basis of race, sex, age or national origin was banned; the only exceptions allowed were provisions of specific jobs which required ordination or active Church membership as a condition of employment. Wages and benefits "befitting human dignity" were required, while every effort should be made to insure that "no person should be deprived of the opportunity to provide for family responsibilities properly because one works for the Church." The diocese affirmed the right of all employees to "freely draw together in associations of their choice," thus recognizing the right to form unions, while encouraging "creative efforts to develop new models of positive labor/management relationships," such as the diocesan School Covenant. Finally, provision was made for due process resolution of conflicts and establishment of grievance procedures throughout the diocese.

These were strong words, and the policy guidelines published along with this statement indicated that they were to be acted upon. These provided that parishes and agencies should insure that all employees had written job descriptions and contracts and underwent an annual review, that the right to strike was recognized, subject to considerations of the common good, and that all administrators would review wages, benefits and grievance procedures to be sure that they accorded with the principles set forth in the statement. The appropriate vicariates would provide assistance and would be called upon to report to the bishop on progress made in implementing these directives.

The bishops did not wait for this process of internal reform to be completed before turning attention to public issues of justice. Indeed, Harrison and Costello were more outspoken on issues of justice and peace than any bishops before them. In 1980, when President Carter resumed draft registration but not induction, the parish council of Our Lady of Good Counsel church in Endicott wrote the bishop praising the statement made by the United States Catholic Conference endorsing the right of the state to conscript its citizens but opposing reinstitution of the draft at that time. They asked for improved materials in religious education to assist in the formation of conscience, and a plan of draft counseling so that "our young men will not be faced with the situation we saw during the Vietnam period where they were unaware of their right to their Catholic belief." Partly in response to such requests, the newly established Justice and Peace Commission drafted

a statement for Bishop Harrison opposing reimposition of the peace time draft, supporting conscientious objection and extension of that right to selective conscientious objection, opposing the drafting of women and upholding with Vatican II the dignity of military service. In 1981 Harrison published "The Formation of a Catholic Conscience on War and Peace," in which he discussed Church teaching on conscientious objection, including its support for selective conscientious objection not allowed in the law. He offered to accept letters to be kept on file from conscientious objectors to be used if and when conscription was reinstituted, and he identified four trained counselors in each of the diocesan regions who were available for personal consultation.

499

Harrison took strong public stands against American policy in Central America, increased arms expenditures and cutbacks on federal spending on social programs, in every case aligning himself with positions taken by the American hierarchy. When the American bishops began preparing a controversial pastoral letter on nuclear weapons, the Syracuse bishops were warmly supportive of a strong anti-nuclear position. In the summer and fall of 1983, protests mounted in Europe and the United States against deployment of new missile systems; in October the two bishops signed a statement lending their "endorsement" to the protests against the "first strike Cruise and Pershing II nuclear missiles," quoting the pastoral's condemnations of first use policies. In January the Diocesan Cabinet considered requests for hospitality for peace activists coming to Syracuse for the trial of seven Catholics charged with damaging property at Griffiss Air Force Base. The cabinet avoided direct comment on the request but St. Andrew's and St. Lucy's, Maria Regina College and Aquinas House all provided accommodations and food for the visitors. On May 24 Costello joined protesters at the Court

Taking his role as Church teacher around the diocese, Bishop Costello logged thousands of miles to speak about some of the controversial Catholic issues of peace, respect for human life, and economic justice. (Photo: The Catholic Sun)

House and led a prayer vigil, for which he was roundly denounced by letter writers to local papers. In an interview he denied that Hope Appeal money was being used for the protesters, but he stoutly defended the right of civil disobedience and indicated that he too wished to sound the alarm against the arms race and nuclear weapons: "you can say I share their concern for the future of this world." Costello was not alone, for Father William Cuddy, Sister Patricia Bergen and several other local Catholics were also on trial for blocking the gate of the air force base.

The diocesan education office prepared an excellent summary and study guide on the peace pastoral for use by individuals, families and groups. Particularly notable about this material was that it was specifically designed for families, with sample conversations on the draft, nuclear weapons and other subjects, and prayers and reflection questions designed for family use. Included too were concrete suggestions for peacemaking activities.

Harrison, like many bishops, had come to his strong position on the arms race in part through his strenuous support of a pro-life position on abortion. That position rested on the principle of the dignity and worth of every human person, a principle that led him to argue not only against the arms race and abortion, but against capital punishment, racial and sexual discrimination, and economic injustice which kept men and women from reaching their full potential and realizing in practice their basic human rights. This position came to be known as the "seamless garment" of pro-life after a term coined by Cardinal Joseph Bernardin of Chicago; it was one which both Harrison and Costello enthusiastically accepted and struggled to put into pastoral practice in the diocese.

On the 10th anniversary of the Supreme Court decision legalizing abortion in 1983, Harrison appealed to the public to pursue every legal avenue "to reverse this dehumanizing national blight." Abortion was an issue for all Americans, he argued, for never would "we be a truly compassionate people" nor a nation of justice and equal rights "as long as this violent denial of human dignity is upheld." Explicitly linking abortion to other issues of human dignity, the bishop appealed to the highest ideals of the nation. "The ideal of a broad view of humanity" could overcome the "destruction of life which is abortion" as it had already helped affirm the humanity and dignity of "the racial minorities, the retarded, the handicapped, the unloved and unwanted, the migrants, the refugees." He remained "hopeful that our developing commitment to humanity will lead us to recognize the unborn child as a human person and to affirm the essential equality and dignity of all human life."

In March 1981, on the anniversary of the assassination of Archbishop Oscar Romero of El Salvador, Bishop Harrison published "Sharing the Light of Faith," a pastoral letter on education for justice. Teachers in schools and CCD programs attended workshops on education for social justice and world peace.

Local Catholic high school students regularly traveled to Nazareth Farm in West Virginia to assist a diocesan priest, Father David Pichette, with his work among the rural poor. Other schools had periodic programs, including poverty suppers and fasts for world hunger. In his letter, Harrison urged "a strong, positive" effort to incorporate "the promotion of justice and peace in all forms of educational ministry in the diocese," promising that the education vicariate was ready to assist in planning and with materials and advice. Harrison spelled out five areas of special concern: hunger; racial and sexual discrimination; violence, the arms race and respect for life; competition and the need for a more just world economic order, and "empowerment/oppression." Under each, his comments showed a passionate commitment to justice and familiarity with the depth of the problems involved. "The ability to determine our own destiny and to take meaningful charge of our lives is daily destroyed by personal and structural oppression," he wrote. "Alienation and escape become ways of life for persons who increasingly sense an absence or loss of power in their individual and communal lives. The erosion of human rights in so many lands is a tragedy of great proportion." To such sins of injustice and violence, "the Gospel says a clear no," Harrison insisted. "To all those problems, humane, Christ-like remedies can and must be found. As followers of Christ, we are called to bring both relief and justice to all those suffering injustice in whatever form it occurs. As Catholic Christians, we have the resources and the clear command to join all men and women of good will to teach and live a better way."

One source of this awareness of issues of international justice was the presence of Syracuse area priests and religious in the missions. A survey in 1979 showed 31 sisters, one brother, 25 priests and one bishop from the region were serving overseas. One of the most prominent was Father Theodore Sizing, who had served at St. Lucy's and Our Lady of Lourdes; he entered a program at Maryknoll in 1983 through which he served in Guatemala. His occasional reports in the *Catholic Sun* helped local people appreciate the problems of poverty and violence in Central America. In 1985 Martha Swann left to serve in Nicaragua as the first lay missionary sponsored by the diocese.

Syracuse, like the whole American Church, had not yet found a way to relate its bottom up approach to parish renewal with the pressing call to serve a struggling humanity. The decline of Catholic schools, the weakening of the ties of ethnicity, and the intense mobility of middle class Americans had made religious faith a more personal matter and parishes more voluntary communities, requiring more attention to adult education, development of lay leadership within the Church and continuing efforts to make the services of the Church more responsive to the needs of its people. Lay people looked to the Church for spiritual nourishment, assistance with the education of their children, and support at times of family crisis. While sympathetic with the principles of charity and justice in Church teaching, they did not generally think of the Church in terms of public issues. In a draft of a pastoral letter on economic justice in 1984, the American bishops called upon lay Catholics to promote human dignity and human rights in economic life and to regard such work as a path to sanctity and holiness. Yet the local Church's pastoral strategy, with its emphasis on the parish, had not yet found a way to forward this approach to the Church's mission or to overcome the gap between the sense of urgency felt by the bishops and the preoccupation with private concerns of most lay people. The bonds of faith and friendship remained strong in the Syracuse diocese; the "We Are the Church" priorities of community

502

As the Church expanded its vision and social conscience, priests, sisters, and lay missionaries were leaving Central New York for work in West Virginia and the Caribbean, and in Central and South America. These LeMoyne College students work in a lay mission project in Mexico. (Photo: The Catholic Sun)

and shared responsibility were well advanced. But the other half of Harrison's dream, a Church turned outward toward the world with a sense of compassion and of social and political responsibility was far from realization.

This was evident in a survey conducted by the Syracuse newspapers in 1984. It reported that 87 percent of those raised Catholics continued to regard themselves as Catholics; those who left the Church to join another were matched by an equal number of converts. In the Syracuse area 47 percent of those surveyed were Catholics. Of that group 68 percent regarded their religion as "very important" in their lives, 27 percent as "fairly or somewhat important." The survey reported that 64 percent attended Mass weekly and an additional 10 percent two or three times a month, higher than national averages and considerably higher than other denominations. Among Catholics, 42 percent gave the church an "A" for meeting their "spiritual needs," 27.9 percent a "B," 16 percent a "C."

On the other hand 65 percent said their

religious beliefs had no effect on their political views, though on most issues the majority of Catholics favored positions taken by the U.S. bishops. For example, 58 percent opposed abortion, 56 percent favored public aid for church-related schools, 58 percent supported a nuclear freeze, 41 percent opposed U.S. policy in Central America (19 percent favored that policy), 58 percent opposed increased military spending, 62 percent opposed cuts in federal spending for the poor, and 54 percent favored increased foreign economic assistance. On the Equal Rights Amendment, on which the bishops did not take a stand, 65 percent of Catholics were in favor. Only on capital punishment, which the bishops strongly opposed, did Catholics disagree, with 55 percent in favor.

Catholics were almost equally divided between Republicans, Democrats, and Independents. Very few were involved in public movements for reform, like the Right to Life and peace movements, though 20 to 30 percent were involved in volunteer service program to the elderly, youth, or the ill. In terms of income, Catholics were now more or less like everyone else — 17 percent earned under $5,000 a year, compared to 19 percent in the area; 22 percent earned over $35,000, while 20 percent each fell between $15,000 to $25,000 or $25,000 to $35,000. In other words, from a poor and working class church, Catholics had moved, not to being a "middle class" Church but to one whose class composition reflected that of the society generally.

503

As the diocese of Syracuse approached its one hundredth birthday, few things were any longer clear. Just as in the old days, diocesan offices prepared carefully designed charts, showing where every activity fit in. Those which did not fit in neatly were few, like the Board of Urban Ministry, largely a cooperative effort of Syracuse inner city parishes. Harrison and Costello, alert to the fact the Spirit moves in many places, maintained personal links to groups like the Plowshares protesters, while restless priests like Father McVey at Unity Acres, Father Schopfer on the streets of Syracuse's south side, and Father William Cuddy with his jail ministry, and any number of sisters, touched the lives of outsiders beyond the reach of parishes and vicariates. Financially, the diocese was prosperous, with the Hope Appeal regularly passing its goal and the various chancery offices staffed by men and women of faith and great professional competence. The remarkable Monsignor Joseph Champlin, a leader of diocesan renewal since the liturgical changes that preceded the council, continued to preside over the vicariate for parish life and worship and was as skilled as anyone in the country in stimulating, encouraging and supporting grass roots movements of renewal. His office, more than any other, served parishes, providing resources for the parish priests, religious and lay leaders as they mastered the art of popular participation in the ministries of the Church. There were in the diocese only a few diehard conservatives bent on turning the clock back, and few sectarian radicals bent upon purifying the messy pluralism of the local Church. Instead, through a new language of ministry and service, and increasingly sophisticated methods of consultation and dialogue, the Syracuse Church was moving towards the ideal of a free Church composed of men an women who cared about each other and kept the faith.

Old problems remained, to be sure. The maintenance and support of Catholic schools and the adjustment of priorities between schools and other works of the Church remained to be resolved, though progress was being made in bringing the whole diocesan Church to accept collective responsibility for its educational mission. New problems were posed by the shortage of priests. At the same time there was a the rising number of lay ministers in a hierarchical church still unsure how far collegiality and shared responsibility should go. A pervasive parochialism also remained, as people still too often found in the local parish the beginning and the end of their Catholic identity and responsibility. Most of all, there was the problem of Church mission, as the American bishops pastoral letters on nuclear arms, the economy, racism, and Hispanic ministry called the Church to engage the deepest problems of the American nation and of the world. The Syracuse bishops spoke strongly about these issues, but they had not yet found their way into the fabric of local Church life, and almost everyone knew it.

Like the rest of the American Church, that in Syracuse stood at a crossroads. One road pointed towards a Church more turned in on itself, reflecting the anxieties of some and the satisfaction of others, in either case marginalizing religion into a matter of personal choice and private life with little significance for the larger society. The other road called the Church to a more vigorous engagement with the problems confronting the world, to the Vatican II ideal of a Church "truly and intimately linked with mankind and its history." Harrison, Costello, the diocesan leadership, and most of the Catholic people of Central New York wanted to walk that road, and to do so while remaining a community of faith and friendship. In parishes with their Renew programs and parish councils, on the Diocesan Pastoral Council, on a number of board and commissions, in neighborhood centers and schools, in all the places Catholics gathered, they were learning what Cardinal Dearden had called a "new way of doing the work of the Church." The conflicts of the last two decades had resulted in a certain modesty, and few claimed to have a blueprint to knit together the strands of the Church's complex life. But after a hundred years the faith endured, the fabric of relationships still knit the Church into one people, hopes were high for Harrison's dream of a united Church working together to be what the Church had always aimed to become — the Body of Christ in Central New York.

EPILOGUE

THE SECOND CENTURY BEGINS

The diocese of Syracuse is a local Church with its own unique history, its own distinctive character. It has not had the problems of the missionary Churches of the American south and northwest, where Catholics long remained a tiny minority of the population. At the other extreme, Syracuse, Utica, Rome, Binghamton and Oswego do not add up to Boston, New York, Chicago or Philadelphia, dioceses among the largest, most wealthy and powerful in the universal Church. In terms of immigrant groups, Syracuse had a cross section of the American Catholic population, while the progress of its members into the middle class after World War II corresponded to the general development of American Catholics. Politically, local Catholics may have been a bit less inclined toward the Democratic party than Catholics in most large urban dioceses, and the absence of the bitter organizing battles of the 1930s made their support of the labor movement less passionate than elsewhere. Overall, the Church in Syracuse has been neither powerful nor powerless, neither liberal nor conservative, neither complacent nor unduly disturbed — a Church confidently Catholic and securely American.

The student of American Catholicism finds some surprising things in the Syracuse diocese. There is the role of lay initiative, from the early days when scattered groups of lay people first formed themselves into communities and invited a priest to visit through the bewildering variety of immigrant groups who found similar leadership from lay people, both from within their community and from outside, to the more recent peace, social justice and charismatic movements, which seemed to spring spontaneously from below at a time when Church reformers were having only mixed success trying to bring about renewal from the top down. Then there is the remarkable success of Syracuse Catholicism as an organization. As organizers, the great founding pastors rivaled the politicians and entrepreneurs of the day in their ability to blend the raw materials of people and money into strong congregations. Their bishops were men noted less for their piety and erudition than for their organizing genius, which went beyond administration and fund raising to building a sense of purpose and high morale among their clergy and religious and a spirit of loyalty and solidarity among their people. There were battles with minority groups within the Church but, until recently, there were few independent lay movements, no Catholic Workers dedicated to Christian perfection in service to the poor, little intellectual life and no cultural dissent. Few priests participated in the liturgical or labor movements, relations with religious communities were peaceful and the clergy after 1900 were loyal, even docile, before episcopal authority. The bishops and clergy handled the problems posed by anti-Catholicism, the new immigrants, the depression and post-war prosperity with remarkable skill, maintaining unity while responding with pragmatic flexibility to each new challenge. At first glance the unity and organized strength of Syracuse Catholicism might have been the result of strong leadership, from the day Bishop Patrick Ludden arrived to draw "the lines tight." But it reflected as well the great, enduring strength of the parishes and religious communities of the diocese. The Syracuse Church was a Church of faith and friendship, knit together by bonds of shared beliefs and networks of families, ethnic groups and parish communities which made Catholics, in fact, one people.

The history of this Church is first of all a success story. To the seven counties and a hundred towns of Central New York came thousands of men and women to begin life anew in a strange land. They built their churches and rebuilt their lives from the bottom up. At the heart of each of these cities and most of these towns are buildings which are monuments to the faith they shared, to the friendships they found, to the dreams they made come true. In the recesses of the memories of today's Catholics are strange

looking people whose language they no longer understand. Most were peasants, who had been told for centuries that they must stay where they were born, that personal freedom, political participation, economic security and the respect of their countrymen were the prerogative of others, born to higher places. Even after they arrived, there were voices, even a few heard in the Church, who said that was still the way things ought to be, that people like themselves were outsiders, born only to build railroads, dig canals and stand 16 hours daily at forges and looms. But those founding mothers and fathers dreamed that things might be different here in America, for their children if not for them. Still who among them could really be sure? The lessons of centuries taught that such dreams were illusions, and unworthy ones at that. Hiding their doubts, they reached out to each other to make a start. Their Church was a center of order and assurance in their lives, at once a community of faith and a network of friendships through which the dream was nurtured and kept alive. When the great pastors arrived, the Beechams, Hourigans, Barrys, Rusins and O'Haras, they said a loud and unequivocal yes to the dream. "Through your own efforts" they said, "you can take charge of your lives, become the architects of your salvation and masters of your history."

But words were not enough, for peasant peoples are realists who distrust rhetoric and value concrete achievements. When Father William Dougherty arrived to begin St. Vincent de Paul parish in 1894, he found a neighborhood filled with shanties, on mud paths, not streets, with people too poor to provide shoes for their children. In less than four years, they had erected — literally from their pennies, nickels and dimes — a magnificent church. When it was dedicated, their joy was so real you could touch it. Towers lifted to the sky expressed their faith in the living God, massive stones gave evidence of their confidence that they were here to stay, decorations evoked cherished memories of a land and people far away. The building spoke a message: "Yes, we can do it, we can become the people we have dreamed of becoming, we can take responsibility for our lives, carve out an equal place for ourselves in this community, open up a future of limitless possibilities for our children. We know it is true, because we have experienced it in the building of this church." American Catholics need look no further for elements of a North American theology of liberation. For here, in the cities and towns and rural villages of Central New York, is the living evidence of a liberation well begun. Things need no longer be as they have been. People have become what they dreamed of becoming. It happened once; it's happening today among newcomers; it can happen again in the future.

The dream of personal dignity, economic security and democratic responsibility, stated in terms of repentance from sin and free commitment to the Church, hard work, self help and sacrifice for family and community, was their theology of liberation. Like all theologies, it came to life in hard, human experience. There was a paradox, too, in that message of liberation. Preachers insisted with passionate intensity that men and women were sinful, that the world around them was filled with greed, materialism and permissiveness, and that the Church alone could guide people to heaven. Catholic clergy too often distrusted freedom; some among them yearned for a more orderly world, "the happiest and most peaceful society" where, among other things, they could be more securely in charge. At times, priests and lay people alike could be maddeningly complacent and self-righteous, harsh in their judgments on non-Catholics and those less ardent than themselves in their support for the Church. But, at their best, they were realists who knew that only commitment, fidelity and

self-discipline could enable the outcasts to claim their place. Sometimes, in spite of themselves, they affirmed the very freedom they feared. Without benefit of a new theology, they taught that men and women could decide for themselves; that their destiny, here and hereafter, was in their hands; that the future was theirs to create; that they were, in fact, responsible.

Yet, as so often happens, the strength of the Church in some areas obscured weaknesses in others. Forced to rely on their own resources, Catholics took pride in what they had achieved, but sometimes looked disdainfully on those who had not accomplished as much. Concentrating on the welfare of their own people, they at times ignored the common concerns of the whole community. Devoting enormous resources to paying for buildings and personnel, they had little time for the life of the mind and little tolerance for criticism. Skilled in organization, their priests and bishops were less adept at theological reflection and moral analysis. As Bishop Cunningham said in 1965, lay people were filled with "wonderment" by the council's liturgical reforms because, they had "little knowledge that all baptized and confirmed members of Christ's body, the Church, share in some way in the priesthood of Christ."

Most of all, there was the question of boundaries. To build a strong Catholic church, it was important to emphasize those things that were thought to be "Catholic" and give less attention to beliefs shared with other churches and other people. To maintain loyalty to the Church, it was necessary to persuade people to spend as much time as possible with other Catholics, limiting the temptation to intermarriage and a too heavy investment of time and money in other organizations. In a free and pluralistic society, strong organizations of any kind, including churches, are not built by men and women who think their particular organization is useful in its way but nothing special. They are built by men and women who think their organization, or their church, is uniquely important — not one among many, but the one that truly stands for crucially important values and ideals, "the one true Church." Bishops and priests, especially diocesan priests, were churchmen first of all; they knew quite well that lay persons must devote considerable portions of their lives to affairs outside of church, but they naturally judged themselves and others by what they did for the Church. Celibate, highly trained, schooled in arguments about the central role of the Church in human salvation, often immersed in ideas about the indispensable role of the Church in human welfare, they measured all things by the standards of the Church, Christ's Church, divinely established to fulfill God's will for the salvation of the human family. They could hardly have avoided thinking that they would be "counted and judged" by the number of people in their assigned part of the world who were members of the Church, faithful to its sacraments and loyal to its teachings.

But it was bound to change — and it did — all at once. Years later many Catholics would look back on the 1960s and use words like "disintegration" to describe their personal experience of those years. Just as the American Catholic Church reached the apex of its long struggle for fidelity and solidarity, the public worship of the Church changed, new forms of pastoral consultation were introduced, priests and religious entered new ministries or even left the active ministry. Schools faced drastic financial problems while new forms of religious education asked more of parents and contained themes different from those in the past. While all this was going on, the Catholic president was killed, new people moved into the neighborhood, demonstrations occurred in the streets, bitter controversies erupted in cities and towns

about housing, education, welfare and civil rights. Students demonstrated against the Vietnam war while other young men went off to serve, some to die, in it. Martin Luther King was assassinated and cities exploded in fire, another Kennedy passed violently from the scene, and crime became a national issue and an all-too-real local experience. The Church, long a source of stability in a rapidly changing society, seemed caught up in the vortex of change, sometimes without apparent direction. Even the pope and many bishops worried publicly about things getting out of hand, and this worry reached into parishes, even into families.

Even in Syracuse, the lines were no longer drawn so tight. Pressure from the left, pushing for more drastic change, was a bit less than in many areas of the country, but the challenges of race, poverty and war had hardly been felt before another, abortion, shook many who had not formerly experienced the shattering of complacency. Gospel faith and Church teaching clearly were difficult to reconcile with violations of human dignity — in racism, poverty, endless war, the arms race, or the growing publicly sanctioned practice of abortion. Yet forging a Catholic response was made difficult by the internal changes in the Church, so that re-discovering the meaning of faith and reestablishing the ties of community while responding to these public challenges proved harder than at first expected. Renewal had come to mean reforging the ties of faith and friendship from the bottom up, almost beginning again at the place where so many pioneers and immigrants had started generations before.

The Church in Syracuse, to its everlasting credit, faced the dilemmas of renewal in an age of rapid social change with honesty and some courage. If the answers were not clear and the future still undefined, that was a measure of the degree to which individual Catholics and local churches meant to dig to the very depths of the tradition, avoiding both a conservatism which would turn the clock back and a radicalism which would forge ahead even if it meant the disappearance of the Church as an institution. Instead, local church people sought the middle ground, responding to the needs of the age, but with an eye toward their commitment to the fundamental truths of faith and their care for one another.

It is no accident that the Syracuse Church in the last generation has rejected the dogmatic righteousness of left and right. Walter Foery, David Cunningham and Frank Harrison sometimes appeared inconsistent. Each of these bishops could sit down with a worried conservative one day and a passionate progressive the next and have each come away thinking the bishop was a friend. They struggled as best they could, these bishops, to hold up a very large tent and invite as many people as possible to come inside. At times their Church indeed did look like a three-ring circus, but somehow it was and remains united. One reason was that, most of the time, the Church's leaders have trusted their people and trusted the Holy Spirit.

In practice, that is the bottom line. In day-to-day human terms, the Church in a free society works well when it is a community of faith and friendship, where the shared beliefs of a people find expression in their simple care for one another. Today the Church does all this a bit more self-consciously, commissioning special people to assist in providing pastoral care; but the reality remains the same. It has something to do with the revelation in Jesus that the Christian God is a God of love, and that faith expresses itself in the ability to love one another, not in a sentimental or a self-denying love, at least in the first instance, but in the kind of realistic acceptance and care which finds its paradigm in Christian marriage. It was this realization that the Church is, after all, a community of

---

THE BISHOPS OF SYRACUSE

Patrick A. Ludden
    May 1, 1887 - August 6, 1912

John Grimes
    August 6, 1912 - July 26, 1922

Daniel J. Curley
    May 1, 1923 - August 3, 1932

John A. Duffy
    June 29, 1933 - January 9, 1937

Walter A. Foery
    August 18, 1937 - August 4, 1970

David F. Cunningham
    August 4, 1970 - November 16, 1976

Frank J. Harrison
    February 6, 1977

509

faith and friendship that gave stability to the Syracuse Church as it moved through the years of renewal. Immersion in local church history brings with it the sobering realization that the love of God and the meaning of faith is communicated more often and more solidly through people than through catechisms or manuals of theology.

To his undying credit Bishop Cunningham understood this. In a sermon at the ceremony marking his installation as coadjutor bishop in 1967, Cunningham admitted that the Vatican Council's call to new life carried risks, but he insisted that the Church need not fear such risks because in the end it did not depend on theological statements or clear lines of authority but on "commitment to Christ whose presence we experience within his Church." That experience took place in the rela-

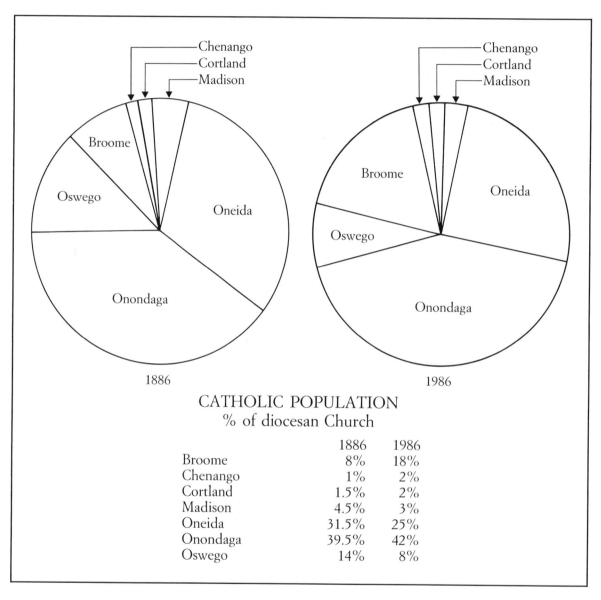

CATHOLIC POPULATION
% of diocesan Church

	1886	1986
Broome	8%	18%
Chenango	1%	2%
Cortland	1.5%	2%
Madison	4.5%	3%
Oneida	31.5%	25%
Onondaga	39.5%	42%
Oswego	14%	8%

tionships among people, Cunningham insisted again and again. The key to successful ministry, he once told his priests, was being "eager to show Christ's love" especially at moments of family and individual crisis. Preaching, worship, education, community decisions all turned on relationships among people. To "show Christ's love" they had to get out of the rectory and into people's lives, they had to like people and enjoy their company. "I love to visit the homes of my people," Cunningham said in a rare moment of self-revelation. "I love to sit at the kitchen table and discuss those things that have a meaning for them, to drink their coffee and have a piece of cake and make them know I am part of their family."

Cunningham and his priests at times seemed to think that only they could do those things, but surely they were right to believe that these qualities of care, of liking people and enjoying involvement in their lives, and bringing the presence of Christ to them at the special events of life, was crucial to the success of pastoral ministry. Out of such experiences of companionship and compassion, friendships are born and faith is renewed. And a community with that kind of faith is equipped to deal with the problems of the larger world. "How does the Church, armed only with apostolic faith, penetrate a society so material, unspiritual and concerned only with the present?" Cunningham asked in a Binghamton speech in 1975. Cunningham thought the "only answer possible" was to "capture the power of the Risen Lord and make that power felt in the pilgrimage the world is part of, the pilgrimage evident when anyone suffers, when the poor reach out for justice, when the hungry cry to us for help, when the unborn are victims of selfishness, when the aged and handicapped are mistreated and almost ignored."

Bishop Harrison's combination of community and collaboration on the one hand and service to those in need on the other reflected well the experience of renewal in the diocese. The reforms initiated by Vatican II came at a time when the maturing of the Catholic population laid the basis for a more independent, self-confident laity. The process of renewal soon interacted with the dramatic upheavals of American society in the 1960s to create a sense of urgency among some and anxiety among others. To manage the rapid changes taking place all around them, Church leaders pursued a variety of approaches. One was simply to try to maintain the institutional basis of Church life, raising money, pacifying those who became upset, accepting just enough change to meet demands for it while

not so much as to divide congregations or upset too many people. This was Bishop Foery's general approach. Bishop Cunningham, more enthusiastic about renewal, hoped to implement the conciliar reforms from the top down, with the help of his staff. People were rarely consulted about the goals which should be pursued, but only about how those goals might be better achieved. A third approach came from those who wanted more drastic reform, from activists in peace and social issues, from charismatics and some younger priests and religious. They looked towards a smaller but more prophetic Church composed of people who had made a deep, personal commitment and were prepared to take a stand against conformity and mediocrity in Church and society.

Gradually it became clear that something more was needed, a deeper approach which would seek to enable people throughout the Church to think and pray about their beliefs and share in the process of defining how the Church would act upon its faith in the concrete conditions in which it found itself. This more pastoral, bottom up approach had been used within religious communities, especially among women religious; each sister reflected on her faith, on the charism of her community and the meaning of her own vocation, and community-wide priorities and policies were reconsidered in response to the personal experience of all members. Behind this bottom up process was not only the call to renewal of the council but the basic structure of a now very American Church. As theologian Richard McBrien put it, renewal had to do with clarifying the mission of the Church, translating that understanding of mission into clear-cut goals and objectives, then mobilizing resources for the pursuit of those goals. Today, in the context of religious freedom and pluralism, the members of the Church are not likely to respond eagerly to goals and objectives which they have no part

511

1886		Broome	Chenango	Cortland	Madison	Oneida	Onondaga	Oswego
470,590	Total population (1)	49,483	39,891	25,825	44,112	115,475	117,893	77,911
62,664	Catholic population	4,893	693	903	2,835	19,698	24,696	8,946
13%	Catholic % of population	10%	2%	4%	6%	17%	21%	11%
50	Parishes	2	1	2	4	18	16	7
24	Dependent Missions	1	2	2	2	8	4	5
847	Average Parish/Mission size	1,631	231	226	473	758	1,235	746
61	Diocesan Priests	4	1	3	4	17	17	15
9	Religious Order Priests	–	–	–	–	3	6	–
1:895	Ratio: Priests-to-laity	1:1,223	1:693	1:301	1:709	1:985	1:1,074	1:596

1986		Broome	Chenango	Cortland	Madison	Oneida	Onondaga	Oswego
1,207,563	Total population (2)	213,648	49,344	48,820	65,150	253,466	463,324	113,811
341,136	Catholic population	61,236	6,013	6,427	11,270	86,653	142,313	27,224
28%	Catholic % of population	29%	12%	13%	17%	34%	31%	24%
172	Parishes	30	7	5	8	47	56	19
19	Dependent Missions	–	1	2	3	4	3	6
1,786	Average Parish/Mission size	2,041	752	918	1,025	1,699	2,412	1,089
	Priests in Pastoral Ministry							
312	Diocesan (3)	50	9	6	10	73	138	26
41	Religious order (4)	11	–	–	–	6	24	–
1:966	Ratio: Priests-to-laity	1:1,003	1:668	1:1,071	1:1,127	1:1,097	1:878	1:1,047
40	Permanent Deacons	7	–	1	–	6	24	2
698	Sisters	104	5	4	8	106	405	66
262	Commissioned Lay Ministers	53	5	8	8	47	107	34

(1) Based on 1880 census
(2) Based on 1980 census
(3) Not included in these figures: 48 retired priests & 24 priests working outside the diocese
(4) Not included in these figures: 12 retired priests & 24 priests working at LeMoyne College

in defining. Therefore, it is necessary to broaden participation in the process of reflection and prayer through which both the mission of the Church and consequent priorities are established and clarified. This was what Cardinal Dearden had meant by "a new way of doing the work of the American Church." It was the direction in which Bishop Harrison set the Syracuse Church, to enlist the entire community in the difficult task of determining exactly what it was God expected from them and to reform the structures and procedures of the Church to enable the whole community to better respond to the call of the Holy Spirit. It was an approach grounded in the process of renewal itself, reflecting the local Church's new diversity of experiences and its continuing desire to remain one people. The challenge to Christians has always been to respond to the needs and experiences of the young and old, the well-established middle class and the often poor newcomers, to form communities open to all and responsive to the needs of individuals, and to remain one people, the Body of Christ. In the atmosphere of freedom and shared responsibility, faced with challenges to Christian faith as severe as those that confronted earlier generations in the barren land and crowded cities of upstate New York, no one person and no doctrinal formula could resolve the historic dilemma. Instead, what the council taught was confirmed by experience — that the people of God must trust one another, trust in the Holy Spirit and find ways to work together to become what they had always dreamed of becoming. The bottom up approach depended on a certain modesty and a remarkable confidence. As Bishop Cunningham once told a priest troubled by the problems of renewal: "Do your best and let the Lord with the Holy Spirit guide your projects to completion. In His own time and in His own way, He will bring clarity out of that which seems to be a mess and success to that which seems to be a failure."

In the late 1970s, rumors circulated that St. John the Evangelist church was going to close, but parishioners rallied around the pastor, reached out into the neighborhood and the parish was saved. One relieved woman told a reporter "if its possible to love a building, I love this church. I've got a little history in this church and if it had been destroyed they would have destroyed a little bit of me." She had a little bit of history in her church, and so do most Catholics. And, it seems, the Church has a little bit of history in them. As Father Edward Terry told the people of St. John's in 1878, "The history of the past is in the very words we hourly use." Catholics are

who they are because they have come from that historic Church. They are a different people because of that history, which is not out there in buildings and legends and stories, but in here, in the thoughts and feelings, the worries and the dreams of the Catholic people. "We are the Church," Bishop Harrison proclaimed in his first pastoral letter. John and Nicholas Devereaux were already the church before the first priests arrived from Albany. Whatever the numbers of priests or sisters, whatever the problems of theology or the politics in Rome, in Washington or on Onondaga Street, the people have been and are the Church, and they will be the Church in the future if they learn what their grandparents from several dozen nations learned before them — that the Church begins when those who share faith in the Risen Christ reach out to one another in friendship.

What is to be done with this Church, with those parishes and schools and hospitals built by yesterday's Catholics? Surely they did not pass them on with only survival in mind, as if people need do nothing more than keep the doors open, the faith intact or the bills paid. And surely they did not expect their children would cast it all aside in the name of some abstract ideal of poverty or other-worldliness, as if the entire historic struggle had been somehow unworthy, only a cheap pursuit of worldly gain and social prestige. No, they probably hoped for more than that, that today's Catholics might build on the foundations they laid to live with integrity as they did. They found in their Church the faith and friendship they needed to live as they knew they should. Of course the future, with less priests, fewer religious, and far fewer schools, will be different. In Renew, with its small groups in living rooms across the seven countries, people are drawing from scripture and their own life experience, the resources they need to create that new future. Around them events are shaping challenges as great as those their immigrant ancestors faced in the muddy canal ditches, isolated railroad sites, dark mills and crowded neighborhoods of upstate New York. Those men and women, out of a shining vision of new possibilities in this newest of nations, forged lives for themselves and futures for their families. As part of that enormous and compelling task, they constructed a diocesan Church, composed of many smaller churches, through which they empowered each other and their children to make dreams come true. In those Renew living rooms, in the sanctuary of St. Anthony's and the sounds of the Voices of Soul choir rising from the hearts of black Catholics, with the native Americans at the Kateri Tekawitha chapel at St. Lucy's, in Hispanic families and Masses around the diocese, in neighborhood centers and rural ministries, in prison cells with Plowshares protesters and in offices and shops and homes and churches of ordinary lay people, at friendly church suppers and not-so-friendly school board meetings, in the chancery and at Unity Acres and the Brady Faith Center — new dreams are being born, new bonds of friendship established, choices clarified and decisions made.

There are as many men and women of courage and vision and strength as there ever were, as many options available as in the 1920s or 1950s. Catholics and their Church can close in upon themselves, becoming once again people like those lay theologian Frank Sheed found too common in America:

We are the sweet, selected few
The rest of you are damned
There isn't room enough for you
We can't have heaven crammed

Or they can turn away from this always sinful world, despairing at the presence of the usual variety of human weakness made more worrisome by modern technology, joining those who think that there is nothing for Christians to do but abandon the world and hold up the banner of truth, awaiting the Lord's return. "Prophets of gloom" Pope John XXIII called such Catholics, people "burning with zeal," but "not endowed with too much sense of discretion" who "in these modern times can see nothing but prevarication and ruin." Or they can allow their Church and themselves to be marginalized, as if religion were only a private affair, while in the rest of life we must trust the experience of the educated and powerful who define the "real world" of science and technology, or dollars and cents. In such comfortable accommodation of Catholics and their Church to the world around them, we find what the American bishops call a "schizophrenic existence" in which the values of Christian discipleship are confined to Church, with little relevance to the rest of life.

There is another choice — more ambiguous, less clear-cut, but closer to the lives and experience of most people. It is a choice for a Gospel which tells of a Jesus who lived in the here and now, cared for the people around him, was a man of faith and a man deeply immersed in the life of his times. He called people to new life, and through his Resurrection suggested the possibility that all men and women might overcome sin and death, and that a new world waits to be born, one in which the hopes and aspirations which quicken the human spirit can be fulfilled. As the bishops put it, in the end we seek "to create a world where love and friendship among all citizens of the globe become the primary goal of all." It will not be easy to be men and women of the Church and men and women of the age, to be good Christians, committed Catholics, and responsible citizens all at once. There is tension between those three ideas of Catholic, Christian and citizen, and there always will be. But none of those poles can be surrendered without a cost — a cost of personal integrity, a cost of human possibility.

The key to living as one should, in Church and in life, is not in the first instance justice, or peace, or sin or death — but love. Perhaps more than any other person in the recent history of the diocese, it was Monsignor Charles Brady who pointed the way. Brady's last days are shrouded in the stories which surround a legend, a man whose life was so special, and whose impact on his friends so great, that every action seemed filled with grace and meaning. His best lay friend, Denny Owen, recalls dining with his wife and Father Brady shortly before the priest's death. Like many others, Owen believes that Brady had a premonition that the end was near. As he helped Brady to the door of the rectory, Owen felt the priest's arm around him and Brady said what Owen called "probably the most beautiful thing that anyone's ever said to me in my life." He said, "I love you Dennis, as Paul loved Timothy." A short time before, news had come that Monsignor Thomas Costello had been named auxiliary bishop. Costello, who lived with Brady, acknowledges that Brady had been "bringing him along" for years, educating him to the plight of minorities and the Gospel call to justice for the poor. He knew that Brady was pleased and excited by his appointment and he asked Brady to serve as one of his two priest-chaplains at the Mass of consecration. When Brady died suddenly he was in the driveway of their home, chopping ice from the driveway — not in front of the garage which housed his own car, but in front of that which housed Costello's. The first man to reach him was Monsignor Charles Fahey, who recalled that it simply did not occur to him to give Father Brady the last rites of the Church; "if he wasn't going to get in without annointing, then we all will be in big trouble." Later, Fahey stood in the back yard with Denny Owen, watching a startlingly

Bishop Frank Harrison (Photo: Office for Communications)

515

beautiful sunset. "That was just such a glorious day," Fahey recalls. "It was March, the sun went down early, and, of course, it was at the end of the afternoon that (Father Brady) was found on the ground. Denny came almost immediately and when we were there in the afternoon, it was just one of those particularly gorgeous March sunsets. We both just looked at it together and, wow, the Lord was saying 'Welcome, Charles' and making sure that we all knew the Lord was welcoming him home. It was just such a fitting thing."

Fahey thought that Brady's "loving personality, as well as the rectitude of what he had to say, brought about conversion of the whole institutional leadership." Bishop Harrison and Bishop Costello agree that Brady had a profound influence on the diocese. Bishop Foery, they thought, loved Brady and admired what he was doing but was occasionally exasperated by his lack of organization and the fact that he did not fit into the well-calibrated chart of the diocese. But when the chips were down on issues of human rights, there was not doubt of where Foery stood, and many believe Brady was the reason. Oral testimony suggests that Brady and Bishop Cunningham were less intimate, yet the latter also became an ardent champion of social justice and racial progress; there were many reasons, but Brady's witness and personal influence were among them. Bishop Harrison came to know Brady well when he served as pastor of St. Andrew's. When he and his assistant, Frank Woolever, signed an open housing petition in 1960, they were still innocents, genuinely surprised at the opposition this effort aroused. Father Brady helped him understand, and to grasp things beyond open housing. For Harrison, Brady's legacy set a direction for the local Church as it moved towards its second century:

One of the great marks of Father Brady was whenever you met him you felt that he cared about you.... It is very hard for many of us to understand the love of God for God loves us for what we are, not for what we have or what we have accomplished. God loves us simply because we are.... When I think of all the people I have known in my life, Father Brady had that notion and understood that notion of divine love, so he had a very deep love for everyone he came in contact with.... The secret, you know, of his whole mission, of his whole work, was tied up in that notion, that ability, that characteristic, that charism, of conveying to people he truly cared for them, that he truly loved them. And in memory of Monsignor Brady, I hope as Bishop of the Diocese that we can keep alive that spirit in all the work that we do so that we might attract people to the Kingdom of God by showing them that we care and that we love them as God truly loves us all.

A faith that evolves and a vision of ever-expanding friendship: That is not a bad outcome for a century of history or a bad angle of vision for the second century that lies ahead. Faithful friendship in Christ might make the final dream of God's Kingdom live for today's Catholics and help them make that dream become a vital part of the lives of their people — the people of the Church, of the nation, and of the world. "We are the Church," Bishop Harrison says. We always were, we are right now, we might yet be once again.

516

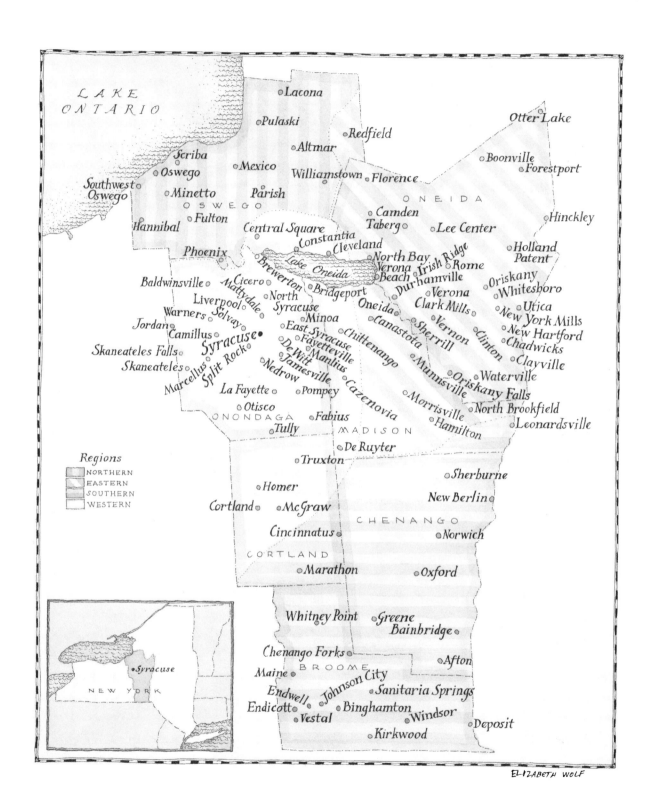

518

LAKE ONTARIO

Lacona

Pulaski

Redfield

Scriba
Altmar

Mexico
Oswego

Williamstown
Florence

Otter Lake

Boonville
Forestport

Southwest
Oswego

Minetto
Parish

ONEIDA

Hinckley

Hannibal

Fulton

OSWEGO

Camden
Taberg

Lee Center

Central Square

Phoenix

Constantia
Cleveland

North Bay
Verona
Beach
Irish Ridge
Rome

Holland
Patent

Baldwinsville

Brewerton
Lake Oneida
Bridgeport

Durhamville

Verona

Oriskany
Whitesboro

Cicero
Mattydale

North
Syracuse

Oneida

Clark Mills

Vernon

Utica
New York Mills

Liverpool
Warners
Solvay

Minoa

Canastota
Sherrill

Clinton

New Hartford
Chadwicks

Jordan
Camillus

East Syracuse
Chittenango

Sherrill

Clayville

Skaneateles Falls

Syracuse
Split Rock

Fayetteville
DeWitt
Manlius

Munnsville

Oriskany Falls
Waterville

Skaneateles

Marcellus

Nedrow
Jamesville

Cazenovia

Morrisville

North Brookfield

La Fayette

Pompey

Otisco
ONONDAGA

Fabius

Hamilton

Leonardsville

Tully

MADISON

De Ruyter

Truxton

Sherburne

Homer

New Berlin

Cortland

McGraw

CHENANGO

Cincinnatus

Norwich

CORTLAND

Marathon

Oxford

Whitney Point

Greene
Bainbridge

Chenango Forks

Afton

Maine

BROOME

Endwell

Johnson City

Sanitaria Springs

Endicott

Binghamton

Windsor

Vestal

Kirkwood

Deposit

Regions

NORTHERN
EASTERN
SOUTHERN
WESTERN

Syracuse

NEW YORK

ELIZABETH WOLF

PARISH BEGINNINGS

Following is a list of each parish or mission within the Catholic Diocese of Syracuse. The dates indicate the earliest known time of establishment. In several cases, Catholics meeting in homes or other facilities and served by visiting priests predate this formal parish establishment; the dates indicated here represent the year in which the bishop formally recognized the community, such as by assigning a priest or dedicating a church building. In some cases, the dates represent the year in which the community was established as a mission; it may have been several decades before they received a resident priest and became a parish.

DIOCESE OF NEW YORK
1819 Utica: St John

1827 Syracuse (then Salina): St John the Baptist

1830 Oswego: St Paul
1831 Irish Ridge: St Mary mission
1837 Rome: St Peter
1838 Binghamton: St Patrick (then St John)
1838 Minoa (then Manlius Station): St Mary of Assumption

1841 Syracuse: Cathedral of the Immaculate Conception (then St Mary)
1842 Little France: St Francis of Assisi mission (then St. Mary) (closed in 1973; incorporated into St Anne at Parish)

1842 Utica: St Joseph (merged in 1966 with St Patrick)
1843 North Bay: St John (then Sts Peter & Paul)
1843 Oneida: St Patrick
1844 Syracuse: Assumption of the Blessed Virgin Mary
1845 Florence: St Mary (then St. Mary of Mount Carmel)

DIOCESE OF ALBANY
1847 Cazenovia: St James
1847 Glenmore (then Annsville): St Anne mission
1848 Forestport: St Patrick
1848 Oswego: St Mary
1848 Rome: St Mary of the Assumption
1848 Solon: St Bridget mission (closed in 1919; incorporated into St Mary at Cortland)
1849 Oxford: St Joseph
1849 Utica: St Patrick (merged in 1966 with St Joseph)
1850 Clinton: St Mary
1850 Colosse (also French Street): St Anne (closed in 1941; incorporated into St Mary at Mexico)
1850 Pompey: Immaculate Conception
1850 Waterville: St Bernard
1851 Deposit: St Joseph
1851 Norwich: St Paul (then St. Patrick)
1851 Syracuse: St John the Evangelist
1852 Baldwinsville: St Mary

1852 Camden: St John the Evangelist
1852 Camillus: St Joseph (then St. John)
1853 Chittenango: St Patrick
1854 Cleveland: St Mary of the Assumption (then St Patrick)
1854 Fulton: Immaculate Conception (then St Mary)
1854 Marcellus: St Francis Xavier
1854 Truxton: St Patrick
1855 Cortland: St Mary (then St Mary of the Vale)
1855 Skaneateles: St Mary of the Lake
1858 Jordan: St Patrick
1858 Sherburne: St Malachy

1860 Dunhamville: St Francis of Assisi
1861 Hawkinsville: St John Chrysostom mission (closed in 1877; incorporated into St Joseph at Boonville)
1862 Oswego: St Peter
1864 Clayville: St Patrick
1866 Lafayette: St Joseph
1869 Fayetteville: Immaculate Conception
1869 Hamilton: St Mary (then Immaculate Conception)
1869 Oswego: St John the Evangelist
1869 Syracuse: St Joseph (French) (merged with St. Brigid in 1964)
1869 Whitney Point: St Patrick

1870 Marathon: St Stephen
1870 Oriskany Falls: St Joseph
1870 Oswego: St Louis
1870 Syracuse: St Patrick
1870 Utica: St Mary
1872 Fabius: St Paul mission
1872 Otisco: St Patrick mission
1872 Syracuse: St Lucy
1872 Utica: St. Peter
1874 Onondaga Hill: St Michael the Archangel
1874 Skaneateles Falls: St Bridget mission (closed in 1984; incorporated into St Mary at Skaneateles)
1875 Boonville: St Joseph
1875 Morrisville: St Anthony mission

(closed; date unknown)
1876 Altmar: St Mary of the Immaculate Conception mission
1876 Taberg: St Patrick
1876 Williamstown: St. Patrick mission
1877 Utica: St Francis de Sales
1878 East Syracuse: St Matthew

1880 Boylston: St Joseph mission (closed in 1933; incorporated into St John at Pulaski)
1880 Phoenix: St Stephen
1882 Holland Patent: St Leo
1882 Syracuse: St Joseph (German) (closed in 1971; incorporated into St. Lucy)
1883 New Hartford: St John the Evangelist
1883 North Brookfield: St. Mary mission (then Maternity of the Blessed Mary)
1883 Whitesboro: St Paul
1884 Canastota: St Agatha
1884 Vernon Center: St Agnes mission (merged with St Catherine at Vernon in 1974 as Holy Family at Vernon)

DIOCESE OF SYRACUSE

1887 Binghamton: St Mary (merged with Assumption as St. Mary of the Assumption in 1967)
1887 Utica: St Agnes
1888 Kirkwood: St Mary
1888 Pulaski: St John the Evangelist
1888 Cicero: Sacred Heart
1889 Greene: Immaculate Conception

1890 Liverpool: St Joseph the Worker
1890 Syracuse: St Peter
1891 Split Rock: St Peter mission
1891 Syracuse: Holy Trinity
1891 Tully: St Leo
1892 Syracuse: Sacred Heart
1893 Oneida: St Joseph
1893 Syracuse: St Vincent de Paul
1895 Hinckley: St Ann
1895 Utica: St Mary of Mount Carmel
1896 Binghamton: St Paul
1896 Utica: Holy Trinity

1899   Jamesville: St Mary
1899   Verona Beach (then Sylvan Beach): St Mary of the Lake mission

1900   Johnson City: St James
1901   Syracuse: St Anthony of Padua
1903   Solvay: St Cecilia
1904   Binghamton: Sts Cyril & Methodius
1907   Binghamton: St John the Evangelist
1907   Chadwicks: St Anthony of Padua
1908   Clark Mills: Annunciation
1908   Endicott: St Ambrose
1908   Homer: St Margaret
1908   Oswego: St Stephen the King
1909   New York Mills: St Mary, Our Lady of Czestochowa
1909   Rome: St John the Baptist
1909   Rome: Transfiguration

1911   Southwest Oswego: St Joseph mission
1911   Syracuse: Transfiguration of Our Lord
1911   Utica: St George
1911   Utica: St Stanislaus
1911   Utica: St Anthony of Padua
1913   Binghamton: Assumption of the Blessed Virgin Mary (merged with St. Mary as St Mary of the Assumption in 1967)
1913   Syracuse: Most Holy Rosary (then Holy Rosary)
1913   Warners: Our Lady of Good Counsel
1913   Verona: Our Lady of Good Counsel
1914   Bainbridge: St John the Evangelist
1914   Binghamton: St Joseph
1914   Binghamton: St Stanislaus Kostka
1914   Mexico: St Mary, Star of the Sea
1914   Sanitaria Springs: St Joseph
1915   Oswego: St Joseph
1915   Syracuse: St Stephen
1917   Cortland: St Anthony
1917   Endicott: St Anthony of Padua
1917   Sherrill: St Helena
1919   Utica: Our Lady of Lourdes

1920   Manlius: St Ann
1920   Otter Lake: St Mary of the Snows mission

1921   Syracuse: Blessed Sacrament
1922   Redfield: St Paul mission
1923   Endicott: St Joseph
1923   Lee Center: St Joseph
1923   Norwich: St Bartholomew the Apostle
1924   Fulton: St Michael
1924   Syracuse: Our Lady of Pompei
1924   Utica: Blessed Sacrament
1925   Binghamton: St Ann
1925   Syracuse: St James
1926   Mattydale: St Margaret
1926   Munnsville: St Therese of the Infant Jesus
1926   North Syracuse: St Rose of Lima
1926   Syracuse: Our Lady of Solace
1926   Syracuse: St Brigid (merged with St Joseph (French) in 1964)
1926   Syracuse: St Therese, the Little Flower of Jesus
1926   Utica: Sacred Heart
1926   Vernon: St Catherine (merged with St. Agnes at Vernon Center in 1974 as Holy Family at Vernon)
1927   Binghamton: St Thomas Aquinas
1928   Central Square: St Michael
1928   Endicott: St Casimir
1928   Oriskany: St Stephen, Protomartyr
1929   Binghamton: St Catherine of Sienna
1929   Syracuse: St Charles Borromeo

1930   Fulton: Holy Family
1931   Morrisville: St Joan of Arc
1932   Minetto: Our Lady of Perpetual Help
1932   Syracuse: St Daniel
1935   Syracuse: Holy Family
1935   Syracuse: Our Lady of Peace (then Lakeland chapel of St. Cecilia at Solvay)
1938   Nedrow: Corpus Christi

1940   Binghamton: St Christopher
1941   Endicott: Our Lady of Good Counsel
1941   Vestal: Our Lady of Sorrows
1943   Dewitt: Holy Cross
1944   Maine: Holy Rosary
1945   Johnson City: Blessed Sacrament

1946 Chenango Forks: St Rita
1946 Lacona: St Francis Xavier Cabrini
1947 Syracuse: Our Lady of Lourdes
1947 Windsor: Our Lady of Lourdes
1948 Endwell: Christ the King
1949 Afton: St Agnes mission
1949 New Hartford: Our Lady of the Rosary

1950 Cincinnatus: Our Lady of Perpetual Help mission
1950 DeRuyter: St Lawrence mission
1950 Liverpool: Immaculate Heart of Mary
1950 Parish: St Anne
1951 Bridgeport: St Francis of Assisi
1953 Syracuse: St Andrew the Apostle
1954 Hannibal: Our Lady of the Rosary
1954 Rome: St Paul
1955 Binghamton: St Andrew
1955 New Berlin: St Theresa of the Infant Jesus

1955 Syracuse: St Ann
1957 New Hartford: St Thomas
1958 Brewerton: St Agnes
1959 Constantia: St Bernadette mission

1963 Utica: St Mark
1964 Baldwinsville: St Augustine
1964 Endwell: Our Lady of Angels
1964 Liverpool: Christ the King
1965 Binghamton: St Vincent de Paul
1965 Whitesboro: St Anne
1967 Brookfield: St Ann mission (closed in 1981; incorporated into St. Bernard at Waterville)
1968 New London (Rome): Holy Cross

1970 Leonardsville: Our Lady of the Valley mission
1971 Liverpool: St John
1972 Scriba: Sacred Heart mission

1985 Baldwinsville: St Elizabeth Ann Seton

NOTES

The archives of the diocese of Syracuse contain an excellent collection of records. Included are the following materials.

1. The papers of historian Thomas O'Connor. These include a manuscript of five chapters of a projected diocesan history, photostats of materials in a variety of archives, and O'Connor's own notes on research in the archives of the New York State dioceses, Baltimore, and other collections around the country, as well as his personal papers.

2. The parish history files. Monsignor David Gildea maintained an excellent collection of published and unpublished histories of individual parishes. In 1936 and again in 1976 the diocese solicited detailed outlines of the history of each parish; the 1976 request drew a 90 percent response, and these outlines are present in this collection. In addition there are miscellaneous clippings, photographs, letters and other materials gathered by Gildea, O'Connor or our own team of volunteers.

3. Papers of individual bishops. These vary in extent and quality. Bishops Foery and Cunningham, for example, kept notes or text from almost every sermon or speech they delivered. Their personal and official correspondence is also extensive, while the materials for earlier bishops are far less complete.

4. The official files. In the vault is kept correspondence with individual parishes, religious communities, institutions and individuals, irregularly arranged. Most useful were the annual reports from parishes, complete from 1887 to the present. The vault also contains reports and records of the various diocesan offices and agencies. Priests' files are less complete, although there is an excellent card file containing vital statistics and information on education, assignments, and special work of individual priests.

5. Miscellaneous collections. These include the papers of Monsignor Gildea, Monsignor Charles Fahey, some of the papers of Monsignor Charles Brady, and a variety of scrapbooks, some dating from the prediocesan period. The archives also shares with the *Catholic Sun* a complete microfilm copy of its publications.

During the course of our work, teams of volunteers visited many parishes, selected on the basis of promising comments regarding records on their 1976 questionnaire. Unfortunately these yielded limited results. While most parishes have official records of baptisms, weddings and funerals, few have additional useful information. Yet some parishes had excellent materials. Worth mention are announcement books from the Cathedral of the Immaculate Conception, St. Matthew's in East Syracuse and St. Vincent de Paul in Syracuse, scrapbooks and minute books of trustees from St. John's in Utica, scrapbooks and letters from St Paul's Oswego and Our Lady of Lourdes in Utica.

In almost all cases the statistics cited in the text come from the parish reports or reports prepared by offices for charity or education. The former, along with vital statistics on clergy and schools, were analyzed on the basis of computer summaries prepared by Rev. Francis J. Case. Quotations come from materials in the diocesan collections or in the parish materials mentioned. What follows are some specific references for each chapter, with special attention to secondary materials which inform the interpretations offered.

Chapter One:
GOD IS EVERYWHERE

This chapter depends heavily on the work of Thomas O'Connor and, in its narrative sections, is an abridgement of his extensive writing on the mission years. The interpretation offered is quite different however. For further reading see the statement of the American Bishops on American Indians in Hugh J. Nolan, editor, *Pastoral Letters of the United States Catholic Bishops,* IV (Washington, 1984), 205-210.

Chapter Two:
A BAND OF BROTHERS

On the social and religious climate of the area see Whitney D. Cross, *The Burned Over District: The Social and Intellectual History of Enthusiastic Religion in Western New York, 1800-1850* (Ithaca, 1950). On the general history of the period see Jay P. Dolan, *The American Catholic Experience* (New York, 1985) and James Hennesey, *American Catholics* (New York, 1980). *The History of the Diocese of Syracuse* published in 1909, edited by William P.H. Hewitt and with an introduction by Msgr. J.S.M. Lynch was particularly helpful on this chapter.

Chapter Three:
A NEW CHURCH MUST BE BUILT

On the formative years of the diocese of Albany see Martin J. Becker, *A History of Catholic Life in the Diocese of Albany 1609-1864* (New York, 1975). On trusteeism see the forthcoming definitive study of Patrick Carey, to be published 1986 by the University of Notre Dame press. Richard Shaw, *Dagger John* (New York, 1977) is a readable biography of John Hughes. For German American Catholics see Coleman Barry, *The Catholic Church and the German Americans* (Milwaukee, 1953).

Chapter Four:
MEMBERS OF THAT
WONDROUS CHURCH

Interpretation here is influenced by the pioneering work of historian Jay P. Dolan. *The Immigrant Church* (Baltimore, 1975) studies parish formation in pre-Civil War New York, while *Catholic Revivalism* (Notre Dame, 1982) presents a fascinating analysis of Catholic parish missions. Anne Taves *The Household of Faith* (Notre Dame, 1986) is a study of popular devotions in the nineteenth century.

Chapter Five:
KEEP THE LINES TIGHT

Thomas O'Connor's notes contain detailed information on the background of the diocesan formation. The general problem has been studied by Robert Trisco in *The Holy See and the Nascent Church on the American Middle West* (Rome, 1962). Ludden's problems with restive priests were not unusual. See Nelson J. Callahan, *A Case for Due Process in the Church* (New York, 1971) a study of the campaign for "priests rights" in the mid-nineteenth century. See also Robert Trisco, "Bishops and their Priests in the United States" in John Tracy Ellis, editor, *The Catholic Priest in the United States: Historical*

Investigations (Collegeville, 1971) pp. 111-292. Ludden sided with the conservative group headed by Archbishop Corrigan in the bitter fights before the turn of the century. See Robert D. Cross, *The Emergence of Liberal Catholicism in the United States* (Cambridge, 1968).

Chapter Six:
NOW YOU ARE A PEOPLE

I am indebted to the oral history collection at the Penfiled Library, State University of New York at Oswego, for some excellent recollections of early immigrant experience. Luciano Iorizzo of that university has explored the early history of Italians in the region in "The History of Italians in Oswego" *Twenty Ninth Publication of the Oswego County Historical Society* (1967-1968) and in "A reappraisal of Italian Leadership in Central New York Immigrant Communities: Some Preliminary Observations" published abroad but kindly made available by the author. General observations on Italian experience can be found in Rudolph Vecoli. *"Prelates and Peasants: Italian Immigrants and the Catholic Church,"* *Journal of Social History*, II (1958-1959). On the struggle to control Italian popular devotions, and the relationship of those devotions to communal and family life, see Robert Anthony Orsi's brilliant *The Madonna of 115th Street; Faith and Community in Italian Harlem, 1880-1950* (New Haven, 1985). On the church and the new immigrants generally see Richard Linkh, *American Catholicism and European Immigrants* (New York, 1975). My interpretation, here and elsewhere, is heavily influenced by the work of historian Timothy L. Smith. See especially "Religion and Ethnicity in America," *American Historical Review* LXXXIII (December, 1978) and "Lay Initiative in American Catholic Life" in Tamara Hareven, editor, *Anonymous Americans* (New York, 1776).

Chapter Seven:
A LADDER FROM EARTH TO HEAVEN

Parish life in the twentieth century has not been studied. The material here is drawn from the archives and is assisted greatly by the announcement books preserved at St. Vincent de Paul parish in Syracuse and by the unique diary kept by Father Bernard Quinn of Deerfield.

Chapter Eight:
TO SUPPORT OUR OWN

This chapter relies heavily on the Grimes and Curley papers and the records of the offices of Catholic Charities. On the national scene, see Donald Gavin, *The National Conference of Catholic Charities* (Milwaukee, 1962) and Aaron I Abell, American Catholicism and Social Action (Doubleday, 1955). The spirit of post-war Catholicism can be studied in two excellent works on Chicago, both of which have influenced my interpretation of the period: Charles Shanabruch, *Chicago's Catholics* (Notre Dame, 1982) and Edward Kantowitz' excellent biography of George Cardinal Mundelein, *Corporation Sole* (Notre Dame, 1983).

Chapter Nine:
THE HAPPIEST AND MOST PEACEFUL SOCIETY

The best work on the interwar years is William Halsey, *The Survival of American Innocence, Catholicism in an Era of Disillusionment* (Notre Dame, 1980). I have examined Catholic response to the depression in *American Catholics and Social Reform: The New Deal Year* (New York, 1968). On Syracuse voting in the Al Smith years see B.R. Andrews, "Religious and Ethnic Influence on Voting Behavior: A Study of the Syracuse

Electorate, 1918-1957," (Unpublished PhD thesis, Syracuse University, 1961).

Chapter Ten:
THE MULTIPLICATION OF NATIONALITIES

Here again the work of Timothy Smith has been helpful. For case studies of immigrant adjustment see Silbano Tomasi, *Piety and Power: The Role of Italian Parishes in the Metropolitan New York Area* (New York, 1975) and Keith P. Dyrud, et al, *The Other Catholics* (New York, 1978)

Chapter Eleven:
PAROCHIAL TREASURE

On Catholic priests in the twentieth century, see John Tracy Ellis, *The Catholic Priest in the United States: Historical Investigations* (Collegeville, 1972).

Chapter Twelve:
REACH EVERY CHILD

The history of Catholic education can be studied in Neil J. McCluskey, ed. *Catholic Education in America: A Documentary History* (New York, 1965), Harold A. Buetow, *Of Singular Benefit: The Story of Catholic Education in the United States* (New York, 1970) and James Sanders, *The Education of an Urban Minority: Catholics in Chicago 1833-1965* (New York, 1977).

Chapter Thirteen:
THE ANSWER TO THE WORLD'S WOES

On Catholics and war see Dorothy Dohen, *Nationalism and American Catholicism* (New York, 1967) and Patricia McNeal Dolan, *The American Catholic Peace Movement, 1928-1972* (New York, 1978). See also Donald Crosy, S.J., *God, Church and Flag:*

Senator Joseph R. McCarthy and the Catholic Church (Chapel Hill, 1978).

Chapter Fourteen:
A FLOURISHING PLANT

On post-war Catholicism, see James O'Gara, editor, *The Catholic Parish* (New York, 1960) and the several volumes of parish studies of Jesuit sociologist Joseph Fichter. See also Andrew Greeley, *The Church and the Suburbs* (Chicago, 1962).

Chapter Fifteen:
NO LONGER A PIONEER CHURCH

The post-war religious revival is analyzed in Will Herberg, *Protestant, Catholic, Jew* (New York, 1955). On the persistence of ethnicity see Norman Glazer and Daniel P. Moynihan, *Beyond the Melting Pot* (New York, 1961). For an analysis of pre-conciliar American Catholicism see Daniel Callahan, *The Mind of the Catholic Layman* (New York, 1965).

Chapter Sixteen:
TOWARD THE ETERNAL KINGDOM

On the U.S. Bishops at the council see Vincent Yzermans, editor, *American Participation in the Second Vatican Council* (New York, 1967). Gary Wills, *Bare Ruined Choirs* (New York, 1968) captures the tensions of renewal while my *The Renewal of American Catholicism* (New York, 1968) attempts to place events in a historical perspective.

Chapter Seventeen:
ADJUSTMENTS IN CATHOLIC EDUCATION

The best works on Catholic schools are Andrew Greeley and Peter Rossi, *The Education of Catholic Americans* (Chicago, 1966) and Greeley, et al, Catholic Schools in a

Declining Church (Kansas City, 1976).

Chapter Eighteen:
NEW WINE, OLD WINESKINS

For an overview of American Catholicism after the Council see Philip Gleason, editor, *Contemporary Catholicism in the United States* (Notre Dame, 1969). My *The Renewal of American Catholicism* (New York, 1972) surveys the post-conciliar scene as well.

Chapter Nineteen:
COUNTED AND JUDGED

For the American bishops response to social issues see the newly issued collection *The Pastoral Letters of the United States Bishops,* four volumes (Washington, 1985). This and the following chapter were greatly assisted by interviews with Frank Woolever, Bishop Thomas Costello, Carl Roesch and Delores Morgan.

Chapter Twenty:
THE REAL WORLD

Here again the interviews mentioned above were helpful. So were the papers of Monsignor Charles Fahey, the taped interviews recorded by members of the Brady research project, and the reports contained in the papers of Catholic Charities. My own assessment of Catholic social action can be found in "Social Teaching, Social Action, Social Gospel," *U.S. Catholic Historian,* V (1986), 195-224.

Chapter Twenty One:
WE ARE THE CHURCH

Here the pastoral letters, speeches and sermons of Bishop Harrison were most helpful, along with the continuing reporting of the *Catholic Sun.* Materials in the archives on "The Church as Employer" project, the studies commissioned by the Priests Senate, and the reports on personnel were most helpful. On the national scene, see Andrew Greeley's various works, especially *American Catholics: A Social Protrait* (New York, 1983) and John Coleman, S.J., *American Strategic Theology* (New York, 1980). See also the pastoral letters of the American Bishops on war and peace and in draft form on the economy.

FAITH AND FRIENDSHIP

528

Designed by Andrea Legg DeRose,
Grafik Communications, Ltd.,
Alexandria, Virginia.

Typeset in Simoncini Garamond by
Printing Dimensions, a division of
Photo Data, Inc., Beltsville,
Maryland, and WTC Goudy
Regular by Type Studio, Ltd.,
Alexandria, Virginia.

Printed on 6016 Booktext Natural
by Bookcrafters, Chelsea, Michigan.